THE SPIRIT OF ST. LOUIS

A HISTORY OF THE ST. LOUIS CARDINALS AND BROWNS

PETER GOLENBOCK

SPIKE

AN AVON BOOK

Readers can reach Peter Golenbock on the web at www.golenbockbooks.com
Readers can reach Ron Stark via e-mail at stark-fam@juno.com

AVON BOOKS, INC.
An Imprint of HarperCollins *Publishers*
10 East 53rd Street
New York, New York 10022-5299

Copyright © 2000 by Peter Golenbock
Interior design by Rhea Braunstein
ISBN: 0-380-97660-9

Library of Congress Cataloging in Publication Data:

Golenbock, Peter, 1946–
    The spirit of St. Louis : a history of the St. Louis Cardinals and Browns / Peter
Golenbock.—1st ed.
        p.   cm.
    Includes index.
    1. St. Louis Cardinals (Baseball team)—History. 2. St. Louis Browns (Baseball
team)—History. I. Title: The spirit of Saint Louis. II. Title.
GV875.S3 G63 2000
796.357'64'0977866—dc21   99-050025

First Spike Printing: February 2000

SPIKE TRADEMARK REG. U.S. PAT. OFF. AND IN OTHER COUNTRIES,
MARCA REGISTRADA, HECHO EN U.S.A.

Printed in the U.S.A.

QPM   10   9   8   7   6   5   4   3   2   1

www.harpercollins.com

This book is dedicated to Barry Halper,
who has given over his life to the Game.

It's amazing that a guy who swings a bat
can affect the country.
—Mark McGwire

ACKNOWLEDGMENTS

One often feels compelled to call upon the generosity of others, in order to write the best book possible. In that this is an oral history, as much as I could make it one, I called upon the assistance of authors who had conducted interviews on tape with a number of key Cardinal players prior to their deaths.

Robert Hood, an early chronicler of "the Gashouse Gang," wrote a really terrific book on the subject back in 1976, and when I called to see if was still in possession of his taped conversations with men long gone, not only did he still have them, but Bob was kind and generous in letting me listen to and use them for this book. Bob, moreover, gave of his own time and memories, and I shall always be thankful to him.

Ditto for William Mead, who readily allowed me to use his taped interviews of a number of Cardinals who played in 1930 and 1968. Tony Salin is a skilled baseball chronicler in his own right, whose wonderful book, *Baseball's Forgotten Heroes,* was published in the spring of 1999. Tony, another Orthodox member of the Baseball religion, not only provided me with a foot-high pile of fascinating reference materials, but he generously permitted me to include his interview of the reclusive Pete Gray in this book. In a cutthroat world and in a hard-nosed profession, such generosity and kindness are rare and appreciated beyond what words can express.

My thanks also to others whose assistance helped me to important research and interviews. To Bernie Levy, an incredible resource, a man who has been fact-checking my books for years. I am privileged and grateful that this time he was able to perform his magic *before* publication. To the friendly staff of the Missouri Historical Society, you were very helpful. My thanks to Bill Borst and David Chavez for pointing me in promising directions. To Betty Grice and her son-in-law Jim Meany for their hospitality and stack of useful research material.

To my esteemed friend Andy Corty, who introduced me to Jack and Katherine Anne Lake, who introduced me to Stan Musial; to my ageless softball buddy John Alderson, who arranged for me to interview his son, Sandy Alderson; to my experts, Cliff Kachline, Al Fleishman, Bing Devine, Fred Saigh, Bob Broeg, Gene Karst, Marvin Miller, David Lipman, Bill Davenport, Gary Froid, Cardinal owner Bill DeWitt, Jr., Gary Mormino, and Bill Miller, for sharing their memories and knowledge. Bob Broeg deserves special mention. Mr. Broeg has written a small library of books on the Cardinals. He was writing a book during the time I was interviewing him. He never once said to me, as others have in the past: "I can't talk to you. I'm writing my own book."

He answered all my questions to the best of his ability, and his generosity will always be special to me.

My thanks to the Cardinals' diligent public relations director, Brian Bartow, for his kind attention. My thanks also to the former major leaguers, including those voices which appear posthumously from their interviews with Bob Hood and Bill Mead: Bennie Borgmann, Bill Hallahan, Joe Medwick, Tex Carleton, Jack Rothrock, Virgil "Spud" Davis, France Laux, Jesse Haines, Bill Walker, Browns owner Bill DeWitt, Sr., Red Schoendienst, and Tim McCarver. Also to the men kind enough to sit for interviews by the author: the late Chester "Red" Hoff, who was a hundred and four years old when we talked, to Max Lanier, Eldon Auker, Angelo Giuliani, Marty Marion, Don Gutteridge, Ellis Clary, Danny Litwhiler, Jim Brosnan, the aforementioned Mr. Musial, Eddie Pellagrini, the late Denny Galehouse, Ned Garver, Nelson Briles, Brooks Lawrence, Rich Folkers, Joe Magrane, Carl Warwick, the late Roger Maris, whom I interviewed back in 1973 for my book *Dynasty,* Enos Slaughter, Gene Oliver, Bill White, Willie McGee, Darrell Porter, and Tommy Herr.

My thanks too to Ron Stark, whose wonderful drawings have made some of the Card stars come alive, and to Frank Bisogno, a great baseball fan, who lent me his collection of print ads for use in this book. Thanks also to George Brace, who in the 1930 World Series stood with his camera along the third base line as Babe Ruth pointed and swore at pitcher Charlie Root. Swears Mr. Brace, now eighty-eight years young, "He didn't call his shot. Root would have knocked him on his ass." George's magnificent portraits have graced a number of my books, and always they are the better for it.

Thanks too to my wonderful family, Rhonda Sonnenberg, our son Charlie, and our basset vite, Doris. Also to Frank Weimann, my hardworking agent, who made this book possible. To Stephen S. Powers, my editor, a sharp mind with a steady hand, and Mark Hurst, my copyeditor. And to Neil Reshen and Dawn Reshen-Doty, without whom I probably would be doing something else.

I also want to thank all the members of Charlie's Fossil Park Youth League team: Dennis Barnes, Travis Dickinson, Steve Garrett, Justin Mortenson, Kyle Mueller, J. J. Richardson, Adam Schultz, Zack Taylor, Mike Vallery, Ricky Williams, and Katie Wright. We might not have won a lot of games, but none of you ever quit, and that's a lot more important. I'm very proud of all of you.

CONTENTS

INTRODUCTION

When Mark McGwire, the Bunyanesque Cardinal first baseman, struck home run number 62 in September of 1998, he left an indelible memory for all who looked on that day. If you close your eyes, you can still see the low trajectory of that ball as it rose slightly, then quickly struck the Busch Stadium façade just beyond the playing area near the left field foul pole. It wasn't typical of McGwire's home runs, which often travel 500 feet, but its significance was monumental. Who can ever forget "Big Mac" crossing home plate and then showing his humanity by hugging his son, his father, his teammates—everyone in that ballpark, it seemed—including the children of Roger Maris as he joined a long list of memorable, mythic St. Louis performers who during the past 120 years or so have taken their rightful place in the annals of American sport.

St. Louis baseball has a rich and storied history. No National League team has won as many pennants as the Cardinals. Few American League teams have boasted as many uniquely quirky and memorable characters as the Browns.

Each generation has its own brace of heroes. Too often I hear: "Baseball isn't what it used to be. The players today don't compare to the ones I rooted for when I was a kid."

I think I know why. Fans become permanently attached to the heroes of their childhood years. As those fans age and advance into their thirties, their heroes retire and disappear from the playing field, leaving the fans with only memories. For the rest of their lives, these fans pine for those lost men. I can't begin to tell you how much Cardinal fans between the ages of fifty and seventy still talk about Stan Musial and Enos Slaughter. Younger fans talk wistfully of Bob Gibson or Lou Brock. Still younger, the talk is of Ozzie Smith and his magic. I can't remember growing older. When did they?

In this book I have attempted to introduce to you the entire cast of St. Louis icons. Before McGwire came "the Wizard of Oz," perhaps the most acrobatic infielder in the history of the game. Equally memorable was his manager, Whitey Herzog, who took over the Cards after years of mediocrity and won three pennants, leaving as a legacy his never-say-die style of play. Vince Coleman, Willie McGee, Tommy Herr, Darrell Porter, and Jack Clark became local heroes for all time on Whitey's teams.

Before Herzog, there was a group of fabled men who won three pennants in the 1960s with a lineup that boasted a whole array of memorable stars: Curt Flood, Bob Gibson, Roger Maris himself, Orlando Cepeda, Ken Boyer, Bill White, Lou Brock, Julian Javier, and Dick Groat. These teams, put together by Bing Devine and run by Augustus "Gussie" Busch, the head man at the

Anheuser-Busch brewery, became a symbol for racial unity during an era of civil strife.

During the 1950s, owner Gussie Busch was searching for the right combination of players that would bring back the glory of the 1940s. The St. Louis Cardinals, owned at that time by Sam Breadon, won four pennants in five years in the forties, coinciding with the heyday of "Stan the Man." Those Cards were put together by Branch Rickey, though "the Mahatma" had already gone on to the Dodgers when the Cards won those pennants. St. Louis old-timers fondly remember their championship players: Terry Moore, Marty Marion, Enos Slaughter, Red Schoendienst, George "Whitey" Kurowski, and the Cooper brothers, Mort and Walker.

Meanwhile, if you are a Browns fan, you may no longer be a spring chicken, but if you still love a team that moved to Baltimore nearly fifty years ago, then you still have a youthful, hopeful heart.

In 1944 the Browns won the only pennant in their history. They faced the Cards in the World Series with heroes such as Sig Jakucki, Vern Stephens, and Mike Kreevich, men who loved the bottle as much as the game. You then rooted for such legends as Pete Gray, who played with one arm; Eddie Gaedel, who was a midget; and Leroy "Satchel" Paige, the ageless Negro League star who sat in his rocking chair between pitching assignments. The owner of the Browns, Bill Veeck, brought these men to St. Louis in a futile attempt to draw fans and stay in business. Veeck, who during one game allowed the fans to plot the strategy, may have been the Browns' biggest character of all.

Some of you may even have watched the five Cardinal pennant winners of the 1920s and 1930s, teams with a roster full of names known to most baseball fans: Jay Hanna "Dizzy" Dean and Paul Dean (known as "Me an' Paul," Leo "the Lip" Durocher, Johnny "Pepper" Martin, Frankie Frisch, Joe "Ducky Wucky" Medwick, "Sunny Jim" Bottomley, Burleigh Grimes, Grover Cleveland Alexander, and Rogers Hornsby, the best right-handed batter who ever lived. I have tried to resurrect them through their words and deeds.

The 1934 team, which won the pennant by a single game on the final day of the season, became known as "The Gas House Gang," and it has become one of the most famous teams of all time. It should be noted that these early winners also were put together by the duo of Breadon and Rickey, the latter of whom may have been the most important and influential team executive in baseball history.

It was the Browns, though, that boasted the earliest champions in St. Louis. They were called the Brown Stockings then, and they won four pennants in a row in the 1880s. Their stars were Walter "Arlie" Latham, "Parisian Bob" Caruthers, and Charlie Comiskey. Their owner was Christian Frederick "Chris" Von der Ahe, a volatile character who made much of his money selling beer in his saloon and who was the first to sell brew at the ballpark.

All of these men had unique skills and personalities—and they made headlines. My job has been to bring them alive between these covers. I have tried as best I could to go behind those headlines to discover what these men were like, how they fit into the fabric of the team, and how they played the game. My primary goal is for you to experience baseball through the players' eyes, to feel whatever they were feeling at the time: their pain, joy, or frustration. Always I am impressed by the consistency of these emotions from era to era.

My lifelong quest has been to save for history as many ballplayer memories as I am able. I live to hear a Marty Marion tell me about Terry Moore, an Ellis Clary talk about Sig Jakucki, see Max Lanier grit his teeth talking about Branch Rickey, hear a Jim Brosnan speak reverentially of Stan Musial, or a Joe Magrane revel in the genius of Whitey Herzog.

I trust you will savor the many stories, incidents, and firsthand accounts as much as I have. For me, baseball history is an endlessly fascinating topic. You can analyze the games themselves. You can try to understand the men who play them. You can look at how the players interact with each other and with their manager and owner. You can learn what life was like during the era in which they played. You can explore the effect of the general manager or team owner on the success of the team. You can discuss changes in the game over the years. You can discuss race, religion, and sociology. I have attempted to do all of this and more.

That I have been afforded the opportunity to interview the men who ran and played the game and who left their mark not just in St. Louis but from coast to coast has left me humble and proud. Here, then, are their stories.

—PETER GOLENBOCK,
St. Petersburg, Florida
July 1999

THE
BROWNS

CHAPTER 1

THE FOUNDING

LONG before the coming of the white man, a hunting party of Fox Indians from the Algonquin tribe spied a caravan of rival Sioux paddling large canoes on a wide river. That night, sitting around the campfire and discussing what they had seen, the Fox warriors discussed their sighting of the "Missouri" — "the Big Canoe People" —who were camped where the river converged with another powerful body of water.

To the smaller of the two rivers they gave the same name, "Missouri," and to the other the name "Mesisi-piya," which in Fox meant "the Big River."

The Indians had this fertile expanse of land to themselves until whites began settling in the area in 1763. Two Frenchmen, Pierre LaClede and Auguste Chouteau, opened a fur-trading post in a log cabin on the west bank of the Mesisi-piya, ten miles downstream from where the mighty Missouri and Mississippi meet.

Back East, wearing a tall hat made of beaver was a sign of elegance. The Indians had an abundance of beaver, for whose pelts the European traders swapped cloth, tobacco, beads, knives, and whiskey. Gradually a village would grow around LaClede and Chouteau's post. It would be named St. Louis in honor of the Crusader King of France, Louis IX.

After explorations by Frenchmen Jacques Marquette and Louis Jolliet, the French claimed territory along the Mississippi stretching from New Orleans at the mouth of the river north over an endless tract of wilderness spreading as far west as the Rocky Mountains and north as Montana. Napoléon I, who ruled France, had intended this land, called the Louisiana Territory, to be France's stronghold in the New World, but he was in a war with England and knew his army's power in the New World was shaky. To consolidate his position, he planned to subdue the rebellious slaves of Haiti, make the Dominican Republic his base of operation from which he would send troops to New Orleans, and then take control of the Louisiana Territory.

President Thomas Jefferson warned Napoléon I that if French troops stepped foot onto Louisiana Territory soil, it would be tantamount to a declaration of war. He asked Napoléon I to cede New Orleans to the United States to prevent any conflict. Napoléon I demurred, but when he lost 40,000 of his best troops in Haiti in a futile attempt to quell a slave rebellion, Napoléon I saw his dreams of empire in the New World crushed. He decided it would be wisest to sell France's land holdings in North America even at a bargain-basement price rather than stand by and watch the Americans take them from him.

In July of 1803, Jefferson negotiated a deal to buy the 828,000 acres of the Louisiana Purchase for $15 million, doubling the size of the United States overnight. France received some much-needed cash, and Napoléon I could take some solace in knowing he had strengthened the United States against their mutual enemy: the hated English. In 1819, when the first steamboat, the *Zebulon Pike,* docked along the wharf, St. Louis had 1,400 inhabitants. These were traders and trappers, many of whom toiled for the St. Louis Fur Company.

By 1850, St. Louis's population had grown to 160,000, including 40,000 Germans fleeing poverty and religious persecution. When gold was discovered in California in 1848, St. Louis became the jumping-off point for thousands of westward-bound adventurers. River traffic grew. Six major rail terminals were built. In 1874 the Eads Bridge was built across the Mississippi River, spurring new railroad construction westward. It wasn't long before nineteen major railroads chugged in and out of St. Louis. By 1870, 310,000 inhabitants had transformed the little trading post into the nation's fourth-largest city.

Among the men who first traveled to St. Louis was a Frenchman by the name of Jean-Baptiste Charles Lucas. He had graduated with distinction from the University of Caen in France, and after going to law school in Paris had become friendly with a man by the name of Roy de Chaumont. Through him Lucas made the acquaintance of the American ambassador to France, Benjamin Franklin. Chaumont was coming to America to live, and at Franklin's urging, Lucas decided to accompany him. Lucas arrived in the States bearing a flattering recommendation from Franklin.

In 1801 one of Franklin's closest friends, President Thomas Jefferson, recruited Lucas to go on a mission. Napoléon I was waging war in Haiti. If he won, his next target would be the United States. He asked Lucas to personally investigate the conditions west of the Mississippi to ascertain the temper of the French and Spanish residents of Louisiana. Would they side with the French or with the Americans if war came? Jefferson appointed him one of the judges of the territory and made him land commissioner.

Lucas traveled by horseback to the fledgling outpost in 1805. Once there, Lucas foresaw St. Louis's future greatness, and he invested heavily in real estate. The war that came was against the British, not the French, and after the British were repulsed, the land boom that followed the War of 1812 enabled him to sell less than a quarter of his substantial holdings for twenty times his investment. At the time of his death in 1843, J.-B.C. Lucas had become a very rich man.

Judge Lucas was survived by his only remaining son, James, and a daughter. James Lucas expanded the family's real estate holdings during the 1850s by developing Lucas Place, the most exclusive residential district in St. Louis. He would go on to own the greater part of the city's entire business district. Upon his death in November of 1873, he left more than $1 million to each of his seven children.

Two of his sons, J.-B.C. Lucas II and Henry V. Lucas, would spend part of their inheritance to start professional baseball teams in separate leagues. And for almost eighty years hence, two St. Louis teams would pull and tug for the loyalty of the citizenry.

*   *   *

According to Shepard Barkley, a judge on the Missouri Supreme Court, it was Jere Frain, a contractor, who introduced St. Louisians to the game.

SHEPARD BARCLAY: "It was in the early fifties that Mr. Frain brought the game to St. Louis. I was a little fellow at the time and with other boys I played all sorts of games on the field located right where Lafayette Park is now. I remember while playing there one day Jere Frain, a great tall boy, came among us. He was a stranger who had come from somewhere in the East, and on our field he laid out a diamond and showed us how to play the modern game of baseball. He built us a diamond much the same as the diamond in use today, and in fact, showed us just how to play the game. That was really the introduction of the game in St. Louis."

Frain, a second baseman, had played for the highly regarded Charter Oak Club of Brooklyn before moving to St. Louis. In 1864 he became captain of the Empire club of St. Louis. Other St. Louis teams, including the Unions and the Reds, were formed, but the Empire club remained St. Louis's best.

In 1869 the immortal Cincinnati Red Stockings paid St. Louis a visit. The Red Stockings, led by the famed Wright brothers, George and Harry, had run roughshod over all opponents in 1869, and the Empires proved no match for Cincy's powerful nine.

The Red Stockings then broke up and were replaced as the country's best team by the Chicago White Stockings, led by star pitcher Al Spalding. After Chicagoans raised $20,000 to fund the team, the White Stockings became the paragons of professional baseball.

The White Stockings came to St. Louis in 1870 and trounced two of the city's amateur teams, the Empires, 36–8, and the Unions, 47–1. In October the White Stockings beat the Empires again, this time by a score of 46–8. In 1871 the White Stockings joined the National Association of Professional Baseball Players. That year they traveled to St. Louis and defeated the Atlantics and Empires by the lopsided scores of 22–2 and 34–8. Other pro teams, the Philadelphia A's, the Brooklyn Atlantics, and the Boston Red Stockings, soundly defeated St. Louis amateur teams. In 1873 3,000 fans attended a game in which the Empires were defeated, 24–4, by the Red Stockings. In 1874 the Chicago White Stockings soundly beat eight different St. Louis amateur teams. Al Spalding, the owner of the White Stockings, further enraged the St. Louis sporting fraternity when he signed two local St. Louis players: pitcher Dan Collins and shortstop Johnny Peters. When the White Stockings defeated St. Louis teams six more times, the cumulative score was Chicago 93, St. Louis 14. The local rooters were embarrassed as St. Louis clubs suffered through a streak of twenty defeats in a row at the hands of the Chicago juggernaut.

The constant losing was hard for the prideful St. Louis boosters to take, and in the fall of 1874 they organized and raised $20,000 of their own to start a professional team to play the next season in the National Association. They sold 450 shares at $50 each.

The president of the St. Louis professionals was J.-B.C. Lucas II, the wealthiest man in St. Louis. Charles Fowle, who owned an establishment called the Dollar Store, also invested. Orrick Bishop, a talented amateur player who ended his career in 1867 when he opened his law practice, was appointed managing director (general manager) of the team, a post he held all three years of the team's existence. Bishop traveled East to sign players for the fledgling St. Louis team. He signed shortstop Dickey Pearce, right fielder Jack Chapman, first baseman Herman Dehlman, who was on the roster of the Brooklyn Atlantics, and Lipman Pike, who had played with the Hartford Dark Blues. (Pike has been called the first professional player. He was paid $20 a week in 1866 by the Philadelphia A's.)

Pearce, who Bishop signed off the roster of the Brooklyn Atlantics, also was a pioneer. When he first began playing baseball, teams played four out-fielders and only one infielder between second and third base. Pearce felt he could help his team more by playing between the third baseman and the second base bag. He cut off a lot of balls that otherwise would have gone into the outfield. Though thirty-eight years old when he joined the Browns, Pearce was still one of the best fielders in the game.

Bishop found the rest of his players in the Philadelphia area. He signed four Philly natives—third baseman Bill Hague, catcher Tom Miller, second baseman Joe Battin, and left fielder Edgar "Ned" Cuthbert, who had been a pro since 1865. Cuthbert, known as an innovator, was credited as the first player ever to slide into a base.

Cuthbert spent all but one season playing in Philadelphia. In 1873 with the Philadelphia Whites he led the National League in stolen bases. In 1874 Cuthbert played for Al Spalding and the Chicago White Stockings. During the winter, Bishop got him to agree to come to St. Louis.

Cuthbert then convinced Bishop to sign a kid pitcher by the name of George Washington "Grin" Bradley. An amateur at the start of the 1874 season, Bradley had been signed by Easton, Pennsylvania, as its batting practice pitcher. But Bradley was so impressive that Jack Smith, the manager and starting pitcher, benched himself and inserted Bradley. When the professional Philadelphia A's sought to sign the boy, the youngster didn't want to share mound duties with pitcher-manager Dick McBride and declined the invitation. When offered the chance to be the number-one pitcher for St. Louis, Bradley jumped at the chance.

When Bishop returned home to St. Louis with his signees, the local papers questioned why he hadn't signed any local talent. Reacting to the criticism, Bishop signed two players to sit on the bench: catcher George Seward and an eighteen-year-old backup pitcher by the name of James "Pud" Galvin. (Galvin should never have been allowed to leave St. Louis. He would go on to win 360 games for Buffalo and Pittsburgh and be elected to baseball's Hall of Fame in 1965.)

The St. Louis team uniform called for brown stockings, and that became the name of the club. (The other explanation is that the team's stockings originally were white but quickly turned brown from the juice from chewing tobacco spat on each other by the St. Louis players.) Shortly after the Brown Stockings announced that they were going to play in the National Association for the 1875 season, another local St. Louis team, the Red Stockings, said that they too had gained a franchise. But the Brown Stockings were a far better team, and the Red Stockings folded before the end of July after a 4–15 start.

The Brown Stockings played their home games on a diamond first laid out in 1866 in the middle of a former German shooting park near the corner of Grand and St. Louis avenues known as the Grand Avenue Grounds (later Sportsman's Park). The highlight of the 1875 season came on May 6 in a game between the St. Louis Browns and the city's longtime nemesis, the Chicago White Stockings. St. Louis baseball fans saw this game as the first decent opportunity for a local team to defeat its rivals, and according to the *St. Louis Democrat,* "a seemingly endless string" of horse-drawn carriages rode down Grand Avenue on their way to the ballpark. Eight thousand fans squeezed into the park, while another 2,000 sought a view from light poles, housetops, and trees. It was a festive occasion, the likes of which was rarely seen before in St. Louis.

Grin Bradley started for the Brown Stockings against Chicago pitcher George "the Charmer" Zettlein. St. Louis scored first when Jack Chapman tripled to the left field fence to score Cuthbert, who had been safe on an error by Zettlein on a ground ball back to the box. The run was all Bradley needed in a shocking 10–0 rout. As soon as the Brown Stockings recorded the final putout, the St. Louis fans gave vent to their emotions, gleeful that the long losing string against Chicago's juggernaut finally had been broken. "Pandemonium" arose in the grandstand. According to the *St. Louis Dispatch,* "The entire assemblage rose to their feet and shouted until they were hoarse, danced, sang and threw their hats into the air as though they were taking leave of their senses. They kissed, wept and laughed over each other, embraced, shook hands, slapped each other's back, ran to and fro like madmen."

The celebration lasted into the night.

"About town last night," said the *St. Louis Dispatch,* "everywhere, the excitement regarding the great victory was most intense. In hotel, shop, restaurant, bar room in the home circle and on the street, but little was talked of save the terrific 'poulticing' the Browns had administered to the Chicago Whites."

In the *St. Louis Republican* the next day, the writer exulted: "Time was when Chicago had an excellent ball club, the best in the West, but that was before St. Louis decided to make an appearance on the diamond field and there, as everywhere else, attest the supremacy of the Western city with the greatest population, the most flourishing trade, the biggest bridge and the prettiest women."

The writer added: "St. Louis is happy. Chicago has not only been beaten in baseball, but outrageously beaten. With all the bragging of that boastful city . . . the result only illustrates once more the old truth that bluster does not always win. In this, as other things, St. Louis proves stronger."

Two days later the teams met again. The traffic jam was infuriating. Every seat in the ballpark was taken. General William Tecumseh Sherman sat in the press box. In the spring of 1861 he had moved to St. Louis from Arkansas, anticipating secession. Before the Civil War, Sherman had worked for the Lucas family, running the North Broadway streetcar system. When the war started, he joined the Union side. His "March to the Sea," which cut the Confederacy in half to help win the war for the Union, became part of American folklore.

In this game Bradley started against Jim Devlin. The Brown Stockings led 4–0 going into the ninth inning, when Chicago rallied for three runs. With the tying run on third, Bradley induced John Glenn to hit a grounder to third baseman Bill Hague, who fielded the ball cleanly and threw to first baseman Herman Dehlman for the final out. Once again the city held an impromptu celebration.

In Chicago the next day, the local papers mocked the importance put on these games by the St. Louis fans. Said the *Chicago Tribune,* "The city of St. Louis [has made] itself ridiculous generally."

A poem in the *St. Louis Democrat* explained just how much the two victories over the hated White Stockings meant to the city. The author, Jack Frost, titled the poem "A Tale of Two Cities—2000 A.D."

This little village seemed accursed;
Soon all her gaudy baubles burst.
She proved what me thought her before,
A wind-bag burgh—and nothing more.
Where this wretched village stood
Now stands a sign of painted wood
On it these words: "Upon this spot
Chicago stood, but now stands not"
Her time soon came, she had to go
A victim, she, of too much, blow.

The two wins over Chicago provided the season's highlights. Led by Bradley and managed by Dickey Pearce, St. Louis finished fourth in the National Association in 1875 behind the Boston Red Stockings.

At the end of the season, the league, badly run, folded.

Chicagoans Al Spalding and William Hulbert met with interested team executives from around the country, including two St. Louisianans, Charles Fowle and Orrick Bishop, to found the National League starting in 1876. Bishop, an attorney and later a judge, helped Spalding draw up the league's constitution, the first schedule, wrote the initial players' contracts, and formulated the entire program.

The St. Louis team, still called the Brown Stockings, played in the National League for only two seasons. In 1876 the team finished second, two games behind the White Stockings with a 45-19 record. Managed by first baseman Herman Dehlman, it was sparked by the superb pitching of Bradley, who finished the season 45-19 with a 1.23 earned run average, best in the league. The highlight was a no-hitter Bradley pitched against Hartford on July 15.

In 1877 team owner J.-B.C. Lucas II decided to begin the season as manager. Lucas would quickly learn a lesson gained by many wealthy men throughout the history of the game: Just because you have a lot of money and you like the game, that doesn't qualify you to run a baseball team.

Lucas's preseason started badly when star pitcher Grin Bradley was lured away by Chicago's Spalding, the smartest and most cutthroat owner in the game.

Lucas sought to strengthen the team at the end of the '76 season by signing four starting Louisville players: pitcher Jim Devlin, outfielder George Hall, third baseman Al Nichols, and shortstop Bill Craver. It was an extremely unusual transaction. Observers wondered why Louisville chose to offer these excellent players for sale. As much as these players strengthened the team, they could not make up for the loss of Bradley, whose replacement, Fred "Tricky" Nichols, proved an unworthy substitute, compiling an 18-23 record despite a 2.60 earned run average. The Browns finished fourth to Boston, led by Harry Wright and pitcher Tommy Bond.

Before the '77 season ended J.-B.C. Lucas II would quit as manager. When it was revealed that the four members of the Louisville team whom Lucas had signed had admitted to throwing games the previous season, they were barred from baseball for life. Lucas, moreover, was accused of knowing about the fixed games and their tainted past at the time he purchased the players. After the 1877 season Lucas resigned as president and the St. Louis team withdrew from the National League.

CHAPTER 2

CHRIS VON DER AHE: THE BEER BARON

AFTER the St. Louis Brown Stockings dropped out of the National League, the team continued as an independent club under the aegis of the St. Louis Sportsman's Park and Club Association. Led by brothers Al and William Spink, the association raised money to outfit and run the team. The Spinks arranged the schedule and wrote up the games in the local newspapers, Al in the *Missouri Republican,* William in the *St. Louis Globe-Democrat.*

The team, skippered by veteran manager Ned Cuthbert, was a popular draw. As many as 2,000 fans attended the exhibition contests despite the amateur standing of the team. In 1880 the team played 21 games and won all but one, losing to the professional Louisville Reds by the score of 14–8.

In 1881 the team again lost only one game. In the fall of 1881 Cuthbert acquired a stylish first baseman by the name of Charlie Comiskey at a salary of $75 a month. For the next decade, Comiskey would star on the team, then he would manage it to greatness.

The twenty-two-year-old was born on August 15, 1859, in Chicago. His father was the first president of the city council and served as alderman for eleven years. He was also deputy United States internal revenue collector under President Andrew Johnson. His father believed it important that the boy learn a trade, and he was apprenticed to a master plumber by the name of Hogan.

When he was eighteen, however, Comiskey's career path changed when in 1877 he pitched on a Chicago amateur team called the Liberties. After high school, Comiskey attended St. Mary's College in Kansas, where he was named captain of the freshman team. At St. Mary's Comiskey met Ted Sullivan, who would become his mentor and his ticket to the big leagues. Sullivan was the St. Mary's shortstop, and when he pitched, at his request Comiskey would catch him.

TED SULLIVAN: "I picked out Comiskey because I considered him the smartest kid on the teams. One incident will show how quickly, even in those days, he grasped an opportunity. I noticed that a runner on third was taking a big lead. Comiskey signaled for a certain ball. I shook my head. He signaled for another and I repeated. Finally I left the box, all the time upbraiding him because of his bonehead strategy. He never said a word but met me halfway, and still bawling him out, I slipped him the ball while I returned to the mound.

"All set behind the bat and Comiskey whipped the ball to third, nailing the runner by ten feet. I did not tell him what to do. I simply wanted to find out if he could think for himself. From that time on, I began to have respect for Charles, and he was only a kid at that."

Comiskey's father had him transferred to Christian Brothers College so he would study more and play baseball less, while Sullivan became player-manager of the amateur Alerts in hometown Milwaukee.

Sullivan needed a pitcher, and when he asked Comiskey to come to Milwaukee and join his team, Comiskey asked for $50 a month. Sullivan knew that owner Thomas Shaughnessy, former president of the Canadian Pacific Railroad, didn't have a budget for salaries, so Sullivan told the team owner he needed $50 to fix a hole in the outfield fence. Sullivan gave the money to Comiskey instead.

When Shaughnessy noticed that the hole had not been fixed, he asked Sullivan what he had done with the money. Sullivan pointed out the hard-throwing pitcher with the underhand motion. Because it was an amateur team, Shaughnessy needed to account for the money somewhere other than "salaries," and he wrote down the $50 under "general expenses."

In the spring of 1878, Sullivan and Comiskey played on the Elgin watch factory team in Elgin, Illinois. The team didn't lose a single game all summer long.

In the fall of '78, Sullivan moved to Dubuque, Iowa, to run a company that supplied newspapers and candy to customers riding the Illinois Central Railroad. Sullivan offered Comiskey $50 a month to play ball during the summer plus a 20 percent commission on newpaper and candy sales. The offer was a lot more than what Hogan was paying him as an apprentice plumber, and it gave Comiskey the courage to tell his father he intended to be a ballplayer. Comiskey quit the plumbing business for good and headed for Dubuque.

CHARLIE COMISKEY
(Courtesy Brace Photo)

In Dubuque, Ted Sullivan not only ran the local baseball team, he organized the four-team minor league pro circuit in which it played, with the other
three teams in Omaha, Rockford, and Davenport. At the end of the 1878
season, Sullivan's league became the first minor league to complete a schedule
without folding.

Sullivan had an unerring eye for talent. In 1879 he added third baseman
Bill Gleason and future Hall of Fame pitcher Charles "Old Hoss" Radbourn
to the Dubuque roster. In addition to his pitching duties, Comiskey played
first, second, third, and the outfield. The team won the league championship,
but still lost money.

In 1880 Sullivan didn't have the money to continue as a professional team,
so he scaled back and played other independent semipro teams. The team was
called the Dubuque Rabbits, in large part because of the speed and skill at
stealing bases of Comiskey and Bill Gleason. That year Comiskey injured his
arm and became the team's regular first baseman, a position he would play
for eighteen years.

On July 16, 1881, the Rabbits were invited to play in St. Louis against
the newly organized Browns at the team's Grand Avenue Grounds. In a game
that St. Louis won 9–1, Comiskey made a dozen plays at first base flawlessly,

hit a double, and showed blinding speed as he ran the bases. When Browns
manager Ned Cuthbert expressed interest in acquiring Comiskey, Al Spink,
who was running the Browns along with his brother William, offered Comiskey
a roster spot.

Comiskey was a dazzling base runner as well as fielder. Although he
wasn't the fastest runner on the team, no one could slide as deftly as he. He
perfected the fadeaway slide that Ty Cobb would become famous for many
years later. Usually, he would slide into a base headfirst. Comiskey once
explained why he recommended the headfirst slide:

CHARLIE COMISKEY: "I started sliding headfirst because I figured that to be
the most advantageous way of getting a close decision. It is true that as the
game developed, the greater number of players went feetfirst into the bag, but
this is risky in more ways than one, even though it is more comfortable than
the other. It sometimes means a broken leg, and in any case the runner is
unable to see the bag. Of course, combining the phenomenal skill and the
extreme speed of a Ty Cobb, the feetfirst slide has certain advantages, but for
all-around efficiency the head slide, in my estimation, has the shade. The
runner knows where he is going, he can watch the movements of the fielder,
and his arms have the edge over the legs in reaching for the bag."

Comiskey was the Brown Stockings' main attraction when in 1882 a local
entrepreneur by the name of Christian Frederick "Chris" Von der Ahe bought
the team and returned it to professional status.

Von der Ahe was born in 1851 in the farming community of Hille, Germany. He came to America at the age of sixteen when tough economic conditions and the likelihood of his being drafted into the Prussian Army prompted
him to emigrate.

In the early 1870s, Von der Ahe opened a bar and meat market at the
corner of Vandeventer and Grand avenues. His beer and knockwurst became
popular items among the many German immigrants living in the area, and
with his profits he began acquiring property after property along the two blocks
stretching from Grand Avenue to Vandeventer to St. Louis avenues. On the
property, he built rooming houses, units he rented to immigrant German labor-
ers. In 1874 he opened a grocery store and the Golden Lion Saloon on the
corner of St. Louis and Grand avenues, close to the ballpark where the
Browns played.

Von der Ahe knew nothing about baseball, and when he first opened the
Golden Lion he was mystified why in the afternoon his bar would fill with
customers and then suddenly empty. An hour or two later it would fill again.
He discovered the reason before that first year was over: His customers were
attending the nearby Browns baseball games. Von der Ahe's Golden Lion
Saloon became a popular meeting place for the St. Louis drinking and sporting
fraternity. Political careers would be launched there. The love of baseball was
was what most of his customers had in common.

At first Von der Ahe didn't pay any attention to the game itself, even
though many of his customers were baseball fans. In 1881 Browns manager

Ned Cuthbert, a regular customer who later became one of Von der Ahe's bartenders, began explaining the beauty and complexity of the game to Von der Ahe. Cuthbert knew of which he spoke. He had been one of the nation's early professionals, starting in left field for the Chicago White Stockings in 1874 and the next year playing in St. Louis with the Brown Stockings. By the 1880s, he had retired as a player, but was well respected as the Browns' manager. Though a knee injury had cut short Cuthbert's career, whenever the Browns found themselves a man short, he would still write himself into the lineup and play.

CHRIS VON DER AHE: "It was Eddie [Cuthbert] who talked me into baseball. That was in 1881. He picked me out, and for months he talked league baseball, until he convinced me that there was something in it."

In addition to learning something about the game, Von der Ahe also came to understand how integral the Browns were to his bar business. During one of their conversations, Cuthbert said to him, "Why don't you bring your beer to them?"

Von der Ahe loved the idea, but he discovered that the management of the St. Louis Sportsman's Park and Club Association was on the side of the burgeoning temperance movement. Al and William Spink, who ran the association, would not allow beer to be sold at the ballpark.

There was only one way out of his dilemma: In 1881 the twenty-nine-year-old Von der Ahe leased the Grand Avenue ballpark from Gus Solari and bought the Browns from the St. Louis Sportman's Park and Club Association. He paid $1,800 for 180 of the 200 shares issued by the club. Von der Ahe later would buy the other 20 shares from the Spink brothers.

Von der Ahe was a quick study and a man of vision. He realized that ballpark fans were a captive and willing audience. In addition to hiring beer vendors who sold tall steins of cold beer to customers in the stands, Von der Ahe converted a two-story home he owned behind right field into a beer garden where fans could sit and drink beer while watching the game. Before long, Von der Ahe could estimate the size of the crowd by the amount of beer he sold there.

AL SPINK: "It was a turning point in the history of sport. Thereafter, beer would provide bucketsful of money for virtually every professional team in the land and for hundreds of colleges as well."

Beer had been popular in America since the Pilgrims landed at Plymouth Rock in 1620. George Washington had a brew house at Mount Vernon. Sam Adams was the son of a prosperous brewer. Francis Scott Key wrote "The Star-Spangled Banner" over a few brews at the Fountain Inn in Baltimore. The melody of Key's anthem even came from an English drinking song, "To Anacreon in Heaven." In 1816 Thomas Jefferson wrote of beer: "I wish to see this beverage become common." By 1821, Jefferson's beer was well known in Virginia.

CHRIS VON DER AHE
(Courtesy Brace Photo)

The beer industry thrived with the influx of hundreds of thousands of German immigrants beginning in 1849. Germans flocked to cities like St. Louis, Cincinnati, and Louisville, and beer consumption grew proportionally.

Some of the biggest breweries in America got their start in St. Louis. In 1859 Adolphus Busch teamed with Eberhard Anheuser to start a brewery, and as American beer drinkers began to show their preference for German beer over the English ale or stout, by end of the 1870s Anheuser-Busch would become one of the top breweries in the Midwest, and before long, in the country.

In the 1870s beer gardens, like Von der Ahe's, began to flourish in St. Louis. One of the finest in town was Schaider's Garden, opened by brewer Joseph Schaider. It featured a bandstand for an oompah band and Strauss waltzes.

By the 1890s, St. Louis breweries were second only to New York in beer sales. In addition to Anheuser-Busch, the firm of Wm. J. Lemp sold beer throughout the Midwest and South. A St. Louis brewery known as the English Cave became popular. (The beer was kept in a cave to keep it cool.) Other St. Louis breweries opened, including the City Brewery, Metcalfe & Son, and the Fulton Brewery. Von der Ahe's establishment was one of the most popular in town because of its clientele: Every night the Browns players would sit and drink in his saloon with the fans.

Along with the rise in beer sales came a surge in the work of the temperance movement. The Anti-Saloon League had no political affiliation. It was the work of religious leaders, mostly from the Baptist and Methodist churches. The founder of the Anti-Saloon League, the Reverend Howard Hyde Russell, considered his leadership to be divinely inspired. Said another leader, the Reverend Purley A. Baker, "It is the federated church in action against the saloon. It has come to solve the liquor problem."

The issue was like the abortion issue today. There was no debate. Each side believed it was right and would brook no argument or compromise.

The debate over the sale of beer in baseball parks was what allowed the St. Louis Browns to become a professional ballclub.

Al Spalding of Chicago, owner of the White Stockings and the reigning czar of the National League, had ruled with a moralistic, tyrannical hand since its inception in 1876. Spalding set the rules, and one of the rules he set was that team owners could not sell beer in their ballparks. The Chicago owner hated alcoholism and made his players pledge not to drink. In addition to the edict against teams selling beer at the park, Spalding also decreed that no gambling be allowed on the premises and that no games could be played on Sundays, in deference to Protestant religious doctrine that the day be preserved as one of rest.

Spalding had the power to eject from the league teams that did not adhere to his rules, and he did so when he saw fit. Before the 1881 season Spalding tossed four teams out of the National League: two for selling beer and two for refusing to finish out the schedule.

Von der Ahe's timing in buying the Brown Stockings was exquisite. Since its withdrawal from the National League in 1877, the team had played on a sporadic, catch-as-catch-can basis against other amateur and semipro nines. What Von der Ahe badly needed was a professional league in which to play, and it was not long after he purchased the team that representatives of two of the four clubs jettisoned by Spalding and the six-year-old National League invited Von der Ahe and his Brown Stockings to join a new league, called the American Association, for the 1882 season.

The new league had been imagined by twenty-eight-year-old Horace Phillips, who had been the manager of the Philadelphia team when Spalding summarily tossed his team out of the league at the end of the 1880 season after the financially strapped Phillips refused to make the final road trip of the year in an effort to cut expenses.

That September Phillips sent postcards to a dozen representatives of professional and semipro teams asking them to attend a meeting in Philadelphia for the purpose of starting a new league. The only invitee to appear was Oliver Perry "O. P." Caylor, a newspaperman who sought a franchise in the new league for the Cincinnati team. The Red Stockings had been tossed from the

National League by Al Spalding because the team owners insisted on selling
beer at the ballpark.

Phillips and Caylor agreed to pursue the notion of a new league, knowing
that once they were taken seriously, other team owners who were chafing at
Spalding's iron grip would join them.

The morning after his initial meeting with Phillips, Caylor sent follow-up
telegrams to Phillips's list of independent team owners, including Chris Von
der Ahe in St. Louis. Each telegram said that the recipient had been the only
one not to attend the initial meeting and requested he attend the next one.

The ruse succeeded. By the late fall of 1881, four team owners including
Von der Ahe joined with Phillips and Caylor to form the new American
Association. On November 2, the league held its first formal meeting in Cincin-
nati, awarding franchises to Cincinnati, Pittsburgh, Louisville, Philadelphia,
Buffalo, Baltimore, and to Von der Ahe's St. Louis Browns.

Three of the teams, St. Louis, Louisville, and Cincinnati, were backed by
beer money, so one of the league's first edicts was to announce that brews
could be sold to spectators. Predictably, Spalding derided the policy by predicting hooliganism by drunken fans. For the German and Irish immigrants,
though, the announcement was met with rousing approval.

The rift between the National League and the American Association mir-
rored the split between the English temperance groups and those of German
and Irish ancestry. Al Spalding was a puritanical purist who believed that the
baseball game should be the primary attraction at the ballpark. Men like Von
der Ahe believed in the very modern notion of doing commerce through baseball. The St. Louis owner saw that baseball was as much a spectacle as it was
a game. Before the game the walrus-mustached Von der Ahe, flanked on either
side by fawn-colored greyhounds, would don a top hat and frock coat and
would lead his players, dressed in silk, in a parade into the ballpark. Von der
Ahe held horse races and fireworks in his park, built lawn bowling lanes on
the grounds, and provided an atmosphere of fun and merriment. The Browns
were part of an amusement park atmosphere. Moreover, Von der Ahe believed
that if the baseball fan was enjoying himself, he would buy a lot of beer.

Spalding understood Von der Ahe's motives.

AL SPALDING: "Mr. Von der Ahe was proprietor of a pleasure resort in the
suburbs of [St. Louis], and he came to be interested in Base Ball from the
fact that games constituted one among other attractions to his place."

But Von der Ahe didn't care at all what Spalding or the temperance lobby
thought. He was a businessman above anything else, and since this was
America, no one was going to stop him from selling his beer.

For the 80-game 1882 season, Von der Ahe hired his bartender, Ned
Cuthbert, to manage the Browns. Cuthbert led the team to a fifth-place finish
in the six-team American Association.

At the end of the season, the Browns' star first baseman, Charlie Comiskey,
persuaded Von der Ahe that his old pal Ted Sullivan could do a better job
running the team than Von der Ahe's bartender. Von der Ahe fired Cuthbert

and sent Sullivan, one of the shrewdest baseball men in the country at the time, to recruit players.

The Browns featured pitcher George "Jumbo" McGinnis, a St. Louis prospect who would win 25, 28, and 24 games the next three years, but to be successful, a team needed three pitchers on its roster. In those days, pitchers completed what they started. Rarely were they relieved. Sullivan signed pitcher Tony Mullane from Louisville, former Buffalo left fielder Tom Dolan, catcher Pat Deasley from Boston, right fielder Hugh Nicol, who had just been released by Chicago, and a young infielder, Arlie Latham, who had played with Buffalo in 1880.

The St. Louis Browns were pennant contenders from the start of the 1883 season. Mullane (35 wins) and McGinnis (28 wins) were two of the better pitchers in the league, and the Browns came within one game of winning the pennant.

If Von der Ahe had left Sullivan and his players alone, it is probable the team would have won the pennant. But from the beginning, Von der Ahe was a distraction. When he first bought the Browns, he made a public announcement that he would not interfere with management (almost 100 years later, another Prussian type, George Steinbrenner, would make the same unkept promise upon his purchase of the New York Yankees). Von der Ahe was an egoist who saw himself as the leader of any enterprise in which he was involved. He dressed like a European nobleman, sporting a flamboyant vest, gleaming top hat, and brilliant shoes. He had a broad-beamed face, in the middle of which protruded a "broad, purpling, mottled, and bulbous" nose. On his lower lip he wore tiny whiskers, "like something he had missed while shaving."

Von der Ahe was so visible that, when writing about the Browns, reporters would refer to him as "der boss president." He was the sort of person who believed he knew far more about the game than he actually did, and reporters enjoyed writing about his ignorance. One time after the Browns won a game when a player hit a ball to right field, he instructed his players to "hit all balls to right field." He insisted he had "the biggest diamond in the world." When someone explained to him that all ball fields were the same size, Von der Ahe said, "Well, I got the biggest infield, anyways."

Von der Ahe saw himself as the brains behind the baseball team to the extent that he built a life-sized statue of himself to make sure that posterity had a chance to savor the living presence of "the greatest feller in baseball." In a public display designed to demonstrate the financial health of his ballclub, he had a daily routine of pouring the cash receipts into a wheelbarrow, and, flanked by security guards with rifles as spectators looked on in admiration, he would personally parade the pile of coins and bills to a nearby bank.

Like many major league team owners who came after him, Von der Ahe was deluded into believing that because he was smart in business, he was equally sharp when it came to baseball. Constitutionally incapable of delegating authority, Von der Ahe constantly made strongly worded "suggestions" to his managers throughout the season. He second-guessed his players and fined them for their failure to perform. Manager Ted Sullivan, who knew the baseball season was grueling and that players had their good games and bad, did what he could to support and protect his boys, but Von der Ahe was the owner, and if Von der Ahe wanted to fine a player, all Sullivan could do was cajole and plead against such action.

Browns players had to put up with Von der Ahe's controlling nature. Any player who signed with the Browns had to live in one of Von der Ahe's rooming houses. This particularly irked third baseman Arlie Latham, who constantly chafed at Von der Ahe's edicts. Latham was a talented comic, and one time he bought a fake nose resembling Von der Ahe's and bought a derby like the owner wore. As the band marched single-file from the train depot to the hotel, Von der Ahe at the head, Latham behind him mimicked the owner, bringing laughter from the crowd. Von der Ahe asked Charlie Comiskey, "Vy do dey laugh at us? Ve lick der stuffings out of dem every time in baseball."

Latham also chafed at Von der Ahe's demand that his players drink only at his bar. His stated reason for the rule was so he could keep an eye on his players' drinking habits. But while Von der Ahe's players couldn't escape him when they were inside his ballpark, they could outside it. To get some privacy, Latham and some of his teammates would sneak into Schmidt's Saloon across the street to drink while Von der Ahe was checking local hangouts in the area, trying to find them. They would sit at the bar watching out the window for him. Von der Ahe, who did everything with flair, liked to walk accompanied by his prized hunting dogs, and when the players saw the dogs, they would escape out the back door of the saloon.

The players resented Von der Ahe's desire to control them, and Sullivan was forced to spend almost as much time trying to mediate between his owner and his players as he did handling his baseball duties. Before the end of the 1883 season, Sullivan quit in disgust.

The loss of Sullivan hurt the team badly, and in 1884 it finished fourth to the New York Giants, led by its star pitcher, Tim Keefe. Jimmy Williams was no better able to handle Von der Ahe's outbursts than Sullivan was, and he too resigned rather than put up with the interference of his flash-tempered, infuriating owner.

At the end of the 1884 season, Von der Ahe turned next to the twenty-five-year-old Charlie Comiskey, who had taken over for Sullivan at the end of the 1883 season, finishing 12-6. Comiskey had the skill, toughness, and smarts to fashion the St. Louis Browns into one of the greatest teams in the history of nineteenth-century baseball. He assembled a championship unit and managed it to four straight pennants and one world championship, while at the same time keeping Von der Ahe under control.

Al Spalding's comment that the only reason Von der Ahe bought the ballclub was to sell beer turned out to be a cheap shot. Von der Ahe grew to love baseball deeply, and in the winter of 1884 Von der Ahe, notorious for his pinchpenny ways, opened his pocketbook in his zeal to bring St. Louis a pennant in '85. He spent money to decorate his office in a baseball motif, covering the walls with "pictures of the diamond's heroes in striking and catching attitudes." During that same winter, Chris Von der Ahe paid the freight as Charlie Comiskey signed the costliest ball team in the country. He paid the fourteen players under contract a total of $32,000.

The Browns could not have succeeded without Comiskey, but Comiskey needed Von der Ahe too. They had a stormy partnership, but they never lost their respect for each other. That mutual affection, moreover, lasted long after their association on the Browns. As a result of Von der Ahe's money and Comiskey's Midas touch, for four magical years the St. Louis Browns became the envy of sporting America, and almost overnight Chris Von der Ahe became one of the best-known and most powerful baseball magnates in the country.

CHAPTER 3

CHARLIE COMISKEY'S HOODLUMS

CHARLIE Comiskey, the manager and first baseman for the St. Louis Brown Stockings, was a mild-mannered, cerebral man off the field, but on the field, he could act like a common thug. He played the game with a controlled aggression designed to ground the opposition into dust. His focus was on victory, and he never permitted anyone to lose sight of the fact that he was there for one reason only: to win. Said Comiskey: "First place is the only subject of conversation."

Comiskey would bait umpires and argue every call that went the other way. He fought as hard as he could on every play and expected his players to act the same way. He was indomitable. Comiskey explained his philosophy about fighting for victory years later: "I have fought every point because, through bitter experience, I learned early that one lost decision sometimes may mean the loss of the pennant. It is the small things in life which count; it is the inconsequential leak which empties the biggest reservoir."

Comiskey encouraged his players to try to intimidate the opposition any way they could. He was a nineteenth-century role model for Leo Durocher and Billy Martin. He encouraged his players to knock over an opponent in the field or on the base paths, and if you didn't like it, that was just too bad. On the base paths, Comiskey was a terror. In one game against Cincinnati, Comiskey threw himself into second baseman John "Bid" McPhee, causing him to throw wild to first, enabling the winning run to score. Ty Cobb, who came to the game twenty years later with a similar nasty disposition, had nothing on Comiskey.

His players followed his example. The next day Curt Welch did the same thing, throwing himself at McPhee "as if hurled from a catapult." Said Welch, "Well, we're playing ball to win."

On defense Comiskey would stand in the path of base runners who were rounding first and heading for second. If the base runner wasn't looking, a hip check would send him sprawling into the dirt. If the opposing player rose to object, Comiskey looked to start a fight. Under Comiskey, the Browns quickly gained a reputation around the league for their "bad boy" attitude. In the press, they were referred to as "demons" and "Von der Ahe's hoodlums."

The Browns' Curt Welch, illiterate and vulgar, was an umpire baiter who was especially despised by opponents for deliberately trying to injure them. In June of 1887, the Philadelphia A's pressed formal charges against Welch for trying to injure pitcher Gus Weyhing as the pitcher ran the bases. Six days later in Baltimore, Welch caused a riot when he smashed into second baseman Bill Greenwood on a steal attempt. Welch was arrested and Von der Ahe had to pay $200 to post bond.

Charlie Comiskey's hard-nosed, trash-talking teammates followed his lead. The mouthpiece of the Browns was third baseman Arlie Latham. Before Latham, players didn't talk it up. There was no "Hey, batter, batter," no encouragement shouted by teammates to the pitcher or batter, certainly none of the endless bench jockeying that became Latham's trademark. The chatter on Little League diamonds across America is the direct descendant of Latham's philosophy of making as much noise for as long as possible.

Latham was an irritant to the opposition. Nicknamed "the Freshest Man on Earth," Latham also was the most popular Brown. He had started playing ball in Stoneham, Massachusetts, at the age of fifteen, played for Buffalo in 1880, and joined the Browns in 1883. Latham was one of the finest fielders in the history of the game, ranking sixth all-time in total chances and eighth in assists. He was acrobatic in the field and on the base paths. Once in a game against Chicago, Latham bunted the ball down the first base line. Adrian "Cap" Anson fielded the ball and turned to tag the batter running up the line, but Latham jumped over the top of the stooped Anson, landed on his hands, did a somersault, landed back on his feet, and ran across the bag. While the crowd hooted, Latham asked, "How do, Anse?"

But it was Latham's mouth that made him famous and drove the opposition wild. He would begin chattering on the first pitch and continue his running commentary on the opposition's sins and weaknesses until they wanted to skull him with their baseball bats. His bench jockeying was so inflammatory that it invited commentary in rival newspapers.

During the 1886 World Series, the writer for the *Chicago Inter-Ocean* wrote the following: "One feature of the St. Louis game might be eliminated with success, and that is the disgusting mouthings of the clown Latham. There was a universal sentiment of disgust expressed by the [Chicago] crowd that left the ball park at the end of the game at this hoodlum's obscene talk on the ball field. One well-known merchant remarked that he never would attend another game that Latham played in. The roughest element that ever attends a ball game in this city could not condone the offense of such a player as Latham. Pres. Spalding should insist upon his being silenced, such coarse mouthings may pass in St. Louis, but will not be tolerated in Chicago."

Shortstop Bill Gleason was another St. Louis ballplayer who bullied the opposition. In the field, Gleason intimidated opposing players by deliberately slamming his knee or hip into base runners as they advanced from second to third. As base coaches, Gleason and Comiskey were reviled for their "offensive coaching" and use of "vile language." The two in tandem so infuriated opponents with their obscenities that team owners called for the pair to be fined

ARLIE LATHAM
(Courtesy Brace Photo)

and/or suspended. At the end of the 1886 season, the American Association passed a rule to establish coaching boxes in an effort to contain Gleason and Comiskey. The coaching boxes became an institution in the game, and they still exist today.

JAMES HART (manager of Louisville in 1885): "The chalk lines which enclose the coaching boxes were added to the field diagram after Charles Comiskey had demonstrated their necessity. Comiskey and Bill Gleason used to plant themselves on each side of the visiting catcher and comment on his breeding, personal habits, skill as a receiver, or rather lack of it, until the unlucky backstop was unable to tell whether one or half a dozen balls were coming his way. Not infrequently the umpire came in for a few remarks.

" 'He's a sweet bird, isn't he, Bill?' Comiskey would chirp.

" 'Never heard of him before, did you, Commy?' would be the direct reply of Gleason.

" 'The cat must have brought him in and put him in the keeping of the umpire or else how could he last more than an inning?' and so to the end of the chapter.

"This solicitous attention did not add to the efficiency of the backstop, so for the sake of not unduly increasing the population of the insane asylums or encouraging justifiable homicide, the coacher's box was invented. This helped out the catcher, but the pitcher and other players on the opposing team were still at the mercy of Comiskey, and I know of no man who had a sharper tongue, who was in command of more biting sarcasm, or who was quicker at repartee.''

Comiskey not only intimidated the opposition, he was also able to use his leadership skills to keep the excesses of owner Chris Von der Ahe in check. But Comiskey, unlike the other managers the owner had second-guessed or the players he had fined, didn't see his owner as a foe, both because he genuinely liked him and also because he knew exactly how to handle him.

G. W. AXELSON (Comiskey's biographer): ''The genius and diplomacy of his manager, and [his] facility of acquiescing in everything that Von der Ahe suggested and then doing the opposite, had the tendency to blunt the barbed shafts directed against 'der boss president.' ''

Comiskey's rough side hid his greatest strengths as a manager: an ability to motivate his players and an intellectual brilliance that allowed him to habitually outthink and outmaneuver the opposition. Comiskey had his rules, but he was not a martinet. His players, aware of his toughness, respected and rarely crossed him.

BILL GLEASON: ''There was always good discipline among the Browns, but occasionally some of the boys would take advantage of the manager. Comiskey was particular about the boys being in bed early, but occasionally they played hookey. [Yank] Robinson, for instance, would ostentiously take his key from the rack and retire only to slide down the fire escape. It was a lively bunch with which 'Commy' had to contend, but they all liked him and loved him as a brother, as he was on the square with everybody.''

Once a game ended, Comiskey would immediately turn his attention to the next contest. He was a perfectionist.

G. W. AXELSON: ''He held himself responsible for the smallest detail, off and on the field.''

Comiskey spent a great deal of time and thought analyzing the strengths and weaknesses of the opposing players.

BILL GLEASON: ''He never went to sleep at night until he had figured out how he was going to win the game the next day.''

At the heart of Comiskey's analytical skills was his remarkable memory. He needed only to meet someone once to remember his name.

G. W. Axelson: "His marvelous memory stood him in good stead. Once heard, a thing was never forgotten. . . . I have yet to meet a human being with the retentive memory of Comiskey. Repeated demonstrations of that faculty have been to me a constant source of wonderment for many years."

This ability allowed him to recall every incident he ever saw on the ball field, going back to his early days in baseball. If he spotted a weak point in an opposing player, he never forgot it.

G. W. Axelson related one example in which Comiskey—who from his position at first base told his pitchers where to aim their pitches—ordered pitcher Bob Caruthers to throw three straight high and inside fastballs to a batter the wily hurler had never seen before.

G. W. Axelson: "A new opponent planted himself at the plate, backed by a big bat and a reputation as a slugger. A signal from first base to the pitcher, and the newcomer whiffed on three high ones close to the breast bone.

" 'How did you know what he was weak on, Commy?' the puzzled Caruthers asked.

" 'Why, didn't I see him put a ball over the fence on a low one on the outside a few years ago up around Galena? I figured he didn't like the insiders.' "

And it was Comiskey who pioneered playing first base the modern way. Until he came along, first basemen stayed close to the base. Comiskey positioned himself instead deep behind the bag and roamed wide and far for balls hit to the right side, with the pitcher covering first to take his throw. Under this system, the second baseman could play deeper and closer to second base, allowing him to get to more balls hit up the middle. He also taught the outfielders to shift, depending on where the batter was likely to hit the ball. On balls hit to the outfield, Comiskey was the first to order the pitcher to back up the base that was most likely to receive the throw.

Commented Hall of Fame second baseman Johnny Evers, "Comiskey won pennants at St. Louis by his inventiveness, and it is a remarkable thing that every team he ever has handled has had great-fielding pitchers."

In addition to his managerial abilities, Comiskey also had the ability to judge talent. After he realized that the 1884 Browns were not skillful enough to be pennant contenders, he made moves during the winter to bolster the team. He added players to the roster until he had a combination that suited his style of play. He signed Bob Caruthers and Dave Foutz to pitch, Albert "Doc" Bushong (he was called "Doc" because he was a dentist) to catch, had an infield of himself at first, Sam Barkley at second, Bill Gleason at short, and Arlie Latham at third. His outfield was composed of slugger James "Tip" O'Neill in left, the speedy Curt Welch in center, and Hugh Nicol in right. This became the regular lineup of the Browns in 1885. Joseph "Yank" Robinson, who subbed that year mostly in the outfield, but also at second, short, and behind the plate, was a top-notch performer wherever he played.

The 1885 Browns quickly ran away from the competition. In the May 2, 1885, issue of the *St. Louis Critic,* a local sports newspaper that was published during only that one year, the unnamed commentator correctly predicted that the Browns would be the class of the American Association. The *Critic* reporter, an opionated sort, didn't mince words. He was a keen observer and an entertaining writer who 100 years later would have been comfortable writing in *Sports Illustrated* or spouting on ESPN. It's interesting to note that after all these years how little sports commentary has changed.

ST. LOUIS CRITIC: "In discussing the chances of the Browns for first place, an argument is sometimes raised concerning a supposed weakness behind the bat—a weakness, by the way, which is purely imaginery. Anyone who is at all posted on the game should be aware that in Bushong the Browns have one of the best catchers in the country, and a man who, for general steadiness of play, reliability and endurance, it is hard to improve upon. Bushong has, so far, done more work behind the bat this season than any other man in the Association, and done it finely, and there is but one thing to fear on his account, viz., that he will be broken down by having too much work put upon him.

"In the matter of pitchers, St. Louis is also in much better condition than ever before. In [Dave] Foutz she has a pitcher who practically stands at the top of the Association record, ranking, technically, second, with 23 games pitched and a percentage of .964, while his batting has improved. [Bob] Caruthers is also pitching a very fine game this season, and shows material improvement, and his conscientious work and careful play have already been instrumental in scoring several winning games for the Browns. Last year Caruthers's record stood eleventh, immediately following [Tim] O'Keefe and [Tony] Mullane, with a percentage of .910, and the end of the present season will see his claim of front rank firmly established. George McGinnis is also a good twirler, though not up to the Foutz standard. McGinnis, by the way, has not shown his best form this season.

"At the willow none of the Browns are weak, while O'Neill, who did well last season, is developing into a veritable slugger, rifle-shot balls and would-be scarers failing to unnerve him. He rarely fails to make a count, and always slashes at the ball in that vicious way which prepares the audience for an over-the-fence. Both [Arlie] Latham and little [Hugh] Nicol are hammering the ball well, though the latter has been somewhat unfortunate in choosing directions, while Foutz has improved considerably, besides running better. Comiskey is doing well at the bat.

"In cunning and base stealing, the boys are great, and can down all the Association clubs, while their fielding is excellent. Comiskey's record at first base is one of the best in the country, while his captaining counts for a good deal. [Sam] Barkley makes an excellent second baseman, and [Arlie] Latham's play at third could be made equal to any in the Association. Last year he ranked seventh out of twenty-six, being practically fifth, and this year he will stand still higher, if he will but give up his fanciful touches of spring-healed agility, to the display of which his muffs are generally attributed. Billy Gleason's shortstop play is equal to any in the Association, while a fly to O'Neill at left, to Welch at center, or to Nicol at right field, is just as good as a putout.

"St. Louis never had as strong a steam in the Association as she has today, and the odds are heavily in favor of the Browns bringing home the championship pennant when they return in the fall."

The Browns started the 1885 season well, but not spectacularly. After moving into first place, however, they became almost invincible. They would win twenty games in a row to finish the season in first place with a 79-33 record and a sixteen-game margin.

Like most top teams, the strength was its pitching staff and defense. Bob Caruthers, who finished the year 40-13 with a 2.07 ERA, was the son of a prominent Memphis lawyer who had moved his family to Chicago in the late 1870s. Caruthers had been sickly through childhood and played baseball against his parents' wishes. When he signed to become a pro, they were aghast. But at age twenty-two he had become a national hero, leading the American Association in pitching percentage and proving himself one of the star pitchers in the league.

The Browns' other pitcher, Dave Foutz, left home as a teenager to pan for gold in Colorado. In 1884 he joined the Browns and would go on to compile a record of 114-48 with the Browns from 1884 to 1887, a record that compares favorably with Caruthers's over the same period: 106-38. Quite a one-two punch.

St. Louis Critic: "[Dave Foutz is] tall, slim, good-natured, and a somewhat bashful young fellow, 24, six feet two inches in height, and weighing 160 pounds, is a brunette and shaves smooth. His first play was with Leadville in 1882, pitching 82 games and losing only one of them. In 1883 he pitched for the Bay Citys, joining the Browns last season when that club went under. Foutz also pitched a fourteen-inning game in Cincinnati and two in Louisville, 14 and 10 respectively.

"Foutz has the longest legs pertaining to any member of the Browns, and gets over the ground slowest. A general impression is abroad that when Foutz is at third it takes a two-base hit to bring him home. Bushong takes second place for slow base running."

On defense the infield of Comiskey, Barkley, Gleason, and Latham were almost as nimble and proficient as the Steinfeldt, Tinker, Evers, and Chance infield twenty years later. In center field Curt Welch was a star player who performed in the style of Tris Speaker, playing shallow, robbing many batters with circus catches of Texas Leaguers. He perfected the play where he'd turn his back to the ball, run to the spot where he figured it would land, and then catch it. Welch had a strong arm, and he threw out many base runners who foolishly tested him.

Welch was a smart hitter who walked a lot. He knew how to get hit by the pitch, and on the base paths he was one of the best of his time, aggressive like Comiskey and Latham.

Years later Charlie Comiskey evaluated his team.

*   *   *

CHARLIE COMISKEY: "I would not be on the level did I not confess that I always have believed that the old Browns were a great team, one of the greatest ever organized.

"The human element alone should figure and taking this into consideration I do not have to apologize for the old Browns. They were composed of the greatest bunch of fighters which were ever brought together, and as for gameness they were surpassed by none. It might be mentioned that our real lineup during the most successful seasons was boiled down to ten or eleven men. Minor hurts never were taken into consideration and it would have to be broken bones to keep anyone out. As everybody on the team wanted to be in the game every day, I had to use some diplomacy in getting the extra man or two to stick to the bench now and then. The pitcher who hurled an extra-inning game one day would feel aggrieved if he did not get a chance to repeat or to play in the outfield the following day.

"Such was the spirit of the men and in that lay the secret of the four championships. I would not seem to underrate the technical skill of such men as Gleason, Welch, Foutz, Caruthers, Bushong, Nicol, Hudson, Latham, O'Neill, Robinson, and others of those who were with me. They were wonderful players, and trained under modern conditions would shine on the field. There was not a slow thinker in the lot, in fact it took some speed to keep up with the bunch in this department.

"The team from 1884 to the close of 1887 had everything it needed. It had speed on the bases and in the field; it had enough sluggers to balance artistic fielding and before it was broken up its teamwork was second to none in the United States. It was not overburdened with signals, as every member was expected to know just what to do in an emergency. The team at the start of the Association played a different style of game from most others. I have been given a certain amount of credit for this, but regardless of that the team never was tied down by precedent. It constantly blasted its way along new roads and thus we got credit for being original."

Beginning in 1885, these Browns would win the American Association championship four exciting seasons in a row.

CHAPTER 4

A DISPUTED CHAMPIONSHIP

IN 1885 Chester A. Arthur was President, and St. Louis had grown such that it had become the greatest manufacturer of chewing tobacco in the world and was second only to Chicago as a railroad center, a rivalry that carried over into the national pastime.

The 1885 World Series was a curiosity, a traveling circus played between the St. Louis Browns, the champions of the American Association, and the Chicago White Stockings, winners in the National League, with games in St. Louis and Chicago, and also in Pittsburgh and Cincinnati.

The competition between leagues had begun in 1882 with two exhibition games between the Chicago White Stockings and the Cincinnati Red Stockings at the Bank Street Grounds in Cincinnati. The teams traded shutouts. In 1883 the American Association champion Philadelphia A's were to meet the National League's Boston Beaneaters, but after Philadelphia lost seven of eight exhibitions, it abruptly canceled any series plans. In 1884 Jim Mutrie, the manager of the New York Giants of the American Association, challenged the Providence Grays of the National League to a three-game series. Charles Gardner "Old Hoss" Radbourn won all three games for Providence en route to a Hall of Fame career in which he compiled a 308–191 lifetime record.

The series of 1885 was the first best-of-seven competition set up like today's World Series. Chris Von der Ahe and Chicago owner Al Spalding arranged to play a series of exhibition games, with the winning team to share a $1,000 purse. Each owner put up $500—small change, considering that far more money than that was bet on the outcome by the players of the two teams.

St. Louis pitcher Bob Caruthers waved a roll of bills at Chicago first baseman and captain Cap Anson. "I'll bet you $1,000," he shouted, "that the Browns can easily beat your nine. And I'll put this money up as a forfeit."

Replied Chicago shortstop Edward "Ned" Williamson, "We White Stockings stand ready to cover all bets the Brown Stockings wish to make."

Though it was just a series of exhibitions, pride was at stake, and the players were not friendly. Chicago, under Anson, boasted a lineup with three future Hall of Famers—Anson, outfielder Mike "King" Kelly, and pitcher John Clarkson—and two other potential Hall of Famers, third baseman Ned Williamson and outfielder George Gore. Outfielder Abner Dalrymple, second baseman Fred Pfeffer, shortstop Tom Burns, and catcher Frank "Old Silver" Flint were among the finest players of the period. The White Stockings, like the Browns, were known for their rough tactics and abuse of umpires.

When the match was announced, the National Leaguers strutted their feelings of superiority. Cap Anson, who with his teammates expressed contempt for the Browns and their "beer league," told one reporter he doubted that St. Louis could have finished fifth in the National League.

Though these were exhibition games for small stakes, the Brown Stockings took their cues from Von der Ahe and the always fierce Charlie Comiskey and played as though these were the most important games of the season. Anson, the Chicago manager and star, urged his teammates to play the games for blood, but some of his players, including pitcher Jim McCormick and hitting stars George Gore, King Kelly, Ned Williamson, and Abner Dalrymple, were weary of the long season and preferred to go home. They did not consider these games part of the season, weren't impressed with the $70 payoff for winning, and didn't dedicate themselves as much as Anson and Al Spalding would have liked, drinking heavily between games. George Gore was so drunk before the opening game that Anson benched him the next day in favor of youngster Billy Sunday and never put him back into the lineup.

The first game was played at the Congress Street Grounds in Chicago before 2,000 fans. St. Louis scored first on three errors, then Chicago tied the game in the fourth on a King Kelly single and two errors. St. Louis scored four runs on three singles and three more errors to take a 5–1 lead, and it stayed that way until the eighth when Chicago came to bat.

It was getting dark, and St. Louis pitcher Bob Caruthers made the mistake of rushing to complete the inning, walking George Gore. Kelly and Anson then singled to make the score 5–2. With two outs, Caruthers threw Fred Pfeffer a pitch that the Chicago infielder hit over the left field fence to tie the game.

At the end of the inning, the umpire called the game on account of darkness.

Both teams took the train to St. Louis, where the series continued before 3,000 fans in Sportsman's Park. In Game 2 the Browns led, 4–2, going into the top of the sixth and final inning. The crowd already was upset with umpire Dave Sullivan for making several calls against the home team.

Billy Sunday, the light-hitting outfielder playing in the place of benched center fielder George Gore, started off the sixth with a double, then went to third on a wild pitch. When King Kelly grounded to Bill Gleason at short, umpire Sullivan looked home to see whether Sunday would score. When Gleason instead threw to first, not home, the umpire had to guess, and he wrongly called Kelly safe at first.

Comiskey and other St. Louis players began ranting. Comiskey told Sullivan that if he did not change his call, he would take his team off the field. After fifteen minutes, Sullivan held firm, threatening Comiskey with a forfeit. Finally the Browns returned to their positions.

With the score 4–3 in favor of the Browns, slugging first baseman Cap Anson came to the plate. Kelly immediately stole second, then Anson singled to knock in the tying run. After a force play at second, Fred Pfeffer stole second and went to third on a passed ball.

Chicago scored the winning run on another controversial call. Williamson grounded a ball into foul territory behind first base, but it began spinning, and by the time it was fielded, it was in fair territory. Williamson ran hard all the way and beat Comiskey's throw to Sam Barkley at second. Sullivan called him safe as Pfeffer scored the go-ahead run. Once again the St. Louis players confronted the umpire. When Comiskey told Sullivan he had heard him holler "Foul ball," Sullivan changed his decision and ordered Pfeffer back to third. Now it was Anson and Kelly's turn to charge the beleaguered official.

Fearing them, Sullivan again reversed his decision, and when he did so, 200 angry, rowdy Browns fans coursed onto the field and headed for the umpire. The police raced to intervene, averting a brawl. The Chicago players had to be escorted off the field.

Later that evening umpire Sullivan declared the game a forfeit to Chicago. Comiskey, declaring that ball games should be won on the field and not in hotel rooms, announced he would not abide by the decision.

So far, two games had been played. One had ended in a tie, the other in a forfeit.

*   *   *

The third game, again in St. Louis, was won by the Browns, who refused to allow Sullivan to work again and selected as umpire Harry McCaffery, who created no controversy as Bob Caruthers defeated the White Stockings, 7–4.

Game 4, the final game at Sportsman's Park, was delayed forty-five minutes when Anson, the Chicago captain, decided he didn't want McCaffery to umpire again. To accommodate him, Von der Ahe selected from the grandstands Harry Medart, a rabid St. Louis baseball fan. It was a bad miscalculation on Anson's part, in that Medart decided every close call against Chicago and even called Chicago's runners out when they were clearly safe.

In the fifth inning, with the Browns leading, 1–0, Chicago's Tommy Burns was on third base and pitcher Jim McCormick was on first. Browns catcher Doc Bushong faked a pickoff throw to first, then fired down to third in an attempt to catch Burns, who was standing on the bag. Medart, who probably hadn't seen the play, called Burns out, cutting short what could have been a big inning for the White Stockings.

With the Browns leading by a run in the ninth inning and one out, the umpire again skunked Chicago. Burns grounded to second and reached base on an error. Then McCormick was safe on another error when Comiskey dropped his pop-up. Before throwing the ball back to the pitcher, Comiskey playfully tagged McCormick, who was standing on the base. Incredibly—shockingly—Medart called McCormick out. Anson had to keep McCormick from beating Medart. The mild-mannered Billy Sunday, who would become one of the most famous American evangelists, doubled his fists and called the umpire a liar. King Kelly had to step in to stop Sunday from striking him. When the next batter made out, the game was over. Medart had handed his beloved Browns the crucial victory.

The series next moved to Pittsburgh, where the two teams agreed to hire a professional umpire, John Kelly, one of the best in the game. The rest of the games proceeded smoothly with Kelly in control.

Before a sparse crowd of 500, Chicago's star pitcher, John Clarkson, pitched a four-hitter against the Browns and won easily. In Cincinnati in Game 6, Chicago won again, behind a two-hitter pitched by McCormick.

After five games, St. Louis had 2 wins and Chicago 2 wins. The question: Did the forfeit count? If so, Chicago would be declared the victors.

Anson was so confident he had the better team, the White Stockings' Cap told the press, "We will not even claim the forfeited game. We each have two victories now and the winner of today's game will be the winner of the series." Comiskey, wanting badly to lay claim to the championship, looked forward to playing a sixth game for the world championship.

When the mercurial John Clarkson showed up for the deciding game five minutes late (and in all probability too drunk to pitch), Anson started Jim McCormick, who needed more rest as St. Louis pounded him and won, 13–4. Where Clarkson was and why he was late no one knows. Apparently no reporter bothered to ask him, or else he didn't feel it was anyone's business to know. His tardiness and/or drunkenness, however, cost the White Stockings the championship, and after the game Al Spalding, a man used to victory, expressed his furor over being jobbed by the poor officiating, Harry Medart especially.

Spalding raved, "Does anyone suppose that if there had been so much as that at stake that I should have consented to the games being played in American Association cities, upon their grounds, and under the authority of their umpires?" Unlike Anson, Spalding refused to ignore the forfeit and declared the series a draw.

Though the baseball world regarded St. Louis as world champions, Browns owner Chris Von der Ahe, who privately rejoiced at the team's victory, publicly declared that the forfeit should count and that the series was a tie, thereby cheating his own players out of the $1,000 prize money and getting out of having to pay his share.

CHAPTER 5

HENRY LUCAS'S ILL-FATED MAROONS

HENRY V. Lucas, the brother of J.-B.C. Lucas II, the first president of the Browns, also loved the American game. According to Al Spink, Henry attended every St. Louis Browns game in 1882 and 1883. An amateur player himself, Lucas thought it might be fun to own a professional baseball team.

In 1884 Henry Lucas applied to Al Spalding for a franchise in the National League, but was turned down by Spalding and the other National League executives. At the time, the National League and the American Association functioned as separate but cooperative baseball leagues. The two leagues made an agreement to uphold the reserve rule, which bound a player to the team that signed him year after year. By adhering to this reserve rule, a team owner was pledging not to sign away players from other teams. The two leagues formed what was known as "the Baseball Trust."

When Lucas's application was rejected, he decided that the best way to get back at the National League was to compete against it. He decided to finance not only his own team, but an entire league, the Union Association, which had been founded the year before by H. R. Bennett. (The sporting press, which was under Al Spalding's influence, called it "the Outlaw Union Association.")

As one of the richest men in St. Louis, Lucas certainly had the means. Like older brother J.-B.C. II, he had inherited more than $1.5 million from his father's estate. He owned a successful barge line that carried freight up and down the Mississippi River. When he married Mies Louise Espenschled, youngest daughter of a wealthy wagon manufacturer, he was considered the Beau Brummel of St. Louis.

When Lucas first came up with the idea of the new league, it was with an eye toward setting it up in a way that would benefit the players most. During the two years in which he got to know the Browns players, what struck him most was the constant harping that they weren't earning the money they deserved for their efforts.

AL SPINK: "He had heard their story that they were being abused and he set out to organize a baseball league that would deliver the players out of bondage."

The players, even back in 1884, felt that the owners made a disproportional amount of money from their labors, and they correctly placed the blame for their situation on the reserve rule, which bound a player to his team in perpetuity. Lucas, who sought to wrest players away from Al Spalding and his National League, called Spalding's reserve clause "an outrageous and unjustifiable chain on the freedom of players."

Lucas figured that if his ballplayers were happy with their salaries and accommodations, they would be more apt to win ball games. With an eye toward Al Spalding and his penury toward the National League players and toward Von der Ahe, who paid well but was constantly fining his players, Lucas's announced goal in starting his league was to revolutionize the way baseball owners treated its players.

He called his team the St. Louis Maroons and stocked it in part by raiding players from the National League by offering these men salaries much higher than the going rate. He lured Charlie Sweeney, the speediest pitcher in baseball, and enticed Fred Dunlap from Cleveland and Charles "Fatty" Briody from Cincinnati.

He outfitted his players in maroon silk stockings and lambs' wool sweaters. The players would march onto the field to the music of a brass band. He built the 10,000-seat Union Park at Jefferson and Cass avenues. The ballpark was called "the Palace Park of America." He also furnished the capital for about half the other Union League teams, with franchises in Cincinnati, Baltimore, Boston, Chicago (which moved to Pittsburgh), Washington, Philadelphia, and Altoona (which moved to Kansas City).

True to his word, Lucas set a salary scale higher than anywhere else in professional baseball. "He treated his players as they had never been treated before," said Al Spink. "They were given carte blanche as to salaries; were allowed to come and go as they pleased and to discipline themselves as they saw fit."

But Henry Lucas discovered that with some players, no matter how hard he tried, it was never good enough. The point was made in an article in the *St. Louis Critic,* a magazine that covered the St. Louis sporting scene in 1885.

ST. LOUIS CRITIC: "There is a class of ball players who are a disgrace to the business, and they are inclined at all times to find fault with the club management for the accommodations with which they are provided while on a trip. The most vigorous kickers are, in nine cases out of nine, the ones that have been accustomed to the commonest kind of fare before they become professionals. For instance, last season several men in a certain club kicked on a three-dollar-a-day hotel and said they would have to have a change, as the food was too greasy for their delicate stomachs. These same men are now, it is safe to say, among the first to grab a plate at some schooner saloon to get a good whack at the free lunch.''

In the same issue, the unnamed author described a train trip that the St. Louis Maroons took from St. Louis to Cincinnati. Henry Lucas had found it impossible to secure lower berths for all his players. One of the players came to him grumbling that he had to sleep in an upper berth. Lucas told him there weren't enough lowers to go around.

"Is zat so?" said the player. "Well, I'm just as good as any one in dis crowd."

"Here, you take my berth. I'd just as soon ride in an upper as a lower."

They made the exchange. According to the *St. Louis Critic,* no player on the team complained about accommodations the rest of the season.

In 1884 the St. Louis Maroons finished first in the Union Association with an astounding 94-19 record. Their second baseman, Fred Dunlap, hit .412 and hit 13 home runs, leading the league in those categories as well as most every fielding category. His fielding was described as "the grandest ever seen at Union Park."

Pitcher Bill "Bollicky" Taylor began the season 25-4 for the Maroons, before he jumped to Philadelphia in the American Association. To replace him, Lucas snaked away Providence's top pitcher, Charlie Sweeney. Sweeney had started the 1884 season with Providence, posting a 17-8 record, but in midseason he got drunk and was expelled from the team for subordination by manager Frank Bancroft. Sweeney jumped to the Maroons, where he compiled a 24-7 record with a 1.83 ERA.

Cincinnati, Milwaukee, and Boston had winning records. Everyone else lost badly. If there was a flaw in Lucas's grand plan, it was that he stocked his Maroons team without regard for whether the other teams would provide any competition. Few teams drew well. By the end of the season, many of the teams had dropped out of the league.

In retrospect, Lucas's one-year experiment may have been only a smoke screen to help him accomplish a primary objective: gain entrance into the National League. At the end of the 1884 season, Lucas met with Al Spalding, et al., of the National League. Lucas made it clear he would carry on his fight indefinitely if they didn't offer him entry into the league. The league moguls had been impressed by the 94-19 record and by Lucas's competitive nature. It was easier and less expensive to include rather than fight him, and so they offered him a franchise if he would agree to disband the Union Association.

Once accepted into the National League, Lucas folded the Union Association immediately. He moved his Maroons to the ballpark at Vaneventer and Natural Bridge and prepared to start the 1885 season as a member of the National League.

The switch in leagues would prove to be Henry V. Lucas's undoing. Lucas was yet another rank amateur who thought he knew enough about the game to manage as well as the pros, and he began the 1885 season as the team's manager, taking over from second base star Fred Dunlap. The Maroons shocked the city of St. Louis when they quickly fell into the cellar and stayed there. The Union Association, it turned out, had been a second-rate league all along. In 1885 the Maroons didn't have a single pitcher capable of taming the other clubs with any consistency. Charlie Sweeney, who had had a drinking problem and a sore arm while with Providence, again suffered from both maladies. He lost his effectiveness and finished the year 11-21. Commented the *St. Louis Critic*: "His present team has been used as a mop frequently."

The Maroons finished the 1885 season with a 35-72 record, far behind Cap Anson's Chicago White Stockings. By September, Lucas realized his deficiencies and quit as manager.

Disaster struck Lucas on July 4, 1885. During the staging of a big fireworks show at the ballpark, a fire broke out, part of the stands burned down, and some of the patrons were injured. He had no insurance. His losses from legal damages won by fans who sued would soon begin to accumulate.

At the same time in 1885, the rival Browns had become a powerhouse. Von der Ahe's team won fifteen in a row en route to a 20-5 start in the American Association as the Browns became the city's darlings. In one season the Maroons went from heroes to zeros. Contributing to the team's financial demise were the National League twin bans on playing ball on Sunday and selling beer at the ballpark. Von der Ahe and the other American Association owners were making a lot of money playing on Sunday and selling beer. The Maroons had become a financial disaster for Lucas.

While the Browns won the American Association in 1885 and would repeat as champions in 1886, the Maroons went into a serious decline in 1886. Managed by Gus Schmelz, the team finished sixth, again far behind Chicago.

One of the highlights of the 1886 season took place on July 3, 4, and 5 at Union Park when Lucas promoted the reenactment of the siege of Vicksburg "as the [Civil War] veterans saw it." Al Spink called it "the grandest and most glorious entertainment in the history of outdoor enterprises." The Busch Zouaves and the Branch Guards appeared. "A fortune's worth of pyrotechnics" were set off. The two games that day drew 12,000 fans, as did the Browns doubleheader at Sportsman's Park. In fact, *The Sporting News* reported that on that day 98,000 fans attended sixteen games at eight sites, disproving "the cranks harping that baseball is dying out."

On the field, the Maroons lost games and began to fight among themselves. One of the low points of the season saw a fistfight between pitcher Charlie Sweeney, abandoned by his fastball, and his catcher, Thomas Dolan, abandoned by his patience.

During a game in which Sweeney was pitching, Dolan taunted his pitcher by calling him "Dead Arm" Sweeney. The next day they collided on a play, and Dolan called him "Dead Arm" again. This time Sweeney responded, calling Dolan "Hamfat." They began duking it out. Dolan suffered a broken hand. Sweeney's eye was bloodied. Lucas released both of them.

Sweeney signed with minor league Syracuse, but his arm never did come around. He never won another game in the big leagues. In 1887, at the age of twenty-four, his career was over. He moved to San Francisco, and in 1894 was accused of killing a man in a saloon. Despite alleging self-defense, Sweeney was sentenced to ten years for manslaughter. He was released shortly before completing his sentence and died of tuberculosis on April 4, 1902, nine days before his thirty-ninth birthday.

The Union Park fire in 1885 was but the first disaster to befall Henry Lucas. Not long afterward, a hurricane-force storm struck the St. Louis area, roiling the Mississippi River and destroying his fleet of barges. He again had no insurance and, in part because of his baseball losses, lacked the means to replace the fleet. The river disaster cost Lucas $250,000, and when the Maroons had another losing year in 1886, he lost another $100,000.

By the summer of 1885, the Maroons were a reported $71,000 in debt, and with his bad team having to compete against the American Association championship Browns for the hearts of St. Louis baseball fans, Lucas held no hope for a turnaround. By August of 1886, the newspapers began circulating rumors: Henry Lucas was either going to sell the Maroons to a Washington group, or sell it to one from Milwaukee in the American Association and have it move to Pittsburgh, or fold. Another rumor had Chris Von der Ahe buying the team and moving it to Pittsburgh. When a writer for *The Sporting News* tried to contact Lucas to find out what he intended to do, the reporter found that Lucas had left town without revealing his plans.

Wrote Spink: "On Monday, Henry V. Lucas, president of the St. Louis League team, left Cullan and Kelly's livery stable on Cass just above Jefferson, on a fishing expedition. He drove a pair of horses hitched to a park wagon with three of his friends. A manservant said they were to be gone ten days.

"Before he left he said the Maroons would travel to Chicago to play. He would not say whether the team would finish out the season."

Within the week, Lucas announced he had sold the team. At the end of the 1886 season, John T. Brush, an Indianapolis merchant, would take over and move the team to the Indiana capital.

With the departure of the Maroons, Henry Lucas's dream of nurturing a new major league had died. Between the fire, the hurricane, and his baseball losses, Lucas had lost most of his money.

"Baseball was the rock on which Lucas's fortunes were wrecked," wrote the *St. Louis Post-Dispatch* years later. "In four years he had lost more than a quarter of a million dollars in an effort to give St. Louis fans a winning ballclub."

After the sale, the well-loved Lucas left baseball for good. His friend Al Spink commented in *The Sporting News* on how much the game would miss him.

AL SPINK: "To his men on and off the field he was always kind and even courteous. . . . It was his disposition that made him welcome wherever he went, and that made friends for him, and that may be the reason that the Maroons and others who know him will regret, and in all sincerity, that they and he have parted company."

During this same time, Henry Lucas's life took a turn for the worse when his wife left him and took their son to New York. From that point on, whatever else Lucas attempted seemed doomed to failure. He tried railroading and started an insurance company, but neither worked for him. He then tried running a coal barge line, a profitable business when steamboats were popular, but as the railroads became the transportation of choice, his profits soon dwindled to nothing.

Henry Lucas built a fancy velodrome and staged national indoor bicycle races by luring the most famous competitors in the country, but that venture too proved a costly disaster. He was said to have lost the remainder of his fortune on bad real estate deals.

Henry V. Lucas, the youngest son, had always been the pet of the family, and he was counting on bequests from older siblings to carry him through his golden years. But when his older siblings died, Henry received no mention in their wills. When brother Joseph Lucas, the master of the 700-acre Goodwill stud farm, died, Henry felt sure he would be left something. Joseph, however, left his entire estate to his wife. Henry sued to set aside his brother's will, but lost, and it was then that he swallowed his pride and went to work as a street inspector for the city of St. Louis at $75 a month. It was a job Henry Lucas performed until three weeks before he died on November 15, 1910, at the age of fifty-three, of heart disease.

Wrote one newspaperman upon his death: "No man started life under more favorable circumstances than the man who ended his earthly existence in such humble circumstances."

CHAPTER 6

THE $15,000 WAGER

THE first issue of *The Sporting News* appeared on the newsstands on March 17, 1886. A one-year subscription initially cost $2.50; a single issue, a nickel. (By May, the former would drop to $2.00.) In addition to covering baseball, the magazine had articles on bicycling and duck shooting. Among the advertisers were the opera house, theaters, and saloons. An ad in the first issue touted Pope's Theater, which featured Kersand's minstrels. The Drum was advertised as "the Most Magnificent Saloon in St. Louis." At Sportsman's Cigars, you could buy "wines, liquors, and cigars." C. L. Webers, "the World's Premium Shoemaker," offered fine shoes at prices ranging from $7.00 to $15.00.

The Sporting News, the brainchild of Alfred Spink, was a pioneer in that it covered professional baseball in more detail than ever before. The paper of May 10, 1886, not only gave the schedule of the upcoming games, along with the league standings, it also printed box scores, which allowed readers to re-create the games in their heads by accounting for every run, hit, putout, assist, and error by each player. Under the line score, you could read who scored the runs, who stole bases, and who hit doubles, triples, and home runs. The final bits of information were the time of the game and the name of the umpire.

The Sporting News did something else. Like the St. Louis Critic, which lasted only through the 1885 season, The Sporting News covered baseball journalistically. The stories and the editorials in The Sporting News were writ-ten by Al Spink, who sought news of the teams and the players not only in St. Louis but around the league, stories you could get only if you hung around the teams.

Spink, for example, covered the machinations of Browns owner Chris Von der Ahe, who, looking to bolster his pitching staff, signed pitcher Tony Mullane toward the end of the 1885 season. That Mullane signed with Von der Ahe was curious because only a year earlier Von der Ahe had lobbied successfully to have Mullane suspended for the entire 1885 season after he had signed with the Browns, and then jumped from team to team to team in four years. (Mul-lane was 35-15 in 1883 with the Browns, then jumped to Toledo, where he starred in 1884.)

Von der Ahe wanted players to honor their contracts, and the league took Von der Ahe's recommendation and suspended Mullane for much of 1885. Now Von der Ahe wanted him for the Browns!

Mullane was expected to be a mainstay of the 1886 staff, but before the season began, he returned Von der Ahe's cash advances and instead pitched for Cincinnati. In an article written in the May 10, 1886, issue of The Sporting News, Al Spink gave his readers the inside scoop on why Mullane didn't pitch for the Browns.

When Von der Ahe purchased Mullane from Toledo, Spink explained, he bought second baseman Sam Barkley from the same club. Both were dating the same girl, and at the time of the sale Mullane promised Barkley he would accompany him to St. Louis, but instead stayed behind in Toledo with the girl, infuriating Barkley.

That winter in New Orleans, Mullane pitched in a game against Barkley, and when the second baseman came to bat, he threw at his head and hit him in the ear. Barkley went after Mullane with his bat held high, but stopped halfway, cursing him. Barkley warned Mullane if he did it again, he would kill him. Von der Ahe got rid of both Mullane and Barkley. Comiskey replaced Barkley at second with Yank Robinson.

In his last paragraph of the article, Spink revealed a personal dislike for Mullane, noting cattily that when the big pitcher was with the Browns, he was the cheapest player in baseball, that he had "worn his $10 suit until the seat of his pants had entirely disappeared." Spink commented that Mullane was not going to buy another one until "the city authorities interfered."

For baseball fans who paid the five cents for the fledgling weekly, Spink was allowing them to eavesdrop on the conversations of their favorite players.

* * *

In 1886, it turned out, the Browns didn't need Mullane. The team was led by pitchers Dave Foutz (41-16, 2.11 ERA) and Bob Caruthers (30-14 with a 2.32 ERA), who were so good that Von der Ahe's team raced off to an early lead, which it never relinquished. It was touch-and-go whether Caruthers would sign with the Browns. It looked like Caruthers was going to sit out the season rather than return to the Browns for the $2,000 salary set by Al Spalding for all players under the new National Agreement.

During their negotiations, Caruthers informed Von der Ahe that he and Doc Bushong were going to visit Paris, France, for the winter and wouldn't be back by April 1. If he didn't get a better contract, warned Caruthers, he would stay in France and skip the season.

Perhaps he did go with Bushong, who had studied dentistry in 1883 in Bordeaux. No one knew for certain. Von der Ahe even received a telegram from Caruthers, purportedly from Paris. But many thought Caruthers had made up the story to make Von der Ahe think he wasn't coming back. When Von der Ahe checked boat passenger lists, he failed to find any listing for his players.

In the end, Caruthers, having nowhere else to go, caved in and signed his contract. Caruthers, who from now on would be called "Parisian Bob," was the first in a long line of St. Louis athletes to complain about subpar pay. It would take almost 100 years for the players to organize and do something about it.

BOB CARUTHERS
(Courtesy Brace Photo)

The 1886 Browns finished the season 93-46, beating out Pittsburgh by twelve full games. In *The Sporting News* of May 10, Spink commented on the seemingly unstoppable nature of the St. Louis Brown Stockings.

AL SPINK: "When last heard from the Boys in Brown had climbed to the top of the mountain and were running downhill again. Nothing can stop them in their wild career short of a hurricane. They will bring that pennant back to St. Louis though the heavens fall and the heavens it should be remarked are not falling at this season of the year."

In addition to their stellar mound staff, the 1886 Browns were a scoring machine. The team hit .273, ten points higher than any other club in the league. St. Louis featured the baserunning circus led by Comiskey, Welch, and Latham. In 1886 the Browns outscored their opponents by 352 runs—944 for, 592 against!

The Sporting News of June 14 reported that George Stovey of the Philadelphia A's tried to stop the Browns' running game by covering the baselines on the field of his ballpark with sand "a foot thick."

Comiskey said the team would not play unless the sand was removed, and the umpire so ordered it. When Comiskey took a shovel and dug into the sand, A's outfielder Henry Larkin tried to stop him. Arlie Latham secured a shovel and began removing the sand, and other Browns removed the sand with their hands.

The Browns won the game, 18–0.

The Sporting News gave details of events behind the scenes, reporting on the battling nature of the Browns. In May Charlie Comiskey was fined for his pugnacious behavior, and it was reported that Chris Von der Ahe announced he would refuse to pay the fine imposed by the league. Commented *The Sporting News,* "It is said the Association will oust the Browns if Von der Ahe does not pay Comiskey's fines. This, however, is the weakest kind of bluff."

In mid-June the paper reported an incident that took place in the dugout between Arlie Latham and catcher Doc Bushong after Bushong accused Latham of playing up to the crowd. "Latham jumped to his feet and called the Doctor all the vile names he could think of," Spink reported in the June 14 edition. Bushong hit Latham in the neck with a punch before teammates intervened. Latham was fined by the league, and again Von der Ahe refused to pay.

The league then sought to collect the fines by strongarming Von der Ahe. During a June meeting of team owners, Charlie Byrne, the owner of the Brooklyn team, opened by saying that Comiskey and Latham hadn't paid the fines. He demanded that the two Browns players be suspended for sixty days.

Von der Ahe argued that no one in the stands saw the punch that Bushong threw at Latham, and he said that if Comiskey and Latham were suspended, he'd pay his players' salaries for the rest of the year and quit the league. The owner of the Louisville team said he would quit the league as well.

On June 15 Bushong and Latham were suspended for thirty days by an order signed by William Wykoff of the American Association. However, if Von der Ahe paid the fines, he was told, the suspensions would be lifted.

A chastised Von der Ahe paid the fines. The suspensions were lifted, and the Browns cruised to the championship of the American Association.

By 1886 the world championship series had become a national phenomenon. Once again, facing each other were the champions of their respective leagues: St. Louis of the American Association and Chicago of the National. The recriminations from the '85 series hadn't been forgotten, and the fans' interest in the series of games was heightened after Chris Von der Ahe challenged Al Spalding, only to be scornfully turned down and then rechallenged by a vindictive Spalding—but only on a winner-take-all basis.

This time it wasn't a measly grand at stake but rather a kingly $15,000. Spalding may well have been trying to scare Von der Ahe off, but the Browns owner called his bluff—if it was one—and accepted. The news of the $15,000 payoff made it the most discussed sporting event in American history up to that point. As Robert Smith described it, the 1886 championship series was "the talk of every ball fan between the Mississippi and the Atlantic Coast."

Spalding, who had taken the loss to the Browns badly in 1885, did everything he could to get his players to take the series seriously. The year before his players had stayed out late, drinking before games. To induce more dedication from them, Spalding wrote to Cap Anson and his players before the series and promised them a suit of clothes and half the gate receipts if the team won. The betting was that Chicago, which had won the National League championship by two and a half games over Detroit, would not lose a single game.

The Browns players were optimistic about winning as they entrained on the Vandalia Special to Chicago for the first game of the series.

The rivalry was fierce. The initial contest was marked by rowdyism and poor sportsmanship by the Chicago fans toward the Browns and their fans. At one point the Chicago newspaper reporters seated in the press box directed the heckling, proving the difficulty of covering a team and not rooting for it. Chicago's ace, John Clarkson, rubbed salt in the wounds of the Browns by pitching a shutout.

Parisian Bob Caruthers, said to be suffering from a "weak heart," played the outfield instead of pitching and went 0 for 4. Chicago fans taunted him with calls of "Bobby's got the heart disease bad."

The next day, again in Chicago, Caruthers took the mound and pitched a two-hitter, giving up two singles. So much for his bad heart.

The loser in the 12–0 drubbing was Chicago pitcher Jim McCormick. After the series, a bitter Al Spalding would complain that too many of the White Stocking players, especially McCormick, had gotten drunk too often during the series—just as they had the year before. When McCormick pitched Game 2, said Spalding, he "was so thoroughly soused, he could not have struck out the batboy."

The Chicago papers were filled with reports that the White Stocking players had been drinking heavily the night before and that this was the reason for their lopsided loss. Cap Anson and Fred Pfeffer angrily denied the reports. (Lying to the press is not a new practice.)

Because Chicago was so heavily favored, the experts figured that if the White Stocking players weren't drunk, then they had to be hippodroming (throwing the game) to prolong the series and increase gate receipts. Rumors to that effect also began circulating in the papers.

Anson defended his players against the hippodroming charge. "I can tell you now positively that these games are for blood, every one of them."

Bob Caruthers, crowing about his dominant performance in Game 2, begged Von der Ahe to let him start the next game despite the lack of rest. Von der Ahe complied. In the first inning, he allowed two runs, and Chicago, behind John Clarkson, roughed him up for an 11–4 win.

Infielder Bill Gleason, for one, was angry that Caruthers had started Game 3 instead of Nat Hudson.

BILL GLEASON: "It was dead wrong to put him in. We all wanted Hudson and we made a special request that Hudson be pitcher. Caruthers insisted on going in, and why they put him in, I don't know. Hudson was anxious to pitch and understood he was going to until the last minute. From the very start we all knew how the thing was going, and when the Chicagos took four base on balls, that settled it. Even then it was not too late, and I heard that Mr. Von der Ahe told Comiskey to bring Hudson in from the field, but why it wasn't done I don't know.''

Jim McCormick was supposed to have started the game for Chicago, but before the game he was so drunk that ''he could not even find his way to the mound and had to be led away to safety.'' Before the third game, Anson would announce that the team would have to play without McCormick, who, he said, had ''rheumatism in his legs.'' The big pitcher wouldn't play in another game for Chicago.

The teams went by train to St. Louis, where several Chicago players were seen in gambling halls on the morning of Game 4. The smart money continued to be on the White Sox.

Ten thousand fans filled the Sportsman's Park grandstands for the game. Foutz started it by walking in a run with the bases loaded and no outs. Ned Williamson then hit a sacrifice fly, scoring a second run and moving Cap Anson to third and Fred Pfeffer to second. When catcher Doc Bushong threw to second in an attempt to pick off Pfeffer, Anson broke for third and scored a third run when Robinson's return throw was wide.

In the second inning, Pfeffer, Chicago's second baseman, made two errors. With Bill Gleason at third and Curt Welch at first, Comiskey called for a double steal. When Welch broke for second, Chicago catcher Mike Kelly threw to second for the out, but Gleason was safe at home. In the third, the Browns scored another run on an error by shortstop Ned Williamson and a long triple into the right field corner by Tip O'Neill. The Browns slugger continued running home and was thrown out, but his hit had narrowed the margin to 3–2.

In the fifth inning, with two outs and runners on first and second, O'Neill came to the plate. John Clarkson wanted to walk him intentionally, preferring to pitch to Bill Gleason. Anson ordered him to pitch to O'Neill, but Clarkson disobeyed and walked him anyway. It was one of the earliest examples of an intentional walk and also of a player showing up his manager.

Gleason, who was batting cleanup, advanced to the plate. After Clarkson threw two strikes, the Browns shortstop then grounded a single between short and third, scoring two runners and giving the Browns the lead.

Chicago tied the score in the top of the sixth, but the Browns won the game in the bottom of the inning when Chicago second baseman Fred Pfeffer dropped a pop-up with the bases loaded and then failed to make the force-out that would have led to a double play. The Browns won, 8–5, in a game shortened because of darkness.

Based on their behavior that night, it's not unreasonable to come to the conclusion that some of the Chicago players, without Anson's knowledge, had bet on the Browns and thrown the game—Pfeffer and Williamson seemed the most likely suspects.

At the Lindell Hotel the evening after the game, according to writer Jerry

Lansche, "The White Stockings, with the exception of Cap Anson, seemed strangely undisturbed by their loss. The team stood around smoking big black cigars, toasting each other with champagne, and joking with reporters. Clarkson was in especially good humor. Shortstop Ned Williamson smiled enigmatically and said, 'Yes, sir, they beat us today on the level.' King Kelly told funny stories to a group of friends."

When the charges of hippodroming resurfaced, Anson, who would have tossed any player throwing a game out of baseball for life, swore up and down that his team had lost fair and square. He got into a shouting match with a *St. Louis Post-Dispatch* reporter who asked how it was possible the White Stockings had lost.

"Didn't you see it yourself?" Anson angrily retorted. "Wasn't you there?"

The reporter said he had been.

"Well, then you know as much as I do about it," Anson said as testily as any modern-day manager to a reporter whose questions were getting under his skin.

The whispers about hippodroming became a roar when Anson started third baseman Ned Williamson on the mound for Game 5. McCormick had been sent home, and Clarkson needed another day's rest, so it should have been the turn of twenty-two-year-old John "Jocko" Flynn, the third fine Chicago starter. Perhaps Anson had discovered Flynn too drunk to pitch. Anson didn't reveal the true story to anyone. But the reporters saw this as a sign that Chicago wasn't trying to win the series, and Anson took a pounding in the press when Williamson was followed on the mound by third baseman Jimmy Ryan. The White Stockings were beaten badly, 10–3, giving the Browns a lead of three games to two.

On October 23, a reporter for the *Chicago News* wrote: "Admitting that baseball is a business conducted for pecuniary profit, there still can be no palliation for the offense of brazenly giving away a game as the game was given away yesterday in St. Louis. . . . The hippodrome was so artistically played that there really was no inclination to cry out against it. . . . The champion League club, having its membership such pitchers as Clarkson, McCormick, Flynn and Baldwin, disdained the services of all these gentlemen and put in the box the very estimable short stop of the nine. . . . We presume to say that if such a shameless face had been attempted here in Chicago the conspirators and co-conspirators would have been hooted off the field."

The sixth and final game was played, according to Robert Smith, "on a warm, cloudy day before a grandstand full of men in high-crowned derbies, plug hats, and odd little round cloth hats like the Rollo hats which in later years used to make small boys wretched on Sunday. There were ladies in the audience, too, and a heavy sprinkling of kids, both in the grandstand and on the bleaching boards, the uncovered benches which became known as bleachers. There was an endless murmur from the crowd, for there was plenty of wagering going on, and St. Louis was an hour or two away from triumph."

Al Spalding came to St. Louis to convince Chris Von der Ahe to start the game early at two so they could get in the entire nine innings before it got

dark. Game 4 had been called after only six and a half innings on account of
darkness. Von der Ahe, confident of victory, complied.

Chicago scored a run in the first and one in the fourth, both by Fred
Pfeffer, to take the early lead. It had drizzled from the start, and as the Browns
were scheduled to bat in the fourth, Charlie Comiskey pleaded with umpire
Dickey Pearce to call the game before it became official. Pearce was going to
go along, but when Von der Ahe saw that the crowd was threatening a riot
if the game was called, he ordered Comiskey to send the players out no
matter what.

In the sixth, Pfeffer scored for a third time. Through six frames, St. Louis
didn't have a single hit against John Clarkson. Tip O'Neill, who walked, was
the only base runner. O'Neill broke up the no-hitter in the seventh, but he was
thrown out running from second to third by George Gore as he tried to stretch
his hit into a triple.

Charlie Comiskey led off the Browns' eighth with a single. Curt Welch,
the speedy center fielder, swung at a Clarkson fastball and hit a slow roller to
Tom Burns at third. When Burns threw wildly past first, Welch sped on to
second and Comiskey reached third. The crowd, on its feet, began to scream
and stamp. Dave Foutz hit a sacrifice fly to deep center to score Comiskey as
Welch went to third. After Yank Robinson popped out, the Browns catcher,
Doc Bushong, stepped to the plate. Clarkson, close to victory, walked him to
load the bases. Bushong represented the tying run.

Arlie Latham, the craftiest bunter in the league and one of the Browns'
best base runners, took his spot at the plate. Latham had annoyed the White
Stockings all series long with his constant stream of invectives.

On this day, according to Robert Smith, "Arlie was oddly silent, and some
of the locals began to tell each other that he couldn't stand the ragging he had
been getting from Anson, that he was obviously too sick to play, or that he
had been ordered to keep quiet because of complaints about his noise."

Anson, who himself was renowned for his tart tongue, spent the game
encouraging his batters to hit the ball to Latham at third. Anson bellowed:
"Knock it down here! This is our puddin'! This is the weak spot."

As Arlie dug in, catcher King Kelly began complaining to the umpire.

"He's got a flat bat," Kelly said. "He can't use that bat."

Latham, an expert bunter, had whittled one side of his softwood bat until
it was flat, so he could bunt with less danger of fouling off the pitch. Umpire
Dickey Pearce examined the bat and sent Arlie back for another.

The St. Louis crowd, estimated at 10,000 fans, derided Anson, Kelly, and
the umpire's decision to bar Latham's bat. It began chanting, "Ten men,"
another way of saying Pearce was on Chicago's side.

Arlie stepped to the plate with his new bat, looked at the base runners,
and yelled to Doc Bushong at first, "Stay there, Doc, and I'll bring you
both in."

The crowd responded with glee.

Suddenly the skies opened and the rains came. Charlie Comiskey called
timeout and asked for a delay. Anson, whose team was leading, 3–1, didn't
think a delay was warranted. Not wanting his pitcher, Clarkson, to have to sit

and take the chance his arm would tighten, Anson raged at umpire Pearce to continue. The crowd, still angry that Kelly had made Latham get a new bat, began pouring onto the field, yelling at both the umpire and Anson.

The ruckus on the field made the protest moot, as the umpire had to call time while the police drove the rowdies back into the stands. When the rain stopped, the game resumed with men on first and third and Latham at bat.

Before Clarkson went into his windup, left fielder Abner Dalrymple moved from his customary spot straightaway to a position not far from the left field line, where Latham often hit.

Robert Smith described what happened next.

ROBERT SMITH: "Arlie did not miss this move. The crowd grew utterly still. The gruff voices of the fat aproned beer vendors, who carried their flowing trays of glass steins about the stands, rang out suddenly with great clearness: 'Give your orders, gents! Give your orders, gents!' "

Clarkson delivered and Latham took strike one. When the fans oohed in disappointment, the little third baseman stepped away from the plate and held up one hand.

"Don't get nervous, folks," Latham called. "I'll bring them in."

ROBERT SMITH: "[Clarkson] took his stance again and, as he did, his alert eye caught the sudden jerk of Mike Kelly's head, which signaled Clarkson to put the next pitch inside. The ball came down straight and fast. Arlie, ready for it, brought his bat around in a half-chopping motion and sent the ball on a line to the very spot where [Abner] Dalrymple would have been standing if he had not been trying to 'play position' on Latham. Dal, a swift-footed fielder, sprinted for the ball, clutched wildly at it, felt it graze his fingertips, and then watched it skim off into the deep grass of far left field. He took after it, and Arlie sped around the baselines. The noise of the crowd seemed to drown all thought. Curt Welch scored. Men beat the wooden railing with their hands. Bushong scored. Ladies jumped to their seats, screaming, and fluttered their tiny handkerchiefs. Arlie pulled up on third.

"The score was tied. Men in curled-brim derbies moved earnestly about the stands to make new bets, to inform each other with solemn excitement that, by golly, that little Arlie Latham was the greatest, yes, absolutely the greatest baseball player in the country today."

The play was the turning point in the ball game, and afterward both Al Spalding and Cap Anson would say that the ball should have been caught by Dalrymple.

That ended the scoring in the eighth, and when no one scored in the ninth, the game went into extra innings.

Chicago failed to score in the top of the tenth, and when the Browns batted, Curt Welch led off.

Welch was skilled at getting hit with pitched balls, and on Clarkson's first pitch, he placed himself in front of a medium-fast pitch and was waved down to first base by umpire Pearce.

Cap Anson came charging in from first, and reminded Pearce at the top of his lungs that Welch was in the habit of getting hit by pitches. Pearce, agreeing, called Welch back to the plate. Few in the stands argued.

Welch, given another chance, lined a single that whizzed past Clarkson's ear into center field. The crowd at Sportsman's Park roared. The winning run was on base.

Dave Foutz, the Browns right fielder, then hit a sharp ground ball to Ned Williamson at short, a ball that should have been an easy double play. But Williamson booted it, so the runners were safe on first and second.

The next man to bat was second baseman Yank Robinson. The crowd was now in a frenzy. Every spectator was on his feet, shouting for Robinson to get a hit.

But Comiskey, coaching at third, ordered Robinson to sacrifice bunt, and the second baseman dropped the ball nicely in front of the plate and was thrown out at first as the two runners advanced. Second-guessers in the stands wanted to know why Comiskey had him bunt rather than allow him to hit away. With runners on second and third and only one out, Comiskey was playing the percentages.

Doc Bushong, the St. Louis catcher, advanced to the plate. Chicago catcher Mike Kelly picked up the bat that Robinson had just dropped. As Bushong came close, Kelly dropped to his knees, in the manner of an acolyte proffering a sacrificial sword, and held out the bat to Bushong. The crowd laughed and yelled nervously as Bushong gravely accepted the club.

There was a moment of tense silence. Clarkson looked at the two runners and turned back to face Bushong. His arm came back slowly, then he snapped it hard and sent a high ball almost at Bushong's head. Bushong let it go. Ball one. Clarkson didn't want the St. Louis catcher hitting anything on the ground. Rather, he was throwing high in hopes of getting a pop-up.

As Clarkson started to wind up again, out of the corner of his eye he saw Curt Welch seeking to steal home. To give Kelly a better chance to tag the runner, Clarkson pitched the ball inside and high. But Clarkson miscalculated. He threw it *too* high.

Kelly sprung to make a grab for it, but the ball skipped off the top of his fingers and bounded off toward the fence.

The crowd screamed as Charlie Comiskey, coaching at third, began trailing after Welch, who could have scored standing up but instead hit the dirt, sliding exaggeratedly across the plate with the winning run with the express purpose of showing up Chicago. Comiskey, pounding on past home, grabbed the ball on the carom off the backstop before Kelly could lay his hands on it. He shoved it in his pocket for a souvenir. Kelly, after shaking both fists in the air, flung his glove and mask high over the grandstand, cursing all the way to the dugout.

The series was over. The St. Louis Browns were the undisputed champions of the world. There was bedlam as the fans rushed onto the field. The players pounded each other for joy. Men flung hats, beer steins, and cushions around the stands. Directly after the game, the St. Louis fans held an impromptu victory parade, marching Von der Ahe and the Browns players around on their shoulders.

Then for an hour and a half a mob of fans hung outside the Browns' clubhouse, giving "three cheers" for Curt Welch, Latham, Comiskey, and Von der Ahe, who ordered champagne for everybody, including the fans who had stayed.

Welch became famous for his victory slide, which became known as "the $15,000 Slide," in that the winning team was supposed to take home the expected $15,000 in game receipts. (The actual total was $13,920.10. Officially the Browns earned $580 each. Von der Ahe earned the other half. According to what Arlie Latham told Robert Smith, what the public wasn't made aware of was that the players on both teams had agreed among themselves before the series to split the money evenly no matter who won.

Chris Von der Ahe, who was able to recoup a full fifth of his season salary with his share of series receipts, asked Spalding to play a seventh game as an exhibition in Cincinnati. Spalding turned him down. WE KNOW WHEN WE'VE HAD ENOUGH, he telegraphed Von der Ahe.

As for White Stockings manager Anson, he was gracious in defeat, though he resented that some of his players had been drunk and caroused too much during the series.

CAP ANSON: "We were beaten, and fairly beaten, but had some of the players taken as good care of themselves prior to these games as they were in the habit of doing when the League season was in full swim, I am inclined to believe that there might have been a different tale to tell."

Chicago owner Albert Spalding, who wasn't as forgiving as Anson, again was furious his champions had lost. He would have to listen to the taunts, like the comment in the *St. Louis Republican* that said, "Chicago should confine itself to the slaughter of hogs as a popular amusement," because "baseball seems to require more headwork." Spalding was in a rage that some of his players hadn't taken the games more seriously, and he was angry that as a result of the loss he hadn't made any money on the series because under their arrangement Von der Ahe took all the owners' profits. When it was over, Spalding spited his players by adamantly refusing to pay their train fare home from St. Louis back to Chicago. His players, who had bet on the games and lost, were so broke that they were stranded in St. Louis. Von der Ahe magnanimously advanced them the money to get home.

As for Von der Ahe, "he was the Boss Manager, his Browns were the Boss Club, and St. Louis was the Boss City of the whole gol-blinking United States."

CHAPTER 7

FOUR-IN-A-ROW CHAMPIONS

THE St. Louis Browns, repeat champions of the American Association, actually improved in 1887. Comiskey's brawling speedsters scored 1,131 runs in 135 games, more than 8 a game. Tip O'Neill scored 167 runs and led the league, Latham scored 163 runs, Comiskey 139, Gleason 135, Yank Robinson and Bob Caruthers 102 each, Curt Welch 98, and catcher Jack Boyle 48. The Browns, who finished the season 95-40, were a powerhouse.

Tip O'Neill led the league with a .435 batting average, the second highest for a season in baseball history. Only Hugh Duffy, who hit .438. with Boston in 1894, hit higher. O'Neill also led the league with 14 home runs, 225 hits, 52 doubles, 19 triples (tied with five others), and in runs scored. Twice in 1887 he hit for the cycle: a single, double, triple, and home run in one game.

O'Neill was one of the first great sports heroes in St. Louis. Even poems were written about him:

TIP O'NEILL
(Courtesy Brace Photo)

O, Jim O'Neill is a slugger bold,
    Yes, a slugger bold is he.
When he taps the ball to the fence it flys
    In a manner good to see.
When he taps the ball the crans all yell,
    All it climbs the far-off fence.
"Bully for slugger Jim O'Neill."
    By gosh, he bats immense.

In addition to their run-scoring ability, the 1887 Browns once again had a top pitching staff. Along with Bob Caruthers (who now was called "Parisian Bob" Caruthers, a nickname based on the story about his going to Paris) and Dave Foutz, Von der Ahe signed nineteen-year-old Charles Frederick Koenig, who had played the year before in Kansas City in the National League. Koenig had huge hands and arms and threw sidearm. The St. Louis papers shortened his name to King, and he was given the nickname "Silver" because of his gray hair. "Silver" King would win his first 7 decisions, and with his 34-11 record, he would lead the Browns' staff in 1887. Caruthers finished the year at 29-9, Foutz at 25-12.

Despite the success of his Browns, Von der Ahe did not have an easy year. Having already angered the leaders of the temperance movement when he began to sell beer and liquor in his ballpark, he now came under attack by the religious lobby, which sought to ban baseball games on Sundays. After municipal judge Edward Noonan ruled that Missouri's blue laws forbade the players of professional baseball on Sundays, Von der Ahe was told that if he played on Sunday, there would be arrests. Von der Ahe, who argued that baseball was fun, not labor, and hence didn't fall under the law, vowed to fight the ordinance.

CHRIS VON DER AHE: "I shall order my men on the field . . . and if they are arrested I shall give bond for them, and see this matter thoroughly tested in a court of justice. Our schedule was made before the Sunday law was put into force, and visiting clubs will require us to play on days scheduled or forfeit games. . . . This might result in my club losing the championship, and I do not propose to let this occur until I have made every effort in my power to bring about a different result."

On Sunday, July 10, 1887, 10,000 fans crammed into the wooden grandstand of Sportsman's Park to watch the Browns play the Baltimore Orioles. Twenty-five mounted police arrived. The game began at three-thirty, and after the first inning the police stopped the game and arrested Von der Ahe, who was seated in his grandstand box.

He was booked at the nearby police station for breaking the Sunday law. He went before Judge Noonan, who set bail at $100. William Medart (the amateur umpire from the 1885 championship series) posted it, and Von der Ahe returned to the ballpark. He announced to the patrons that he was calling off the game to prevent his players from going to jail.

Five days later Von der Ahe argued his case before Judge Noonan. He pleaded not guilty. A close friend, United States Representative John J. O'Neill, spoke on his behalf.

After hearing both sides, Judge Noonan ruled in Von der Ahe's favor, saying that baseball was recreation, not labor, and could be played legally on Sundays in St. Louis.

Another antagonist, Charlie Byrne, the Brooklyn owner, sought to oust Von der Ahe's ally, league president William Wykoff. Byrne wanted changes in the way revenues were divided. Under the present rules, the visiting team received a flat fee of $65. Byrne wanted 30 percent of the gate. Byrne also pushed for one day when women would be allowed in the American Association ballparks for free. He also proposed a rule stating that if a manager pulled his team off the field before the end of the game (something Charlie Comiskey did frequently when it drizzled and the Browns were behind), the team would be fined $1,500.

Von der Ahe realized that the changes would hurt him the most, in that his team was the biggest draw. He was determined to stop Byrne. In late September the Browns had a four-game series with Cincinnati. The Browns lost all four games. Immediately the sporting press accused Von der Ahe of ordering his players to deliberately throw the games in order to allow Cincinnati to finish in second place over Baltimore. The charge was that Von der Ahe needed the Cincinnati owner on his side in his fight against Byrne. The charges were denied, but the smell never did go away.

Von der Ahe also had a major war with his players over exhibition revenues and World Series pay. When eight of the Browns refused to play an exhibition game against an all-black team in New York in September of 1887, Von der Ahe lambasted his players—not for their racism, but because their refusal to play had cost him in gate receipts.

Just before the 1887 World Series against the Detroit Wolverines, Von der Ahe arrogantly took away much of the players' incentive for the series when he told them that instead of receiving half the take he gave them the year before, this year they would get exactly $100 per man. What made his penury even harder to stomach by the players was that Von der Ahe had agreed to play the Detroit Wolverines in a grueling 15-game championship series circus to be played in Detroit; St. Louis; Pittsburgh; New York; Boston; Philadelphia; Washington, D.C.; Baltimore; Brooklyn; and Chicago. The Browns owner figured that since he had made significant money playing six games against Chicago in 1886, he could make at least twice that playing a fifteen-game series.

Though the Browns players had to play the games, they had lost all incentive to play hard or well. The Wolverines won eight of the first eleven games to clinch the world championship. In those first eleven games, the Browns hit .181 and scored just three runs a game. Curt Welch led the team with but 6 RBIs. Tip O'Neill and Yank Robinson each drove in 5.

Few Browns players stood out. Bob Caruthers won the opening, fifth, and tenth games. Arlie Latham played outstanding defense. Otherwise the team appeared flat.

After the third game, the teams left Detroit by train for Pittsburgh. The Detroit players went to bed early. Some of the Browns, including Charlie Comiskey, stayed up late, playing poker. Yank Robinson and Curt Welch, who were drinking, got into a fistfight after one of the hands. When Welch looked in the mirror the next morning, his nose was black and blue.

After losing the next day by 8–0, on the train to New York City the Browns players again stayed up late, drank, and played poker.

The *St. Louis Post-Dispatch* commented, "The Browns stay awake all night gambling and fighting and squabbling over the cards. In a recent game Caruthers lost $80, and he was so excited over the loss that he dashed down the pasteboards and cursed the man who invented them. Comiskey stays up all hours playing poker with his men, and the majority of the club never knows what sleep means till 2 and 3 o'clock in the morning. Seven o'clock in the morning finds them awake at the poker tables again, and the loss of sleep, combined with the excitement of the game, shows itself in weak, nervous, sulky dispositions and poor eyes when they begin to play ball.''

The paper went on to report that the Detroit players "are as sober as judges, sleep ten hours to the night and play a strong game of ball."

After Detroit took a 5–2 lead in games, Charlie Comiskey expressed his disappointment that despite Caruthers's excellence and the fine play of Arlie Latham, Detroit was winning most of the games.

CHARLIE COMISKEY: "Individually the team is playing strong ball, but when it comes to a whole we can't win. Why, I don't know. There's a screw loose someplace."

When the Browns lost again, this time by a 9–2 score, Arlie Latham spoke out more strongly.

ARLIE LATHAM: "That was no game we played today. The men were like a lot of amateurs in a vacant lot. I never saw them go on like that before. It made me sick. It disgusted me. It made me wish I was dead. We were a regular custard pudding for Detroit and they ate us without any sauce. We are not ballplayers, we are chumps."

When Detroit won its eighth victory in Baltimore on October 21, the players from both teams figured that since the series was clinched by Detroit, they were going home. But Von der Ahe and Detroit owner Fred Stearns agreed to play the final four games as exhibitions, and the games dragged on for another five days. When the players learned they would have to play the extra four games, they were justifiably angry.

When the series was over, Von der Ahe announced that his team had played so badly, he refused to share any of the gate receipts with them. Charlie Comiskey pleaded with Von der Ahe to pay them the $100 he promised, but the Browns owner refused, opening a wound between Von der Ahe and his players that would never heal.

Dave Foutz had even predicted that Von der Ahe would do this.

DAVE FOUTZ: "You see how it is. If we won the series from the best baseball club in the world outside ourselves, we would get our little $100. If we lost it, we wouldn't get a blank cent."

Caruthers and Dave Foutz were both so disgusted that they demanded to be traded. Von der Ahe obliged. He ordered Comiskey to sell several important players. Von der Ahe was so upset with shortstop Bill Gleason's poor performance that he ordered him sold too. At the end of the 1887 season, Von der Ahe sold Foutz, Caruthers, and catcher Doc Bushong to Brooklyn for a total of $20,000 and sold Curt Welch to the Philadelphia A's for $3,000. Von der Ahe also traded his star shortstop Bill Gleason to the A's for catcher John "Jocko" Milligan and infielder James "Chippy" McGarr.

The St. Louis fans were furious that Von der Ahe was dismantling his great team. But according to Charlie Comiskey, real estate losses were at the heart of his actions.

*   *   *

CHARLIE COMISKEY: "Von der Ahe had built a row of apartment houses and named them after his star players. It was surmised by some that when his buildings ceased to be a paying proposition he took a dislike to five of his stars and sold them to make up the difference."

The Sporting Life, a magazine founded in 1883, reported that Comiskey was behind the dealings more than he let on.

THE SPORTING LIFE: "Very few people know that the sale of Welch, Foutz, and Caruthers was made more at Comiskey's request than at Von der Ahe's desire. Comiskey wants no man on the team who does not obey him."

Critics were certain that the Browns would finish in the second division in 1888, but they had not taken into account Charlie Comiskey's ability to rebuild a ballclub. Comiskey was able to acquire Louisville's excellent short-stop, Bill White, after White got into a dispute with his manager. The player had requested a day off on a hot Louisville day, and when the manager refused, White made some errors on purpose. Louisville owner Mordecai Davidson sold White to St. Louis.

Although the Browns had lost Doc Bushong, Bill Gleason, and Curt Welch, they still had the heart of their lineup: Arlie Latham, Yank Robinson, Tip O'Neill, and Charlie Comiskey, and they were joined by one of the greatest base runners in the history of the game, Tommy McCarthy. In 1888 McCarthy would steal 93 bases, hit 20 doubles, and score 107 runs. In 1889 he would steal 56 bases and score 136 runs. And in 1946 he would be elected to the Hall of Fame.

The Browns struggled some in the spring to stay with the rejuvenated Brooklyn team as the Browns worked the new players into their lineup, but in August the Browns won eighteen of twenty-one games and sprinted to their fourth straight pennant. The four in a row would set a record that would stand until the New York Giants tied it between 1921 and 1924. The New York Yankees between 1949 and 1953 and again between 1960 and 1964 set the new record of five in a row.

The one bump in the road occurred during July, and it was brought on by Chris Von der Ahe's paranoiac meddling. When Tip O'Neill played poorly in a series of games against the Brooklyns, owned by Chris Von der Ahe's nemesis, Charlie Byrne, Von der Ahe became suspicious that this was a repeat of the Bill White incident. He accused former teammate Doc Bushong of getting O'Neill to play badly so that Von der Ahe would trade O'Neill over to Brooklyn so he could rejoin his friend. Von der Ahe suspended O'Neill, who hit .335 in 1888 to again lead the league and knocked in 98 runs to lead the team. He also fined Silver King $1,000 for pitching poorly against Brooklyn (the game was played on July 10, 1888). This despite a season in which King pitched in 66 games, compiling a yeomanlike 45-21 record with a 1.64 ERA, leading the league in wins, games, innings pitched, and ERA.

The other star Browns pitcher, Nat Hudson, was 25-10 when he left the team in July to get married. He never returned that year. It was clear that as relations between the players and Von der Ahe were breaking down, manager Charlie Comiskey was having a harder and harder time keeping his team together. A potential disaster was averted when Comiskey was able to purchase Elton "Icebox" Chamberlain, Louisville's top pitcher, in August, after Louisville owner Mordecai Davidson refused to meet Chamberlain's salary demands. Chamberlain, 14-9 for Louisville, finished the year with St. Louis 11-2. Thanks to the acquisition of Chamberlain, one of only three pitchers known to pitch both lefty and righty in a game during the nineteenth century, the Browns led the league with a 2.09 team ERA.

The Browns faced the New York Giants in the 1888 championship series. The Giants were led by six future Hall of Famers, including "Orator Jim" O'Rourke in left, catcher William "Buck" Ewing, shortstop Montgomery Ward, first baseman Roger Connor, and pitchers "Smiling Mickey" Welsh and Tim Keefe.

The team that won six games first would be declared the champion. The Browns won only twice against Tim Keefe and Mickey Welsh. The Browns might have won had they won Game 4 and tied the series at 2 games apiece, but with the Browns ahead, 4–1, in the eighth inning of the fifth game, a costly error by shortstop Bill White turned the tide and allowed the Giants to come back and win. Von der Ahe never forgave White, and in the next game Von der Ahe's frustrations came to the surface when he accused umpires John Kelly and John Gaffney of betting on the Giants. By the time the train from New York reached St. Louis, the umpires had read Von der Ahe's charges in the papers. When both umpires threatened to quit, Von der Ahe claimed he had been misquoted, and the umps agreed to go back to work. The Giants won their sixth and final victory on a home run and a three-run triple by the legendary catcher Buck Ewing.

With the Giants declared the world champions, Von der Ahe obligated his players to perform in three more exhibition games against the New Yorkers, and when it was all over again, he refused to pay them a penny because they had lost, pocketing all the receipts for himself.

CHAPTER 8

THE DEMISE OF VON DER AHE

WHEN St. Louis won the pennnant over second-place Brooklyn in 1888, the Browns rooters, who had resented Brooklyn owner Charlie Byrne for buying Bob Caruthers and Dave Foutz, rejoiced. When a fan spotted Byrne on the street, he yelled to him, "You can spend $50,000 on players and buy all the stars in the Association and put them on your team. Then next year Charlie Comiskey will come along with his gang of Job Lots and knock you out of the pennant again."

But after 1888, that fan, and the other Browns fans, would suffer deep disappointment as Byrne's Bridegrooms, as they had been dubbed for finishing second so often, would win the American Association pennant in 1889 and the National League flag in 1890.

The animosity by the embittered players toward owner Chris Von der Ahe continued to fester, and in 1889 it almost seemed to some observers that Comiskey and his teammates were throwing the pennant, perhaps to spite their owner for his penurious, dictatorial ways. There was some strange behavior on Charlie Comiskey's part, including two forfeited games. During one game, Comiskey withdrew his team from the field, and another time he refused to play on the Sabbath.

Before another game in 1889, Von der Ahe leaned over the railing and began berating second baseman Yank Robinson, who had chewed out an elderly gatekeeper at the ballpark for not allowing an errand boy to bring him a new pair of uniform pants he had requested.

That night, after Von der Ahe, son Edward, and Charlie Comiskey boarded the train for the next series, Robinson and some of his teammates remained on the platform, talking about going on strike. They thought better of it and took a later train. Then they lost three games in a row—each, suspiciously, in late innings.

The Browns finished the season two games behind Brooklyn.

In 1890 the players of both the American Association and the National League staged a shooting war. Spalding had set a $2,000 a year salary cap, and the other owners had been only too happy to go along. Von der Ahe kept his salaries low and made it harder for his players to make ends meet by his habit of fining them on days they performed poorly.

Deeply dissatisfied league-wide, the players decided to desert their owners and start their own league, which they called the Brotherhood League. Along with hundreds of other professional players, Charlie Comiskey joined the new league, moving to Chicago. He took Latham, O'Neill, Boyle, and King with him. The severely weakened Browns dropped into third in the American Association.

Said Comiskey on why he deserted the Browns for the new league, "I couldn't do anything else and be on the level with the boys."

The Brotherhood League lasted but one season, costing everyone involved in the game great sums of money. Comiskey, who in ten years would become owner of the Chicago team in the American League, learned up close the importance of strong ownership.

After the league folded, Von der Ahe agreed to take Comiskey back as the Browns manager for the 1891 season. The magic, however, was gone. Von der Ahe had gotten a taste of what it was like to run the team with Comiskey gone in 1890, and he was reluctant to turn the reins back to his former manager. Though the team finished second, throughout the year Comiskey fought with an owner who was becoming too irrational and headstrong for even him to handle.

In 1891 Von der Ahe and the owners of the National League got into a war over stealing players. Al Spalding, the ruthless gutter fighter who led the National League, hired former American Association pitchers Mark Baldwin and Guy Hecker to contact American Association players with the purpose of getting them to switch leagues. Baldwin had succeeded in getting former Philadelphia A's second baseman Lou Bierbauer to jump clubs and sign with Pittsburgh. The clubs's tactics were branded "piracy," and from then on the team would be called the Pirates.

In March of 1891, Von der Ahe made a complaint to the St. Louis authorities, accusing Baldwin of bribing his star pitcher, Silver King, to join the Pittsburgh team. Baldwin was arrested and jailed. The move would come back to haunt Von der Ahe.

At the end of the 1891 season, the Cincinnati Reds of the National League offered Charlie Comiskey a salary of $7,500 to switch leagues. Comiskey asked Von der Ahe to match the offer. Von der Ahe refused. At the same time, John T. Brush, now the owner of the New York Giants, argued that one ten-team league was the only way professional baseball was going to survive. Von der Ahe, wishing to maintain the integrity of the American Association, objected. But the National League went ahead with its plan, and on October 29, all of the Browns stars, including Charlie Comiskey, Tip O'Neill, strikeout pitcher "Happy Jack" Stivetts, Tommy McCarthy, and Denny Lyons, announced that in 1892 they would play for National League teams. Comiskey was said to be the ringleader.

After the players defected, on December 18, 1891, the two leagues merged. Von der Ahe held a secret meeting in St. Louis with National League owners and worked out an agreement for the Browns and Louisville, Washington, and Baltimore, three other profitable American Association teams, to join the National League.

Von der Ahe was optimistic he could replace his star players. He always had done it before. But this time he didn't have Charlie Comiskey to show him the way, and when he sought to fill the holes, he discovered that the good players had already been signed.

Von der Ahe might have survived the merger if he hadn't lost Charlie Comiskey as player-manager. After Comiskey's departure, Von der Ahe decided he had the ability to manage the team himself, and from an 86-52 record under Comiskey in 1891, in just one year under Von der Ahe the Browns dropped to 56-94 and sank like a stone into the second division.

Von der Ahe had set a course headed for ruin. He didn't have the knowledge or temperament to manage, and he wasn't qualified to judge talent. Scout Bill Gleason recommended to his manager-owner a young, hard-nosed third baseman. The man wasn't tall, but Gleason saw that the player had talent and fire. When Von der Ahe saw him, he wasn't impressed. He exclaimed, "Dot liddle feller? Take him over to der Fairgrounds and make a horse yockey oudt of him." Gleason sold the player to Baltimore, where John McGraw began his Hall of Fame career.

In 1892 Von der Ahe emphasized flash over substance. He moved the Browns to their new modern ballpark at Vanderveer and Natural Bridge. In addition to baseball games, Von der Ahe also featured a carnival and horse racing in the off-season. A new ballpark, however, could not mask the poor showing by his team, which continued to be mediocre under Bill Watkins in 1893 and George Miller in 1894. In 1895, under three managers, the Browns sank back to eleventh as the city of St. Louis, the other National League owners, and the sporting press turned on Von der Ahe.

After Al Spink's brother Charles took over *The Sporting News,* he became Von der Ahe's biggest critic. He began referring to the Browns owner as "Von der Ha Ha." He called him "maggot" instead of magnate, and later he referred to him as "the tricky Teuton." One time he called Von der Ahe an "ignorant boor" and editorialized that "baseball should rid itself of the thing that smells to heaven in the nostrils of every honest lover of the game."

At the time *The Sporting News* was in financial trouble. The paper was not attracting advertisers, and Charlie Spink even hocked a diamond ring to meet the payroll. But when Spink went after Von der Ahe, still one of baseball's most powerful figures, circulation picked up. Spink called Von der Ahe's private life "an affront to the community" and suggested "dalliances with young ladies not his wife."

That same year, perhaps a result of Spink's writings, Von der Ahe's personal fortunes took a turn for the worse when his wife sued him on grounds of infidelity and his son joined her in the suit. But Von der Ahe, who was resilient and seemingly impervious to criticism, remarried and stubbornly refused to quit baseball.

The more Von der Ahe was attacked, the more paranoid he became and the more hostile he acted toward his fellow owners. He publicly called them "thieves and crooks, porch-climbers and sandbaggers," and one year he even complained that they had arranged the schedule so that most of his attractive dates would be rained out. Von der Ahe's abuse of his ballplayers, moreover, worsened. He had five managers in 1896, including himself for two games. In 1897 the team became a laughingstock. Four managers, including Von der Ahe for the final fourteen games (2-12), headed a team with a 29-102 record. The Browns finished in the cellar, twenty-two and a half games behind eleventh-place Louisville!

The Browns had become an embarrassment. The other National League owners were desperate to get rid of Von der Ahe.

Edward "Ned" Hanlon, who would lead a dynasty in Baltimore from 1892 to 1898, tried to buy the Browns from Von der Ahe in 1897. His offer was $75,000. When Von der Ahe demanded $125,000 and wouldn't budge, the deal fell through.

Von der Ahe's downfall came not long after fire raced through the ballpark in 1898. The grandstand, half the bleachers, his Golden Lion Saloon, the club offices, most of the gate money, his trophies, his fancy clothes, and his correspondence files were left in ruins. Moreover, 100 people were burned or trampled in the panic, so Von der Ahe was bombarded with lawsuits as well. In addition, Von der Ahe was still facing the wrath of the other National League owners, who were desperately trying to figure a way to boot the irrational Von der Ahe and his disgraceful Browns out of the league.

Von der Ahe unknowingly provided them with the means when in 1890 he had ordered the St. Louis police to arrest Mark Baldwin and throw him in jail. Four years later, as Von der Ahe was leading his players into the Pittsburgh ballpark before the game, two policeman came up to the Browns owner and arrested him. Baldwin had pressed charges against him for false arrest. Freed on bail, Von der Ahe returned to St. Louis, stiffing W. A. Nimick, the president of the Pittsburgh team, who had posted the bail.

When Von der Ahe didn't respond to his requests for the return of his bail money, Nimick became worried. To collect the judgment against Von der Ahe, he needed to find a way to get the Browns owner into a Pennsylvania court.

Von der Ahe was asked to attend a secret meeting with a wealthy financier at the St. Nicholas Hotel on business that the caller said would very much be to Mr. Von der Ahe's advantage. Von der Ahe rushed to the front of the St. Louis hotel, where two well-dressed men ushered him into a horse-drawn cab, ostensibly to meet the principal in the deal.

The cab rode to the railroad station just before the train was pulling out. The two men hustled him aboard and managed to keep him quiet. On the train, the men revealed themselves as detectives hired by Nimick.

"Von der Ahe was thrown into an Allegheny County jail where, disheveled and disgraced, he reposed for several days."

Led by Nimick, in 1899 the other National League owners stripped Von der Ahe of his franchise. In an auction held on the steps of the Court House, G. A. Gruner bought the franchise for $33,000 and quickly sold it for $40,000 to Edward Becker, who was acting on behalf of brothers Frank and Stanley Robison, the owners of a Cleveland streetcar line and the Cleveland Spiders of the American Association. They immediately transferred the best of the Cleveland players, including pitcher Denton "Cy" Young, to St. Louis.

To change the laughingstock image of the team, they changed the design of the uniform. The stockings were no longer brown, but bright red. A reporter for the *St. Louis Republic,* Willie Hall, has been credited with giving the red-stockinged team its new name in 1899: the Cardinals.

Von der Ahe took the National League and its officials to court in an attempt to recapture ownership of the once Browns/now Cardinals. Von der Ahe argued he had not given up his franchise, that the league had stolen it from him, and demanded $25,000 from each team owner. But during the trial Al Spink and others who testified against him convinced the judge that Von der Ahe had given up his rights to the team, and it was ruled that the auction of the Browns had been legal.

On January 29, 1899, *The Sporting News* chortled, "Chris Von der Ahe is a baseball corpse." Years later Charlie Spink would proudly call himself the man who drove Von der Ahe out of baseball.

Von der Ahe returned to the saloon business, where he worked as a bartender, an unknown to a new generation of baseball fans. His drinking became worse and worse. In 1908 he filed for bankruptcy, listing his assets at $200. That summer Charles Spink, of all people, staged a benefit game between the

National League Cardinals and the American League Browns to raise money for Von der Ahe. Five thousand dollars was raised to help get him through his last years. Von der Ahe's creditors immediately moved to attach the money, but Charles Spink managed to forestall them, keeping Von der Ahe from poverty for a few more years.

When Von der Ahe died on June 5, 1913, of cirrhosis of the liver, he was penniless. Charlie Comiskey returned to St. Louis from Chicago to make sure his old boss had a fitting burial at Bellefontaine Cemetery. Among the pallbearers were Comiskey, Al Spink, Ted Sullivan, George McGinnis, and Bill Gleason.

The next day a newspaper headline gave Von der Ahe his proper due, referring to him as THE MAN WHO PUT ST. LOUIS ON THE MAP. The life-sized statue of himself that Von der Ahe had commissioned to memorialize "the greatest feller in baseball" was placed above his grave.

CHAPTER 9

THE ARRIVAL OF MR. RICKEY

DURING the period between 1899 and 1902, when there were no Browns in St. Louis, Al Spink, the sports editor of the St. Louis Post-Dispatch, pined for their return. When Spink learned that Ban Johnson, a well-connected journalist from Cincinnati, was proposing the organization of a second major league, the powerful Spink enthusiastically supported him in the founding of the American League.

Johnson awarded the Milwaukee franchise, which finished the 1901 season with a 48-89 record, to a friend, thirty-three-year-old Cincinnati resident Robert Lee Hedges, who immediately moved the team to St. Louis and changed its name to the Browns.

Hedges was native of Missouri, born on a farm not far from Kansas City. When he was ten, his father died, and his mother, two brothers, and he moved to Kansas City. He attended school there until his brothers were killed in 1886 by a deadly tornado. After working for three years in Kansas City in the office of the recorder of deeds, he moved to Cincinnati, where he took a job working for a buggy manufacturer. He became an executive with the company, married a Cincinnati socialite whose beauty was praised in the papers, and in 1901 paid $35,000 for the Milwaukee franchise in the American League and transferred it to St. Louis.

Hedges, a businessman, opted to play at Sportsman's Park on the corner of Grand and Dodier. When Hedges first bought the team, the new owner was horrified at the rowdiness of the fans at the ballpark. A fan by the name of Theodore P. Wagner described fifty years later what it was like to go to his first Browns game after the turn of the century.

                    *   *   *

THEODORE P. WAGNER: "Looking back through the haze to our own boyhood, we remember a Sunday afternoon. The time was 1903 and the scene was the squat, rundown wood grandstand of Sportsman's Park.

"The game was between the Browns and the Cleveland team. The occasion was my first big league game, to which I had been escorted by my uncle Paul, an amateur baseball player and ardent fan. I sensed as soon as we took our seats on the hard wood benches that I was going to like baseball.

"Saloons were open on Sundays in that period, and many fans had stopped for refreshments on their way to the park. Pregame activity consisted largely of a lively selling and drinking of brew, and horseplay resulting from same.

"Women fans were a rarity in those days. Very few possessed the hardihood to attend the games. Those who did, and their red-faced escorts, received a raucous and often ribald welcome from the beer drinkers. There were cries of 'Wouldn't she let you out?' and similar witticisms.

"The unfortunate escorts suffered more than the women, who, apparently fired with the zeal that made suffragettes, appeared determined to brazen the thing through. Their escorts, who had no such zealous inspiration burning in their breasts, slunk to their seats and hoped that the unwelcome attention would be transferred elsewhere.

"The beer drinkers had a special weapon. It was a 'brew bomb' fashioned by pouring beer into a peanut bag, and hurriedly hurling the sopping missile at an unsuspecting target some rows below. The splatter and foamy deluge that accompanied a direct hit on a new straw hat was the occasion for a great outburst of innocent merriment by everyone except the target and his immediate neighbors.

"The Browns had a fleet-footed player named Harry Niles, a champion base stealer. Among the Cleveland players was the immortal Napoleon Lajoie, a stylist in the field and an excellent man with the bat. The Cleveland catcher was a squatty individual named [Jay] 'Nig' Clarke. Mr. Clarke was a good player, if somewhat short on the niceties now propounded by Emily Post.

"As the game progressed, beer continued to flow, and 'brewbombs' to fly. Along about the fifth inning, there was an incident resulting in conduct which would have been classified as a riot these days—even in Brooklyn. But in 1903, it was just part of Sunday afternoon at Grand and Dodier.

"The fleet Mr. Niles, having gotten on base and around to third by means not now remembered, tried to steal home. He found the way blocked by the irritable Mr. Clarke, who thoughtfully stepped on Mr. Niles while sinking the ball wrist-deep into his anatomy. Flying bottles immediately darkened the air as threats and profanities were hurled at Mr. Clarke and the unfortunate umpire, who had called Mr. Niles out. Even the ladies in the assemblage stood up and with upraised arms beseeched heaven itself to take note of Mr. Clarke's outrageous conduct.

"It was not long before Mr. Clarke of the Cleveland team received his just deserts. No mean batter, he wanged a ball into the outfield for a double. His triumph was brief. As he slid into second base, one or more Brown infielders, bent on revenging the insult and injury to their Mr. Niles, danced a vigorous buck and wing on Mr. Clarke's shins.

"Mr. Clarke was not one to take such indignities lying down. Scrambling to his feet, goaded by the spiked shoes of his assailants, he began swinging his gnarled fists. Other Browns swarmed in for the kill. Minions of the law, wearing the pot helmets, handlebar mustaches and long blue costs of their day, hurled their bulk into the fray. Shoving and breathing Gaelic oaths, the blue-coats broke up the melee, but not before the hysterical and beer-inspired spectators laid down another bottle barrage.

"The game came to an end all too soon. As the sun swung deep into the West and bluecoats escorted Mr. Clarke and his perspiring associates off the field, I realized that a new world had opened for me. A world of marvelous Sunday afternoon filled with 'brew bombs,' fisticuffs and excitement. I had been converted to baseball in one exposure at Grand and Dodier."

Hedges's goal was to improve attendance by attracting businessmen rather than hooligans. He cleaned up the park and planted grass on the diamond. To stem the rowdiness, he outlawed the selling of beer and whiskey at the ballpark. To attract more women, Hedges inaugurated Ladies' Day, a promotion that allowed women customers to come to the park for only the price of the sales tax.

Hedges hired Jimmy McAleer as his manager, and to build the team he lured outfielder Jesse Burkett and shortstop Bobby Wallace, two future Hall of Famers, from St. Louis in the National League and catcher Joe Sugden from Chicago in the American League.

The Cardinals sued in court, arguing that the reserve clause provided that when a player signed a contract, his obligation continued into the next season at the club's option. The judge ruled otherwise, holding that a contract ran out at the end of the season, despite the clause. The legal wrangle was bitter and split the city of St. Louis into two camps. The ill feeling of one team for the other lasted another fifty years until the demise of the Browns.

Jumping leagues was common the first few years the National and American circuits competed with each other. Davy Jones, who played in Milwaukee the first year of the American League, moved to St. Louis with the team in 1902, then jumped leagues and signed with the Chicago Cubs.

DAVY JONES: "I played six weeks in the summer of 1901 with Rockford in the Three-I League, hit .384, fielded like a blue streak, and before the season was over I was sold to the Chicago Cubs. However, the Milwaukee Brewers in the brand-new American League made me a good offer, so instead of reporting to Chicago, I jumped to Milwaukee. See, the American League was an outlaw league in 1901, and Milwaukee was one of the eight teams in the league that very first year.

"The next year, 1902, the Milwaukee franchise was transferred to St. Louis, and we became the original St. Louis Browns. So not only did I play in the American League the very first year of its existence, but I'm also a charter member of two of the teams in that league. Neither one of which exists any longer, a fact for which I assure you I can in no way be held responsible.

"I'd been with the St. Louis club about two or three weeks. After the game that day, I got a phone call from James A. Hart, the owner of the Chicago Cubs. He'd been pretty sore ever since I'd jumped from the Cubs to the American League the previous August. Mr. Hart said he'd like me to come over and talk with him at his office the next morning. Well, why not?

" 'I see you're going pretty good,' he said to me after I got there.

" 'Yes, that's right,' I said. 'We've got a good club.'

" 'You know,' he said, 'I've lost a lot of good ballplayers to the American League, men like Clark Griffith and [James] 'Nixey' Callahan, not to mention yourself. I'd like to try to get some of you fellows to move the other way. What would you think about jumping back to the Chicago Cubs?'

" 'Well,' I said, 'what have you got to offer?'

"So he thought a minute, got up, walked into the next room, and sent the clerk for some cash. I guess he thought I'd find green cash more tempting than a check. (He was right.)

"Finally he came back. 'How about a two-year contract for $3,600 a year, the highest salary on the club, plus a $500 bonus that you can have right now. Here's the $500!'

"Well, what could I do? I was playing for $2,400, and here was a 50 percent raise plus $500 in cold cash stacked right up right in front of me. And, after all, I wasn't even twenty-two years old yet. Besides, everybody was jumping all over the lot in those days: Sam Crawford, Larry Lajoie, Clark Griffith, Willie Keeler, Cy Young, Jack Chesbro, Ed Delahanty. You name him, he was jumping from one league to the other.

"So I signed.

"I didn't want to go back to my hotel while the Browns were still there, because I wasn't particularly anxious to see any of my teammates. My former teammates, that is. After I was pretty sure they'd all gone out to the White Sox park, I went up to the room, packed my grip and bat bag—in those days, you know, we carried our own bats in a little bag—and took off for the Cubs' West Side Grounds at Lincoln and Polk streets."

Hedges's team was financially successful during his reign. In 1903, his second season, he was reported to have made $168,000, money that he used to build bleachers in Sportsman's Park. In 1907 and 1908 the Browns had two record-breaking seasons. The eccentric George "Rube" Waddell struck out 232 batters in 1908 and pitched the Browns to a fourth-place finish, earning profits that enabled Hedges to remodel Sportsman's Park and build the first concrete grandstand in baseball.

Waddell, who was elected into the Hall of Fame in 1946, had begun his major league pitching career with Louisville in 1897, played for Pittsburgh and Chicago in 1901, and then pitched for Cornelius "Connie" Mack and the Philadelphia A's from 1902 through 1907. Mack tolerated Waddell's penchant for chasing after fire trucks, for being unreliable, and for drinking too much too often because in those six years the big pitcher won 24, 21, 25, 26, 15, and 19 games. At the end of the season, Mack sold his troubled star to St.

RUBE WADDELL
(Courtesy Brace Photo)

Louis, where he won 19 games in 1908, then quickly slid downhill, winning 11 in 1909 and only 3 in 1910 before receiving his release. Acquiring star players on the downward slide of their careers would be a trademark for the entire history of the new Browns.

Jimmy Austin, who was the regular third baseman for the Browns from 1911 to 1919, had played with the New York Highlanders in 1910 when he faced the Browns in one of Waddell's final appearances. He remembered a drinking problem that the talented pitcher couldn't overcome.

JIMMY AUSTIN: "When I was with the Highlanders, Rube [Waddell] was with the St. Louis Browns. He'd left Connie Mack by then and was near the end of his career. This day I'm thinking about we were riding to the ball park in the tally-ho to play the Browns, knowing Rube was going to pitch against us. As we got near the park, somebody yelled, 'Hey, look, there's Rube.'

"And darned if it wasn't. He was scheduled to pitch that day, but there he was, standing out in front of the swinging doors of a saloon with a mug of beer that big. He's waving and yelling to us, and while we're yelling and waving back and forth, he holds up a beer, like as to say 'skoal,' and downs the whole thing, chug-a-lug, right like that. And as the tally-ho continued on, we saw Rube go back into the saloon.

"Doggone it, though, when game time came, darned if Rube wasn't out there, ready to pitch. I'll never forget it as long as I live. He went along all right for three innings, but in the fourth we got two men on base, and then Rube grooved one to me, which I promptly hit over the fence. As I'm trotting around the bases, Rube is watching me all the way, and as he kept turning around on top of the mound, he got dizzy, and by golly he fell over right on his rear end. Fell over right flat on his can!

"Oh, that started everybody to laughing so hard we could hardly play. Some guys laughed so much they practically had a fit. All except the St. Louis manager, Jack O'Connor. He came running out and yelled, 'Come on out of there. You didn't want to pitch anyhow.' Somehow that made everybody laugh all the more. Good old Rube. In his life he gave a lot of people a lot of enjoyment."

As Waddell sank, the Browns sank with him. In 1909 Waddell finished 11-14, and the Browns finished seventh; in 1910 Waddell won 3 games and then left baseball. The Browns that year finished dead last with a 47-107 mark.

Jack O'Connor, the manager of the 1910 Browns, had been a tough catcher-outfielder during a career that began in 1887 in the American Association with Cincinnati and lasted a total of twenty-one seasons, including his last three with the Browns.

Hedges gave O'Connor a two-year contract for 1910 and 1911, but at the end of the 1910 season, the Browns manager was involved in an unsavory incident that cost him his job and his career.

On the final day of the 1910 season, the Browns played Cleveland in a season-ending doubleheader. For a team squarely in last place, the game ordinarily would have had no meaning, but Larry Lajoie, the star second baseman for the Naps, was fighting it out for the batting title with Ty Cobb of the Detroit Tigers. The winner was to receive an expensive, luxurious automobile (back then they were known as "benzine buggies") called a Chalmers 30.

At the start of the day, Cobb, a fierce loner who was despised by almost everyone, was hitting .380. The gregarious Lajoie was at .372. If Lajoie could get a hit every time up and if Cobb made out a couple of times, "the Fabulous Frenchman" had a shot at catching "the Georgia Peach."

Albert "Red" Nelson started on the mound for the Browns, and he gave up a triple to Lajoie in his first at-bat. The next time up Lajoie saw that Browns rookie third baseman John "Red" Corriden was playing very deep, and he bunted for a hit. The next two times up Corriden remained deep on the grass, and twice more Lajoie laid down bunts for base hits. Lajoie was in the hunt.

In the second game against Browns rookie Alex Malloy, Lajoie bunted for a hit his first time up. The second time up he feigned a full swing, then bunted again for a hit. By this time, the fans were catching on to the fact that the Browns were conspiring with Lajoie to help the Cleveland star win the batting title against Cobb. Offended by the breach of integrity of the game, they began to boo.

The next time up, with a man on first, Lajoie again bunted. When the third baseman bobbled the ball, the official scorer ruled it a sacrifice. The Cleveland players, who wanted it ruled a base hit, reacted strongly.

An unsigned note was passed to official scorer Dick Collins that he would get a new suit of clothes if he would change his ruling. Harry Howell, a Browns pitcher who knew Collins, went to the press box to plead on Lajoie's behalf. Collins sent him away.

That night Cleveland manager Jim "Deacon" McGuire also badgered Collins to change his ruling, saying that the batting title would not only get Lajoie the Chalmers but a better contract for the next year as well. Collins told McGuire to watch himself. He said, "It's dangerous business, and I'm not so sure that there won't be a lot of hell over what has already happened."

Collins was prophetic. American League president Ban Johnson conducted an investigation. *The Sporting News* said, "There's something rotten here," and assailed Browns manager Jack O'Connor for allowing the tainted hits.

As a result of the probe, third baseman Corriden was cleared, on the assumption he was only following orders in playing so deep. So was Lajoie. But Harry Howell, a thirteen-year veteran, was released at the end of the season and never played again, and Browns manager O'Connor, who had once helped Ban Johnson recruit players for the American League, was fired, despite having a year left on his contract.

Years later O'Connor looked back on the incident.

JACK O'CONNOR: "I got the rap for that Lajoie affair, but it wasn't all my fault. I suppose as manager I might have directed my infielders differently. Still, it was the last day of the season and I let the players run things pretty much to suit themselves. Sure, I knew Lajoie was due to get whatever breaks could be passed his way. All of the players wanted him to beat out Cobb. In fact, there was nothing basically crooked about it and it so happened that the hits credited to Larry had no direct bearing on the result.

"We won the first game and in the second game there was no chance for the Browns, because they were shut out. The truth is that the games, having no bearing on the pennant race, were more genuinely contested than usually are the wind-up games of a schedule, when it used to be the custom to do a lot of horseplay, clowning, and switching about of the players. I do not present this as a defense for what happened, but there are things that occur to me now, nearly thirty-two years later. Mind you, not a nickel was waged on the games."

O'Connor said that if he had been given another chance, he would have done things differently and expressed regret over the incident.

JACK O'CONNOR: "I'll never forget my conference with [Ban] Johnson. He, of course, put the blame on me for permitting the players to be out of position, but as much as admitted to me that the evidence showed that I had not directed my men to help Lajoie. It was their own doing. So it was that I left the conference feeling pretty certain that no drastic punishment would be handed out to me. In fact, I had been led to believe that a fine or reprimand would be all there was to it.

"I got on the train to St. Louis that night. Remember, I was under contract for 1911 as manager. When the train reached Springfield, Illinois, the Pullman porter came to me and asked me if I had seen the morning newspaper. I told him I hadn't. 'Well,' said the porter, 'there's bad news for you. You've been fired.' And sure enough, there was the story of my dismissal in big type.

"I might have been well fixed today, perhaps still in the game, had I squashed that thing before it had a good start. I had just become a big league manager and had another year to go on my contract. That damned automobile was behind the whole thing and I might add that Lajoie probably was given hits before he ever came to St. Louis with the Naps for that final series.

"I wish I had it to do over again."

O'Connor sued the Browns for $5,000, the amount of his contract, and received judgment. But his baseball career was over. Such odd occurrences would also be a trademark of the St. Louis Browns. The team rarely finished in the first division, but as for bizarre moments, the Browns would have many. Another came two years later, during the 1913 season, when a second Browns manager, George Stovall, was cast from the league.

JIMMY AUSTIN: "When I went to St. Louis [in 1911], Bobby Wallace was the manager. One of the greatest fielding shortstops who ever lived, you know. It was a delight to play third base next to that fellow. Bobby played most of his career with the Browns. He was their regular shortstop from 1902 to about 1914 or so. Anyway, they made Bobby a playing manager in 1911, but he wasn't very happy as a manager, and in the middle of the 1912 season they got George Stovall to replace him. Bobby stayed at shortstop, though, for a few more years. George was a playing manager too. He managed and played first base.

"However, George spit himself out of job the next year. Yeah, that's right, he expectorated himself right out of a job. He got into an argument with an umpire by the name of Charlie Ferguson. It was an awful rumpus. They were hollering at each other and one thing and another, and finally Ferguson threw George out of the game.

"Well, before he left, George had to go back to first base to get his glove. Our dugout was on the third base side. So Stovall walked, as slow as he could, all the way around behind the umpire and to first base, picked up his glove, and then started back the same way, maybe even slower. Well, the longer he walked, the madder he got. And the longer he took, the madder the umpire got.

"As George came around behind Ferguson on the way back to our dugout, the umpire told George to hurry it up. I guess that was the straw that broke the camel's back, because George let fly with a big glob of tobacco juice— ptooey—that just splattered all over Ferguson's face and coat and everywhere else. Ugh, it was an awful mess. It was terrible. George always did chew an uncommonly large wad, you know.

"Well, they suspended George for that. In fact, they threw him clear out of the league. I don't believe he ever played another game in the American League, although I think that George did manage the Kansas City club in the Federal League later on.

"So there we were in the middle of the season—that was 1913—without a manager. So who did Mr. Hedges, the president of the club, ask to be temporary manager until they got a new one? Of all people, me.

"Mr. Hedges called me in after Stovall was suspended and said, 'Jim, will you come out to my apartment tonight?'

" 'Sure,' I said, 'where is it?' How was I supposed to know where the devil he lived?

"He told me, I went out there, and when I got there here's this Branch Rickey fellow. He'd been a second-string catcher years before with St. Louis, but since then he'd become a lawyer and was at the University of Michigan as a teacher or a baseball coach or something.

" 'Jim, I want you to meet Mr. Rickey,' said Mr. Hedges. 'Mr. Rickey is going to be the manager next year, but we'd like you to finish out as manager for the rest of this season.' Which, of course, I did.

"So that's how I met Branch Rickey. A year or two later, Branch brought George Sisler to the Browns. Branch had been his coach at the University of Michigan. And you know the tremendous ballplayer Sis became. One of the very greatest who ever lived. Golly, he hit like blazes, .407 one year and .420 another. He was unbelievable with that bat. Really, you had to see it to believe it.

"I was Branch Rickey's Sunday manager, you know. He'd promised his mother and father he'd never go near a ballpark on Sunday, so I managed the team for him every Sunday all the time he was with the Browns."

When Robert Hedges hired Branch Rickey to be manager of the Browns in 1913, it was the resumption of a friendship that had begun back in 1906 when Rickey caught for the Browns. Rickey was studying to become a lawyer, and baseball was merely a sideline then. At the end of the 1906 season, Rickey returned to Ohio Wesleyan University to study and to coach football and act as the school's director of athletics.

In mid-October, from out of the blue, Rickey received a check for $320 from Hedges. He had been voted a full share of their city series victory over the Cardinals. Rickey was touched by Hedges's generosity.

During the winter, New York Highlander manager Clark Griffith acquired Rickey to catch Jack Chesbro, the great knuckleballer. But when he left Ohio to join the Highlanders, Rickey discovered he had a sore right arm. In a game on June 28, 1907, his arm aching, the Washington Senators stole 13 bases against him. The record stands to this day. He caught only one more game, then packed his bags to study law in earnest at Ohio State University.

In April of 1909, Rickey came down with tuberculosis. He and his wife Jane spent ten days at the Trudeau Sanitarium at Saranac Lake, New York,

CATCHER BRANCH RICKEY
(Courtesy Brace Photo)

and he stayed in bed until August, when the fever subsided. After recovering, he arrived at Ann Arbor, Michigan, the day before the first day of law classes. He had enough money for only the first semester, so when he saw that the baseball coach had resigned, he applied and got the job. His team did well, and in June of 1911, he graduated from law school.

In September of 1911, he and two classmates passed the Idaho bar. They settled in Boise because they liked the climate, but Rickey made little money, and he returned to Ann Arbor to start the university's intramural program and to continue to coach varsity baseball.

One of his players was a freshman engineering student by the name of George Sisler. Sisler couldn't play on the varsity because he was a freshman, but Rickey let him work out with the regulars. In one scrimmage Sisler struck out 20 of the 21 batters he faced. Against the alumni, a team featuring six former All-Americans, Sisler threw a four-hit shutout and struck out 15.

George Sisler always was one of Rickey's favorites. When in 1965 Rickey wrote the closest thing to his autobiography, *The American Diamond,* with illustrator Robert Riger, he named Sisler as one of the sixteen immortals who changed the face of baseball. Rickey recalled his first meeting with Sisler when he coached at the University of Michigan in 1912.

BRANCH RICKEY: "As the baseball coach at the University of Michigan, I had asked for varsity baseball candidates through notice in the *Michigan Daily*. While registering and interviewing applicants in Waterman Gymnasium, I was confronted by a handsome boy of eighteen with serious gray-blue eyes. He was well-built, about five feet nine inches tall and weighing about 160 pounds. He wore a blue sweater and a well-used fielder's glove on his right hand. He introduced himself as George Sisler, a pitcher from Akron, Ohio, and an engineering student in the freshman class.

" 'Oh, a freshman,' I said. 'Too bad. You can't play this year. This inside work is only for the varsity.'

"Silent and crestfallen, he reflected deepest disappointment as he turned away. A moment later the team captain, Norman Hill, came up to ask if I knew about 'that kid in the blue sweater you were just talking to.' Norm then told me about his high school record and asked that I take another look at the boy before dismissing him. I inquired immediately for a catcher. Lo and behold, young Sisler had his high school catcher right with him, a boy named Baer, and a good catcher too.

"It was a one-minute workout, all that is needed when coaches meet greatly impressive youngsters. This boy was something in grace and delivery on the very first pitch. The freshman battery was made an exception and stayed out with the varsity during the entire practice period. The 'workouts' were unforgettable. George pitched batting practice inside the cage regularly and created no end of varsity embarrassment, although restricted to the use of his fastball. His left-handed speed and control made him almost unhittable.

"He was a major league pitcher right there!"

Rickey, always mindful of the kindness of Robert Hedges, had seen three players he felt were good enough to play for the Browns, and he wrote the Browns owner and recommended them. But Hedges didn't act quickly enough, and one of the prospects, catcher Frank "Pancho" Snyder, signed with the Cardinals.

It was Hedges's turn to be grateful, and in the winter between the 1911 and 1912 seasons, Hedges contacted Rickey and told him of his intention of purchasing the Kansas City team in the American Association. Hedges asked Rickey if he would run the team as its president and general manager.

There had been a long-standing rule against stockpiling players in the minor leagues. But many of the owners got around the rule by loaning players out to minor league teams surreptitiously with gentleman's agreements. The one drawback was that sometimes a minor league owner would go back on his word and sell the players out from under the major league owner.

Rickey turned Hedges down, saying he was setting up a law firm in Idaho. Hedges then suggested Rickey scout for him. He could study the players in the Pacific Coast League and make recommendations. Hedges would pay all expenses for Rickey and his wife.

Rickey agreed, and during one trip to Los Angeles, he recommended three players to Hedges, including catcher Sam Agnew and pitcher Walt Leverenz, who both played for the Browns in 1913.

Hedges asked Rickey to meet him in Salt Lake City, and in their meeting asked Rickey to be his second-in-command on the Browns. He would be in charge of acquiring players, making trades, and of strengthening the Browns in every way. He was offered a $7,500 salary and he could continue as coach of Michigan one more season. This time Rickey accepted.

In January of 1913, Rickey came to St. Louis, where he was named second vice president and secretary. There was no fanfare and no official announcement of his exact status and duties. He had no private office, and he returned to Ann Arbor for his final baseball season. He returned to St. Louis on June 1 to begin one of the most significant careers in the history of baseball.

Hedges was an astute businessman, and he realized that he did not have the kind of money to spend on prospects like the teams in New York and Chicago had. It was Robert Hedges, along with Branch Rickey, who devised a way to sign and develop young players for their major league team.

BRANCH RICKEY: "Let's get right, once and for all, the really early beginning of the farm system. Nobody had fabulous amounts of money to spend for finished ballplayers from the minor leagues or from one another. Our Browns club was so-so, though not the worst team in the league. I brought to Mr. Hedges a wide acquaintanceship in college circles throughout Ohio, Indiana, and the Western Conference, and beyond those universities through Kentucky, Tennessee, and even Georgia, because of the annual spring vacation trip of our Michigan team. I had coaching friends also throughout the East. I cultivated those contacts and kept in close touch with them when I went to St. Louis.

"They told me about players, more than I could take care of because of our low player limit. With no place to put these recommended players, I had to find minor league clubs to take them and sign them on a title basis. They owned the contracts and, in return for recommending and signing the players, we tried to have a gentleman's agreement on later purchase. There was no rule against it at the time. There shouldn't be any rule against it. It was the only way for a major league club to get players except by outright purchase.

"It was very easy to place players with a minor league club on an arrangement that gave you the right to purchase them later at a fair price. If that kind of arrangement could have been maintained and kept realistic and honest as just that, there is no reason for the gentleman's agreement not being in use and entirely legal today. Unfortunately there was a disposition of the minor league clubs owning these college contracts to find a market far in excess of anything we could pay. Indeed, they sometimes manufactured a market to realize the highest dollar.

"For that reason, some clubs where I first placed my players—Montgomery, Alabama, was the chief repository and later party to the first written working agreement—took the players and refused to be honest about it. Since the verbal agreement could not be proved, they simply sold the players to another major league club at a higher price. That didn't pay, and it wasn't right. It occurred to me that I had to have something more than an oral understanding. Friendship was vital and friendship is the best thing you can have, but when a man who is your friend has controlling or determining interest in a minor league club, and dies or sells out, then all your agreements amount to nothing. This complex problem arose and begged for solution all during my first year with the St. Louis Browns.''

Rickey and Hedges tried to buy one or more high-classification minor league clubs to season their players but were foiled when the National Commission declared that ownership by a major league team of a minor league team would be outlawed after January 1, 1914. Hedges and Rickey were stopped cold.

The original no-farming rule had been passed in 1903, decreeing that no player could be sent down from a major league club. Despite the rule, seven years later Brooklyn had 61 players under contract to Philadelphia's 31. Cleveland had 60 under contract, Washington 29. Gentleman's agreements made this possible. In the winter of 1912–13, rulemakers raised the big league player roster to 35, with a reduction to 25 a month after the season began.

Hedges and Rickey thought they had solved their problem by devising baseball's first open and aboveboard working agreement. In July of 1913, they loaned four Montgomery, Alabama, businessmen $12,500 to buy the ballclub. Hedges and Rickey agreed to supply the players at no expense to the club in exchange for the privilege of buying any or all of the player contracts for a flat $1,000 at the end of each season. But at the last minute one of the merchants tried to change the financing agreement, and Hedges and Rickey canceled the deal.

The American League held a draft meeting shortly after Labor Day in 1913 in order to combat the Federal League, which was signing up their players. The meeting was held in Cincinnati. Of the 108 minor league players selected by the sixteen clubs, the Browns selected 30 of them. The Browns paid more than $100,000 for these players. Observers said it was a poor gamble.

BRANCH RICKEY: "Poor nothing. Two outstanding players will be worth that. Meanwhile, we'll look at twenty-eight others besides our regular team of thirty-five."

A third of the 30 players ended up in the major leagues, some for many years. The top prize was Bill James, a right-handed pitcher, and Leon Cadore, who became a star after leaving the Browns. Rickey had come up with a revolutionary new concept. It violated no existing rule. Here was the birth of the farm system.

When Jack O'Connor was barred from managing at the end of the 1910 season, Hedges replaced him with Bobby Wallace, just as the star shortstop's productivity in the field and at bat was coming to an end. In a season when Connie Mack's Philadelphia A's won 96 games behind such marquee players as Jack Coombs, Eddie Plank, Eddie Collins, and Frank "Home Run" Baker, the

Browns found themselves mired deep in the cellar in a dismal 45-107 effort. Only 207,000 fans turned out for the 77 home dates at Sportsman's Park. As the fortunes of the Browns fell precipitously that 1911 season, Robert Hedges discovered that owning a baseball team could be a very expensive proposition.

In 1912 the Browns finished 53-101 under Wallace and George Stovall. and in 1913 they went 57-96 under Stovall, 2-6 under Jimmy Austin, and 5-6 under Rickey.

It was at the end of the 1913 season that Robert Hedges decided he should hire the scholarly and knowledgeable Branch Rickey to dig him out of his hole. Hiring a manager with so little experience was a dramatic move, but Hedges could see that Rickey had an encyclopedic knowledge of the game. Rickey, now the general manager and manager, for the first time had real power to make a difference.

CHAPTER 10

PHIL BALL'S FATAL MISTAKE

STOVALL returned from his suspension and remained on the team as a first baseman, and after a while he began to resent Rickey and demanded his release. Rickey wouldn't give it to him. By the end of the season, unsurprisingly, Stovall had become a thorn in Rickey's side and at the intercity postseason series with the Cardinals, managed by Miller Huggins, Rickey decided he no longer could afford to keep Stovall on the team.

BRANCH RICKEY: "I didn't wish to make it known at the time, but Stovall cast his lot with the Federal League while still under contract to the Browns and then began tampering with players on my club. I refused to permit him on the ball field during the fall series. Prior to that, having learned that he was not working for the best interests of the club, I asked him to stay away from the games. When he refused, I did the only thing possible. I removed his uniform from his locker."

Stovall was not the only person with whom Rickey was feuding. Near the end of 1913, Rickey entered into open warfare in the press with Miller Huggins, who like him was a lawyer. Rickey was a theorist, and among his interesting, novel theories was that a team could prepare for the regular season better if it traveled to a warm weather site and practiced for a couple of months just prior to the start of the season. To implement his idea, he arranged for the Browns to travel to St. Petersburg, Florida, to work out under the sun in February and March of 1914. A newspaperman wrote an article about Rickey's plans, noting the type of drills he intended to use in working out his players.

A writer for another paper interviewed Huggins, who scoffed at his ideas of practicing sliding in a sand-filled pit.

Rickey, sensitive to even the mildest criticism all his life, could not let Huggins's comments go unanswered. He harangued Huggins in the papers and defended his theory that players can learn techniques and fundamentals and be developed. He stressed that raw ability is important, but that any athlete can be schooled to be better. Rickey predicted that Huggins would copy his theories before he left St. Louis.

In mid-February of 1914, Branch Rickey and the St. Louis Browns traveled to St. Petersburg, in large part due to the persistence and civic-mindedness of Al Lang, who openly courted baseball teams to visit the city in winter. Once there, Rickey opened baseball's first all-purpose training camp, the most novel and rugged of all time. George Palfry, the team photographer, and five newspapermen, accompanied Rickey and the players. Rickey described his first training camp site.

BRANCH RICKEY: "After a prolonged struggle among real estate promoters, the training grounds site was located on Snell and Hamlett's Coffee Pot Bayou district, a select residential area. The sandy stretch, cleared of pines, cabbage palms, and palmetto bush, contained a large wooden grandstand, handball courts, three net-covered batting cages, sprinting lanes for speed tests, and sliding pits."

One of Rickey's best-imitated innovations—one that would be used and copied for generations by teams everywhere—was his "pitching strings." Rickey placed two upright poles at either side of home plate and connected them by two horizontal white cords across the front edge of the plate at average knee height and shoulder height. Cross strings were then connected by upright cords 17 inches apart to indicate plate width. The thin white rectangle outlined the strike zone. The catcher squatted behind the strings and plate. The pitcher stood at the regulation distance and tried to "hit the strings."

Rickey, who wanted his players to be in top shape when the season started, made the Browns players walk a mile and a half from Fifth Avenue North to what is now North Shore Drive and 30th Street. After a strenuous workout, they walked back. Everyone had to be up and eating at 8:30 A.M.

Rickey made certain his Florida excursion received plenty of local publicity. The *St. Petersburg Independent* published an extra. Sportswriters wrote 15,000 words. Special trains brought crowds from Tarpon Springs and excursion boats sailed into Coffee Pot Bayou for the first exhibition game against the Chicago Cubs. The National Leaguers made the two-hour trip across the bay from Tampa on the steamer *Manatee*.

Three thousand spectators jammed the stands to see Rickey's Browns beat the Cubs, 9–5.

In 1914 the Browns improved dramatically, finishing in fifth place with a 71-82 record. The team had no stars, no drawing power, and no prospects on the horizon. What it had was Branch Rickey's rare baseball intellect.

An article in the *St. Louis Post-Dispatch* in June of 1914 accurately described Rickey's influence on the Browns.

"Manager Branch Rickey's team is arousing the interest of the country with its remarkable spurt from last place in 1913 to a near-championship position. He is no longer referred to as a baseball theorist. He has put to flight penners of the sarcastic criticism and skeptics who predicted that practice, not theory, won ball games. His applied theories have made the Browns one of the country's best and most exciting teams. He has shown himself a master of the science of the game, a capable handler of men and a man who can practice what he preaches."

In 1914 the Browns also improved at the box office, drawing 335,000 fans, only 11,000 fans fewer than the crosstown Cardinals, but the attendance of both teams was cut by the Federal League "Sloufeds," owned by refrigeration magnate Philip De Catesby Ball. The Federal League, which took the field in 1914 and 1915 before folding, set Ball back $182,000 in its two years of existence. Hedges, meanwhile, was beginning to lose more money than he could afford. With three teams in St. Louis, there weren't enough fans to go around.

In 1915 the Browns held spring training in Houston. As rumored defections to the Federal League by Browns players swirled around the team, Rickey fought to keep his players in line and also to tutor his youngsters.

The one bright spot came in late June of 1915, once Rickey's star ballplayer at Michigan graduated.

When freshman George Sisler had reported to coach Rickey in 1912, he had acknowledged that he had signed a contract with Akron in the Ohio–Pennsylvania League. He was under the legal age of consent, and the paper was not signed by his parents. He never took any money. When Sisler learned his high school catcher, Russ Baer, was going to Michigan, he decided to go to college instead of going pro. Rickey, who knew contract law, assured him the contract was not binding.

Sisler as a sophomore had pitched 57 innings and struck out 84. When he didn't pitch, he played the outfield and first base. He hit 46 for 104, a .443 batting average. Sisler, captain of the 1914 championship team, finished his college career with a 13-3 pitching record, and 120 hits in 297 at-bats for a .404 career average. When he graduated, he chose to play for Rickey and the Browns in St. Louis.

Akron, meanwhile, sold the "contract" to Columbus, and Columbus sold it to the Pittsburgh Pirates, owned by Barney Dreyfuss, who insisted Sisler be suspended from playing ball for Michigan as a result of signing the contract and be ordered to report to the Pirates.

Rickey went before the National Commission and, using his great oratory powers, urged it not to enforce an illegal contract. He predicted that if Sisler's contract were upheld that parents, colleges, and even high schools would be alienated from professional baseball forever.

He intoned, "For who is going to trust you, if you cajole minors into signing contracts and then declare them suspended—as you have tried to suspend Sisler—when they change their mind?"

GEORGE SISLER
(Drawing by Ron Stark)

Chairman Garry Herrmann, the owner of the Reds, cast the deciding vote against Dreyfuss, ending a long friendship.

In 1915 Rickey had assembled the best crop of young players in baseball. Rickey's protégé, George Sisler, pitched and won 4 games for the Browns in 1915.

BRANCH RICKEY: "Within a week after he came to the majors in late June 1915, he pitched against Cleveland in St. Louis. He struck out 9 and beat their ace right-hander, Guy Morton, 3–1. It was a great day for George when he beat Walter Johnson, his boyhood hero, 1–0—in fact, a second time 2–1."

Bill Stern, for fifty years a nationally renowned sports commentator, recalled Sisler's rookie season with the Browns.

BILL STERN: "It all began back in the season of 1915, when [George Sisler] graduated from the University of Michigan. He reported to the St. Louis Browns (the manager was Branch Rickey, who had been the boy's baseball coach at Michigan).

"In that year, the most feared pitcher was Walter Johnson, who tossed them for the Washington Senators. The season before, Johnson had won 27 games, the season before that, 28 games, and still another season before that, 36 games. So you can see how great a pitcher 'the Big Train' was in the season of 1915.

"In this same year, the rookie hurler for the St. Louis Browns also proved his worth. The first time he pitched against the great Johnson, the youngster won a shutout decision by a 1–0 score. It created a tremendous sensation. Then this kid straight from a college campus proved that his victory over the magnificent Walter Johnson was no fluke, for the second time he faced the old master he licked him again, winning a great pitcher duel by a 2–1 score.

"It was an amazing beginning for a college kid. But the manager of the Browns, anxious to use the youngster every day, made him give it up and become a first baseman. A potentially wonderful pitcher was lost, but baseball gained a player who was among the greatest first basemen of all time."

Rickey was faced with the same dilemma as Ed Barrow when the Red Sox manager had pitcher Babe Ruth. Rickey saw that Sisler hit as well as he pitched, and the baseball man extraordinaire decided that the boy would be more valuable to the team as an everyday player.

BRANCH RICKEY: "He showed such promise of greatness as a hitter while pitching that he was returned to first base, where he had been tried briefly, and finished his first year with an average of .285. During the next seven years playing first base, he surpassed practically all records, both as batsman and fielder. His average assists per game have never been equaled, and his league mark of 140 for a 154–game season remained for twenty-nine years. That figure came in 1920, the year he set the record 257 base hits for a single season that still stands. He led American League hitters with a mark of .407 in one of the greatest seasons any player ever enjoyed. [In 1922 Sisler hit .420!]

"In his first eight seasons, 1915 to 1922 inclusive, Sisler was in a class by himself as a symbol of individual achievement. His every move on the ball field reflected the artistry of physical perfection. During those eight years, he batted .361 and averaged 1 stolen base every 3.7 games. He climaxed the period with 51 steals in one season. But the cold statistics cannot do justice to the full scope of his baseball life. They cannot, for example, reflect the coordination and artistry of a matchless defensive move that Sisler made at first base in Fenway Park, Boston, shortly after joining the Browns.

"When none out and Boston runners on first and third, Burt Shotton, our left fielder, caught a fly ball, conceded the run and made a surprise throw to Sisler, beating the runner returning to first base for a double play. Without an instant of hesitation or lost motion, Sisler whirled and rifled the ball with bullet speed and accuracy to [Hank] Severeid, our catcher, who tagged the runner trying to score from third base. It was the most amazing triple play I ever saw.

"Sisler once fielded a routine grounder deep behind first base. Running forward, he lofted the ball toward the bag to meet the approaching pitcher covering. It was a high toss. Then, realizing the pitcher wouldn't arrive in time, Sisler raced in, caught his own throw, and stepped on the bag to retire the hitter.

"And it was a climax, because an insidious eye affliction all but ended his career and made play in 1923 impossible. But Sisler fought back and returned as playing manager of the Browns in 1924 by dint of raw courage and determination. He contributed seven more years of fine major league play, but those marvelous reflexes and the keen eyesight were not as before.

"George Sisler was fortified with the ideal temperament for a baseball player, for his will to win was not a savage uncontrolled emotion. It stemmed from an orderly, regulated mind always subject to his reflexes and will. His intelligent daring, versatility, contagious spirit in contests, his refusal to condone mistakes which were controllable in advance, his brief yet effective words of instruction, and, above all, his marvelous aptitude made him a nonpareil."

Branch's boy would become the greatest player in the history of the St. Louis Browns and would be rated with Lou Gehrig as the finest first baseman in the history of the game. The lifetime average of the fifteen-year veteran was .340.

The Browns finished the 1915 season 63-91, but the future looked brighter than the team's record indicated. George Sisler hit a respectable .285 in 81 games as a twenty-two-year-old rookie and looked brilliant in the field. Robert Hedges rewarded Rickey with another contract at the same $7,500 salary.

In December of 1915, peace was declared between Organized Baseball and the Federal League. As part of the treaty, the St. Louis Federal League team went out of existence, and Robert Hedges sold his interest in the Browns to one of the owners of the St. Louis Feds, Phil Ball.

Hedges had given a purchase option on his 90 percent of the shares to John Bruce, secretary of the National Commission, and Walter Orthwein. They sold the option to Ball for $525,000 and cleared a $90,000 profit. Hedges made more than $400,000 on his original investment, giving him the distinction of being the last man ever to make money owning the St. Louis Browns.

Phil Ball was a gruff and growling Iowan of fifty-six who had been a cowhand, a construction worker on a Tennessee railroad, and a killer of buffalo for hides in Texas. He had played baseball in Louisiana and lived in many states until he settled down in St. Louis and made a fortune making machinery for the ice business. Ball manufactured ice machines for companies like Armour and Swift and for the biggest breweries in the country.

When the new Browns officers were named, Branch Rickey was not one of them. Ball informed the press that Rickey was not going to be part of the new organization. Ball, the former cowhand, despised the do-gooders who were pushing the country toward Prohibition. Rickey, while studying law at Ohio State, had traveled the state, stumping in favor of a national ban on alcohol. Because Rickey was a teetotaler, he was not to be trusted. Arthur Mann, Rickey's biographer, described the first meeting between Ball and Rickey.

ARTHUR MANN: "Roscoe Hillenkoetter [Rickey's secretary] brought Ball in to see Rickey for the first time at Sportsman's Park. Branch looked up and saw the fleshy, pear-shaped face twist slightly. Ball rubbed a stubby hand through his iron-gray, brush-cut hair and bellowed, 'So you're the God-damned prohibitionist!' "

In 1916 Ball replaced Rickey as manager with Fielder Jones, who had managed Ball's Federal League team. Rickey continued to work in the front office, spending long hours placing the Browns' excess players.

At the league meetings in February of 1917, Rickey was visited by James C. Jones, attorney for the crosstown St. Louis Cardinals, a team that had had little success since their inception in 1899. Jones told Rickey that their financial plight was desperate. Six years earlier Helene Hathaway Robison Britton (daughter of Frank Robison and niece of Stanley Robison) had inherited the club and had lost a lot of money. It was likely an out-of-town owner would come in and move the Cards franchise. She wanted $350,000 for the team.

BRANCH RICKEY: "Many wanted the club, but no one had the fair price that Mrs. Britton asked—$350,000. What I didn't know, and Jones told me, was that several businessmen had just met at his home to discuss his own plan for buying the club and keeping it in St. Louis. His partner was Mrs. Britton's personal attorney, and easily got a purchase option, which was good until March third. Jones then explained to me his Knothole Gang idea. It was based on the public sale of stock at a nominal price per share, with two shares entitling the holder to sponsor a full season of free admission for one boy. I thought the idea splendid and suggested the age limit.

"Then Jones said, 'If we go through with the plan, will you be president?'

I said I couldn't reply, being under contract to the Browns. However, Mr. Ball and I had discussed the possibility of improvement when I last signed, which is usual, and he said he wouldn't stand in my way if anything came up. So, I told Jones I would speak to Ball as soon as possible."

When Rickey told Ball of the offer, Ball said, "Why, those sonsabitches want to buy that ballclub?"

"It's to be financed by a public sale of stock," said Rickey.

"If you've got a chance to go with them," said Ball, "I wouldn't keep you down for the world."

Rickey thanked him and asked, "Do you want me to pursue it?"

"Let me know what they offer you," Ball said. "I think I can get them to beat it, and I will help you on that contract."

The Cardinals offered Rickey a contract for $15,000 for the 1917 season. Rickey reported back to Ball. Ball asked if he had it in writing. Rickey said he didn't. Ball told him, "Get it. I'll help you with the contract. Have another meeting with those bastards and get enough to make it good."

BRANCH RICKEY: "He had made rough language a part of his gruff nature. The idea, I suppose, was to disarm you by shock, or something. But he was very kind and cooperative during the several meetings we had on the subject. Our final talk lasted a half hour and he promised to 'loop up three or four of those so-and-sos' among the purchasers and tell me whether or not they could be trusted. That was from ten-thirty until eleven.

"At noon I was in Jones's office. We went over the contract, and I signed. Just as we were about to leave for lunch at the Noon-day Club, a call came for me from Sol Swartz. He said Mr. Ball was at the Missouri Athletic Club and wanted to see me immediately. It was very important. I was completely mystified and told Mr. Swartz it was too late, that I had signed [with the Cardinals]. Jones said to go over, since everything was all set now."

When Rickey met with Ball, he was shocked to discover that the Browns owner had radically changed his position. Ball had spoken with league president Ban Johnson, who was horrified to learn that one of the brightest, ablest young executives in the American League was about to switch to the other league. Johnson told Ball, "Under no circumstances must this fellow be lost to the great American League."

When Ball changed directions and suddenly refused to approve the move to the Cardinals, Rickey was in a bind. He told Ball, "But I have no choice now. I only signed after you said it was all right. You gave me your word. We shook hands."

"I don't care," said Ball. "Just tell those bastards you can't go through with it."

Said Rickey, "You can't go back on your word. They're giving it to the press."

"If they do, I'll deny I ever said it."

Rickey replied, "Mr. Ball, whether or not I ever go with the Cardinals, I'll never work another day for you.' "

Years later Rickey commented on his predicament. He said, "I wish I had gone out of baseball at that moment. I was overwhelmed by mortification and shame at hearing a man of big business and responsibility feel obliged to say such a thing. I learned later that Ban Johnson had raised the devil on the telephone with Ball, who was very much under his thumb. I didn't speak to Mr. Ball for many years."

The loss of Branch Rickey from the Browns would create a seismic shift in power for baseball in St. Louis and in America. Within a few short years, Rickey would team up with Cardinal owner Sam Breadon to perfect his farm system concept and would create one of the great dynasties in the history of baseball.

The Browns, without Rickey's genius, would sink into the second division during most of their dreary history as Phil Ball lost hundreds of thousands of dollars trying to stay afloat. At his death in October of 1933, Ball's estate would inherit a woefully underfinanced franchise, one that would struggle and ultimately fade out of existence twenty years later.

THE CARDINALS

CHAPTER 11

RICKEY RESURRECTS THE CARDINALS

BEFORE Branch Rickey joined the St. Louis Cardinals in 1917, the National League franchise had had little success and its future seemed limited. The Robison brothers, who had purchased the franchise in 1898 after the league wrested it from Chris Von der Ahe, boasted several future Hall of Famers, including pitcher Charles "Kid" Nichols and slugger Jesse "The Crab" Burkett, but could not finish higher than fourth. The team was hurt badly in 1901 when Baltimore of the new American League wrested away two of the Cards' famed players: John McGraw and Wilbert Robinson.

The two had been traded to the Cards by Baltimore for $16,000 in 1900, when Oriole owner Harry von der Horst agreed to drop out of the National League in exchange for $30,000 plus whatever he could get for his ballplayers. McGraw and Robinson, the team manager and captain, were Baltimore fixtures who hated the idea of abandoning their hometown. Both swore to quit the game rather than move to St. Louis.

When the spring of 1900 came around, Frank Robison kept after the two men. Robison was a fighter. He had once been swindled out of more than $1 million by a corrupt broker, but he had pursued his legal remedies and recovered the money in court. Robison desperately wanted to add McGraw and Robinson to a team that already featured Cy Young and Jesse Burkett.

Robison met the two stars in Cleveland. In addition to raising their salary, the Cardinal owner granted them two concessions. He allowed them to return to Baltimore to clean up some personal business, and he agreed to allow them to become free agents at the end of the season. Robison insisted this clause remain a secret. As long as the other players didn't find out, he figured, what was the harm? It was a serious mistake on Robison's part.

McGraw and Robinson had hated their year in St. Louis and could not summon the old fire that had pushed them so hard in Baltimore. They would purposefully get themselves ejected from games and then go across the street to the racetrack. The team was floundering in sixth place in August of 1900 when manager Patsy Tebeau was fired. When asked to take his place, McGraw refused.

At the end of the season, McGraw and Robinson were wined and dined by Ban Johnson, who was starting the fledgling American League. The notion was that McGraw and Robinson would return to Baltimore to start a franchise. They signed Joe McGinnity to pitch for them and were in business. Robison tried to argue they would still be bound by the reserve clause despite his promise to let them out of their contracts at the end of the year.

When McGraw left for Baltimore, the Cards had let slip away their best chance for instant success.

McGraw did not last long in Baltimore either. He fought bitterly with American League commissioner Ban Johnson over umpiring and the signing of former teammate Hughie Jennings.

In May of 1902, McGraw got into a fight with Detroit left fielder Dick Harley and broke his jaw. Then he was thrown out of a game for arguing with the umpire. Johnson suspended McGraw for the second time in two years. During his sentence, he met with the owner of the National League's New York Giants, Andrew Freedman. For $10,000, he agreed to ditch the American League and manage the Giants. McGraw would lead the Giants to twelve National League championships and three world championships, while it would take the Cardinals almost thirty years to win their first pennant. The team would get a lot worse before it would become better.

In 1905 ill health forced Frank Robison to step down as Cardinal president, and in 1911 Stanley Robison died, leaving the team to his niece, Helene Hathaway Robison Britton. Late in 1916, Mrs. Britton and her husband Schuyler divorced. World War I was in its third year, and the last-place Cards were playing to empty houses. Mrs. Britton called in manager Miller Huggins, a favorite of hers, and James C. Jones, her attorney, and told them to put the team up for sale. She fully expected that Huggins would buy the team. Mrs. Britton set the sale price at $350,000, but allowed the purchasing group to buy it over time. The first payment was to be $75,000.

Huggins returned to Cincinnati, where he joined with Julius and Max Fleishmann, the yeast moguls. Jones worried that Fleishmann would move the team from St. Louis, and he organized a civic-minded group of fan-stockholders. The group could raise only $50,000, but Mrs. Britton accepted the offer, to the consternation of a disappointed Miller Huggins.

James Jones, in charge of the ownership group, assembled seven of St. Louis's sports editors and baseball writers in his office. He asked each to write down the name of the person who would make the best team president. When he looked at the slips of paper, all had the same name on them: Branch Rickey. Jones himself had been impressed with Rickey's manners and business sense and hired him away from the Browns to be the team's vice president and general manager.

Rickey had been part of the contest to find stockholders to buy the Cardinals. He had enlisted more individual stockholders, but Jones's allies, who were wealthier, raised three quarters of the money, giving Jones control.

The incorporation papers filed on May 2, 1917, indicated that Rickey had bought 200 shares costing $5,000. To pay for it, his parents, J. Frank and Emily Rickey, had mortgaged their farmland and buildings and had wired him the money.

To get altruistic fans to purchase Cardinals stock, James Jones came up with what he felt would be a clever incentive: Anyone who bought a share of stock at the price of $25 had the right to give a season's pass to a deserving underprivileged youngster. The goal was for wealthy benefactors to give kids who couldn't afford it passes to Cardinal games. But the plan initially was a failure, and Rickey knew why.

BRANCH RICKEY: "Unfortunately, the men who bought the shares knew boys with ample spending money and hardly any who needed to be taken off the streets. Because the overprivileged boys, so to speak, declined the gratuitous admissions, we had no Knotholers at all at the first half dozen games for the first season."

Rickey, who was enamored of the concept of the Knothole Gang, figured out how to fix the flaw in a program he believed would provide an invaluable public service. At several board meetings, Rickey convinced the stockholders to sign over their rights to the free tickets to the club. Rickey then contacted nine or ten large organizations serving St. Louis youth and had them appoint adult Knothole Gang committee members to select and invite boys between the ages of ten and sixteen to attend Cardinals games for free. The committee agreed on two rules for attendance: (1) No boy could attend without his parents' consent; (2) No boy could skip school to attend.

Before long, this innovative and effective program would be largely responsible for the heavy shift in loyalty of the St. Louis baseball community over the years away from the Browns, as thousands of youngsters would flock to Cardinals games and become lifelong Redbird fans.

The other, more important, program Rickey intended to implement when he joined the Cardinals was his ingenius farm system. To find players for the Cards, Rickey had hired a former minor league teammate of his by the name of Charlie Barrett to be his chief scout. Barrett had been a scout since 1909, when he was hired by Robert Hedges of the Browns. He had gone to work for the Detroit Tigers in 1917 and then was lured to the Cards by Rickey to help sell shares of stock. When Barrett began with Rickey at the start of 1917, the club was so broke that Barrett made no salary and his office had only one chair in it.

When World War I broke out in 1917, Rickey had to postpone his plans to place promising young players in quantity on minor league rosters until after the war's end. The Cardinals' cause also suffered when, after the team finished third in 1917, American League president Ban Johnson got revenge on Rickey for jumping to the National League by inducing Miller Huggins to leave the Cards and to jump to the New York Yankees in his league. After Johnson planted the idea in the head of Colonel Jacob Ruppert of the Yankees, the American League president then asked his good friend Taylor Spink, editor of *The Sporting News,* to go to Huggins and offer him the Yankee job. It paid twice the salary. Huggins headed East.

Huggins was a Hall of Famer, a top-quality manager, and his loss cost the team dearly. After Huggins's departure, the team's fortunes sank. The 1918 season began with very little cash, barely enough to buy new uniforms. The stockholders owed Mrs. Britton $175,000. The team was mediocre, finishing eighth under manager Jack Hendricks at the end of the attenuated season, which closed up shop on Labor Day, 1918, with the War Department's Work or Fight order.

Shortly after the end of the season, Percy Haughton, Boston Braves president and the former Harvard football coach, enlisted Rickey to join him in a U.S. Army program to devise new ways of launching surprise attacks using gas warfare.

Over Jones's protests, Rickey left the Cardinals to join the Army. He reported to Washington, D.C., and then, while making a voyage aboard the ship *President Grant,* he contracted pneumonia. Rickey trained twenty men in the field of chemical warfare. The Armistice came on November 11, 1918, and by December of 1918, Rickey was home in Lucasville, and in mid-January of 1919, he was back with the Cardinals, a team now so deeply in debt that the stockholders feared for the life of the franchise. When Rickey returned, they looked at him as their savior.

Head scout Charlie Barrett, meanwhile, was feeling the frustration of competing under the current system that enabled flush teams like the Giants, Cubs, and Red Sox to continually outbid him for young players. Part of the problem was that Barrett's reputation was so good that if he offered money to a minor league team for a player, that team's GM would call other major league teams and tell them of Barrett's interest. Anyone Barrett wanted automatically became a target, and Barrett usually was outbid. Barrett asked Rickey what the use was of scouting under those circumstances.

James Jones realized there was only one way out of the team's financial hole: to implement the plan Rickey had spelled out to the board before the war—to sell their surplus players to the minor league teams and in return get an option on their entire teams in the fall.

When spring training opened in February of 1919, the Cardinals' coffers were empty. There was not even money in the budget for railroad fare, so rather than head South for spring training, Rickey had the team work out at nearby Washington University in St. Louis. Stockholder A. M. Diez, who had made money selling shoemakers' tools and supplies, agreed to house the players and buy equipment for spring training. The coaches assiduously guarded the baseballs. The uniforms from the year before that were salvageable were sent to seamstresses for patching. Rickey found a sporting goods store that would make the rest and extend him credit.

Meanwhile, the vultures began circling. The richer teams called to offer money for the one outstanding Cardinal player, a young second baseman by the name of Rogers "Rajah" Hornsby.

Hornsby had come to the Cards before Rickey. After a season in the Texas–Oklahoma League, the eighteen-year-old phenom was promoted to the Cards in 1915 for a cup of coffee. He was brash, outspoken, sure of his ability, and something of a loner. The veterans considered him strange, in that he didn't drink, didn't smoke, and refused to go to the movies, insisting that moviegoing was injurious to a player's eyesight.

In his first full big league season in 1916, Hornsby batted .313, standing out on a roster of mediocre talents. That winter he worked as a checker on a packing house loading dock, gaining muscle and strength. The next year he would bat .327, second highest in the National League. Though a big man, Hornsby had exceptional speed, and he led the league in triples with 17. In 1918 he slumped to .281, driving in 60 runs.

During the summer of 1919, Charles A. Stoneham, the new owner of the New York Giants, asked Rickey to meet him at a café at 110th Street and Broadway in New York City. Stoneham came prepared. He brought with him John McGraw, his manager; Francis X. McQuade, a Giants stockholder; and Oscar Cooper, his banker. During the meeting, Stoneham offered Rickey $150,000—the amount of the Cardinals' debt—for Hornsby.

Rickey had seen what had happened to teams that had sold their best players for cash. Connie Mack had sold his stars following the 1914 season and was doomed to years in the second division. Meanwhile, Boston and Chicago, the teams that had paid him the money for Eddie Collins, Jack Barry, and Herb Pennock, had become powerhouses. Once Boston began selling all its stars to the Yankees beginning in the early 1920s, the Red Sox became doormats, while the Yankees rose to prominence.

Rickey refused to consider Stoneham's offer.

Stoneham called Rickey "irresponsible."

"Your board of directors will hang you for betraying their trust," Stoneham told him. "You must have a price. What is it?"

"Half a million dollars," said Rickey. Stoneham upped his offer for Hornsby to $200,000. Rickey said no.

Stoneham asked Rickey what his stockholders would say. Rickey, who always sought to deal from a position of strength, even when he had none, said, "I'll tell you what I'd do. You do have a player I like."

"I think that can be arranged," said McGraw, thinking Rickey was offering a trade.

"Not so fast, Mr. McGraw," said Rickey. "This is a young college fellow. He's green and only played a few games."

"Who is he and what about him?" asked Stoneham.

"His name is Frisch, and I'll give you $50,000 for him right now."

Stoneham flushed. "What's going on here!" he bellowed. "You haven't got $50,000. You haven't a quarter, Rickey. What are you trying to do, insult us?"

Stoneham made a final offer. He would give Rickey $300,000 for Hornsby, and Rickey could keep him until the end of the season. And if the Giants won the pennant, he would pay an additional $50,000. McGraw snapped at Stoneham that his offer was too generous, but Rickey still said no. He wanted Frisch for cash. But McGraw would not part with the youngster. The meeting broke up. No deals.

Rickey was concerned about what the other members of the Cardinals' board would say when they found out he had turned down $300,000 for Hornsby. But he also realized that as its appointed "savior," he was in a strong position on the team, so Rickey had no qualms about calling reporters to tell the baseball world about Stoneham's $300,000 offer for Hornsby. In doing so, the cagey Mr. Rickey would make both Hornsby and his team seem that much more valuable.

The next day Cards shortstop Johnny "Doc" Lavan took a grounder and without looking threw to second, hitting Hornsby in the head and knocking

ROGERS HORNSBY
(Drawing by Ron Stark)

him unconscious. Rickey, the manager of the team, covered his eyes, fearing the worst.

BRANCH RICKEY: "I'll never forget those moments on the bench. Three hundred and fifty thousand dollars suddenly mobilized out there on the turf at the Polo Grounds. There were large silver dollars. They had arms and legs and wings and faces that mocked at me. They did squads right and squads left, and right oblique and left oblique. They turned cartwheels, and as they rushed on their way out, toward the exits and over the fences, each one laughed at me."

When the Giants came to St. Louis for their first road series, McGraw came at Rickey with a different proposition. He offered five players for Hornsby and even wrote out a lineup card showing Rickey what the new Cardinals lineup would look like.

"They're yours for Hornsby," McGraw said. Frisch was not included. Again, Rickey turned down the offer.

When Rickey considered how much money was being bandied about for two players—Hornsby and Frisch—he resolved even more strongly to implement his farm system idea.

BRANCH RICKEY: "I said to myself that I could find other Hornsbys and other Frisches. I would find them young, but I could find them and develop them. Pick them from the sandlots and keep them until they became stars. All I needed was the place to train them."

In the summer of 1919, Rickey spread the word that the team was looking for young players and the Cardinals began holding workouts. Though he was team manager, Rickey nevertheless somehow found the time to attend the several tryout camps in the St. Louis area. Among the boys in the very first group who tried out for Rickey's Cardinals were three exciting prospects: Ray Blades, Clarence "Heinie" Mueller, and Jim Bottomley. Blades, from Mount Vernon, Illinois, was signed as a pitcher. Mueller, eighteen, told the Cards scouts he could "run like Ty Cobb, hit like Home Run Baker, and field like Tris Speaker." Bottomley was recommended by the principal of his high school in Nokomis, Illinois. When he arrived for the tryout, the nineteen-year-old wore his father's street shoes with spikes nailed to the front and a tattered uniform.

Rickey commented on the three youngsters years later.

BRANCH RICKEY: "Blades's speed could be built on because he was a natural athlete. Mueller had the stolidity and stubbornness of the indefatigable German. Bottomley, properly shod, had the grace and reflexes of a great performer. Had he been unable to walk, I'd have taken him on."

By Labor Day of 1919, the fortunes of the Cardinals continued to sink. The team was in seventh place, and that year the team would draw but 170,000 fans. Owner James Jones wanted Rickey to step down as manager and concentrate on what he considered the most important task: building the team. Rickey, who loved being on the field, preferred being field manager. Since his contract gave him control over his players, he didn't care whether he gave up the vice president's title. Jones, however, saw the bigger picture and wouldn't let him step down as GM.

In November of 1919, Rickey scouted a pitcher by the name of Jesse Haines, who had pitched for Cincinnati in 1918. Kansas City, who now owned the young right-hander, wanted $10,000. Rickey told Jones to borrow the money to get him. Jones did. Haines, who entered the Hall of Fame in 1970, pitched for the Cards for eighteen seasons. Haines would be the last player purchased by the Cardinals for more than twenty-five years. All the rest would reach the big leagues through Branch Rickey's farm system.

Through the winter of 1919, Rickey fumed because the team's lack of funds was preventing him from setting up the farm system that he was envisioning—a string of minor league teams at every level, with the best players rising to the Cardinals. Rickey would sell the rest to other major league teams to help pay the system's cost.

Rickey knew his plan was crucial to the success of the Cardinals, because under the current system, if he signed a player and sent him to the minors for development under an option agreement, he had no control over whether that player would be handled decently or not. If the minor league manager overworked Rickey's pitcher or if a player was neglected, abused, or taught the wrong techniques, there was nothing Rickey could do about it. And because minor league teams made money from selling their own players, players on option didn't always get the best attention.

In his mind, Rickey knew exactly what he needed to do to build a dynasty in St. Louis. Money was needed to give him the opportunity to make that happen.

To that end, Rickey sold 4,000 more shares of stock, raising $100,000 in capital. Among the investors was Sam Breadon, a car dealer who initially paid $200 for four shares of St. Louis Cardinals stock in 1917 as a favor to his friend and cohort Fuzzy Anderson, who was crazy about the game. Later that year James Jones gave a dinner at which the stockholders were able to meet the players. That evening Breadon bought another $1,800 worth of stock.

At the behest of Fuzzy Anderson, Sam Breadon kept increasing his holdings in the Cardinals as the team's fortunes sank until he became one of the larger stockholders in the team. First Breadon was named director and then in December of 1919 was offered the presidency of the St. Louis Cardinals. Breadon told James Jones that if the team would lower the number of its directors from twenty-five to five, he would take the job. They compromised at seven directors, and Breadon was elected president in January of 1920. After becoming president, Breadon then started buying all available stock, including a large block owned by his friend Fuzzy Anderson, who became angered and willing to sell when he wasn't named team vice president.

All his life Breadon had worked for what he owned. He was born in Greenwich Village in lower Manhattan in 1879, the son of a poor truck driver. He completed grammar school and then went to work as a bank clerk. A handsome

SAM BREADON
(Courtesy Brace Photo)

man, Breadon never lost his lower Manhattan accent. He'd say, "The Cah-dinals finished foist."

In 1902 a friend named Gus Halsey invited him to come to St. Louis to open a garage and sell automobiles. He lived in a dollar-a-week room in St. Louis, working as a mechanic and learning all he could about the new invention. One of his customers was Marion Lambert, a pharmaceutical mogul, owner of the company that makes Listerine. Lambert offered Breadon a $10 tip, which he refused.

Said the young Breadon, "I might want to see him in an automobile some day, and I wanted to be able to walk into his office with my head up, on equal terms with him."

When Gus Halsey heard that Breadon intended to go out on his own, he was fired. For months during the following year, Breadon had to borrow money to eat.

In 1904 St. Louis was host to the World's Fair. That was the year everyone was singing the popular lyrics "Meet Me in St. Louie, Louie, Meet Me at the Fair." Breadon talked a confection firm into giving him three cases of Honey Boy popcorn on credit. He stored the popcorn under a grandstand erected by two old ladies and hired a dozen boys to go out and sell Honey Boy.

He made some money. Not a lot, but it was a start. When Breadon decided he wanted to go into the fledgling automobile business, he went to Marion

Lambert, who had been very impressed by his integrity, and Lambert suggested they become partners. Lambert lent him $10,000 to begin selling the newfangled horseless carriage invented by Henry Ford. Breadon became president of the Western Automobile Company, distributors of the fashionable Pierce-Arrows and the affordable Fords.

According to William DeWitt, Sr., the Cards treasurer under Breadon, Marion Lambert thought the automobile business was "terrible," and so after two years, he sold out to Breadon, who became the sole owner of the firm.

Breadon, though a drinker and a tough talker, was a serious, dedicated businessman. The 1904 World's Fair gave the St. Louis automobile business a tremendous lift, and by the end of the year he made $20,000.

With this money, he was able to buy his shares in the Cardinals. Unlike the Browns' Phil Ball, who was alienated by Branch Rickey's professorial demeanor, his WCTU stance, and his strong belief in himself, Sam Breadon was captivated. They were an odd couple. Breadon was a Democrat, a barbershop quarter singer, and a straight shooter. His word was his bond. Rickey was a Republican, a teetotaler, a Bible thumper, and slick around the corners of rules.

But Breadon saw that Rickey had great ideas, and Breadon loved the way his mind worked. When Rickey explained to Breadon what he was planning to do to make the Cardinals a powerhouse, Breadon gave him carte blanche to begin building his farm system.

At the end of the 1919 season, Breadon made a deal to sell the dilapidated, ramshackle League Park and to rent Sportsman's Park from the Browns. To do so, he had to convince the Browns' Phil Ball, who still was smarting over Branch Rickey's departure years earlier. When Ball turned him down, Breadon told Ball he would build a brand-new park not far away. After a month, the stubborn Ball finally gave in. Breadon then tore down the grandstands of League Park and sold the real estate to the Board of Education for $200,000. He sold the rest of the acreage for $75,000 to the Public Service Corporation for a loop for their streetcars.

With the team in the black, Mrs. Britton was paid in full, and Rickey was able to continue to expand his farm system. "Without [that money]," said Breadon, "we never could have made our early purchases of minor league clubs."

Rickey's first step in creating his farm system was the purchase of a part interest in a team in the low minors, despite the inherent dangers of making such a transaction. No one had tried such an arrangement before. Rickey would be bringing his best prospects to the farm team, and Rickey had to be sure that no farm team executive would double-cross him and sell those prospects out from under him. If Rickey had been able to buy a farm team outright, he wouldn't have had to worry about perfidy on the part of his partners, but because Rickey didn't have the money to buy more than minority shares of ballclubs, he worked hard to find people he felt he could trust.

Not long after Breadon became president, Charlie Barrett, Rickey's head scout, informed him that Blake Harper, one of Barrett's friends and the owner of the Class C Fort Smith, Arkansas, franchise in the Western Association, was willing to work with Rickey and sell half of the team to the Cardinals. Rickey made the deal.

With the Cards owning a share of Fort Smith, Rickey now had a minor league team where players like Heinie Mueller could train. But Rickey knew that if Mueller succeeded at that level, he would have to field a team at the next rung, and then the next, and he began to seek out other teams with which to make similar arrangements at every level up the ladder to the major leagues.

To secure a team for Mueller after he graduated from Fort Smith, Rickey bought a minority interest in the Houston team in the Texas League. Rickey had known the owners. He had met Doak Roberts, the business manager, at the minor league meetings. He knew Al Bridwell, the field manager. The Cards bought an 18 percent interest in the team for $15,000, no money down, but Rickey gave his word that the Cards would make good on the deal.

Rickey could not have succeeded if he had not had a stellar reputation for keeping his word. Most minor league executives didn't trust the arrangement Rickey was proposing. Rickey worked hard at building trust between himself and the owners of the Memphis team in the Class A Southern Association before the Memphis owners finally agreed to work out an arrangement. He needed Memphis because it was there that he wanted to send prospects Ray Blades and Oscar Tuero, a pitcher from Cuba.

Sam Breadon, meanwhile, was making his own friendships as a way of adding to the Cardinals' farm system. In December of 1920, he attended the annual meeting of the minor leagues in Kansas City. Though Prohibition had begun, the Meulebachs, owners of the Kansas City Blues, had made their business manufacturing beer. George Meulebach supplied the beer, and that evening Breadon sat and drank with Ernie Landgraf, the owner of the Syracuse team in the International League. According to Bill DeWitt, Sr., "They got drunk together one night," and before they parted company Ernie had agreed to sell Breadon a 50 percent interest in the Syracuse team for $25,000. When Rickey saw the Cards couldn't afford to spend money on both Memphis and Syracuse, he let the Memphis deal go and sent Blades and Tuero to Syracuse. Rickey had opposed going into partnership with Landgraf, and two years later the Cards bought the team outright.

Rickey then increased his holdings in the Houston franchise from 19 percent to 59 percent, but he was forced to put ownership in the name of a third party because Texas League owners objected to ownership by teams in higher leagues.

Since the true ownership of the team was kept secret, Rickey found himself in a bind when the Houston president wanted to sell Chick Hafey, a young prospect, for $35,000. Rickey had signed Hafey as a pitcher and quickly turned him into an outfielder when he saw the boy hit. Rickey knew that Hafey would become a star, and he was appalled when he was forced to match the offer to keep Hafey.

Pressure from the office of the baseball commissioner also made it clear to Rickey that he needed to own his farm teams rather than have secret agreements.

In 1921 Judge Kenesaw Mountain Landis, for the first time in what would be a twenty-five-year war between them, accused Rickey of covering up young ballplayers. Both Rickey and the Browns were claiming ownership of a young first baseman, Phil Todt. Rickey had signed him to a contract off the sandlots when he was seventeen. He was released first to Sherman, Texas, and then to Houston, but never played on either team. He didn't sign a contract with either team. Neither club ever told the league that Todt had been released.

Then in 1920 the Browns signed him. In Landis's very first ruling as commissioner, he declared Todt to be a Brown, saying that Rickey had had secret agreements with both Sherman and Houston, and therefore the transfers were void.

Rickey saw that since Landis intended to stop the handshake agreements with minor league teams, he would need to own the teams outright for his farm system plan to work. In 1922 he bought the other 50 percent of the Syracuse club. When the Cards increased their holdings in the Houston team to 90 percent, there were objections from other Texas League team owners. Rickey called their bluff. He told the league to pay him fair market value for the team—$500,000—or keep quiet. That silenced them.

In 1922 the Cards challenged for the pennant. The star of the team was Rogers Hornsby, who showed the baseball world why Stoneham and McGraw of the Giants had been willing to offer $300,000 for his services.

Hornsby had won the batting title for the first time in 1920 with a .370 average. Then he repeated in 1921 when he hit .397. In 1922 the right-handed slugger had one of the greatest seasons in the history of baseball when he won the Triple Crown, leading the league with a .401 batting average, 42 home runs, and 152 RBIs. He also led the league with 46 doubles and 141 runs.

Hornsby, a large man, was a vicious line-drive hitter, and he had power. One of the classic stories told about him came from Arthur Daley, a veteran *New York Times* writer. According to Daley, a rookie pitcher for the Brooklyn Dodgers was facing Hornsby for the first time. He asked Jack Fournier, a former Cardinal and now the Dodger first baseman, how to pitch to him.

"Just feed him inside pitches," said Fournier.

In his first confrontation, the pitcher threw inside as instructed, and Hornsby hit a line drive so hard he almost took off the head of the third baseman.

"I thought you said his weakness was inside pitches," said the pitcher to the first baseman.

"I said nothing of the kind," said Fournier. "I just didn't want him hitting outside pitches on a line to me. I'm a married man with a family."

Hornsby once hit a line drive back at Art Nehf of the Giants. The ball caromed off his chest, leaving the name A. G. SPALDING stenciled on his skin like a tattoo for a full week.

The lyrical Ogden Nash wrote about Hornsby in his "Line-up for Yesterday: An ABC of Baseball Immortals":

H is for Hornsby
When pitching to Rog

The pitcher would pitch,
Then the pitcher would dodge.

Experts said of him: His only weakness is base on balls.

LES BELL: "Hornsby was the greatest right-handed hitter that ever lived. I can guarantee you that. Maybe even the greatest hitter, period. He had the finest coordination I ever saw. And confidence. He had that by a ton.

"There was another thing that Hornsby could do that a lot of people don't realize—he could run. When he was stretching out on a triple, he was a sight to see. If he had hit left-handed, he probably would have hit .450. He was a streak going down the line.

"In '28 Hornsby led the league with .387. Paul Waner was chasing him most of the summer—I think Paul ended up around .370 or so. [He hit exactly .370.] Anyway, toward the end of the year Pittsburgh came in for a series and the batting race was pretty close at the time. The papers made a big fuss over it. Rog really went to town and got a carload of hits in the series, while Waner didn't do too well. When it was over, Paul and Hornsby happened to be going back together through the runway underneath the stands to the clubhouse.

" 'Well, Rog,' Paul said, 'it looks like you're gonna beat me.'

"Rog scowled at him and said, 'You didn't doubt for a minute I would, did you?' "

Jim Bottomley, who lived life with a perpetual smile, came up in 1922 and hit .325 in 37 games. He became the idol of the Knothole Gang youngsters. Born in 1900, he was raised in Nokomis, Illinois. His father was a coal miner, and he would have been one too had Rickey not offered him a contract in 1919. His younger brother had been killed in a cave-in shortly after the end of World War I. He had been working as a blacksmith's apprentice at the mines and playing semipro ball when he caught the attention of Rickey's head scout, Charlie Barrett.

As one of Rickey's first farmhands, Bottomley began at Sioux City in the Three-I League, graduated to Houston, and in 1922 played for Syracuse before the Cards bought him and Ray Blades. In 1923, his first full season, he hit .371. Bottomley set a major league record on September 16, 1924, when he drove in 12 runs in one game. He had three singles, a double, and two home runs.

Bottomley was regarded as the finest first baseman the Cardinals ever had. He was certainly one of the most popular. He was an old-fashioned, old-time player, a guy who played mostly for the love of the game. When he was named winner of the League Award in 1928, he was given a $1,000 bag of gold from league president John Heydler. More than 10,000 Knothole Gang members attended the ceremony. For his day in 1936, he was asked what he wanted for a gift. He asked for a Jersey cow. "They're the best milkers," he said. He was given a cow named "Fielder's Choice," named by the fans in a contest. Teammate Les Bell remembered "Sunny Jim."

LES BELL: "I'll never forget my first big league game [in 1923]. The club wasn't going anywhere, so they loaded the lineup with kids, me at short,

JIM BOTTOMLEY
(Courtesy Brace Photo)

another fellow at first, and so on. The first ball that was hit down to me I picked up cleanly and threw with everything I had. Listen, I had a strong arm. I sure did. I think I must have broken a seat ten or fifteen rows behind first base with that throw. A couple of innings later I had my second chance. This time that ball really flew, and I must have broken a seat twenty rows behind first base. When I came into the dugout after that inning, I was feeling pretty blue. Who sits down next to me but the regular first baseman, Jim Bottomley. All he did that year was hit .371.

"Jim put his arm around me and said, 'Now, kid. Old Jim will be out there tomorrow playing first base. So when you throw the ball, just throw it in the direction of the base, and Old Jim will get it.'

"That made me feel better, but I got to laugh now when I think of it. I was twenty-one and 'Old Jim' was all of twenty-three. They called him 'Sunny Jim' and he sure was all of that. What a fine gentleman he was, and a great ballplayer. He could do it all."

Hornsby and Bottomley's heroics brought solvency to the Cardinals, as half a million home fans paid to see him hit in 1922. Arguments arose in bars all over St. Louis as to who was the better hitter: George Sisler of the Browns or Hornsby of the Cardinals.

Aided by the additions of Rickey's crop of prize rookies, Bottomley, Heinie Mueller, and George "Specs" Toporcer from Syracuse and Ray Blades
from Houston, the Cardinals finished the 1922 season with a 85–69 record, 8
games behind McGraw's victorious New York Giants

The Cards might have had a shot at the pennant had Horace Stoneham and
John McGraw of the Giants not shored its pitching staff by paying $100,000 to
the Boston Braves for starting pitcher Hugh McQuillan. At the same time, the
Yankees stole the 1922 pennant from the St. Louis Browns when the New
Yorkers purchased the great third baseman, Joe Dugan, from the Boston Red
Sox. With Dugan, the Yankees overtook the Browns and won the flag by a
single game.

Complained Rickey, "What chance have we ever to win a pennant in St.
Louis if such conditions are permitted to go on?"

The furor was so great that Commissioner Landis issued an edict preventing player deals after June 15, except for waiver transactions.

Under Breadon and Rickey's brilliant management, the three-year overall
profit of the Cardinals for the years 1920–22 was $374,000. Only the New
York Giants and the Pittsburgh Pirates had been more profitable.

During the winter of 1922, Breadon offered Rickey a ten-year contract at
$25,000 a year plus 10 percent of the profits of the team before taxes. (This
was in a period when the average player's salary was about $2,500.) Rickey
asked that the contract be for only five years. The pact would make him the
highest-paid executive in all of baseball. Before long, Branch Rickey would
lead the Cardinals to become one of the most successful and exciting teams
in the history of baseball. And he would make a higher salary than anyone
in baseball.

CHAPTER 12

RAJAH DELIVERS A PENNANT

ALL the while Branch Rickey was working to build the Cardinals' franchise
by buying farm teams and evaluating prospects, he also held the position of
field manager. While a player, he had studied what made players succeed and
why they failed, and he had learned the fundamentals of the game inside and
out. As manager, Rickey saw himself as a teacher; the man knew every aspect
of the game of baseball and could spend hours talking about bunt strategy, the
hit and run, how to pitch, when to steal, etc. The game between the lines held
endless fascination for Rickey, and he would get animated when expounding
on an aspect or two of the nuances of the game to one of his players. While
he enjoyed the challenge of assessing the ability of young prospects, as the
player behind the plate or as manager, he loved being the leader of men
even more.

He continued using spring training to teach his players the game's fundamentals. During his whole life in baseball, he had his pitchers throw through
strings and his base runners practice in running pits. His methods are still
taught and used today. As he sat in the dugout, managing the game, he kept
a fat scorebook with all sorts of relevant notes and statistics. He would write
down the speed of each batter, where any batter was mostly likely to hit the
ball, and how far each batter hit against each pitcher. This use of statistics
and probabilities, widely used today, was another of Rickey's innovations. The
players, however, most lacking his education and his computerlike mind, were
cool to his bookish ways. Said Roy Stockton, who covered the team for the
St. Louis Post-Dispatch, "Rickey's players could not understand his ideas or
execute them. The majority either became wanderers in a labyrinth of theories
or took to scoffing at it all."

The player who did the most scoffing was Rogers Hornsby, an anti-intellectual
and a lifetime second-guesser of anyone with and for whom he played. The
star second baseman almost never read books, magazines, or newspapers because he felt reading would hurt his eyesight. He was a man who knew what
he liked and didn't like, and he wasn't afraid to express his opinions. Hornsby
was a constant irritant, but he was such a great hitter that men who managed
him and others who played for him when he managed usually took his vitriolic
abuse in silence in deference to his superstar status.

In 1923 Hornsby was having another stellar season, hitting .384 with 17
homers and 83 RBIs in August, when the Cards traveled to New York to meet
the Giants at the Polo Grounds.

Hornsby was on third base with the count 3-1, when Rickey gave the
batter the take sign. Hornsby, who later would become one of the most hated
managers in baseball history, in large part because of his love of giving his
hitters the take sign, indicated his displeasure with Rickey's order by making
a show of his disgust. Rickey noticed and yelled out to Hornsby, "Stay in the
ball game."

In the clubhouse after the game, Rickey took Hornsby aside and reminded
him that in order to win, a player must show respect for the manager, regardless
of how he feels personally. Hornsby's answer was a vulgarity that offended
the mild-mannered Rickey.

Rickey went at Hornsby, who pushed him away. Rickey came at him a
second time, as teammates broke them up.

When the incident appeared in the papers the next day, Hornsby decided
to teach Rickey a lesson; he told Rickey he had developed a skin infection
and couldn't play. Rickey tried waiting him out, and after a time asked Hornsby
to return to the lineup. When Hornsby refused, Rickey asked Sam Breadon to
suspend him for the rest of the season. To Breadon's credit, the owner decided
that Rickey was the more important figure in his organization, and he backed
his GM-manager over his star.

The vindictive and egotistical Hornsby, a man who was never wrong in
his own mind, told reporters a fictitious story that made it look as though

Rickey had picked on him for no good reason. Hornsby, who had the same sadistic need to go for the jugular that Ty Cobb had, blasted Rickey. The Cardinal manager, who was psychologically incapable of ignoring the slightest criticism, never mind public insults, eloquently responded.

BRANCH RICKEY: "I have just read of Hornsby's statement in Friday morning's paper. It is incorrect in many particulars.

"In one particular, the articles were particularly incorrect. He knows and everyone knows that I should not have resentment without very unusual cause. I have been in charge of baseball teams in one capacity or another for twenty years. And for the last ten years in major league baseball. In that time only one player has ever spoken disrespectfully to me. I am not a 'fighting manager.' However, I am not sorry I resented the vile and unspeakable language used by Hornsby in New York.

"The present suspension of the player is absolutely unavoidable. He not only refused to play in the game—he refused to work out in practice. Finally, I suggested that he might win the game, or enter the game as a pinch hitter.

"He simply persisted in forcing discipline. It was a part of the plan. Most people will understand that it is not really possible to fail to discipline the star and expect good services from other players. In some respects, all players must be understanding as well as obedient."

Hornsby was fined $500 and suspended for the rest of the 1923 season. At the end of the press release, Rickey wrote: "Rogers Hornsby will not be sold or traded." Hornsby was back at his home in Winters, Texas, when he won his fourth batting title in a row with a .384 average.

In 1924 the Cardinals fell from fifth to sixth. They were a lackluster 65-89 under Rickey, who kept releasing veteran pitchers despite the lack of replacements to take up the slack. In 1924 Hornsby, who returned unrepentant, batted .424 (the highest single season batting average in the 1900s) with 25 home runs and 94 RBIs, his fifth National League batting title in a row. He also led the league in runs (121), hits (227), doubles (43), and walks (89). Hornsby felt cheated when Dazzy Vance, who won 28 games for the Dodgers, was named league MVP. Asked Sam Breadon, "What does one have to do in this league to win that prize? All Hornsby did was to hit higher than any man in the major leagues in forty years and he loses out to a pitcher who was in less than 50 games. That isn't right."

During the spring training of 1925 in Stockton, California, Breadon informed Rickey that he wanted him to step down as manager. Rickey told Breadon he would quit and hire Burt Shotton as his replacement. Breadon agreed. When the announcement didn't come, Rickey told Breadon he had changed his mind about quitting.

When the Cardinals began the 1925 season 13-25 and advance orders for a May 31 doubleheader were too few, Sam Breadon forced Rickey to do what James Jones couldn't: step down as field manager, so he could concentrate on running the off-the-field operations. Breadon felt he needed a manager with the personality to bring back some of the fans lost when the colorless Rickey suspended their hero, Hornsby. Breadon, who tended toward panic over the future of the ballclub whenever attendance dropped, knew he needed a gate attraction. In what had to be one of the more complicated realignments in Cardinal history, he appointed as manager the most popular player on the team and Rickey's bête noire: Hornsby.

When Breadon told Rickey he was fired as manager, Rickey told him, "You can't do this to me, Sam. You are ruining me."

"No," said Breadon, "I am doing you the greatest favor one man ever has done to another."

Rickey asked who would replace him. Breadon said Hornsby. Rickey suggested Burt Shotton, his coach and right-hand man. Breadon said no, that the fans knew Shotton was close to him, that the team needed a new direction.

According to sportswriter Fred Lieb, Breadon told Rickey, "If Hornsby won't take [the manager's job], I'll go outside the club. I hope you will stay with us, but if at the end of the season you wish to make a change, the club will not stand in your way."

The exchange between Breadon and Rickey perfectly explains their relationship. They were associates, not friends. Rickey was a valued employee, but he was nevertheless an employee. The way Breadon handled Rickey also showed Breadon's hard side. The Cardinal owner had an utter disregard for public relations. He could turn cold and unyielding to his players during salary disputes, and he received a lot of bad press over the years because of it.

Once while Breadon was swimming off the coast of Bradenton, Florida, it was remarked that Breadon should be concerned with sharks. Replied *New York Times* sportswriter John Drebinger, "Sam taking a chance, hell. How about those poor sharks!"

The twenties was the era of star player-managers. Ty Cobb led the Detroit Tigers, Tris Speaker the Cleveland Indians, Dave Bancroft the Boston Braves, Eddie Collins the Chicago White Sox, George Sisler the Browns, and Bucky Harris the Washington Senators. If these men could do it, Breadon figured, so could Hornsby. (At the same time, he didn't have to pay two salaries.)

Hornsby recalled the day when Breadon approached him to become the manager.

ROGERS HORNSBY: "I told Breadon the only way I would be interested in becoming manager would be if I could buy Rickey's stock, which was 1,167 shares and second only to Breadon's. Then baseball could be my business for life.

"I bought Rickey's stock [Breadon lent him the money] and became manager for the first time on Memorial Day. We had only one way to go—up. We were in the cellar. I suggested some changes. We strengthened ourselves at catching by getting Bob O'Farrell from the Cubs, and recalled shortstop Tommy Thevenow from Syracuse, our farm club in the International League.

Managing was new to me, and I felt the players really hustled for me. We climbed out of the cellar and finished fourth.

"I won the batting championship for the sixth straight year with a .403 average, led the league in runs batted in (143) and home runs (39)."

Breadon's move proved popular. Attendance rose dramatically, by 125,000, and the Cardinals earned $80,000 for the season.

Freed from his managerial duties, Branch Rickey was able to concentrate full-time on his farm system and administration. One of his legacies was his ability to hire trusted executives who would one day rise to become baseball's leaders. He hired twenty-three-year-old Bill DeWitt, Sr., who later would own the Browns, as the Cards' treasurer and appointed Warren Giles, who would one day be president of the National League, as head of the St. Joseph team in the Western League. After Rickey and Giles became closer friends, Rickey made him president of the Syracuse Triple A farm team.

In 1925 Rickey was forced to buy the majority interest in the Houston team when one of the owners, a man named Crooker, demanded that Houston sell its players to the highest bidder, regardless of the arrangement the general manager had made with the Cardinals. The Cards bought out Crooker and now owned 75 percent of the stock. Rickey made his friend Fred Ankenman president and gave him 5 percent of the stock as an incentive not to double-cross him.

Rickey now owned or controlled teams at every minor league level from Class D to Triple A. On a chalkboard in Rickey's office was a list of every player in the organization. Rickey kept track of the status of every one of them.

Things were going smoothly for the 1925 Cards when in midseason Hornsby incurred the wrath of team owner Sam Breadon, who after a game walked into the clubhouse to make small talk and see his players. Manager Hornsby, in a foul mood, swore at him, using typical Hornsby vile language, and ordered him out of the clubhouse in front of the players.

Breadon went straight to Branch Rickey. "He's got to go, Branch," said Breadon. He's got to go. Nobody can talk to me that way."

Rickey didn't even ask Breadon about whom he was talking. "What did he say?" asked Rickey.

"I'm ashamed to repeat it," Breadon replied. "But he also told me to get the hell out of his clubhouse. *His* clubhouse? Practically threw me out. He's got to go."

"If you really feel a that way, Sam, he'll go."

"Can a trade be developed?"

"For Hornsby? Oh, yes."

"When? How? What can we get? You name the deal, and he goes."

When Rickey heard what had happened, he felt for Breadon but inwardly sided with Hornsby. He felt that it *was* Hornsby's clubhouse, that Breadon should not have gone in there unannounced, and that for Breadon to argue with

Hornsby in front of the players was wrong. Rickey stalled, hoping Breadon's ill will toward Hornsby might dissipate. As much as Rickey may have disliked Hornsby, he knew it was in the team's best interest to keep him in the Cardinal lineup. When the 1926 season rolled around, Rogers Hornsby was still playing manager of the Cardinals.

The New York Giants, led by John McGraw, were the early favorites that year. The Pittsburgh Pirates, the defending champions, also were rated highly. During spring training, Hornsby told his players that the team could win the pennant. No one snickered. Les Bell, the Cards' third baseman, recalled Hornsby's intensity with admiration.

LES BELL: "In 1926 we went to spring training in [Terrell Wells, outside of] San Antonio. Hornsby was never much of a guy for holding meetings, but he held one on the first day of spring training. I'll never forget it.

" 'If there's anybody in this room who doesn't think we're going to win the pennant,' he said, 'go upstairs now and get your money and go on home, because we don't want you around here.'

"That's the attitude we all started with, right from the first day of spring training. And it carried us all the way, to the pennant, to the world championship. And for me, personally, it was a great year. I hit .325, knocked in 100 runs, was up among the league leaders in a lot of departments. I even outhit Rog that year, believe it or not—that was the only time over a ten-year stretch that he was under .360. Yeah, when I think of baseball, I think of 1926."

The team battled the Cincinnati Reds for the top spot, when in June of 1926 Rickey and Hornsby made several moves that would change the course of baseball history. In mid-June John McGraw approached Breadon and Rickey with a trade offer. McGraw wanted Heinie Mueller, one of Rickey's earliest signees, even up for classy outfielder Billy Southworth. A year and a half earlier McGraw had given up two excellent players, shortstop Dave Bancroft and outfielder Casey Stengel, for Southworth. But with the Giants, McGraw played Ross Youngs in right field, Southworth's usual position, and switched Southworth to center field, where he wasn't comfortable. McGraw needed a pure center fielder and asked for Mueller. It would turn out to be the worst trade John McGraw ever made.

A week later Rickey made headlines when, at Hornsby's insistence, he claimed Grover Cleveland Alexander on waivers for $4,000 from the Chicago Cubs.

Alexander in one respect was a lot like Hornsby. On the field, he brought a world of talent. Off the field, he could be trouble with a capital T. While Rajah had difficulty with civility, Alexander had trouble with drink. "Pete" or "Alex," as his teammates called him, had come up to the majors in 1911 with the Philadelphia Phillies, and over the next twenty years won a total of 373 victories against only 208 losses, tied for third in wins in baseball history with Christy Mathewson behind Cy Young (511) and Walter Johnson (416). His 90 shutouts rank him second in major league history behind Johnson's 110.

In his first seven years with the Phils, Alex won 28, 19, 22, 27, 31, 33, and 30 games, but when he was drafted into the Army after the 1917 season, Alex asked Phils owner William Baker to pay $500 to his then-girlfriend (and future wife), Aimee Arrants, every other month for three years to take care of his mother, family, and Aimee. Baker, afraid Alexander would be killed or wounded in the war, responded by trading Alex to the Chicago Cubs.

Cubs owner William Wrigley agreed to Alex's demands, and when Alex returned from the war, he spent eight productive seasons with the Cubs. He wasn't quite so dominating, but in 1920 he won 27 games and in 1923 won 22, so he could still pitch effectively. His problem was that while he was fighting in Europe during World War I, Alex had suffered from shell shock.

In France, he had fought in the front lines as an artillery sergeant. The roar of the guns made him deaf in one ear. Within a few weeks of his returning to the States, Alexander's wife Aimee discovered that the effects of the war had somehow caused him to have epileptic seizures, which often appear after head trauma. During his first

GROVER CLEVELAND ALEXANDER
(Courtesy Brace Photo)

year in pro ball while pitching for Galesburg, Illinois, in 1909, he had been struck on the side of his head by the relay from the shortstop. After lying unconscious for two and a half days, he awoke. He suffered from double vision for months. Certainly he had had a serious concussion. The subsequent concussions of the big guns so close to him brought on the epilepsy. Alexander was haunted by the disease, which could strike him at any moment.

AIMEE ALEXANDER: "Sometimes a fit would strike him while he was out on the mound. He always carried a bottle of spirits of ammonia with him. They would have to carry him off the field. Some thought he was drunk. They would take him into the locker room, Alex would whiff the ammonia, fight to get control of himself, and then go right back out and pitch again.

"We were never certain when they were going to happen. Sometimes he'd get three or four in one month. Then he'd go months without anything happening. I remember once in Pittsburgh, I saw Alex signal the umpire suddenly and call time. I knew what was happening. He went into the dressing room for about fifteen minutes, came out again, and pitched the entire game. That takes a great deal of courage. They always left him so weak and, well, sort of helpless."

"PINKY" WHITNEY (his teammate in 1930): "Sometimes he'd have one of those spells out on the mound and we'd get around him and pull his tongue out. And then he'd get up and throw the next ball right through the middle of the plate.''

When Alexander returned after the war, he suffered from another problem even more serious than epilepsy: alcoholism. They great pitcher lived every day in fear, and to make those fears tolerable, he drank, and as the years went on, more and more often he drank so hard, he would end up passed out in the gutter.

AIMEE ALEXANDER: "Alex always thought he could pitch better with a hangover, and maybe he could, at that. I did my best to keep him straight. When he was with me, he was all right. But then he'd wander off. Even so, he did pretty well as a pitcher, didn't he? I don't see any reason to hide the fact that he drank—everyone knows it.''

And yet despite the twin curses of epilepsy and alcoholism, Grover Cleveland Alexander in 1925 had finished 15-11 with a 3.39 ERA for Chicago. Then in 1926 a rookie manager by the name of Joe McCarthy joined the Cubs. McCarthy didn't want prima donnas on his team, and Alexander, who had his own way of doing things, didn't respect the new manager. When Alex arrived in spring training, he told reporters, "I'm not going to be bossed around by a bush league manager.'' But Alexander was wrong about McCarthy, who was no lightweight. In the spring Alexander broke an ankle. Even though Alex wasn't playing, McCarthy forced him to make the painful trip from L.A. to Catalina Island on crutches every day. Alexander deeply resented his treatment.

Their tug-of-war ended on June 22, 1926, when McCarthy banished Grover Cleveland Alexander from Chicago, releasing him on waivers. Alexander's former catcher, Bill Killefer, had become a coach for the Cardinals. Killefer convinced Rogers Hornsby to sign him. Hornsby convinced Rickey. Years later Roger Hornsby recalled the details behind Alexander's availablity.

ROGERS HORNSBY: "In June of 1926, Joe McCarthy, manager of the Chicago Cubs, thought that Grover Cleveland Alexander was dissipated, drank too much, and was finished as a major league pitcher. Then too, Alex had suffered a broken ankle in spring training. They say that McCarthy and Alexander didn't like each other. McCarthy liked to tell Alexander what to pitch to certain batters, and Alex didn't want anybody to tell him how to pitch. The big blowup came in Brooklyn when the Cubs were talking about how they were going to pitch to the Dodger batters. They brought up the fact that the Dodgers' 'Rabbit' Maranville had been traded away by the Cubs.

'' 'We'll have to switch signs whenever he gets on second base,' McCarthy said. 'He's smart enough to remember signals from last year.'

'' 'Well now,' Alexander said and sort of grinned, 'if we thought there was much chance of this guy gettin' on second base, we wouldn't have got rid of him, would we?'

"The Cubs moved on to Philadelphia, and Alexander was finished with them. He had been put on the waiver list.

"Even though Alex—that's what I always called him, though his nickname was Pete—had been in a sanitarium at Dwight, Illinois, the winter before to try to quit drinking, I knew he still had a fastball. Even if it was only half as good as it once was, it was still good. He had the greatest control I've ever seen. Could almost nick the corners of a soft drink bottle cap. He won 30 games a season for three straight years while pitching for the Philadelphia Phillies in the smallest park in the big leagues. He once pitched four consecutive shutouts, including sixteen in one season; twice he won two games in one day.

"I was playing manager of the Cardinals, so I asked Branch Rickey, who was the general manager and had been the manager before me, to claim Alexander. I had heard of all those newspaper stories about Alex—that he carried a gin bottle more often than his glove—but I wanted him on my team. The Cardinals were in fourth place at that time, so that meant the four teams under us in the standings got a chance to pick him up for the $4,000 waiver price before we got to him. All four teams figured he was washed up, or figured something, because none of them took him. We got him on June 22.

"All I said to Alexander when he reported was 'Glad to have you on the team. Think you can help us. Just follow the curfew like the other guys.'

"The next Sunday we played the Cubs, the team that had released Alexander. I don't think he ever pitched a better game in his life. He beat the Cubs, 3–2, in ten innings and only gave up four hits. After the game he sort of tipped his cap, which was always too small for him, when he passed by McCarthy."

Alexander had been one of Bill Hallahan's boyhood heroes, and Hallahan marveled at what he saw.

BILL HALLAHAN: "I was a rookie on the Cardinals in 1926 when we bought Alec from the Cubs in midseason. I'll never forget the first time he pitched for us. I was sitting on the bench with another young pitcher, and naturally we glued our eyes on Alec when he went out to warm up. He flipped a few in to the catcher, then stopped, put his glove under his arm, took out a piece of chewing gum, very casually took the paper off, put the gum in his mouth, looked around through the stands, then put his glove back on and started throwing again. He threw just a few more pitches, very easily, with no effort. Then he was through. He came back to the bench, put on his sweater—we wore those big red-knit sweaters on the Cardinals—and sat down.

"I looked at this other fellow and said, 'This is going to be murder. He isn't throwing anything.' Well, Alec went out that day and stood the other team on its ear. Control, that's how he did it. Absolute, total control. He had this little screwball that he could turn over on the corners all day long. Amazing fellow. Born to be a pitcher."

JESSE HAINES: "I never saw a machine like him. Every pitch he threw was the same. Low outside. To every hitter. The only thing he adjusted was the position of the infield and outfield. he'd shift the fielders around. He didn't care who the batter was. He'd pitch him low and outside. Throw him that fading fastball. Or curve him. I saw a lot of pitchers in my time, but I never saw a machine that worked any better than he did.''

Rogers Hornsby knew what he was getting when the Cardinals acquired Alexander. On days when he knew he wasn't going to pitch, Alexander would drink. In their game of cat and mouse, Hornsby spent a great deal of time trying to curtail the big pitcher's imbibing. Sometimes he didn't succeed.

BILL HALLAHAN: ''[Alexander] liked to go out before a game and work in the infield, generally around third base. One day we were taking batting practice and there's Alec standing on third, crouched over, hands on knees, staring into the plate. A ground ball went by him and he never budged, just remained there stock-still, staring in at the batter. Then another grounder buzzed by and same thing—he never moved a muscle. Then somebody ripped a line drive past his ear and still he didn't move. That's when Hornsby noticed him.

''Hornsby let out a howl and said, 'Where in the hell did he get it?' Meaning the booze, of course. 'Get him out of there before he gets killed.'

''So one of the coaches, Bill Killefer, I think, went out and brought Alec in and sat him on the bench. Hornsby was fuming. 'Where did he get it? Where did he get it?' he kept yelling. He ordered a search made and they found it, all right. In old Sportsman's Park in St. Louis, there used to be a ladies' room not far from the corridor going down to the dugout, and that's where he had stashed it, up in the rafters of the ladies' room. One of those little square bottles of gin.''

ROGERS HORNSBY: ''I knew Alex liked his highballs. He liked to go out and drink with his friends, and he had a lot of friends. But he never showed up drunk [on a day he was scheduled to pitch], and I don't think we could have won the National League pennant that year without him.''

They also could not have won it without Hornsby, who hit only .317 and 11 homers, but drove in 93 runs and provided the leadership the team needed to take it to the pennant. Alexander, for one, loved the tough-talking Texan. They formed a mutual admiration society. Alex had faced Hornsby ever since the Rajah had come into the league in 1915. With his uncanny control, Alexander liked to throw pitches just off the plate, inducing batters to swing at less than ideal pitches. Hornsby, he contended, was the one hitter who wouldn't bite.

GROVER CLEVELAND ALEXANDER: ''[He was] the greatest man with a bat I ever faced. And he'd stand from this bed to that door [Alex was in the hospital during this conversation in January of 1937] away from the plate. Always did. Looked like a sucker for an outside pitch, but it really was his alley. He'd just step forward and bang . . . away she'd go. You know, I'd figure if I got him 0-2, which was seldom, I'd come so close on the next one he'd have to bit, bad ball or not, but he wouldn't move a muscle.

"That ball'd come up maybe this far [indicating an inch between his thumb and forefinger] from the plate, but Hornsby would watch it go by and then call back: 'Come on, get the ball over the plate, Alex. I haven't got all day.' Oh, he was a tough guy."

Hornsby, moreover, didn't play head games with Alex the way Joe McCarthy did. Alex once told his wife, Aimee, "You know, I sure like that young fellow. He don't tell me nothin', except to go in there and throw 'em the way I see fit."

Les Bell, who had the distinction of playing for manager Hornsby on the Cardinals, Braves, and Cubs, also loved the guy.

LES BELL: "I've heard a lot of ballplayers say he was a tough man to play for. I never found him that way. All he ever asked of anybody was that they give him all they had out on the field. 'You're only out there for a couple of hours,' he would say. Well, I don't think he was asking too much. Yes, I got along with him fine, wherever I played for him.

"He was a lone wolf, you know. Even as a player, he never roomed with anybody. And you would never see him anywhere outside the hotel lobby. He wouldn't go to the movies because he said it was bad for the eyes. And about the only thing he would read was the Racing Form, because he said reading was bad for the eyes too. Was he neurotic about his eyesight? Well, maybe he was. But there was a stretch over five years where he averaged around .400. So maybe Rog knew what he was doing.

"You know, that infield in St. Louis cost him a lot of hits. Around the Fourth of July it had been baked out of concrete, and Rog always hit bullets—he seldom put his bat on the ball that it didn't whistle off. On that infield, those ground balls were in the infielder's glove in no time."

Hornsby had his team in contention coming down the stretch in 1926 when he had another serious confrontation with team owner Sam Breadon. This time it was over a Sunday exhibition game with New Haven, one of three exhibitions Breadon had scheduled. Hornsby didn't want to play any of the games. Breadon refused to cancel them. The result was another Hornsby eruption. Many years later Hornsby showed he was still furious with Breadon about it.

ROGERS HORNSBY: "I ran into front-office bossing the second year I was manager—in 1926 with the Cardinals. It was near the end of the season and I told Sam Breadon, the owner, that it looked like we could win the pennant and that he should cancel three exhibition games we had scheduled. It was a tight race, too. We led the Reds by only a game. Breadon said he would do what he could to get out of the exhibitions, which was the right thing to do if he wanted to win the pennant instead of having a nice exhibition schedule.

"We played morning and afternoon games in Pittsburgh and lost the morning game 1 to 0 when Allen Sothoron made a throwing error at first base. We were having sandwiches and milk between games when Breadon came into the clubhouse and said belligerently, 'You're going to play those exhibitions, Hornsby, and that's final.' All the players heard him.

"Hell, that's all right with me,' I said back. 'We get a total of $3,000 for three games and take the chance of getting some players hurt on those minor league fields. But if you want to take a chance of kicking away a half million dollars for winning the pennant for those silly exhibition games, then I'm not going to play all my regulars.'

"We played those three exhibitions, against Syracuse, our farm team; Hartford; and New Haven. Sure enough, one of my top players, left fielder Chick Hafey, got all banged up and had to miss the next three-game series with Boston. Nearly cost us the pennant.''

Gene Karst, now ninety, was an eighteen-year-old reporter for the *St. Louis Globe* at the time. Not too much later, when he was hired by Rickey as the first-ever public relations man in sports, he worked with Hornsby. He remembered the various tirades that gave Hornsby a bad name and caused him to wear out his welcome wherever he went.

GENE KARST: "Rogers Hornsby was, in my opinion and in that of many others, the most blunt and tactless guy in the world. That takes in a lot of territory. He reportedly had a big argument with Jack Fournier, a hard-hitting first baseman for the Cardinals, a pretty good hitter. Jack was a Catholic. Hornsby didn't like Catholics and Jews. He was really prejudiced against blacks and Jews, Catholics, and everyone else. They were supposed to have had a religious argument.

"It was 1926, the Cardinals had never won a pennant, and times were tough. It wasn't yet into the Depression, but on an open date the Cardinals would book an exhibition game with another team—Hartford, Connecticut, wherever. And they had a big argument about that, and at one point Breadon went to the clubhouse to discuss something with Hornsby, the manager, and the first thing you know, they got into a hot argument, and Hornsby said, 'Get the hell out of my clubhouse.' How do you think that sat with Breadon? Well, he left the clubhouse, and that certainly didn't help relations.''

No, indeed. Hornsby had made Breadon angry. Years later Breadon talked about the incident. He said, "I came to the decision that if I was president, my chief must work with me. If he didn't, either he or I must get out, and I wasn't ready to leave the club.''

After the Hornsby incident, there was still a pennant to win. The Cards needed to win one game to win the first pennant in the history of St. Louis since the string of pennants won by the Brown Stockings from 1885 through 1888.

LES BELL: "We finished up in the East, in the Polo Grounds. We opened up there on a Thursday and Cincinnati was playing in Philadelphia. All we needed was one win or one Cincinnati loss to clinch it. We kept watching the scoreboard all afternoon. I think we must have paid more attention to the Red–Phillie game than to our own. Anyway, we lost and the Reds won. So we still needed that one game.''

The star of the pennant-clinching game was McGraw's "impure" center fielder, Billy Southworth. Southworth played thirteen years in the big leagues and batted .297 lifetime. His best single season was in 1926, when he hit .320, hit 16 home runs, and drove in 99 runners. Southworth, a student of the game, felt extra pleasure in that the home run he hit to clinch the pennant was won at the expense of John McGraw.

BILLY SOUTHWORTH: "We came to the Polo Grounds on September 24, needing just one more victory to clinch the pennant. I couldn't have asked for a better setting, in the Polo Grounds, against the Giants who had traded me and who were settling for a fifth-place finish. And there was an added thrill to being with the Cardinals, for of the squad only four of us—Alexander, Bob O'Farrell, Bill Killefer, one of our coaches, and myself—ever had been in a World Series.''

Bill Terry of the Giants hit a three-run home run in the first inning against the Cards' Flint Rhem. "Handsome Hughie" McQuillan, the Giants pitcher, was a tough right-hander, and the Cards' chances appeared dim.

BILLY SOUTHWORTH: "Hornsby poured acid on us as we came back to the bench. He told us we hadn't been taking our full cuts at the ball for several games and to get out there and swing. We went out and proved he was wrong, and in a hurry.

"Lester Bell led off for us in that second inning and drove a double down the left field line; where he loved to hit the ball. Bell went to third when McQuillan made a wild pitch and scored when O'Farrell singled to center. That left us two runs behind. Then Thevenow doubled and so did George Toporcer, who batted for Rhem, and the score was tied. [Taylor] Douthit flied out and that brought me to the plate.

"Our bench was yelling for me to get a hit and break the tie. McQuillan's first pitch was outside. The next one looked in there. I started to swing but checked myself. Then Hornsby was yelling from where he stood waiting to bat, and I can still hear his rasping voice, 'Have your cut, Bill. Have your cut. We need that run. It can be the pennant.'

"I dug my spikes in a little deeper. I wanted that hit more than any of our gang. The pitch was coming and just where I liked it. I swung, and hard. The ball took off and so did I. As I neared first base, Otto Williams, our coach, was jumping up and down like a madman, jibbering and pointing to the right field stands. The ball was bouncing around the upper tier and Torporcer was rounding third.

"That was the timeliest home run I ever hit and to have hit it against the Giants, with McGraw snarling his defiance from the bench, made it double thrilling and satisfying. We never gave up our lead and backed [Bill] Sherdel, who replaced Rhem, with some of the greatest defensive play you ever saw. McGraw kept on playing the hit-and-run, but O'Farrell was a sheer genius that afternoon and three more times he called the play and flagged Giant runners at second.''

LES BELL: ''[During the game we clinched against the Giants], there was no score showing up for Cincinnati and Philadelphia. We figured they had been rained out. Well, we won, and then found out later that Hornsby had felt we had been too distracted by the scoreboard and he asked that no Cincinnati score be shown until our game was over. Sure, ballplayers watch the scoreboard in a close pennant race. Don't think they don't.''

CHAPTER 13

ALEXANDER'S MAGIC MOMENT

THE combination of owner Sam Breadon, general manager Branch Rickey, and manager Rogers Hornsby had brought the Cardinals their very first pennant in 1926. Either as reward or punishment, the Cards would have the opportunity to play one of the greatest offensive teams in the history of the game, the New York Yankees, ''Murderer's Row.'' Led by Babe Ruth and Lou Gehrig, the Yankees also boasted Bob Meusel, rookie second baseman Tony Lazzeri, and speedy center fielder and leadoff man Earle Combs, who would earn the third-highest career batting average in Yankee history. Their three top pitchers, Urban Shocker, Herb Pennock, and Waite Hoyt, each dominated. When the Series opened, the Cardinals were 15–1 underdogs.

Hornsby, undeterred, was as convinced the Cards would win the Series as he had been in spring training when he predicted his team would take the National League pennant. Before the Series, Hornsby made a speech to his players.

ROGERS HORNSBY: ''They've got a good ballclub; that guy Ruth is always tough, but he isn't going to get many good balls to hit. The only pitchers they have who will bother us are Pennock and Hoyt. But we can take them—just as we took the best in the National League. And no matter what the score is, we're going to keep fighting and hustling.''

When some of those Cardinal players walked into Yankee Stadium before the first game and saw the sea of 60,000 faces, they were awestruck.

LES BELL: ''I'll never forget what a thrill it was walking into Yankee Stadium for the first time, on the opening day of the '26 Series. That ballpark was up for only a few years at that time, but already there was a magic about it. It was big and beautiful and important-looking. And of course Babe Ruth played there. Maybe that was it: Babe Ruth.

"I'd never seen so many people in my life—there were over 60,000 packed in there. In those days, you had to come out through the Yankee dugout to get over to your own, and I guess when I walked onto the field and saw all those people I must have started shaking. Bill Sherdel, our little left-hander, put his arm around my shoulder and he calmed me down by saying, 'Hey, Les, I'll tell you what to do.'

" 'What's that, Bill?'

" 'You count 'em upstairs and I'll count 'em downstairs, and we'll see how much money we're gonna make today.'

"I think a lot of people underestimated our ballclub in that Series. The Yankees were top-heavy favorites. But we were fired up and we nearly won that doggone first game. Sherdel pitched beautifully, but Pennock was a little bit better and beat us, 2–1."

Hornsby started Alexander in Game 2. Alex allowed two runs in the second inning, but not a hit afterward. He struck out 10 as the Cards won, 6–2.

After the game, his wife Aimee asked Pete how he felt.

GROVER CLEVELAND ALEXANDER: "Fine. May win another for Hornsby. You know, I sure like that young fellow. He don't tell me nothin', except to go in there and throw 'em the way I see fit."

LES BELL: "Billy Southworth hit a home run with two on in the seventh and that was the clincher.

"Alec had them beating it in the dirt all day. I don't think there was more than one putout in our outfield. Alec was really on his game that day. When he was pitching like that, the outfielders might just as well have set up a card table out there and played pinochle, for all they had to do."

Game 3 was played back in St. Louis. Because the Cards had played most of their September games on the road, the team had not been home in almost four weeks. When the Cards returned, they were the object of a celebration not seen on the city streets since the Armistice.

LES BELL: "Man, what a parade they had waiting for us when we got back! So in the middle of the World Series, St. Louis turned out for us, to celebrate the winning of the pennant. It was no ordinary pennant, you understand—it was the first ever for St. Louis. The Browns had never won one and neither had the Cardinals.

"The train pulled in around three o'clock in the afternoon and they had a line of open touring cars waiting for us. We piled into the cars and they had this parade along Olive Street through downtown St. Louis. The streets were so packed there was just room enough for the cars to get through. Everybody was cheering and yelling and the ticker tape was pouring down like a blizzard. Why, we had trouble getting out of those automobiles into the hotel, what with everybody crowding around, wanting to pat us on the back and shake our hands.''

Game 3 the next day pitted Cards knuckleballer Jesse Haines against Walter "Dutch" Ruether. The game was scoreless going into the bottom of the fourth. Les Bell started the inning with a single over second base.

LES BELL: "[Then] Bob O'Farrell walked. Then there was an error in the infield on a double play ball that Tommy Thevenow hit to Lazzeri. Lazzeri flipped it to [Mark] Koenig, but Koenig's throw to first was wild, and I scored the first run. Then Jess Haines, of all people, hit a home run into the right field bleachers. He went on from there to shut them out, 4–0.

"I'll tell you a funny story about that game. We scored those three runs in the fourth inning. Okay. Well, the inning before, Haines had led off with a hit, and he got around to third base with one out and Hornsby and Bottomley coming up. Pretty good spot, wouldn't you think? But neither one of them could get him in. Now, there was a jewelry store in St. Louis that had put up as a prize a pocket watch for whoever scored the first Cardinal run in St. Louis. It was a beauty of a watch too, with a baseball on it surrounded by diamonds. So there was old Jess standing on third with one out and Hornsby and Bottomley the hitters. Jess said later he could just feel that watch in the palm of his hand. But they never got him in. Then an inning later I score the first run. So I got the watch, and every time I showed it to Haines he would scowl and say, 'Yeah, that ought to be mine.' ''

Game 4 belonged to Babe Ruth. The Yankee slugger struck three mighty home runs to sink the Cards, 10–5, setting eight new World Series records. His third home run, off Herman Bell, traveled more than 500 feet into the center field bleachers of Sportsman's Park.

LES BELL: "He was something to watch that day. What a show! Flint Rhem started for us. Do you know about Flint? Well, he came from a well-to-do family down in South Carolina. As a matter of fact, I think the town was even named for his family: Rhems, South Carolina. Flint was Alexander's drinking buddy, which meant he had to be pretty good. One time we had a couple of off-days between Pittsburgh and Boston, and Rog sent Flint and Alec to New York to rest up there and wait for the club to come in. Well, those two guys went on a binge that was unbelievable. When we pulled into New York, Flint, in particular, was so gassed up he could hardly see. When he sobered up, his explanation was a beauty: He said he didn't want Alec to get drunk, so he had kept drinking all the whiskey around them, just to keep it away from Alec.

"Flint won 20 games for us that year, but all the same it was a mistake to start him in the Series. In fact, Bill Killefer, one of our coaches, begged Hornsby not to do it.

" 'The Yankees will murder him,' Bill said.

" 'Maybe,' Rog said, 'But he won for me all year. I'm a game up and I can afford to take the chance. He's earned it.'

"Flint's control wasn't that good, you see. You had to have control to pitch against the Yankees, otherwise they'd kill you, I don't care who you were. To give you an example, Flint started off the game by striking out Combs and Koenig. Then he got Ruth two quick strikes and decided he would throw the next one right on by Babe. Well, you couldn't pitch Ruth like that. He hit that ball over the doggone pavilion. Next time up he hit one out even farther. Then in the sixth inning—Flint was gone by this time—he hit the granddaddy of them all. He hit one out to center field that Taylor Douthit started in on. But that ball just kept rising and rising and ended by ricocheting in the top row of the center field bleachers, 485 feet away. If the bleachers hadn't been there, I think that ball would have torn down the YMCA building across the street."

The Cards then lost the fifth game of the Series in extra innings by the score of 3–2. The Cards could have won, but they let the game get away late.

LES BELL: "We were leading, 2–1, going into the top of the ninth. Gehrig led off with a little Texas League double into left-center that just fell away from Thevenow, [Roscoe] 'Wattie' Holm, and Hafey. Lou eventually came around to tie it, and they went on to win it in the tenth."

When the Cards returned to New York, behind 3-2 in games, few thought the Cards could come back against the New Yorkers. Hornsby, sounding a lot like Knute Rockne, gave a pep talk to his players:

ROGERS HORNSBY: "If we don't do it today, there ain't any more Series. But, there is going to be more Series. We've got to win today, and we've got to win tomorrow. So get out there, fight your heads off; knock the ball down the pitcher's throat, and don't concede a thing."

To win, the Cards would have to win two in a row at the Stadium. The Cards had Grover Cleveland Alexander to start Game 6. They would take their chances. Les Bell would turn out to be their star.

LES BELL: "When we got into New York, we saw in the papers that Miller Huggins was going to start Bob Shawkey. Bob was a good pitcher, but we figured we could hit him, and we did. Started right off in the first inning. We scored one run and had men on second and third and I lined a hit over Joe Dugan's head to score them. Alec was pitching and we were never headed. It was still fairly close going into the seventh, 4–1. We scored a few more and then I came up against Urban Shocker. I caught one and hit it into the left field bleachers. That was the icing. Alec kept tooling right along, and we won it by 10–2.

"I'll tell you something else about that Ruth. He could throw. In the ninth inning, I lined a hit into right-center. I figured I could get two out of it because Ruth had to go to his right and then turn around to throw. I thought it was a cinch double, but he came around and fired a strike right in there on one hop and got me. It came in with a zing, too. I had heard that you didn't take liberties with his arm, but there's always that little space between hearing something and believing it, and sometimes you just have to have it filled in for you, don't you?''

The Series was tied at three apiece. The next morning dawned dark and dreary. Before the day would end, the Cardinals and the Yankees would play what is arguably the third-most-famous game in baseball history. Bobby Thomson's home run off Ralph Branca to win the 1951 National League pennant probably is the most famous, and Don Larsen's perfect game in the 1956 World Series may be second. After that comes the final game of the 1926 Series, when Grover Cleveland Alexander would make his long walk in from the bullpen to strike out Tony Lazzeri and elevate himself from great to legend.

The legend was that Alexander got himself good and drunk the night before and was sleeping off a hangover in the bullpen when Hornsby called him into the game. Alexander may have been a drinker, but he was a tough competitor who never let down his teammates. The Cards of '26 remember the events of the day.

ROGERS HORNSBY: "It was October 10, a Sunday, cold and drizzling in Yankee Stadium. So cold in fact, that only 38,093 persons turned out in New York for the seventh game of that Series.''

LES BELL: "We were staying at the Alamac Hotel, at 71st and Broadway, and when we woke up and looked out the window we didn't think there would be a game. It was a miserable day. Ordinarily we would have been out at the ballpark by eleven-thirty, but the day was so gloomy we just sat around the lobby, waiting for word. Then Judge Landis called up and said, 'Get your asses out there, boys. We're going to play.' So we piled into taxicabs and headed up to the Stadium.

"[Jesse] Haines started the seventh game for us and he pitched just fine. We got three runs in the fourth inning and I'll tell you, I should have got credit for a base hit on the ball that Koenig got his hands on. Why, sure I remember it. You certainly do remember those hits that they took away from you. I can tell you just what happened. We were losing, 1–0, to Ruth's home run. Then in the top of the fourth Jim Bottomley got a hit. I came up and hit one way over in the hole on the left side. Koenig went far to his right and fumbled the ball. They gave him an error on it, but there was no way he could have thrown me out, even if he had handled it cleanly. No way.

"Then Chick Hafey lifted a little fly ball that fell into short left for a hit and the bases were filled. And then came a big break. Bob O'Farrell hit a fly ball to Meusel in left-center, and Meusel dropped it. Just like that. Easiest fly ball you ever saw. What must have happened was he had set his mind on getting that ball and throwing home to try and catch Bottomley—Meusel had an outstanding arm. So he might have been thinking more about throwing it than catching it and maybe that's what brought about the error. But, gee, when that ball popped out of his hands, the silence in that big ballpark was really stunning. It was a hometown crowd, of course, and they couldn't believe what they had seen. Nobody could.

"Then came the last of the seventh. The score was 3–2 now. With two out, they loaded the bases against Haines and Tony Lazzeri was up. Haines was a knuckleball pitcher. He held that thing with his knuckles and he threw it hard and he threw it just about all the time. Well, his fingers had started to bleed from all the wear and tear, so he called a halt. Rog and the rest of us walked over to the mound.

" 'Can you throw it anymore?' Rog asked him.

" 'No,' Jess said. 'I can throw the fastball, but not the knuckler.'

" 'Well,' said Hornsby, 'we don't want any fastballs to this guy.'

"You see, we had been throwing Lazzeri nothing but breaking balls away and had been having pretty good luck with him.''

ROGERS HORNSBY: "He had worn the skin off his index finger of his right hand, throwing knuckleballs. He had to come out of the ball game. Willie Sherdel, a left-hander, was already warming up in the bullpen.

"We didn't have any telephones to the bullpen like they do today. I just waved and motioned for the guy to come on in. I wanted Grover Cleveland Alexander, who was thirty-nine years old, had pitched and won a complete game the day before for us. Some people figured Alexander might even be drunk during the game.

"There was a little delay before anybody came out of the bullpen, which was so far down the left field corner you could hardly see it. I yelled, 'Alexander,' and when he didn't come out real quick, people thought he was asleep or something. Then he came out, walking real slouchy-like. Alexander could have been drunk for all I cared, but he certainly wasn't. Hell, I'd rather have him pitch a crucial game for me drunk than anyone I've ever known sober. He was that good.''

BOB O'FARRELL: "I had caught Alex for years on the Cubs before we were both traded to the Cardinals. [In 1925, while O'Farrell was a member of the Chicago Cubs, a foul tip crashed through his mask and fractured his skull. With Charles "Gabby" Hartnett behind him, the Cubs traded him to the Cards at the end of the season. In 1926 O'Farrell was voted the League Award.] I think he was as good as or better than any pitcher who ever lived. He had perfect control and a great screwball. He used to call it a fadeaway, same as Mathewson.

"I don't believe Alex was much of a drinker before he went into the Army. After he got back from the war, though, he had a real problem. When he struck out Lazzeri, he'd been out on a drunk the night before and was still feeling the effects. See, Alex had pitched for us the day before and won. He had beaten the Yankees in the second game of the World Series, and again in the sixth game, pitching the complete game both times. He was thirty-nine years old then, and naturally wasn't expecting to see any more action.

"However, after the sixth game was over, Rogers Hornsby, our manager, told Alex that if Jesse Haines got in any trouble the next day, he would be the relief man. So he should take care of himself. Well, Alex didn't really intend to take a drink that night. But some of his 'friends' got hold of him and thought they were doing him a favor by buying him a drink. Well, you weren't doing Alex any favor by buying him a drink, because he just couldn't stop.

"So in the seventh inning of the seventh game, Alex is tight asleep in the bullpen, sleeping off the night before, when trouble comes.

"So Hornsby decides to call in old Alex, even though we know he'd just pitched the day before and had been up most of the night. So in he comes, shuffling in slowly from the bullpen to the pitching mound.

" 'Can you do it?' asks Hornsby.

" 'I can try,' says Alex.

JESSE "POP" HAINES: "They said Alex was drunk when he came to the mound. I don't think he was. I don't know, though, because I didn't stay there. I went into the clubhouse. He couldn't have been drunk, not the way he pitched those two and a third innings. They never gave the old fellow the credit he deserves."

LES BELL: "In came Alec, shuffling through the gloom from out of left field. You ever see him? Lean, long, lanky guy. An old Nebraskan. Took his time at everything, except pitching. Then he worked like a machine. Well, Alec was a little bit of the country psychologist out on that mound. I guess a lot of your great pitchers are. He knew it was Lazzeri's rookie year, and that here it was, seventh game of the World Series, two out and the bases loaded and the score 3–2. Lazzeri *had* to be anxious up there. This is not to take anything away from Lazzeri—he later became a great hitter—but at that moment he was a youngster up against a master. And don't think when Alec walked in it wasn't slower than ever—he wanted Lazzeri to stand up there as long as possible, thinking about the situation. And he just knew Tony's eyes would pop when he saw that fastball."

GROVER CLEVELAND ALEXANDER: "I don't think I'll ever forget that day. The biggest moment I ever had. You know, they say I stopped to pick daisies on my way from the bullpen that day. I didn't, but hell, what did they want me to do, run for the mound? I'd a been all out of breath.

"But you know when I started out, and you know how far that bullpen is, I could see Lazzeri already at the plate. He was knocking the dirt from his spikes and hopping around, and I just thought to myself, 'Well, I'll give you plenty of time to get more dirt in those spikes.' So I did stop to look at the center fielder's glove, and I paused to take a squint at the shortstop's glove, but eventually I got there.

"I wasn't worried about the spot I was in. Naw. You know, I always had one motto, and it was this: 'I'm a better pitcher than you are a hitter.' I carried that idea into every game. Besides, Lazzeri hadn't bothered me in the Series. Of course, if he'd a hit one, it would have been too bad. But he didn't."

ROGERS HORNSBY: "I trotted about halfway out to the outfield to meet Alex. 'Well, the bases are full,' I told him. 'Lazzeri's up, and there ain't no place to put him.' "

The droll Alexander replied to Hornsby as catcher Bob O'Farrell listened in, "There just don't seem to be no place to put Lazzeri. Guess I'll have to get him out."

ROGERS HORNSBY: "Alex threw only three warmup pitches. He didn't need to throw fifteen or twenty minutes like most pitchers to get warmed up. Then he fixed his little cap, fooled around with his belt, and looked to see if everybody was ready."

LES BELL: "There are so many legends associated with that strikeout. For instance, they say Alec was drunk, or hung over, when he came in. And they say that Hornsby walked out to left field to meet him, to look in his eyes and make sure they were clear. And so on. All a lot of bunk. It's too bad they say these things. Now in the first place, if you stop to think about it, no man could have done what Alec did if he was drunk or even a little bit soggy. Not the way his mind was working and not the way he pitched. It's true that he was a drinker and that he had a problem with it. Everybody knows that. But he was not drunk when he walked into the ball game that day. No way. No way at all, for heaven's sake. And as far as Hornsby walking out to meet him, that's for the birds too. Rog met him at the mound, same as the rest of us.

"He wanted to get ahead of Lazzeri. That was his idea. But it had to be on a bad ball. He was going to throw that first one fast to Lazzeri, high and tight, far enough on the inside so that even if Lazzeri hit it solid it would have to go foul, because in order to get good wood on it, Tony would have to be way out in front with the bat. If he didn't get good wood on it, then he would be hitting it on the handle and maybe breaking his bat. What made him think Lazzeri would be swinging at a bad ball?"

ROGERS HORNSBY: "Alexander's first pitch to Lazzeri was wide for a ball. Lazzeri took the next one for a strike. Then Lazzeri laid into the third pitch and it was a home run all the way. The Yankees were on top of the dugout steps to run and meet Lazzeri at home plate. And I was going to be the biggest bum in the history of the World Series. I knew it, too. But just before the ball went into the left field stands, where it was supposed to go, we got a break. The wind pushed the ball a little more to the left. Enough left to make the drive foul by about ten inches."

LES BELL: "After the conference on the mound, we all went back to our positions and Alec got set to work. Sure enough, the pitch to Lazzeri is the fastball in tight, not a strike. Well, Tony jumped at it and hit the hell out of it, a hard drive down the left field line. Now, for fifty years that ball has been traveling. It has been foul anywhere from an inch to twenty feet, depending on who you're listening to or what you're reading. But I was standing on third base, and I'll tell you—it was foul all the way. All the way.

"And then you should have seen Tony Lazzeri go after two breaking balls on the low outside corner of the plate. He couldn't have hit them with a ten-foot pole.

"Then Alec shuffled off the mound toward the dugout. I ran by him and said something like, 'Nice going, Alec.' He turned his head toward me and had just the shadow of a smile on his lips. Then he took off his glove and flipped it onto the bench, put on his Cardinal sweater, and sat down.

"You know, a lot of people think that Lazzeri's strikeout ended the game. You'd be surprised how many people I've spoken to through the years think it was the ninth inning. But hell, we still had two more innings to go."

ROGERS HORNSBY: "Alexander didn't let anybody get on base in the eighth inning, retiring the tail end of the lineup in order. He got the first two Yankees, Combs and Koenig, in the ninth inning. But the tough part was next—Ruth, Meusel, and Gehrig.

"Alex worked the corners carefully on Ruth and had a 3-2 count on him. Alex had better control than anyone in history. He wouldn't walk over a half dozen batters all year unintentionally. Then he thought he caught the outside corner of the plate with a curve and started off the mound. But the umpire, George Hildebrand, called it ball four. Ruth got his eleventh walk of the Series.

" 'What's wrong with it, anyway?' Alex hollered at the umpire.

" 'Missed by this much, Alex,' the umpire said, holding out his hands to show it had missed by four or five inches.

" 'For that much,' Alex said, 'you might have given an old sonofagun like me a break.' "

LES BELL: "Ruth got to first and then, for some reason I've never been able to figure out, tried to steal second."

ROGERS HORNSBY: "Meusel was up. He hit .315 during the regular season and could hit the ball out of the park to either field. The Babe was the tying run, standing over on first base.

"Alex came in with a low curve to Meusel. Then it happened: Babe Ruth, the slowest regular on the Yankees and a guy who ran like he was pulling a trailer, was trying to steal second.

"Bob O'Farrell, my catcher, made a perfect throw to me at second base and I just held my glove out. Babe slid right into it for the final out. We were the world champions. Babe Ruth saw to that—it was the only mistake I ever heard of him making in about twenty-five years of baseball. After Ruth was out, he got up and shook my hand to congratulate me.

"For years, sportswriters said that Ruth probably thought there was but one out. And Miller Huggins, the Yankee manager, said he sure didn't give Ruth any signal to steal. 'That's right,' Babe said later. 'Nobody did anything. I just decided to go. So I went.' "

Bob O'Farrell: "You know, I wondered why Babe tried to steal second then. A year or so later I went on a barnstorming trip with the Babe and I asked him. Ruth said he thought Alex had forgotten he was there. Also that the way Alex was pitching, they'd never get two hits in a row off him, so he better get in position to score if they got one. Well, maybe that was good thinking and maybe not. In any case, I had him out a mile at second."

Grover Cleveland Alexander: "I'll never know why the guy did it but on my first pitch to Meusel, the Babe broke for second. He (or Miller Huggins) probably figured that it would catch us by surprise. I caught the blur of Ruth starting for second as I pitched and then came the whistle of the ball as O'Farrell rifled it to second. I wheeled around and there was one of the grandest sights in my life. Hornsby, his foot anchored on the bag and his gloved hand outstretched, was waiting for Ruth to come in. There was the Series and my second big thrill of the day. The third came when Judge Landis mailed out the winners' checks for $5,584.51."

Les Bell: "We all froze for a second, then rushed at Alec. We surrounded him, the whole team did, and pounded him around pretty good. He kept nodding his head and smiling and saying very softly, 'Thanks, boys, thanks.'

"That number seven was a good ball game. In fact, it was a great Series, any way you look at it, what with some good pitching and some very heavy hitting. But it was also a dramatic Series, for the simple reason of Alexander in that last game. I think it's one of the most dramatic things in all of baseball history, because it was Grover Cleveland Alexander who was involved. Anytime you have a really great athlete who's at the twilight of a long career come in and rise to the challenge, it's truly something to see and to remember."

Alexander's gritty performance in the 1926 World Series would make him a national hero. It would take the historic first flight by Charles Lindbergh across the Atlantic Ocean a year later to eclipse his fame. A couple days after Alex struck out Lazzeri, Sam Breadon called Alex's wife Aimee and told her he wanted Alex to attend an important banquet in honor of the world champion Cardinals. Pete was at the governor's mansion, explaining to Governor Reid the pitches he used to strike Lazzeri out. Aimee, who worked very hard to control Alex's drinking, asked Alex to leave with her before the party had broken up.

Aimee Alexander: "The governor got real mad when I wanted to take Alex away. You see, everybody loved him, all sorts of people."

During the World Series, Branch Rickey was visiting a friend, Gene Mudd. When the Cards won the final game, Rickey told Mudd, "Gene, you can't possibly realize what this means to me . . . to the club. Not only vindication of all I've dreamed of and fought for, but it means capital to reinvest and

spend for expansion and scouting and large training camps and more teams
for developing the finest players.''

Vision was part of Branch Rickey's genius. What he foresaw often came
to fruition. This would be the first of eight pennants attributable to Rickey's
ingenuity and planning. What the New York Yankees were to the American
League, the Cardinals would become to the National.

CHAPTER 14
▬▬▬▬▬▬

THE RAJAH IS SENT PACKING

Rajah Hornsby had captivated the city of St. Louis by leading the Cardinals to
their first world championship since Chris Von der Ahe and Charlie Comiskey
were in the championship series back in 1888. But no sooner had the city celebrated when less than two months later Hornsby, perhaps the city's most celebrated
hero, was traded away in December following a salary dispute with Sam Breadon.

Throughout the fall, Branch Rickey hoped Breadon would change his mind
about trading his star after his first order to peddle him. Before leaving for
the winter meetings in New York in early December, Rickey again asked
Breadon if he wanted a trade. Breadon said he did.

"I can handle him, Sam," said Rickey. "If you two can work something
out, I can handle Hornsby." But Breadon was adamant.

GENE KARST: "After they won the pennant and the World Series, Hornsby
was the big hero. He had led the Cardinals out of the wilderness. He was also
a wonderful hitter, though he had had an off season as a hitter. He hit only
.317, and he had been hitting .400 for some time, so he thought he had Breadon
by the balls, and so he wanted a three-year contract at $50,000 a year. Babe
Ruth made $80,000 maximum salary. But nobody else was worth that kind of
money. Breadon said, 'I can't do it. This is a small city, and for three years?
Who knows what's going to happen?' He said, 'I will give you $50,000 for
one year. Or I will give you a $40,000 contract for three years.' Breadon and
Hornsby had another blowup, and this history of friction between them was
still in Breadon's mind, and of course, the Giants and the Cubs particularly
had been offering a lot of money and players to get Hornsby, so Breadon
knew that he had a market. Frisch, meanwhile, had had a big argument with
John McGraw that summer, and he was unhappy with him and left the team.

"Around the twentieth of December, Hornsby stalked out of Breadon's
office and slammed the door. He wanted $50,000 or else for three years. And
when he left, Breadon picked up the telephone and called the Giants."

Rickey could not make the deal himself. He made Breadon do it. Rickey
told Breadon to get a good pitcher in addition to Frisch. Breadon didn't even

do that. Breadon called Horace Stoneham of the Giants and told him, "Well, you've wanted Hornsby for a long time. You can have him now for Frisch and [pitcher Jimmy] Ring."

Jimmy Ring had won 11 games for the Giants but would not win a single game for the Cards. Infielder Frankie Frisch in 1926 had had a decent but not spectacular season, hitting .314 with 5 home runs and 44 RBIs. At the time, Rickey was very unhappy with the trade.

BRANCH RICKEY: "Had I been in sole charge, Hornsby never would have left St. Louis. Depriving the Cardinals of a known quantity of greatness in batting and competitive spirit wasn't right. Whether Frisch was good or better, personal affront is never enough to justify a move of such magnitude."

The trade also left the team's fans furious and resentful toward both Breadon, the owner, and Rickey, who they saw as his henchman.

GENE KARST: "The fans did everything they could to try to reverse the deal— one of the sportswriters, Jim Gould, swore he would never go to a Cardinal ball game again. There was wide criticism, the fans were furious. They went to the chamber of commerce. They called on Judge Landis, wanting him to throw the deal out, and of course, they wanted to crucify Breadon. They hung crepe on his door at home and at his automobile business. They said if Frisch didn't have a good year, Breadon better get out of town.

"But the joker in this deal was this: When Hornsby became manager in 1925, one of the inducements that Breadon gave him at that time was some stock in the Cardinals. So here this guy owned stock in the Cardinals, and he was now a member of the New York Giants. That can't work, especially with Landis in office, so Breadon offered to buy the stock back. A lot of money was involved, and Hornsby wanted top value. They had an impasse, and somebody had to solve the problem or Hornsby couldn't play. He's a big star in the National League. As I understand it, they worked it out where the other seven National League teams put up the money to meet Hornsby's price. He got what he wanted for that stock. A lot of money. [The amount was reported to be $118,000.]

"Hornsby went to the Giants, and he lasted one year. Tactlessness shortened his career. He went to Boston, and they made him manager, and then the Cubs got him, and he was with the Cubs a few years, and meanwhile he had a spur on his heel, and he went backward as a hitter, couldn't play regularly, and he was gambling all over the place. Hornsby was one of the biggest gamblers who ever lived. He was with the Cubs during the 1932 season, and I was with the publicity man for the Cardinals, and Breadon at this point decided to take this broken-down ballplayer, Hornsby, who was somewhat contrite by this time, and he was broke! He was on the Cub payroll for twelve months a year and he was actually broke after his Cub experience! The Cardinals lent him some money for the rest of 1932, and they signed him up as a substitute on the Cardinals, trying to mollify some of the anti-Cardinal fans. He couldn't play regularly, but he could still hit.

"My job was dealing with the radio stations, and I set Hornsby up for a radio appearance. I was talking to him in the office. He said, 'What do we talk about? I'll say anything you want, anything Rickey or Breadon wants me to say.' He was very contrite. On the radio we talked about the positive aspects of his career, and we went on. It was not a sensational interview, but I had no trouble with the guy. Hornsby would make brutal remarks to anybody and everybody, but I had that pleasant interlude. It was interesting."

Hornsby, for one, never knew what struck him when he was hit by the Cardinals' swinging door. Hornsby figured his many accomplishments should have allowed him to name his price. But he had underestimated the anger Breadon and Rickey directed at him. Both considered themselves gentlemen, and Hornsby's behavior toward them had been crude and tactless. Hornsby also didn't understand how concerned Breadon was about money. When Hornsby called Breadon's bluff, the Cardinal owner played his hand. Many years later Hornsby's bitterness remained.

ROGERS HORNSBY: "Even though I had managed the Cardinals to their first pennant and World Series in history, Breadon only offered me a one-year contract. I made up my mind that I wasn't going to take anything less than a three-year contract. He definitely had made up his mind that he was only going to sign me for one year.

"After we won the World Series, I learned that Breadon offered my job to Bill Killefer, one of my coaches, and Killefer turned it down and told me so. I then took a train to Texas for my mother's funeral.

"I loved St. Louis, had a house there and everything. Planned to spend the rest of my life there. Being the second-largest stockholder in the Cardinals, I felt fairly secure. I had won six straight batting championships and managed the team to the pennant and World Series championship. Then five days before Christmas, 1926, the phone rang. It was the traveling secretary of the Cardinals. 'We've traded you to the New York Giants,' he said. The owner—the guy who traded me because I had stood up for my decisions—didn't have the nerve to call.

"The St. Louis fans tried to bring all kinds of pressure on Breadon. Even wrote a letter to the commissioner, Judge Landis, trying to get Breadon to change his mind.

"There was a lot more howling. I made a simple statement to the press:

" 'If they want to trade me, it's all right with me. But it doesn't seem right that I should be traded from a club that I just managed to a world championship. I gave the Cardinals all I had, and I asked for a three-year contract that I believed I was entitled to. I had always been playing under a three-year contract. I wasn't paid a thing for managing the club—not even a word of congratulations or a complimentary remark. The players weren't even congratulated.' "

The Cardinal players were just as upset as the fans when Hornsby was sent packing.

BOB O'FARRELL: "That winter the Cardinals up and traded Rogers Hornsby to the Giants for Frankie Frisch and Jimmy Ring! They trade away the manager of the world's champions, who also happens to be a guy who had hit over .400 in three of his last five seasons! Boy, that really shook us up. Traded away a national hero. And to top it all off, who do they make the new St. Louis manager? Me!

"What a position to be in, huh? Hornsby couldn't get along with the owner, Sam Breadon, and in a way I wound up as the goat. I didn't want to be the manager. I was in the prime of my career, only thirty years old, and managing always takes something away from your playing.

"Nevertheless, we almost won the pennant again in 1927. Lost out to the Pirates by only one and a half games. But we didn't win it, so the following season I wasn't the manager anymore, and I found myself traded to the Giants early in 1928."

After leaving the Cardinals, Rogers Hornsby's career quickly went downhill. After a season with the Giants, he was dealt to the Boston Braves, where he replaced Jack Slattery as manager, then quickly was dealt to the Chicago Cubs, where he spent three seasons before wearing out his welcome. His problem was a gambling addiction. Though he was player-manager, he borrowed money from most of his players. When owner Phil Wrigley learned how much money Hornsby owed, he fired him. His next stop was the St. Louis Browns, where owner Don Barnes figured Hornsby would be a draw for a team perpetually in last place. In five years, Hornsby did little to raise the fortunes of the Browns, and he was fired in 1937. Once again, his gambling addiction brought him down.

BILL DeWITT, SR.: "Hornsby used to bet on the horses a lot. Judge Landis was against anybody betting on the horses or anything else; he thought you might become involved in some kind of scheme or subject yourself to some bribe. [Browns owner Donald] Barnes talked to Hornsby about gambling before he ever went to spring training in 1937. He said, 'Look, you can't gamble, you can't bet on the horses and have your mind on the ball game at the same time. There's no way you can do it. Why don't you go one season and not bet on the horses at all. Just forget it.' Hornsby said, 'All right, sure. I'll do it.'

"Hornsby was about through as a player then, although on Opening Day, 1937, he hit a ball into the bleachers. He would go to the park in the morning very early, something like nine or ten o'clock, and the ball game wasn't until around two-thirty. He would always go into one of the phone booths in the ballpark. Then during the game, the clubhouse boy would go out two or three times and spend ten or fifteen minutes away. We couldn't figure out what he was doing. So we finally checked around and found out that he was running bets for Hornsby to a saloon across the street, where they used to make book on the horses and the ball games and everything else. He'd come down and give Hornsby the results on the bench. Jesus, here he is supposed to be running the ballclub. Isn't that something?

"Barnes got the idea of tapping the telephone, and we hired some Pinkerton's guy to get on the other end of the line to see what was going on. The guy gave us a report every day; we had all Hornsby's bets: what he lost, what he won, everything. Listen, he was a big bettor. He'd bet $50 across the board or $100 across the board. Sometimes he'd bet $1,500 on a race. He'd bet eight or nine different races. And he was placing bets all over the country.

"I think he owed us something like $4,800; as an incentive to invest in something besides horses, Barnes had loaned him the money to buy stock in Barnes's company, American Investment Company. And one day Hornsby had a hell of a day at the tracks, won about $3,000 or $3,500. So he came in the office and he said, 'I want to pay off some of that money, about $2,000.' Barnes said, 'You must have had a windfall.' Hornsby said, 'Well, a guy owed me some money and paid me.' Of course, we knew where he got it, so he and Barnes got into an argument. Barnes wound up firing him, right then.''

CHAPTER 15

CASUALTIES

WHEN the 1927 season began, the Cards fans were cool toward their new second baseman, Frankie Frisch. He didn't put up gaudy numbers like Rogers Hornsby did. He wasn't even the star of the New York Giants at the time of the trade to St. Louis. But they would soon learn that few played the game with the intensity of the man who became known as "the Fordham Flash."

Frank Frisch was born on September 9, 1898, in the Bedford Park section of the Bronx. Frisch played baseball on a dozen or more teams around New York City and went to Fordham University, where he played football and baseball. His baseball coach at Fordham was Art Devlin, who had played third base for the New York Giants. One of Fordham's opponents was the Baltimore Orioles, owned by Jack Dunn, who had sold Babe Ruth to the Yankees. There was a rumor Dunn was interested in signing the kid. But Devlin had contacted his close friend, John McGraw, who was managing the New York Giants, and after McGraw sent a scout, signed him for a $200 signing bonus and $400 a month. It was 1919, and right after his final semester ended at Fordham, in June, Frisch joined McGraw and the Giants directly, taking the train to Pittsburgh to begin his big league career.

Frisch played nine years in New York. From 1921 through his last year there in 1926, Frisch hit no lower than .314 and in 1923 hit .348. He helped lead the Giants to four pennants in a row between 1921 and 1924.

But by 1926 McGraw had become unbearable. Frisch was the captain, and he bore the brunt of the manager's abuse. In Cincinnati in early summer, one of the Giants booted a ball, and McGraw started calling Frisch names, including "cement head." In late August in St. Louis, Frisch was the second baseman on a hit-and-run play, and when the ball shot through the hole he had just created, McGraw asked him, "Are you trying to give away the ball game?" Frisch retorted, "You don't mean that." But after the game McGraw continued his abuse.

That night Frisch vowed to quit the club and bought a train ticket back to New York.

McGraw fined him $500. The Giants called, but for a few days he refused to answer the phone. Eventually, Frisch did come back, but McGraw was not the sort of person to let something like that go. When Breadon called to discuss the trade of Hornsby for Frisch, McGraw was only too happy to ditch his captain. Frisch wouldn't speak to McGraw again for many years.

When Frisch came to St. Louis, he was met by manager Bob O'Farrell, who told him he could train at his own speed and play his own game. "I know what you can do, and it's great to have you on the ballclub," said O'Farrell.

When Frisch arrived for spring training in 1927, he marveled how different the Cardinals atmosphere was in comparison to the Giants'.

FRANKIE FRISCH: "Spring training with the Cardinals at Avon Park [Florida] in 1927 was the most pleasant experience of my young baseball life. What a difference! After those stern years with the regimented Giants, to be in a baseball group where everybody was happy and relaxed, having a good time, enjoying their work.

"We worked hard, all right, but it was different. There was nobody standing there over you with a whip in his hand, telling you to do this and do that and do it his way, or else. It was a new picture for me, human beings enjoying their baseball, instead of mechanized underlings."

Frisch fit in immediately. He was determined to do everything in his power to prove that Breadon didn't make a mistake when he traded Hornsby for Frisch. And he did so in style.

If Breadon, Rickey, and O'Farrell had to thank anyone for saving their skin in 1927, that person was Frankie Frisch, who showed everyone why Rickey had been so high on him. Frisch handled 1,037 chances, including 641 assists—records that stand to this day as the most ever by a second baseman—had 208 hits, hit .337, led the league with 48 stolen bases—a Cardinal record at the time—hit 31 doubles, 11 triples, 10 home runs, and scored 112 runs. He did as much as humanly possible to make the fans forget the loss of Rogers Hornsby, and by the end of the 1927 season became as popular with the fans as Hornsby had been. Never again would Sam Breadon be afraid to trade anyone. Said Breadon, "I knew after that year that what the fans want is a winner, and that a popular player is quickly forgotten by one who is equally popular."

BOB BROEG: "Frankie Frisch was my favorite player. He was getting prematurely bald with silver hair. I'd tease him: 'How can you keep a round cap on a square head?' He had small hands. The index finger of his right hand was jammed while he was a catcher playing at Fordham, so the finger was short, but he was such a cat. He had stocky legs and small feet. He was a strong, sturdy switch hitter. He would punch the ball over the third baseman's head,

FRANKIE FRISCH
(Drawing by Ron Stark)

and he galloped when he ran. And he was a great slider. When he played second base, his cap would come off a lot of the times. He was exciting and the greatest clutch hitter I ever saw.''

Grover Cleveland Alexander, in his first full season with the Cards, won 21 games and Jesse Haines won 24 in 1927. Bill Sherdel won 17, but Flint Rhem, Alex's drinking partner, fell to 10 from 20 the year before. During a road trip, the Cards were in Boston, quartered at the Elks Club, which had just been converted into a hotel. Though it was Prohibition, a nightclub had been set up on the third floor, and without manager O'Farrell's permission, Rhem, Alexander, and some of the other players were partying late into the night. Rhem got very drunk, and the next day he was called to task. His explanation: "They were passing drinks at Alec so fast, I had to drink 'em up. I wanted to keep him sober; he's more important to the club than I am." Rickey, trying to keep both Rhem and Alexander sober, fined Rhem $1,500.

Among Rickey's finds was his starting shortstop, Tommy Thevenow. The boy couldn't hit very well—he hit 3 home runs in his entire career, 1 in the 1926 World Series, and all inside the park—but in the field he was a magician.

FRANKIE FRISCH: "I had played with some fine shortstops in New York—Art Fletcher and then the great Dave Bancroft—but I believe Tommy Thevenow, the Cardinal shortstop who helped so much to make the club world champions in 1926, might have developed into the greatest of them all if it hadn't been for the injury he suffered in the summer of 1927. Tommy was a master at giving you the ball on a double play. He got the ball away without the slightest delay. It came to me at chest-high and he had the softest throw of any shortstop I ever teamed with."

But in June of 1927 Thevenow was involved in an automobile accident, broke his ankle, and ruined his career.

FRANKIE FRISCH: "We'd have won the pennant by a dozen games that year if it hadn't been for the [automobile] accident to Thevenow and another to manager O'Farrell, our catcher, who suffered a broken thumb. Bob was one of the best catchers I ever saw. He was quiet and a gentle sort of a guy off the field, but on the field, he was a piece of granite.

"While it's not fair to second-guess, we always felt that if the Cardinals had done something about that shortstop gap as soon as Thevenow was hurt, we could have won easily in 1927, but it was too late when they finally brought up Rabbit Maranville."

The Cards lost the 1927 pennant to the Pittsburgh Pirates by a scant game and a half. The final game of the series in Cincinnati was rained out, so the Cards had to stay in Cincy an extra day. It would prove to be a fortuitous delay. That day a tornado struck St. Louis, flinging the roof of the right field pavilion of Sportsman's Park out to Grand Boulevard, bending the flagpole in center field, and heavily damaging houses in the neighborhood.

If the Cards had won the pennant, they would have been hard-pressed to have played the Series in their park.

At the end of the 1927 season, Sam Breadon—for the third year in a row—fired his manager. Though the Cards had lost by a very small margin, Breadon felt that Bob O'Farrell suffered behind the plate because of his added managerial duties. He hired as his new man O'Farrell's right-hand man, Bill McKechnie, who had once managed the Newark Federal League team in 1915 for oil tycoon Harry Sinclair and who had led the Pittsburgh Pirates to a World Series win over the Washington Senators in 1925.

McKechnie was recognized early in his career as a student of the game. When he played for the brilliant Frank Chance on the Yankees in 1913, Chance paid him the highest of compliments. McKechnie was hitting below .200 that year in a part-time role, and a reporter asked Chance why he was on the team. Said Chance, "Because he's the only man on the club with whom I can talk baseball. He has brains and knows what it's all about."

The 1928 pennant race could have been won by the Cards, Cubs, Reds, or Giants. All fought for the lead through June, when the Cards took over first place and held on to the finish.

In early May, Branch Rickey traded away catcher Bob O'Farrell to the Giants for outfielder George Harper, and the next day traded Virgil "Spud" Davis to the Phillies to acquire an excellent receiver, Jimmy Wilson.

McKechnie's specialty was working with pitchers, and in 1928 he coaxed 21 wins out of Bill Sherdel and 20 out of Jesse Haines. Grover Cleveland Alexander won 16, despite more frequent epileptic fits and a greater propensity to drink. During the tight pennant race, Alex was pitching against the Cubs when in midgame he crumpled to the ground. He came to in the clubhouse, and pleaded with manager Bill McKechnie to let him go back out and finish the game. "Just a dizzy spell," he said. He went back out and won.

Sherdel clinched the 1928 pennant on the second-to-last day of the season with a 3–2 win over the Boston Braves. The star hitters of the team were two of Branch Rickey's farm team signees: Jim Bottomley, who hit 31 homers and drove in 136 runs, and Chick Hafey, who batted .337. Frankie Frisch hit .300 and anchored the infield.

This was 1928, just one year before America's economic bubble would burst. The team drew 778,147 fans at home, an all-time record. Sam Breadon should have been very happy. But in the World Series against the New York Yankees, the Cardinals were swept when Babe Ruth and Lou Gehrig put on one of the greatest two-man exhibitions in Series history. McKechnie made the mistake of pitching to Ruth rather than walking him. Ruth hit .625. He hit 3 towering home runs. Gehrig hit .545 with 4 home runs and 9 RBIs. There were no Cardinal highlights, as the Yankees swept the Redbirds.

Shortly after the end of the Series, Breadon took out his frustrations on McKechnie, demoting him to the minors. Billy Southworth, the playing manager at Rochester, was hired to replace him, Breadon's fourth choice in four years.

But Southworth, who one day would lead the Cardinals to victory, quickly lost the backing of his players in his first try as manager, and that failure would cost the team the pennant in 1929. Roy Stockton, sportswriter for the *St. Louis Post-Dispatch,* recalled why.

ROY STOCKTON: "Billy Southworth had been one of the gang only two springs before. As right fielder, he had helped those Cardinals to their spectacular World Series victory over the Yankees in 1926. And he hadn't ever been averse to burning a candle or two at any number of ends. But now he was their manager. As a manager in the minors, he had won the 1928 International League pennant at Rochester and had been called in for promotion by Sam Breadon, because the Cardinals, after winning the pennant that year under Bill McKechnie, had lost four straight games to the Yankees in the World Series. Breadon was burned up. He wanted a winner. Southworth knew what Sam wanted—an aggressive, well-disciplined club. He'd give Sam what he wanted.

" 'Now get this straight,' Southworth said, 'We go to Miami tomorrow and all you men will ride the train. There won't be any riding in motorcars with families or friends.'

"Big Chick Hafey, who always grinned at authority and did about as he pleased, because he could field so well and hit the ball so hard, brushed away a grimace with his sleeve. Jimmy Wilson broke the silence.

" 'Look, Bill,' he said, 'that won't work. My wife's down here and she's been looking forward to this trip. And I'm telling you here and now that I for one am going to drive my own car to Miami.'

" 'All right,' snapped Southworth. 'As long as you've gone on record, I'll go on record. If you drive to Miami, it will cost you $500.'

"Wilson didn't drive to Miami, and Southworth probably felt that he had scored a victory. But he hadn't. 'Don't look now,' Hafey whispered to Bottomley, 'but there's a heel on the job.' And soon all the Cardinals in 1929 were muttering to each other that they certainly had come up with a lousy so-and-so for a manager. Yes, there surely had been a big change in their old pal Billy Southworth. What harm was there in grown men driving with their wives and families across Florida to the East Coast?

"Early that season, while the club was on the road, there was an after-curfew knock at the door of those inseparable roomies, Hafey and Bottomley. Something had made Southworth suspect that they were out skylarking, but there they were in their room, snug in bed, wide-eyed, amazed, and in no small measure pained at what they deemed unnecessary espionage. No more doubt about it. 'Billy the Heel' was the name."

By July of 1929, the team was out of contention. Breadon fired Southworth and sent him down to Rochester, where he won four straight International league championships, including 1930 and 1931. He wouldn't return to manage the Cards for another eleven years.

Grover Cleveland Alexander was another baseball casualty in 1929. Pete was drinking too much and squandering all his money. He was so irresponsible that his wife Aimee, so long devoted, finally lost patience and divorced him.

The Cards suspended him, and after a short stint with the Phils the following season, he retired.

In the 1930s, during the heart of the Depression, Pete drifted. In 1934 he pitched for the House of David, a barnstorming team featuring players who wore long beards in an attempt to emulate the look of Orthodox Jews. Aimee married him again that year. He pitched relief for three years, but when he kept on drinking, Aimee left him a second time.

In 1938 Alexander was elected to the Hall of Fame. He was given a job as guard at the Hall in Cooperstown, New York, but he became bored, resenting the inaction, and couldn't keep it. The National League paid $50 a month to his sister to care for him, but then, a vagabond at heart, he wandered away and disappeared.

In 1939 Pete was found on exhibit at Hubert's Museum on 42nd Street in New York. He held court between a snake charmer, penny slot machines, and a shooting gallery, recounting his famous strikeout of Tony Lazzeri in the 1926 World Series. He remained there several years, and during World War II worked as a guard in a gun factory. He disappeared again, then popped up working in a Washington, D.C., hotel. He later moved back to St. Louis, lecturing kids and giving clinics.

Aimee lost track of him. She wrote to sportscaster Bill Stern, who on national radio asked listeners to report Pete's whereabouts. Stern was informed that Pete was in a veteran's hospital in the Bronx, undergoing an operation for an old war wound. Aimee stayed with him until he got better. She got him a room in a nearby hotel. The National League gave him a pension of $100 a month. Until he again vanished.

The day before Christmas, 1949, Pete was found behind a small hotel near Hollywood Boulevard in L.A., coatless and crumpled on the pavement. One of his ears had been severed. Blood tricked from a gash above it, split open by a fall.

When the ambulance arrived, Alexander seemed near death. He was taken to the emergency room of Los Angeles General Hospital. He had no money but carried a battered Social Security card. On his fingers were two rings. On the gold band of one it said: ST. LOUIS CARDINALS, WORLD CHAMPIONS, 1926.

Pete was taken to a county hospital. Shortly thereafter, Aimee went to see him. Three other out-on-their-luck male patients were in the same room. Pete was deaf, his hearing gone. Aimee had to write notes on a piece of paper for Pete to understand. He began to cry.

Aimee found Pete a small apartment to live in back in Nebraska, where he lived out the rest of his days.

Alexander once had had friends in high places, luminaries such as actor John Barrymore, World War I hero General John Pershing, Governor John Tener of Pennsylvania, and New York Mayor Jimmy Walker. He used to play golf with William Jeffers, the president of the Union Pacific Railroad, and with John Heydler, president of the National League. Once America's hero, Grover Cleveland Alexander died on November 4, 1950, in St. Paul, Nebraska, broke and alone.

CHAPTER 16

RICKEY VS. LANDIS

WHAT was most remarkable about Branch Rickey's organizational successes was that he was operating in naked defiance of baseball Commissioner Kenesaw Mountain Landis. From the start, Rickey sought to convince Landis of the fairness of the farm system. Without it, the richer teams like the Yankees, Cubs, and Red Sox—teams owned by multimillionaires Colonel Jacob Ruppert, the beer baron, William Wrigley, the chewing gum king; and Tom Yawkey, one of the richest men in the country—had the luxury of signing any minor leaguer they wished merely by paying a few dollars more than the less financially stable teams felt they could afford.

The Yankees had opened their wallet to strip the Red Sox of their top players in the 1920s. Fifteen years later Yawkey spent more than $1 million for players in his quest to win. Wrigley had paid $200,000 to acquire Rogers Hornsby from the Boston Braves. Sam Breadon didn't have that kind of money, and neither did most of the baseball owners, who were very concerned with the escalating cost of minor league prospects.

Rickey couldn't understand how Judge Landis could be against his farm system, and at the same time he had to fight him, year after year, as the battle between the two men turned to enmity.

Rickey would say of Landis, "What did he ever do for baseball?" And according to Taylor Spink, the publisher of *The Sporting News,* "From the start, the commissioner regarded [Rickey] as the colored boy in the baseball farm's woodpile. I think I tell no secret, either in baseball or outside the game, when I say that Landis had little love for Rickey and his methods, and dislike grew in intensity with the passing of the years."

After Rickey's Cards won pennants in 1926 and 1928, Landis began to increase the pressure against the farm system. On December 13, 1928, during a joint meeting of the two leagues held in the Congress Hotel in Chicago, Landis made it an issue. He quizzed each owner individually as to how many farm teams were in each system. Rickey, unwilling to put himself in the position of having to defend himself, refused to go to the meeting. Breadon went in his stead, and at the meeting he read telegrams from minor league owners praising the arrangement with the Cardinals.

Landis was temporarily stymied, but in December of 1929, he acted, nullifying the transfer of catcher Gus Mancuso from St. Louis back to Rochester. Mancuso had gone from St. Louis to Minneapolis and then to Rochester the next year. Landis declared the third transfer to be illegal. In his decision for the first time he used the term "chain gang."

Rickey, correctly, complained that there was nothing in the rules that made such a transfer illegal. Said Rickey, "This is neither ruling nor decision. It has no basis of fact in baseball law. It is simply an edict."

As he had done in many of his earlier federal cases, Landis made a ruling based on emotion, not fact nor logic. But unlike his federal cases, most of which were overturned on appeal, Rickey had no court of appeal.

Landis didn't want a major league team owning a minor league player. He wanted a free and unobstructed draft. In 1930 he ruled that any player who dropped back from the majors to the minors would be eligible to be drafted. The minor league teams, however, rebelled. They wanted players owned by the major league clubs to be allowed to play in the minor leagues as long as possible, and why not? The major league teams were paying the players' salaries. It was a lot cheaper than having to go out and sign their own players.

Eventually, Landis had to give in. The case that forced Landis to recognize the legality of the farm system came after the czar freed Fred Bennett, a player owned by the Browns. Bennett had gone from the majors back to the minors several times. When Landis freed him, Phil Ball of the Browns sought a restraining order in court.

Federal Judge Walter Lindley, sitting in Chicago, ruled that Landis had the right to free Bennett, but he also recognized the legality of the farm system. Lindley ruled that there was nothing in the baseball bylaws to stop a major league owner from also owning a minor league team.

But, said Judge Lindley, a major league team could not use a farm team to cover up a player and keep control over him indefinitely. He ruled that Bennett was free.

When Ball announced he would appeal, Landis tried to muscle him. Landis called in a group of owners and threatened to quit as commissioner if Ball didn't drop his suit. Clark Griffith, the owner of the Washington Senators, and Bob Quinn, owner of the Philadelphia Phils, pleaded with Ball to drop his appeal. In late December of 1931, Ball finally bowed to the pressure and did so. It was the first and last challenge to Landis's authority, but it accomplished its purpose: The farm system was legal. Rickey could continue as before.

In 1932 in a unanimous vote of National League owners, Landis was officially barred from trying to interfere with transactions involving their minor leaguers.

It would take a few years, but Judge Landis, who held grudges, would get his revenge—in a big way. Landis would poison the working relationship between Rickey and Sam Breadon and change the course of baseball history.

In October of 1929, prosperity in America came to an end. On "Black Thursday," the twenty-fourth, the Stock Market crashed, and the country's financial health would not return for another decade. Most baseball players, who made between $3,000 and $10,000 a year, were not affected. They owned little or no stock, and so they were not wiped out when the bottom dropped out of the market. But the crash hurt some of the owners badly. Connie Mack, for instance, lost almost everything he had, hundreds of thousands of dollars. Mack, owner of the Philadelphia Athletics, had to sell most of his great stars, including Mickey Cochrane, Jimmie Foxx, and Al Simmons, to save his franchise. Branch Rickey lost more than $300,000. Though a seemingly conservative man, he was a speculator who bought blocks of stock on margin. Like many wealthy Americans, he was was caught unaware when the ten-year run of profits suddenly and unexpectedly came to a shocking halt, and the value of America's companies plunged precipitously. Who could have anticipated that the Stock Market would crash? When the house of cards tumbled, Rickey's portfolio was worth only the paper it was written on. Unlike a lot of high rollers, he was fortunate not to lose his house.

For a while, Rickey tried to keep his troubles from his wife and children. Baseball became his sanctuary from his malaise over his financial plight.

The Depression was killing the minor leagues, and Rickey knew the only way they could survive was with the help of the big league clubs.

At the minor league convention of December of 1930, Rickey was again faced with having to defend his farm system. Landis would be on him, he knew, but Rickey also knew he had circumstances on his side. The five leagues that refused to participate in the player draft were not getting the high prices they were asking for their players and were going under. The small clubs without working agreements were also going under.

Rickey made a historic speech. It wasn't reported, but it kept Landis off his back and allowed his farm system to flourish.

BRANCH RICKEY: "Three Class D leagues, two in B, and one in A may not open this coming year. Thirteen leagues have closed down since 1926. Not one of the thirteen that failed has had major league affiliation. And what are we doing about this?

"The farm system is not an ideal system, and nobody is talking about whether it is ideal or not. When people are hungry, they eat food which may or may not be ideally cooked and served. No questions asked because it is not an issuable point. The point is, do we have food and can we live on it? Is there sustenance in it? Yes. Then eat it and don't complain too much about where it came from, who cooked it, how it is served.

"It is all right to have a physician [he looked directly at Judge Landis here] who will feel your pulse and look at you and say, 'You are a sick man, I think you are going to die.' He offers you no medicine, none at all. He gives you no change of climate. He just says you are sick, he's awfully sorry. Then along comes somebody else who says you've got epizootic and he can cure epizootic and he doesn't have to cut off the epi. He doesn't have to take out an eye. He can make you live. 'Here's pill number one and here's pill number two and when you get through with one you can take number two.'

"I claim that such a doctor in a hopeless case should be acceptable both to the patient and to the helpless doctor who has had the case. In no way should it be said, in my judgment, that anyone should say to the new physician who is offering assurance of a cure, if, in a rational hope a thousand held interest, 'You can't give him those pills. You can't give him anything!'

"Ladies and gentlemen, the Cardinals are interested in eight minor league clubs: Rochester, Houston, St. Joseph, Danville, Fort Wayne, Laurel, Fort Smith, and Scottdale. We are minor league conscious. Our minor league interests are two to one over our major league interests and we are the National League champions as of now. Golf, motoring, economic conditions, and bad management have played havoc with minor league operations. Our farm clubs have been hurt, of course, but we have not suffered at all in comparison with those who are unable to continue, and those champions of local interest who may fail in midseason. I deplore the philosophy of indifference to what is going on.

"For without the minor leagues, baseball can get nowhere. When the majors get to the point where they think they do not have to consider the status of the minors, then a great danger exists to the structure of baseball.

[Again he looked at the commissioner.] "Baseball is bigger than one club. I owe much to this game. It is bigger than I am. It is bigger than any one man!"

Those in attendance applauded loudly. When Landis spoke, he did not reply. He made no reference to Rickey or to the minor leagues at all. He spoke on how baseball helped make kids into good citizens.

Whenever anyone would commend Commissioner Landis for his integrity, Rickey would hiss, "Saying a person has integrity is like saying he breathes. What's so unusual about having integrity? It's common. It's so usual that you don't have to keep repeating it."

"Is there any doubt about Landis's sincerity?"

"Absolutely no doubt. But a person can be so sincere about rules and law as to blind himself to justice."

"He's a self-made man."

"That relieves God of a tremendous responsibility."

CHAPTER 17

EARLY DEAN

As part of his plan to stock a farm system, in 1930 Branch Rickey set up a series of innovative tryout camps manned by Cardinal scouts. Announcements were made all over the South and Midwest for youngsters to arrive and display their baseball skills. Rickey ran one camp at Shawnee, Oklahoma, which attracted hundreds of kids from the Sooner state and Texas. He and scout Pop Kelcher were watching prospects when they saw a tall, hunch-shouldered pitcher throwing strike after strike. After a couple of batters, Rickey told the boy to stay in and face a few more hitters. He would throw eighteen strikes to six batters without a batter hitting even a foul ball.

Later that day the boy approached Rickey in the lobby of the Aldredge Hotel. "Hello, Branch," said the pitcher.

"I'm sorry, but I don't know you," said Rickey, who of course knew him, all right, but was trying to cut him down a peg or two.

"Yes, you do. I'm the pitcher that struck out all them batters an' you asked me to stay in and strike out more. I'm Dean."

"How do you do, Mr. Dean?"

"When's you an' me goin' to St. Louis?" asked the boy.

"To where?"

"To St. Louis. When're you takin' me to join the Cardinals? I can win the pennant for you up there, Branch."

Rickey, a formal person, was upset that the boy was being so familiar. It also bothered him that this hayseed had such a high regard for himself. Rickey preferred his players to be more humble.

"Mr. Dean," said Rickey, "I don't know when or where you're going. The men in charge will decide and let you know. Meanwhile, Mr. Dean, I'd like to continue reading my paper."

"Okay, Mr. Rickey," said Dean.

That's how it began, with a conversation that annoyed if not disturbed Rickey and probably upset Dean as well. For the next eight years the pitcher, whose nickname appropriately was Dizzy, would give Branch Rickey one headache after another and live up to his nickname. Dean, the greatest pitcher in the history of St. Louis until Bob Gibson came along forty years later, from the start would prove to be a royal pain in the behind for Rickey and the Cards. But, like Rogers Hornsby, he would also provide Cardinal fans with some magical, exciting moments and one very memorable world championship.

Dean's father picked cotton, and sons Dizzy, Paul, and Elmer picked cotton by his side until a back injury disabled the father. Paul, at age seventeen, supported his father with a job as a pump jockey at a filling station. Dizzy joined the Army and made $21 a month.

Don Curtis, who worked as a brakeman on the Waco to San Antonio run of the Missouri, Kansas, & Texas Railroad, was the man who discovered Dizzy Dean. Curtis saw him pitch semipro ball for the San Antonio Power & Light Company in San Antonio, and before he finished pitching the first inning, Curtis knew he was looking at something special.

Curtis was a friend of Dean's manager, Riley Harris, and he arranged with Harris to bring Dean to the Hamilton Hotel, where Dean signed a contract worth $300 a month to play for Houston. Curtis was ecstatic until he discovered an important lesson about Dizzy Dean—nothing ever was at it seemed with Dean. Curtis learned that Dean would not be able to report anywhere. He was still in the Army.

After he received his discharge, Dean traveled to the Shawnee camp to try out with the Cardinals. He had neither money nor decent clothes. Despite his braggadocious nature, Rickey was taken with the boy's talent, signed him, and sent him to his St. Joseph's farm club in the Western League.

In his first game, Dean threw a shutout. At the same time, his behavior was embarrassing. He would taunt opposing batters, making fun of them at times, even laugh at them. When one hit a single and yelled at him, "How do you like that, you SOB?", Dean wanted to fight him. Though the first baseman got between them, Dean connected with a hard right to the chin.

Gene Karst worked for Branch Rickey when Dean was in the minor leagues. He recalled the troubles Dean had as a youngster.

GENE KARST: "Dizzy went as far as the third grade in school. He had no book learning at all. He had a great body, a great arm, and an awful lot of self-confidence. He was sent to St. Joe's in the Western League, and there he won a lot of ball games and began to manifest his nature. This was common knowledge: He roomed with a shortstop named Emmett 'Heinie' Mueller. Emmett was five foot seven, a sturdy, husky guy, and here was Dizzy, at six feet two, and Dizzy had no concept of civilized living. He figured that whatever was in the room was his. He borrowed shirts and anything that was available, and that resulted in a big argument with Dean and Mueller, and Mueller reportedly gave him quite a thrashing, despite the size difference. That changed his attitude a little bit."

At St. Joseph's Dean won 17 games by mid-August. Off the field, he found himself in terrible financial difficulties. Dean, always poor, now found himself in a position to buy whatever he desired, and he ran up huge bills at the hotel, at clothing stores, at the U-Drive-It car rental. "Charge it to the ballclub," he'd say.

He owed so much money he told St. Joe's business manager Oliver French, "Just get me [to Houston], and I'll pitch for nothing."

The Cards promoted Dean to Houston, where he finished the 1930 season with an 8-2 record. He struck out 95 batters in 86 innings. Rickey knew Dean was a rare find. But he wondered whether Dean would survive off the field.

Rickey brought him up to St. Louis so he could get his feet wet. Jesse Haines clinched the pennant on September 26, 1930, and Dean was given his first major league start two days later. Dean told manager Gabby Street, "Just tell the boys to get me a couple of runs, Charlie." Dean beat the Pittsburgh Pirates, 3–1, on three hits.

Once Dean arrived in St. Louis, he was under the impression that because he was a major league pitcher and something of a celebrity, he didn't have to pay for anything. That night he bought dozens of papers featuring the account of the game. He crossed the street to a fruit stand and took an apple. When the vendor asked to be paid, Dean showed him a copy of the paper and replied, "Don't you know who I am?"

Rickey was concerned about the boy's welfare. He had no home, no mother, no girlfriend, no money. The baseball season was over and wouldn't resume for five months. He needed someone to look after his twenty-year-old protégé, and he got Oliver French to take Dean in for the winter in his home in Charleston, Missouri.

Oliver French recalled the hours the restless Dizzy spent tossing small pieces of coal into their furnace.

OLIVER FRENCH: "As long as we heard the clink of the coal, we knew he was happy and all right. It was hard on our fuel supply, but it helped. Dizzy used to open the furnace door and stand at the other end of our long cellar to throw. A piece of chestnut coal into the furnace was a strike. Missing the opening was a single. Missing the furnace was a double. When the house got unbearably hot, we knew Dizzy had set another strikeout record."

While with the Frenches, the restless youngster learned to play bridge and shoot quail. Only a teenager, he wanted a car, and a local car dealer lent him one. When he drove down the middle of the road, everyone else had to get out of his way. He wanted to fly in a Piper Cub—and could have been killed when the plane crashed through a fence and plummeted into a field.

More than anything, Dean wanted to shop for whatever caught his fancy. Impulsive and demanding, Dean never felt he had enough money. But because it burned a hole in the boy's pocket, Oliver gave him only small sums. He also warned local merchants not to give him any credit.

Dizzy was so unhappy about his financial situation that Oliver drove him to see Rickey at his home. If Rickey had a blind spot, it was that, like Dean, he also liked the good things in life. The difference was that Rickey, despite his financial reversals, made close to $100,000 a year in salary from the Cardinals, so he could afford a large house and a fine car. When Dean saw Rickey's mansion at Country Life Estates, his eyes popped. When he entered the living room, he exclaimed, "Wow! That's be a pretty fur piece to hit a ball!" Dean figured that because Rickey was rich, he wouldn't mind giving him some. Dean didn't yet realize that Rickey made his money in part from keeping players' salaries low.

When Rickey and Dean were done talking, Dizzy was disgusted that Rickey turned down his request for a little spending money.

"A fine friend you are," said Dean to Oliver French.

"What did he give you?"

"All I wanted was $150, and all I got was a lecture on sex. Golly, Oliver, when he first began talkin' about the facts of life, I thought for sure he meant money!"

While living with the Frenches, Dean was smitten with a sixteen-year-old girl he immediately wanted to marry. At Christmastime, he presented her with costly silk pajamas, which shocked her parents. Dean wrote to Rickey about her. Rickey said he would give Dean $500 if he married, but it had to be the *right* marriage.

By the new year, the kid's amorous intentions were making Oliver French nervous. French felt he needed to get Dean away from the girl and out of his house as soon as possible, and he sent the boy to training camp even before the reporting date. French hoped baseball would take his mind off his romance.

Dean apparently did not want to leave his true love, and he hid before the train to Houston arrived. But French finally got him on the train.

Dean was a disruption in camp. He didn't follow any of manager Gabby Street's training rules during his Bradenton stay. On the third day of spring training, Dean didn't show up for the morning workout. He had overslept. Street ordered him to turn in his uniform.

Dean, continuing his free spending and running up debts, finally was reined in by Rickey, who put him on a $1-a-day budget. Being broke liked to drive Diz plumb crazy.

GENE KARST: "I was in Florida with Rickey before the 1931 season. I'm rooming with Rickey, and on this particular occasion he had left me at the hotel. Dizzy was very unhappy. He wanted a new contract. He came to the room and said, 'I want to see Mr. Rickey.' I said, 'He's not here. Come back this afternoon.' See, Dizzy had piled up maybe twenty-five hundred dollars in debts when he was with St. Joe's in 1930. He'd check into the hotel, and then not check out. He'd just leave. 'Charge it to the Cardinals.' He had a debt that was larger than his upcoming salary. Rickey had set up an arrangement where in order to reduce his debt, Clarence Lloyd, the traveling secretary, would give Dizzy a dollar a day for spending money.

"A dollar then was a lot more than it is today. For several days Lloyd gave Dizzy a dollar a day, and Dizzy and the other Cardinals would shoot pool, buy a Coke, and Dizzy would run out of money. He wasn't very happy. He was with the veteran players, and he couldn't buy his way. So he was looking for Rickey. He wanted more money. He said he could make more money pitching for an oil team in Houston than the Cardinals. But this was all talk. The newspapermen were sitting around outside the Dixie Grand Hotel in Bradenton, listening to Dizzy complain, and finally Rickey drove up. Rickey was in the habit in those days, when he went on a trip, of getting $100 from the bank in crisp one-dollar bills.

"As Rickey drove up, all the newspapermen were curious to see what would happen, waiting to get Rickey's reaction to Dean's complaining.

"Dizzy approached the car, and Rickey asked him to sit beside him. Dizzy got in, and he began to tell him his woes, how he was embarrassed that he didn't have enough money.

"Rickey told me he reached down in his pocket and silently counted in his pocket ten crisp one-dollar bills. He said to Dizzy, 'Here, don't tell Lloyd I'm giving you these.'

"Dizzy was somewhat mollified, and they readjusted their arrangement. But then Diz was sent to the Houston club for that '31 season.''

Cards manager Gabby Street sent Dean to Houston just to get him out of his hair. When Dean first arrived at the Cardinal training camp, he immediately announced that he would win 30 games. The day pitcher Jim Lindsey heard that Dean was getting sent down to the minors, he commented sarcastically, "It's the first time that a ballclub ever lost 30 games in one day."

Pitching for an outstanding Houston ballclub in 1931, Dizzy Dean would

DIZZY DEAN
(Drawing by Ron Stark)

win 26, strike out 303 in 304 innings, and post a 1.53 ERA. On the field, he oozed greatness. Off the field, he bragged to anyone who'd listen about how good he was. He told tall tales. He spent money he didn't have. The quirky, Bunyanesque Dean even went by two different names: Jay Hanna Dean and Jerome Herman Dean.

Many years later Dean explained how he came to do so.

DIZZY DEAN: "I just can't help doin' favors for people. Sometimes I'm afraid this heart is gonna bust right through this sweater. Always been that way. You know how people follow me around now; when I couldn't see over a cotton field, it was the same way. I was very popular with the neighbors, and especially with a man who had a little boy about my age—six or seven, I guess. I often wondered whether that man thought more of me or his own boy. Then all of a sudden the boy took sick. My name, in the first place, was Jay Hanna Dean and this boy's was Jerome Herman Something or Other. I was named after some big shot in Wall Street [Jay Hanna], or he was named after me, I don't know which. Anyhow, this boy Jerome Herman took sick and died, and we sure did feel sorry for his dad. He just moped around and didn't care for nothin' no more. So I went to him and told him I thought so much of him that I was goin' to take the name of Jerome Herman, and I've been Jerome Herman ever since. He perked up right away, and I guess wherever he is he's mighty proud."

Nothing Dean did was ordinary—and rarely was it sensible. While at Houston he met a beautiful young woman named Patricia Nash in a clothing store. After a one-day courtship, they were married. Dizzy wanted the ceremony to be at home plate at the Houston ballpark. Prefering normalcy, she refused. From that day forth until the day he died on September 17, 1974, Pat took care of Dizzy and their finances. She couldn't always control his mercurial, sometimes irrational behavior, but she was his anchor when the seas became rough.

CHAPTER 18

PEPPER'S YEAR

BRANCH Rickey and manager Gabby Street had felt they didn't need the tumult that came with the great arm of phenom Dizzy Dean. But early in the 1930 season when the Cards started slowly and fell behind Brooklyn, it appeared they had made a mistake in not promoting Dean to the roster.

Manager Wilbert Robinson's Dodgers raced to a big lead behind the pitching of Clarence "Dazzy" Vance and the hitting of outfielder Floyd "Babe" Herman. The Cubs, led by the extraordinary home run hitting of Hack

Wilson, also were in the race, as were John McGraw's Giants, led by Bill Terry and Mel Ott.

But just before the deadline, Sam Breadon engineered an important trade that would ultimately bring the Cardinals the 1930 pennant. It came after a group of St. Louis sportswriters pushed Breadon into making it. On June 16, Breadon had some hard-to-get Prohibition Scotch, and in his New York hotel room he was sharing his cache with Sam Muchnick, who covered the team for the *St. Louis Times,* Red Smith, who was with the *Star,* and J. Roy Stockton, the longtime sportswriter from the *St. Louis Post-Dispatch.* The reporters were admonishing Breadon about the Cards' needing one more good pitcher. "Why don't you get Grimes? He's having contract problems." Burleigh Grimes, a solid pitcher as well as a tough bargainer, was with the Boston Braves. Muchnick added, "I'll bet you ten dollars if you get Grimes, you'll win the pennant."

Breadon excused himself and went into the bedroom. When he came back out, he said to Muchnick, "All right, Sammy. You got your wish. I just got Grimes for Sherdel and [Fred] Frankhouse. But you'll have to give me ten-to-one odds."

Grimes, the last of the legal spitball pitchers, began his career in 1916 with Pittsburgh, but his career blossomed after going over to Brooklyn two years later. Grimes five times won 20 games, twice won 19, and over a nineteen-year career won 270 games. He was elected into the Hall of Fame in 1964. Four times he led teams to pennants, including the Cards both in 1930 and 1931. When Grimes joined the team in June of 1930, Breadon told him, "I want you to win 12 games for us." He won 13. The next year he was 17-9, his last great season.

Grimes also was known for his toughness. He once got into a scuffle with Chicago reporter James Kilgallen, father of 1950s gossip columnist Dorothy Kilgallen. According to Sam Muchnick, Kilgallen called Al Capone and asked him to kill Grimes. Muchnick intervened on Grimes's behalf. No hit was ordered.

Grimes battled his team owners for money every year. Despite his excellence on the mound, he was traded or sold nine times. Grimes also fought on the field. He believed in throwing at batters, and did so, often. One of the hitters he threw at frequently was Frankie Frisch, the Cardinals' second baseman.

BOB BROEG: "Frisch was a high-ball hitter right-handed and a low-ball hitter left-handed. Grimes was a spitball pitcher, and Frisch a low-ball hitter, and that's why when Frankie was with the Giants he wore him out. Burleigh would throw at him, trying to intimidate him. I know Frisch thought Zack Taylor, a young catcher, was involved. Frisch would throw the bat at Zack as he was running."

Getting thrown at angered Frisch, and one time when Grimes threw at him, he decided to do something about it. His next time up, Frisch bunted and when Grimes came over to field the ball, Frisch spiked him on his foot. A severed Achilles' tendon almost ended Grimes's career.

Grimes recovered. Before his next at-bat against him, Frisch apologized to the big pitcher. Grimes knocked him down anyway. "You didn't smile when you apologized," said Grimes.

When Grimes came to the Cards, he and Frisch roomed together. For two seasons, they were the heart and soul of the Cardinals.

VIRGIL "SPUD" DAVIS: "Frisch was the best money player I ever saw. If he had been on a tail-end ballclub or low down, he couldn't have done as well. It had to mean something. He could throw, he could field, he was smart, he knew how to play the hitters, he was just a baseball player.

"He couldn't stand to lose. He was a tough loser. And that's all he could talk about: baseball. Frisch couldn't stand mistakes, because he was so perfect himself. He could do everything, and he thought everyone else could do it the same way."

At the time of the Grimes trade, the Cards were in fourth place with a 53-52 record. As late as August 9, 1930, Grimes's accomplishments didn't seem to matter, in that the Cards were twelve games behind the Brooklyns.

Behind the rotation of Bill Hallahan, Pop Haines, Syl Johnson, Flint Rhem, and Grimes, the Cards began winning, but when the team lost a pivotal series to the Chicago Cubs in late August, the pennant seemed lost. Even Breadon had given up. There was an open date in the schedule, and the Cards owner threw a party for the St. Louis writers. He commented to the reporters, "Too bad we didn't get started a little earlier."

But by mid-September the team began to win consistently, and they closed in on the Dodgers. The Cards were in Brooklyn for a crucial three-game series when on September 16, pitcher Flint Rhem disappeared from the New York hotel in which he was staying. When he returned, he told manager Gabby Street this story: He had been watching the crowds go by in front of the hotel when a big black limo pulled up to the hotel entrance and someone inside beckoned to him. He walked toward the car and was shoved into it. The men inside pointed pistols at him and drove away.

Rhem told of having to drink cups of whiskey at gunpoint. The other Cardinal players all knew the story was made up. Everyone on the club was laughing over that one.

But there was no laughter when they found out that his roommate, pitcher Bill Hallahan, had hurt himself badly that same night when someone slammed the door of his cab on the fingers of his right hand.

Known as "Wild Bill," Hallahan was a big left-hander who threw with a classic overhand motion. He was very fast, and his curve broke sharply. He had some problems with his control, but at the same time he used his wildness to his advantage.

BILL HALLAHAN: "Nobody was up there digging in against me. Because—what the hell—they didn't know whether the first ball was going to knock them down.

They were glad to get out of there. Other pitchers would come close to a guy, and there'd be a fight. The batter figured he was being thrown at deliberately, because the pitcher had good control. With me nothing was said, never got put out of a game or nothing. They never told me to knock anybody down. No manager. The manager always said, 'What the hell's the use of telling you to knock anybody down. They aren't going to stand up there anyway.' "

Hallahan specialized in winning the tough games. Said teammate Tex Carleton: "The tougher the going, the better he pitched." Added his catcher, Virgil Davis, "If I was manager and I wanted one ball game that meant the pennant or World Series, I would rather have Hallahan than any of them. He was wild, but if he got the ball over the plate, they didn't beat him too often."

Though he pitched left-handed, he was in great pain as a result of the car-door incident. Hallahan didn't seem in shape to pitch the opener against Brooklyn.

BILL HALLAHAN: "Ray Blades and I and another player went downtown to a movie that night. Afterward, at about eleven o'clock, I got into a cab and was going to move over to let the last guy in. Well, he slammed the door! Jeez! He caught the fingers of my right hand. Probably broke one of them. Hell, you didn't go to the hospital in those days. I was up nearly all night with Doc Weaver, the trainer, working on it.

"Branch Rickey came in. 'Do you think you'll be able to pitch tomorrow?' he said. 'You probably won't be able to pitch.'

"I said, 'Well, it's on my right hand, and I pitch left-handed.'

"Well, I've got to tell you what else was going on at the same time. It became one of those stories they're still talking about to this day. Sometime late that night somebody noticed that my roommate, Flint Rhem, hadn't shown up. Do you know about Flint? Well, he was a pitcher and a pretty good one too. But he had the same problem Alec did—a fondness for the booze. He was a very nice fellow, but now and then he did some strange things.

"Flint never did show up that night, nor did he show up the next night either. When he finally did reappear, the reporters asked him where he'd been. Flint kind of hemmed and hawed, until one of the reporters jokingly asked him if he had been kidnapped.

"You could see Flint think about it for a minute, and then he said, 'That's right. I was kidnapped by some gamblers who wanted to make sure I didn't pitch.' Hell, he wasn't even scheduled to pitch.

" 'Is that so?' somebody asked.

" 'That's right,' Flint said. He was really getting warmed up now. 'They kidnapped me and took me to a room someplace. Then they held a gun to my head and made me keep drinking whiskey until I passed out.'

"That was the best part of the story, and one of the writers remarked in the paper the next day: 'Imagine kidnapping Flint Rhem and forcing him to drink whiskey?'

"What happened, we found out later, was some friends of Flint's had come up from South Carolina to see the games in New York and Brooklyn.

After the games in the Polo Grounds, they went out for a few drinks and just kept going.''

When Hallahan told manager Street that he could pitch despite the pain, he was given the start.

BILL HALLAHAN: ''Meanwhile, I was still in considerable pain the next morning. But there was never any doubt in my mind that I was going to pitch. It was an important game and I wanted to be in it. Two fingers on my right hand were packed in some sort of black salve and I had to cut my glove so they could protrude on the outside.

''Dazzy Vance started for the Dodgers. You had to be at the top of your game to beat Vance. When Dazzy had his stuff, he was almost unhittable. He was one of the greatest pitchers I ever saw. He could throw hard. And he had an exceptional curve too. I saw many a right-handed hitter fall away from that curve and then be highly embarrassed when it was called a strike.

''Dazzy was really firing that day, but so was I. I had a no-hitter until the eighth inning. At one point, I retired twenty in a row. At the end of nine, there was no score. In the top of the tenth, we got a run on a couple of hits by Andy High and Taylor Douthit. In the bottom of the tenth, the Dodgers gave us a scare. They loaded the bases with one out. Then Al Lopez hit a ground ball to Sparky Adams at short. Sparky threw to Frisch at second, and Frank made the fastest pivot I ever saw in my life, and we just did nip Lopez at first. There was a full house at Ebbets Field that day and the crowd was just stunned, absolutely stunned. You didn't hear a sound.

''I would say it was probably my best game, and not just because I pitched well but because it meant so much. We were right at the end of the season and really needed that one.''

When relief pitcher Jim Lindsey helped beat Brooklyn in the second game, the Cards moved into first place by percentage points over the Dodgers.

The Cards clinched the pennant on September 26 in St. Louis by beating the Pirates. They won the 1930 pennant by two games over the Cubs. The Giants were third, the Dodgers fourth. The Cards had come from farther back than any team in the history of the game, including the 1914 ''Miracle Braves.''

FRANKIE FRISCH: ''I know that when I call the Cardinals' drive down the stretch to a pennant in 1930 the greatest, people will remind me of 1914, the year when the Boston Braves won after being last in July. But I didn't see that. I did see the Cardinals accomplish their remarkable feat of 1930, winning 39 of the last 49 games of the season, winding up with 92 victories and 62 defeats after being just one game over .500, 53 won and 52 lost, as late as August 9.''

Winning the pennant was a team effort, as each of the eight starters in the Cards lineup hit over .300. They were: 1B Jim Bottomley .304, 2B Frankie Frisch .346, SS Charlie Gelbert .304, 3B Sparky Adams .314, LF Chick Hafey

.336, CF Taylor Douthit .303, RF George Watkins .373, and catcher Jimmy Wilson .318. From the bench Ray Blades hit .396, Gus Mancuso .366, and George "Showboat" Fisher .374. As a team, the Cards hit .314 in a season when the entire league hit .303. Hack Wilson, who hit 56 home runs and drove in 190 runs for the Cubs, led all batters that year.

The opposition in the World Series was the Philadelphia Athletics, owned and managed by Connie Mack. Like Rickey, Mr. Mack had lost everything he made in the crash of 1929, and his three pennants in 1929, 1930, and 1931 would be his swan song. He would sell off his players, as he had done a dozen years earlier, only this time the A's would sink into the cellar and remain there in perpetuity. But before his fire sale, the A's lineup featured some of the greatest hitters in the history of the game, including Hall of Famers Jimmie Foxx, Al Simmons, George "Mule" Haas, and Mickey Cochrane.

Bill Hallahan remembered those great A's.

BILL HALLAHAN: "In the 1930 World Series, we went up against one of the greatest teams of all time: the Philadelphia Athletics. Jimmie Foxx, Al Simmons, Mickey Cochrane, Mule Haas, Bing Miller, Max Bishop, and so on. We were underdogs. God—that Simmons. He was a guy who stood with his foot in the bucket. Cripes. You wouldn't think he could hit the ball away from him. But that was his power. He could. Boom! Right over the fence. And that Foxx could wind up—pow!

"Not to mention three of the best pitchers you'll ever want to see on one staff—Lefty Grove, George Earnshaw, and Rube Walberg."

"We ran up against Grove and Earnshaw in the first two games and lost. I started the third game and drew Rube Walberg. I had a rugged first inning. They filled the bases with two out and Bing Miller came up. He was a very tough hitter. As a matter of fact, they didn't have a soft spot in their lineup either. I went to a full count on Miller, and I can remember standing out there on the mound, rubbing up the ball and thinking to myself, 'Well, what do you do when you've run the count full and the bases are loaded?' The answer was easy: 'You put everything you've got on the ball and hope he doesn't hit it.' That's just what happened. Miller was one of the most deadly curveball hitters that ever lived. So I threw him my best fastball and he swung and missed. I went on from there to pitch a shutout, which was a pretty good trick against that team."

The Cards lost the Series, in part due to Grimes's bad luck in the two games he lost.

After the Series was tied at two games each, Grimes faced George Earnshaw at Sportsman's Park. The game was scoreless until the ninth when Mickey Cochrane led off with a walk. Grimes retired Al Simmons, but Jimmie Foxx hit a line drive into the bleachers to end it. In the year of the lively ball, the home run cost Grimes the game, and the Cards the Series.

BURLEIGH GRIMES: "Oh, Connie Mack had sweet teams in those years. We'd heard about Lefty Grove, how hard he could throw. But I'll tell you, the guy we thought threw the hardest was Earnshaw. Big George Earnshaw. But Grove could throw hard, no doubt about that. He beat me in the opening game and then again later on, in relief. That game was a heartbreaker. It was 0–0 to the top of the ninth. I walked Cochrane on a 3-2 spitter with two out. Geez, that pitch didn't miss by much. It was just a little tight. Then I threw Jimmie Foxx a curveball, and he knocked the concrete loose in the center field bleachers. He hit it so hard, I couldn't feel sorry for myself.''

BILL HALLAHAN: "They came back to beat us in six games. Grove and Earnshaw each won two. That was the second straight world championship for them, and people were saying that nobody was going to be able to stop that team for years to come.''

The experts were wrong. Other Cardinal teams received more ink, but the 1931 Cardinals, one of the finest ever to play in St. Louis, went on to defeat those powerful A's and keep Connie Mack from winning his third World Series in a row.

Frankie Frisch, who played second base, in 1931 hit .311, drove in 82 runs, led the league with 28 stolen bases, and was named National League Most Valuable Player. He looked back on the 1931 team with fondness.

FRANKIE FRISCH: "There's no question in my mind that the best club I ever played with was the happily efficient Cardinal team of 1931.''

Manager Gabby Street agreed.

GABBY STREET: "I've seen a lot of great ballclubs in my day, but for pitching, hitting, spirit, and all-around balance, I would back my 1931 Cardinal team against any of them.''

It was the year of the deader ball. The baseball brass, concerned there was too much hitting in 1930, produced a mushier, harder-to-hit baseball, and averages dropped precipitously around the league, though not that much in St. Louis. The star of the Cardinals' offense was outfielder Chick Hafey, who led the league, batting .3489. Bill Terry of New York finished second at .3486, and the Cards' first baseman, Sunny Jim Bottomley, was third at .3482. It was the closest batting race in baseball history.

Manager Gabby Street insisted from the very start of the season that the team would win the pennant, and that's just the way it turned out. The Cards drove to the front at the start and never were seriously threatened. The team won 101 games, the first National League team in eighteen years to win 100 or more, and finished thirteen games ahead of McGraw's Giants.

One reason Frankie Frisch won MVP honors was his ability to perform in the clutch. In one game against the Philadelphia Phillies in St. Louis, Burleigh Grimes gave up a first-inning home run to Chuck Klein, and going into the bottom of the ninth, the score was still 1–0 when right fielder George Watkins pinch-hit for Grimes and hit a 3-2 pitch into the right field pavilion in right to tie the score. Frisch then hit the next pitch onto the pavilion roof to win the game, 2–1.

Hafey, Bottomley, and Frisch became known as "The Three Musketeers," and joining "the Big Three" in midseason was a center fielder by the name of Johnny "Pepper" Martin, a talented .300 hitter who had tired of sitting on the bench. During the spring, he had burst into Branch Rickey's office and said, "I want to get into the game or I want you to trade me to some club that will play me." Rickey traded Taylor Douthit to Cincinnati on June 15, and Martin became the regular center fielder.

From the farm system, Rickey also brought up a right-handed pitcher by the name of Paul Derringer, a Kentuckian who would go on to win 18 games his rookie year. Derringer joined Burleigh Grimes, Bill Hallahan, Jesse Haines, Syl Johnson, Flint Rhem, and Jim Lindsey as the Cardinals carved up the league.

The A's that year were no slouches themselves. They won 107 games, the most in their long history. Al Simmons was batting champion of the American League with a .390 average. Lefty Grove had his greatest year, earning 31 victories against only 4 defeats. He had one winning streak of 16 in a row. But they met their match over 7 games in the Series against the Cards.

The stars were Burleigh Grimes, Bill Hallahan, and Pepper Martin. Grimes won two games, and Hallahan won two more and saved Grimes in Game 7. Big Bill allowed one run in eighteen and a third innings. His ERA was 0.49.

The flamboyant Martin hustled his way into baseball history with an extraordinary Series. He had 12 hits—the official scorer denied him a thirteenth by giving Jimmie Foxx an error on the play—and 5 stolen bases. In Game 5, a 5–1 win, Martin had a home run and two singles and drove in four of the runs. He handled ten balls in center without an error. By the end of the Series, Martin had gained immortality with his spirited play. Though he was from Oklahoma, his nickname was "the Wild Horse of the Osage," an area that is in Arkansas. Bob Broeg, who grew up a Cardinal fan, recalled the rube from Oklahoma's dust bowl.

BOB BROEG: "Pepper was a mess, you know. He didn't wear underwear or a jock strap. He was wide-shouldered and very awkward. When he was playing third, he'd pick the ball up, and Rip Collins wasn't very tall at first, and he'd throw it down the right field bullpen. Oh, Pepper could throw. Rip would see it coming and retreat.

"Everything with Pepper was awkward. He would try to hit the ball to left, and he'd hit a line drive to right. Once in a while he'd swing that bat and miss a pitch and sling the bat, and one day he slung it into the box and hit Mrs. Breadon, the wife of the owner. If he was playing in the outfield, I'd see him run in to get down on one knee and catch the ball cross-handed, and it looked like he would catch the ball with his bare hand. Pepper was a good ballplayer, just awkward.

"He'd run to first base real hard, and he'd stop instead of running through the play and slowing down. I'd think, 'Jeez, you're going to tear your knee ligaments.' "

*   *   *

Burleigh Grimes remembered the 1931 Series, in which Pepper Martin almost beat the A's by himself.

BURLEIGH GRIMES: "We got hunk with [the A's] the next year, beat them in seven games. That's the one they call the Pepper Martin World Series. Pepper went hog-wild, got 12 hits and stole a passel of bases. They blamed [A's catcher] Cochrane for it, but the truth was he was running on Grove and Earnshaw, because neither of them knew how to hold a man on. Cochrane never had a chance. Every time poor Mickey looked up, there was Pepper sliding around to one base or another."

BILL HALLAHAN: "The Series didn't start too well for us. We opened with Paul Derringer, and the A's hit him hard. They beat us, 6–2."

PEPPER MARTIN: "I'm not a dignified man myself, but when I look back over the World Series between the Cardinals and Athletics, I always remember how the fans booed President Herbert Hoover in the first game at Philadelphia.

"They cheered me—me, a rookie from Oklahoma who could run a little— and booed the President of the United States.

"It just didn't seem right, and I sure felt sorry for Mr. Hoover, and I was kinda put out with the fans because, after all, being President of the United States is a pretty big job and should command respect.

"You know I was a pretty lucky fellow that year. I don't think the Cardinals were gonna play me regular at all in '31, even though I'd hit .363 at Rochester, so finally one day I got hold of Branch Rickey and I said, 'Look, Mr. Rickey, I'm a little tired of chasin' up and down these minor leagues and if you can't use me here, why don't you trade me so I can play every day?'

"Well, ol' uncle Branch looked at me through those glasses and chewed on his cigar and finally said that he'd see. So I did, all right, but I sure never looked for no Series hero role and, anyway, my stealing five bases wasn't because I wanted to show off or anything.

"No, we decided to run whenever we could against catcher Mickey Coch-rane because he wouldn't be looking for it and Gabby Street told both George Watkins and I to 'limber up' right from taw.

" 'I don't know how much hittin' we'll get off Grove and Earnshaw,' said Gabby, 'so we better not waste time on the bases. Let's run everything out.'

"We lost the first game to Grove, but Hallahan gave up only three hits in the next game and we won, 2–0. I scored both runs. I came up in the second inning and hit a single in front of Al Simmons in left. Now Al could throw pretty good, but I figured he wouldn't expect me to try for second, so I kept right on going. As I hit second in a cloud of dust, I turned my head around to look at Simmons and he was standin' there, lookin' at me as much as to say, 'Oh, a smart busher, huh?'

"I took a quick glance at our bench, and Street looked sort of happy, so just as Earnshaw threw the next pitch to Jim Wilson, I lit out for third.

"Cochrane almost threw the ball into left field, tryin' to get me, and I

PEPPER MARTIN
(Courtesy Brace Photo)

was safe again. Wilson flied, and I scored easily. Then in the seventh I singled again, and Wilson was up once more, and I stole on the first pitch. I took third when Wilson grounded out.

"Street decided to put the squeeze play on, figuring Earnshaw was pretty apt to get Charles, so he told Charley to lay one down. I was all set and slid under Cochrane while Earnshaw was trying to field the bunt.

"It's a good thing we did a little runnin' that day, because we weren't hitting."

BILL HALLAHAN: "We won the next day with Burleigh Grimes and then lost the next one. In the fourth game, Jimmie Foxx hit a home run over the left field pavilion that was hit just as hard and as far as any ball I've ever seen. One of our bullpen pitchers, Jim Lindsey, said later, 'We were watching that ball for two innings.' "

PEPPER MARTIN: "I bet Earnshaw got good and mad at me before the Series was over, 'cause four days later he'd had a no-hitter in the fourth game if I hadn't got both blows off him."

BILL HALLAHAN: "I started the fifth game, against Waite Hoyt. I beat them, 5–1, and again I had a little help from Pepper. Just a little. All he did was drive in one run with a fly ball, two more with a home run, and another with a single. It was after that fifth game that he had all of his hits. There was a story that was to come out later, about Mr. Mack asking Earnshaw what Pepper was hitting. 'Everything we throw,' George said. He was just about right."

PEPPER MARTIN: "The day we beat 'em 5–1, we started out with a run in the first inning. Sparky Adams singled past third to open the game, but he pulled a leg muscle turning first base and Andy High replaced him. This turned out to be a good move because, after Watkins flied, Frankie Frisch singled and High went to third. Adams wouldn't have been able to make it. I got a long fly and High scored.

"In the fourth inning, both Jim Bottomley and I singled, but Wilson lined into a double play. We were still in front, but only by one run, so we didn't feel too safe and ol' 'Sarge' [Gabby Street] kept tellin' us on the bench, 'Let's get some power at the plate. This ain't Earnshaw or Grove today.' [It was Waite Hoyt, on the downside of his long, illustrious career.]

"We finally sewed up the game in the sixth. Frisch doubled to left with one gone and I was up again. I think Hoyt got a little careless with me . . . or maybe he figured I'd try to get Frisch to third by laying one down . . . because he put a pitch right down the middle and took a couple of steps as if to field the ball.

"It looked so good I couldn't help swinging, and the ball went into the left field stands for a homer, my first in my first World Series.

"Frisch waited for me at the plate and held out his hand. 'If you'd a bunted that ball and made me run, I'd a died between third and home,' he said. 'That's the way to hit, so old man Frisch can walk home.'

"I got a single in the ninth to score Watkins and then I tried to steal another base, but this time Cochrane nailed me easy. But we won the game, that was the main thing.

"[In that fifth game] I got two singles and a home run and drove in four men. That made it twelve hits for me in five games, and if I'd only got one more I'd a broken a Series mark, but they horse-collared me in the last two games. It's probably just as well things didn't go on because my sombrero mightn't a fit me after all the luck I had."

BILL HALLAHAN: "We went back to St. Louis on the train that night, and Doc Weaver was putting ice packs on my leg to try and keep the swelling down. [Foxx had hit a line drive off his shin.] Pepper and some of the fellows were sitting around, watching. Pepper was by this time a national hero. Judge Landis was making the trip with us, and he came walking through the car. He stopped to ask me how I was and then somebody introduced Pepper to the judge.

" 'Well, Mr. Pepper Martin,' the judge said with a big grin, shaking hands with Pepper. 'What I wouldn't give to be in your shoes.'

"Pepper looked at him and said, 'I'd be happy to make the switch, Judge. I'd trade my sixty-five hundred a year for your sixty-five thousand any day.'

"We all laughed, the judge the loudest.

"The next day Lefty Grove came out firing bullets and they beat us, 8–1. That made the Series three games apiece.

"Burleigh Grimes started the seventh game for us against big George Earnshaw. We jumped off to a 4–0 lead by the third inning and Burleigh nursed it along until the top of the ninth. Then he got some rough waters and gave up two runs and had men on first and second with two out. Burleigh decided he had better come out right then and there. You can be sure he must have been in great pain, because he was a tough customer, that Grimes, and he hated to come out of a game."

GENE KARST: "Burleigh had appendicitis. This had come up during the month of September, and Doc Hyland would use ice on him. They didn't want to operate during the pennant race. As I remember, he was pitching into the ninth inning of that seventh game, and you could tell he was taking an awful lot of time between pitches. He was obviously in pain, and finally they had to take him out. Bill Hallahan went in and finished the ball game for him. Burleigh was a gutsy guy."

BILL HALLAHAN: "So they brought me in to pitch. The batter was Max Bishop. They used to call him 'Camera Eyes,' you know. He used to average a hundred walks a year. Besides that, in our short park in St. Louis, it didn't take much for a left-hander to hit against the screen or over right field. Again, here was this fellow I didn't like to pitch to.

"I went to a full count with him and burned one in there. He lifted an easy fly ball to Pepper in center, and that's how the Series ended—the Pepper Martin Series—with a fly ball right into the glove of the man himself."

Not only did the Cardinals win the World Series, but Rochester and Houston also won their titles.

After the Series, the heroic Martin insisted that the impetus for his great Series was a speech made by Branch Rickey.

PEPPER MARTIN: "The National League hadn't beaten the Americans in the last four tries. The National League officials' pride was hurt. Mr. Heydler, the league president, talked to us first; then Mr. John McGraw spoke; but then came Mr. Branch Rickey. His theme was: The greatest attribute of a winning ballplayer is a desire to win that dominates! I have never forgotten those words. He brought every single Cardinal off his seat with an address that beat anything I ever heard. He reminded us that we had dreamed of this moment from boyhood. We had schemed and scratched and fought and gone hungry to get here, and here we were, and what in heaven's name were we going to do about it?

"Well, we rushed out of there cheering, and I personally got down on my knees in front of our dugout and I kissed the ground, and I actually prayed to God to help me have the desire to win that dominates. And I meant every word I prayed. I really did."

*   *   *

Gene Karst was the Cards' director of publicity when Pepper Martin made history. Karst recalled that the national adulation never did affect him.

GENE KARST: "Pepper was the great national hero. He had all the headlines. Mickey Cochrane was outguessed on his steals, and Martin hit .500. The fan mail poured in by the bucketful. Some were mash notes and simply admiring fans, and as head of the Cards' public relations department, I'd go through them.

"Pepper was an outdoors guy, rough and ready. He didn't pay much attention to the adulation. After the World Series, he was signed up for an appearance onstage, though he certainly was not an actor. He'd go on the stage and imitate Will Rogers, twirl a rope and tell a few stories. He said he was getting $1,500 a week, which was a lot of money. He was only making around $4,000 a year with the Cards.

"Anyway, this mail pours in, and I go through it, and there's a lot. Anything involving financial offers, endorsements, money, was to be turned over to the club treasurer, Bill DeWitt, Sr. Bill would talk to Pepper.

"I had the rest of this mountain of fan mail, and we filled out a form letter or postcard to acknowledge the fans. I had a great big box full, probably two by four by four, and after Martin ended the stage deal, he said, 'I'm no actor. I want to get back to Oklahoma and go hunting and fishing.' We loaded up this pile of mail on a small trailer on the back of his car and he drove on to Oklahoma.

"The following spring training, I said, 'Pepper, did you read all that fan mail?' He said, 'You know, Gene, I never got around to reading any of it.' He never opened the package.

"Pepper was plain folks. He was not braggadocious, but rather confident. He had a wonderful arm.

"After being that great hero in 1931, in 1932 everything went wrong. He was nature's boy, didn't use pajamas, slept in the outdoors, got bitten by bugs, and developed a rash. He broke a finger, and he had a miserable season in 1932. He had been the big hero, the best hero since Hornsby, with all this World Series adulation, and after a subpar year in '32, in 1933 he lost his job in center field to Ernie Orsatti. Gabby Street was the manager, and that year everything went wrong. They were losing frequently. Sparky Adams got hurt, and shortstop Charlie Gelbert shot himself in the leg before the season in a hunting accident, and the Cardinals' infield was a mess. Pepper had played some infield way back, and Gabby Street put him on third base and moved Adams to short. At first Pepper fumbled a lot of balls, and then he threw wild, and at the bat he was very ineffectual. One Sunday afternoon in late April of 1933, Martin was playing third base, and he couldn't do anything. He struck out two or three times, and made an error or two, and after this second or third strikeout on the afternoon—in those days they had the bats laid out horizontally in front of the dugout—he threw the bat to the dugout area and got back to the batrack area and kicked at the batrack, and one of the bats acted as if it were alive, and it bounced up into the stands into the box seats, and landed, in all places, in the lap of Mrs. Sam Breadon. And when the fans saw that, they booed the heck out of him. It was a sad commentary on the speed with which a guy could go from a great hitter to a bum.

"That was a Sunday. Gabby Street kept him on third base, and the Cardinals went on the road, and by the time Martin got back to St. Louis, he had calmed down and become a pretty fair third baseman. And here comes the claimer: 1933 was the first year of the All-Star Game in Chicago. The Chicago sports editor Arch Ward promoted it, and John McGraw was named manager for the National League. Who was on Pepper's team but Pie Traynor, the best third baseman in the league. And who was on the All-Star team by vote? Traynor for third base. Pepper Martin for center field. However, McGraw played Martin at third the entire game. Pie Traynor rode the bench. He was used as a pinch hitter. The ups and downs. These are the things behind baseball which intrigue me."

CHAPTER 19

GABBY CUTS HIS OWN THROAT

THE year 1932 marked the rookie season of Jay Hanna Dean. He would win 18 games with a 3.30 E.R.A. He led the league in innings pitched, and his 191 strikeouts would be the first of four straight seasons in which he would lead the league in that category.

But as at St. Joseph's and at Houston, Dizzy Dean would have to be handled. Part of the problem was that the youngster was a rube. He had little or no frame of reference.

Frankie Frisch recalled just how much of a hayseed Dean really was when he first came up.

FRANKIE FRISCH: "On an Eastern trip, Mrs. Dean and he shared a taxicab with a newspaperman and his wife in the ride from the railroad station in Boston to the club's hotel.

"Mrs. Dean asked how the newspaperman's wife had been enjoying the trip and she said they had been doing a lot of sight-seeing, visiting historic spots in various towns. They had been in the church where George Washington had worshiped, they had seen Independence Hall in Philadelphia, etc., etc.

" 'Diz,' said Mrs. Dean, 'that's what we ought to do.'

" 'Yeah, let's go sight-seeing, but we can't start here. There ain't no historic spots in Boston.' "

At the same time, the young pitcher was ambitious. He had a burning need to be the center of attention, and he always seemed to need more money. It was the depths of the Depression, and Dean's $3,000 salary didn't go far. Though he had little book learning, Dean was sophisticated enough to see that he drew more fans than other players and that he won more games than most pitchers in the league. His logical conclusion: He deserved more money than he was earning.

In his rookie season of 1932, he threatened to jump the club in Philadelphia if Branch Rickey didn't give him financial help. Teammates thought Dean was bluffing until reporter Red Smith learned that Dean had purchased a train ticket back to St. Louis. Manager Gabby Street, a disciplinarian, wanted to fine and suspend him, but Sam Breadon and Branch Rickey needed his box office appeal, gave him a little more money, and kept him playing.

Later in the season, Dean was scheduled to play in an exhibition game between the Cardinals and their Elmira farm team. The players hated to play these exhibitions, which Breadon booked for added revenue. Instead of going to the game, Dean took the train to Pittsburgh with the players not listed to play that day. The Elmira fans were sorely disappointed. Dean, though a rookie, quickly had become a marquee draw, and when the game wore on and Dean didn't appear, their disappointment was great. Dean tried to sell manager Gabby Street on the story that he had gotten on the wrong train by mistake. He was fined $100. But Street also knew that the rookie was capable of giving less than his best when feeling economically challenged. A few days later, Street said he'd return the money if Dizzy won his next game. Dizzy pitched a shutout.

Bob Broeg remembered that Dean would sometimes lose concentration and that his rookie catcher Bill DeLancey would scream at him to get back in the game.

BOB BROEG: "I always ranked DeLancey as one of the three greatest catchers ever to play the game, even though he only played parts of four years in the big leagues. He was a knock-kneed left-hander, had a good throwing arm, and was tough. He'd be catching Dean, and he'd walk out to the mound and say, 'You big cocksucker, don't you jake on me.' Diz loved it. He was like a slap in the face."

What Gene Karst recalls about the irrepressible Dean at the time he came up to the Cardinals at the beginning of the 1932 season was just how difficult it was to deal with the big pitcher. Though Dean had pitched exactly one game for the Cardinals in 1930, Dean's reputation for heroics preceded him to the extent that though Dizzy was an untried rookie in the spring of 1932, he was still the most sought after personality on the team. Anyone who was throwing a luncheon, dinner, church picnic, or bar mitzvah wanted the chance to meet boy wonder Dean. It was Karst's job as director of publicity to push Dean to fulfill his commitments. Karst, no match for the elusive pitcher, admittedly was a dismal failure.

GENE KARST: "I had no powers to enforce public appearance requests. Here was this guy who had gotten a lot of publicity in the minor leagues, having pitched only one ball game in the majors, and he was surrounded by veterans like Frankie Frisch, Jimmy Wilson the catcher, and the rest of the team, and he's getting all the headlines, all the notoriety, so in that first full season all these local people wanted Dizzy to speak at their meetings. Their requests came to me.

"One man called me early in the '32 season, and he said, 'We're having a dinner,' it was a Jewish organization, and this was a month in advance, and he said, 'We'd like to have Dizzy Dean speak at this dinner.' I said, 'I cannot promise. I have no power over him. I will talk to him.' So I got in touch with Dizzy, and arranged a meeting with this fellow, and Dizzy said, 'Sure I'll go.' I said to this man, 'Listen, confirm this in a letter, and I will remind him from time to time before the dinner.' Each time I saw Dizzy, once a week or so, I'd say, 'Dizzy, remember you have this dinner.' He'd say, 'I'll be there.'

"We had a game around twelve-thirty in the afternoon on the day of the dinner, and this man came to see me to make sure Dizzy was coming. I said, 'I'll take you to the clubhouse, and you and Dizzy make your arrangements to pick him up.' I took him there, and they agreed he would wait at the clubhouse door after the game to give Dizzy a chance to shower. It was out of my hands.

"After the game, I went back home and sat down to dinner, and the telephone rang. It was this fellow, who said, 'Hey, Gene, can you get me some ballplayers for this dinner?' I said, 'What about Dizzy? I thought that was under control.' He said, 'I was at the clubhouse door to meet Dizzy and so was his wife, and she said to me, 'He can't go like this. He has to go back to the hotel and get on a clean shirt.' She had a lot more on the ball than he had in that respect. He said, 'We went to the Forest Park Hotel, and when I got to the hotel, I was ready to take him, and Dizzy said, ''Some people have come from out of town who I didn't expect, and I'm going to go with them. I'm not going to go to the dinner.'' '

"This was forty or fifty minutes after the ball game. I said, 'Hold everything and call me back in ten minutes. I'm going to talk to Dizzy.' I got Dizzy on the phone and I gave him a mild lecture. I said, 'Dizzy, you made a commitment to this man for at least a month, and we reminded you again and again. You're starting your career. You don't want to have the reputation of going back on your word at this stage.' And he seemed contrite. He said, 'Gee, tell that guy I'll go.' I said, 'That's fine,' and I talked the fellow again and said, 'Before he changes his mind, you get hold of him and take him to the dinner.'

"Well, another fifteen or twenty minutes later, this guy called me again, and he said, 'I need some ballplayers.' I said, 'What about Dizzy?' He said, 'I was at the hotel, and by the time I got to the desk and telephoned his room, the desk clerk said that he and his wife and other people had gone. I said, 'It's unfortunate, but I'll do the best I can.' The players were staying at the Fairgrounds Hotel, which was not too far from Sportsman's Park, and I knew that Frisch and Jimmy Wilson were staying there, so I telephoned there and got ahold of Frisch, and they realized they were pinch-hitting for Dizzy Dean, the rookie, but nevertheless one or two of them said okay, and they went to the dinner.

"It was during the Depression. We had an arrangement with a packing client in East St. Louis, National Stockyards. We'd take ballplayers to a noon luncheon every week or ten days for the employees of this stockyards company, and there was no such thing as speaking fees in those days.

"It had been the custom that when the ballplayers would go to these luncheons, the stockyards people would give them a ham or a tongue or a side of bacon, but no cash. The ballplayers in those days were welcoming gifts of that type in lieu of cash. It so happened that Dizzy was going to go the very next day after this fiasco, and I went to pick him up in his hotel. I knew the situation. I said to Dizzy, 'How was that dinner last night?' He said, 'I sat in my hotel room all night, and that guy never did show up!' So I gave up at that point.

"On another occasion I had Dizzy lined up for an interview at KMOX, a 50,000-watt station, the leading station. Dizzy was staying at the Fairgrounds Hotel, and the program was scheduled for eight on a Saturday night, and they had programmed it. So I went to pick him up around seven o'clock, wanted to get him down there in plenty of time so he could catch his breath at the station before the broadcast started. I finally went there, and he was not in his room, he was in the basement, playing pool. Fine. I said, 'Come on, Dizzy, we have this radio appointment.' He slowly finished his game of pool and went up to his room to see his wife Pat, and she decided she wanted to go too, and that was further delay, and instead of going in my car, they decided to go in their own car. And they didn't know St. Louis. Dizzy didn't know where KMOX was, maybe fifteen or twenty minutes away. I said, 'Dizzy, you have to follow me.' We started out, and I was looking in my rearview mirror, trying to make sure he was following me.

"First thing you know, I lost him. What was I going to do? I turned around, and I found Dizzy and Pat at a filling station, filling up with gas and having the tires checked. It was pushing toward eight o'clock, and I finally got him on the road, and we got to KMOX about five minutes late. They had made other arrangements and gone on. But that was typical of Dizzy."

In 1932 the Cardinals finished a disappointing seventh under manager Gabby Street. The team was in transition. Rip Collins took over at first base for Jim Bottomley, and Charlie Gilbert, a slick-fielding infielder with a gun for an arm, became the shortstop. While Dean pitched brilliantly, Paul Derringer, Tex Carleton, and Bill Hallahan had only fair seasons.

In 1932 the Cards lost $73,895, in large part because of cost overruns from building the new ballpark in Columbus, Ohio. Because the team was in the red, Rickey wondered whether Breadon would let his contract expire. Rickey lined up a job with his friend Sidney Weil, owner of the Cincinnati Reds. Rickey had traded Chick Hafey to Weil for two players and $50,000 on an IOU. Weil offered him a job as general manager and vice president—just in case.

The cautious Rickey was being overly concerned. Under Rickey, the Cards had won pennants in 1926, 1928, 1930, and 1931. The farm system was producing, and despite the Depression, the team itself was making money. When Rickey brought up the subject of his dismissal to Sam Breadon, the Cards owner said, "Branch, if you leave me, I've got to get out of baseball."

They came to terms quickly, at $50,000 a year for five years, plus a clause giving him 10 percent of operating profits.

Gabby Street went into the 1933 season with a serious disadvantage. During the off-season, his talented shortstop, Charlie Gelbert, shot himself in a hunting accident. He tripped over a bramble, the shotgun went off, and the load struck him just above the ankle. The doctors wanted to amputate, but Gelbert fought them. Gelbert had had a strong arm, sure hands, and a powerful bat. He would miss the next two seasons. When he returned, he would be only a utility player.

FRANKIE FRISCH: "Gelbert would have been a Hall of Famer sure shot. [He] was the closest [shortstop I played with] to Dave Bancroft, and before he almost shot his foot off, he had remarkable range, a powerful arm, and was a stout hitter, able to hit to all fields."

With Gelbert gone, Branch Rickey was desperate. He sought to acquire an old nemesis-employee, Rogers Hornsby, to play second while Frisch moved over to short. Hornsby was available because the Cubs had fired him. Rickey needed infield help and a pinch hitter, and Hornsby seemed the most likely candidate. But Judge Landis, wary of the slugger's raging gambling addiction, at first refused to approve his contract, declaring that he was a bad influence. Rickey, however, refused to accept Landis's decision and demanded concrete reasons, not emotion. "If he's such a bad influence, why has he been in baseball for so long?" Rickey asked.

Rickey told Landis, "I will write a contract and I will describe the gambling that Hornsby will not do, and he will sign it. Will you then deny this man the right to earn a living as a baseball player?"

As usual with Landis, Rickey prevailed. Hornsby signed a contract in October, played in 46 games for the Cardinals in 1933, and hit .325 before finishing the season as playing manager for the Browns.

The makeshift double play combination of Hornsby at second and Frisch at short was subpar. "As a double play combination, they were murder," said pitcher Tex Carleton. Frisch, playing out of position, knew he did not have enough range to his right, and he pushed Rickey to trade for a shortstop so he could return to second.

Rickey tried to buy "Rowdy Dick" Bartell from the Phillies but failed. His friend Weil offered to trade him Leo Durocher, but wanted pitchers Paul Derringer and Allyn Stout and utility infielder Sparky Adams. Rickey countered by asking for pitcher Jack Ogden, and Frank "Dutch" Henry, along with Durocher. Weil also sought some badly needed cash.

After winning 18 games as a rookie in 1931, Derringer had started the first game of the World Series and lost, 6–2, and in Game 6 was shelled early. In '32 he won only 11 games, and then early in 1933 the big pitcher pushed Rickey over the edge during a salary negotiation. According to Gene Karst, who witnessed the outburst, Rickey was "cursing Derringer with vocabulary that would have shamed the proverbial trooper. As Derringer descended the stairs, the air was blue with the most violent profanity most witnesses had ever heard.''

On May 7, 1933, Rickey agreed to the trade, one that would contribute to the explosive chemistry of the Cardinals in an important way: the fiery Leo Durocher was coming to St. Louis.

But when Durocher learned he had been traded to the Cardinals, he was adamant. He didn't want to leave Cincinnati and his friend Weil. Durocher, like Dean, was a bright man who lived by the seat of his pants, making statements and offering opinions not based on anything but his gut-sense and his emotions. Durocher knew of Rickey's reputation: he was a stuffy religious fanatic who didn't drink, and he didn't pay his players very well. Durocher told Weil, of whom he was fond, "I won't go, Sid. I won't play for any chain gang, and especially for Rickey. I know all about him.''

"Take it easy, Leo," said Weil. "So you don't want to play for Mr. Rickey. All right, but I made a deal. At least we owe him the courtesy of telling him why we can't go through with it.''

When Durocher went to meet Rickey at his hotel, Rickey, who had a cold, sat up in bed, wearing a flannel nightgown and holding a Gideon Bible in his lap.

Said Durocher, "I'll tell you what I told Mr. Weil. I won't play for your chain gang. In Mr. Weil I found a friend, the only one I've had in this world since Miller Huggins died. He's treated me like a son, and I'm not going to leave him. I just won't play for you.''

Durocher kept talking, dredging up every nasty story he had ever heard about Rickey, and adding some personal invective. When Durocher finished, Rickey stuck a fresh cigar in his mouth and stared at his new player. He put on a performance that wowed even the cynical Durocher.

BRANCH RICKEY: "You said a lot of things about me since you sat down in that chair. You know something, son, I've heard a lot of things about you, too. You know, it has always been my opinion, as it seems to be yours, that where there is smoke there is generally a little bit of fire connected with it somewhere.

"But I'm not interested in that. Your reputation doesn't worry me one bit, son. I made this trade because I think the St. Louis ballclub can win a lot of pennants with you at shortstop. This deal was made because in my opinion *you're* just what we need. *You* can do it for us, *you* can turn this trick for us, *you* can make us go, *you* can be the spark. With *you* on the team, we can win pennant after pennant after pennant.''

Durocher was hooked. As he later explained, "The more this man talks, the smarter and the nicer he becomes. In fact, I'm beginning to become just a little indignant about all the vicious slanders that certain people have been spreading about this brilliant baseball man, this keen judge of talent. This biblical scholar.

"Before long, I was regarding Mr. Rickey with such affection that, although I was obviously being underpaid, I decided it would be in very poor taste to ask for anything more than a $1,000 raise in salary. But somehow, you know, Mr. Rickey kept waving all talk of money aside, as if $1,000 was too insignificant to worry about with all that World Series money I was going to be collecting."

Added Durocher: "Three days after a session with Mr. Rickey, you suddenly snap out of the trance and say to yourself, 'Hey, wait a minute.' "

When Leo joined the Cards, he came with a good-field, no-hit reputation. Off the field, he was known as a bad check artist, a thief, and an all-around bad guy.

Leo Durocher grew up in a seedy tenement in West Springfield, Massachusetts, a close friend of a boy named Gerald Chapman, who in 1926 was hanged in Connecticut for killing a prison guard. As a teenager, Durocher worked in a battery factory in Springfield, and to supplement his income, he hustled pool at Smith's Billiard Academy. He became the house player and rarely lost. He also developed an unsavory reputation, hanging out with low-level mob guys, card sharks, hustlers, and gamblers.

When Durocher was signed with Hartford in 1925, his manager, Paddy O'Connor, caught him stealing money from one of the other players. His

LEO DUROCHER
(Courtesy Brace Photo)

teammates wanted him banned from baseball, but O'Connor needed him to win the pennant and promised them he'd be traded at the end of the season. True to his word, O'Connor sold Durocher—to the New York Yankees, for whom he became the regular shorstop in 1928 under manager Miller Huggins. He annoyed his teammates with his flashy clothes and high lifestyle.

He was ruthless with women, and showed that same fanatical drive on the field. He showed deference to no one, including the game's greatest stars. He once shouted at Ty Cobb that he was "an old man." With the Yankees, he antagonized his teammates, who saw him as a thug. Even Babe Ruth, who liked almost everyone, hated Leo. Once, when Ruth lost his wristwatch, he accused Durocher of stealing it, though he never had any real proof that Durocher had done the deed. For years opposing players would stand in the dugout during a game, swinging a pocket watch back and forth, taunting Durocher for stealing the Babe's watch.

With the Yankees, Durocher spent many of his off-hours hanging out in pool halls up and down Broadway. He became close friends with two young punks named George Raft and Billy Rose. Raft became a famous actor in Hollywood and Rose became one of the nation's top songwriters and showmen.

Other nights he visited such establishments as Jimmy Durante's Club Durant, hangout for such mobsters as Al Capone, Waxey Gordon, and Lucky Luciano; the Partridge Club, the classiest gambling house anywhere in the world; and Larry Fay's El Fey Club, where society's cream, such as the Vanderbilts, the Astors, and the Whitneys, dined alongside such gangsters as Arnold Rothstein, who was accused of being involved in the fixing of the 1919 World Series, Dutch Schultz, and Louis Lepke.

Making no more than $5,000 a year, Durocher lived way above his meager salary, and his reputation as a deadbeat grew when he began writing bad checks to several shopkeepers near Yankee Stadium. As a public rebuke, some of those shopkeepers taped the bad checks on their walls for all to see.

Durocher's one ally was manager Miller Huggins, but "Hug" became ill early in the 1929 season and died on September 25. The new manager, Bob Shawkey, put Durocher on waivers, even though he was arguably the best shortstop in the league. Leo went to Cincinnati, where he continued to postdate checks and fail to make them good. He was called on the carpet by Landis. Later he dated a young girl who became pregnant and forced him to marry her. A couple months later she recanted, said it was not his baby, and the marriage was annulled.

But Cincinnati owner Sid Weil loved him anyway. Leo may have been something of a con man, but he was charming and street smart and fun to be around. A baseball player, moreover, can get away with anything short of murder if he excels on the field, and Durocher played superb shortstop for Weil for three years and part of the fourth, until Cardinal shortstop Charlie Gelbert shot off a piece of his foot.

When in St. Louis, Branch Rickey made him a personal project.

BRANCH RICKEY: "When he came to St. Louis, Leo was in trouble. No fewer than thirty-two creditors were breathing down his neck, suing or threatening to sue. An impossible situation. I proposed that I go to his creditors and arrange for weekly payments on his debts. This meant a modest allowance of spending money for Leo himself. But Leo agreed.

"There was other matters to be straightened out. Leo's associates at this time were hardly desirable ones. But he was not the kind of man to take kindly to criticism of his friends. I thought a lot about Leo's associations, but I didn't see what I could do about them."

Durocher, the latest in the saintly Rickey's collection of talented bad boys, was now a Cardinal. In St. Louis, a conservative city, his rogue image would enhance, not detract, from the team's take-no-prisoners image.

When Paul Derringer went to Cincinnati in the Durocher trade, Branch Rickey filled the spot in the rotation with pitcher Tex Carleton, who had languished in the Cardinal minor league system for seven seasons. Carleton was born in Comanche, Texas, in 1906, and at the age of eleven moved to Fort Worth. He played high school ball and went to Texas Christian University for two years. He first signed with Texarkana in the East Texas League in 1925, then quit when the club wanted to cut his $275 a month salary. After he was released, he pitched semipro ball throughout the South. He signed with the Cards. In 1929 he led the International League in ERA, but because he lacked stamina, Rickey was reluctant to promote Carleton to the big team.

TEX CARLETON: "I was allergic to the sun, and during the hot months of July and August, I used to weaken about the sixth and seventh innings. Then I had to come out of the game."

Carleton was a sidearmer with a deceptive delivery. His best pitch was a low sinking fastball. In 1931 with Houston, he was 20-7 with a 1.89 ERA, teaming with Dizzy Dean to lead one of the greatest minor league teams in history. Rickey was able to make the Derringer-for-Durocher trade because he knew Carlton was ready to step in for Derringer.

TEX CARLETON
(Courtesy Brace Photo)

In 1933 Carleton, a worrier, began to lose weight. Dr. Hyland, the team physician, could find no reason for his condition. In an era before tranquilizers, Dr. Hyland recommended that Carleton have a few drinks before bedtime.

TEX CARLETON: "He recommended three highballs before dinner each night to stimulate my appetite. I used to get prescription whiskey—it still being

Prohibition—and carry it with me on the road. I'd have a couple of highballs and go around blowing my breath in the other guys' faces."

In the 1930s the Cards used to travel by train. Summers were stifling, and there was no air-conditioning. Carleton remembered what that was like.

TEX CARLETON: "You sat in the station, waiting to get on the Pullman. They had great big old units that blew cool air into the Pullman. But the minute the car started—there was no refrigeration—and it got hot again, you just had to open up the window—and work your way out of the cinders the next morning. We had long trips of ten to sixteen and eighteen hours, all overnight trips. We used to play cards and fool around before going to bed."

Rickey seemed intent on assembling a cast of colorful characters. In fact, it was Rickey, like Charlie Finley fifty years later, who provided the players with colorful nicknames and who filled reporters' notebooks with stories about his men.

Rickey always talked of how fast Pepper Martin was. The Rickey example: "He was so fast, when he went rabbit hunting, he'd outrun the rabbit, overtake it, reach down, and feel how plump it was before deciding whether to put it in his sack or not."

Rickey told stories about outfielder Ernie Orsatti, who was a stand-in stuntman for silent screen actor Buster Keaton. Rickey was the one who first told St. Louis reporters about Dizzy Dean. He told how Dean ran into Houston president Fred Ankenman in the lobby late one night. According to Rickey, Dean told Ankenman, "This is kinda late for us to be turning in, Mr. President, but if you don't say nothing about it, I won't either."

And it was Rickey who told reporters about another of his minor league phenoms, an outfielder by the name of Joe Medwick. According to to what Rickey told St. Louis reporters, a girl in the stands said that Medwick walked like a duck, and she thought that was good because he was "Ducky Wucky." Even before Medwick came to the Cardinals in September of 1932, he was "Ducky Wucky" Medwick to the St. Louis fans.

The fans also loved him because of his intensity on the field and because he was one of the most talented hitters ever to play for the Cardinals. In seventeen years in the major leagues, Medwick batted .324, claimed the RBI title three consecutive years, and in 1937 won the Triple Crown and was named Most Valuable Player. During his era, only John Mize and Mel Ott outslugged him.

Medwick was of Hungarian extraction. One of his parents came from Buda and the other from Pest, and he was fluent in Hungarian. He hailed from Carteret, New Jersey, and was such a great natural athlete that he earned four varsity letters as a freshman in high school. He played baseball, football, basketball, and track. While still in high school, he played semipro ball for $15 a game under the alias Mickey King.

JOE MEDWICK: "After riding two buses and a streetcar, when I came home, I was even. They didn't give you no money. Actually, you weren't supposed to take money. I played under a different name. I went to Scottsdale, Pennsylvania, and played under the name Mickey King. I was a credit and a half short of graduating high school, and Notre Dame wanted me to go to LaSalle Preparatory School in Chicago. I said, 'No, I want to play baseball.' They said, 'You can't go to school and play pro baseball.' I said, 'I have a name I'd like to play under: Mickey King.' I played in the Middle Atlantic League under Mickey King and hit .419. I drove in 100 runs in 75 games. I was still in high school.

"I tried out with Newark when I was still in school. Tris Speaker was the Newark manager. Jack O'Connor was playing center field at the time. I hit the ball out of every part of the field, and after the tryout was over, Speaker said, 'You're too young.'

"Meanwhile, Tom Kelster signed me for the Cardinals. The Yankees soon after that sent Jack Onslaw to find out who this Mickey King was. He went to Eddie Dyer, my first and last manager. He said, 'Where is that Mickey King?' 'Over there.' Onslaw said, 'We could have had him.' Eddie said, 'You don't get him no more.'

"I would have played alongside Joe DiMaggio."

Medwick played in the Cards' system for Houston in 1931, and according to Medwick, Rickey wanted to bring him up in the fall of that year, but Medwick insisted he remain in the minors to get more seasoning.

JOE MEDWICK: "I could have come up my first year. Rickey wanted me to. I said, 'No, I want to learn more about the game, throwing to the right bases.' He said, 'That's fine.'

"When I was with Houston, they announced on the loudspeaker it was going to be my last game, and the first pitch I hit a home run. And seventeen years later I came back to Houston, supposedly to manage, and on my first pitch, I hit a home run! In Houston they even had a candy bar named after me, the Ducky Wucky candy bar.

"When I was with Houston, I didn't room with anyone. I always roomed alone. When I came with the Cardinals, I roomed with Durocher and with Bill Hallahan. When I joined the Cardinals, some of the players gave me a hard time. They used to do that to a rookie. See, they were jealous of the young fella, see. They were afraid I was going to take somebody's job, and that's exactly what happened. I took Chick Hafey's job. He was traded to Cincinnati.

"Gabby Street was then the manager. It was his last year. When I joined the Cardinals, he said, 'You're my left fielder,' and that was it. Nobody said nothing. They didn't have coaches like they do now. They didn't have hitting instructors. I'm one of the first to start hitting instruction. I've been doing it for eight years now [the interview was conducted in 1974]. There aren't too many major league hitting instructors. They don't want someone making $15,000 telling someone making $65,000 how to hit. But they listen to me.

"The first year I came up to the Cards, I had to work on my own hitting. I'd take a lot of batting practice. In fact, one day Tex Carleton tried to stop me. They tried to scare me. Fifteen minutes before the pitchers were to hit, I

JOE MEDWICK
(Courtesy Brace Photo)

went to Frisch and said, 'Frank, I want to go out and hit.' He said okay. I started to go into the batting cage, and Tex said, 'I don't think so.' I said, 'I think so. I'm hitting.' And I punched him. That was it. They never stopped me again. I said, 'I got permission from the manager, and that's good enough for me.' And nobody ever said another word after that.

"These baseball fights, if you're going to get into a fight, you'd better hit first. A young fellow has to learn how to protect himself. If you didn't, they'd run you out of the batter's box. One time Carl Fischer was pitching batting practice for Newark, and he knocked me down! Wally Pipp, the old first baseman, said, 'Give the kid a chance.' And then I got angry, and I hit the baseball out of the park. He thought he was going to show me up. See ya!

"When they threw at me, I knew they belonged to me, that they were afraid to pitch to me."

In the fall of 1932, Rickey brought him up to St. Louis for the proverbial cup of coffee, and in the spring of 1933, he became a regular outfielder.

The 1933 Cards had a lot of talent—Dean, Hallahan, Carleton, Rip Collins, Frisch, Durocher, Pepper Martin, Rogers Hornsby, and Joe Medwick—but finished only in fifth place, behind Bill Terry's New York Giants. According to Frisch, the primary reason the team plummeted in 1933 was that in prior years Gabby Street had allowed some of the other veterans to share in the decision-making, leading to a cooperation and camaraderie that brought two pennants in 1930 and 1931.

By the spring of 1933, reporters began writing about Street's "board of directors," and the prideful manager began to feel that he was being slighted, that he wasn't getting the credit for his leadership that he deserved. When during the spring of '33 Street blew up in a clubhouse meeting, declaring the end of his managerial board, he forever alienated himself from the vets who had been such a big help to him. There was a mutiny. The players came to see Street as weak. The ringleaders referred to Street derisively as "Old Sarge," and talked of their desire to get rid of him. "I can manage better than he can," was what they said. Without their cooperation, the Cardinals sank quickly. Frankie Frisch, who was a member of Street's "board," recalled what happened.

FRANKIE FRISCH: "The baseball writers soured Gabby on the ballclub [in 1933], and I'm not criticizing the writers. They wrote what they saw and what they thought. They were entirely within their rights.

"They wrote about Gabby, but they also wrote about the players. They mentioned what finally they got around to calling the 'board of strategy' on the ballclub. They wrote of how Grimes took charge when he was on the mound. They told about how Jimmy Wilson, our catcher, handled a ball game. They wrote about the alertness of the entire team and how no possible move in the interest of winning a ball game was ever overlooked.

"Gabby didn't like those stories about the Cardinal 'board of strategy' on the ballclub. There wasn't going to be any such board of strategy from there on. He'd crack the whip, he'd make all the decisions, he'd take all the responsibility, and maybe after the next pennant the Old Sergeant would get just a little bit of credit as manager of this outfit.

"The Cardinal squad took the speech silently, although there were many surprised glances of disbelief. Nobody protested, although everybody was amazed. We had gone all out throughout his term as manager, for the team, for ourselves, and for Gabby. We had become intensely fond of him.

"Leaving the clubhouse immediately after the explosion and while making his way to the dugout at the Bradenton ballpark, Street met a newspaperman, and he couldn't keep what he had said and done a secret.

" 'I just told those so-and-sos off,' he volunteered almost gleefully, and when asked what in the world he meant, he elaborated. 'I told them there wasn't going to be any blankety-blank board of strategy this year. I told 'em I'd crack the whip and maybe I'd get a little credit for running the ballclub.'

" 'Gabby,' Roy Stockton pleaded, 'go right back into the clubhouse and tell the boys you were just fooling, just playing a joke. If you don't do that, you have just cut your own throat.'

"But Gabby was adamant, and I firmly believe that then and there he did ruin his chances of having another winning ballclub. He completely lost control of his players, players who had held him in such affectionate esteem and who had enjoyed helping to make him a successful manager.

". . . The old mutual respect was gone from the picture. One group of players—and I was not a member of that group—rented a cottage on the outskirts of town, hired a cook, stocked the icebox with beer, wine, and stronger beverages, and made the place a spring training country club. The players would put in an appearance at the club hotel, but would go their personal ways at dinnertime.

"Spoken or not, the sentiment was: 'We'll let him manage the ballclub, we'll let him crack the whip, we'll let him get all the credit, and we'll just keep our damned mouths shut.'

"It hurt me to see the absolute divorce between manager and squad. I got him alone one day and asked him why in the world he had lost his temper and popped off like that to a club that thought so much of him.

" 'Frank,' he said, 'I just got so damned sick of that junk in the newspapers that I couldn't stand it any longer.' "

The Cards were in the pennant race for a couple of months, but in June the team slumped, then sank. Without his board, Gabby Street did a mediocre job. During the final days of his regime, a distraught Street was taking regular walks to Branch Rickey's office. On July 24, 1933, he made a final visit.

"They won't obey my signs, Branch. One said only yesterday, 'We're runnin' this team.' "

"But you're running out, Gabby. On them . . . on me. You fine them. I'll make it stick. Just name the players, Gabby. You know I won't. Name the players and I'll trade them. If you don't discipline them now, they'll run you right out of your job."

But Street realized the folly of naming the five or six players and having them traded.

"I'm through, Branch," said Street. "I'm pushed."
Frankie Frisch tried to get Breadon to let Street finish the season.

FRANKIE FRISCH: "I said, 'Mr. Breadon, why don't you let Gabby finish out the season? We've only got about two months more and it wouldn't be such a blow to him if the change were made in the winter months.'

" 'I am going to make a change, Frank. The club is out of hand. Gabby doesn't have control of the situation as he did in 1930 and 1931. I'd like you to try your hand at it. During the remaining two months, you can be studying what you'd like to do next year. I think it is the wisest course.' "

The team would finish fifth, nine and a half games behind the Giants. Under Frisch, who learned the game from the tyrannical John McGraw, the Cardinals began playing hard-nosed, winning baseball. They won six in a row and sixteen of the next seventeen. As a penalty for his egotism, Gabby Street would miss one of the most exciting pennant races in the history of the National League. Frankie Frisch, not Gabby Street, would go on to gain renown as the leader of the legendary Gashouse Gang.

CHAPTER 20

TRAVELS WITH BRANCH

WHEN Gene Karst was seventeen, he was hired by the *St. Louis Globe-Democrat* to work as a summer intern. He wrote general assignment articles, a little bit on sports, and worked rewrite. While on the job, he noticed how poorly the PR releases that crossed his desk were written. He figured that the sports departments on the many small-time newspapers on a path from Galesville, Illinois, to Champagne-Urbana, to Danville, through southwestern Indiana, western Kentucky, south through Missouri to St. Louis were undermanned and that if someone on a professional baseball team could provide interesting stories and articles, the newspapers would publish them. He figured he should be that person.

Around Thanksgiving of 1930, Karst wrote a letter to Branch Rickey, explaining his idea. After a month, he received a phone call. Rickey wanted him to come to his office for an interview.

Early in January of 1931, Karst went to Sportsman's Park, where Rickey had his office, for an interview reminiscent of the one he had with Jackie Robinson fifteen years later. When Rickey hired him, Gene Karst became the first PR man to work for a professional sports team. In the three years he worked for the Cardinals, he accomplished much of what he had proposed to Rickey. He started the *Cardinal News*, which was distributed on Thursdays to promote upcoming Sunday doubleheaders. Karst sent questionnaires to players, and then he wrote articles about them for the local newspapers. Karst had another job: Branch Rickey's confidant.

GENE KARST: "When I applied for the job, he asked me, 'Can you take the third degree?' I said, 'Shoot.' He asked me every question under the sun. 'How many are in your family? Are you married? Do you go to church? Do you smoke? Can you type?' He must have talked to me well over an hour, and finally he said, 'Can you drive a car?' I said, 'Yes.' He said, 'If Mr. Breadon approves, I'll hire you.'

"My opening salary was $160 a month. This was the Depression. It was tough. If you were making $5,000 a year salary, you were in the bucks, on easy street. Rickey had a lot of ballplayers in Class D and C making $50 or $60 a month. I was lucky I got that job.

"Rickey worked for Sam Breadon, who was the money man. He was a millionaire, but he worked really hard to accumulate his money. Breadon didn't want to waste any money. He was a very nice guy, but he was very conscious of money. He was afraid he would lose what he had. It's a matter of personal judgment: Was he trying to squeeze his employees or was he just trying to survive?

"I didn't have a staff. I was my own mimeograph operator, and I stuffed my own envelopes. I also made personal contact with the editors of the various newspapers in and around St. Louis. I remember calling on the editor of the *St. Louis Angus*, a black newspaper. I was born and raised in St. Louis, and I had not had any social contact with any blacks. I shook hands with that man, and I realized it was the first time I had ever shaken hands with a black. Here I was, in effect, saying, 'Please consider using some of our articles boosting the Cardinals in your newspaper.' And I promised to send him passes, but it bothered my conscience that he could use the passes but he couldn't get into the grandstand [not until World War II]. He had to sit in the bleachers. I wasn't going to take on a crusade, but it did bother me. As I understand it, every place else in the majors but St. Louis let blacks sit in the grandstands.

"Rickey had to travel quite a bit by train or by car. I would usually go to Florida with Rickey, occassionally drive with him to a farm club: Springfield, or Danville, or Columbus.

"Rickey was an interesting guy, a man of many paradoxes. You know how he didn't go to ball games on Sunday. He did not like to discuss it, not with newspaper people or anybody else, except to say that as a kid when he left home to go play baseball, he promised his mother he would not go to a ballpark on Sunday. Of course, he was criticized for that many times by sportswriters who thought it was hypocritical because he shared in the profits of the Sunday doubleheaders, all right.

"When I rode in the car with him, I did an awful lot of the driving. He would sleep. He was a man who worked eighteen hours a day. He'd be sound asleep, leaning on my shoulder, while I was driving.

"We had plenty of time to talk. He would question me. I had been to Mexico, and one of his questions was about sex in Mexico. He wanted to know about it. I had been there several months, and I was young and inexperienced, so I didn't know much about sex in Mexico, and I wasn't able to give him very much information.

"At one point, I was driving with him, and he said, 'You know, today is my fiftieth birthday, and looking back, I always thought I'd have a career in law.' Instead of law, he was making $80,000 a year running the Cardinals, which is those days was great big money.

"Rickey had a very healthy interest in world affairs. He read widely. He was a devout member of the Methodist Church, a deacon. He probably was a virgin when he married his wife. He read widely. I remember we had a league meeting in Bradenton, Florida, and it was well after midnight when the meeting broke up. I was rooming with him. I said, 'I'm exhausted and going to bed.' I was a young guy. But Rickey propped himself up in bed and said, 'I haven't been keeping up with my reading during this trip.' He sat up until late in the morning, reading another chapter or two of a bestseller of the time.

"In the spring of 1934, I was in Florida with Rickey. On a number of occasions, he would think out loud in my presence. This time he said to me, 'Gene, you know what I should do? I've been thinking about this. Frisch has lost a lot of speed at second base. And I don't think I can win the pennant with Frisch at second base. Also, I don't like Virgil Davis as my catcher.'

"Planes were not commonly used then, but he said, 'What I really should do is fly to St. Louis and convince Sam Breadon to trade Frisch. I think I can make a deal with the Boston club to send them Frisch for Al Spohrer,' who was the Boston catcher. 'I would have Burgess Whitehead play second base.'

"Rickey knew Frisch really was Breadon's pet. Frank had had that wonderful year in 1927 after Rogers Hornsby was traded. Frisch was a great second baseman that year, stole a lot of bases. After thinking it over, Rickey dropped the idea. He said, 'I don't think I can do it.' His not doing it changed history.''

CHAPTER 21

DIZZY GOES ON STRIKE

IN 1933, the depths of the Depression, the Cardinals lost $83,000, and Branch Rickey announced across-the-board salary cuts. The mood of the veteran players during spring training was tight-lipped outrage, which blackened further when opposing bench jockeys from the New York Giants and other teams taunted them by calling them "cheap coolie labor." One of the Cardinal players forced to accept a low salary was Dizzy Dean's younger brother, Paul Dean, a rookie who had been a pitching star for Columbus in '33. Breadon and Rickey offered him $3,000, which was a slight raise over his minor league pay. Paul, who was as quiet and sober as Dizzy was loud and outrageous, twice turned it down, threatening to work at a local cotton mill instead. Paul Dean, confident that he would be successful in the major leagues, felt his minimum worth was $7,500. To earn that, he countered with a proposal: he would pitch for nothing at the start, but if he won 15 games or more, the Cards would have to pay him $500 for each win. Rickey turned him down. Because of the wording of the reserve clause in every player's contract, Paul Dean's choice was to sign for what Rickey offered or sit out. Finding himself in an untenable bargaining position, Paul Dean finally was forced to accept the $3,000–a-year salary, but he and Dizzy deeply resented both the offer and Rickey's hard-nosed bargaining tactics.

Even the St. Louis press expressed scepticism over Rickey's low-ball salaries. Roy Stockton of the *St. Louis Post-Dispatch* wondered whether college men would shy from playing baseball because of such low wages. In response, Rickey righteously defended his salary structure in no uncertain terms.

"We have more young men than we can use," said Rickey. "We are swamped with applications. We have organized the Nebraska State League and equipped every team with players, and no salary will be above $50 a month."

"But, Mr. Rickey, won't better-educated men hesitate to go in for baseball with the drastic reduction of salaries?" asked Stockton.

"No, indeed. We can get all the college graduates we want. Baseball still is attractive financially to young men."

Stockton asked Rickey about the average salary and baseball life span.

"The average should be $6,500 for a star player. And he should be able to play for eight years."

"Well, Mr. Rickey, the player gives baseball the years in which, in other businesses, he would build up his earning capacity, with prospects of a steady income through his life. At $6,500 a year, would a man have much to show for his baseball labors?"

"The thrifty man should leave baseball with a snug savings account. Out of $6,500 a man should be able to save $5,000. Thus, after eight years, without interest on his money, a player should be able to retire with more than $40,000."

"Do you know any players who could save $5,000 out of $6,500?"

"Yes, we have many players who will save more than that."

"Mr. Rickey, do you save $5,000 out of each $6,500 you earn?"

"I do not."

"You have help at your house, your children go to the best schools, you eat well, travel, and have automobiles."

"Well, of course a player could not expect to save $5,000 if he lived like that."

For the rest of his career, Rickey would be remembered bitterly by his players for his low salaries. For several generations of Cardinal and later Brooklyn Dodger players, the name of Branch Rickey would be spoken as though uttering a curse.

If the players thought to enlist manager Frankie Frisch in their salary disputes, they needn't have bothered. Frisch, who was tight with owner Sam Breadon, was a company man all the way. He was making a lot more money than anyone else on the team and seemed to think that because other teams paid poorly, that made it right.

FRANKIE FRISCH: "Rickey and his business associate in St. Louis, Sam Breadon, have been accused of being 'tight' when it came to paying players' salaries. I don't subscribe to that at all. Those were struggling days for ballclubs. There was no night baseball, crowds were small, and the baseball operators had to be shrewd businessmen. And the Cardinals didn't pay salaries any lower than were paid in many other cities. I happen to know that when Breadon and Rickey were being criticized and panned around the circuit for paying Paul Dean, Dizzy's brother, a meager salary, Paul was getting the same first-year pay that Hal Schumacher received in his first year with the Giants.''

In addition to their resentment over the low pay, the Cardinals had other distractions in the spring of 1934. Some players were still upset over the firing of Gabby Street, and Tex Carleton, for one, hated to pitch under new manager Frisch.

Though Frisch had hated the way McGraw bossed his players around, once Frisch was handed the Cardinal managerial reigns, he ran his team with the same control-all-aspects-of-the-game attitude that McGraw had employed. Frisch called every pitch from his position at second base, and it drove Tex Carleton crazy.

TEX CARLETON: "Frankie was a New Yorker who thought everything west of the Hudson was camping out. Frisch was one of the worst managers I ever played for. He was very set. He wanted to be McGraw, but he wasn't McGraw.

"I didn't care whether a guy was a low-ball hitter or not, because I challenged him. I figured my pitch, my strength, was better than his strength. If I raised the ball up, I lost a lot of effectiveness.

"Frisch, like McGraw, thought pitchers could get most hitters out with curves. Frisch would call the pitches, putting a fist in the glove for a curve, and his hand outside for a fastball. Everybody in the league knew what his signs were all year long. It's pretty hard to pitch out there when they know what's coming.''

Carleton, a quiet, thoughtful man, also was offended by the behavior and big mouth of 23-year-old Dizzy Dean, who produced reams of copy for the reporters and who was quick to tell everyone how good he was. Dizzy was as entertaining in his homespun way as Will Rogers. With his Southern drawl and quick mind, he could spin yarns and tell tales that could keep everyone amused for hours.

In addition to going by two names, Dean listed his birthday as either January 16, February 22, or August 22, 1911. He listed three different places of birth: Lucas, Arkansas; Holdenville, Oklahoma; and Bond, Mississippi. When Roy Stockton of the *St. Louis Post-Dispatch* asked Dean to clear up the confusion, he did. The kid, it turned out, was sly and clever. Who would have thunk it?

DIZZY DEAN: "I like Brooklyn. They got good guys writin' for the papers over there. I like Tommy Holmes and Bill McCullough and that [Roscoe] McGowan. They says nice things about me and I'm nice to them.

"I give 'em each a scoop last time we're here. It's funny, but their bosses all comes up with the same idea the same day. Told 'em to get a piece about old Diz. Well, Tommy come first and wanted to know where I was born, and I told him Lucas, Arkansas, January 16, 1911. Then it wasn't two minutes after he leaves that McCullough comes along, and doggone if he don't want the same piece. Now, I wasn't going to have their bosses bawl 'em out for both gettin' the same story, so I told Mack I was born at Bond, Mississippi— that's where my wife comes from—and I pick February 22, which is giving George Washington a break. McGowan was next. He's with the *Times*. I guess me an' Paul has helped to get jobs for a lot of guys. Imagine a New York paper sendin' a man way over to Brooklyn every day. They're doin' that now, ever since we're in the league. McGowan wanted the same story, but I give him a break, too, and says Holdenville, Oklahoma, August 22. They each wanted to know how many games me an' Paul was goin' to win, and I gives 'em each a different number, so each goes back and can tell their editor they got a scoop about old Diz.'

"What is your official birthday?

" 'I'll swear I'm mixed up myself now. I always thought it was January 16 at Holdenville, but, do you know, my dad stood up in Branch Rickey's office and said it was Lucas, Arkansas, August 22. Can you imagine that? I told him if anybody ought to know, it was me. I was the one bein' borned, for pity's sake. But I believe I'll keep 'em all. I got lots of friends at all three places and it kanda makes my wife feel good to say it's Bond, Mississippi, and maybe I'll add Bradenton, Florida, before I get through, especially if they changes the name to Deanville, like they said. Four birthdays shouldn't ought to be too many for me, do you think?"

With younger brother Paul Dean added to the roster, Dizzy now began bragging about the two of them. At a press conference in March announcing Paul's signing, Dizzy Dean announced, "We're going to win between us 40 or 45 games this year."

"How many will Paul win?"

"I don't know, but I guess he'll win more than me. You know, Paul's a great pitcher, has lots of stuff, haven't you, Paul?"

The always somber Paul Dean nodded. At the time, no one was sure Paul would even make the starting rotation. Dizzy's boast seemed empty and ludicrous until reporters saw Paul's fastball. Sid Keener of the *St. Louis Star-Times* predicted that "Paul will be another Walter Johnson."

Mike Ryba, a catcher trying to make the team when Paul Dean joined the Cards during spring training in 1934, recalled how green the youngster was during his initial outing.

MIKE RYBA: "We used basically simple signs, one finger for the fastball, two fingers for the curve, and three fingers for the change of pace. The first inning was kind of long, but we got out of it all right. Paul didn't have too much. In the middle of the second, he called me out to the mound.

" 'What's the matter, Paul?'

" 'Mike,' he said, 'call for that two-finger ball more. I can get more on it.'

"Then I realized that Paul had been gripping the ball with the number of fingers I put down. On the one-finger grip, which called for a fastball, he had been throwing a one-finger pitch."

After Paul Dean won his fourth straight decision in late May of 1934, Dizzy in New York again complained to manager Frisch and to Roy Stockton of the *St. Louis Post-Dispatch* about Paul's low salary. Frisch, who as manager never much liked Dean's antics, responded, "If anybody doesn't want to play on this club, they can go home."

On May 31, Dizzy Dean met with Frisch and again asked for more money for Paul. Again Frisch told the big pitcher, "If you don't want to pitch, go home."

Replied Dizzy, "If Paul had my nerve, we'd both be back in St. Louis. I don't need a second invitation to leave when I'm not appreciated."

When Dizzy announced he had a sore arm, Paul told reporters he had one too. Said Dizzy: "Paul must get $1,000 cash in the hand, and there will be no compromising." He accused Frisch of turning his back on them. Dean explained that he was making $7,500 and Paul $3,000, and how fair was that, considering that Bill Hallahan was making $12,500.55? [How happy could Hallahan have been about this revelation?]

Dizzy said he was satisfied with his own pay but that if Paul didn't get another $2,000 more, the Cardinals wouldn't win the pennant. "Neither Paul or I will pitch any more under the present circumstances."

For baseball this was a stand as revolutionary as Lenin's. A player who sat out over pay during spring training was called a "holdout." This was different. This was a player airing his grievances and threatening disruption of the team and game *after* signing a contract and *during* the season. In one stroke, Dizzy Dean was attempting to buck the reserve clause, outmaneuver Branch Rickey, extort Sam Breadon, and shake up the underlying foundations of the Game itself.

If ever Breadon, Rickey, and Frisch had their nuts in the wringer, this was it, because Dizzy Dean had become the finest pitcher and most famous player in baseball, and at least throughout 1934, Paul wasn't far behind. Dizzy would go on to win 30 games that year, and Paul 19. If the Cardinal brain trust wanted to withhold the $2,000 from Paul Dean, it would do so at the risk of losing a thousand times that in revenue, not to mention the goodwill and excitement Dizzy and Paul were generating for the Cardinals both home and across America. But to give in, that would signal weakness to the rest of the players.

Despite a nickname that suggested he was a little flaky, when Dizzy Dean stood on that mound, there was nothing at all funny about him. If anything, he stood on that mound as a tall picture of fury. Few had his competitiveness

or his meanness. Leo Durocher recalled what happened if a batter dared dig
a hole with his back foot as he stepped into the box.

LEO DUROCHER: "Diz would just stand there nodding his head until he was
finished and then he'd yell, 'You all done? You comfortable? Well, send for
the groundkeeper and get a shovel because that's where they're gonna bury
you.' And—boom—down he'd go.

"I once saw Diz dust off seven straight Giants in Miami early in the
exhibition season, because the Giants had had the nerve to score seven runs
off him in one inning. Diz was so mad he was stomping all over the place.
'They're not gonna hit *the master* that way.' The last hitter was Bill Terry,
the manager. Terry got as far out of the box as it was legal to get and kept
looking down at our catcher, Bill DeLancey. 'Come on,' he said. 'What's the
matter with you guys? Are you guys crazy?'

" 'Because you're the manager, you're no better than the rest of them,'
DeLancey told him. 'Get up here, because you're going to get yours too,
you know.'

"Diz got him twice. Hit him in the back and the ball bounced up and hit
him again in the neck. When Cy Pfirman, the umpire, finally went out and
told Frisch he was going to have to take Dizzy out, he was almost apologetic
about it. 'I got to do it, Frank,' he said. 'He's gonna kill somebody.' "

Dizzy Dean employed this same toughness with respect to his negotiation
on his brother's behalf with Rickey. If striking was the only way to get his
attention, then that's what he would do. It was a stance only a great player
could take.

Frankie Frisch recalled the trouble Dean made for him.

FRANKIE FRISCH: "There were times when members of the Gashouse Gang
were very angry at Dizzy, to put it mildly. The Deans caused me many vexa-
tious moments, days and weeks. I'll never forget one Eastern trip we made—
a journey of bickering, threats, and conferences. Dizzy, who has a greater-
than-average regard for his brother Paul, got the idea that the younger boy had
not been compensated properly in the contract that had been signed in the
spring. I heard rumblings that he wasn't going to pitch unless Paul's contract
was reopened and the salary increased, and finally the thing came to a head.
He declared himself.

"I talked to Dizzy and told him that it was not the time or place to start
a controversy over a contract that had been signed a long time before. I
suggested that if he and Paul thought they had a complaint, to wait until they
returned to St. Louis and take up the business with the proper officials.

"Time and again I thought I had the situation under control, but each time
I was mistaken. Finally coach [Mike] Gonzalez brought Paul to my room and,
in front of the coaches and a player, Paul said that he had no complaint, that
he had signed his contract and was going through with it, and that he wasn't
going to go on any strike. I summoned Dizzy to hear that, and it struck me
that it ought to be convincing. But after listening to it all and saying that

everything was all right, Dizzy decided that Paul really didn't mean it, and he guessed he'd better keep on with his strike for Little Paul. Each night, it seemed, there was an endless argument which led nowhere and, remember, on each next day I had to go out and play a ball game and manage a ballclub.''

Neither Rickey nor the Deans revealed the outcome of "the strike," but when the Deans returned to the team after being AWOL for five days, the reporters of the day felt they had enough information to tell readers that Paul and Dizzy had won, that Rickey had lost.

What is interesting about the incident is that usually when a player or players go up against management, the national and local sporting press is quick to bury the player under a mound of vicious criticism and invective suggested and supported by management. But Dean's opponent was Branch Rickey, who many reporters disliked because he wrapped himself in religion and then often acted anything but godly by skirting their questions with aphorisms and obfuscation, or worse, lying to them when it suited his needs. Rickey, moreover, drove a fancy car and lived in a ritzy mansion while paying his proud players a relative pittance. Dean won sympathy if not support around the country, especially in the New York papers.

Wrote John Lardner in the *New York Post:* "There is reason to suspect that the players would be stronger under a unified front than either they or the magnates imagine, for the present rules of the industry put the individual player at the mercy of others.''

Commented Joe Williams in the *New York World-Telegram*, ''The outcome seems to indicate that the Deans are neither dizzy or nuts. They know what they want and, more important, they seem to get it.

''There are no standards for baseball values. Mostly, the size of the paycheck is determined by geography and expediency. A third base coach in New York is likely to be paid more than a star in St. Louis or Cincinnati.

''Mr. Dizzy would be getting twice as much pitching for the Giants, and he'd be worth it. And he is worth it in St. Louis, but because salaries have never been high there, he doesn't get it. Mr. Nutsy (Paul) was started at a beginner's pay as it is figured in St. Louis. By now it is apparent that he is a real pitcher worth much more than $3,000.

''I am glad the Deans struck, and I think this sort of striking should be encouraged. . . . That the Deans were not permitted to walk out is proof enough that the management recognized their value and realized it all the time. Without the Deans, St. Louis would be lucky to finish in the first division.''

By the end of June, the Deans were 20-4: Paul 10-1 and Dizzy 10-3. The rest of the staff was 17-21. Bill Hallahan, the pitcher whose salary Dizzy had used as a comparison to show how badly Paul was getting paid, was 2-7. Wrote Tom Meany in the *New York World-Telegram*: "The Deans are not only keeping the Cardinals in the race—they're keeping them in the league.''

Grantland Rice, the sportswriter who once wrote, ''Outlined against a blue, gray sky, the Four Horsemen rode again . . .'', was equally smitten with the talent of Mr. Dean. Rice, who wrote some of his columns in the form of poetry, waxed eloquent about the Cardinal pitcher on the pages of the *New York Sun*.

He wrote a poem called "Dizzy Gunga Dean (If Mr. Kipling Doesn't Mind)":

> You may talk of throwing arms that come up from Texas farms,
> With a hop upon the fast one that is smoking;
> But when it comes to pitching that will keep the batter twitching
> I can slip you in a name that's past all joking;
> For in old St. Louis town, where they called him once a clown,
> There's a tall and gangling figure on the scene,
> And of all that Red Bird crew, there's one bloke that pulls 'em through,
> Just a fellow by the name of Gunga Dean.
>> It is Dean—Dean—Dean
>> You human coil of lasso—Dizzy Dean
>> If it wasn't for old Dizzy
>> They'd be worse than fizzy-wizzy,
>> Come on and grab another—Gunga Dean.

By the summer of 1934, the entire country was plumb Dean crazy. On August 9 Dizzy pitched in relief in the tenth inning and held the Cincinnati Reds until the Cards could win the game. It was Dizzy's 20th win. Commented the *St. Louis Post-Dispatch*, "What the Cardinals need is more Deans."

Behind the scenes, though, Dizzy and Paul were feeling sorely unappreciated by Breadon and Rickey. One of Branch Rickey's promises to Dizzy and Paul was that he would give their third brother, Elmer, a job in the Cardinal organization. The brothers were figuring Rickey would give him a decent-paying, substantial job.

On August 10 the *St. Louis Post-Dispatch* announced that the Cardinals had signed Elmer. Blake Harper, the head of concessions at Sportsman's Park, was given credit for "scouting" him. The punch line of the story was that Rickey had hired Elmer Dean to sell peanuts in the grandstand! But on the day he was supposed to appear, Elmer was a no-show. A few days later he told reporters he didn't like the looks of St. Louis and decided to remain in Houston to be with his father. Dizzy and Paul felt humiliated and betrayed by Rickey. "What kind of job was that?" they wanted to know.

In midsummer the Deans had yet another run-in with Frisch. Dizzy and Paul each lost games to the Chicago Cubs on August 12, as the Cards fell seven and a half games behind the New York Giants. The next day the Cardinals took the train to Detroit to play the Tigers in an exhibition game. The Deans were not on it.

That evening a wealthy friend who lived in suburban Chicago was having a barbecue at his estate. The friend said to Diz, "Too bad about that exhibition game in Detroit. Otherwise, you'd have been able to come tonight."

The angry Deans skipped the game and went to Belleville, Illinois, to eat fried chicken.

Frank Navin, the owner of the Tigers, was furious that the fabulous Deans were not available to play in the game. Frisch also was angry. When the Deans finally met up with the team, Dizzy said he had a sore arm. Paul, who was celebrating his twenty-first birthday, said his ankle was bothering him. Frisch didn't believe them and fined Dizzy $100 and Paul $50.

Dizzy, who was feeling unloved and unappreciated by Frisch and the Cardinals, said they would not play again unless the fines were rescinded.

The next day Dizzy asked Frisch, "Do the fines stick?" Frisch said they did. "Well, then, we'll take off our uniforms," said Dizzy. Paul concurred.

The bell rang for batting practice. Dizzy refused to get off the rubbing table. Paul sat half-dressed nearby. Frisch said to them, "Come on, boys, this is a big league ballclub. Let's go."

Said Diz, "We're not going out on the field."

"You're not?" said Frisch. "Well, then, take off those uniforms. You're both suspended."

Dizzy leaped off the table and announced he would never play for the Cardinals again. He tore to shreds both his white home uniform and the gray road uniform. Dean, a master mimic, did a one-man show imitating how Branch Rickey had tried to hoodwink the Detroit Tigers out of the $3,800 guarantee Rickey had promised for playing the game. Playing Rickey, Dean tore at his hair and carried on in a Rickeyan way.

Tex Carleton, who never liked the Deans, and Rip Collins took offense. To them, Dean's ripping the Cardinal uniform was like burning the American flag. They warned the brothers that they would be sorry for their outburst. Dizzy and Paul shouted back and swore at them.

About the fourth inning of the ball game, Pat Dean said to her husband, "Come on, Diz. Let's go."

"Where are you going?" a teammate asked Dean.

"Florida," said Diz.

Rickey told Dizzy he would pay for their transportation.

Despite their announcement that they had quit the team, the Deans stayed in St. Louis, waiting to be asked to return. But Frisch, backed by Rickey and owner Sam Breadon, insisted that the Deans pay their fines. Breadon, moreover, charged Dizzy $36 for the two uniforms he destroyed.

Said Paul, "They will take the fines off, or the Cardinals will finish the season without us."

Replied Frisch, "Those fines stick. Take it or leave it. Go to Florida if you want and stay there. I don't want you back unless you meet my terms."

The issue, of course, was over who was going to run the team: Frisch or the Deans. Even the other ballplayers sided with Frisch. So did the reporters. Wrote John Wray: "It must take a mighty ego to produce a frame of mind where, for no particular reason, a man can cause twenty others to suffer [financially.]"

Pat Dean would break the impass. She announced that the Deans were returning and also explained why they had skipped the exhibition in Detroit in the first place. Pat Dean was an expert spin doctor long before the phrase even was coined.

PAT DEAN: "Diz will never admit it, but the reason he didn't go to Detroit was that he was heartbroken over the doubleheader [loss] Sunday. Diz was so disgusted, he simply didn't want to see anyone. He wouldn't even have a soda with me after the game. Diz hates to lose. It hurts his pride. If he had won, he could have gone to Detroit a hero, but losing, he felt he would be a heel.

"It was expensive, $100 for a day's vacation, but I feel that if he wanted the vacation he should accept the fine and go back to the club. He wasn't trying to flaunt the rules; he was just heartbroken."

When asked why she was so sure the brothers would be back, she replied: "The Dean family needs the money." That evening on a radio show, Dean said he would pitch for the Cardinal fans, but not for the Cardinals. Paul, though, wanted to go home. A still-furious Frankie Frisch suspended the brothers for an additional ten days.

Dizzy was sure Judge Landis would uphold the righteousness of his stand. Landis held a hearing on August 19. Dean presented his side. He told the same story Pat Dean told reporters. He said he was angry that everyone from the batboy on up knew about the fines before he did. He apologized and asked that the ten-day suspension be lifted. He concluded, "I'll leave it to you and the sports fans. What else can I do?"

Rickey and Frisch allowed the Deans to return to the team on August 16. On the following day, Dizzy defeated the Phillies, 12–2. Sam Breadon made it clear how much Dean had angered him with his actions. Said Breadon, "Dizzy has been a source of worry on each of the teams he has been with since joining our organization." Then he added, "I believe he'll be a good boy after this latest affair."

The final blow for Dizzy Dean was Landis's report, which was issued after a four-hour meeting between Landis, Frisch, Rickey, and Breadon. Landis backed Cardinal management, saying that Rickey and Frisch were within their rights to fine and suspend the brothers.

The meeting was closed to the public, but the reporters heard every word over the open transom above the door. All the participants—Breadon, Rickey, Frisch, and Dean—were righteously indignant. Each thought himself justfied. The arguments made by management and those made by Dean were arguments made many times in the past and would be made many more in the future. There would be no middle ground. Breadon and Rickey knew that either Dean's revolt had to be crushed totally, or anarchy (free agency and market-value salaries) would result. Frisch needed to squash the Deans to maintain control of his ballclub. For their part, Dean and his backers were justifiably convinced that paying $7,500 for a pitcher who could win 30 games and bring 5,000 to 10,000 extra fans per game to the ballpark wasn't in the least bit fair, and paying $3,000 for a 19-game winner was downright exploitative. Management, of course, didn't—and never would—see it that way.

Sam Breadon told Judge Landis, "Dizzy has the wrong idea about this business. He goes around knocking the owners, the manager, and the club. When he does that, he's knocking his own business. He says we're cheap. Well, last year our payroll was the second-highest in the National League. I believe we're no lower than third this season. Does that look like we're cheap, Dizzy?"

Breadon added, "I'm not saying that we are always right, and Dizzy is always wrong. But we have been extremely lenient and generous with him. We developed him from a raw rookie to a great pitcher by putting him through our system of development. I am not saying we are entirely responsible for making Dizzy what he is, but we have gone a long way in bringing him around."

Frisch too spoke out against his star pitcher. He said to Dean, "There are ten million people out of work in this country, yet Dizzy Dean is willing to sacrifice a daily income of approximately $50 to fill the role of playboy. Baseball may be considered an amusement by the fans, but with us it's a business. It gives us our livelihood and nets us a comfortable income. Now we come to Dizzy's flair for causing a rumpus. He refused to abide by the club decision and decided to go on strike that cost him $50 a day for each day he is out of uniform. He's too deep for me to solve.

"He's a great one. I can't take that away from him. But we've given him considerable support. Dizzy feels that he's the only one who wins his games. In fact, we have scored 114 runs for him in 16 of his full-time victories. That's an average of 7 per game. That's giving your pitcher a lot of assistance.

"Dean won a game from the Reds, 3 to 0. In that game Ripper Collins and Burgess Whitehead turned plays that prevented the Reds from scoring at least four runs. So you'll see that while the box score gave Diz credit for the game, some of the other boys helped. That's baseball—a pitcher can't do it all by himself."

During the meeting, they heard Dizzy Dean express bitterness toward Rickey. The pitcher said to the Cardinal general manager, "How did you treat my brother? You told me you'd get him a job at Sportsman's Park, an' what kind of a job did you pick for him—selling peanuts."

Rickey replied, "Yes, but wasn't it at your invitation that the club brought Elmer from Texas? You knew he wasn't making much money in Houston, and you asked us to see what could be done for him."

Said Dizzy angrily, "Don't give the impression that you're taking care of Elmer. You're hardly taking care of me an' Paul."

" 'Hardly taking care' of you?" said Rickey. "Your salary is $7,500, a pretty good salary, I would say, for a young man only twenty-three years of age."

The meeting lasted four hours and five minutes. Rickey suggested the ten-day suspension be cut to eight. Breadon said, "I'll cut it to seven and make Dean eligible to return to uniform tomorrow—if this meets with manager Frisch's approval." Frisch nodded his consent. Dean, understandably, was not appreciative or forgiving. He knew full well that Rickey and Breadon—and Frisch too—were giving him and his brother a royal screwing and were using flowery language in their justification. In the end the holdout cost the Deans $486.

After the meeting, Dizzy Dean sat sullenly for ten minutes while photographers took pictures of him with Landis, Frisch, and Breadon. It was supposed to look like a truce had been reached, but Dizzy let everyone know that surrender was more like it. When he was asked to smile, he refused. When Frisch went to shake hands, he refused that as well.

Dean told the *Star-Times*, "I got a raw deal. It was unfair, but what can I do? I'm whipped."

Four days later Dizzy went out and shut out the Giants, his fifth win over the New Yorkers and his 22nd of the season.

The Cards could make Dizzy eat crow, but they could not shut him up about it. As September rolled around, the Cardinals continued to trail the New York Giants. They were five games back on September 3, and the next day Paul and Dizzy lost a doubleheader to the Pittsburgh Pirates. The day after that the Cards were to play an exhibition game against their Greensburg, Pennsylvania, Class D farm club. This time Frisch ordered Dizzy to skip the exhibition and go directly to New York. In an attempt to show up his manager, Dizzy refused to go to New York and insisted on going to the exhibition game.

Dizzy was so upset about the salary situation that two days later he was back in the news again. He told Bill McCullough of the *Brooklyn Times-Union* that if his pay didn't increase significantly in 1935, he would not pitch in the big leagues. He again complained that Bill Hallahan was making more than the two Deans combined: "a pitcher who can't hold Paul's glove, let alone mine."

Said Dizzy, "The St. Louis club advertised Paul and me to pitch a doubleheader against the Cubs. They ballyhooed us all week, and nearly 39,000 fans, the largest in the history of the St. Louis club, came out to see us. The people know class when they see it, and I'm not kidding when I say Paul and I have it."

Dizzy raised eyebrows when he concluded the interview by talking about his reluctance to be in the spotlight. He contended that the reason he made headlines was that writers insisted on quoting him. "Writing about Dizzy Dean is what keeps the papers from going out of business," he said.

More than a week later Dizzy repeated his raise demands to the *New York Herald Tribune*. He told reporter Richard Tobin enigmatically, "I'm getting $7,500 now. I'm worth $100,000 or more in a trade or a sale. If we don't get good dough next season, there will be a walkout that will make Rhode Island laugh theirselves [*sic*] sick."

On September 16 Dizzy and Paul proved the worthiness of their salary demands. They won a doubleheader against the Giants in New York before the largest crowd in the history of the National League. The crowd was announced at 62,573. (It had never seated more than 55,000 before.) When the fire department ordered the gates locked, another 15,000 were turned away. Fans crowded the aisles, sat two to a seat, and clung to the rafters. Dizzy left the opener losing, 3–0, but Frisch's base hit with the bases loaded in the seventh inning gave the Cards the lead in a 5–3 victory.

Paul won the second game, 3–1, in twelve innings. Pepper Martin beat Carl Hubbell with a home run into the lower right field stands. The Giants' lead was cut to three and a half games.

Two days later Dan Parker of the *New York Mirror* wrote about the precarious financial condition of the two St. Louis ballclubs. But Parker made it clear in their dispute with management, he sided with the Deans against those cheapskates, Breadon and Rickey.

DAN PARKER: "The owners blame it on the town, but I think it would be nearer the truth if the town blamed it on the owners. Take the case of the Dean boys. Instead of being encouraged to outdo themselves as they probably would if shown the least bit of consideration, they are underpaid and treated like striking mill hands whenever the flagrant injustice of their case leads them to register a protest.

"Any other club would recognize the value of this colorful brother act and pay them at least twice as much as the Cards. But the nickel-nursing Cardinal owners only look at it from the angle of how much they can save by underpaying the brothers. This case is typical of the policy followed by the two St. Louis clubs for years until they have almost succeeded in killing off baseball interest in what used to be one of the game's strongholds."

On September 21 the Deans again made a mockery of their salaries with a doubleheader sweep of the Brooklyn Dodgers. In the first game, Dizzy pitched a three-hitter in a 13–0 win. In the nightcap Paul Dean pitched a no-hitter in a 3–0 whitewash.

Cards pitcher Jim Mooney remembered that afternoon. As usual, in addition to his brilliant performance, Diz caused some commotion, first by getting on the wrong New York subway and showing up late, then by trash-talking manager Frankie Frisch during a pregame meeting to go over the Dodger hitters.

JIM MOONEY: "The day Paul pitched the no-hitter in Brooklyn, we were in the clubhouse, and Diz was late getting there. He got on the wrong subway, he told Frankie, went the other way. Well, anyway, when Dizzy walked in the clubhouse, we were all dressed, ready to go out onto the field. We happened to be talking about Sam Leslie at the time, going over how to pitch to Sam Leslie. Diz walked in, and he said, 'Aw, hell, don't pay any attention to Frankie. He doesn't know how to pitch.' Well, that broke up the meeting. Frank looked at him and said, 'Who the hell are you to tell me?' Diz said, 'I reckon I ought to know. I won 28 ball games.' "

Dizzy Dean loved to drive Frisch crazy. He too remembered his antics on this famous day of triumph for the Dean brothers and the Cardinals.

DIZZY DEAN: "I sure was having a picnic with Frisch. You oughta seen the fellows in the clubhouse when I was puttin' him on. They was duckin' behind posts, tryin' to keep Frank from seein' how they was laughin', an' I had a time keepin' a straight face myself. I hope Frank manages the Cardinals forever. I sure love to drive that Dutchman nuts!"

After the meeting, Dean then went over to visit with the opposing Dodgers. He broke everyone up by going into the Brooklyn clubhouse and announcing how he intended to pitch to the Dodger batters that afternoon. It made Frisch furious, but since Dean was perhaps the best pitcher in baseball, Frisch had little recourse but to shake his head.

TEX CARLETON: "Diz didn't pitch but one way, and that was a high fastball. Whether they were high-ball hitters or not, hell, he was going to pitch to his strength. I pitched to my strength too. I was a low-ball pitcher, and I didn't care if the batter was a low-ball hitter. If I let the ball get up, I was exposing myself.

"When we'd start our meetings, we'd go over the opposition, every day. Old Diz was going to pitch his strength, and then he went into the Brooklyn clubhouse and told them how he was going to pitch to him. He was going to pitch a high fastball. High inside to right-handers and high and outside to left-handers.

"I got a big kick out of Diz doing that. Of course, we all knew Diz. We knew he was just mouthing off. We knew he was going to pitch high. We all laughed about it."

Dodger manager Casey Stengel asked Dean if there were any more brothers back home.

Dean said he had a brother Elmer. Dean told him, "Casey, you oughta grab him. He's down at Houston, burnin' up the league, an' I know the Cardinals ain't figurin' on him. They got more Deans than they can handle. You might get him cheap."

Stengel told the reporters of his intent to seek out Elmer Dean. When the Dodgers inquired, they learned that Elmer Dean worked in the Houston ballpark, but as a peanut vendor. Apparently Elmer took the proffered job after all.

Jim Mooney recalled the legendary afternoon against the Dodgers at Ebbets Field.

JIM MOONEY: "Then we went out on the field, and Diz pitched the first game. He was warming up with [Bill] DeLancey in that old Brooklyn park. The catcher stood right in front of the backstop, and Diz was out there warming up, he throws the ball up on the screen. That's the way he was warming up. We didn't know whether he was going to get ready or not. He started that ball game, and he pitched a beautiful ball game. They got two or three hits off him, and then Paul followed him and pitched a no-hitter. Diz went over to Paul and patted him on the back and said, 'Why didn't you tell me you wuz going to pitch a no-hitter? I would have too.' And I believe he would."

*   *   *

Paul Dean remembered how good his arm felt that afternoon against the Dodgers.

PAUL DEAN: "My curve was breaking good, and as the game went along, I felt looser and better. I got faster as I went along, and the funniest thing was that I wasn't a bit tired when it was over. I didn't feel like I'd done no work at all. The other fellows acted like they'd been under a great strain, and they kept a-sighing and heaving that they was glad it was over. But I didn't feel none of that. I could have pitched a couple more games. I guess my arm was just right."

On Tuesday, September 25, Dizzy Dean defeated the Pirates, 3–2. When the Phillies beat the Giants, the margin was down to a single game to New York. Three days later Dean started against the Cincinnati Reds and pitched his sixth shutout of the season. No Cincinnati player reached third base. When the Giants lost, the race was tied.

As the Cards crept close to the top, Dan Parker unloaded another barrage at Breadon and Rickey. He wrote sarcastically, "If they win the pennant for St. Louis, the Dean boys, you may be sure, will be handsomely rewarded. Sam Breadon probably will give them a day's rest before the World Series, pat them on the back and [hand them] two of the best five-cent cigars that can be bought in St. Louis."

CHAPTER 22

A TOTAL SURPRISE

THE Cardinals found themselves in the thick of the 1934 pennant because of the right arms of the Dean brothers and because of a callous, nasty remark made by the arrogant Bill Terry, manager of the New York Giants. That January, Terry was in New York City, meeting with some of the local sportswriters, when he was asked to predict the order of finish for the National League.

"I'll start with the same team that won the pennant," he said. His Giants had won the pennant in 1933.

"You mean the team we picked for sixth place last year?" a reporter kidded.

"The same team. Anybody want to bet a hat that we don't win again?" Terry said. He then picked the Pittsburgh Pirates, the St. Louis Cardinals, and the Chicago Cubs as the other teams to beat.

"Do you fear Brooklyn?" he was asked.

"Is Brooklyn still in the league?" he replied.

A month later Casey Stengel, who never forgot a face or a barb, took over as manager of the Dodgers. He told those same reporters, "The first thing I want to say is that the Dodgers are still in the National League. Tell that to Bill Terry."

With two days left in the 1934 season, the Cardinals had two games to play against the Cincinnati Reds. Bill Terry's Giants had two games left against "Professor" Stengel's Dodgers.

On September 29 Paul Dean defeated the Reds, 6–1, his 19th win, on two days' rest. James Gould of the *St. Louis Post-Dispatch* was impressed by the Cardinal's lack of exuberance afterward. When Dean came into the clubhouse, the players quietly shook his hand and said, "Nice work, Paul." There was no cheering, no horseplay. Another game remained. Without a mention of the World Series, everyone knew what the final game might mean.

The Giants, meanwhile, lost to the Dodgers, 5–1, proof that the Dodgers, indeed, were still in the National League. Wrote Bill Corum of the *New York Evening Journal,* "It is amazing—the attitude New York City has taken toward the Giants' desperate battle to save the pennant. Instead of rooting for them, three fourths of the fans are laughing at them. I can't understand it."

Frisch, who employed a two-Dean rotation coming down the stretch, chose Dizzy Dean to start the final game. Like his brother the day before, Dizzy was pitching on two days' rest. In front of 37,402 shrieking fans at Sportsman's Park, Dean shut out the Cincinnati Reds, 9–0. It was his 30th win.

Jack Rothrock, an outfielder on the '34 team, remembered the day the Cards clinched the pennant.

JACK ROTHROCK: "We're going into the ninth inning, leading. All of a sudden, factory whistles were blowing, and horns were tooting. Then we knew for sure that the Giants got beat."

When the Dodgers defeated the Giants, Bill Terry was made to eat his words, and the Cardinals were champions. When Terry told reporters he wouldn't be going to the World Series because it would be too humiliating, Dodger manager Casey Stengel replied, "So he feels bad, huh? How do you think I felt when he made fun of my ballclub last spring?"

It was the end of one of the most spectacular pennant drives in baseball history. Only the Cubs' chase and capture of the Giants in 1908 was more dramatic. That was the year of Fred Merkle's boner, when Johnny Evers forced the Cubs' first baseman at second base for the third out of the inning after everyone thought the winning run had scored for the Giants. For the Cardinal players and their fans, the pennant came as a total, wonderful surprise.

Damon Kerby of the *St. Louis Post-Dispatch* recorded the Cardinals' celebration.

DAMON KERBY: " 'We're in the mon-ey! We're in the mon-ey!' sang James 'the Ripper' Collins when he charged into the clubhouse a few seconds after a pop foul from Sparky Adams's bat landed in Billy DeLancey's catcher's mitt to end the Cardinals' nerve-racking National League season. Jim's song may have been off-key, but it sounded the Cardinals' keynote of victory.

"In they filed through the clubhouse door, a shouting, happy gang, these new league champions. Yelling? Yes—but wait, one among them did not add his voice to the pandemonium. That man was—Frank Francis Frisch, who dropped astride a bench and sat with the look of a man off whose head an anvil had just bounced. He was bowed down. The letdown from the strain of the pennant race had him on the ropes.

"Dizzy Dean was among the first to grab the manager's hand, and, boys and girls, there was nothing dizzy about the greeting. They shook hands quietly, and Frank moved over to make room for Jerome Herman, and they sat talking until interrupted by photographers."

Frankie Frisch explained to Sid Keener of the *St. Louis Post-Dispatch* how his discipline helped win the pennant for the Cards that season. Notice that nowhere in his discussion does he mention the 49 combined wins of the Dean brothers.

FRANK FRISCH: "Sit down. I'll give you some inside stuff. We won this pennant because I wouldn't let the fellows give up. There are times during a season when a player loses his fighting spirit. That's when the manager enters the scene.

"I kept after them day after day. I guess they thought I was pretty tough. Well, I was.

"I couldn't afford to let them go into a tailspin. My job was to keep the fellows moving. I had to jack them up. I had to keep after Joe Medwick about playing in certain spots in left field. I had to keep talking to Ripper Collins. I had to do this and that.

"When we'd lose, they'd come into the clubhouse filled with gloom. They'd moan in the hotel lobby that night. They'd come to the park the next day, cussing about the line drive that was caught. They'd be ready to sag. I had to hold 'em up.

" 'We ain't going to win the pennant if we continue beefing about bad luck' is the way I'd talk to the boys.

"In the first week of September, we lost a doubleheader to the Pirates. That was the end of the pennant boom, most everyone believed. The players were ready to give up. I never saw such a dejected bunch of athletes as my boys riding into New York. I sat alone. I was hot—I was boiling. I realized that this wasn't the time to chuck it up.

"I sent orders to the players that we would hold our meeting in the Brooklyn clubhouse one hour earlier than usual. I burned them like they'd never been burned before. 'Are you fellows going to quit?' I shouted. 'It ain't over. If you fight to the finish, we won't be beaten.'

"The change was remarkable. They started kicking the benches. They dressed with fire in their eyes.

" 'We ain't giving up, Frankie,' growled Dizzy. 'I'm pitching today an' I'll show you we ain't beat.'

"I can hardly describe the change in my club. From then on, they were a great club. There you have the Cardinals. They tried to count us out when we were seven games behind the Giants on September 6. We wouldn't be counted out.

"That's why we won the pennant."

Of course, the 1934 Cardinals also won the pennant because they had an extremely talented if strange team. Jim Mooney, who lost his spot in the starting rotation when Paul Dean joined the team, recalled the eccentricities of his teammates from the 1934 champions. He also remembered the Depression and the low salaries.

JIM MOONEY: "Take the ballclub we had. What I call big men like they had now, we didn't have any. There weren't any big men on that team. Virgil Davis was tall but slender. Rip Collins wasn't six feet. Frisch wasn't, and Durocher wasn't. Most were five foot ten, five foot eleven. But they were devoted fellas to their job. They'd go out there and gave you all they had.

"They were together. They really were. And if they weren't fighting the enemy, they were fighting each other! It was really an experience to be with that bunch. They were so different.

"Of course, there was no one like Dizzy Dean. He was the greatest competitor I ever saw. He could do it, and he'd tell you he could do it. He was a smart fellow out on that hill. He'd pitch just as hard as he had to. If we made a lot of runs, Diz would kind of coast along, but if he had a tough ball game, he'd bear down.

"One time Diz goofed off in Pittsburgh, and Medwick got mad at him, went after him with the bat. Oh, listen, Diz was all the time getting in fights after ball games if he'd lose one. He'd come in that clubhouse. We'd be taking a shower, and he'd be griping about someone not getting a base hit at the right time, something like that, and Rip Collins and Pepper Martin would jump all over him. I saw them beat him up many a time. Never hurt him, but you know, they didn't like him blaming the other players.

"Paul Dean was a pretty good pitcher. He believed in Dizzy, and Dizzy believed in Paul. One of them would be out there pitching, and the other would be sitting on the bench as the game was going on, and he'd say, 'Boy, there's the best pitcher in baseball.' And the next day, why, the other one would say the same thing about the one on the mound. Diz would get his glove and go out to the bullpen and warm up in the latter part of Paul's ball game. He was always ready to go get him. Frisch would never tell him to do it. I'd be sitting down in the bullpen, waiting to get into the ball game, and here's Diz coming down while Paul was struggling, and he'd warm up, and he was always ready. They were two very close boys. They really were, and they were good pitchers. They had their record.

"I was disappointed I didn't get to start more games. I had been a starting pitcher everywhere I had ever been. The first year I was with the Giants, I won six straight ball games. But they were trying to build Paul Dean up, and they kept starting Paul, kept starting Paul, and he'd get his ears beat, and they kept up until he finally got his feet on the ground and had a pretty good year, won 19 that year.

"I don't think Paul was faster than Dizzy. In my estimation, Paul couldn't carry Dizzy's glove in comparison in pitching. He'd just throw. But I was disappointed because I didn't get to pitch. What the heck. I relieved a lot.

"Pepper Martin was a great ballplayer. I enjoyed just watching him play. Pepper was a boy who gave you all he had. I still say he fielded more balls with his chest than he ever did with his glove. They'd hit that hard ball down there to him at third base, and he'd get down and block it, pick it up and throw the man out. He had a strong arm, and once in a while he'd throw one about the third row in the stands, and they'd kid him about it. He'd say, 'If you're going to throw them away, you might as well throw them away good.' Nothing fazed him. And he was a great slider. I liked to see him get a double or a triple and watch him slide, always headfirst. Little puffs of dirt would come out from under his feet as he ran around the bases. A daredevil. He proved that in the World Series against the Athletics. He liked to have drove Cochrane and Earnshaw and Grove crazy.

"Pepper had a little midget racer. He raced that thing. He liked to hunt. He was just an all-around sportsman.

"I had been with the Giants, and with John McGraw and Bill Terry as managers, you had to dress up when you went out. With the Cardinals, it didn't make any difference what you had on. Pepper Martin always wore his Texas boots and his ten-gallon hat, had on a suit of clothes. It wouldn't be twenty minutes before that suit was dirty. One time in St. Louis, he came down with a brand-new suit on, looked nice, had his pockets full of cowboy magazines. By the time we got to New York, you'd have thought he'd a slept in that suit. I don't know what happened to it! He was just that type of a fella. His baseball uniform was the same way. He'd put on a clean uniform, and the first thing he'd do was go and lay down in the dirt.

"Pepper and Dizzy were always into mischief. Pepper Martin and two or three others went out and got sneezing powder, and they'd go around slinging that, and everybody had tears in their eyes. That was just good fun. I remember one time the temperature was 110 in St. Louis, and here comes Dizzy Dean and Pepper Martin with big blankets on. They picked up scraps and built a fire and set down there like Indians, before the ball game started. The crowd went crazy over it. They'd do anything to please the crowd.

"Rip Collins, my roommate, was kind of a playboy-type boy. He liked the-a-ter-type people, and we'd go round at night in New York and talk to the the-a-ter people. He was a good ballplayer, a switch hitter. Rip was a nice, ol' ballplayer. He used to have nightmares. I'd wait till he went to sleep before I went to sleep, because he'd get up and run around. One time I caught him going down the hall of the hotel in New York. He was getting ready to get on the elevator. He didn't know a thing about it.

"There really wasn't much carousing on our team. Everybody was in their room the time they were supposed to be. We enjoyed having a good time.

Back then, they had a different attitude. You were hungry, there was a Depression, and you wanted to eat.

"Joe Medwick never did say too much. He was just quiet. He had a funny attitude. I never could figure him out. I hit fungoes to him all the time, and shoot, you had to hit them right in his hand almost. He wouldn't even run to catch them. But he was a pretty good fielder. And he could swing that bat, too. Funny thing about him and his hitting, you might fool him on the pitch and come right back with that same pitch, and he'd knock it out of the park. He swung at anything. He was a bad-ball hitter. If they threw a high curve, he was liable to knock it out of the park.

"He was a moody-type boy. I remember one time Medwick was in a slump, and the pitchers always come out and hit before the regulars. You get your practice, and we were out hitting, and Medwick came out and he was nice enough about it. He asked if he could get with us, and nobody said anything but Tex Carleton, who made some remark, and Medwick cold-cocked him, like he was shot.

"When Medwick was in a slump, you'd better leave Medwick alone. As long as Medwick was hitting, everything was fine and dandy. If he was getting his base hits, everything was fine, but if he was in a slump, boy, just leave Joe alone. He'd sit over in the corner and come in and sit by himself. His hittin' was where his bread and butter was coming from, I reckon. He had to have his hits.

"Our manager, Frankie Frisch, also was quite a ballplayer. He was always out there giving his best. He'd play around a little and have fun. I was pitching one day. I heard this commotion going on behind me, and Bill Klem and Frisch were out there, arguing at second base.

"One time they got in an argument up at home plate. Klem drew a line. He dared Frankie to cross that line. He said, 'If you come across that line, you're out of the ball game.' Frisch got down and looked and there wasn't any line.

"We were always doing something to entertain the fans. The players put on a show before the game. That pepper game was something to see. They really put that on. Jack Rothrock, Pepper Martin, Rip Collins, and Ernie Orsatti were in on it. [It was the baseball version of the Harlem Globetrotters' warm-up routine.] They'd put that on almost every day before the game, have fun with it. You can't do those things anymore. They won't let you.

"Orsatti was a great little ol' outfielder. One time we were playing in Chicago, and someone hit a line drive out into center field, and he went out there and caught it and turned two or three somersaults, and that ended the inning. And usually what happens when a fella makes a good play, then he's the first man up at bat. Well, that crowd went crazy. They gave him a big hand. So he went back the next inning, a little lazy fly he could have put in his pocket, he dropped it! He was a great little fellow. I enjoyed watching him play. Orsatti was a showman. His brother was a movie director. He came to St. Louis when they made that picture *Death on the Diamond*, and he followed us around to get the scenery for that. Ernie played the boy who got shot. He took a dive coming in from third base. This fellow shot him. I don't imagine

FRISCH, MARTIN, COLLINS, MEDWICK, DEAN
(Courtesy Brace Photo)

you ever saw that picture. They showed it around the World Series time, in
'34. I never heard of it since.

"Our catchers were Spud Davis, a great big ol' strong boy, and Bill
DeLancey. Spud was a good catcher. A fair hitter. He was slow. He was a
big fellow, the biggest man on our ballclub. Spud could hit that ball when he
got ahold of it.

"DeLancey took over from him. He was young. He had his future before
him. Bill would sit in the bullpen, and I could tell every pitch the pitcher
threw. He followed it with a whistle, whistle through his teeth. If it was a
curveball, his whistle would be a little longer than if it was a fastball. It was
interesting. I don't know whether the opposing team knew what he was doing
or not. He was a good hitter. It was a shame that he got sick.

"And there was Leo Durocher. The thing about it, no one liked Durocher.
When he got his street clothes on, no one would associate with him. He was
a prima donna. He brought a couple of trunks of clothes on road trips. Every
time you'd see him, he was dressed differently. The rest of us carried our own
luggage. He had bellboys. When we'd get off the train in New York, we'd
stay in the hotel opposite Penn Station. We'd get our bags and take them off
to the hotel. Not Leo. He had bellboys do it.

"This was during the Depression. We'd come into a town on the train
and see people asleep out in the parks and the doorways early in the morning.
The trains always went through the slum section anyway. That impressed me
more than anything, seeing these old men in a park or even in a doorway with
a newspaper over him, sleeping.

"We didn't see too much poverty in St. Louis. The people are more self-sustaining around here. Farms. You didn't see too much in the smaller places like this. They weren't affected as much as the big cities, metropolitan areas.

"The team was owned by Sam Breadon, a tight-fisted man, and he had the right man to work for him, that Rickey. In my estimation, Branch Rickey could make salt taste like sugar. He had a tongue that wouldn't quit. He could paint a beautiful picture for you. They tell some good ones about him, like the time Preacher Roe had a good year, and Rickey gave him two bird dogs for a raise. Two days later the bird dogs ran back home to Rickey, and Preacher never saw them again.

"They were always tight with the money. They sure were. Someone should write about the salaries we made that year. It was pathetic. Jack Rothrock was making $3,500. Some of the others were making $3,000. That's why Diz kept striking. I made $4,000.

"I don't know, but even though we were much more successful than the Browns, St. Louis was always a Brownie town. They'd go in for the Browns. The Browns never won. You know, I guess it was the personality of the man who runs the club. I don't know whether the fans went too much for Rickey."

CHAPTER 23

THE TIGER FANS THROW GARBAGE

ROY Stockton was Dizzy Dean's ghostwriter for a series of articles before and during the 1934 Series. Stockton asked Dean who was going to win the Series. Dean responded with his usual bravado, angering both the Tigers and the rest of the Cards pitching staff. As far as Dean was concerned, he and Paul constituted the staff. "Me an' Paul will take care of the Tigers all by ourselves," he said. What made his teammates even more furious was that Diz turned out to be right.

DIZZY DEAN: "I don't want to make the people think I'm a big windbag, but I want to tell the truth, so just say that the Cardinals will take them Tigers like a bulldog takes a pussy cat, and that if they get a good foul off me an' Paul, they can consider themselves lucky. I'll pitch the first game, of course, because pitching is duck soup for me an' I'll knock 'em off easy.

"That won't sound like braggin', will it? The way I sees it, braggin' is where you do a lot of poppin' off an' ain't got nothin' to back it up. But I ain't braggin'. I know me an' Paul is gonna win four games in this here Series—if Detroit is good enough to win a couple when we ain't pitchin'—an' you might just as well be honest an' tell the public all about it. They pays our salary an' it's nothin' but fair that we tell 'em just what's goin' to happen."

*   *   *

The question Frisch had to face was who to start in the first Series game against the Tigers. Dizzy Dean assumed Frisch was holding back in informing him he was starting as a psychological ploy. Frisch, who had fought with Dean all year, may well have been trying just to rankle his arrogant star.

DIZZY DEAN: "Frisch is sayin' that he don't know who's goin' to pitch that first game. But he ain't foolin' me none. I told him this afternoon there wasn't no use kiddin' hisself. There's only one man to pitch the first game, an' that's old Diz. Frank, I guess, is tryin' to use what Doc Weaver calls 'Psy-chology.' He don't want old Diz nervous on the eve of battle. But he's silly if he thinks he can fool me. I ain't no kleptomaniac or whatever you calls it, what goes around gettin' nervous. Who won the pennant? Me an' Paul. Who's goin' to win the World Series? Me an' Paul. Certainly. Psy-chology, my foot!"

Before the opening game, Dean ran into Hank Greenberg. That year the Tiger slugger hit 26 home runs and had 139 RBIs. Dean was not impressed.

DIZZY DEAN: "Hello, Mose. What makes you so white? Boy, you're a shakin' like a leaf. I get it; you done heard that Old Diz was goin' to pitch. Well, you're right. It'll all be over in a few minutes. Old Diz is goin' to pitch, an' he's goin' to pin your ears back."

Dean pitched and won that first game, 8–3. Joe Medwick homered. So did Greenberg.

Before the second game, Dean stood on the field with a tuba draped around his neck and a big grin. He had never played the instrument before. He told the owner of the tuba, "Shucks, this ain't hard. I can play this as good as you if you give me ten minutes."

Bill Hallahan started Game 2, and the Cards' Bill Walker lost to Lynwood "Schoolboy" Rowe in the bottom of the twelfth inning by the score of 3–2 on a single by Leon "Goose" Goslin. Paul Dean started the third contest and defeated the Tigers, 4–1. Eldon Auker and slugger Hank Greenberg then defeated Tex Carleton and the Cards, 10–4.

After the fourth game of the 1934 Series, two strangers offered Dizzy a ride in their car back to his hotel. Dizzy got in. Sam Breadon, who saw him get in the car, was afraid that he might be kidnapped and sent a messenger to tell him to take a cab instead. He did. Breadon then arranged for Dizzy to have a police escort, which thrilled him. He introduced his escort to anyone within earshot, then whispered, "He's guarding me."

As unbelievably naïve and kidlike as Dizzy was, his wife Pat was as mature, savvy, and moneywise. During the 1934 World Series, Vera Brown of the *St. Louis Star-Times* interviewed her. Pat Dean showed the reporter a new carat-and-a-half diamond ring.

PAT DEAN: "It's my 'pennant trophy.' Dizzy got it last week, and it celebrates a lot of things besides the victory. In the first place, we just paid off the last of the mortgage on our home in Bradenton, Florida. It is free and clear. That is one thing we've worked for. We have annuities and government bonds. Dizzy is never going to be a 'has-been,' pushed about as a down-and-outer.

"I wouldn't let Dizzy buy me a ring when we were married—I said, 'No ring until our home is paid for.' And here's the ring. Isn't it beautiful?

"When we were first married, Dizzy got $3,000 a year and we saved $1,800. I did my own washing and cleaning—and was glad to do it. Now we have our home! That means as much as the pennant to us. It's been a hard road up for Dizzy. Just look at his hair sometime. He's only twenty-three, and he is almost white. He won't last more than five years at the rate he's going, and I want to make those five years glorious.

"Sometimes, if Diz gets a little obstreperous, I just say, 'Dizzy, you're the world's greatest pitcher on the diamond, but here at home you're just a husband.' Then he laughs and says, 'Okay.' "

Dean almost cost the Cards the Series when he ran to first base to pinch-run for Spud Davis in the fourth inning of Game 4.

FRANCE LAUX: "Dizzy Dean talked Frisch into letting him go in as a pinch runner. He was running down to second base, when the batter hit the ball to Charlie Gehringer, and Gehringer scooped it up and threw it to Billy Rogell at second, and Rogell fired it down to first base and hit Dizzy right between the eyes. It knocked him colder than a cucumber. He had to be carried off the field."

GRANTLAND RICE: "The speeding ball . . . struck Dizzy Dean squarely on the head with such terrific force that it bounced thirty feet into the air and more than 100 feet away into Hank Greenberg's glove in short right field. The impact of the ball and glove sounded like backfire of an automobile. Rogell crowded everything he had into a fast throw, and when the leather struck Dean's skull, the great Dean crumpled and fell like a marionette whose string had snapped."

FRANKIE FRISCH: "Fortunately, Dizzy wasn't hurt badly. In fact, he regained consciousness when we got him into the clubhouse, and he had one quick question: 'They didn't get Pepper at first, did they?' "

Dean recovered sufficiently to start the next day, but he was not his dominating self, and when Tommy Bridges won, 3–1, in Game 5 over Dizzy to take a lead of three games to two, it looked like the Tigers would be champions. Thanks to the Deans, however, it didn't turn out that way.

FRANKIE FRISCH: "The Dean boys came through in storybook fashion in the final two games of the Series. The sixth game was a little too close for comfort, but we broke a 3 to 3 tie with a run in the seventh inning and Paul Dean protected that through the rest of the game to whip Schoolboy Rowe, 4 to 3."

Radio announcer France Laux remembered that before Game 7 manager Frisch wasn't sure who he was going to start. Dean would have had to go on but one day's rest, and that was asking a lot. Bill Hallahan had beaten the Philadelphia A's twice in 1931, and the consensus was that the left-hander would start. Others like John Carmichael of the *Chicago Daily News* knew better.

JOHN CARMICHAEL: "It will be Dizzy, you can bet all the tea in China. Wild horses won't keep him on the bench. In the end, Frisch will say yes because he can't say no. It's his best bet, and after tomorrow there is no tomorrow at all."

FRANCE LAUX: "We went back to Detroit to finish up. Dean had pitched the first game and won it. Paul Dean pitched the second game and won it, and Paul Dean came back in the sixth game and won that one in Detroit, and that tied up the Series. And going into the seventh and final game, Frisch didn't know who he was going to pitch. He was worried because he wasn't sure that Diz was able to go. And everyone was in the meeting except Diz, who was out there watching Detroit bat, and finally Frisch said, 'Hallahan, you start. Walker, you're in reserve.' Just as he said that, the door opened, and here's old Diz. He called Frisch 'Franco.' He said, 'Franco, you know what the problem is? You're going over the batting order, trying to decide who's going to pitch. You want to win, don't you?' He said, 'There's only one man to pitch, an' here he is.' Frisch said, 'Are you sure you're able to go?' He said, 'You let me pitch, an' you won't have any more problem.' Frisch said, 'Okay, you start, and, Hallahan, you're in reserve.'

"Diz got up and ran out of the meeting. The first guy he bumped into was Hank Greenberg. He said, 'Hey, I'm pitching this afternoon. You know what that means. You won't touch me.'

"He was trying to get Greenberg a little hot under the collar. The game started, and the first time Greenberg came up to the plate, Diz struck him out on three pitches. Greenberg waltzes back to the dugout, and Diz walks halfway over to the sideline, and he yells out, 'What did I tell ya?'

"Meanwhile, the Cardinals went crazy in that ball game. And it came Greenberg's turn to bat again. DeLancey was catching. He gave the signal, and Diz shook him off. He gave him the signal again, and Diz shook him off. Five times Diz shook him off. Finally DeLancey starts out to the mound, and Frisch comes charging in from his position at second base, and Frisch says to DeLancey, 'What's the trouble?' 'I keep giving Dizzy signals, and he shakes me off.' Frisch says to Diz, 'What's the matter with you? You struck the man out. Aren't you satisfied?' Diz says, 'Yeah, I know, Skipper, but they say if I pitch him high and inside, he'll hit it a mile. I want to see if that's true.'

"Frisch said, 'Yeah, if you pitch him high and inside, he'll hit the ball over the bleachers in left field.' Frisch threw up his hands and went back to second base. DeLancey got back behind the plate and gave him the signal, and he shook him off. He shook him off a second time. DeLancey decided, 'If he wants it high and inside, that's what I'll call.' So he calls the next pitch high and inside, and you never saw a ball hit so hard in your life that Greenberg hit that thing. They had temporary bleachers back of left field, and lucky for Diz, the ball curved foul by about that much. You know what he did? He turned around and walked over to Frisch at second base, and he said, 'You know, by golly, you're right. He can do it!'

"That's the kind of thing Frisch had to put up with."

LEO DUROCHER: "We had to come out through the Detroit dugout, and I look back, and [Dizzy's] standing behind the Detroit pitcher, Eldon Auker, watching him warm up. Auker was an underhanded pitcher. Not sidearm, but all the way under, like a softball pitcher. He had already beaten us a game, the game where Diz got hit on the head, but Diz is standing there with his arms behind his back as if he's scouting him. He hollers down to [Mickey] Cochrane, 'Are you going to pitch *this* guy today? You must have given up.' Then he breaks out laughing, the most insulting laugh I've ever heard in my life. 'Is that the best he's got? He's nothing. Nothing. My slow stuff is better than that.'

"Auker turns around and hollers, 'Get out of here, you blowhard. You loudmouthed . . .' Auker is ready to pop him, he's so mad, and Cochrane is screaming at me. 'Get him out of there!' He's ready to come charging up and take a whack at him himself."

Leo dragged him away from there.

Game 7 was a Cardinals rout. Dizzy Dean pitched a shutout, giving the Deans all four Series wins. Frankie Frisch, the player-manager, drove in the first runs of the seventh game, an 11–0 Cardinal rout. Twenty-eight years later Frisch still enjoyed the memory.

FRANKIE FRISCH: "Don't think I don't still get a kick out of that last World Series game of mine. In that third inning spot, I worked the count to three and two. I wasn't counting, of course, but the press box told me afterward that I fouled off seven pitches before I finally got the wood on one and hit to the right field corner of Navin Field for a double, sending three runs over the plate.

"We were off and flying and before the inning ended, we had driven four more runs over the plate, knocking out Auker, Rowe, and Chief Hogsett before Bridges came in and got the third man out."

It was 7–0 Cardinals before anyone knew it. By the seventh inning, the score was 11–0. At this point, catcher Bill DeLancey called for several pitches, only to have Dizzy Dean shake off all of them. DeLancey called timeout and went to talk to Dean. Frisch and Durocher joined the conference on the mound.

LEO DUROCHER: " 'Frank,' Diz says, 'Do you think Hubbell is a better pitcher than me?'

" 'No, Diz, Hubbell's no better than you. Nobody's no better than you. You're a better pitcher than God. Come on, you're going great. Throw the ball and let's get this game over with.'

"Diz is satisfied. 'If Hubbell's no better than me,' he says, 'then I ought to be able to throw a screwball.'

"He never threw a screwball in his life, and he wants to experiment in the seventh game of the World Series."

Diz recalled the ninth inning of the final game. Diz was just being Diz, driving Frisch crazy.

DIZZY DEAN: "Eleven–nothing I got 'em, an' that Billy Rogell on base an' Hank Greenberg came up. I already struck him out twice, no trouble 'tall, an' when he came up in the ninth, I hollered over to the Tiger bench. I said: 'What, no pitch hitter?' An' Hank looked at me like he'd a liked to break one of them sticks over my head, but hell, he was my meat. He was easy.

"You know what that Frisch did? I put two fastballs right past the letters on that Greenberg's uniform an' when he missed the second one, I hadda laugh. I put my glove up to my face to keep from laughin' right in his face, he looked so funny, an' before I could throw any more, Frisch came out. He was mad. He said, 'Cut out the foolin', we got a lot at stake,' an' I just stood there an' looked at him like he must be outta his mind . . . me leadin' 11–0 with one out in the last of the ninth. Just then Leo Durocher came in from short an' he said: 'Aw, what the hell, Frank, let the guy have his fun. What's the matter with you?' Well, you know what Frisch told me? Yeah . . . he said, 'You lose this guy and you're through.' Eleven–nothing . . . I can't get over that yet. He was gonna pull me.

"That Greenberg couldn't a hit that next pitch if he'd a started to swing when I wound up. Gonna pull me. He didn't even see it an' the next guy was Owen, an' he forced Rogell an' the whole thing was over. Them Tigers weren't bad; they gave us a good battle, but they were just pussycats with me. I don't like to brag a lot, 'cause folks think I'm a lunkhead or somethin', but when I had my fastball, nobody could hit me . . . much."

Throughout the Series, there was bad blood between the two teams, whose bench jockeys continued a steady, vicious patter.

FRANKIE FRISCH: "There probably never has been a Series in which there has been more bench jockeying than there was in that battle with the Tigers. We had some pretty good country jockeys on our side and they gave the Tigers a rough going-over. It was all good, clean fun. [Sure it was, Frank.] For instance, Rowe, a fairly new bridegroom, made the mistake of saying, as he concluded an interview on radio, 'How'm I doing, Edna?' Schoolboy got mighty tired of hearing about that from our dugout."

In the sixth inning of the seventh game, Joe Medwick hit a two-run triple against the center field fence to run up the score, and he came into third with his cleats pointed for Tiger third baseman Marv Owens's chest.

PAUL GALLICO: "There was no mistaking Medwick's ideas as he lay on the ground on his back and suddenly began [lashing] out at Owens's legs with his spiked feet. One-two-three, his feet flashed, and then he kicked with both together like [pro wrestler] Joe Savoldi.''

Owen, angry, kicked Medwick. Medwick, as was his nature, swung and hit Owen in the face. They tangled. The Cardinals swarmed from the dugout.

Medwick held his hand out to Owen to apologize, but Owen refused to accept it. As a result, when Medwick went back out to his position at the end of the inning, the Tiger fans showed their frustration—the Cards were winning big—and, without warning, the raging mob sitting in the bleachers began booing and then throwing fruit, beer, and soda bottles at Medwick, who was just out of range.

Three times Medwick tried to take his position. Each time garbage rained down on him. The crowd chanted, ''Take him out!''

FRANCE LAUX: ''It was really dangerous out there, because they were throwing everything you can think of. Finally Judge Landis called Joe in from the outfield. Landis decided to take him out of the ball game. Of course, Medwick blew his top about that. He was pretty hot. But it didn't make much difference. The Cardinals had already taken a pretty good lead in the ball game.''

According to Bob Hood, who idolized Joe Medwick and eventually wrote a fine book on the '34 team, Medwick always held his being taken out of the seventh game against Landis. Medwick was one hit short of tying Pepper Martin's record of 12 hits in a Series when he was yanked. In Medwick's conversation with Hood many years later, his anger remained.

JOE MEDWICK: ''That goddamn Commissioner Landis, the son of a bitch took me out of the Series. I could have broken the Series record for hits. I had 11 hits. He had no right to do that. I would have broken that record.''

What Dizzy Dean remembered best after the Cards won the Series was manager Frankie Frisch's criticism of him. The Cards had won everything, but Dean's behavior had taken a toll on Frisch's nerves.

DIZZY DEAN: ''We're in the clubhouse, see, celebratin', an' I got a rubber tiger, all blown up, an' I'm twistin' his tail an' hollerin' like the rest, an' Frisch came by an' stopped and you know what he said?

'' 'Anybody with your stuff should have won 40 games this year instead of a measly 30. You loaf. That's the trouble. Thirty games! You ought to be ashamed of yourself.' Imagine that, an' me just winning the Series for him: ole Diz out there pitchin' outta turn too, don't forget that.''

Frisch recalled how angry Tiger fans were over their defeat.

FRANKIE FRISCH: ''I never knew a city to take a World Series defeat so bitterly. We had to have police escorts to get back to the hotel and to get out of town. And those fans in the bleachers weren't the only ones who were mad.

Twenty-five years later, our center fielder, Ernie Orsatti, was in Detroit on a business trip and he registered at the Sheraton–Cadillac Hotel, where we were housed while playing the 1934 World Series.

"The desk clerk looked at the name on the register, then looked at Orsatti. He told Ernie he didn't believe he could give him a room. Orsatti thought he was joking, but he wasn't.

"Ernie had to go over the clerk's head to get a room at the hotel."

CHAPTER 24

THE GASHOUSE GANG

At no time during the 1934 season did anyone ever talk about this team as the "Gashouse Gang." The only reference to the nomenclature came in September of 1934 after a rough-and-tumble doubleheader with the New York Giants at the Polo Grounds. The next day there was a cartoon in the *New York World-Telegram* by Willard Mullin. It showed two big gas tanks on the wrong side of the railroad track, and ballplayers crossing to the other side of town carrying clubs over their shoulders. The caption read: THE GAS HOUSE GANG. That was the first reference. Though it would be the name the '34 Cards would be remembered by, it was not until the 1935 season that the name was firmly established and the team memorialized.

The Cards in 1935 were playing a doubleheader in Boston. It rained during the second game, and several of the Cards had had to slide, and their uniforms were caked with dirt. The team had to grab a late train to New York for another doubleheader against the Giants. There had been no time to dry-clean the uniforms, and they were mud-stained and wrinkled when the Cards took the field against the Giants.

FRANKIE FRISCH: "The next afternoon we played before a large crowd at the Polo Grounds in the worst-looking uniforms I ever saw. They were grimy, stained, and wrinkled, and the New York writers completed the job of tagging us 'the Gashouse Gang.' "

A reporter in the press box commented that the Cardinals looked like they came from the other side of the tracks. New York reporters Frank Graham and Bill Corum wrote about the "gashouse area" in their stories. Around that time, Warren Brown, who wrote for the *Chicago Tribune,* accused the Cubs of being afraid of "that Gashouse Gang."

Frisch's team of characters, featuring the antics of Dizzy Dean, Pepper Martin, Rip Collins, Leo Durocher, Joe Medwick, and the fiery Frisch himself, was one of the most famous teams in baseball history, but ironically, as great a team as they were, the Gashouse Gang would win but one pennant and one championship.

The Cards didn't lose the pennant in 1935. Rather, the Chicago Cubs, with 100 victories, won it by four games over St. Louis. Dizzy Dean won 28 games and Paul Dean again won 19. Joe Medwick recalled the color and unpredictability of his teammates.

JOE MEDWICK: "You never knew what would happen. You might go to sleep and find a match in your shoe. We'd open the paper, and there'd be a hole burned right in the middle of it. You'd go in the hotel and sit in the lobby, and you'd have a sneezing powder attack. Something was always happening. Pepper would walk down one side of the street, and Diz would walk down the other. 'Hey, Pepper, you going to play today?' 'Yeah, Diz, you gonna pitch?' 'No, Paul is gonna pitch.' They were very, very colorful. You never knew what was going to happen."

Leo Durocher also remembered the craziness of this band of rogues, which was led by Dizzy Dean and Pepper Martin. The two, posing as workmen, got the Cards thrown out of three hotels in Philadelphia. One time they invaded a society luncheon at the Bellevue–Stratford Hotel. First they exploded smoke bombs, then they impersonated firemen, producing pandemonium. Another time Dean, Martin, Rip Collins, and another player, all wearing carpenter overalls, invaded the lobby of the hotel and announced they were going to redecorate the kitchen, which had just been done in copper. "We're here to do it in aluminum," said Martin. After they were thrown out of the kitchen, they headed for the biggest banquet room in the hotel. Leo Durocher was a witness to what happened next.

LEO DUROCHER: "A Boy Scout meeting was in progress, with a mixture of adults and kids. Pepper and his crew cleared everybody away from the very first table they came to—'Excuse me. Excuse me.'—threw the chairs back, and stood the table on its end. While the head speaker was being introduced, Pepper was hunched down, taking sightings along the table with his micrometer, Dean was slapping a level here and there, and the others were arguing noisily and pointing up to the ceiling and down at the floor.

"Finally a couple of men came down from the head table to find out what was going on. 'We're redecorating,' Rip Collins told them. 'Gonna do over the whole place. Go right ahead with your speech, though. You're not bothering us.'

"Through it all, the main speaker was just standing there. Speechless, you might say. 'Well,' Diz said, 'if you're not going to make a speech, I will. Sit down. I'll take care of this.'"

When Diz got up to speak, everyone recognized his famous face, and he made a speech that entranced both the kids and adults. Afterward, the "crew" was thrown out of the hotel. They were also thrown out of the Governor Clinton Hotel for tossing sneezing powder into the large wind fan. Then they were tossed

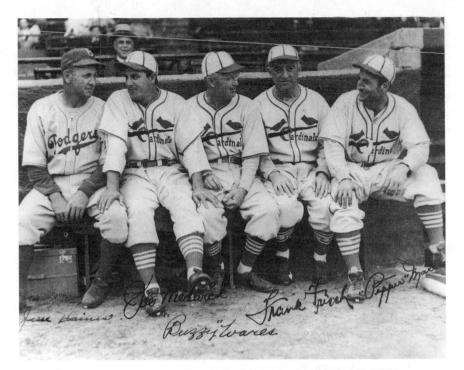

JESSE HAINES, MEDWICK, WARES, FRISCH, MARTIN
(Courtesy Brace Photo)

from the Benjamin Franklin Hotel for throwing water balloons out the window of their rooms on a high floor. Frankie Frisch had his hands full every day.

Infielder Don Gutteridge joined the Cardinals in 1936. He remembered the strong personalities of Dizzy, Pepper, Leo, and Ducky. Every day, it seemed, was an adventure.

DON GUTTERIDGE: "When I joined the team in '36, Dizzy Dean was still on the team. He was always complaining about his salary, and he was the highest-priced ballplayer by far. We always wanted him to get more, because if he did, we'd get more. It brought us up a little bit. Plus the fact that we wanted him to be satisfied, because then he'd pitch better, and we'd win. If Dizzy didn't win, we didn't win too many games without him.

"When I first went up there, Pepper Martin was playing third base, and he hated it. He wanted to play the outfield. So when I came up there, Pepper told everybody, 'Leave this kid alone. He's going to play third base.' And Pepper protected me. No one got on me. He wanted me to play third base so he could play in the outfield.

"Pepper and Dizzy Dean were the best of buddies. They always hung out together. Both of them kidded one another, and they were always up to pranks. They were always doing something, doing it together.

JEROME and PAUL DEAN
(Courtesy Brace Photo)

"When I came up, Leo Durocher was our shortstop. Leo really took good care of me. He really went to front for me. In the field, Leo would place me. He'd holler over to me at third, 'Get a little over. Protect the line on this guy.' Or 'Come this way a little bit.' He told me, 'Buddy, you just play closer to the line all the time, because I'll take care of the hole.' And he did. He could go in the hole and throw anybody out. He was a fine, fine fielding shortstop. He didn't get the credit for being as fine a shortstop as he was.

"I'll tell you another incident. We were playing in Chicago, and they had a big ol' guy by the name of Frank Demaree, an outfielder. Dizzy was pitching. We got a batter out, and Demeree was next up. At that time, they threw the ball around the infield, and I was standing pretty close to Dizzy. I tossed him the ball, and I started back to third base. And Dizzy always pitched quick. So about the time I got to my position and turned around, a line drive went past me like a shot. It nearly knocked my head off. Frank Demaree hit it, and I just got a glimpse of the ball.

"When I came in the dugout, Frank Frisch met me there, and he started reaming me out for not being ready to play. And Durocher jumped up and said, 'Don't get on that kid. Get on the big dumb pitcher of yours. He never gives us a chance to get set.' Leo took the heat off me and got on Frank Frisch something terrible, just on my account.

"Leo would fight for you. He knew what to do. He was a very intelligent baseball man.

"Leo was a very astute dresser. He and Joe Medwick would wear the latest styles. Pepper always wore a dirty shirt. That's where the rift came in. It was not on the ball field. They played together on the field. Off the field, they didn't like one another.

"In '36 we were three or four games behind the Giants, still in the hunt. We really wanted to win, but I don't think we had that good a ballclub. They were trying to replace their veteran players with players like me to see if we couldn't give a little spark to get a winning streak. But our club wasn't that good overall. They were frustrated, and some of the players resented Frisch. Dizzy and Frisch were at odds, and that was hard on Frisch. But if Diz didn't win, who was going to win? So they argued back and forth. Dizzy would tell Frisch off. Dizzy would want to pitch more, and he'd want to go relieve—if Paul was in trouble, Dizzy would go down to the bullpen and start warming up. And maybe Dizzy was supposed to pitch the next day or two, and Frank would want to save him for the next game. But Dizzy wanted to save Paul's game for him. And they got into some problems with that.

"Paul Dean was very silent. He was the opposite of Dizzy. He didn't

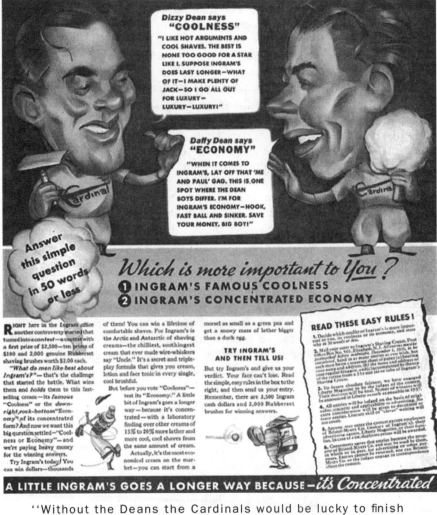

DIZZY & DAFFY talk INGRAM'S Shaving Contest
and its $2,500 FIRST PRIZE

ALSO 10 PRIZES OF $100 EACH AND 2,000 RUBBERSET SHAVING BRUSHES—2011 PRIZES IN ALL

Dizzy Dean says "COOLNESS"

"I LIKE HOT ARGUMENTS AND COOL SHAVES. THE BEST IS NONE TOO GOOD FOR A STAR LIKE I. SUPPOSE INGRAM'S DOES LAST LONGER—WHAT OF IT—I MAKE PLENTY OF JACK—SO I GO ALL OUT FOR LUXURY—LUXURY—LUXURY!"

Daffy Dean says "ECONOMY"

"WHEN IT COMES TO INGRAM'S, LAY OFF THAT 'ME AND PAUL' GAG. THIS IS ONE SPOT WHERE THE DEAN BOYS DIFFER. I'M FOR INGRAM'S ECONOMY—HOOK, FAST BALL AND SINKER. SAVE YOUR MONEY, BIG BOY!"

Answer this simple question in 50 words or less

Which is more important to You?
1. INGRAM'S FAMOUS COOLNESS
2. INGRAM'S CONCENTRATED ECONOMY

RIGHT here in the Ingram office another controversy started that turned into a contest—a contest with a first prize of $2,500—ten prizes of $100 and 2,000 genuine Rubberset shaving brushes worth $2.00 each.

"What do men like best about Ingram's?"— that's the challenge that started the battle. What wins them and holds them to this fast-selling cream—its *famous* "Coolness" or the *down-right,rock-bottom* "Economy" of its concentrated form? And now we want this big question settled—"Coolness or Economy"—and we're paying heavy money for the winning answers.

Try Ingram's today! You can win dollars—thousands of them! You can win a lifetime of comfortable shaves. For Ingram's is the Arctic and Antarctic of shaving creams—the chilliest, soothingest cream that ever made wire-whiskers say "Uncle." It's a secret and triple-play formula that gives you cream, lotion and face tonic in every single, cool brushful.

But before you vote "Coolness"— test its "Economy." A little bit of Ingram's goes a longer way—because it's concentrated—with a laboratory finding over other creams of 15% to 20% more lather and more cool, cool shaves from the same amount of cream.

Actually, it's the most economical cream on the market—you can start from a morsel as small as a green pea and get a snowy mass of lather bigger than a duck egg.

TRY INGRAM'S AND THEN TELL US!

But try Ingram's and give us your verdict. Your face can't lose. Read the simple, easy rules in the box to the right, and then send us your entry. Remember, there are 3,500 Ingram cash dollars and 2,000 Rubberset brushes for winning answers.

READ THESE EASY RULES!

1. Decide which quality of Ingram's is more important to you, its coolness or its economy, and state why in 50 words or less.

2. Mail your entry to Ingram's Shaving Cream, Post Office Box No. 501, Elizabeth, N.J. All entries must be postmarked before midnight, December 1, 1936, to be considered. Send in as many entries as you wish, but each must bear a separate sheet of paper (a) bearing your name and address, (b) the name and address of your regular druggist, (c) the facsimile reproduced by the top of the carton from a 35¢ size jar or tube of Ingram's Shaving Cream.

3. To insure absolute fairness, we have engaged Liberty Magazine to be the judges of the contest. Their decision in Liberty as soon as possible will be final.

4. All entries will be judged on the basis of originality, sincerity and applicability to advertising. No extra consideration will be given to decorated or fancy entries. Literary skill of "clever" writing will not count.

5. Anyone may enter the contest except employees of Bristol-Myers Co. Owners of Ingram's, their advertising agents, Liberty Magazine, their families. In case of a tie, duplicate prizes will be awarded.

6. Contestants agree that entries become the property of Bristol-Myers Co. and may be used by them in whole or in part, for advertising or other purposes. Entries cannot be returned, nor can Bristol-Myers Co. or the judges engage in correspondence about the contest.

A LITTLE INGRAM'S GOES A LONGER WAY BECAUSE—*it's Concentrated*

''Without the Deans the Cardinals would be lucky to finish in the first division.''—Joe Williams

have very much to say, just kind of grinned and went ahead. Finally Paul ended up with a sore arm. That really hurt him. And I really think Diz took it personally. Because he really wanted Paul to win so much. 'Cause he and Paul were really close. They really liked one another. The fact was, Paul kind of followed Dizzy around. Whatever Diz wanted to do, Paul was for it. But that year our whole pitching staff wasn't that good. Dizzy was good, but when we said that, you just about said everything. The rest of them were mediocre .500 pitchers. You can't win pennants with .500 pitchers.

"Bill DeLancey was the catcher at the time. He had a lung replaced. He tried to come back in '36, but he didn't have the stamina he used to have. He was a good hitter, but he lost some power. I think his medical condition got the best of him. He was a nice guy, a fun guy. He and Diz hit it off real good, too. They bantered with each other. They'd get together and pull a trick on somebody. They liked to agitate Joe Medwick all they could.

"Truthfully, Medwick was a sour disposition. He just was not a real likable guy. He was a little bit of an egotist. So Dizzy kind of put the needle to him all the time. I would laugh. I thought it was great. "But nobody liked Joe. For a while, I thought his personality might keep him out of the Hall of Fame.

"I liked him because he drove me in all the time. I liked to score runs, and he'd drive me in. "In '37 Joe won the Triple Crown. That year he couldn't do anything wrong. I saw him actually swing at balls that bounced, seen him hit balls up over his eyeballs, up high, outside, but he hit them so hard. He was very strong. He had very strong wrists and arms, and he could hit a ball as hard as anybody, and when he hit it, it just sailed.

"Both those guys like to play jokes. They never did anything to me. I was a meek little lamb. They didn't pay any attention to me. But I saw Pepper Martin drop a water balloon and just miss Frankie Frisch when he stepped out of the hotel. We were staying at the Kenmore Hotel, which had a porch on top next to the sidewalk where you could sit down. So Pepper got a balloon and filled it with water, and he went to his room overlooking where Frankie was standing, about four or five stories up. He punched the button on the elevator, and when the elevator came he told the elevator boy to hold it right there. Don't go away. I'll be right back.'

"He dropped the balloon and just missed Frisch. If he had hit him, Pepper might have killed him. And Pepper ran and got in the elevator. 'Take me down. Take me down.'

"Frisch suspected who it was. He ran for the elevator. It opened, and Pepper walked out and said, 'Hi, Frankie,' and kept on walking. Frankie knew who did it, but he couldn't prove anything because Pepper had planned it so well. I don't think Pepper wanted to hurt anyone, but he sure wanted to deal him a lot of misery! He did it just to create fun.

"You know, when Pepper wasn't playing, you had to watch him, because in St. Louis our bench had two tiers. You could sit in the front row or the back row. And if you were sitting in the front row, Pepper'd sneak up behind you, crawl underneath there, and hotfoot you. The ball game would be going on, and you'd hear a guy go, 'Aaahhhh!' And it could hurt you. Sometimes

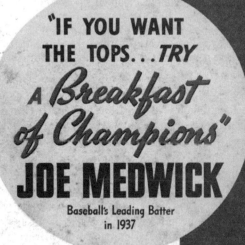

"As long as Joe Medwick was hitting, everything was fine and dandy."—pitcher Jim Mooney

it would even burn a hole in their shoe. If you weren't careful and you were sitting in the front row, Pepper would get you sooner or later.

"Another thing he did, he did to me. Pepper chewed tobacco. I wasn't playing, so my glove was laying down. He picked it up, and he spit into all the fingers with tobacco juice. Late in the game, Frisch called me to play, and I grabbed my glove and started out there, put my hand in the glove, and 'Oh my God!' I turned that glove upside down and tobacco juice oozed out of it. I could have killed him. But he laughed. Pepper thought that was so funny. And Frisch would get mad. He'd say, 'What happened?' 'Cause you'd look silly going out there, yelling, shaking your glove.' Then I'd explain what happened, and Frankie didn't know what to say. He figured Pepper was the guy who was guilty of it. He'd say, 'Why did you let that guy do that to you?'

"And gum. Pepper'd shake hands with you and have gum on his fingers. Or he'd pat you on the back and put gum on the back of your hair. He was always doing that. Nobody ever got angry.

"Pepper and I were buddies. He played little tricks on me all the time. We were riding on a train, going from St. Louis to New York, and you'd sleep part of the time. I went to sleep in my chair, and during a stop he got out and took some grease off the wheel, and he came back in and got a straw, and my hand was drooped down, and he put a little grease on my fingers. Then he tickled my nose like it was a fly, and I'd knock the fly off my nose, and I ended up with grease all over my face. He did that to several guys, of course. It was fun. We liked that.

"Pepper was a very competitive ballplayer. He would do anything to win. When he went out there, you had to beat him. He wasn't going to beat himself. You were going to have to be better than he was. He liked to win, and he never let up. He ran out everything. Some guys would run hard to first base. He ran hard all the time. When he went to steal, he did it headfirst. He was an advocate of it. He talked to me about it. 'You ought to slide like that.' And I did once in a while.

"I never will forget, I was on base and I was going to score, and Jimmy Wilson was the catcher with the Phils. It was a close play at the plate, and I dove headfirst. He blocked me with both knees, and liked to knock my head off. He had the ball in his hand, and he reached down and hit me on top of the head. He said, 'Next time, kid, don't slide headfirst.' After that, whenever I went into home plate, I slid feetfirst.

"On one ballclub, we had Pepper, Dizzy, and Medwick. They were not ordinary people."

CHAPTER 25

THE GANG BREAKS UP

THE Cards in 1935 were strengthened by the addition of a young center fielder by the name of Terry Moore. When he came up, writer Roy Stockton said about the fleet rookie: "Terry Moore could throw a baseball into a barrel at 100 yards, run 100 yards in ten seconds, and hit a ball a country mile."

DON GUTTERIDGE: "Terry was absolutely great. Terry could come in or go back on balls quicker than anybody I have ever seen. He had a sure hand, and his arm was powerful. When I was playing third base and the ball came in from Terry in center field, I could stay on the base and I knew the ball would come to me.

"Terry didn't get a lot of ink because at that time everybody liked to talk about hitters, and Terry wasn't really a good hitter. That didn't come for another six or seven years. Everybody likes to see hits, hits, hits, and defense didn't get much attention. But he was the best defensive outfielder."

In 1936 Branch Rickey's farm system added another rookie sensation to the team. Johnny Mize, "the Big Cat," was a distant relative of Babe Ruth. He was big like Ruth, left-handed like Ruth, and in his rookie season he impressed everyone with his home run prowess.

Branch Rickey was lucky with Mize. He had grown up in Demorest, Georgia, and after attending Piedmont College there, he played for a lumber company in nearby Helen, Georgia, for $10 a game. A bird dog told Warren Giles, who was running the Rochester farm club, and Giles sent Frank Rickey, Branch's brother, to scout him. Mize signed when he was seventeen.

In 1934, while playing for Rochester, Mize tore a muscle from his pelvic bone, and in the spring of 1935, Rickey offered him to Cincinnati on a trial basis. Larry MacPhail, who was running the Reds at the time, had just bought several players from Rickey, including Ival Goodman, Billy Myers, and Lew Riggs, and MacPhail didn't want to take a chance on buying a player with a bum leg. He sent Mize back to the Cards.

When Mize joined the Cards in '36, he beat Rip Collins out of the first-base job. After the season, Collins was traded to the Cubs. From the moment he arrived in 1936, Mize dominated the National League as a slugger. For seven consecutive seasons, he finished among the top three players in slugging average, leading four times. He also finished among the top five in batting average five of the six years between 1937 and 1942.

In a fifteen-year career, Johnny Mize had a lifetime batting average of .312 and hit 359 home runs. Only Jimmie Foxx and Lou Gehrig are rated

more prolific sluggers than "Big John" Mize. With the Cards, he led the
league in homers in 1939 (28) and 1940 (43). Later in his career, playing for
the New York Giants, The Big Cat again led the league in homers with 51 in
1947 and 40 in 1948. That he had to wait almost twenty years to enter the
Hall of Fame (in 1981) was a terrible miscarriage of justice.

Despite the addition of Moore and Mize, in 1936 the Cardinals would
suffer two crippling blows that would keep the team from challenging for
the pennant.

FRANKIE FRISCH: "The first big blow was the loss of the services of Bill
DeLancey. Bill was one of the greatest young catchers I ever saw break into
baseball. He played in 103 games in 1935, but he wasn't the same young man.
He was listless, not at all like the ball of fire he had been as we battled through
the 1934 season. Shortly after the season's end, a physical checkup showed that
DeLancey had contracted tuberculosis. He was ordered to a Western climate.

"How many clubs could stand the loss of a catcher like that? What would
have happened to the talent-rich Yankees if they had lost Bill Dickey when
Bill was at his prime? The Cardinals had one of the most productive farm
systems in baseball, but no talent factory can replace a man like DeLancey."

JOHNNY MIZE
(Courtesy Brace Photo)

"The second big wallop from Lady Luck was the sore arm that plagued Paul Dean throughout the season. Paul, after winning 19 games in [1934 and] 1935, could win only 5 in 1936 and he lost the same number.

"Actually, we were lucky to finish in a tie for second place in 1936, after losing a great young battery like Bill DeLancey and Paul Dean. And from then on, we went from bad to worse.

"We dropped to fourth place in 1937 and the 'Old Flash' began to see the writing on the wall."

In 1937 disaster struck the Cardinals again. This time the victim was Dizzy Dean, and it was a blow from which the team wouldn't recover for five years.

At the time, Dean was still a rebel, but he was beginning to understand that his salary battles were hurting him financially. He no longer was the extroverted braggart he had been when he first came to St. Louis. He was settling into the role of veteran leader. Several years of turmoil and repercussions had chastened him.

In 1934, the year he told everyone that "me an' Paul" were going to win 45 games, Dean announced he had signed for a salary in excess of $40,000. This was the salary he should have been making in his mind. As Dean then let everyone know during his first work stoppage, his real salary was $7,500. When in 1935 he announced he had signed for between $24,000 and $26,000, the real figure was $17,500. Because of his greatness and his fame, Dean made twice that off the field, endorsing sweaters, shirts, caps, hats, toothpaste, gloves, shoes, watches, school writing tablets, and cigarettes.

But Dean never stopped campaigning for more money from Breadon and Rickey, and he kept insisting he and his brother were being cheated by the Cardinals. Dean publicly called Sam Breadon "cheap" and said it was a "disgrace that me an' Paul had to work for such measly salaries."

During the 1935 season, Diz and Paul reluctantly went to an exhibition game in St. Paul, but as a protest they adamantly refused to appear in the game. They sat in the dugout and never left it, much to the displeasure of the adoring crowd. Adverse publicity rained down on Dean. Shortly thereafter, the sale of Dean-related products came virtually to a halt.

When Dizzy failed to honor a commitment to play in an exhibition game in Chattanooga, Commisioner Landis held a hearing and fined him $100. Then Dean told Breadon and Rickey he no longer would pitch to catcher Spud Davis, and that too angered both his bosses and the public.

In the off-season prior to the 1936 season, Dean once again held out.

In response, Rickey wrote Dean a stern letter, telling Dean he would have to be a better soldier, take orders from the manager, and not "arrogate to himself the prerogotives of Frank Frisch," that he "would have to show a willingness—nay an eagerness—to be just a soldier in the ranks, always with his shoulder to the wheel, striving for the common cause."

Dizzy, ever the wordsmith, told Roy Stockton that "the president of Constitute of Tecknological would have had a tough time finding out what it was that Mr. Rickey wanted to say."

He had won 96 games over the past four years, plus 2 more in the World Series. "Wasn't that enough?" he asked Stockton.

DIZZY DEAN: "I am lopsided on one shoulder from that wheel, an' the grindstone has my nose as flat as a policeman's foot. What the heck does Mr. Rickey want me to do—play the outfield or lead the boys' band?"

Rickey ordered Dean to answer by January 23, 1936, or face a suspension without pay. Rickey and Breadon considered doing without him for 1936. Dean asked a friend to ask Roy Stockton to answer. The letter, approved by Diz and Pat, was another surrender. In it he vowed to do everything Rickey asked of him. But Stockton, who was close to both Breadon and Dean and whose loyalty was split, also wondered whether Rickey *really* wanted Dean to be dull or whether it was financially beneficial to the club for Dean to be eccentric.

Rickey, whose focus was on winning his salary negotiation with Dean, said he was satisfied with the reply. Dizzy verbally promised to let Spud Davis catch when he pitched. He promised to be good. He signed for $24,000.

Dizzy was as entertaining and popular as Will Rogers. In this cartoon the heroic Dizzy helps round up the bad guys.

But his holdouts and money demands were beginning to sour the public on him. By 1936 his outside income had dropped to almost zero.

Dizzy was suspended in '36, but this time it was by National League president Ford Frick, not the Cardinals. Dean was pitching against the New York Giants in Sportsman's Park. He led late in the game, when umpire George Barr called a balk for not coming to a stop before he threw. Diz, rattled, allowed three runs and lost the game. That night at a banquet, Dean, who was a sore loser, called Barr and Frick "a couple of crooks."

The remark made the papers, and when the Cards arrived in Brooklyn, Frick announced that Dean had been suspended until the pitcher apologized. He refused.

DIZZY DEAN: "I was in a hell of a spot, an' don't you forget it. Frisch was crazy. I got so many laughs listenin' to him I wouldn'ta signed [a letter of apology] even if I'd been wrong, an' once I told him I had a notion to sue the National League for slander an' Frank hit the ceiling. All he wanted me to do was get back in uniform.

"So Frick finally saw the error of his ways, an' I got back, but I had a great time not workin' for a few days. Night-clubbin' every night an' a couple of times I ran into ol' Frisch an' gave him a big cheery hello an' I didn't pitch neither until I made sure I got paid for that time out. Well, it was June 9, 1936, when I put on the uniform, an' Hubbell'd beaten me May 19 in St. Louis. So here we were again, an' that Polo Grounds was a madhouse. I was afraid to come out of the dugout. Everybody was yellin' and throwin' things down at our bench, an' I waited until Frisch said: 'You only got five minutes, you better warm up,' so I dashed out there by home plate an' warmed up, an' I was almost deaf from the noise when I got through.

"I just went out there an' pitched a cool three-hitter in the first game of a doubleheader an' beat Hubbell, 8–1, an' I'd had a shutout, only Durocher booted one near the end. Yes, sir, ol' Jay Hanna Dean was just in ripe form that day an' there was nobody gonna make a monkey outta him. I told that Durocher after the game, I said: 'You oughta been more careful on that ball, I wanted to rub it in [against the Giants],' an' he said, 'You rubbed it in enough, don't worry about it . . . the time to boot 'em, if you have to, is when you got runs to spare,' which I guess is probably right."

Then in 1937 disaster struck. Dizzy had his toe broken by a line drive hit by Earl Averill during the All-Star Game in Washington. But the real damage would be done to his arm when he tried to come back too soon.

DON GUTTERIDGE: "I was at the game when Dizzy hurt his arm. After he got hit, we opened in Boston against the old Boston Braves. Frisch didn't think his toe hurt that much. And Branch Rickey was another one. Branch Rickey told Frisch to make him pitch.

"Doc Weaver didn't want Dizzy to pitch. Doc said, 'He has a broken toe.' Then Diz went out and tried to pitch, and instead of pushing off the front of his foot, his toe—like he'd always done—he turned his leg some and pushed off his heel, and that put a strain on his shoulder and arm, and he never did recover from it. I heard those stories that Frisch didn't wanted him to pitch and Diz did, but that's not what happened. Branch Rickey and Frisch didn't think Diz was hurt that bad. Doc Weaver said he was, and that proved out to be. It was criminal what they did to him. Criminal what they did to the whole ballclub.

"It wasn't long before we could see that his ball wasn't moving, wasn't fast, that he wasn't the same pitcher. He was getting hit more, too.''

According to Jesse Haines, who was on the pitching staff that year, Dizzy didn't need prompting to pitch. Haines says he was impatient to get back on the mound.

JESSE "POP" HAINES: "After the All-Star Game in '37 when [Earl] Averill hit him on the foot with that line drive, we rode back from Washington together on the train. Diz's berth was right across the aisle from me. He says to me, 'Pop, you know my toe's sorer than thunder. It hurts.'

"I said, 'Put her up here once and let's take a look at her.' So he puts his foot on my berth, and I took ahold of his toe and worked it until I heard a grit. Then I said to him, 'That toe's broke.'

" 'Naw,' he says.

" 'It is,' I said. 'When you get back to St. Louis, go out and see Doc Hyland.'

"Well, he did, and the toe was broken. Doc, he splinted it, but Diz wouldn't pay any attention to the splints. Dizzy was the kind of pitcher who wanted to pitch every day. He'd pitch today, and tomorrow he'd go to the bullpen. 'If you need me, I'll be ready,' he'd say. I'd tell him, 'Look, Diz, this is your bread and butter. You can't do that.'

" 'Ah, yes, I can,' he'd say. 'She's rubber,' he'd say, pointing to his right arm.

" 'All right,' I'd say. 'Your rubber is gonna snap one of these days.'

"After a week or so after Doc [splinted his toe], he told Doc to take them off. 'I'm gonna pitch,' he says. He started pitching, and he hurt his arm. Didn't throw natural. He would have been a great pitcher if he'd a listened and laid off for three or four more weeks. He was a character, though.''

Frankie Frisch stoutly defended himself from allegations he had pitched Dean too soon after the injury. Contradicting Gutteridge, Frisch also laid the blame at Dizzy's feet.

FRANKIE FRISCH: "It was my judgment that Dizzy ought to wait several more days, possibly weeks, before trying to pitch in a ball game.

"I explained this to Diz, but he laughed off my caution.

" 'There ain't nothing wrong with Old Diz,' he insisted. 'You don't think a little old broken toe is going to keep me out of action.'

"If he pitched too soon, it was because he insisted on pitching. And if you think imposing your will and what you consider your superior wisdom on Dizzy Dean is an easy task, you didn't know that man Dean.

"I believe it was reasonable to assume that it was impossible for him to use his natural, smooth pitching motion, with that fractured toe paining him each time he braced his right foot against the rubber on the mound. To ease the pain, he probably used an unnatural pitching motion. The old rhythm was gone and Dizzy's arm became sore and it was never the same arm after that.

"The arm was still bothering Diz during spring training at St. Petersburg, Florida, the following year, and his work during the exhibition season was not at all impressive. So on the eve of the 1938 season, Breadon and Rickey traded the great pitcher to the Chicago Cubs for two pitchers, Curt Davis and Clyde Shoun, an outfielder, Tuck Stainback, and $185,000.

"That deal didn't hurt the Cardinals, with Dean in the shape he was. Davis and Shoun did some fine pitching for St. Louis. But what did hurt the St. Louis club was the loss of the services of 'the Great Dean.' "

DON GUTTERIDGE: "I loved playing with Dizzy. So did everybody else. The players all liked Dizzy. They were crazy about Dizzy. Even when he held out, they found no fault with him.

"After we traded Diz to Chicago, we went up there to play, and there was a big crowd because Dizzy was going to pitch against the Cardinals. Pepper told Frankie Frisch, 'Frankie, I got a headache. I can't play.' So Frankie knew immediately.' He said, 'You've got to play, Pepper.' Pepper said, 'I don't want to hit against ol' Diz. I'm liable to hurt him. He ain't got enough out there. Somebody is going to kill him.'

"Well, Pepper went to bat, and the first time, sure enough, he hit a ball right back at Dizzy, and he hit Dizzy right in the belly with a line drive. Instead of running to first base, Pepper ran out to the mound. 'Hey, Dizzy, you all right?' Diz was his friend, and he didn't want to see him hurt."

On the day Dizzy Dean was traded, Branch Rickey went into the Cards clubhouse to tell the players he had traded Dean to the Cubs. Rickey knew the players would be upset. He told them, "We don't want you players to feel we're letting you down, because we've got a man to replace him and we'll still win the pennant."

The man Rickey got to replace him, Curt Davis, would go 12-8 in 1938 and would improve to 22-9 in 1939, but Dizzy would gain further immortality as he won on the final day of the 1938 season to lead the Chicago Cubs to the pennant.

DIZZY DEAN: "Hell, I knew they couldn't win any ol' pennant without Diz, even if I was only a half a pitcher then, so when they asked me to say somethin' for the newspapers, I said, 'Well, Mr. Rickey, I predicted we'd win the flag right here in St. Louis, but now that I'm gone, we'll win it in Chicago, an' I'll see you get into the World Series.' [In other words, Dean was going to get Rickey tickets!]"

At the end of the 1937 season, in another damaging trade, Rickey sent Leo Durocher to Brooklyn for five players (Joe Stripp, Johnny Cooney, Roy Henshaw, Jim Bucher, and Tony Malinosky) who never did help the Cardinals. Leo had decided he could manage the team better than Frankie Frisch, and in his undiplomatic, blustery way, he said it loud and often enough that Frisch, who was as abrasive and strong-willed as Durocher, told Rickey there wasn't room on the team for both of them.

Don Gutteridge saw the constant sniping.

DON GUTTERIDGE: "Leo and Frisch battled all the time, literally argued all the time. They just didn't get along. One guy would say one thing, and the other would say the other. I think Leo had aspirations of managing, and that's how he was building himself up to it."

Durocher, who tended to live his life with blinders on, never saw the cause and effect between his big mouth and his departure.

LEO DUROCHER: "I was traded because Frisch demanded that Rickey get rid of me. And I couldn't understand why. Frank and I had always been close. Almost from the first, I had been his captain.

"Mr. Rickey called me in a couple of months into the season to tell me that Frank had given him an ultimatum at the end of spring training. Either I went or he went. Rickey had been sitting on it for two months, hoping that he'd be able to get Frank to change his mind. All Frisch would say, Rickey told me, was 'It's me or Durocher.'

" 'I think,' Rickey said, 'that he's afraid you're after his job.' "

Frisch had a right to resent Durocher's undermining of his authority, but the departure of Durocher cost the Cards a splendid infielder and perhaps a future Hall of Fame manager. And the next year, in 1938, Frisch was fired anyway as the team fell to sixth.

DON GUTTERIDGE: "Frisch treated me very well. He thought I was young and innocent. He never got on me much. But he was on the other guys all the time. He tried to drive them a little bit better. He tried to get more out of them.

"One time we were having a meeting—they have a meeting every once in a while—and Frankie was really ripping us good, everybody. 'You guys are a bunch of bums.'

"Pepper Martin held up his hand like a kid in school, and said, 'Frankie, Frankie.' Frank said, 'What do you want, John?' [Frisch called Pepper by his given name, John.] Martin said, 'Do you know what? This is like the Kentucky Derby. You can't win the Kentucky Derby with a mule. You got a lot of jackasses here who can't play.' And that broke up the meeting. Frisch just walked out. What can you say after that? Pepper was right, too, because at that time we just didn't have that good a ballclub."

According to Don Gutteridge, there was friction that year between Frisch and Branch Rickey.

DON GUTTERIDGE: "During the latter part of the season, all of us were thinking Frankie might get fired. There was an article in the newspaper that he and Branch

Rickey weren't getting along too well. You suspect when that starts to come out, you expect things to happen. My guess is that Frisch wanted to play certain players, and Rickey wanted him to play somebody else. Also, if you're a major league manager, he looks at who's in the minors and says, 'I want that guy up here.' And Rickey had a policy. He didn't break up a minor league club in order to help the Cardinals, 'cause if you brought up the best players from the minor league club, you hurt the minor league club, and it would lose money.''

Eventually Sam Breadon had to blame someone for the team's lethargic sixth-place performance, and as was his habit, the man who took the fall was the manager, this time Frisch.

FRANKIE FRISCH: "As manager of the Cardinals, I made it my daily practice to call at [Sam] Breadon's office at Sportsman's Park every day before a game, or after the day's play. He liked to talk baseball and I was very fond of him as a person. And he always was warm and friendly to me."

In one meeting, Frisch asked the Cards owner about his plans for the next season. Breadon said he hadn't made up his mind. He spoke of the poor season financially and the necessity of reducing expenses and said that the manager would have to take a pay cut as a condition of employment. Frisch told him he would not do that.

On Sunday, September 11, 1938, Breadon called Frisch into his office and told him he was fired. With a 61-72 record, Sam Breadon decided he needed a new man to bring out a better performance in his players. Frisch said he saw a tear trickle down Breadon's face.

Despite having been fired, Frisch was asked to manage that afternoon. Paul Dean, just back from the Texas League, won that day.

After the game, Frisch said goodbye to his players, then was mobbed by fans who had heard the news. May Ott, "the Queen of the St. Louis Cardinal rooters," was in the front row of the waiting crowd. She threw her arms around him and cried.

The next day the "Fordham Flash" headed for his home in New Rochelle. For the first time in his life, Frankie Frisch was unemployed.

CHAPTER 26

LANDIS GETS HIS REVENGE

DON Gutteridge was playing in the low minors with Hartford, Connecticut, when the league went belly-up in 1933. To keep playing, he signed with a team in the Nebraska State League. Gutteridge, a fine infielder, was about to be unemployed for a second time, when Branch Rickey invested Sam Breadon's money to save his league from going under. Gutteridge remembered what it was like playing in the Cardinals farm system during the Depression days of the 1930s.

DON GUTTERIDGE: "This was 1933. The Nebraska State League was going to go busted. There were four teams in the league. Branch Rickey came in and said, 'I'll pay each team $2,000 so you can finish the season, and for that $2,000 I get two players from each team.' Well, they agreed to that, and I was one of the players who was bought. In fact, out of the eight, six of us— Nelson Potter, Johnny Hopp, Tom Seats for a short time, Cotton Pippen, Lynn King, and I—ended up in the major leagues. That was right in the heart of the Depression. Everybody in the league got $50 a month. Everybody. Nobody got any more or any less. We got a dollar a day to eat when we were on the road.

"The Cards had a large farm system. If I had to guess, I'd imagine he had 200 or 300 players under contract. When I went to spring training with the Cards in '34, there were gobs of players there. It wasn't discouraging, really. I guess it made us play a little harder.

"That spring they sent me to Houston, Texas. We had a good team in Houston. We finished way up in the standings. The manager was Ray Blades, who was very thorough. He wanted perfection. He wasn't very popular with the ballplayers, and I don't know why. I liked him a lot. He was a very serious guy, but I got along with him fine.

"The next year I went to Columbus. The Cardinals had a lot of Triple A ballplayers. They needed two clubs to have all of them. They would shift players back and forth between Columbus and Rochester.

"When I went to Columbus, my manager was Burt Shotton. He was fun, a very nice man and very good handling men. Everybody liked him. When he'd say something, he'd say it in a low tone, and you did it.

"Traveling in the minors was kind of tough. We'd travel by bus at Houston, and with Columbus we traveled mostly by train. We would have delays and get into a town at four in the morning and have to play that day. At that time, there wasn't air-conditioning on the train. You'd work yourself dead, and then you'd spend some hot, hot nights on the train. They wouldn't put us in Pullman if it wasn't a long trip. To save money they put us in the chair car. The Cardinals were a cheap organization. They squeezed the dollar until the eagle screamed. We were known as 'Rickey's hoboes.'

"They said he got a budget from Sam Breadon to sign ballplayers and anything he saved out of that was his. That was a known fact. [Though many players thought that, Rickey's deal with Breadon was his salary plus 10 percent of net profits at the end of the year. Of course, the lower the players' salary, the greater the net profit, of which he earned 10 percent.] In the minor league system, they had a chart they went by. If you played in Class D, you got so much, in Class A, so much more. It was a scale.

"When I signed with the Cardinals for the first time, I got $325 a month [$1,950 a year]. If you stayed with the Cardinals until June 15, which used to be the trading deadline, then you got a raise to $500 a month.

"They called it the farm system. They wanted to keep you down on the farm all they could. The players resented it, because we felt we were not getting paid like players of other teams. But we couldn't complain, because the owners were so powerful that you better not complain too much or they'd send you back down to the [low] minor leagues, and you couldn't do anything about it.

"And if you made it to the majors, Rickey would bring you in for a salary talk, and the first thing you know, he'd bring up all your negative points, instead of agreeing with you that you had a good arm or were a good runner. It made us furious, because he was always negative. You'd come out of a meeting like that, and you'd think, 'That guy . . .' You didn't realize what he was doing to you.

"I learned that instead of going in and seeing him, I just wrote a letter, and he'd write a letter back. I knew not to go in and negotiate with him face-to-face. I knew I wasn't capable of competing against him. I figured if I wrote a letter, he couldn't influence me."

By the late 1930s, the St. Louis Cardinal farm system was a well-oiled moneymaking machine. Rickey would sift through hundreds of prospects in the hunt for one or two players a year to help the Cardinals, then he would sell dozens of lesser players to other major and minor league teams.

His farm system was so fruitful that other teams—with Rickey's help—copied it. In the early 1930s, the New York Yankees bought the Newark franchise. They then hired George Weiss to design and run a farm system like the Cardinals.

BRANCH RICKEY: "This was one of the best things that happened to baseball. We welcomed another strong operator in the other league and wished there were more. The farm system had finally ended the undercover work of gentleman's agreements, which were bad because they were covert. The farm system caused the aboveboard optional agreement. The working of the optional agreement was the outcome of trial and error. Down through the years, I sat with many business managers or major league clubs in a discussion of the details of working agreements. I have given many printed copies of my working agreement to other clubs in both leagues."

When Eddie Collins joined the Boston Red Sox as Tom Yawkey's right-hand man, Collins came to St. Louis and spent two full days with Rickey, learning his system.

"We helped wherever and whenever we could," said Rickey, who knew the more clubs had farm systems, the less chance Commissioner Landis would sanction him.

If one could be critical of Rickey's system, the biggest complaint was that after 1934 the pennants had ceased. Players like Johnny Mize swore that the main reason for that was Rickey's refusal to bring up needed players to the Cardinals in the middle of the season.

JOHNNY MIZE: "We always had good ballclubs in St. Louis, but most of the time we needed just a little bit more help. They had plenty of good ballplayers in the minor leagues in those years, but they kept selling them off. Guys like Bob Klinger, Bill Lee, Fritz Ostermueller, Cy Blanton. Those guys were good pitchers. Bill Lee especially. He was a great one for the Cubs [who helped lead the Cubs to pennants in 1935 and 1938]. If the Cardinals had brought them up, we might have won a few pennants during those years. I heard later that Rickey got 25 percent [it was 10] of whatever he sold a player for. [That's what a lot of players erroneously thought.] That's why every year he was selling these players. He sold Johnny Rizzo, too, and those other fellows I mentioned, Riggs, Goodman, Myers."

Mize was a cynical man, and like many of his teammates, he disliked Rickey intensely because of Rickey's constant pressure to keep salaries low. Mize once told me a story of how when he married, Sam Breadon gave him $500 as a gift. The next year when salary negotiations rolled around, said Mize, Rickey tried to include the $500 as part of his salary, in order to keep his raise to a minimum.

Mize surely was off-base when he charged that Rickey was trying *not* to win pennants to keep salaries down. But Cardinal fans expressed the same notions about the way Rickey did business as Mize did.

JOHNNY MIZE: "I'll tell you what the talk used to be about Rickey: Stay in the pennant race until the last week of the season and then get beat. I heard some talk to the effect that that was what he preferred. That way he drew the crowds all year, and then later on the players wouldn't come in for the big raise for winning the pennant and maybe the World Series. I don't know if it's true or not, but that was the talk."

It may have been the talk, but Rickey didn't bring up his minor league prospects in mid-season for a very good reason. He needed full cooperation of the owners of the minor league teams with whom he did business, and part of his dealings included the promise not to raid minor league teams in the middle of the season and hurt their chances to win a league title.

Rickey believed that it was important to keep the goodwill of his minor league customers, and so he refused to take an important player from a team during the season, no matter how badly the Cards may have needed him. Only after the pennant race was over would a player move up. It was a philosophy that, while financially sound, infuriated managers and fans of the parent Cardinals and caused players and fans alike to wonder about Rickey's will to win.

By 1938, Rickey again came under attack by Judge Landis. Taylor Spink, who wrote Landis's biography with the help of journalist Fred Lieb, saw how much the commissioner disliked both Rickey and his farm system. Part of his dislike for Rickey stemmed from Landis's distrust for anyone who purported himself to be religious. Landis had a distrust of "religious hypocrites and those who went around with pious looks on their faces and larceny in their hearts."

TAYLOR SPINK: "He always seemed to think that Rickey, a Sunday school teacher, was trying to put something over on him six days in the week. As a player, Rickey refused to play Sunday ball, and as a manager, he turned the team over to a coach on Sundays. One of the judge's favorite references to Branch was 'that sanctimonious so-and-so.' "

According to Taylor Spink, "Landis bided his time and waited for the proper moment to strike." The first inkling that Landis was investigating Rickey's operation came during spring training while the Cards were in St. Petersburg. Landis called in Sam Breadon, Rickey, and some players to his suite at the Bellaire–Biltmore Hotel to discuss the way Rickey ran the farm system. Frankie Frisch, in his final year as Cardinals manager, was called in and questioned about a player by the name of Dick Siebert. At the time, Frisch didn't know what Landis was angling for. Later, after Landis lowered the boom on Rickey, he found out.

FRANKIE FRISCH: "Was I being used as a stool pigeon by the commissioner? Were he and Branch Rickey on the outs and was he trying to get something on Rickey or the club? One of the first calls I got from him was when he asked me about Dick Siebert, whom the Cardinals were going to send to Rochester or Columbus. Landis asked me if Siebert could play big league ball. I answered him honestly, saying that I thought surely there must be some big league club that could use Siebert. Then the roof caved in. He declared Siebert a free agent or issued an order that the Cardinals couldn't keep him. I felt sure then that Landis was using me as a stoolie."

Sam Breadon, who was becoming alarmed about Landis's inquiries, questioned Rickey about his operations.
"I'm absolutely in the clear, Sam," Rickey replied. "I've kept within all the rules and regulations. Landis has nothing on me."
But Rickey didn't understand that Landis had the animosity and the power to hurt him and his organization, even if he was within those rules and regulations. In March of 1938, Landis punished the Cardinals and Rickey, their farm director, when in what came to be known as the Cedar Rapids case, he freed 91 Cardinal farmhands, including Pete Reiser and James "Skeeter" Webb.
Taylor Spink recalled Landis's determination to get Rickey.

TAYLOR SPINK: "Landis had Leslie O'Connor work on the Cedar Rapids case for weeks, digging deeply into Rickey's Class D and C farms and doing the preliminary spade work. No penalty was inflicted on Farmer Branch, but the Sacramento Pacific Coast League club and Cedar Rapids of the Western League were each fined sums of $588 and Springfield of the Western Association $1,000. The commissioner permitted clubs having players declared free agents to dicker again for the services of these players, but added the provision that none could be transferred to the St. Louis club, or affiliate, or to Cedar Rapids within a period of three years.''

Landis found that Rickey had had ''secret understandings'' with these minor league teams and berated the minor league teams for subverting and circumventing the rule against one club having a working agreement with more than one team in a minor league. In documents he handed out to the press, Landis said that Rickey's manipulations were ''big as the universe.''

According to Spink, Sam Breadon rushed to Rickey's defense. In a rebuke of Landis's allegations, Breadon praised Rickey as the savior of the minor leagues.

He wrote a long treatise on how Rickey saved the minor leagues from extinction in constant opposition of the commissioner's office. Breadon questioned how Landis could have freed certain players ''if he knows the facts.''

The answer lay in Landis's egotistical nature. He was vain, and he held grudges. He couldn't stand it when in 1942 journalist Stanley Frank wrote an article in *The Saturday Evening Post* calling Taylor Spink ''Mr. Baseball.'' Landis thought of himself as ''Mr. Baseball.'' In the article, Frank wrote glowingly of Spink's role as Baseball's watchdog. Landis believed himself to have that role.

Spink for years had published baseball's *Official Record Book and Guide*. After the article ran in the *Post,* Landis in a meeting berated Spink, sarcastically referring to him as ''Mr. Baseball.'' He told one of his associates, ''Be very careful what you do. That's Mr. Baseball. He'll watch everything you do in this office.''

Spink tried to reason with the commissioner. He told Landis he had had no knowledge of the statements made in the *Post* article. Landis as much as called him a liar to his face. When Spink asked if he would be allowed to publish the *Official Record Book and Guide,* Landis barked, ''No,'' and walked out in a huff.

American League president Will Harridge called Landis to intervene. Harridge told Spink that Landis would see him again. This time Landis treated him even more harshly. At the end, Spink asked Landis, ''Am I still a friend of yours, or am I not a friend?''

Landis replied, ''I have no friends, and you're just the same as you were before.''

Spink asked him to shake hands. He did. Spink left his office hurt and humiliated.

Spink had to put out the 1943 *Guide* without the word ''Official'' on it. To spite him, several months later Landis published his own ''Official'' guide, edited by Leslie O'Connor.

Wrote Red Smith, ''Judge Kenesaw Mountain Landis is a fool. And if that be treason, let him go ahead and fine me $29,000,000.''

After discussing the fact that Landis published his guide after Spink had put his out, Smith wrote, ''The Judge's deep and abiding disaffection for Mr. Spink is strictly personal and has been attributed to various causes, all of them petty. The Judge himself never gave any reason for going into the publishing business. Maybe he noticed how the newspapermen he deals with quake and cower at the mention of the sports editor's name and decided he'd like to be an editor so he could be all-powerful, too. The old guy has got a dictator complex.''

Landis's pursuit of Rickey seemed to be a personal vendetta. Rickey had saved many minor league teams from going broke during a period when Landis did nothing to stop the erosion of the minor leagues. Rickey had outsmarted and outargued him so often, it was just a matter of time before Landis would get even.

Landis's verdict stuck, of course, because he had absolute power over the owners. But this was a kangaroo court with Landis acting as judge and jury. Neither Breadon nor Rickey ever received a formal statement of charges. They were not permitted to present their side of the case and offer evidence, the right to witnesses, counsel, and cross-examination. The Cardinals could have challenged him in court, but didn't.

Shortly after Landis's decision, there was an incident that may well have been an attempt by Landis to further sully Rickey's name and drive him out of baseball. It began with an allegation by Dizzy Dean, who charged that he had signed his original Cardinal contract when he was a minor and without his parents' approval. Called to Chicago for a hearing, Landis told Rickey, ''Dean's charges sound rather conclusive.''

Rickey pulled from his inner jacket pocket a copy of Dean's marriage license that proved Dean had lied to Landis about his age, that Rickey had been aboveboard.

It marked the end of the persecution of Rickey by Landis.

Despite the loss of star outfielder Pete Reiser to the Dodgers and shortstop Skeeter Webb to the White Sox, the only 2 of the 91 freed farmhands to reach the major leagues with other teams, the Cardinals maintained their farm system at full throttle.

A year later in December of 1939, the major league owners sought legislation that would codify relations between big league teams and minor league teams. Landis ridiculed the idea, charging that the proposal was the work of the teams with big chains: the Cards, Yankees, Dodgers, and Browns. ''The minors are just pawns of the majors,'' said Landis.

But then on December 11, 1940, Landis surprised everyone by throwing in the towel and relenting on his former stand. He accepted the right of associated clubs to recommend and sign players for each other. Rickey—at last—could run his farm system without having to worry about Landis.

In 1942, when the Cards again won a World Series, every regular on the team was a product of the farm system that Branch Rickey had conceived and developed. But because Judge Landis had taken out his wrath on Rickey, his days with the Cardinals would be numbered.

CHAPTER 27

SOUTHWORTH RETURNS

In 1938 Branch Rickey brought up to the Cardinals a young outfielder by the name of Enos Slaughter, who would prove to be one of the toughest, most durable, and most exciting players ever to wear a Redbird on his sleeve. In nineteen years in the major leagues, thirteen with the Cards, Enos would hit .300, consistently score and drive in runs, and play with a ferocity and a hustle not seen again until Pete Rose came on the scene twenty years later.

Slaughter's accomplishment would be overshadowed by one Stanley Frank Musial, much as Lou Gehrig was outdone by one George Herman Ruth. For the ten years between 1939 and 1949, Slaughter's .313 batting average was second in the National League only to Musial's .347. Enos was also the fourth best in slugging percentage in the league during that period, behind Musial, Johnny Mize, and Mel Ott.

Slaughter in 1939 led the league in doubles (52), and in 1942 led it in hits (188) and triples (17), and led the league in RBIs in 1946 with 130. He should have been awarded the batting title in 1942 when he hit .318. It was given instead to Ernie Lombardi, who hit .330 but came to bat only 309 times. An excellent fielder, Slaughter ended his career with 2,383 hits. Had he not missed three full seasons because of World War II, he probably would have finished his career with the magical 3,000 hits.

Enos, who ran to first after a walk, who even ran to his position in the outfield, was a player who loved the game of baseball with all his heart and soul.

When Slaughter arrived for spring training in 1939, however, he was suffering from rabbit fever. On New Year's morning, he and his father had gone rabbit hunting. As they waded through the underbrush, they were scratched by sharp thorns, and then they shot and handled infected rabbits. That afternoon his father became ill and was bedridden. Eleven days later he died of the disease, called tularemia. Enos contracted the same disease.

Rabbit fever strikes its victims with a high temperature that comes and goes. Weakness, black depression, and abscesses develop. Six weeks later, when it was time for Enos to go to spring training, his mother and his doctor pleaded with him not to go. But the Cardinals had appointed a new manager, Ray Blades, and Enos felt that if he didn't go and be productive, he would lose his chance at a starting spot in the lineup.

During spring training, Slaughter shivered under the hot Florida sun, and he suffered from the pain caused by the abscesses when he swung the bat.

"But he wouldn't tell Blades, and he swore me to secrecy," said his roommate, Terry Moore. "He was afraid Ray would send him home and that way he might lose out."

In 1939 Slaughter batted .320.

ENOS SLAUGHTER: "I finished high school in Roxboro, North Carolina, in 1934. Fred Haney, a sportswriter over at the *Durham Morning Herald,* recommended me along with two or three other boys to the Cardinals. We were playing on a mill team. They wrote us a letter and said we could come to Greensboro for fall of '37 practice. If they signed us up, they would pay our expenses. But if they didn't sign us, we'd pay our own way. Two of us boys signed. I signed as a second baseman for $75 a month.

"But in working out at second up there, Bob Rice, the old Pittsburgh traveling secretary, he was the manager, and Oliver French was the business manager, and they had several more scouts at this training camp, and I was hitting the ball good, and they moved me back to the outfield. They said, 'You're so clumsy, you're liable to break your neck at second base trying to make the double play.' They signed me up.

"One of the turning points in my career came the next year. They had a question mark beside my name. The Cardinals had five teams. Billy Southworth and Hap Bowie, my first manager at Martinsville, Virginia, asked me, 'Did anybody ever try to teach you how to run?' They said, 'If we can't improve your running, we're going to have to let you go.' That's why there was a question mark next to my name. Well, they took me in the outfield, and they said, 'We want you to practice running on your toes.' And for three days I practiced running on my toes, and I increased my speed by four steps to first base. And that's what I try to emphasize to a lot of young boys today: Anybody can get up on their toes and learn to run a little bit faster. It kept me in the game for twenty-seven years. And running turned out to be one of my greatest assets. Lou Miller, who wrote for the *World-Telegram* in New York, was a track man, and he kept statistics and times, and when I was forty years old, I was still going from home to first in 3.6 seconds, and to think they were going to give me my release in 1935 because I couldn't run! So just by getting on my toes, running kept me in the game.

"In 1937 I hit .382 for Columbus and won the batting title. I played right field, Lenny King played center, and Johnny Rizzo played left. The Cards owned that club. When Dizzy Dean was traded to the Cubs, Clarence Rowland offered the Cardinals $100,000 for me in the same deal, but Mr. Rickey kept me and sold Johnny Rizzo to Pittsburgh instead.

"When I joined the Cardinals, to me all of them really liked to play ball. They enjoyed it. The boys back in those days talked baseball among each other all the time. On the trains. In the hotel lobbies. You would see more ballplayers sitting around the hotel lobby, talking baseball, than you do today. When I played ball, regardless of what uniform I wore, I gave them 100 percent. I gave them 100 percent, and any ballplayer who gives 100 percent, the fans will have no problem with."

*   *   *

ENOS SLAUGHTER
(Drawing by Ron Stark)

Don Gutteridge, the third baseman in 1939, remembers the comings of Slaughter and Blades as positive ones. It wasn't too long, though, before the martinet manager outwore his welcome.

DON GUTTERIDGE: "We won 92 games that year and finished second to the Cincinnati Reds. Rickey had strengthened the team in '38 when he brought up Enos Slaughter to play right field. Enos was like the rest of us when we started. He was young, and all of us farm boys are alike. We don't push ourselves too much right quick. He didn't make a real impression right on, but he worked in and played very well after he got his feet on the ground a little bit. Some of us were getting better all the time, and another thing too, Blades had been in the farm system, and he knew all the players. He managed me at Columbus. Most of the Cardinals had played with him, and maybe they responded to him better. He was a different kind of guy than Frisch. Ray was intent and serious. Frisch was intent, but he had a humorous side. Ray Blades never did.

"We didn't win in '39 and '40 because of [Cincinatti's] Paul Derringer, who was one of them that Rickey had got rid of [in the trade for Leo Durocher]. He came back and beat us all the time. [Derringer was 25-7 in 1939 and 20-12 in 1940.] We resented that just a little bit. Paul was a big, strong overhand pitcher. He had a good, good fastball. I don't know why they ever traded him. It wasn't only us. He beat everybody else.

"The Reds had a good ballclub. They had a good defense: Frank McCormick at first, Lonnie Frey at second, Billy Myers at short, and Billy Werber at third. If you keep the other guy from scoring, you're liable to score yourself. I think defense is the key to it, and that's what they had.

"We fell behind early in 1940, and in June, Ray Blades was fired. The players got to where they didn't like Blades. They were criticizing him. I don't think Blades was a very good major league manager. He was great in the minor leagues but not in the big leagues, all the difference in the world. In the minor leagues, you take what players you get, and it's more teaching because your job as a minor league manager is to send kids to the big leagues. When you get to the big leagues, you ought to know how to play, and after that it's all strategy and managing men. And Blades was not popular at all with the press. He just didn't know how to do it. Period.

"Breadon saw we were dropping behind and we weren't drawing anybody, and he got a little nervous. He said, 'Hey, let's get someone else so we can draw some more people.' "

The manager the Cardinals hired in 1940 to replace Ray Blades (after coach Mike Gonzalez filled in for 6 games) was Billy Southworth, who had failed so badly as the Cardinal manager back in '29. What was unusual about this hire was that Sam Breadon made it without Branch Rickey's knowledge or approval. Rickey found out when he read about it in the papers. The day before Rickey had told reporters that the rumors about a change in managers was untrue. When the change was announced, Rickey felt embarrassed. It was the first major public rift between Breadon and Rickey.

Alienating Rickey further, as part of Southworth's deal to manage the

1940 CARDINALS INFIELD
(Courtesy Brace Photo)

Cardinals, Breadon agreed to two important Southworth demands: (1) No player would be added or subtracted from the roster without his approval; (2) No player could go to the front office to visit or talk over things without permission from the manager. Southworth, who learned the importance of political maneuvering, protected his flank from the start.

ROY STOCKTON: "Through the Rickey years, it had been the custom for players to call at the front office for chats, frequently behind closed doors, with Rickey. Managers and managerial methods were discussed by player and Rickey. Occasionally rumors reached the dugout that the manager of the day wasn't so sure of his job as he'd like to be. Occasionally managerial changes followed these dugout rumors."

According to Stockton, Sam Breadon gave Southworth permission to post his rule about going to Rickey behind his back on the wall of the Cardinals' clubhouse. Breadon knew that Rickey would be furious, but by 1940 Sam Breadon didn't feel as dependent on Rickey as he once had—and he didn't care.

In 1940 Branch Rickey added another of his minor league phenoms to the Cards roster: shortstop Marty Marion. The Cardinals were able to sign the lanky youngster only because the Washington Senators' owner, Calvin Griffith, petulantly released him.

Like so many Cardinals who came out of Rickey's farm system, Marion was a Southerner. Born in Richburg, South Carolina, in 1917, Marion was the son of a cotton farmer. When he was two, his family moved to Atlanta. "Back then, they all hated the Yankees, and I don't mean the baseball Yankees," said Marion. "Everybody who lived up North was a Yankee, and they were very opinionated against them."

Marion played high school and American League ball. When he graduated in 1935, his brother Johnny was playing for Chattanooga in the Washington organization. After he tried out with Chattanooga, Calvin Griffith paid him a $500 bonus to sign with Washington.

He reported to Chattanooga, but the team was on the road. When no one told him what to do, he drove home to Atlanta to see his girlfriend. When he returned several days later, he walked into Griffith's office. "Why did you leave town?" he was asked. "Nobody told me to stay" was Marion's reply.

"We're going to release you," said Griffith.

Marion returned to Atlanta.

There was a Cardinal tryout camp in Rome, Georgia, about seven miles from Atlanta. Marion's American Legion coach suggested that he and several of his teammates attend. Marion went and impressed everyone with his third-base play. He and teammate Johnny Echols were asked to take the train to St. Louis to try out for Branch Rickey.

The two worked out for several days, but initially didn't sign. Branch Rickey, in signing Marion, would acquire an All-Star infield and also one of the savviest and shrewdest employees. No player could fend off Rickey's salary manipulations, but Marion did better than most.

MARTY MARION: "I could tell that Rickey was really more interested in Johnny than he was in me. Johnny and myself made a deal that we weren't going to sign unless both of us signed. Pretty soon they got to dickering around—they didn't offer us any money at first—and we did not sign. We went back home to Atlanta.

"Then Frank Rickey came down that winter and started taking us out to dinner. He started negotiating with us, telling us what he could do for us. I finally came up with a deal, and Johnny agreed to it, that we would sign a four-year contract—this was back in 1935. Nobody heard of something like this—first year we were to make $125 a month wherever they sent us. Second year we made $175 a month. Third year we make $3,000 a year, and the fourth year $5,000 a year. And hell, we weren't that good a ballplayers. We were just high school kids, though, hey, I had experience. I had been fired already! Hadn't played a game yet, but gollee, I was an old experienced guy. I was seventeen.

"We wrote the deal down on a piece of paper. On an old envelope, I wrote down what we were going to get, what they promised to do.

"We signed, and I went to Huntington, West Virginia, our first year. They sent Johnny to the Piedmont League. I was the only one on the Huntington team who made anything of himself. I remember the first notice I ever got as a ballplayer. Dukes Rigsey was the sports editor of the *Huntington Times*. He said, 'That kid Martin Marion looks like a girl playing shortstop just learning how to wear her first pair of high-heel slippers.' And then, before the year was over, he said I was the best prospect in the whole league!

Bennie Borgmann was a Cardinal scout and minor league manager. He remembered the time Branch Rickey determined that Marty Marion would switch from third base to shortstop.

BENNIE BORGMANN: "I was managing in the Southern League, and Mr. Rickey came into the clubhouse and pointed his cigar. 'I want you to play that boy at shortstop tomorrow,' he said.

"There were two kids standing where he pointed. One of them was well-built and strong-looking. The other was skinny and frail. I thought Mr. Rickey meant the husky one.

"The next afternoon I had the husky one at short when Mr. Rickey came onto the field. 'I told you to play *that* fellow at shortstop,' he said. I had picked the wrong guy. Mr. Rickey wanted the tall skinny kid. That kid, of course, was Marty Marion."

The next year Marion was promoted to Triple A Rochester. He played there for three years, learning how to play shortstop under managers Ray Blades and Billy Southworth. When the Cardinals released Johnny Echols in spring training of his fourth season, Marion showed Rickey just what a sharpie he was.

MARTY MARION: "We were having spring training in St. Petersburg, Florida. We stayed at the old Detroit Hotel. Johnny came into my room and told me he needed to shack up in my room. 'Mr. Rickey fired me,' he said. 'He can't do that,' I replied.

"Mr. Rickey called Johnny and me over to his office. 'What do you mean I can't fire you? I can fire Medwick. I can fire Mize. I can fire great stars. I can fire anybody I want to.'

"I said, 'Yeah, Mr. Rickey, but you can't fire us. We have a contract.' I said, 'The piece of paper I wrote down promises us this.'

"Judge Landis called me and Johnny over to Clearwater. That's where he stayed, over in a big ol' wooden hotel [the Bellaire–Biltmore]. He was sitting on the front porch, leaning up against the bannister. I don't think he liked Mr. Rickey anyway. He said, 'What did Mr. Rickey promise you?' I told him. He asked me, 'Do you have any proof?' I told him, 'I wrote it down.' I said, 'He promised us we would have four-year contracts.' And I told him the details. He said, 'Thank you, boys.'

"So he called Mr. Rickey over there, and they had to resign Johnny at $5,000, and they sent him to Pocatello, Idaho! They sent him to the ends of the earth! He finally wound up with the Cardinals, pitching batting practice

MARTY MARION
(Drawing by Ron Stark)

for them in St. Louis. After that year, they released him, and he was gone, but he got his $5,000 dollars.''

In 1939 Rickey returned Marion to Rochester. Marion told Rickey, ''I can play shortstop a lot better than the guys you got.'' Rickey wasn't swayed. When he arrived in Rochester, he was greeted by the arrival of Sammy Baugh, who had begun his stellar football career with the Washington Redskins two years earlier. Baugh had played shortstop at Rochester in '38, and Rickey was giving him a shot at making the team.

MARTY MARION: ''Oh, he was good. But he finally decided he was a better football player. I'll never forget the quote he made one time. He said, 'I knew I was never going to make that baseball team with Marty Marion there.' ''

Marion came up to the Cardinals in the spring of 1940, replacing Jimmy Brown. Don Gutteridge, who played third that year, recalled Marion's ability.

DON GUTTERIDGE: ''Marty was very, very skilled. He was big and tall and very agile, and everybody said you can't be a tall shortstop. That was the old adage. But he could stretch out and reach and field more balls than anyone. He could cover a lot of ground. He was a fine, fine shortstop. I don't know why he isn't in the Hall of Fame. I always thought he should be.''

What Marion recalled most vividly his rookie season was how poorly the Cardinals drew and hard it was for players to find housing. The reputation of the Gashouse Gang apparently gave home owners an idea that renting to a ballplayer was not a smart idea. Marion also recalled the rivalry between the two Cardinal power hitters, Johnny Mize and Joe Medwick, and remembered the uncertainty of playing on the Cardinals, how Rickey, through his far-flung farm system, made the players feel insecure and eminently replaceable.

MARTY MARION: ''Baseball wasn't that popular at the time. We had a litle ballpark. Only 32,000 people could sit out there in Sportsman's Park. But boy, we sure didn't fill it up much either. What did we draw, 300,000 people? You had two teams in St. Louis, so that divided it up a little bit. We didn't draw, and as a result, hell, $5,000 was a big salary when you came to St. Louis. I remember when Whitey Kurowski came to St. Louis, his first year he made $2,800.
   ''St. Louis was a nice town, a friendly town. Not particularly glad to have ballplayers. See, baseball players didn't have a good reputation. A lot of people who rented houses thought baseball players were ruffians, so back in those days we had a hard time renting houses. They thought we were drunkards. Baseball had a bad reputation for a long time. Oh yes. They thought baseball players were rowdy. Matter of fact, my grandfather, a Methodist preacher, God, when he found out I was going to play baseball for a living, he liked to have gone crazy. He said, 'They're just a bunch of ruffians.' So baseball people were not highly regarded in the neighborhood like they are today.
   ''The kids loved you. The grown people didn't. I can remember on a lot of different occasions, the players would say, 'I'm having a tough time getting

housing, because of the past reputations of ballplayers.' We weren't the big heroes like they are today. Baseball has come a long way in that respect. And they make more money, too. That helps a little bit.

"I'll never forget my first year with the Cardinals when Johnny Mize and Joe Medwick were there. They were jealous of each other. Every time Mize would get a cheap hit, you'd be sitting next to Medwick, and he'd say, 'They never give me those cheap hits.' And the same thing with Mize. He'd be sitting there. 'They never give me cheap hits.' They were jealous of each other all the time! Good ol' Joe. You know, Joe had a mean streak in him. Even in batting practice, he used to see if he could hit the pitcher! We didn't have those screens in front. He'd hit the ball off the shins and laugh about it. He'd hit a line drive through the box and just laugh. Later in life, Joe mellowed. Everybody loved Joe then, after he came over to the Dodgers. He was practically a has-been then. He was on the way down. Joe got to be a real nice guy. He died too soon.

"It's funny what a nice guy you can be, hitting .250. And a son of a bitch when you're hitting .350! That's baseball.

"As for ol' John, all he wanted to do was rub his bats down. All John cared about was hitting. He had forty-two bats in the batrack, and we had two! And he could hit that ball! He was left-handed, but he had a lot of power to left-center. And he was from Georgia, too, like I was. But what I remember

SLAUGHTER, MOORE, MEDWICK
(Courtesy Brace Photo)

were those forty-two bats. Back in those days, you didn't get to order many bats. I'd go up to the secretary of the club and say, 'I need some bats.' Well, they'd issue you two. But they gave Mize all he wanted.

"They were jealous of each other all the time, so the Cardinals finally traded both of them. Medwick first. He went to the Dodgers. The Cardinals had so many players coming up, they could trade you and not miss you, and they needed the money all the time. Mr. Rickey believed in trading a player at the peak of his career, not when he was going down. That was one of his philosophies. As a result, we kept our bags packed all the time. You wouldn't believe the things they could do to us then. 'If you don't do good, we're going to send you to Rochester.' Or Columbus. Honestly, they had guys who could replace me like nothing. No problem at all. They always had somebody who could replace you. Don't think you're so good that you can't be replaced. You *can* be replaced. Don't forget it.' Baseball is never a one-man sport. I don't care how good Musial is, or Babe Ruth. They can't carry a team. You gotta have twenty-five players who want to win."

In 1941, after two straight pennants by the Cincinnati Reds, the Brooklyn Dodgers became the new kids on the block, led by former Cardinal bad boy Leo Durocher and his two young protégés, ex-Card farm product Pete Reiser and Harold "Pee Wee" Reese. Marion recalled the ribbing the Cards would give Durocher. He also remembered how fierce was their rivalry.

MARTY MARION: "In '41 the Dodgers were led by Pete Reiser, who was one of those players who got released by Landis in that deal where the Cards owned the whole Nebraska State League. I don't know what the Cardinals were doing wrong, but Landis freed everybody. We used to laugh about it. The Cardinals owned the whole league, so how could they lose?

"The Dodger manager was Leo. You remember the incident of Babe Ruth and his watch? [The story was that Durocher had stolen Ruth's watch when they were teammates on the Yankees in 1929.] Well, Walker Cooper had a watch, and every time we'd get in an argument, he'd just wave the watch at ol' Leo. 'Leo, look at the watch. Ruth's watch.' We were vicious. We were pretty bad. We didn't take anything laying down.

"We had a rivalry, but it wasn't anything special, except that we seemed to battle them every year for the pennant. That was the only reason it was intense. Leo had his pitchers throw at us a lot, but let me tell you something: Everybody threw at us. And we threw at them, too. That was no sacred cow. They'd say, 'You're going down,' and boy, any time we went down, the next guy up for the other team, he went down too, real quick. If you don't want to lose the respect of your players, you just don't let someone knock your player down without retaliating. Now it's against the law to do that. But they still do it.

"We had a tough ballclub. We had a rugged ballclub. We'd fight our way through anything."

But before they could win a pennant, they first would have to finish higher than Leo Durocher's Dodgers. That day would soon come.

CHAPTER 28

MAX

IN 1941 the Cardinals under Billy Southworth won 97 ball games, normally enough to win a pennant, except that Durocher's Dodgers that year won 100 games, edging them out. Leading the Cards pitching staff were Lon Warneke, Ernie White, Mort Cooper, and a wiry left-hander by the name of Hubert "Max" Lanier, a hardworking farmer's son who began playing ball in a Carolina cow pasture. Like so many Cardinal farmhands, Lanier resented the way he was being treated, but unlike most of the others, he was not the sort to suffer ill treatment in silence. After Cardinal executive Frank Rickey broke a promise to him, he quit and pitched semipro ball for a cotton mill.

Three years later Frank Rickey got Lanier to return by meeting his financial demands, and after pitching for Triple A Columbus, he came up to the Cards in '38. He got to play for Frisch, Blades, and Southworth. Lanier, who fought for a fair salary his entire career, remembered what it was like to play for the Cardinals before the war.

MAX LANIER: "We had a 120–acre farm, and I plowed corn and I picked cotton until my back killed me. We put the cotton in the sacks and took it to the gin, and they made bales out of it. When I was sixteen, I started pitching semipro ball, playing for Rock Hill, and one of the batters I faced was 'Shoeless Joe' Jackson, who was playing for Greensville, South Carolina. He was fifty years old, white-headed, and shucks, he could still hit those line drives, I'm telling you. He could hit just about anything you throwed up there. They had good ballclubs back then. Most all of them were professional ballplayers.

"I started pitching in high school when I was seventeen. We played Pilot High School, and I shut them out, 3–0. When the game was over, this scout, Frank Rickey, Mr. Rickey's brother, met me at the gate—I was going to take a shower, and he said, 'I'd like to talk to you. You get your shower, and I'll take you home.' I said, 'I don't know you.' He pulled out his card. He was a scout for the Cardinals. So I got in the car, and he took me back to the high school, and I took a shower and went home, and he sat down and talked to me and my parents. He said, 'How would you like to play baseball for the Cardinals?' I said, 'I love to play baseball.' He said, 'Will you sign a contract?'

"I finally signed. I was only seventeen. That contract looked as big as the room when they showed it to me. I didn't know the Cardinals had thirty farm teams. They didn't want you to know it until after they got me signed.

"He said, 'We'll send you to Greensboro.' That was only thirty miles from my home. He said, 'We'll pay you $100 a month. If you don't make the club, we'll release you.'

"I was there ten days, and they wanted to send me to Huntington, West Virginia, for $70 a month. And I quit. I said, 'You told me you'd release me if I didn't make the club.' And I played semipro ball for three years. I played over in Asheboro, North Carolina, working for a hosiery mill, and I won 16 straight ball games.

"Rickey came back, and he said, 'I've been seeing you pitch, and we'd like for you to go to Columbus in the American Association.'

"I said, 'The only way I'll go is if you pay me what I'm making here, pay me in spring training, and guarantee I'll still be on the ballclub. And I want it in writing.'

"He said, 'How do you know you can play there?' I said, 'Most of these clubs I'm playing against have fellows who have played pro ball before.'

"He said, 'I'll give you $350 a month, pay you in spring training, and you'll be on the ballclub.'

"In 1937 I went to spring training with Columbus. Frank Rickey came by to pick me up, and before we got to Deland, which was where Columbus trained, we had six other guys in the car. He'd stop in different places, Atlanta, picking up players, and when we got to Florida, we got to an orange orchard, and he asked us to go out and pick some oranges. That was stealing them. I said, 'I'm not going out. Somebody'll have a shotgun.' I didn't get out of the car.

"We won the pennant at Columbus, and I won 10 and lost 4. And I didn't get to start until the middle of the season. I won the third game against Newark, the New York club, in the Little World Series. The Cardinals called me up to the majors in 1938. They paid me $400 a month, $2,000 dollars. And I never got more than a $500-a-year raise from then on for five or six years. Branch Rickey would say, 'You had a good earned run average, but you didn't win many games.' The next year I won more games, and he'd say, 'Your earned run average was up.' That was him.

"In 1938 I spent a little time with Frankie Frisch. He was the toughest manager I ever played for, but he knew his baseball. He wouldn't be tough with guys like Pepper Martin and Dizzy Dean and those guys, because they'd talk back to him. Us kids, we were afraid to talk back. He had Enos Slaughter scared to death in right field. Enos couldn't pick up a ground ball. Frisch'd be in the clubhouse, and the game would be over, and he'd walk up and down the aisle and say, 'Ballplayers, my ass.'

"We were in Philadelphia, and I got beat, 2–1. I had a cousin who lived there, Johnny Lanier, and he wanted me to come out to dinner with him. And Clyde Shoun and I were in the shower a little too early. He came over and started getting on us. He asked me, 'Is your daddy a goddamn fireman?' I turned around and didn't answer him.

"One time when he was managing the Cubs, he was coaching third base as managers did back then. He looked over into our dugout and said, 'Hey, Lanier, why don't you go down to the bullpen?' I said, 'You had me down there all the time anyway.' Then I said, 'I'd rather be at Columbus than play for you.' But Pepper and them would talk back to him. It didn't bother them.

"We had some tough guys on that team. Joe Medwick was hard to get along with. I was in the bullpen in '38, and the first game I went in to relieve he was going out as I was going to the mound. He always stepped on third base going to left field, and we met, and he said, 'Come on, Lanier, get them out, or you'll go back to Columbus.' That was a heck of a thing to say. He was a great hitter, and he knew it, and he could do anything he wanted, just about.

"We also had Johnny Mize on our team. I liked John. He was a laid-back guy, didn't have a lot to say. He could hit, and he wasn't a bad fielder. The only thing Mize couldn't do was run. I remember he had thirty-six bats in the dugout at one time, and he didn't want nobody to use them. I think he had a bat for every pitcher.

"Terry Moore was one of the greatest guys in the world to play with, a great center fielder. I played with Willie Mays, and Terry was as great an outfielder as I ever played with. Terry was the captain of the ballclub. He'd get on you if you did something wrong. He always praised you when you did something good, too.

"Pepper Martin was still there. He was the most colorful ballplayer I ever saw. He did something funny every day, just about. Like he'd slide into second, and the fielder would have the ball, and he'd knock the ball out of his glove and would be called safe, and he'd laugh. I swear they couldn't tag him out. He'd stick his feet in the ground and go the other way quick as they run him, until they got so tired they had to drop over.

"I remember we had a coach, Buzzy Wares, who smoked cigars and cigarettes, and Pepper'd put powder in them, and they'd blow up. I never will forget: We were in New York. We lost a doubleheader, and we came into the clubhouse. Ray Blades was managing the club then. Pepper had one of his cigarettes. He started to light it, and Buzzy said, 'I'll get my own matches,' and he lit the cigar, and it blowed up right in his face. Even Blades had to laugh at that—after we lost a doubleheader. Pepper'd tie up the manager's uniform in knots, nail your spikes to the floor. He was a great guy. We had the Mudcat Band in '38. Bill McGee played the fiddle. He was the best musician of any of us. [Stanley] 'Frenchy' Bordagaray played the washboard, and Bob Weiland played the bass with a big jug, and I played the harmonica and a little bit of guitar, and Lon Warneke and Pepper took us on tour. We had a booking agent, went to Cincinnati. We just played country songs. We played on 'Ripley's Believe It or Not' program in New York. We played one song and got $750 for that—we had to split it up. We were staying at the Lincoln Hotel, and we had to slip out. We slipped away and went down the lower level and went out to Radio City to be on Ripley's program.

"I made as much money doing that as playing ball, about.

"When Frisch was fired, that didn't bother me too much. Ray Blades wasn't near as tough as Frisch, and he was the one in '39 that started me pitching, and that's where I really got started good. When they let him go, Billy Southworth took over.

"I remember we had a doubleheader against the Reds in '40, and Mort Cooper pitched the first game, and the next time I was supposed to pitch the first game. Well, this one time we were sitting in the Netherlands Plaza, having lunch, eating with Cooper, and Southworth came over and said, 'I'm going to flip a coin to see who's going to pitch the first game today.' I said, 'It's my turn,' but Cooper won the toss, and he beat Paul Derringer—we must have scored ten runs for him—and I had to pitch against Bucky Walters, and he beat me, 1–0. I didn't make any comments, but I sure thought a lot! The Reds had some tough ballplayers. They won the pennant in '39 and '40. They had Johnny Vander Meer, Walters and Derringer, Whitey Moore, Junior Thompson, a good infield. Frank McCormick, the first baseman, was one of the toughest hitters I've had to get out. You got to pitch him away, because he's strictly a pull hitter, but he hit one somewhere all the time. He must have hit .500 off of me.

"Ernie Lombardi was tough. Only thing he couldn't do was run. If he could have run, he would have hit .400 every year.

"In '39 Leo Durocher took over as manager of the Dodgers. He was the best bench jockey. He'd holler, and you could hear him from the dugout. 'Stick it in his ear,' he'd yell, and they'd throw at you. We had fights with the Dodgers three straight nights in '41.

"The ball was hit to the second baseman, Jimmy Brown, and he threw to get a double play, and Medwick, who was playing for the Dodgers, slid into him and

MAX LANIER
(Courtesy Brace Photo)

his spike was almost to his face. Marty [Marion] slapped at him, and here came all of them off the bench. Dixie Walker made a diving tackle at Whitey Kurowski, and before it was over, Jimmy Brown had Dixie down on the ground, and he got hurt somehow. He didn't play the next day. We had fights all the time.

"The Dodgers had a good team. Dolph Camilli could play first base. He was a big guy, and he could tag you the quickest on a ball thrown over from the pitcher. And he could hit the long ball, too. Reese was a good shortstop, Cookie Lavagetto was good at third, and Pete Coscarart and Billy Herman could play second.

"St. Louis was a great place before the war. They had some wonderful fans there. I know I made a lot of mistakes, but I never once heard a boo. Sportsman's Park wasn't in good condition because of the simple reason that the Browns played there, and they couldn't keep any grass on the infield. It was all sand and dirt. But they had some great fans there.

"There wasn't a lot to do in St. Louis. Only thing I'd do after a ball game, I'd go and have a root beer float and then go and get a half a watermelon over at Sal's watermelon place.

"When we had a day off, we were a close ballclub, and we'd go take the kids down to the picnic grounds on the Mississippi River. We really enjoyed it, had a lot of fun.

"After I married Betty, we had an apartment in the Fairgrounds Hotel, only three blocks from the ballpark. We'd invite the other players up there and have sandwiches after a ball game. I'd play the harmonica, and they'd get out the other instruments. But that's all forgotten. They don't do that anymore.

"In 1940 Marty Marion became our shortstop. Marty should be in the Hall of Fame. He's on a par with Rizzuto and Pee Wee Reese. He had long arms and he caught a lot of balls that would have gone for triples if he hadn't caught them. The only thing he couldn't do was run. He was a great guy, too. He never cursed. If we made an error, he'd say, 'Oh, chickenbutts.'

"In '41 we added Harry Walker, Whitey Kurowski, and Stan Musial. When Harry first came up, he pulled the ball against the right field fence, and then he got to be a slap hitter, and that's the reason he was hard to get out. I loved to pitch against guys who swung hard. Those guys who punch the ball, they were tougher to get out.

"Kurowski was the most underrated player we had. He had a throwing arm that didn't have any bone in it, just gristle. I don't know if he was born that way or not. He was a gutty player, I'll tell you. He was strictly a pull hitter because his right arm was shorter, and he got his bat around quick.

"Now '41 is when Musial came up. I know because he had just joined the club from Rochester, and he brought Lil, his wife, down to my favorite clothing store to buy him some clothes. I bought a brown pair of suede Stetson shoes, and I still got them. I save them, because it was the day Stan joined the ballclub.

"Stan is one of my favorites. He's the same guy he was when he came up. Stan and Lil used to come over after a ball game a lot of times. Lil is a wonderful person, too.

"In every league Stan played, he hit more. He kept getting better. When Stan first came up, he hit over .400. He had a funny stance, but it all unwound when he swung. I'll tell you, he was a great, great hitter."

CHAPTER 29

NUMBER 6

STAN Musial, who is as much a St. Louis monument as the Gateway Arch, for decades has been the embodiment of the Midwesterner: solid, undemonstrative, strong. A sculpture of him swinging a bat stands outside Busch Memorial Stadium, a tribute to his stature in a town that rarely goes out of its way to glorify or deify. And yet despite his fame, Musial is the kindest, most modest famous person I have ever met.

How good was he? In Stan's case, his numbers speak for themselves: He is fifth in games played with 3,026, behind only Pete Rose, Carl Yastrzemski, Hank Aaron, and Ty Cobb; he hit .331 over twenty-two years; is second only to Hank Aaron in total bases with 6,134, second behind Aaron in extra base hits with 1,377; is fourth in hits with 3,630, behind only Rose, Cobb, and Aaron. He is third all-time with 725 doubles, behind Tris Speaker and Rose; his 475 home runs is sixth in runs scored with 1,949; he was the Most Valuable Player in the National League in 1943 and 1948; he was elected to the Hall of Fame in 1969.

Musial and Ted Williams were head and shoulders above all other left fielders, and Musial was a far better outfielder than Ted. What was amazing about both Stan and Ted was that every year in which they accumulated enough at-bats to qualify for the batting and slugging championships, they finished among the top ten in the league in both categories. Both players led their league in batting average seven times. Each led his league in slugging percentage six times.

In his first four seasons in the big leagues—1942, 1943, 1944, and 1946 (in 1945 he was in the armed services)—Musial helped lead his team into the World Series. And though he would come into Brooklyn and regularly beat the Dodgers with his bat, his skill and demeanor were so appreciated in the enemy camp that it was from Brooklynites that he received the nickname "Stan the Man."

With his arrival coming around the same time as Branch Rickey's departure, Stan Musial came to symbolize the Cardinals through the 1940s and 1950s. During a pennantless dry spell that lasted from 1947 through 1964, Cardinal fans could always count on being entertained by the left-handed batter with the corkscrew swing. Like Ernie Banks of the Chicago Cubs, Al Kaline of the Detroit Tigers, Mickey Mantle of the New York Yankees, Willie Mays of the New York Giants, and Richie Ashburn of the Philadelphia Phillies, Musial was a fixture who could be counted on to be a hometown hero to children and adults alike.

Older fans can't remember when Stan wasn't out there playing. Despite the Cardinals' perpetual financial woes, which made trading or selling him very attractive, Stan managed to play his entire career in St. Louis. He has also stayed married to childhood sweetheart Lillian Labash for more than fifty years. And when he retired, he remained in St. Louis, where he continues to greet former fans with a smile and sign autographs for anyone who asks.

He has been a friend to Presidents from Harry S Truman to Bill Clinton. He even campaigned for John F. Kennedy. He has grown rich from successes in and out of baseball, and through it all he has maintained the demeanor of the quiet, hardworking country boy that he displayed when he first burst onto the big league landscape just as America was about to enter World War II.

Stan Musial was born and raised in Donora, Pennsylvania, downwind from the Pittsburgh blast furnaces, galvanizing mills, and zinc plants that for years blanketed the town with poisonous fumes. Stan's father, Lukasz, and his mother, Mary, were immigrants from Poland and Czechoslovakia. After three girls, son Stanislaus was born on November 21, 1920. That he became a famous baseball player was most unlikely because Stan's father, like most immigrants, thought baseball was a foolish pastime. Stan was a Pirates fan,

STAN MUSIAL
(Drawing by Ron Stark)

but he never went to a game for several reasons: (1) the price was too steep; (2) he had a summer job; or (3) he was playing ball.

A neighbor, Joe Barbao, once a semipro ballplayer, gave Stan a job as batboy on his team. It was on Barbao's team that Stan first began to show his talent. In high school, Stan once hit a 450–foot home run, but no college offered him a scholarship. He could have gone to the University of Pittsburgh on a basketball scholarship, but during the summer of 1937, he decided he wanted to try out with the Monessen team in the Class D Penn State League instead.

His father was adamantly against his decision. Lukasz didn't want his son working in the steel mills. He wanted Stan to go to college to have a better life than he had. During his senior year in high school, his hoop coach took him to meet H. C. Carlton, the Pitt basketball coach. Carlton, who was an able recruiter, told Stan's father that Stan would probably throw out his arm in the low minors and end up back in Donora, working in the mill. His father bought the argument, but Stan wasn't impressed. When his father wouldn't let the boy sign with the Cardinals, Stan began to cry.

"Lukasz," said his wife, "why did you come to America?"

"Because it's a free country, that's why."

"That's right. And in America a boy is free not to go to college too."

The Cardinals' Andrew French signed Musial to a Class D contract for $65 a month. When Judge Landis freed 91 Cardinal farmhands, Musial seriously wondered whether he had made a mistake signing with Rickey and St. Louis. He worked out with the Pittsburgh Pirates, but when Pirate manager Pie Traynor learned the boy had signed with the Cardinals, he knew he had no chance.

During Musial's first three years in the minor leagues, he gave little or no indication of what was to come. He began as a pitcher at Williamson, West Virginia, in 1938 and 1939. His manager, Harrison Wickel, recommended releasing him. "The only place he can win is Class D," said Wickel.

In 1940, pitching for Daytona Beach in the Florida State League, Musial finished the season 18-5 with a 2.63 ERA. Because the Cardinals were saving money wherever they could, the team had only seventeen players on the roster, and when he didn't pitch, he played the outfield. In a game in Orlando during the final week of the season, he fell on his left shoulder while he was trying to catch a fly ball. When he tried to pitch, his arm was sore.

Musial figured it would heal by the time he went to spring training in 1941. It didn't. Pitching for Albany, Georgia, Musial faced the major league Cardinals. In his second inning of work, Terry Moore and Johnny Mize each hit long home runs. In his next start against the Philadelphia Phillies, he allowed seven runs. A betting man might have predicted an end to Musial's career.

At the end of spring training, Rickey asked his minor league managers if anyone wanted to take Musial on his team. Only one raised his hand. Ollie Vanek, who liked the way he hit, volunteered. Knowing that Musial had a sore throwing arm, Vanek put him in right field because the fence in Springfield, Missouri, was short. Vanek batted him cleanup and taught him how to play the outfield. Almost twenty-one, Musial began to show some power, and in one game against Topeka hit three home runs.

He was hitting .379 with 26 homers and 94 RBIs when in late July he was ordered to report to Rochester. With Musial in the lineup, Rochester won sixteen of the last twenty games and made the playoffs.

In 1941, Enos Slaughter hurt himself, and the Cardinals needed another left-handed bat for the pennant drive. When the Rochester season came to an end in September, eleven Cardinal games remained, and Branch Rickey called up pitcher Hank Gornicki, infielder Whitey Kurowski, and outfielder Erv Dusak—three players with pedigrees—and the unknown youngster, Musial.

The other Cardinal players were dumbfounded when they learned who Musial was. On the train leaving St. Louis to go to Pittsburgh, he was sitting with Terry Moore in a Pullman car. Musial mentioned the home runs that Moore and Mize had hit off him in spring training. Moore called over to Mize, "Hey, John, you won't believe this. Musial is the left-hander who threw us those long home run balls this spring."

Manager Billy Southworth loved the way the young Musial played the game. In a doubleheader against the Cubs, Musial was 6 for 10. In the first game, he scored the winning run on a dash from third when catcher Clyde McCullough failed to cover home on a topper. Said Southworth to one of his coaches, "That kid was born to play baseball."

Nineteen forty-one was the year that Joe DiMaggio hit in 56 straight games and Ted Williams hit .406. Stan Musial's improbable one-year journey from the depths of the minor leagues to the starting lineup of the St. Louis Cardinals may have been just as amazing.

Stan Musial and I sat on the veranda of the Vinoy Hotel in St. Petersburg, Florida, looking out over the marina and the bay, as Stan discussed his twenty-two seasons in the big leagues with the Cardinals. For more than an hour and a half, he never uttered a single harsh word, and you had the sense that those words were not part of his vocabulary. Everything he had to say seemed pure gold.

STAN MUSIAL: "Any time you have the best arm in high school, they always want to make you a pitcher. I was a wild left-hander. I walked a lot of batters, didn't have a lot of confidence pitching. But I could always hit. Why the Cardinals didn't sign me as a hitter I don't know. I saw some of my high school records—I hit .450, hit home runs with the bases loaded, triples. I was a fantastic high school hitter. Of course, I did very well in pitching too, but why someone didn't see me as a hitter? I was surprised.

"After I signed with the Cardinals, I didn't hear from them for a while. I wondered if they had forgotten about me.

"That spring Judge Landis released 91 Cardinal minor league players. I honestly hoped I had been among them. If the Cardinals really were as bad as Judge Landis said they were, I didn't want to be part of their organization. I had a friend in Donora, Irv Weiss, who knew Pie Traynor. He took me to Pittsburgh, and I worked out with the Pirates a couple of days. I was pitching batting practice to the Pirates when I got a notice to report to their [the Cardinals'] farm club at Williamston, West Virginia. Well, I had to tell Traynor. He said, 'Did your dad sign your contract?' I said, 'Yeah.' He said, 'That sort of makes it official, but if you're ever out of a job, come back and see us.' Pie Traynor liked me.

"I played two seasons at Williamston, and in 1940 played for Dickie Kerr at Daytona Beach. Dickie and I talked a lot about baseball. We got to be good friends. [Musial bought Kerr and his wife a home after he became a Cardinal star.]

"I hurt my arm the last week of the '40 season at Daytona. I was playing the outfield, and I dove for the ball and landed on my shoulder. I tried to pitch one game after that, and my arm was sore. In those days, they didn't send you to a doctor for examination. I figured my arm would get better over the winter.

"The next spring I was assigned to Columbus, Ohio, and we trained at Hollywood, Florida, and when I started warming up, my arm was still sore. What happened, the pitchers came down early. We had an exhibition game between us pitchers. Burt Shotton was our manager. I hit a long drive, there wasn't a fence out there, and Rickey was there, and they told me he stepped off how far the ball was hit, and so he said from then on I was going to be an outfielder. Rickey sent me to Ollie Vanek in Springfield, Missouri. Class C. That was '41.

"I went from Class C to the majors in one year. That was amazing to be able to do that. I played 87 games in two and a half months at Springfield, and I was hitting .400, driving in a lot of runs, and in midseason they sent me to Rochester, which was Triple A. I was there a couple months, and I led the league in hitting, hitting well over .300, and at the end of the season I came home [to Donora, Pennsylvania]. I got a wire from the Cardinals saying to report to St. Louis. This was mid-September. So I went to St. Louis, and

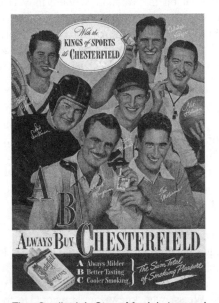

The Cardinals' Stan Musial (second row center) was truly one of the "Kings of Sport" in the 1940s. That's the Boston Red Sox' Ted Williams front right.

we were playing a doubleheader against the Boston Braves. In the second game, Southworth put me in the lineup. Well, I got a couple hits, and we won the game, and I hit over .400 the last couple weeks of the season.''

In twelve games, Musial lashed out 20 hits and batted .426. It was not enough, however, to wrest the pennant from the Dodgers. Johnny Mize, a clubhouse lawyer who was not a fan of Branch Rickey, fumed that Rickey should have brought up Musial sooner. Said Mize, who missed the last two weeks with a bad leg, "We might have gone ahead and won the pennant."

Pearl Harbor was bombed on December 7, 1941, but none of the Cardinal players with the exception of pitcher Johnny Grodzicki were called into the American military during the 1942 season.

In the spring of 1942, Branch Rickey summoned Stan to his office. His contract called for him to make $400 a month. Said Rickey, "I'm tearing it up, boy. We're going to pay you $700 a month." His new wife had not joined him for spring training because his pay was so low. With the extra money, she was able to join him in St. Louis.

CHAPTER 30

THE DROUGHT ENDS

MARTY Marion, the Cards' regular shortstop, didn't think 1942 was going to be anything special when he arrived in St. Petersburg, Florida, for spring training. The Japanese had attacked Pearl Harbor the previous December, signaling the entry of the United States into the war, but at least for the first year, everything remained status quo.

MARTY MARION: "When I heard the news about Pearl Harbor, I was sitting in my old Chevrolet in the driveway of the front yard of our farm in South Carolina. We were getting ready to go to Anderson, South Carolina, on a shopping trip. It was wintertime. When I heard it on the car radio, I thought, 'Uh-oh, everything is going to break loose.'

"But when spring training came, nothing had changed. We went back to St. Petersburg as usual. I didn't have any idea that 1942 would be any different than any other year. Rickey added some rookies: Stan, Harry Walker, Whitey Kurowski. Stan and Whitey were regulars, and Harry was behind Terry Moore. But I didn't think about whether we'd have a good team or not. Players just think about having to play a game every day. It isn't until you get into the middle of the season that you begin to think about it."

One of the decisions manager Billy Southworth had to make was whether to play the rookie Stan Musial full-time. Southworth never hesitated. Beginning in '42, he started an outfield of Musial in left, Terry Moore in center, and Enos Slaughter in right. The three would patrol the Cardinals outfield for the next half decade.

STAN MUSIAL: "I owe a lot to Southworth. He gave me a lot of confidence by playing me often. He let me play, put me in the lineup. I'll tell you what happened: After I came to St. Petersburg in '42 for spring training, everybody expected me to keep like I did in '41. Well, I never did hit well in Florida because in those days we didn't have a hitting background. They had palm trees waving, and with my stance I couldn't pick up the ball very well. So I didn't have a very good spring in Florida.

"When we got to St. Louis, we played the Browns in an exhibition series. The first game Billy said to me, 'You're playing in left field.' I'm glad Billy didn't judge me by my hitting down in Florida. And with a better background, I got a couple of hits that day, and I started hitting again. So I'd have to say that Southworth gave me a lot of confidence."

When the 1942 season began, it appeared that the Dodgers, led by former Cardinals Leo Durocher and freed farmhand Pete Reiser, would run away with the pennant. But during a doubleheader with Brooklyn in St. Louis in July, Enos Slaughter hit a long fly toward center field, and Reiser, who played with no regard for his safety, smashed his head against the Sportsman's Park concrete wall, knocking himself unconscious. Reiser, who was hitting .350, would never be the same again.

STAN MUSIAL: "I remember the day Pete Reiser ran into the wall. He ran into a lot of walls, but this time he hit his head against the right-center field wall and he really got hurt. It was a pretty serious injury.

"The Dodgers had had a big lead. We got started slowly in '42, and we were about thirteen games out in early August. But without Reiser, the Dodgers started to slide, and our club started to jell. We had a young veteran club. We had good speed, good defense, good pitching, and we won forty-two of our last fifty-two games. We went to Brooklyn and beat them two out of three, and went to Philadelphia and kept on winning.

"That '42 club was a great club because Billy Southworth handled the pitchers so well. And everybody got along. Whitey Kurowski, myself, Harry Walker, and Johnny Beazley were rookies, and Terry Moore and Enos Slaughter were veterans, along with Marty Marion, Jimmy Brown, and Walker Cooper. As I said, it was a young veteran club, and we jelled together. We spent a lot of time together. We went out to have dinner and talk baseball.

"I spent a lot of time with Terry Moore, Slaughter, and Marty Marion. We used to drive together to the ballpark every day. And I was close to Whitey. We didn't have many oddballs on that Cardinal team. Walker Cooper liked to play practical jokes. We'd go to New York, and someone would fall asleep in the lobby, and he'd give him a hotfoot, put a match in his foot and light it. In those days, we wore belts, and Walker used to put a lit cigarette in there. He used to carry on. Other than him, we were a pretty serious group.

We had a good spirit among us. We had a spirit where after a while we didn't think we could be beat by anybody. We were tough. We were a tough club.''

In mid-August, the Dodgers had a lead of eight and a half games, but when Reiser began to feel the effects of his concussion, he stopped hitting, and the Dodgers began to slip. But after the Cardinals took the lead, the Dodgers rarely lost.

MARTY MARION: "We were hot. We knew we had a chance to win, and the newspapermen kept building it up about how well we were playing. Anyway, the players don't think about things like that. They're anxious to get to the ballpark. When you're going good, you're glad to get there. When you're going bad, you don't want to go.''

On September 11, the Cardinals, two games behind, traveled to Brooklyn for the final two games with the first-place Dodgers. Mort Cooper, seeking his 20th win, defeated Whitlow Wyatt, 3–0. Southworth told Max Lanier he wanted to hold him for another day and pitch Beazley instead. Max talked him out of it.

MAX LANIER: "I'd had a little trouble with my elbow. Southworth came to me and said, 'I believe I will pitch Beazley today and give you another day's rest.' I said, 'No, I've beaten them four times. I can beat them once more.' And he let me pitch, and I beat Max Macon, 2–1. Whitey Kurowski hit a two-run home run.

"The last batter of the game was Billy Herman. I had two strikes on him, and I know he was looking for a curveball. I pitched him a fastball right on the outside corner and struck him out. I never will forget it. He was a good hit-and-run man, hard to strike out.

"We tied the Dodgers.''

Both teams had 94-46 records. A confident Sam Breadon ordered World Series tickets to be printed. The team left for Philadelphia. When the players detrained, pitcher Johnny Beazley got into a fight with one of the redcaps. When it was over, he was bleeding profusely from his right hand.

MARTY MARION: "We got a scare in Philadelphia. We were at the Broad Street Station, waiting for the train, when Johnny Beazley got in a fight with a porter, who pulled a knife and cut his right thumb. I didn't see the fight. I heard about it. The porter wanted to carry his bag, and Beazley didn't want him to. Beazley was that sort of guy. [Translation: He didn't like blacks. All the porters were black.] He was a hard-nosed pitcher. He would knock you down. He had good stuff, and he was a cocky guy. Very cocky. Oh yeah. He thought he was the best.''

MAX LANIER: "Johnny Beazley won 21 games in '42. He had great stuff and good control, but he did have a temper. Johnny never had a dad. His mother was always up there with him. Beazley was nice to all the players, got along with them good. But he was more a loner. He had an awful temper when things went wrong out there, which a lot of guys do.

"I never will forget, Eddie Dyer was the manager, and I liked him as good as any manager I ever played for. One year a couple weeks before the season started, he said, 'Max, I want you to be Opening Day pitcher.' I said, 'Great.' Later he came to me and said, 'Would you mind if I give it to Beazley? He's down in the mouth.' I said, 'Sure. I've pitched Opening Day before. I doesn't bother me a bit.' He pitched and got knocked out and came in and raised holy hell. I felt sorry for Eddie Dyer. He never opened his mouth. I pitched the next day and pitched a two-hit shutout. I struck out Ralph Kiner three times and Bob Elliott twice.''

With two weeks to go in the '42 season, the Cardinals led the Dodgers by a scant game. A short losing streak could have defeated them, but the Cardinals won nine of their last ten games. At the same time the Dodgers finished ten and two. The Dodgers could not catch up as the Cardinals finished 106-48, the best record in the National League since the 1909 Pittsburgh Pirates. To win, the Cards had won forty-three of their final fifty-two games.

MARTY MARION: "We were not a home-run-hitting team, and we didn't steal a lot of bases. We weren't a running team, although we were fast. We stole very few bases. We didn't even try to steal. We were a first-and-third team. We got a walk or a single, and if we got another hit, we took the extra base. We were aggressive on the base paths. And we had speed in the field for defense.

"If you look at our players, they weren't really aggressive in a certain way. Stan wasn't aggressive. Terry wasn't. Neither was Whitey Kurowski. I wasn't. Jimmy Brown wasn't. Johnny Hopp wasn't. Enos was aggressive in a way, but his aggression was mostly running somewhere. He had that false hustle. We always gave him hell. We didn't let him get by with anything. He always said the reason he ran to first was that in the minor leagues his manager told him he wasn't running, and Enos said, 'I've run ever since.' That's his story. But Enos wasn't aggressive. He wasn't the type of player who'd slide hard into you.

"Terry Moore was a lovable person. He was so good that Harry Walker named his son after him. And yet Terry taught us that if you get in a fight, make sure you get in the first punch. He said when he first came to the big leagues, he got in a fight with a guy, and while he was asking a question, the guy popped him. So he told me, 'Pop first and ask questions later.'

"Terry was a well-respected person on the Cardinals team. Nobody ever wrote a lot about him. He was just a good steady ballplayer, and one of the greatest center fielders you'd ever want to see play. Terry liked everybody. He was number one with reporters. Everybody loved Terry. But he was a player who was in the background. He meant a lot to the club, a lot to other players. He never got a lot of publicity like Enos got, or Medwick, but he was good. No question about it.

"Harry didn't get much of a shot here in St Louis, playing back of Terry. Harry didn't get famous until he got over to Philadelphia, where he led the league in hitting. He was noted for those loopers. We used to call them 'Banjo hitters.' But Harry was a good ball-player, a lot better than everybody gives him credit for.

"Whitey was another one. Whitey was a good hitter. He was one of our power hitters, though I'll bet he didn't hit 20 homers a year. At third base he used to say, 'Now Marty, back me up.' I was always catching balls he missed over shortstop. 'Back me up, Marty.'

"The tough reputation of the Cardinals was built on our catcher Walker Cooper saying, 'Knock him down. I'll get him before you get him.'

TERRY MOORE
(Courtesy Brace Photo)

That was our reputation. I'll never forget the time Mickey Owen was catching for the Dodgers, and Walker stepped on the Dodgers' first baseman, and Mickey was coming down the first base line, backing up. Well, after Cooper stepped on the first baseman, Mickey ran and jumped on top of Cooper's back and gave him a bear hug, and Cooper flipped him off real quick, and when Mickey came through the dugout the next day, he said, 'I won't do that again.'

"We didn't play dirty, but if you wanted to play dirty, we could play dirty. I guarantee you, nobody didn't do anything that we didn't get back at you. That was just the way we were taught to play baseball.

"It's kind of funny trying to explain what makes a winning team: twenty-five guys with the will to win and the ability to do so, plus a lot of things bouncing your way.

"I played on a lot of good ballclubs, but the '42 team was the best I ever played on. We had everything. We had good pitching, good defense, and good hitting, even though we were not particularly a running team or a power team."

Stan Musial, who caught a fly ball hit to left field by Clyde McCullough to end the clinching game, remembered the excitement of catching the Dodgers and winning the Cards' first pennant since 1934.

STAN MUSIAL: "On the final day of the season, we played a doubleheader against the Chicago Cubs at Sportsman's Park. We needed to win one of the games to win the pennant. We won the opener easily, 6–2. I caught the last out, and it was a great thrill. We had worked so hard, came from eight and a half games back. We had to win every game at the end, and we did. That club in '42 was one of the best Cardinal teams ever. We had great pitching with Johnny Beazley, Harry Gumbert, Murry Dickson, Lon Warneke, Ernie

White, Mort Cooper, Max Lanier, Howie Pollet, and Howie Krist. We had good balance in our lineup with Kurowski and Cooper from the right side and Slaughter and I from the left.''

After winning the National League pennant in '42, the Cardinals had the task of facing the seemingly unbeatable New York Yankees, led by Joe DiMaggio, Bill Dickey, Phil Rizzuto, Red Rolfe, Frank Crosetti, and Joe Gordon. The Yankees, winners of 103 games, had been victors in thirty-two of thirty-six World Series games in eight straight World Series triumphs since 1927. The Cardinal players, however, were not impressed.

STAN MUSIAL: ''In '42 we played the New York Yankees during spring training and beat them three out of five games. We played against them all the time in the spring, and that was a plus. We knew they were a tough club, a good club, but the Yankees didn't faze us.

''In the first game [of the World Series], we faced Red Ruffing. We didn't do much against him, and the Yankees took a big lead, but we scored four runs in the ninth. I came up with the bases loaded and two outs, and I hit a hard ground ball to first base, but that ended the game. [The Cards lost, 7–4.]

''The next day Johnny Beazley pitched, and it was 3–3 in the eighth. I drove in the winning run, and Slaughter made a terrific play throwing out a runner at third, so we won that game.

''We went to New York, and we beat them three in a row with good pitching. Ernie White, Mort Cooper, Harry Gumbert, Howie Pollet, and Max Lanier, and then Beazley. We were tough.''

MAX LANIER: ''Beating them four in a row after them beating us the first game, we didn't think it was possible. But once we got started, we didn't stop. Terry Moore made some great catches. Slaughter caught a ball that [Charlie] Keller hit that would have been a home run. Marty Marion and Kurowski made great plays. It was a team effort.

''Mort started that first game and was knocked out, and I came in in relief in the ninth and gave up two runs. I was nervous, to be honest with you. Rizzuto bunted the ball down the third base line, and I had him throwed out, but I made a quick throw, and I threw it over the first baseman's head. I had pitched against Rizzuto when he was at Kansas City and I was at Columbus, and I got him out pretty good then. He was a great bunter. You didn't know whether he was going to bunt or swing until the last second.

''We rallied in the ninth and had the tying run at the plate. Musial was up, and he grounded out. They beat us, but from then on it was a different story, I'll tell you. Stan drove in the winning run to tie the Series, and Slaughter saved the game when he threw out Tuck Stainback going from first to third. Slaughter had a great arm. The ball was hit to right field on the ground, and he threw him out by ten feet.

''We traveled to New York for Game 3.''

MARTY MARION: ''It was a thrill to play in Yankee Stadium. Let me tell you something about playing in Yankee Stadium. Of all the places to play in baseball, that's it. 'The House That Ruth Built.' It was just awesome. It was just a thrill to be in Yankee Stadium. It felt like you were in a mammoth arena, and it made you feel that you wanted to do better than you really could. Playing in Yankee Stadium made you feel important. Sportsman's Park was a little downtown crackerbox, but a great place to play. But there was never a place that awed you like walking into Yankee Stadium.''

MAX LANIER: "I had never been to Yankee Stadium before. Seventy thousand people. It impressed me, all right. Ernie White beat Spud Chandler. Ernie had great stuff. Later on he had trouble with his arm in back of his shoulder, but that day he was right on the button, shutting out the Yankees, 2–0. Terry Moore made some great catches in that outfield. Against Joe DiMaggio, he caught one almost against the 400-and-something-foot sign with his back to the grandstand.

"And then Joe Gordon hit one to left-center, and him and Musial crossed, and I didn't know who caught that ball, but Terry had it. Then Enos made a catch to rob Charlie Keller.

"In Game 4, Southworth decided he wanted to use me in relief, and he started Mort Cooper. I don't know why, but Mort had trouble in big games: the World Series, All-Star Games. He'd lose stuff on his fastball and didn't make the good pitches he made during the season. The score was 6–6 going into the seventh, and we scored two runs, and Southworth brought me in.

"I just happened to have a good curveball that day and good control. I don't think they got a hit off me in the three innings. I struck out Keller on a 3-2 pitch to end it. I threw him a curveball, and he took it for strike three.

The closest they came to getting a hit off me was a pitch I threw to Joe DiMaggio. There ain't no way you as a left-hander can pitch to him. He hit left-handers good, but I got him out that day. I threw him a curveball low and inside, and he hit the ball pretty good, but Marty Marion made a good save of it.

"In the final game, Beazley held the Yankees down. Red Ruffing was pitching, and he threw Whitey Kurowski a change of pace, and he hit it into the left field bleachers. He hit it good, too. I told Kurowski a dozen times, 'You won the pennant for us.' He'd say, 'Everybody won the pennant.'

"In the ninth inning the Yankees had runners on first and second with nobody out, and Walker picked Joe Gordon off second base. Walker had a good arm, and he wasn't paying attention to what the catcher was doing. And Gordon didn't have too good a Series with the bat. We'd pitch him up and inside.''

MARTY MARION: "There was a man on first and second. It was the ninth inning, and the Yankees could do anything. They had a hell of a ballclub. It was a bunting situation. Gerry Priddy was the hitter. Joe Gordon was at second base.

"We had no play on. It was one of those things, when he breaks too far, I break in back of him, and Walker Cooper just threw the ball down to me, and ol' Joe was out. It was a perfect pickoff play. But it wasn't a planned

play. It just happens every day if a guy gets too far off second base. He tried
to scramble back to second base, but he just dusted himself off, walked off,
didn't say a word.''

The pickoff of Joe Gordon put an end to the Yankee threat, and Beazley
completed his 4–2 victory, giving the Cardinals the Series. It was considered
the biggest upset since the "Miracle Braves" won in 1914 over the powerful
Philadelphia A's.

After the final game, Whitey Kurowski lifted Judge Landis off the floor,
tore National League president Ford Frick's hat to shreds, and sang the
Cardinals' anthem, "Pass the Biscuits, Miranda."

Most important, each Cardinal took home $6,193 for winning the Series.
For many, it doubled their yearly salary.

MARTY MARION: "I was walking around the clubhouse the last day of the
season, telling everyone I had read in the paper that if we won the Series, our
share would be $6,193. I was going around bragging about winning the money
when Terry Moore got me. He was our captain. He was kind of the leader on
the club. We respected him. He said, 'Marty, don't talk like that. That's a
jinx.' I said, 'The hell it is.' He said, 'Don't talk like that.'

"We weren't a club to jump up and down and scream and pour champagne
on you. We laugh and say the only thing we had was a Coke. We didn't
celebrate. Everyone shook hands, took off the uniform, and went home.

"We were not an emotional team at all. I can never remember shaking
somebody's hand coming into the dugout. So winning that last game against
the Yankees was like another game. When you win, everybody's kind of
happy. And we won $6,193. And it was all ours. That was more than what
we made all year. Yeah.

"I came up making $5,000. I was the highest-paid rookie they ever had.
And I made $5,000 the next year, and I wasn't that great, and it went up
$1,000 every year. You didn't get a jump, not with Mr. Rickey and Mr.
Breadon. They didn't have the money to pay you.

"Can you imagine drawing 300,000, no television rights, concessions were
five cents a Coke and ten-cent hot dogs. There wasn't much money around.
What was admission, a dollar? Where did the money come from? Back in
those days, they didn't have any money."

MAX LANIER: "The money I was making wasn't much. Winning the Series
meant a little bit more money in the bank. It gives you a great thrill, and you
feel good about the ballclub. There's hardly nothing like it. Everybody was so
tickled we won, there was nothing else to talk about but the ball games.

"Sam Breadon, the owner of the team, was about as stingy as they come.
I never will forget, when we beat the Yankees, we got on the train for the
ride home, and Breadon's wife bought us one round of drinks. That was
the thanks."

CHAPTER 31

RICKEY DEPARTS

THROUGH 1942, Rickey's farm system continued to supply the Cardinals with great players. Frank Crespi, for instance, was called the "best-looking second baseman since Rogers Hornsby" by *Post-Dispatch* writer Roy Stockton. Catcher Walker Cooper, moreover, looked to be a potential star in the spring of '42. Marty Marion was an All-Star. Ernie White and Howie Krist were the best of a fine crop of young pitchers. And with the addition of Musial, Harry Walker, Erv Dusak, and infielder Whitey Kurowski, the Cardinals had the finest collection of young players west of Brooklyn.

In addition, Rickey made hundreds of thousands of dollars for Cardinal owner Sam Breadon. Farmhands who were stuck behind more talented vets or who didn't meet Rickey's high standards were dealt to other teams for substantial amounts of money. He also continued his policy of trading away vets just before they started to fade, adding to Breadon's coffers.

After the 1939 season, he sold Mickey Owen to the Dodgers.

Then in the summer of 1940, Rickey sold $385,000 worth of players. He traded Joe Medwick and Curt Davis for cash and players. Brooklyn paid $15,000 more for infielder Herman Franks. Herb Bremer was sold to New Orleans for $3,500. Pitcher Bob Weiland went to Los Angeles for $7,500. The Giants paid $70,000 for Bob Bowman and Joe Orengo and paid Rickey $20,000 more in a deal for pitcher Harry Gumbert. The Red Sox paid $17,500 for Rochester pitcher Mike Ryba. Stu Martin went to the Pirates for $15,000. Forest "Tot" Pressnell was purchased by Brooklyn for $10,000, and Ernie Koy cost the Reds another $20,000.

As a result, Rickey's salary in 1942, including 10 percent of the Cardinals' net profits, was reported to be close to $90,000. And by putting a World Series trophy on Sam Breadon's mantel in 1942, Rickey silenced all those critics who said his team couldn't win it all.

Nonetheless, Rickey knew for some time that there was little likelihood that his contract would be renewed when it expired at the end of the 1942 season. The schism between Breadon and Rickey had become irreparable when Landis freed the 91 Cardinal farmhands in 1938.

ROY STOCKTON: "Breadon, a stickler for the rules, sensed that something was wrong in the Cedar Rapids affiliation and suggested that it be cleaned up. Rickey looked at it from a lawyer's viewpoint, insisting that the setup was within the law.

"[When Landis ruled against the Cardinals,] Breadon took that decision to heart as a reflection on his personal integrity."

*   *   *

Once Breadon no longer considered Rickey indispensable to the running of his ballclub, he began to second-guess other transactions. Breadon, for example, was angered when Rickey sold Joe Medwick to Brooklyn.

But Rickey had reason to be angry with Breadon as well. When Breadon announced a 10 percent wage reduction for all Cardinal employees not under contract, Rickey told him, "Sam, I will dig ditches at a dollar a day rather than work for you one minute beyond the expiration of my contract."

The final issue to come between him was Breadon's insistence that Cardinal radio broadcasts be sponsored by a beer company. Rickey, ever the teetotaler, was appalled. When Breadon did it anyway, Rickey made plans to leave.

Rickey thought of quitting baseball altogether. He pondered running for either the U.S. Senate or governor of Missouri, but he was sixty years old and declined. A political man, the Republican Rickey spoke out against Franklin Roosevelt and his packing of the Supreme Court, but he angered the GOP when he stumped against the isolationism that his fellow Republicans preferred to war. Rickey considered joining the Mutual Benefit Life Insurance Company as vice president for public relations, but the president of the company rejected that notion.

On October 19, 1942, Branch Rickey resigned from the St. Louis Cardinals. His resignation surprised a lot of people. The players, however, were not sad to see him go.

MAX LANIER: "Branch tried to sign you for as little as possible. He met me in North Carolina once and took me for a little ride. Despite everything I had done, he said, 'Your earned run average wasn't like it was last year.' And the year before he said, 'Well, you didn't win enough ball games.' He said, 'We just can't pay you any more than what you're making.' I didn't make $10,000 until the last year. I made $7,000 or $8,000 at the most.

"I never will forget, we were in Pittsburgh. We were staying at the Schenley Hotel, and Rickey was there. He'd go on the road with you. He called up Slaughter and myself, wanted us to have breakfast with him up in his room. We went up. Rickey didn't have money to tip the bell captain. Slaughter and I had to pay for it. He never took any money with him.

"It was the first of the year, the weather was cold, and he said, 'I hope it gets hotter because you and Slaughter ain't been worth a shit so far.' He was tough, I'll tell you. Then after we signed the contract, he'd say, 'Oh, you're going to have a great year.' He wouldn't go to Sunday ball games. Instead, he stayed home, trying to figure out how he could get his players to play for less money."

MARTY MARION: "When I was playing, Mr. Rickey was kind of a phantom. Not many ballplayers talked to Mr. Rickey in his presence. The only time he got involved with you was during contract time, and he would send you letters. Mr. Rickey didn't go around looking for conversation with ballplayers.

"I was kind of glad when Mr. Rickey left. The players always talked bad about him behind his back. He was a demon. He was the law. We respected him, don't forget that, but we didn't like him. He was keeping us from getting the money. And he was kind of a villain in a way: He was the guy who'd send you back to Rochester.

"I figured I could get more money from Mr. Breadon, which I did. But times were changing, getting better then.

"Mr. Breadon was a businessman. He loved baseball, and he always liked me. I used to give him trouble, contract-wise. But unlike Rickey, he didn't send you two pages of silver-toned oratory telling you how lousy you were and give you a cut for not being able to hit 25 home runs rather than hit .300. Mr. Breadon would just send you a contract, and he'd always say, 'Dear Marty, Please sign the contract and return it. See you in spring training.'' That was about it. I'd always write him back, 'Dear Mr. Breadon. I'm not signing for that.'

"I'd go up in his office and talk to him, and he was always drinking milk and eating crackers. He had a very bad stomach. They thought milk was good for your stomach back in those days. He was always nervous, a very nervous man. During my time with the Cardinals, Mr. Breadon took advice from Mr. Rickey. We were all surprised when Rickey left. I don't know the circumstances why he left. Did Mr. Breadon fire him, or what?''

BOB BROEG: "There was obviously more than one reason Breadon let Rickey go. Breadon knew areas of Rickey's hypocrisy and double-talk. Enos Slaughter told me that Breadon said to him, 'How does it feel to be in five figures?' Enos said, 'What do you mean, Mr. Breadon?' 'To make $10,000.' 'I'm not making $10,000.' Enos said, 'He kind of looked at me real funny, and soon thereafter I got my $10,000.' Obviously Rickey and Breadon had agreed to pay Enos $10,000, and Rickey had chiseled it down to $9,000. The players would ask for a raise and be lucky they didn't get cut through his eloquence.

"Rickey was not as honorable a man as Breadon was. Breadon could not lie to the press. As an illustration, it was November of '45, and I was on the *Post-Dispatch,* a young guy out of the service. I suspect Taylor Spink of *The Sporting News* must have had a tip, and he had me call Breadon to ask whether Billy Southworth was going to the Braves. Breadon said, 'No comment.' I hung up and thought, 'It's true.' So Breadon was offended by Rickey's getting caught covering up ballplayers in the minors. And also the attendance was poor. In 1939 the Cardinals finished second and drew just over 400,000. It was tough making a go of it, and Rickey was getting a big salary and 20 percent [actually, 10 percent] of all the profits. And with the war clouds forming as early as '40 and the draft in the fall of '40 and swords rattling, by the time he was making the decision on Rickey, he felt sure there was going to be a war, and that was one way to get rid of a *big* salary.''

After Rickey and Breadon mutually ended their relationship with the Cardinals, Rickey was offered the reins of the Philadelphia Phillies and the St. Louis Browns. Instead, he accepted a job as Larry MacPhail's successor with the Brooklyn Dodgers—the Dodger board of directors was happy to see the boisterous MacPhail leave for a post in the military, despite his having engineered the 1941 pennant. One of the reasons Rickey went to Brooklyn was that Branch Jr. was there, unhappily working with MacPhail. Going to Brooklyn gave Rickey a chance to reunite with his son.

Breadon was happy to be free of Rickey, and after Rickey's departure, he began firing Rickey's loyalists. Many of them followed their leader to Brooklyn. After Rickey's departure, his players would win Breadon three additional pennants in 1943, 1944, and 1946, but then the pennants would stop, and a long skein of Brooklyn pennants would begin. In Brooklyn, Rickey would single-handedly break the color line, bringing Jackie Robinson, Roy Campanella, and Don Newcombe to the Dodgers. Brooklyn pennants would follow in 1947, 1949, 1952, 1953, 1955, and 1956.

The great irony was that Judge Landis, a virulent racist, had been the one mainly responsible for Rickey and Breadon splitting up. When Rickey went to Brooklyn, he found the liberal New York community the perfect milieu for bringing Jackie Robinson up to the major leagues. This after so many years of Landis keeping blacks out of major league baseball, even forbidding the white major leaguers from barnstorming against black players. After Commissioner Landis died in 1945, his replacement, Happy Chandler, gave Rickey his blessing to bring up Robinson.

Had Rickey stayed in southern St. Louis (with the Cards or the Browns), rather than going to Brooklyn, it's possible that Rickey might have been reluctant to break the color barrier, and not only baseball history but American history might have turned out differently. It's also possible that Robinson and "Campy" and Newcombe might have ended up playing for the Cardinals (or the Browns), bringing another string of pennants to "the Mound City."

One thing is certain: When Breadon let Rickey go, the team and the city lost an important asset. While Brooklyn celebrated the alliance between Rickey and Jackie Robinson, St. Louis would have to wait some twenty long years before the Cardinals would win again behind the strong right arm of Bob Gibson.

CHAPTER 32

THREE IN A ROW

AFTER Branch Rickey's departure, if some players thought the days of poor pay would be over, they were underestimating the fear and penury of Sam Breadon, who tightened the financial screws on all Cardinal employees as the war dragged on and attendance stagnated. When Stan Musial returned home to Donora, Pennsylvania, after the 1942 World Series, he was making so little money that he took a job working in the zinc mills. When Breadon offered Musial a $1,000 raise from his $4,200 salary for '43, Musial replied that he thought he deserved a raise to $10,000. He reasoned that both Enos Slaughter and Terry Moore would be in the service, making him the Cards outfielder with the most seniority. (He was twenty-one.) Breadon took a hard line. He told Musial he could either accept his offer or sit out the season. When Musial refused to report for spring training, farm director Eddie Dyer was sent to Donora to sign him for $6,250. (He made $1,050 more than if the intractable Rickey had been in charge. Rickey would have made Musial sign for the $5,200 or sit out until he capitulated.)

With a war on, the big league teams decided to hold spring training at sites close to their hometowns, rather than spend the extra money traveling to Florida. The Cardinals trained in Cairo, Illinois. In addition to Terry Moore, Enos Slaughter, and Frank Crespi, among the players lost to the war effort were two young pitchers, Johnny Beazley and Johnny Grodzicki. Neither would be effective again for the Cards.

MARTY MARION: "Beazley was in the Army, and we played his Army team an exhibition game in Memphis. Ol' Beazley hurt his arm pitching against us. He tried to beat us, I guess. He babied it for a couple of years, and it never did come back.

"Johnny Grodzicki, a good ol' Polish boy, was one of the best prospects the Cardinals had. He was a pitcher, and then he went to the war. He was a paratrooper, and he came back with a bad leg. He tried to pitch on that bad leg, and he hung around for a couple of years. They were hoping he'd come back, but he never did."

The year 1943 saw the rationing of tires, cars, sugar, gasoline, bicycles, rubber boots, fuel oil, coffee, shoes, meats, and fats. When rubber became scarce, the major leagues began the season using what became known as "the balata ball." It was mushy. Home runs became scarce. The dead ball hurt the teams with home run hitters. It didn't hurt the run, run, run Cardinals.

MARTY MARION: "They were saying the ball was made the same as always, but we said it was a dead ball. We never knew for sure when we were playing. We just thought it was a dead ball. We were always kidding about it. But nobody really questioned it. If that's what we were going to play with, that's what we were going to play with."

The Cardinals took the lead right from the start in 1943 and except for a few days in July when they were tied with the Brooklyn Dodgers, led throughout the season. It was the way Marty Marion preferred it.

MARTY MARION: "If you had your choice, you'd lead from day one to the end of the season. It was more exciting the way we won it in '42, when we came from behind, but if you had your druthers, you'd rather win the whole thing from start to finish.

"You get into winning ways. You go out there and feel, 'We can't lose.' You have that feeling.

"We had a very good pitching staff in '43. Our two aces were Mort

Cooper and Max Lanier. Mort was kind of a rounder, didn't take good care of himself. When he first came up, he had a good fastball, but nothing else. He came up with a forkball, a change of speed, came up with control, and he got to be a real good pitcher. And he had a good team behind him. He used to love me. He used to say, 'Marty, you're my best friend. Those double plays!'

The year after I won the Most Valuable Player in 1944, the Cooper boys were in their glory. Mr. Breadon promised the Cooper boys that they would be the highest-paid players on the team. I don't know what he had promised Mort and Walker, but he sent me a contract for $13,000, and I wouldn't sign it. I kept dickering with him, and he told me, 'Marty, I promised the Cooper boys they would be the highest paid players on the team.' I said, 'I don't care what you promised them. I won't play for this.' I said I wanted $15,000. It wasn't much more, but it was more that the Cooper boys were making. I said, 'All you have to do is call them and give them more money.'

"Well, what happened, they were going to strike because I was making more than they did. I understand Mr. Breadon called them in the office and offered them the same thing he had offered me. But they weren't satisfied with that, so they went on strike. They didn't suit up. After it was all over, they both got a raise. Mort bought me a new hat. He said, 'You got me a raise!' The Cooper boys were the backbone of the club.

"Mort won over 20 games in '42, '43, and '44. When Mort would pitch, we'd get him all kinds of runs. Every time Max Lanier would pitch, we never could get him any runs. Max used to beg us, 'Please get me one run.' So he pitched a lot of tight games, because we sure didn't get him many runs. He let us know it too: 'Get me some runs.'

"Max had a stocky build, had short arms. He had good curveball, a good fastball, had a herky-jerky move. He was a tough competitor and a pretty good hitter at the plate. All our pitchers were good hitters. Harry Brecheen, Murry Dickson, Johnny Beazley. We used ol' Mort as a pinch hitter. Most of them were pretty good athletes.

"Harry Brecheen was a left-hander, and his claim to fame was a screwball. Not many people other than Carl Hubbell were noted for a good screwball. Well, Harry had a good one and was sneaky fast. Harry wasn't a big man. We called him 'the Cat.' He had a good change of pace, a good curveball, and good control. He had everything. He wasn't overpowering, but he was a damn good pitcher.

"Al Brazle was a herky-jerky left-handed pitcher. He threw a sinker. We always thought George Munger would be a better pitcher than he was. George wasn't mean enough. He was a likable redhead, smiled all the time. Everybody loved George, and we always wished he was a little bit meaner. He didn't want to knock you down, but he would if he had to. But you'd have to rile him up to make him do it. George had a good fastball, a good curve. He was a good pitcher, not a great pitcher."

Nineteen forty-three marked the blossoming of Stan Musial as a hitter. That year he got 220 hits and won the batting championship with a .357 average.

STAN MUSIAL: "I had a good year in '43. I led the league in hitting. I was the Most Valuable Player. I had a year under my belt, and of course, the caliber of baseball went down somewhat, as a lot of guys left for the service.

"I was a good fastball hitter and could get the bat on the ball. I had a feeling that nobody could throw that fastball by me. After they found out I could hit the fastball, they started throwing me more curves, and they found out I could hit the curve as well."

MARTY MARION: "Stan used to be quiet when he was younger. Now he's not quiet at all. He's so famous now, anything he says, everyone laughs at. If you don't like Stan Musial, you don't like nobody. Tell you the kind of kid he was, I can remember when the '42 World Series was over, Stan didn't come back to St. Louis to celebrate. He went from the New York station back home to Donora, and he was telling everybody goodbye, and he was crying like a baby. Stan had a good heart.

"Stan was just a good ol' country boy. We had a lot of good ol' country boys on our team. Naturally, it didn't take Stan long to become famous. He was the topic of conversation because of his stance. Everyone asked, 'How can he hit with that stance?' curled up like a corkscrew at bat, and all the time he was whacking the ball all over the place. No, if you don't like Stan, you don't like anybody.

"Stan didn't have a good arm, but he could throw the ball all right. Stan could run. He was a good base runner. He didn't steal a lot of bases, but he didn't have to. He knew how to play. And he had good power.

"If you ever saw Stan undressed, he had a lot of muscles in his shoulders. I asked him one time, 'Stan, how does the ball look to you? It looks like an aspirin tablet to me.' Stan said, 'It looks like a grapefruit!' He wasn't lying. He had good eyes.

"I never saw Stan get mad with anybody. He was always kidding, a jovial person. He liked to tell jokes and play that damn harmonica. Stan's a very popular man."

With Musial moving over from left field to right, Sam Breadon made a trade with the Philadelphia Phillies to acquire left fielder Danny Litwhiler on June 1, 1943. Two years earlier with the Philadelphia Phillies, Litwhiler had hit 18 home runs, but what impressed Cardinal manager Billy Southworth more were Litwhiler's hustle and determination. Before he was traded, Phillies owner Bill Cox had promised him a $2,000 bonus if attendance rose in '43. It did. Litwhiler, who after his pro career went on to become a famed collegiate coach, recalled that when he arrived in St. Louis, Sam Breadon refused to honor the promise.

DANNY LITWHILER: "Philadelphia was coming along pretty good. We got Bucky Harris as manager. Bill Cox came in. He bought the club—he's the one who got in trouble with gambling and horse racing—and he said, 'If attendance is up, I'll give you a $2,000 raise.' I said to myself, Oh man, this is going to be all right. He talked a big game. We got near the end of May, and I got traded to St. Louis. I felt pretty bad about it, because I really liked Philadelphia. In fact, I cried. It broke my heart, because I was leaving Philadelphia—I really liked the fans, and I thought, 'If I go over to St. Louis, they got a million ballplayers. Rochester and Columbus are loaded with talent who can probably play in the majors, and I'll be in Columbus and Rochester, and I won't get my $2,000.'

DANNY LITWHILER
(Courtesy Brace Photo)

"When I got there, I said to Mr. Breadon, 'That's not my contract. My contract is for $10,000, not $8,000.' He said, 'No, your contract is for eight.' I said, 'I was promised ten if the attendance was up, and it was up substantially, and I think I deserve that raise.' He said, 'It isn't up here. Besides, they didn't want you anyway. Billy [Southworth] wanted you. I thought, 'That's a nice thing to tell me.' But I was happy Billy wanted me. I never got the $2,000.

"But it turned out Billy was the reason I got to St. Louis. The last week of the 1942 season the Cardinals were playing the Phillies, and they were going for the championship tied with the Dodgers, neck and neck, and we were down one run, and it was the ninth inning, and I got a base hit at the end of the bat right over the second baseman, and I stretched it into a double. The next batter hit a ball to Terry Moore, who had a great arm, a really good fielder, and I just made up my mind to head for home, and the ball and I got to home plate at the same time. Walker Cooper was the catcher, and I hit him and knocked him out, and I was knocked out, and I was safe.

"When I got over to St. Louis, Billy said, 'Do you know why I traded for you?' I said, 'I have no idea, but I'm glad you did.' He said, 'You remember that game where you got the base hit stretching that double and scored?' I said, 'Yeah, I do remember.' He said, 'Anyone who can hustle on a last-place club like that would really do a first-place club a lot of good.'

"I said, 'Thank you.' So Billy and I started off in pretty good shape. He was a great teacher. He taught us how to play. I didn't know how to slide until I got over with them. Nobody had taught me how to slide. He was the best teacher. Every spring we'd go through the complete fundamentals, everybody—pitchers, catchers, infielders, outfielders—all the fundamentals. He had an alarm clock out there. He'd say, 'We have fifteen minutes . . .' And when the alarm rang, we'd go on to something else. He was a great teacher. I learned to slide. I actually learned how to bunt from Debs Garms, my roommate at St. Louis. Neither one of us did any running around. We did a lot of talking. We'd go up and eat in the club car and talk baseball. He said he played for Casey Stengel, and he said Casey taught him how to bunt. He said, 'The whole theory of bunting is to get the top half of the ball to beat the bottom half of the bat, and have the angle of the bat meet the ball where you want it to.' I said, 'That makes sense.'

"Billy's offensive philosophy was to bunt the ball and get the runner over. That's why we won. He taught the fundamentals. I don't care if you were Musial, if that winning run gets on first base, he's bunting. Billy always bunted with no outs and a runner on first or runners on first and second. You could bet on it.

"You ask, 'How did you win?' It was bunting, and learning how to slide, even the pitchers, and we would take the extra base. If you were on first base, everybody would go to third on balls hit to the outfield if they weren't hit to left. You knew you could slide and get in.

"He didn't believe in big innings. We didn't have a lot of power. We played for one run. We did more extra base running than we did hitting home runs. Billy didn't go for the home runs. But he did want you to take the extra base.

"The Cards were pretty fast. The only one who wasn't was Walker Cooper. He could run before he started catching and his legs started to go. The older he got, the slower he got.

"I remember we were playing against Cincinnati in Cincinnati, and Clyde Shoun was their pitcher. Walker Cooper hit a home run. Whitey Kurowski got up and hit a home run. I got up and hit a home run. Three in a row! Then Marty Marion got up and got knocked down! Marty said, 'This is terrible. I don't hit the home runs. They hit the home runs, and they never get knocked down. I get knocked down.'

"Marty Marion, as far as I was concerned, if it was an important game, the most important game you have, and you need a base hit, I would take Marty over anybody I ever played with. He had something about him in a clutch—he was tough. He was not a real good hitter, but in a clutch he was tough.

"He was also the best shortstop I ever saw. I've seen some shortstops who were quicker or who had better gloves, but Marty was the best I ever saw as a player. I didn't realize how good he was until I played left field behind him. Balls would be hit that I just knew were going to be base hits, and I'd go in to make the play, and his arm would come over and grab it and give it the flip to first base. He just had fantastic hands.

"Stan Musial was a silent team leader. He never said anything derogatory, never was in any arguments. He just did the job, and he was *so* good at it. He had hit a home run, and someone said, 'Nice going, Stan. What is that, your fourteenth or fifteenth?' Stan said, 'I don't know. I'll hit them. You count them.' And that was the way he felt.

"He was the nicest gentleman you'd ever want to play with.

"In 1942 Stan hit .315. In '43, he hit .357. After the '44 season was over, I was asked to go on a USO tour with some other ballplayers over Christmas and New Year's, and Frankie Frisch, Dixie Walker, Hank Borowy, Stan, and myself went up to Alaska. While we were up there, we answered questions. This one GI asked, 'Stan, how come you hit .315 in '42 and the next year you led the league? What was the big difference?' And Stan pointed to me and said, 'Because of him.' I said, 'Because of me?' And everybody laughed. Stan said, 'I'm serious. When we got Litwhiler, I moved from left field to right field. The throw from right field was perfect for me. When I was in left field I was always throwing across my body, and I kind of three-quarter-armed, particularly going into second base. And he had a sore arm. That's the reason he got to be a hitter instead of a pitcher in the first place. Stan said, 'I played the whole year in '42 with a sore arm, and in 1943 I didn't have a sore arm because Litwhiler played left, and I played right.'

"We didn't argue on that Cardinal ballclub. There were no arguments. None at all. It was pretty much a team. I had a friend who had a cabin on the lake, and every off-day we'd take the families out there, and just about the whole team would go, a big bunch, ten players. Musial was always with that group. And Harry 'the Cat' Brecheen. And after a night game, it was so hot in St. Louis, so Stan and 'the Cat' and I would go out to this lake and we'd gig frogs and have frogs' legs. We'd go out until two, three, four in the morning, and we'd come in and it would be cooler, and you could sleep.

"We got along good. We really did. You'd go on a road trip, and one of the players would be in the lobby of the hotel, and you'd say, 'What are you doing?' 'Nothing.' 'Let's go to a show.' That didn't happen on a lot of clubs. You couldn't go out with anybody. With the Cardinals, you could go with anybody. We were a family.

"Around that time, all the clubs were starting to get beer in the clubhouse after the game. We said to Southworth, 'Hey, Billy, how about getting us some beer in the clubhouse.' He said, 'Nah, I don't know.' Finally he said okay. We were in Brooklyn to play a twi-night doubleheader. After we won the first game, and we had a little time off before the evening game, it was 'Okay, can we have beer in the clubhouse?' And Whitey Kurowski and another player had a beer. Well, we lost the second game, and Billy said, 'Okay, no more beer in the clubhouse from now on.' We never got a drink.

"You know the difference between the Cardinals and any team I ever played with? You knew you were going to win. Every day you knew you were going to win. And if you lost, it was 'Okay, we'll win tomorrow.' And it didn't really bother you. And you usually won the next day.

"I remember in '43 we finished up in Pittsburgh, and Southworth was saying, 'We're getting too lackadaisical. You gotta fight. You gotta fight.' Well, they beat us three games in a row, and boy, that was unusual. And Southworth was really ticked off. 'Oh man, we're going to lose.' It really bothered him.

"I really liked Walker and Mort Cooper. Liked them a lot. I played with Walker at Cincinnati and also at the Cardinals. We were together in Cincinnati during spring training. Ed Bailey was a cocky young kid, always popping off, so Cooper said, 'You say you're so fast. I'll race you any time for 100 yards. Ten bucks.' Boy, Ed couldn't get enough of that. He gives the money to the trainer, and Walker gives his, and Walker said, 'Wait a minute. Did I say 100?

Ed, I don't think I can go 100. Make it 75, and the bet's on.' Ed said, 'Go ahead. That's fine.'

"We go out, and they race, and Ed jumps out to the lead, and Walker is running—boomp, boomp, boomp, boomp—and he loses by a long way, and Ed says to the trainer, 'Give me the money.' The trainer says, 'No, it's not your money. It's Walker's.' Walker comes over and says, 'Ed, we said we'd race for $10. We didn't say win. I raced you for 75 yards.' Walker said, 'Give it to the clubhouse man. All right, everybody gets Cokes.'

"When I joined the Cardinals in '43, I was making $8,000 a year. The highest-paid player on the club was Marty Marion at $12,000. The Coopers were getting $10,000. Musial was getting $9,000. Can you imagine Musial getting $9,000? It seems crazy. His wife told my wife that they thought I was rich, because I had a car. Stan couldn't afford to buy a car.

"Rickey was no longer there, but it didn't matter. Breadon had learned how to do it.

"We won 105 games in '43. Even though we had been winning, they made the Yankees the Series favorites. We were surprised. We were sure we were going to win it."

Part of the reason the Cardinals felt they were going to win was that the Yankees had lost a number of key players to the armed services, including Joe DiMaggio, Red Ruffing, Phil Rizzuto, John "Buddy" Hassett, and George Selkirk. Each team was able to replace its stars from large productive farm systems.

Because of the restrictions of the war, Judge Landis declared that the first three games would be played in New York, the remainder in St. Louis. Marty Marion remembers the Cards as being less up for the Series than in '42.

MARTY MARION: "I don't know what happened, but we didn't have the intensity, the desire to win like we had in '42. It was a war year. I don't think our minds were on it, to tell the truth, and that's a poor excuse, because they beat us. And they played under the same circumstances. But we didn't seem to have the same feeling. Our minds were on something else, but that was a poor excuse."

Spud Chandler, who posted a 20-4 record and won the American League MVP in 1943, started the opener for the Yankees. Billy Southworth didn't start Mort Cooper, the logical choice, because Cooper had been ineffectual in the '42 Series and in the All-Star Game. Instead, he pitched his talented lefty, Max Lanier.

MAX LANIER: "I pitched the opening game in New York and got beat in the sixth on two hits and a wild pitch. The final score was 4 to 2. Terry Moore had been in the service all year. He was in the Panama Canal. After the game, he said to me, 'You pitch another one like that, and I guarantee you'll win.'

"I don't think the Yankees had near as good a club as they had in '42. But we just weren't hitting, that's all.

"In the fourth, I was covering first on a ground ball, and I had already crossed the bag when Frank Crosetti knocked the ball out of my hand, and the umpire called him safe. He had already called him out. And he done it on purpose. I know he did. And it cost us a run. Billy Johnson singled, moving him to second. I threw a wild pitch that let Crosetti score from second. It hit in front of the plate, and Walker Cooper thought he had it blocked, and he was looking for it while I was hollering to him, 'To the right! To the right!' And he just didn't get it quick enough. Crosetti kept running. I was at home plate, waiting on the ball, but he didn't get it in time to tag him out."

DANNY LITWHILER: "I'll tell you a memory of that first ball game. Spud Chandler was the pitcher. The first three times up, I ran the count to 3 and 2, and I never swung the bat, and I walked three times in a row. The fourth time up I was 3 and 2 again, and he made a pitch that looked like it was going to be close, and I hit it off the end of the bat, back to Chandler, and the game was over.

"That night at the hotel the phone rang. The caller said, 'Danny?' I said, 'Yeah.' He said, 'Take that bat off your shoulder. Don't be a wooden Indian.' And he hung up. I just about went through the telephone to get at him. I thought I had done a great job walking three times!

MAX LANIER: "The morning after that first game, Mort and Walker's dad died. Walker was my roommate. I don't remember them saying much about it. Mort told me, 'My dad would have wanted to see me pitch.' Walker said, 'I'll do the catching.' I know his dad would have wanted them to do it that way, 'cause he was a great baseball fan. I got a picture of them when they were both kids, with their dad in between them. Mort beat the Yankees, 4–3."

DANNY LITWHILER: "We had thought, and Southworth had thought, that both Mort and Walker were going to go home. But they talked it over and said that their dad wouldn't want them to do that. So they played, and Mort won, 4 to 3. He pitched one super ball game.

"I'll tell you something about that ball game: In Yankee Stadium when the sun is out and everybody is smoking in the stands, there's a blue haze in left field, and you have a tough time seeing the batter. You almost never, ever see the ball leaving the bat. You see the swing, and maybe you hear the crack of the bat, but you have a tough time deciding where it is. You're not too sure.

" 'King Kong' Keller was the batter, and he hit the ball to left field as good as any right-hander, so I played him fairly deep. Well, he hit the ball, and I just could not see it right off the bat, and it went over my head. No way I could get that ball. It bounced against the fence. If I had seen the ball and played it right, I was deep enough to catch it.

"I came in, and I said, 'Mort, I'm sorry. I just couldn't see the ball leave the bat.' He said, 'Hell, that's all right. I made a lousy pitch.' He took it right off of me."

MAX LANIER: "The Yankees won Game 3, 6 to 2, beat Al Brazle, and in the fourth inning Johnny Lindell ran over Whitey at third. Kurowski was really hurt, but he wouldn't let on. The big outfielder really hit him hard."

DANNY LITWHILER: "When Lindell came in and knocked Whitey Kurowski out, that blow knocked a kidney stone loose. That night we got on the train and left for St. Louis. And that night he passed that kidney stone. And Whitey was not in real good shape the rest of the Series."

MAX LANIER: "I started the next one against Marius Russo in St. Louis. We were losing, 1 to 0, when Southworth took me out in the seventh inning. He brought in Frank Demaree to pinch-hit for me, and he hit into a double play and we scored one run. I just hated to come out as a hitter. I thought I could hit anybody. I didn't care how hard they threw.

"It went nine innings, and Brecheen got beat, 2 to 1. Russo hit a double to win the ball game. Russo wasn't an overpowering pitcher, but he pitched with control and he changed it up. I thought we were going to score four or five runs about every inning. We had the bases loaded once and nobody out. We just weren't hitting. You have to give the other pitcher credit once in a while.

"In the final game, Spud Chandler beat Mort, 2–0. He allowed ten hits, all singles. Bill Dickey won it with a two-run home run. Dickey was a great hitter and a great catcher. So we lost, four games to one, which was a real disappointment to all of us, because Southworth had said, 'We should beat the Yankees.' "

DANNY LITWHILER: "Like the rest of us, I was disappointed. We packed up and went home. It was a long ride home to Pennsylvania."

After winning the National League pennant in 1942 and 1943, the St. Louis Cardinals managed to keep from losing five of its starters to the war as the team gathered for spring training in 1944. Osteomyelitis kept Whitey Kurowski from the draft. Walker Cooper had an old leg injury, Danny Litwhiler had a bad knee, and Marty Marion had a back injury, conditions that moved them down the draft list. Stan Musial at twenty-three was healthy, but he supported his father, who had contracted black lung disease working in the zinc mines. Musial, moreover, had a child born before Pearl Harbor. In addition, Stan worked in a war plant during the winter.

The Cardinals had the best lineup by far, and everyone knew it. The Dodgers, their chief rivals, had been decimated. Dolph Camilli, Billy Herman, Arky Vaughan, and Kirby Higbe were gone. Whitlow Wyatt suffered from a sore arm and had to quit in midseason. Cincinnati, the other contender in '43, lost its two best pitchers: Johnny Vander Meer and Elmer Riddle. The Cards began the '44 season with a 45-15 record, one of the best starts ever in National League history, then went 60-34 the rest of the way, finishing the season with a 105-49 record.

MARTY MARION: "We scared 'em that year. Common sense had to tell you the competition wasn't as good as it was before. But as a player, you don't notice that sort of thing at all. I don't ever remember playing a game where we said, 'I wish we had Enos and Terry.' We just played the game like that was it. We never mentioned the war. You put out nine players, we put out nine players, and we play.

"In 1944 I won the Most Valuable Player Award. Right after the World Series, somebody called me up and said, 'You won the Most Valuable Player Award. I didn't know what the hell it was. I never was impressed with it at all. That's right. I didn't think about things like that too much. Now, after years passed, that's pretty nice. But back then, it didn't mean a thing to me.''

Led by stellar shortstop play by Marion, the Cards made 112 errors in the field, fewest in the league, and 162 double plays, most in the league. On offense, the Cards were led by first baseman Ray Sanders, who drove in 102 runs; third baseman Whitey Kurowski, who hit 20 home runs and drove in 87 runs; Danny Litwhiler, who hit 15 home runs and drove in 82 runs; and Stan Musial, who hit .347 and drove in 94 runs. As a team, the Cardinals led the league in hits, runs, batting average, doubles, and home runs.

The pitching staff, moreover, was superb, leading the league in winning percentage, shutouts, and ERA. Mort Cooper won 22 games and had a 2.46 ERA, Max Lanier won 17 with a 2.65 ERA, rookie Ted Wilks had his finest season, producing a 17-4 record with a 2.65 ERA, and Harry Brecheen won 16 games with a 2.85 ERA. The Cardinal staff recorded 26 shutouts and had a *team* ERA of 2.67.

DANNY LITWHILER: "In 1944 we played the same Billy Southworth baseball. He never went for the big inning. Get a man on and get him over. At the time, we defined National League baseball.

"What I remember most about '44 was that every day you knew you were going to win. Like I said, if you lost, so what? 'We'll get them tomorrow.' And we did. It was so easy. And it wasn't one person who did it. It was always someone new.

"Billy was the kind of manager who was tough to play for sometimes because you didn't know for sure if you were going to play. He played hunches. He would pick up the ball for the pitchers during batting practice, and he'd watch you hit, and if you looked good, you'd be in the lineup. If you didn't swing good, you might not be in the lineup. And that was tough. He might substitute Augie Bergamo or Pepper Martin, who the Cards brought back in '44. Pepper was fairly old, but he was still agile. Do you know the trunks they use for traveling? He could take two of them, lay them side by side, and jump

BILLY SOUTHWORTH
(Courtesy Brace Photo)

over them without a run. And then he'd put one on top of the other, and he'd jump up on top of them without a run. Pepper just had tremendous legs. He still ran pretty good.

"I remember one day Pepper got a base hit, and it looked like a triple. He hit the ball between the outfielders, and as he rounded second base, one stocking came down, and by the time he got to shortstop, the other stocking was done, and the first one was over his shoe. And he's running. The sock is flopping, and he went headfirst into third.

"Pepper was a good man on a ballclub. He paid me one of the nicest compliments I ever had. He said, 'Danny, you're the greatest two-strike hitter I've ever seen.' And I got to thinking about it, and I thought, 'Maybe I am,' so he made me a tougher hitter with two strikes."

On September 1, 1944, the Cardinals had 91 wins. Pittsburgh, which finished second under Frankie Frisch, recorded a total of 90. The final margin of victory was fourteen and a half games. (Pittsburgh did not win another game that season, while the Cards won fourteen more.)

The St. Louis Cardinals from 1942 through 1944 were the first team in National League history to win 100 games for three consecutive seasons. However, because they played during the war, when most of the major leaguers were in the armed services, this team does not get the same glory and recognition as the 1934 Gashouse Gang. Nevertheless, during those three glorious seasons, the wartime St. Louis Cardinals were the most dominating team in National League history.

Making the 1944 season even more special, the American League team that the Cardinals had to face was a shock and a surprise: The St. Louis Browns, who played in Sportsman's Park when the Cards were on the road, edged out the Detroit Tigers on the final day of the 1944 regular season.

MAX LANIER: "It was good in a way. We didn't have to travel. And I had people come up from North Carolina. We only got ten tickets, and I done give them away or sold them. Here comes six guys from North Carolina, some of them cousins. And they wanted tickets. I said, 'I don't have any.' I went to the Cardinals. They said, 'We don't have a ticket left.' I went to the Browns, and they said, 'How many do you want?' I said, 'Give me nine tickets!'

MARTY MARION: "We didn't know them much, and they didn't know us, because when we were at home, they were on the road. We'd play them in exhibition games in spring training. They had a good ballclub. The town of St. Louis, from the fans' standpoint, everybody loved the Browns, but they went to see the Cardinals play. Nobody went to see the Browns play, except that year. Although we didn't draw a lot either. But the Cardinals were a better ballclub, a more famous ballclub, a ballclub with more tradition, although the Browns were there first.

"I was very interested in the Browns' last series, whether they would beat the Yankees. We were on the road, so we couldn't watch. I never did see them play, but we were interested in them, because we might have to play them. I don't think we had any special feeling about them, except when we were in the World Series together, we knew very well we could beat the Browns. They wasn't nothing, we felt. But after we played them that first game, we changed our minds. Hey, they were a pretty good ballclub. And we were lucky to beat them.''

STAN MUSIAL: "Everybody thought we had a better club, and we did too, but that was one of the toughest Series we played. They played tough, and we were always having to play catch-up. We had a hard time winning against the Browns. They had [Denny] Galehouse, [Nels] Potter had that screwball, and Jack Kramer and [Sig] Jakucki.

"The funny thing about that World Series, the fans were rooting for the Browns, and it kind of surprised me because we drew more fans than the Browns during the season. The fans were rooting for the underdog, and I was surprised about that, but after you analyze the situation in St. Louis, the Browns in the old days had good clubs. They had great players like George Sisler and Kenny Williams, and the fans who were there were older fans, older men, old-time Brownie fans. But it was a tough Series.''

DANNY LITWHILER: "We lost the first game of the '44 Series, 2–1. Denny Galehouse was tough. He had great control. I was surprised we didn't do better.''

MARTY MARION: "About all I remember is they beat us. George McQuinn hit a two-run home run to beat Mort, 2–1. You know that whole Series, I guarantee ya, you couldn't even see that damn baseball in that ballpark. They had people sitting in the center field bleachers, all those white shirts out there. I never saw such a horrible background in a ballpark. You could hardly see the ball. A lot of sunshine, a lot of bright shirts, in the field even getting the ball off the bat was very difficult to see. A lot of white shirts. And very glary. And a lot of sunshine, particularly when you were hitting. The pitching wasn't that good, even though the hitting was horrible. We always claimed that we couldn't see the damn ball.

"I remember very well that I had the flu. My second child was being born, and my wife had gone home, and I was staying at the Melbourne Hotel. I had a temperature of 104. I played every game, but as soon as the game was over, I'd go back and get in bed, and for three days all I had was orange juice. I'd get up and go to the ballpark, and I was weak as hell. I played that whole Series sick as a dog. I didn't tell nobody. Nobody knew I was sick. I had a temperature the whole Series, taking medicine and drinking orange juice. But I played all right. I didn't play great, but I played all right.

"After we played the Browns, we had a lot more respect for them. See, they had Junior Stephens, a hell of a ballplayer. McQuinn was at first, and they had Chet Laabs, a good hitter. Their catcher, Red Hayworth, wasn't that strong.

"Emil Verban hit well [for the Cardinals]. Sam Breadon would say, 'Verbin? Who's Verbin?' Mr. Breadon didn't even know who Verban was when he joined the club. He kept asking, 'Who's Verbin?' "

DANNY LITWHILER: "In the second game, Blix Donnelly came in in relief [of Max Lanier in the eighth inning]. They had runners on first and second, and they bunted the ball right near the line. Blix went over and fielded the ball, spun around and threw it to third base, and got the out, and then he finished the inning off. He did a fantastic job. That was a great play. Blix was a three-quarter sidearm pitcher, and he had a good strikeout ball. He was cocky in a nice way. He was good, very confident. We won the game in the eleventh, 3–2."

STAN MUSIAL: "I had played with Blix Donnelly in Springfield. He was a little guy with a good fastball, pretty good control. In the second game, the batter laid down almost a perfect bunt, Blix went down and fielded that ball and threw to Kurowski, and pow, just got the runner, just like that. Blix made a fantastic play on the bunt, and that got us out of trouble.

DANNY LITWHILER: "The Browns won the third game behind Jack Kramer [who won, 6–2, striking out ten], but in Game 4 Stan Musial hit a two-run home run to beat Jakucki, and Marty Marion made some unbelievable plays at shortstop, and the Browns didn't win another game."

After the third game, Cards infielder Emil Verban went to Browns owner Don Barnes and complained that his wife's tickets were obstructed. Verban had been lifted for a pinch hitter in each of the first three games. Verban said, "My wife is sitting behind a post, and I'd like to have you do something about it."

According to Verban, Barnes laughed at him and said, "The way you're playing, you ought to be sitting behind a post." Barnes's friends sitting with him laughed. Verban was furious. His anger was assuaged some when the Cardinals won Game 4 to tie the Series at two games apiece.

DANNY LITWHILER: "In Game 5, Denny Galehouse pitched against us again. Billy Southworth had me lead off. Even though my knee was swollen, he said, 'I'd just like to have you lead off.' I said, 'What do you want to do, win the game with the first hitter?' He said, 'Yeah.' It so happened, the first time up I hit a double against the center field wall, and Denny struck out the next three guys. We all thought, 'He's going to be tough again.' And then Ray Sanders hit a home run, and in the eighth inning, I hit a home run, and we won the game, 2–0. And what was funny about that, during the Series when a Brown would get up and do something, there would be a terrific roar, and when the Cards did something, it would be the same thing, so you really wouldn't know what happened sometimes. Like in that fifth game when I hit my home run off Galehouse, the fielder jumped up, and I heard this terrific roar. I thought, 'Oh Christ, he jumped up and caught it.' But I looked out, and I saw the ball bouncing in the stands. I thought, 'My God, it's a home run!' I don't even remember touching the bases after that. Max Lanier won the final game, 3–1.''

MAX LANIER: ''I won the final game of the Series, but it was because of the good relief pitching of Ted Wilks. I had them beat, 3–1, and he came in and retired the next eleven hitters in a row.

JOE GARAGIOLA: ''Ted Wilks's temperament was perfect, his makeup ideal—strong, durable, without fear. His only words when he came into a tough situation were 'Use the second sign.' (Meaning that of all the finger signals I flashed only the second sign counted.) Then he would rear back and throw. His fastball was his money pitch, and many was the time he threw it right into a hitter's power and struck him out. The hitters knew it was his bread-and-butter pitch, but they had to beat him with the bat. He never walked himself into trouble, and he never thought himself into trouble. He threw strikes and knew no fear.

''Being named 'the Big Cork' (because he was the stopper) appealed to him. Like all good relief pitchers, his attitude became 'Don't worry, just give me the ball.' ''

MAX LANIER: ''The Browns had some power, but you could pitch to them. The shortstop, Stephens, was a good high-ball fastball hitter, but he couldn't hit a curveball real good. Same thing for Laabs. He got a base hit off me. He was a low-ball hitter, and I thought I made a good pitch on him, and he hit it to right-center for a double. I struck him out the other times.''

Verban, the Cards' weakest hitter, turned out to be the hitting star of the Series. He hit .412, including three hits in the final game.

DANNY LITWHILER: ''Emil Verban, who had a nice Series, had been angry at Don Barnes, the owner of the Browns, because his wife got a bad seat. In fact, none of the wives got good seats, but his wife evidently got a worse one: behind a pole. When the final game was over, as soon as we won, Emil went over to Barnes's box and told him, 'Now you go sit behind the pole.'

''And we were kind of happy he did.''

MARTY MARION: ''I can see Emil running right now. After the final out, he didn't go into the dugout. He ran right over to Don Barnes's box, and he told him off. Emil was a feisty little devil, and he gave Don hell after the series was over. He said, 'That will teach you to put my wife back of a post!' ''

DANNY LITWHILER: ''Winning the World Series was a great feeling, one you'll never forget. If about think about it, there are so many really great ballplayers who never won a World Series. Coming from the Phillies and winning a World Series, for me that was really special.''

THE
BROWNS

CHAPTER 33

BALL'S PLAYERS

PHIL Ball, the owner of the St. Louis Browns, was a hard drinker and a tough talker who constantly feuded with managers, players, and even the baseball commissioner. Once he accused two of his players, Del Pratt and Johnny "Doc" Lavan, of not giving their best, and the two sued him for slander. Ball responded by trading them away.

After a game the Browns blew in the ninth, his manager, Fielder Jones, told Ball he felt like quitting. Instead of showing sympathy, the Browns owner became enraged. Said Ball, "So you want to quit? You haven't an ounce of courage. Get out of my office. I wouldn't take you back if you'd work for nothing. I want men who like to tackle a tough job. Quinn [general manager Bob], get me a new manager." Quinn hired Jimmy Burke to replace him.

If Ball doomed his franchise by offending Branch Rickey and allowing him to move to the Cardinals, he compounded his mistake by then allowing the Cardinals to move into Sportsman's Park as tenants. The Cardinals were on shaky footing. It was Ball who put them back on their feet with their rental deal.

Shortly after Sam Breadon took control of the Cardinals and hired Branch Rickey from the Browns to run the team, Breadon came to Ball and asked if he could move to Sportsman's Park and play there when the Browns were on the road. Ball, still smarting from what he saw as Rickey's betrayal, said, "Are you crazy, Sam? I wouldn't let Branch Rickey put one foot inside my ballpark. Now get out yourself."

Breadon tried a second time and again was refused. Breadon tried again. He explained to Ball, "I was a poor boy—a very poor boy—in New York. I came here in St. Louis, nearly starved at first, but eventually made some money in the automobile business. I got into the Cardinals with that fan group—soon got in over my head—and much of my money is in the club. We're heavily in debt, and our only chance to salvage what we put into it is to sell the Cardinals' real estate for $200,000, get out of debt, and move to Sportsman's Park. You're a rich man, Mr. Ball. Money doesn't mean anything to you, but I'm about to go broke, and only you can save me."

Ball relented. "Sam," he said, "I didn't know you were hooked so bad. I admire your frankness, and what's more I admire a fighter, a man that doesn't quit easily. Get your lawyer to draw up a contract, insert a rental figure you think is fair, and I'll sign it. Even if it includes having that Rickey around the place."

Once Ball said he could play in Sportsman's Park, Breadon sold his ballpark for $300,000, allowing him to buy an interest in the Houston and Fort

Smith ballclubs and get out of debt. He paid Ball $35,000 a year rent, plus half the maintenance expenses.

Ball then aided the Cardinals' bottom line further when in 1925 he decided to double the seating capacity of Sportsman's Park to 33,000 seats. He increased the capacity of the wooden stands down the first and third base lines and added bleachers from foul line to foul line, with a pavilion in right field, so sure was he that his Browns, third-place finishers in '25, would reach the World Series in 1926. History, however, would prove it would be the Cardinals, and not the Browns, who would play in the '26 Series, helping Sam Breadon's bottom line instead.

Through his ownership, Phil Ball had a penchant for making enemies. He picked fights, and one of his longest-running was with Commissioner Kenesaw Mountain Landis. It had started when Landis was a federal judge in Chicago. Ball had owned the St. Louis Federal League team, and when the Federal League sued Organized Baseball, charging it with being a monopoly, Landis was given the case. But instead of deciding it, he held it and did nothing. He stalled, waiting for the league to fold, making the lawsuit moot. Ball, who believed the Federal League owners should have won the suit, never forgave him. When Landis was asked to take the commissioner's job after the Black Sox scandal of 1919, eleven owners went to his courtroom in Chicago to pay homage. Ball refused to go. When the owners held a ceremony celebrating Landis's appointment, Ball again refused to attend. When it came time to sign the document making him commissioner, Ball even refused to sign that.

When Landis declared his dislike for Branch Rickey's farm system, Phil Ball was one of the owners to fight him. In 1930 he even went so far as to take Landis to court, angering the other owners who had hired Landis specifically to keep Organized Baseball out of the courts.

The case concerned Fred Bennett, an outfielder in the minor leagues. The Browns had acquired Bennett from the Ardmore, Oklahoma, team, and from there he went to Muskogee, Tulsa, Wichita Falls, and Milwaukee teams controlled by the Browns. Several times Bennett was brought up to the Browns for a look-see.

When the Browns sent Bennett to Milwaukee after spring training of 1930, Landis decided to get involved. That's when Milwaukee took Landis to court to keep Landis from interfering.

Bennett spent the 1930 season in Milwaukee and came up to the Browns in 1931. On September 3, the Browns asked for waivers on him, and the Pirates claimed him for $7,500. The Browns then withdrew their waivers. Bennett then asked Landis to declare him a free agent, and Landis complied, prompting Ball to sue Landis.

Ball's attorney argued that Landis had no right interfering with the relationship between Milwaukee and St. Louis. Landis argued that as commissioner he had the right to do anything he pleased.

Federal Judge Walter Lindley ruled that Landis had the right to act. He also ruled that the relationship between Milwaukee and St. Louis was legal. He ruled that nothing in the baseball bylaws prevented a major league team from also owning teams in the minor leagues. Finally Lindley ruled that the owners could not use the farm system to hide or cover up players, or to control them indefinitely. He set Bennett free, and Bennett signed with Pittsburgh.

Ball announced he would appeal. Landis, frustrated and angered by Ball, summoned to his office a group of American League owners, including Ball, and demanded the owners live up to their agreement giving him dictatorial powers. He asked the other owners to condemn Ball for his renegade actions and put a leash on him.

Ball didn't comply until late December of 1931, when he withdrew his appeal. Both Washington owner Clark Griffith and Ball's general manager Bob Quinn feared that Landis would quit the job if Ball didn't stop challenging his authority. It was the one and only attempt to have one of Landis's rulings overturned in court.

Ball's temper and arrogance contributed greatly to the Browns' lack of success. Ball was the sort of man who was easily offended, and he let his emotions get in the way of the team's success.

Bill Stern, who for years entertained sports fans with his radio broadcasts, recalled one of the worst trades in Browns history—Heinie Manush, who was hitting .328, and Al Crowder, 17-15 in 1929, to the Washington Senators for Goose Goslin—a deal engineered on the instructions of an angry Phil Ball.

BILL STERN: "One morning, when Ball happened to be in the neighborhood of Heinie Manush's hotel, he decided to drop in and have a friendly little chat with his famous outfielder. He walked into the hotel lobby and rang the room where lived the famous ballplayer. The hotel operator sweetly cooed: 'Sorry, sir, but Mr. Manush was rather tired this morning and is having breakfast in bed. He doesn't want to be disturbed for an hour.'

"When the club owner heard that, he blew his top.

" 'Breakfast in bed'! screamed Phil Ball. 'Breakfast in bed! I'm a millionaire ten times over. I own the ballclub. He works for me. He has breakfast in bed—and I can't.'

"Fuming with rage, the club owner stalked from the hotel.

"That afternoon Ball took several prominent guests to the ball game and sat them in his own private box close by the first base line. That afternoon Al Crowder was pitching. Ball was pleased because 'the General' was his best pitcher and he wanted his friends to see the best.

"Early in the game, Crowder became vexed at the umpire's decision on an important pitch, and in a blind fury, he took the ball and flung it into the stands. It struck the rail in front of Phil Ball's private box, and all, including the amazed club owner, ducked in fright.

"A moment later, Ball, burning with anger, left his friends, marched straight to his office and put in a long distance call to Clark Griffith in Washington.

"When Griffith answered the phone, Ball quickly said, 'Hello, Griff, do you want Heinie Manush and Al Crowder?'

"Without any surprise in his voice, he replied, 'Well, I don't want your players particularly, but to help you out . . .'

"[Ball] roared into the phone, 'I just don't want them anymore. I want to get rid of them—both of them. You can have them—what'll you give?'

"Griffith gulped in surprise and slowly said, 'Well, you can have Goose Goslin . . .' Griffith was going to name several more players in addition and toss in maybe $50,000. But he never got a chance to finish his offer, for Ball said, 'Goose Goslin! Did you say Goslin? Okay, it's a deal—Goslin for Manush and Crowder.' "

Under Ball's leadership, the Browns were neither successful nor colorful enough to attract much of an audience. Attendance was dismal. The Browns played 77 home games, and after reaching a peak of 339,497 fans in 1929 and 280,000 fans in 1930, the Depression reduced those figures dramatically to the point that the Browns averaged only 3,500 fans a game in 1931 (179,126) and never came close to reaching that figure throughout the 1930s. Attendance in 1933 was 88,113 (that year only 34 fans showed up for one game), in 1935 it was 80,922 (1,050 fans a game), and in 1936 it was 93,267 (1,200 a game).

Ball died in 1933. His last act midway in the season was to fire manager Bill Killefer and hire Rogers Hornsby. In his five seasons, Hornsby could raise the team no higher than sixth. The highlight came on September 18, 1934, when Louis "Bobo" Newsom pitched a no-hitter for nine innings against the Red Sox, only to lose in the tenth on two walks and a single.

When Ball died, no one wanted to buy the team. The executor of the estate, Louis B. von Weise, in desperation turned to Ball's former enemy, Branch Rickey, asking him to find a buyer.

Rickey turned to a man who sat across the desk from him in the offices of the Cardinals, team treasurer Bill DeWitt Sr. DeWitt was married to socialite Margaret Holenkamp, whose best friend, Anita Barnes, was the daughter of Donald Barnes, president of American Investment Company.

The price of the team was $325,000. Barnes sold stock at $5 a share. He put up $50,000, as did a man named Al Curtis. DeWitt, who spent $25,000, left the Cards and became the Browns' general manager. Barnes became the president. In all, there were 900 Brownie stockholders, almost as many owners as fans. Rickey received $25,000 for putting the deal together. As a strategy, Barnes and DeWitt decided to hire ex-Cardinals to try to attract Cardinal fans. Ball had done that when he hired Rogers Hornsby. But Barnes and DeWitt discovered what other owners had known before him: Hornsby had a gambling addiction that made his employment difficult to justify.

BILL DeWITT SR.: "Hornsby used to bet on the horses a lot. Judge Landis was against anybody betting on the horses or anything else; he thought you might become involved in some kind of scheme or subject yourself to some bribe. Barnes talked to Hornsby about gambling before he ever went to spring training in 1937. He said, 'Look, you can't gamble, you can't bet on the horses and have your mind on the ball game at the same time. There's no way you can do it. Why don't you go one season and not bet on the horses at all. Just forget it.' Hornsby said, 'All right, sure. I'll do it.'

"Hornsby was about through as a player then, although on Opening Day, 1937, he hit a ball into the bleachers. He would go to the park in the morning very early, something like nine or ten o'clock, and the ball game wasn't until around two-thirty. He would always go into one of the phone booths in the ballpark. Then during the game, the clubhouse boy would go out two or three times and spend ten or fifteen minutes away. We couldn't figure out what he was doing. So we finally checked around and found out that he was running bets for Hornsby to a saloon across the street, where they used to make book on the horses and the ball games and everything else. He'd come down and give Hornsby the results on the bench. Jesus, here he is, supposed to be running the ballclub. Isn't that something?

"Barnes got the idea of tapping the telephone, and we hired some Pinkerton's guy to get on the other end of the line to see what was going on. The guy gave us a report every day; we had all Hornsby's bets: what he lost, what he won, everything. Listen, he was a big bettor. He'd bet $50 across the board or $100 across the board. Sometimes he'd bet $1,500 on a race. He'd bet eight or nine different races. And he was placing bets all over the country.

"I think he owed us something like $4,800; as an incentive to invest in something besides horses, Barnes had loaned him the money to buy stock in Barnes's company, American Investment Company. And one day Hornsby had a hell of a day at the tracks, won about $3,000 or $3,500. So he came in the office and he said, 'I want to pay off some of that money, about $2,000.' Barnes said, 'You must have had a windfall.' Hornsby said, 'Well, a guy owed me some money and paid me.' Of course, we knew where he got it, so he and Barnes got into an argument. Barnes wound up firing him, right then. We made Jim Bottomley manager. He had been sort of a player-coach with the Browns.''

Angelo "Tony" Giuliani was a member of the St. Louis Browns in 1936 and 1937. He remembered the chaos caused by the managerial dicta of Rogers Hornsby. He also recalled that though it was a sorry team, he preferred playing for the Browns than for the Cardinals.

After a seven-year major league career, Angelo Giuliani became a scout for the Minnesota Twins, and over the years signed thirty players, including Jim Eisenreich, John Castino, Kent Hrbek, Jerry Terrell, and Tim Laudner.

TONY GIULIANI: "I was born on November 24, 1912, in St. Paul, Minnesota. My father was in the statuary business. He and his three brothers formed the Giuliani Statuary Company in the late 1890s in Tuscany, Italy, which is world-famous for artists and sculptors. Michelangelo, for one, came from there, and so did Leonardo da Vinci. My father's name was Giocando, and when I was thirteen months old, my mother got a letter from Italy that her father was in his last days. My mother and I took a steamer to Genoa, and we arrived in time for her father to have his eternal rest. But unfortunately, in 1914, World War I started, and we were trapped there until it was over in 1918. The Germans were invading. We went to my grandpa's place in Tuscany, and when I was six and seven, I stomped grapes in the fall.

"When the war ended, we returned to St. Paul, and I'll never forget the sight of seeing the Statue of Liberty in New York Harbor. We took the train up to West Point and then crossed over, so I got to see Niagara Falls. As the train went over the bridge above the falls, I remember my mother saying to me in Italian, 'Angelo, Angelo, *guarde aqua.*' 'Look at the water.'

"We went to Chicago and took the Great Northern and Northern Pacific to St. Paul. I lived three blocks from the old Lexington Park, where the St. Paul Saints played. While I was in Italy, my dad had become a baseball fan. He took me to my first game in 1924. The starting pitcher for the Baltimore Orioles was Alphonse Thomas. He was from the same era as a younger Lefty Grove and George Earnshaw. The bug bit me. I used to play a game against the steps with a rubber ball. 'The Bambino' was hitting home runs. I would throw a rubber ball against the steps, have a lineup, and Babe Ruth would hit a home run every time he came to bat. My mother would hear the noise of the ball against the steps, and she'd say in Italian, 'Angelo, what's all the noise?' And I'd say, 'The Bambino hit another home run.'

"I played in grade school, went to St. Thomas Military Academy, and I went one year to Catholic University in Washington, D.C., where I played quarterback, and broke my collarbone, and that was the end of my football career.

"I signed with the St. Paul Saints in 1932 when I was twenty. The Browns drafted me from the St. Paul club in 1936. My first major league manager was Rogers Hornsby, the greatest right-handed hitter of all time, but not too great a manager at all times.

"I married my wife in '36, my honeymoon year, and where did we train? In West Palm Beach. The reason was that Hornsby liked it. There's a racetrack around there and horses, which he was addicted to. I loved the horses, but not to the extent of being addicted. I would see him, right at the finish line, especially in Louisville, at Churchill Downs. He was addicted to the gambling of the horse races, no question about it. Later on, Judge Landis tried to ban that. He was one of them who he was shooting at.

"The George Washington Hotel was right on the intercoastal. You could see Palm Beach across the bridge, and the ocean, and it was a beautiful view, and after my wife and I checked in, got our things upstairs in the room, we were looking out at the beautiful view when the phone rang. The clerk said, 'Sorry, Mr. and Mrs. Giuliani, you will have to move.' I said, 'Why? We just got here.' He said, 'Your manager doesn't like this hotel.' So we didn't stay there, not even one night. We moved to a rattletrap farther inland, closer to the ballpark. That was one of my first experiences with Mr. Hornsby. What could you say? He was the manager. We had to follow his orders.

"Hornsby liked to take the bats away from you. 'Take. Take.' I could see it in my case, but most of the others offensively just had no chance. They always accused him of not wanting anyone to hit .358 or higher. That's what we used to get after him on. Not to his face.

"Julius ['"Moose"'] Solters was a dead left field hitter, and Hornsby was managing on third base. The take sign on the road was touching the *S* on the uniform with his thumb, and at home it was the *B* for Browns. Solters was a dead pull hitter, and we were in Boston—the Monster fence with the net on top of it was only 315 feet. And Hornsby kept giving him the take sign.

"Solters got so upset, he said, 'I'll show that so-and-so how to take.' He took the bat out of that bat rack, stood at attention, marched to home plate with the bat upside down on his shoulder, one strike, two strikes, three strikes, you're out, and he was the third out. He flipped his bat over his shoulder and started to march out to his position in left field. And Hornsby whistled him out of the game and fined him. But Julius did what a lot of us would have liked to do. At the end of the year, Solters was traded to Cleveland.

"The next year Hornsby was fired, and he was replaced by Sunny Jim Bottomley. Jim was a great player. He held the record for many years, 12 RBIs in one game. He had good power, but he wasn't a home run hitter like Ruth or Gehrig or Foxx. He had a great glove. When he took over as manager, we became a different club immediately. Jim didn't take the bat out of your hands.

"I was a catcher behind Rollie Helmsley, and he was a character. In 1936 we had 'the Four Horsemen': Rollie, Julius Solters, Lyn Lary, and one other. After a ball game, they'd have a glass of beer, and if you recall the Four Horsemen, that's when they really started to move! Curfews were in vogue then, and sometimes they were caught away from their rooms. Hornsby had a coach checking. They would raise a little cain, but nothing bad.

"Hornsby was not a drinker. Back then the Pullman cars weren't air-conditioned. As we traveled East, we looked for a glass of ice water. The cars would have ice cubes in coolers. But Hornsby knew the Four Horsemen would make a highball out of the ice cubes in the coolers in the Pullman cars, so Hornsby went to the point of declaring, 'No ice in the coolers. Orders from the boss.'

"Nineteen thirty-six also was the year Mr. Barnes and Mr. DeWitt bought the ballclub. Both of them were very wonderful fellows. Of course, they had the lowest winning club. The Cardinals were number one. That was during their heyday with Branch Rickey, the formulator of the farm club. But we didn't mind. We didn't want to belong to a chain gang. The Cards were bringing players in on one train and shipping other ones out the other way to the farm system. So we felt a lot better about being with the Browns. At least we had a home. Rollie was first-string catcher, and I was second-string. I learned a lot from Rollie, and I did quite well with the glove but not with the bat. I had a .233 lifetime batting average, which is a good bowling average but not in baseball. And I made more money than they did on the Cardinals. I was a second-stringer, and I was making $3,500 a year. I had a winter job.

"When you ask what I made, you know that Ruth made $100,000. Jacob Ruppert, a wonderful man who owned the Yankees and Ruppert's beer, sat with Ruth under the palms in St. Petersburg. The writers and cameramen were watching the signing of Ruth. You know what had happened? The crash. So Hoover was the President, and Jake Ruppert was on one side of the table, and he has the contract all made our for Ruth, but he asked him first in a very beautiful German dialect, 'Vat the hell is the matter vit you, Ruth. Vat you vant this year?' And Babe said, 'Without any question, $100,000.' 'My Got,

Ruth, you want more than the President of the United States.' And Ruth answered, 'The President didn't have a very good year.' That's a true story.

"However, the next one to him, Herb Pennock, was at $17,500, and Jimmie Foxx, who the home run hitter Harmon Killebrew more or less copied, was making $12,500. Now all the rest of us were below that. I'm confident I knew because I played with these players, and we'd talk.

"We just didn't have the talent to beat the other clubs. When we played the Yankees, that was quite a mismatch. I played against Lou Gehrig the day they honored him, and that was one of the saddest moments I've ever been in, without any doubt. There were 65,000 people in Yankee Stadium, and there wasn't a dry eye in the place.

"I saw Gehrig lose coordination the year before in '38. My wife and I were going to spring training in Orlando, and I said, 'Jen, let's stop and see the Yankees work out.' They had started already in St. Pete. So Lou came up to the plate, and it looked like he was swinging an iron bat. He just couldn't get around on the ball. There was something radically wrong, and I told her that. I said, 'This isn't the Lou Gehrig I caught behind the last couple of years.' He then went to the Mayo Clinic in Rochester, Minnesota, and they diagnosed him. They didn't know what it was, but they named it 'Lou Gehrig's disease,' which is [amyotrophic] lateral sclerosis. That was very sad.

"In 1936 the Browns drew very few fans [80,500]. St. Louis had the west of the Mississippi, that's about it, but that was farmland. The population wasn't there. And the Cardinals were winning, and the Browns [57-95] were losing."

CHAPTER 34

BARNES BUILDS HIS TEAM

IN 1939 Will Harridge, president of the American League, urged the other teams in the league to help the sad-sack Browns. Every club offered to sell Bill DeWitt a player for $7,500, but only two teams offered players who had talent. Don Barnes and Bill DeWitt bought outfielder Walt Judnich from the Yankees and acquired pitcher Eldon Auker and outfielder Chet Morgan from the Boston Red Sox for infielder Michael "Pinky" Higgins and pitcher Archie McKain. Auker had pitched valiantly for six seasons with Detroit, helping the Tigers to a pennant in '34 and a world championship in '35. But Tiger owner Walter Briggs hated Auker's underhand delivery and traded him to the Boston Red Sox in 1938.

One of the best pitchers ever to perform for the Browns ended up in St. Louis because he could not get along with Boston manager Joe Cronin, who insisted on calling every pitch from his position at shortstop. Auker's 1939 season in Boston was a terrible strain for him emotionally, and he vowed he would quit the game if he wasn't traded. As a result, when he was sold, Auker was one of the few players who looked forward to playing with the Browns, and from 1940 through 1942 Auker won 16, 14, and 14 games, an excellent record, considering a less-than-stellar supporting cast. During the winter of 1940, the Browns and Cards split the cost of building lights for the fourteen night games each team was allowed to play. Auker pitched the nighttime opener.

ELDON AUKER: "Fred Haney, the manager of the Browns, called me at the end of the '39 season. I knew Fred. He had heard I was going to quit, that I didn't want to play for Joe Cronin anymore. Maybe he got it from Tom Yawkey, maybe from Eddie Collins. But he called me on the phone, and he said, 'Eldon, I've talked to Tom Yawkey, and it's all right for me to talk to you. Tom tells me you do not want to play for Boston anymore and there's a possiblity you're quitting baseball.' I said, 'That's right. I will not play in Boston. I'm wasting my time. I don't want to play like that. I won't put up with it.'

"He said, 'Would you play for me if I traded for you?' I said, 'Great.' He was the first one to call. He said, 'I'll make the deal.' I think they bought me for $30,000 and an old baseball.

"With St. Louis, I had three of the most enjoyable years I ever had, and the reason it was enjoyable, we had a nice bunch of ballplayers. They weren't great ballplayers, but we had a good ballclub, a good little team. Fred Haney, our manager, was one of the nicest guys you've ever seen. He was a great manager. Like Mickey Cochrane, who was my manager with Detroit, he was one of us. He was with us all the time. He loved to win. He knew how. He was a player himself. He knew what the game was all about. And when you walked out on that mound, he'd say, 'It's your game. You go get 'em.' That was it. He never bothered you or said one single thing. You knew when you were going to pitch. You were in the rotation whether you won or lost. You were pitching, and you were on your own.

"And Don Barnes, who owned the ballclub, was one of the nicest guys in the world. He was very wealthy. He owned the Public Finance Corporation of America. It was the largest small-loan corporation in the United States. He had started with $300 as a youngster and built it into a fortune.

"I pitched a ball game in Cleveland one night against Mel Harder. I beat him, 2 to 1. In the ninth inning, we were leading, and I had the bases loaded with nobody out. The stadium in Cleveland was packed. This was 1940, and the Indians were fighting for the pennant with Detroit. Haney came out to the mound. He said, 'You want to get out of here, or you want to stay?' I said, 'Just leave me here. I think I'm going to be all right.'

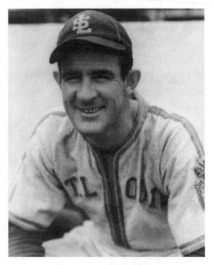

ELDON AUKER
(Courtesy Brace Photo)

"Ben Chapman was the next batter. I knew damn well I'd get him out. I struck out the next two batters, and the next guy popped out to the infield, and the game was over.

"The crowd was so loud you couldn't hear yourself think. You never heard anything like it in your life. The crowd was crazy, because they were driving for a pennant, and we stopped them.

"When the game was over, I went in the clubhouse, and Don Barnes was there, and he had peed in his pants. He reached into his pocket, and he handed me five $100 bills. He said, 'That's the greatest ball game I ever saw in my life.' He was the owner, and he had wet his pants. Never saw anything like it. But that's the way he was.

"I really don't know why the Browns weren't better. They had a good farm system. Of course, the people didn't come out. As a club, the Browns weren't wealthy. See, Barnes owned the club, but it was separate from his business, a separate entity, and he had only put in so much money. And he did put money into it. We finally got people coming out in St. Louis in 1940 when they put in the lights [attendance was 239,591, the highest since 1929]. We drew pretty good crowds.

"I pitched the first night game at Sportsman's Park. Bob Feller beat me, 3 to 2. He hit his first home run in the major leagues off me, over the right field stands. You could spit over that stand out there. It was only about 230 feet. But he hit it.

"When I came to St. Louis, Sportsman's Park was in bad shape. See, they played 154 games at that ballpark. The groundskeepers worked their tails off trying to keep it in shape, but it was hot in the summertime. The field was just baked. You walked out on that field with your steel cleats on, and your feet would almost burn off.

"I pitched a ball game there in 1936 on the Fourth of July, the first game of a doubleheader, and I was in perfect physical condition. I pitched nine innings. I changed my uniform three times, and I lost eleven pounds pitching that ball game. It was 110 when I walked onto the pitcher's mound.

"But St. Louis was a great town. It was a highly industrialized town. They made textiles. They had a steel mill and foundries. They were on the Mississippi River. St. Louis was an old town. They had all kinds of industries: leather and breweries. A lot of manufacturing. Fisher Body had a plant there. Ford had a plant.

"We stayed at the Chase Hotel. Terrific, first-class. We went to picture shows in our spare time. They had theaters. We played cards: bridge, hearts.

"In 1940 we finished sixth, and then in the winter Don Barnes bought Denny Galehouse, George Caster, Johnny Allen, and Fritz Ostermueller to strengthen our pitching staff."

Galehouse recalled the circumstances behind his trade to the Browns. He also remembered the low pay, how hot it was in the summer in St. Louis, and how hard it was to make a living playing baseball.

DENNY GALEHOUSE: "Donald Barnes and Joe Cronin were at the winter meetings in Atlanta, and it was the last day out at the Coca-Cola plant, where they were serving more than Coca-Cola, and Donald Barnes, the owner of the Browns, got to Cronin. They were leaning on the bar, and he said, 'Doggone it, I haven't been able to make a trade of any kind the whole time I've been here. What will you take for Galehouse and Ostermueller?' And Cronin put up quite a high price for us, figuring he would end it, and Donald Barnes said, 'I'll take them.' And that's how I went to St. Louis. Cronin himself told me the story later on.

"I was very disappointed going to St. Louis. I liked to be on a winning team. It's just natural for most people. It was not a very good club, actually. We had a few good players, of course, a couple of decent players. George McQuinn at first was a damn good first baseman and hitter. But there weren't too many real good ones. [Don] Heffner, [Johnny] Berardino, [Harlond] Clift, they were big league players, but they were not big league championship players.

"What I remember about playing in St. Louis was how humid it was. The humidity was worse than the heat, even at night. Of course, you'd have cooler days and days when the humidity wasn't so high, but it was mostly that way.

"In fact, when I was pitching for St. Louis, I'd warm up before the game, and five minutes was enough to get loose, but I'd change sweatshirts before I started the game. I'd sweat that much. Then about the third inning, I'd change sweatshirts and top shirts. Later on in the game I would change the whole uniform. It would be so much lighter, it would give you a little relief. One time I lost sixteen pounds pitching a ball game.

DENNY GALEHOUSE
(Courtesy Brace Photo)

"We weren't making much money to begin with, and in '42 we had to take 10 percent of our pay in war bonds. You could cash them in, but you didn't get much money out of them. It was a hardship. It made it tougher to live. You had to draw in the belt a little bit. I worked in the off-season for Goodyear Aircraft in Akron. I wrote up job descriptions to keep people working there. If their jobs weren't necessary enough, they were placed in 1–A and taken in the draft. Most war plant people had necessary jobs. We made the Corsair airplane, and all the workers made the parts and assembled them. We made a lot of planes."

ELDON AUKER: "Denny Galehouse was a very soft-spoken guy, very quiet, a first-class gentleman. He was a good pitcher, a workhorse. He just went out, did his job, never said much. And Fritz Ostermueller was a damned good left-handed pitcher. When I was with Detroit, Hank Greenberg almost killed him once. Fritz had good stuff, but Cronin was driving him crazy 'cause he never knew when he was going to pitch. Greenberg was at bat, and Fritz had a delivery where he finished very low, and he followed completely through, and he had a lot of stuff on the ball. This day he put the ball on the outside, and Hank hit it right directly back at Ostermueller, and the ball hit him in the face, shattering his jawbone and loosening his upper teeth. He laid on the mound and began to tremble. We thought Hank had killed him. We didn't think he'd ever pitch again, but he did.

"Hank turned white. Hank was so upset about it I didn't know whether Hank was going to finish the game or not. That scared Hank. It was the first time he realized how dangerous he could be.

"I never forget Johnny Allen because he was one of the most competitive pitchers you ever saw. And boy, he could throw. Right through a wall. And he'd throw it through your head if you got a solid hit off him. He broke Gerald Walker's wrist one day. He'd knock you down as soon as look at you. He was mean. When he went out there, he went out to win that ball game. And off the field, he was the nicest family man you ever saw. His wife was a lovely person, and he had a son he just adored.

"After forty games in 1941 [actually, forty-four], Fred Haney quit as manager. I guess he became disgruntled. He left the ballclub and went to California as an announcer. He went into the radio business. He had managed Hollywood on the West Coast for several years, and he had a lot of friends out there. He and Barnes were very good friends. There were no hard feelings between the two of them when he left. He became the announcer for the Hollywood Stars. Later he was the manager of the Milwaukee Braves when they won the National League pennant in 1957 and 1958, and then he went to work for Gene Autry when he bought the California Angels.

"When Haney left, he was replaced by Luke Sewell, who was a good manager. He was a technician. His personality left something to be desired. He was not a big leader, not aggressive, a quiet guy. Luke had been a good catcher.

"Under Luke in '41 we played .500 ball. We had a pretty good ballclub. Before he came, they didn't have any confidence. In '40, the guys didn't think they could win. We had a little team, little Brownies. We didn't have any Greenbergs or Ruffings or Dickeys or Groves. They were all little guys: We had George McQuinn, a good first baseman, and Don Heffner at second, a good little ballplayer, Johnny Berardino at shortstop, he was good, and Harlond Cliff at third. No big home run hitters, but good fielders. We had Walt Judnich in the outfield, and they got Rip Radcliff from the White Sox, and Chet Laabs, the power hitter on the club, but still a little, chunky guy. God, I was the biggest guy on the ballclub!"

Pitcher Denny Galehouse also recalled the skills of the cast of players behind him.

DENNY GALEHOUSE: "Vern Stephens had fairly good range. His toughest play was a ball right at him. It was a matter of judging the speed and the hop of the ball. He had more trouble doing that than anything else. At bat, he was a very erratic type hitter in that he would look real bad on a pitch, and they'd come back with the same pitch, and he'd hit it out of the park. So he was inconsistent in that respect, but still a good runs batted in guy.

"Don Gutteridge was at second. Nothing real outstanding, but okay. He made all the plays necessary. In addition to Stephens, our two best hitters were Walt Judnich and Chet Laabs. Judnich was a left-handed hitter, a pretty good hitter, hit 17 home runs, wasn't the greatest outfielder in the world as far as range was concerned. He was a nice guy. Chet Laabs wasn't a very big guy, but he had very big wrists, hands, and forearms, and he could whip that bat around. As long as nobody threw close to him, he could hit the ball out of the ballpark.

"I can remember one incident, Bob Swift was catching for the Athletics, and Chet was hitting the ball out of the park, and finally Swift told one of his pitchers, 'We have to stop this,' so he had the pitcher throw one close to him, and he didn't get another hit the rest of the series. Scared him a little bit. Some guys will dig in a little harder when that happens. They get mad. Other guys get a little scared of the ball. In fact, I was that way. I was always afraid of getting hit.

"We had George McQuinn at first base. He had a good range, saved a lot of bad throws, and was a good guy all the way around, and Rick Ferrell became our catcher in '42. He was a good, smart catcher, not mechanical in his pitch calling. He wouldn't always call for a fastball when you got behind. He was a good guy, good to pitch to. It helps your confidence to know a guy will catch a ball in a tough situation when you don't want a passed ball, or enough for a guy to go from first to second. If you get a guy who can block the ball good, it helps your confidence."

Nineteen forty-one was extraordinary for the performances of two American League stars: Ted Williams and Joe DiMaggio. Browns pitcher Eldon Auker recalled what it was like to have to face them.

ELDON AUKER: "In 1941 Ted Williams hit .406 for the Boston Red Sox. He beat me in Boston one day, broke my heart. I was working the ball game against Lefty Grove and had the Red Sox beat, 2 to 1, going into the bottom of the ninth. One of the Red Sox speedsters came up. We knew he could bunt and run like a rabbit. On the first pitch, he bunted it down the third base line and beat it out.

"The next hitter was Williams. Bobby Swift was my catcher. He came out to the pitcher's mound and asked, 'What do you think Williams'll do? Is he hitting him over? Hitting straightaway? What?' I said, 'Christ, I don't know. With Cronin managing, he might have him taking.' I said, 'We'll just have to wait and see. I'll keep the ball low and outside, keep it away from him to see whether he's going to square around and bunt or whether he'll hit.'

"I threw a pitch about two feet off the ground, off the plate by a good six to eight inches, and Ted hit it into the center field bleachers for a home run. It was a line drive like a two-iron. And the ball game was over. He jogged around the bases. He was waiting for me down in the dugout when I came in. I said, 'Get out the way, you son of a bitch. I'll kill you.' He started laughing. Ted put his arm around me and said, 'You know what you said to Swift? You said, 'We'll keep the ball low and outside and see if he's going to bunt or hit.' He said, 'I was reading your mind. I knew exactly where you were going to throw that ball.' That was Ted Williams. That was the way he thought. He said, 'You couldn't have thrown a ball in any better place than where I knew goddamn well you were going to throw it.' Ted was thinking all the time. That's how I lost the ball game.

"That same year Joe DiMaggio of the Yankees hit in 56 straight ball games. I used to pitch him in on his fists to keep him from getting the good part of the bat on it. I had very good luck against Joe. He didn't like my style of pitching. 'Cause I threw underhand. I had him stopped during that streak at about Game 27 or 28. We were playing at Yankee Stadium, and I had gotten him out three times. His last time at bat if I'd a walked him or hit him, the streak would have been stopped. But I pitched to him, because streaks didn't mean anything to us. Nah. What the hell did we care? We were just trying to get him out. And I had struck him out twice before that. He came up that last time, and he hit a ball down to third base to Harlond Clift. It was hit hard, and it skipped and hit Harlond on the shoulder and went into left field, and Joe got a double and drove in a run to tie the score.

"They beat me the ball game, and in the paper the next day the story was about how the streak was continued. But that streak didn't mean anything to me. I was just trying to get him out. Joe was tough, a great ballplayer and a great guy. [He was a] wonderful gentleman.

"What I remember about playing in St. Louis in '41 was how few fans came to the ballpark. [141,000, less than 2,000 fans a game. The Cards drew 646,000.] It was hot in the summertime and they had to leave the grandstand open, because if they had closed it, people would have suffocated. The people who came sat in the shade. The 600 people who came were all Brownie fans, but they never did have much of a following. The people didn't support it. The owners never put any money into the club. Barnes and DeWitt were operating hand-to-mouth. They just couldn't afford to have a good ballclub. It's a wonder they even survived."

During the 1941 season, Don Barnes concluded that he could not successfully fight the Cardinals for attendance. Five years after buying the team, he negotiated to move the team to Los Angeles, a transfer that would have brought major league baseball to the Left Coast seventeen years before the Dodgers moved West from Brooklyn after the 1957 season.

At the minor league convention held on Sunday, December 7, 1941, in Jacksonville, Florida, Barnes made an agreement with Sam Breadon of the Cardinals. Breadon would pay Barnes a substantial sum to move out of town. The plan was for the Opening Day Browns game of 1942 to be held in Wrigley Field in Los Angeles, which was owned by Phil Wrigley of the Cubs. Wrigley gave his blessing. Barnes had made arrangements with Jack Frye, president of Trans World Airlines, to fly two ballplayers on each of twenty-one Chicago to Los Angeles daily flights to avoid the possible loss of an entire ballclub in a crash.

Official approval of the transfer was set for Monday, December 8 at the major league meeting held in Chicago.

In faraway Hawaii, squadrons of Japanese zeros that left from aircraft carriers near a tropical island in the middle of the Pacific Ocean bombed the American fleet docked in Pearl Harbor. The date was December 7, 1941.

If the Japanese had attacked one day later, the St. Louis Browns' existence would have ceased at the end of '41. A great deal of craziness and wonderment, including a Browns pennant, would have been lost. Instead, Pearl Harbor prolonged the existence of the Browns franchise for another dozen years.

Bill DeWitt, Sr., who was in on the negotiations, recalled what happened.

BILL DEWITT, SR.: ''It was kept very quiet. In fact, the Browns' directors didn't even know about it. Barnes and I were the only ones who knew at first. Barnes worked out a deal with Sam Breadon; if Breadon would pay him $350,000, he would vacate St. Louis. And he went to Chicago and made a deal with Phil Wrigley to buy Wrigley Field in Los Angeles—a nice ballpark, the same as Wrigley Field in Chicago, only a little smaller—and the franchise. I think the price was $1 million. We talked to Will Harridge, the president of the league, and he talked to the other club owners—confidentially.

''The clubs were working on a three-trip schedule at that time, two four-game series and a three-game series in each city. I sat down in the New Yorker Hotel with the guy who wrote the American League schedules for fifty years, an old man who was in charge of the safe-deposit department of a bank in Boston. He had these long sheets and wide sheets; we had to get a card table in there to spread things out. We'd try it this way and that way, trying to work it out so the other clubs could get out to the [West] Coast and get back again. On the train; there was no flying then. We figured that we'd open up out there and play about four clubs, and we'd only have them make two trips out there. They'd take the Super Chief out of Chicago. We had the schedules made out.

''December 7, 1941, screwed up the whole thing. We were in Comiskey Park, watching the Bears and the Cardinals play football that day, and it was cold as the devil. Somebody came in and said, 'Gee, they just had a flash on the radio that the Japs have bombed Pearl Harbor.' Me, I didn't know where the hell Pearl Harbor was; I never heard of Pearl Harbor. Everybody started, 'Buzz, buzz . . .'

''Well, we had the meeting the next day and killed the whole thing.''

Unable to move, Don Barnes went in the opposite direction. He decided to spend some real money on players and try to compete with the Cardinals head-to-head. In February of 1942, Barnes convinced several angels, including board member Richard Muckerman, to buy stock in the team. Muckerman bought $300,000 worth of stock and was named team vice-president. His arrival kept the team afloat, and with his money the team bought Don Gutteridge and Vern Stephens to play second and short.

The added expenditure of money, as it often does, paid great dividends.

In 1942 the Browns finished a surprising third with an 82-69 record. This was the best Browns team since 1922. The hard-hitting Stephens, twenty-one, was the star, Gutteridge played well, and Chet Laabs hit 27 home runs, second only to Ted Williams in the American League, and drove in 99 runs. Elden Auker finished the season 14-13, his last in the major leagues. He retired at the end of the year to work in a Detroit factory to help the war effort and never looked back.

ELDON AUKER: "I had heard talk about the Browns moving to L.A. in *The Sporting News*. I would have gone, but once the war started, I decided I wasn't going anyplace. I would have quit wherever they would have gone.

"December 7 was a Sunday, and I was sitting in my apartment in Detroit. The couple who lived right below us were Freddie and Edith von Bonham. He was a German baron who was in the motion picture business. My wife and I went to their apartment for a late breakfast. And while we were sitting there, the news came on the air over the radio. I'll never forget it. I couldn't believe it.

"Barnes was the president, and he was getting together a group that had some money, and he tried to get the team going. Barnes was the one who got the others interested. I remember a fellow named Johnson who was the president of the Buster Brown Shoe Company. He was very wealthy and on the board too. And another man who made women's shoes. He was president of the International Shoe Company.

"Both of them came to spring training in '42. My wife Mildred and Fritz Ostermueller's wife used to play bridge with them. And Barnes also got Muckerman in. I knew Richard Muckerman. He was on the board of directors, a wealthy guy and a great baseball fan. He put some money into the team when he came in.

"We were pretty happy with our team. Vern Stephens was a good ball-player, a hard hitter, a good fielder, had a great arm. He was a very quiet guy, one of those old country boys doing his job. And Gutteridge did a good job, and Harlond Clift was great at third for a long time. I don't think he ever played on an All-Star team. The Browns never got much publicity. Everything in those days came out of New York. George McQuinn was a very good first baseman, but they had a lot of good first basemen in the league, of course. Our players never got any publicity. Even in St. Louis, we never got as much publicity as the Cardinals.

"I finished the season 14-13, and I said I was going to quit. The war had started. I started in 1938 working for a factory in Michigan. I lived in Detroit. I was working on an antiaircraft gun project. I was a specialist on antiaircraft guns, and this was a hot issue. We were grinding 20 mm shells, grinding airplane parts. I was in charge of the antiaircraft guns department. I had two other guys working for me.

"In the winter of 1941, I was hardly home. I was all over the United States. When the '42 season ended, I went back to my work immediately. The next day I was working. That winter Mickey Cochrane, who had enlisted, was in charge of the athletic program at Great Lakes, and he wanted me to come over. I went out to see him. Great Lakes was in North Chicago, a big operation where all the sailors were being trained. They had the best football team and the best baseball team in the country. Mickey was in charge of it.

"I called Mickey and told him, 'If I'm going to fight a war, I'm not going to fight it in North Chicago. Hell, I can't contribute anything over there. I'm on a job here where I feel I'm contributing. I'm too old for the draft.' I was thirty-one. I had a child. I thought I could do more for the war effort doing what I was doing than I could in the Navy.

"So I announced I was going to quit. Then I got a call from Clark Griffith, the owner of the Washington Senators. He said, 'I've just talked to President Roosevelt, and he said we want all the older players who are not going into the service to keep playing. I understand you said you were going to retire from the game.' I said, 'That's right.' He said, 'We'd like to have you stay in. We have to keep up the morale of the country.' Mr. Griffith said, 'He's given me the job to do it. We'd like you to continue to play.' I said, 'Mr. Griffith, I can't do it. I wouldn't feel right playing baseball while the guys are over there getting killed. I'm not going to go to North Chicago to coach baseball or football. I can contribute more where I am, and that's where I'm going to be.' The Browns offered me $27,500 to come back to St. Louis. I was getting $500 a month from the antiaircraft company. I said no.

"I never went to the ballpark for five years. I didn't want to be seen there. If I went, sportswriters see you and you have your name in the papers, and I didn't want that. I just didn't feel right. Many of the guys had gone to war. It wasn't anybody's business what I was doing. But I knew. I did what I thought was right. I stayed away."

CHAPTER 35

LUKE

WHEN Fred Haney quit as Browns manager in the middle of the 1941 season, they asked coach Luke Sewell to replace him. Sewell, who was with Cleveland, didn't want the job, but Indian owner Alva Bradley convinced him to at least talk to Browns owner Don Barnes. Since Sewell didn't really want the job, he figured he might as well make some demands and see just how committed Barnes was. Sewell demanded absolute authority over personnel. He wanted authority to make trades and move players up and down to the minors. Barnes agreed. Sewell took the job.

LUKE SEWELL: "I felt then that I could take practically any ballclub and, given the authority to do what I wanted, within three years make a winner out of it or at least get it into contention.

"One thing we needed badly, among others, when I took over the Browns, was a shortstop. Well, we had Vern Stephens playing at Toledo. Fred Haney was managing there. That shows you what kind of shape the Browns were in then—they couldn't afford to pay Fred for not working, so after they fired him, they sent him to manage Toledo and sent me the Toledo manager, Zack Taylor, as my pitching coach.

"I saw Haney after the season and asked him what kind of ballplayer Stephens was.

" 'No good,' he said.

" ' Can he play shortstop?'

" 'No,' he said. 'He'll never be a shortstop.'

" 'Well,' I said, 'we'll take a look at him in spring training.' "

Sewell worked with Stephens all through the spring of '42. He wouldn't let anyone else teach him. By the time the season began, Stephens was one of the top rookies in the league.

The Browns also needed a second baseman, because Johnny Berardino was going into the service, and Sewell contacted Branch Rickey, who was still with the Cardinals, to ask about Don Gutteridge, his former third baseman who had spent an unhappy season in Sacramento. Rickey knew that Gutteridge

VERN STEPHENS
(Courtesy Brace Photo)

was going to quit, and he figured he would make a quick $500, and he sold Gutteridge to the Browns. If the Browns kept him, the Browns would have to pay an added $250.

Sewell called Gutteridge on the phone. "Don, I need a second baseman. Can you play it?"

"Yes, I can play second base," said Gutteridge, who felt he could play anywhere.

"You're going to be my second baseman. Come to spring training and figure out how to play it," said Sewell.

Gutteridge recalled how he went about finding out how to play this new position.

DON GUTTERIDGE: "In spring training, we played against Bobby Doerr. I knew Bobby, and I talked to him a long time about playing second base. And I talked to Joe Gordon. I figured they were the two best second basemen.

"Doerr showed me how to pivot, and where I should play, and so did Joe. Both of them were very good to me. They took time with me. I took what I thought was the best of both of them, and I tried different ways of doing things and used what worked best for me.

"I started with the Browns in '42. Let me give you a little background. The Browns were never a contending ballclub, never a good ballclub. The Browns were a bunch of guys who would get released from another club and they just wanted to get in one more year. All they wanted was a paycheck. Winning didn't mean anything to them. They were a so-so ballclub, and if they won, all right,

DON GUTTERIDGE
(Courtesy Brace Photo)

and if they got beat, all right. It didn't matter to them, because they were players about to quit anyway. And they didn't have any farm system to replace them.

"When Luke Sewell took over, he said, 'This is going to change.' The very first day I met him, he kept saying to the whole team, 'We can win.' We'd have a team meeting, and he'd tell us this. He'd give the winning spirit. He traded off some ballplayers, guys like Harlond Clift, who had a losing attitude. Luke installed a winning attitude, and that made the difference on the ballclub. Instead of taking any old guy who wanted to finish out the year just to get another paycheck, he didn't take that ballplayer. He didn't claim anyone on waivers. Instead we got players like Vern Stephens, who should be in the Hall of Fame. He was the strongest shortstop, physically a very strong man. He was the type like Joe Medwick. He could be fooled, but he had the strong arms and strong wrists, so he could hit the ball hard anywhere, no matter where you threw it.

"I had a terrific season in '42. I led the league in putouts and assists. You don't know the satisfaction I had of doing that and proving Rickey wrong. And Rickey was next door too. He saw everything I did. If I had been a vengeful fellow, I would have written him a couple of letters, but I didn't. I just wanted to show him that I could play in the major leagues, and I did. I proved him wrong.

"He never came up to me and said, 'I was wrong.' And he never spoke to me from then on. And I never spoke to him. I just kept on, because I was enjoying my years so much playing with the Browns. I enjoyed playing under Luke Sewell, and I liked the idea of winning. In all the years I played in the major leagues, I only finished in the second division a couple of times. I wanted to win. Winning was my big thing, and I was willing to sacrifice myself if we could win a ball game. That gave me the satisfaction. Another thing too, Sewell gave me a free rein. He said, 'You're it. No other second baseman is going to take your place. I want you there.' I was the captain— not officially, but if anything came up, he'd come to me—Luke and I talked a lot. I had a little bit more experience than most of them. Not so much about strategy, but how to handle these different ballplayers.

"For instace, Vern Stephens liked the night life very much. I didn't drink or fool around, and the second year I was in St. Louis, Sewell said to me, 'I want you to room with Vernon and keep him sobered up and keep him on the beat.' Well, that didn't last too long because all I did was room with his suitcase. Literally sometimes. I only saw him at the ballpark. He was drinking. He would come and tell me. We were very good friends.

"I don't know why he drank so much. Tell me. But he enjoyed it, and he liked the lady friends. He always had lady friends. He was married to a nice girl, and he had a nice young son, but that wasn't enough for him.

"Luke knew how to handle men. He could do it better than anybody. He knew how to get the most out of everybody and do it really in a sneaky way. He would be managing you, and you wouldn't know it.

"Of course, we had George McQuinn at first base and Mark Christman at third, and they didn't need any discipline. They had played on second division teams, and they were so tickled to get on a good ballclub and start winning. They fell right into it. And Chet Laabs could hit the ball farther than anybody. He was a little guy who was just as strong as the devil with his arms. He wasn't a really good outfielder, but if the ball came to him, he'd catch it. He couldn't go ten steps and catch a ball. He was very slow. But he sure could swing a bat. We had Mike Kreevich in center field, and he took care of left field too for Chet. He did such a good job and made Chet a better ballplayer.

"Chet was from Milwaukee. He liked that Milwaukee beer. 'Get the ball game over, let's win, and I can have three beers and go home.' He wasn't excessive. He was a nice guy, and a real good ballplayer.

"In '42 we had the best attendance in many, many years. We drew 250,000 fans. It was terrible. You could almost shoot a shotgun into the grandstands, and you wouldn't hit anybody. But what can you do? You get paid for playing and doing the best you can. That's why Sewell wanted to win. He

figured if we won, the fans would come
out and see us play. Because everyone
loves a winner.

"With the Browns, I talked contract
with Bill DeWitt. He was a protégé of
Rickey's. Bill didn't want to pay you
either, but he didn't have the money to
pay you. If you haven't got the money,
you can't pay. And we didn't think we'd
get very much if we didn't win ball
games. So I don't blame DeWitt. I
didn't resent him the way I resented
Rickey. DeWitt was truthful with you.
He said, 'I can't pay you. I'd like to.
You had a good season, but I can't raise
your salary because I haven't got the
money.' I said, 'Well . . .' So I liked
Bill DeWitt. I liked to play for him. I
have no fault with him at all. His brother
Charlie was the traveling secretary. You
know what, we traveled better than the
Cardinals. 'Cause we always had a good

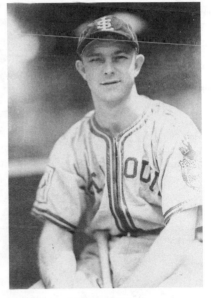

CHET LAABS
(Courtesy Peter Golenbock)

Pullman car, always stayed in good hotels. The Cardinals were always pinching
pennies. The Browns were a better club to play for than the Cardinals. I think
Rickey was at fault for that. And Breadon could pinch some pennies too.

"In 1943 we trained at Cape Girardeau, down the Mississippi from St.
Louis. The United States government put a restriction on travel, and all the
ballclubs had to play within 200 miles of their hometown.

"It was cold most of the time. Missouri that time of the year still had
wintertime. There's a college down there, and they had a field house, and so
they'd haul in four or five inches of dirt to put on that thing, and we took
infield in there. It wasn't big enough for a diamond, but we took ground balls.
On a good day we'd go outside. It was the best of a poor bargain.

"It was a college town, and there were bars all over. College towns have
places for young people to drink. Our ballplayers, a lot of them, did just that.
They liked to go out at night.

"One of the guys who had a tremendous drinking problem was Mike
Kreevich. He was the same type of guy as Stephens. The Philadelphia A's
had released Mike because he drank so much. Sewell had played with him
and picked him up. Mike had tremendous talent. He was a good, good outfielder. And he hit well enough to play outfield. Sewell took him. He said,
'Take care of yourself,' but he didn't ride him about it. Sewell would talk to
him. He'd say, 'Listen, Mike, we have a big, important series. Why don't you
take care of yourself?' Luke would do that all the time. Sometimes Luke would
say to me, 'Go talk to Mike and see if you can't get him to let up a little bit.'

"One night Sewell went out thinking he'd catch a few of them. He went
into this one bar, and Mike Kreevich was settin' in there, and he said, 'Kree-

MIKE KREEVICH
(Courtesy Brace Photo)

vich, go on home.' He sent him home in a taxi. Pretty soon he came back in, and there was Kreevich. The taxi driver took him to the hotel, he went up to his room, and then he went back to the bar! He was back thirty minutes later!

"Luke liked Kreevich, in spite of everything, because he wouldn't harm anyone. He didn't try to get in fights. He just liked to drink. And he was a very likable guy. When he wasn't drinking, he was a lot of fun. Mike came and did a good job for us. He had talent.

"Another player we picked up in '43 was Nelson Potter. He had won 19 games in the Cardinal minor league system, and Rickey let him go. I knew Nelson from way back in the early thirties when we played together in the Nebraska State League. I was tickled to death to see him. 'Cause I thought he was a good pitcher.

"I'll tell you why Rickey let him go. Rickey liked great big guys who could throw fastballs, and Nelson wasn't a fastball pitcher. He didn't throw hard. He used a screwball or curveball. But Potter turned out to be a really good pitcher for us. Our ballclub was made for Potter, because our infield was solid. If you hit the ball on the ground, you got thrown out. All of us were good infielders. McQuinn and Christman and Stephens and me. We were a great infield. We could have played with any ballclub. We were that good.

"In '43 the Browns also traded for pitcher Bobo Newsom. He had played with all sixteen ballclubs [ten, actually, but many clubs more than once]. I thought he was completely nuts. He was an extreme egotist. He just irritated everybody. I don't think Bobo was a winning pitcher. He could pitch on a club that didn't care if they won, but he rarely pitched on a pennant-winning ballclub. And there are players who can't do that. They can play on a losing ballclub but not on a winning one.

"Bobo was always talking. He talked from the time he got up in the morning until he went to bed at night. And he always had a story to tell. He had a pretty good arm, but he would always make a mistake at the wrong time. He couldn't win tight ball games. That's the losing part. Luke didn't have anyone else, so he put him out there, figuring sooner or later he'd win for us. [It never happened. Newsom was 1-6 with a 7.39 ERA for the Browns in '43, and he was quickly dealt to Washington.]

"Ellis Clary was another player we picked up that year. He was another player who Luke wanted. He traded Harlond Clift to Washington to get him. Ellis was a good ballplayer. He filled in in the infield quite a bit, and he'd fight for you. Nobody would bother his buddies. Talk about a fighter! Ellis would fight for you in a minute. You want to be amused? Call Ellis Clary. I'd just follow him around all day long and listen to him talk."

ELLIS CLARY: "I was born in Valdosta, Georgia, in 1916. My dad was a lawyer. I had no intention of doing that. I didn't want no part of it. As a boy, we played baseball and football on the sandlots every day. In the winter, if it was cold, we'd play football in the morning and baseball in the afternoon when it was a little warmer. When I was eighteen, I was playing semipro baseball every day but Sunday. I was playing in the summertime in a place called Vienna, Georgia. Bill Peer, a scout for the Tigers, was living in Birmingham and scouted for the Birmingham Barons, which was an independent team. Most of the Southern League teams were independent teams.

"My manager was Clyde Milan. He had played for Washington. He was a super man. Everyone loved Clyde. My second year I got into the Washington chain. Early Wynn was on my team. He was seventeen years old. He walked into the ballpark for a tryout in Florida. He was barefooted with a T-shirt and a pair of blue jeans and a Coca-Cola cap. He said he could play. They said, 'We'll find out.' Early wound up in the Hall of Fame.

"Our manager was Bill 'Raw Meat' Rogers, and he was the greatest human being that you could ever imagine. We were horseshit. That's the only word that fits, and Early was worse than I was. He walked everybody. And this man, in a word, bullshitted us into thinking we could play. He was the best man in the world for young players to be with. He put up with us. And we were terrible. But he kept sticking with us. Anybody else would have released both of us. Wynn couldn't throw a strike. And I was horseshit. He hung in there with us. I led the league in stolen bases that year. He let me run when I wanted to. One game I bunted, and I stole second on the next pitch, stole third on the next pitch, and he just yelled out where everybody

ELLIS CLARY
(Courtesy Brace Photo)

could hear, 'Hell, go on home.' And on the next pitch, I stole home. He was
a super man. Everybody thought the world of 'Raw Meat' Rogers.

"In 1938 I was playing for Charlotte. Calvin Griffith was the manager. I
beat Jesse Owens in the fifty-yard dash in Richmond, Virginia. I stayed ahead
of him halfway, anyway. But it didn't count 'cause we were racing in the
hundred. I thought I had him beat. Of course, I jumped the gun and cut over
into his lane. The sprint champion of the Southern Conference also was in the
race, and at least I beat him. But I stayed ahead of Jesse Owens about halfway.
About the fifty-yard line, I was envisioning getting a telegram from Adolf
Hitler for beating Jesse Owens! And I didn't see Jesse for thirty years after
that. And one day I'm out at Tempe, Arizona, in the lunchroom during spring
training. Milwaukee was training there at the time. I was sitting in the dining
room with a group at the table, and I looked over across the room over in the
corner. This black guy was sitting there with some other people, and I asked
who it was. 'It's Jesse Owens.' I walked over there, and I said, 'Hey,' and he
looked up at me and knew immediately who I was. I said, 'You know what,
Jesse, you broke every bookmaker in Richmond. They had me 9 to 1 to beat
you, and you lucked out on me.' He said, 'Man, get out of town. What you
talking about?' He remembered the race. He remembered me cutting into his
lane and elbowing him as he went by. You couldn't beat that son of a bitch.

"On that team, I played with Bobo Newsom. I was with him at Washington, the St. Louis Browns, and Chattanooga. Bobo played with everybody. He would have played on more if they had had expansion like they got today. When we were in St. Louis, Dizzy Dean was getting all the ink with the Cardinals. Bobo put him in the shade. I knew both of them. Bobo was so full of shit you wouldn't believe it. A marvelous guy. He died early. He was only fifty-five. He had cirrhosis of the liver. He wouldn't drink anything else but beer. He stood at Harper's Bar in Orlando, over near Rollins College, and he wore a hole in the tile standing at the end of the bar until the tile wore out. That was his hangout, and he had a special parking place there.

"Bobo would come to spring training, and he would wind up and throw a 90-mile-an-hour fastball without warming up. He was a good-natured guy who loved to have a good laugh. He could wear out his welcome, no question about that. Mr. Griffith got him five times, you know. He would talk hisself off of any club after a while, but he was a drawing card. Every time he'd get released, Mr. Griffith would get him back. And he got to throwing that bloofer ball, you know. Like that guy in Pittsburgh, Rip Sewell, he got to throwing that thing.

"When I was with the Browns he was pitching for Washington, and they

BOBO NEWSOM
(Courtesy Brace Photo)

came to town, and he started the game throwing that damn bloofer ball, which was showing up our players to a certain extent. He'd embarrass you. If you couldn't hit fungo flies to the outfielders as a coach, you couldn't hit it.

"Anyway, he had a shutout with a no-hitter until the fifth inning, and then Al Zarilla got a hit to right field. And all at once, he couldn't get us out. We scored five or six runs, and we beat him. The next day he told me, 'That's another thing I am going to stick up my ass.' 'Cause it beat him. He kept throwing it until we finally tuned into it.

"But Bobo was such a lovable character. He was a pitiful, terrible hitter. He would take one strike left-handed, then switch over and take one right-handed, get back over and take the third one left-handed, and sit down. He couldn't knock the ball out of the infield. He occasionally would hit a ground ball. The bench was on the first base side, and he would run no more than halfway and turn and go set down in the dugout. Today he would get suspended for doing that. He would almost run out of the batter's box straight to the bench and sit down.

"And he was as big as a horse, you know. He was so big, and pitching in St. Louis on a hot day, you could actually hear his feet sloshing in his shoes, coming off the mound going back to the bench. I never heard that before on anybody else. He could sweat like a mule. In St. Louis on a day game, it was intolerable.

"In 1943 I was playing with the Senators. We were in second place. In the middle of the summer, I got traded to the Browns. I felt like committing suicide. Course, you never know what's down around the corner. Turned out to be the finest thing ever to happen to me. But when I was traded, I felt terrible. I mean bad. I get over there with all them clowns, and it was the greatest group of all. The fun we had and the characters on that team, there will never be an assemblage like that again. Never.

"The player I was traded for was Harlond Clift. Harlond was very popular. In 1938 he hit 34 home runs for the Browns. Anybody who hits 34 for the Browns is doing something, because that fence in old Sportsman's Park was 350 feet down the line. You had to kill the ball to get it up in the seats, and he hit 34. And so when I learned I had been traded for Clift, I was upset— until I tuned in with all those meatheads over there.

"You know about a month before I went over there, we had a little scuffle with the Browns in Washington. They came in, and they were red-hot. They had been going good and were stopping in Washington for four games on the way back to St. Louis. We beat them badly all four games, and then in the last game we got to throwing at each other. You could do that back then.

"Somebody in front of me hit a home run, and the next pitch was right behind my head, and I hadn't hit no damn home run. And back then you wore a cloth cap, not a helmet. I said to myself, 'I will get that son of a bitch.' I bunted the ball to first base, and one of the best people I have ever met in my life was Denny Galehouse, and he was pitching in relief. We had slammed everyone around, and he was out there, and I didn't know Denny Galehouse from Joe Blow.

"I pushed a bunt down first, and he covered, and I hit-slammed into him and knocked him out into right field, and he made the third out. I jumped up and headed for third base, because the inning was over, and Bill Grieve, who was umpiring, thought I was charging Galehouse, and he grabbed me, and I said, 'You son of a bitch, I'm going over there to get my glove. Get the hell out of the way.'

"A month later, maybe even less, I went over to St. Louis, and I was scared to walk into the clubhouse. And Rick Ferrell was the catcher for the Browns then, and our dressing room in St. Louis was upstairs. I came up those steps, and I dreaded it. To tell you the truth, I was scared to walk in there. I walked in the door and looked around.

"Rick Ferrell spotted me. He jumped up and came to the door and shook my hand. This is exactly what he said: 'Welcome to our nine.' And that was the greatest thing. Rick was a fine man. Many years later I visited him in his office in Tiger Stadium. I said, 'I want to thank you again.' That was the greatest relief I ever had when he said, 'Welcome to our nine.' And that was the greatest thing in the world to get over there with all them guys, 'cause you couldn't believe it unless you were there.''

CHAPTER 36

1944

DESPITE Luke Sewell's additions, the Browns in 1943 finished in sixth place, twenty-five games behind the Dickey–Gordon–Crosetti–Keller-led New York Yankees. But during the season there had been indications that the Browns were capable of winning ball games. In June, for instance, the Browns had a winning streak of eighteen of twenty-six games. But the Browns' greatest victories, it would turn out, would be before the Selective Service Draft Board. Both George McQuinn and Vern Stephens were declared unfit for service when they flunked their physicals.

One of the weaknesses Bill DeWitt knew needed shoring up was catching. He found two rookies, Red Hayworth, brother of the talented Ray Hayworth, who was a longtime Detroit Tiger, and Frank Mancuso, brother of the Giants' Gus Mancuso, a former Card. Frank Mancuso had joined the Army in '42 and then broke his leg and hurt his back in a parachute jump.

By the start of the 1944 season, about 340 major leaguers were in military service, along with 3,000 more from the minor leagues. But not one Brown was taken in 1943 and in 1944 only one pitcher was taken: Steve Sundra, who left early in the year.

To give you an idea of the advantage this presented the Browns, as a comparison, the New York Yankees, in addition to losing Joe DiMaggio, Tommy Henrich, Buddy Hassett, Phil Rizzuto, and Red Ruffing in 1943, after dependency deferments were knocked out, lost Marius Russo, Roy Weatherly, Billy Johnson, Charlie Keller, Bill Dickey, and Joe Gordon in 1944.

The Red Sox were without Ted Williams, Johnny Pesky, Dom DiMaggio, catcher Frankie Pytlak, and pitcher Charlie Wagner. Detroit had lost Hank Greenberg, Barney McCosky, Pat Mullin, Hoot Evers, Birdie Tebbetts, Fred Hutchinson, Al Benton, and Charlie Gehringer.

Bill DeWitt needed more pitching, and he signed two of the more renowned alcoholics ever to wear a major league uniform: Alvis "Tex" Shirley, a drunk and brawler who had been released by the Philadelphia A's, and a large fighting Marine by the name of Sig Jakucki. Sig had last pitched in the majors for the Browns in 1936, then drank and slugged his way around the minor leagues.

When Shirley and Jakucki joined the other carousers, Vern Stephens and Mike Kreevich, manager Luke Sewell, who had personally assembled this team, *really* had his hands full. Ellis Clary, Don Gutteridge, and Denny Galehouse recalled the highlights of the most momentous season ever compiled by the St. Louis Browns.

ELLIS CLARY: "We opened spring training in 1944 at Cape Girardeau. Joining our team that year were Tex Shirley and Sig Jakucki. Both of them were drinkers. The first night the whole club was in the bar there. The whole team was drinking beer. And they weren't bringing it to Tex Shirley fast enough. He got up and went to get his own beer, and when he came back, Jakucki was sitting in his chair. Everybody was about half in the bag.

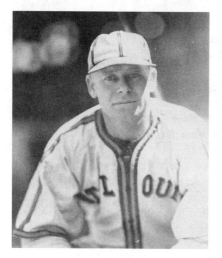

SIG JAKUCKI
(Courtesy Brace Photo)

"Shirley didn't know who Sig was, and he figured he would pour a little beer on Jakucki's head. He figured he'd give him a little shampoo. And Jack got up and hit Tex Shirley right in the mouth and damn near knocked the wall down with him. Tex's mouth the next morning looked like a freight train had run through it. He had it all patched up. And he told Luke that he had been riding at the riding academy and that a horse threw him against a fence. And Luke didn't know any better. But that was their introduction: Jakucki smacked him right in the mouth.

"Every night something would happen. They would get in a barroom brawl somewhere."

DENNY GALEHOUSE: "Shirley was a rugged guy. He was bald, and he wore a cowboy hat on his head real tight, and one time he got in trouble in the clubhouse, and they threw him out head over heels, but he never lost his hat.

"Sig played with a pinochle deck. He had about the mentality of a twelve-year-old. He fought at the drop of a hat. He used to get in a lot of fights while we were on the road. I never paid any attention.''

DON GUTTERIDGE: "Tex was a good pitcher. He could throw the ball hard. An overhand pitcher and a little bit of a character. He liked to drink a little bit, like Jakucki, but he wasn't quite as good a pitcher. We used Tex a lot of times as an extra pitcher, to finish games, pitch relief, and if we were in a pinch and we needed a starting pitcher, he did a good job for us. You get characters like that on a club when you have a lot of people gone. Tex helped us. He won some important games.''

ELLIS CLARY: "We had three guys on the team who ought to have been preachers. Each had been in seminaries somewhere: Gene Moore, Don Gutteridge, and George McQuinn. They'd just sit in the lobby. They didn't drink. They'd sit and watch the shit. The others would come in all hours of the night, skinned up and bleeding, fighting, every damn thing. Nowadays they don't fight. If you're making $8 million, you can't get in no fight. Back then, it was part of the game. And them three would sit there and look at that shit. They didn't take part in that nightlife.

"One time the drinkers were in a bar right across the street from the New Yorker Hotel, where we stayed in New York. What they called the Travelers' Bar, a huge bar. Jakucki would go all over town working those bars at night. Some thug came in and was sitting on a stool next to him, and they started jawing at each other, and this guy pulled a gun, stuck it right in Jakucki's ribs and threatened to blow him off the stool.

"Jakucki grabbed that pistol and hit him right over the head with his own gun and knocked the guy flat on his back. Jack threw the gun down beside him and walked out.

"Jack had served time in the Army. I don't know which branch, but they tell me over before the war in Japan where he was stationed, they got places marked where he hit long home runs. I don't know that that's true. That's what they said.

"We were over in New York one day, and he was pitching, and the Yankees were beating us by a run in a close game in the eighth inning. You didn't take Jack out for no hitter. The son of a bitch could hit. He used an old Hornsby-model bat, not much of a knob. And this day he done broke his bat. He done walked up to me, and I was setting there right next to the batrack. He said, 'Where is that chickenshit bat you use?' I reached over and pulled it out and handed it to him, and he hit a home run with it and won the game and never used it again!

"After he pitched a game, Jack would disappear. You might not see him for two or three days. After a home game, when he'd pitch, I'd take a shower, and McQuinn would always be one of the last ones to leave after the game, but Jakucki'd be gone in ten minutes. He was heading out to work the bars. Jakucki'd head out that door, and McQuinn would say to him, 'See you Thursday, Jack.' And Jack'd turn around, laugh, and take off. And if it was a Thursday, McQuinn would say, 'See you Monday, Jack.'

"Luke couldn't do anything about him. If he tried, what good would it have done him? You couldn't do that today, and you couldn't do it then. In fact, if you tried to stop it, the some who didn't drink would start. Just to show they could do it.

"Another fine, fine guy we had on the club was Mike Kreevich, who we got from the A's because he drank too much. His wife used to have to watch him like a hawk. In St. Louis she had him staked out with a one-foot rope so he couldn't drink. But on the road, man, he let it fly.

"That's why damn near every night on the road—we were the same size, the same height, he was heavier than me—he would want to wrestle me. He'd be half-loaded. And if a man wants to wrestle you, you have to wrestle back or he'll kill ya. We wrestled in the Pullman cars up and down the aisles, rolling over and over. A carpet in a Pullman car is like sandpaper. It's rough, and I stayed skinned up.

"I would try to trade rooms with somebody, try to hide from him. We had two private cars, and he would just part them curtains looking for me, and when he found me, I'd have to wrestle him. Or he'd come find me in my hotel room to wrestle.

"One night in Washington in that Shoreham Hotel where we were staying, he found me, and I had to start wrestling, and the whole club laughed all night. We broke the bed. I used to dread him, but he was a wonderful guy. He never did get mad. I loved Mike Kreevich. And he was the most underrated ballplayer I ever saw, and I've spent fifty-nine years in the game.

"He could hit! The index finger of his left hand was cut off, and one day he got 4-for-4 off of Hal Newhouser. He came to the bench, and held his hand near his jaw, and he said, 'I got me a whole handful.' He had three fingers and a thumb.

"One night in Philadelphia Jack and Tex Shirley tore up a barroom. They turned it over. Everybody was drunk. The rest room was up a flight of stairs, a little mezzanine deal, and somebody in there took a piss right over that damn banister, and peed on the people down below. Jakucki and Shirley went up there and got him, turned over the tables, chairs, everything, and busted down the door to get him. But something like that was common with them guys.

"Another player who stayed out all the time was Vern Stephens. I had to room with him one year on the road. You'd wake up the next morning, and his bag would be there at the foot of the bed, wouldn't even be opened. The bed wouldn't be touched. And women—every gal who looked at him wanted to hop in bed with him. He had three names, Vern, Stevie, and Junior, and the phone would ring all night. Nobody could put up with that shit for very long. 'Is Vern there?' 'No, he ain't here.' And she'd think you were lying. 'Is Stevie there?' 'Is Junior there?'

"One day in Philadelphia he came out to Shibe Park, and his locker was right next to mine. He came up to me, and this was when I was rooming with him. He said, 'Roomie, I don't think I can make it today. I haven't slept a wink all night.' He had been fooling around with some woman. This was a day game in Philadelphia and Russ Christopher, a big tall sidearmer, was going to pitch for the A's. Right-handers didn't like him nohow.

"But Vern got out there to play after he told me he didn't think he could make it, and that guy struck him out three times, and he ain't fouled out. Three times he got him swinging, and the fourth time up in the ninth inning Stevie hit the façade of the roof of the upper deck and the ball bounced back in the ballpark. Beat Christopher the ball game! Now ain't that something! He hit a rocket out of there.

"Vern was a better-than-average shortstop. He wasn't up there with Aparicio, Pesky, Reese, Rizzuto, Appling. He wasn't Marty Marion, I'll put it that way. Who was at the time? But he had good range and good speed. When he first got up there, he could fly to first base. And he had a rifle arm. Jesus Christ, he could knock the first baseman down.

"They always said Vern would die young, and he did, at forty-eight. But he was a wonderful guy. They tried putting Don Gutteridge in there to room with him. Gutteridge was a teetotaler. I kidded Don. I said, 'You couldn't stop Junior from drinking, but he got you to start drinking! It was the only way you could stay in there with him.' But Gutteridge never did drink. I don't think he's taken a drink yet.

"They even sent Don to watch over Jakucki. But he couldn't do it. Everybody tried to straighten up somebody. You couldn't do it.''

DON GUTTERIDGE: "In the spring of '44, we knew a lot of regulars from other teams were missing, but we didn't dwell on it. We realized a lot of guys were gone. On the very first day, Luke Sewell said, 'We can win. We've got as good a ballclub as anybody. We can win. We can win. We can win.' He said, 'We're going to win the pennant.' He drilled that into us.

"We thought, 'Maybe we can.' He said it so many times we began believing him, then things started to happen.''

ELLIS CLARY: "When the 1944 season began, we didn't know how good our team was, but we did know that we had four pretty good pitchers. Like them guys in Atlanta today. We had Jack Kramer, Nelson Potter, Denny Galehouse, and Bob Muncrief. Those four bastards, when they went out there, you'd think you could win the game. And we had as second-liners Jakucki, Sam Zoldak, Al Hollingsworth, Tex Shirley, and a relief man, George Caster.

"But the Big Four, hell, they were good pitchers. They could beat anybody. And that's what won for us, those four pitchers. This was a pretty good team when you put those four pitchers out there.

"You always heard people say, 'It was the war years,' but shit, you play the ball games. It don't matter who we're playing. If you beat them, you beat them. Hell, you got a game to play. It don't make a damn bit of difference who is over there. You're not concerned with who they are. I don't give a shit who he is. Knock his ass off!

"The season began, and we won nine in a row.''

DON GUTTERIDGE: "I was quoted as saying, 'I don't think we're going to get beat all year long.' I actually thought we could win every ball game. Of course,

no one is going to win 150 games. But we thought we could win. We'd talk
to each other. 'Hey, we can win this thing.' "

ELLIS CLARY: "I remember telling them, 'If we keep going, we may get a
Sugar Bowl bid or if we go undefeated, we may get a Rose Bowl bid!'
Everybody was running their goddamn mouth. In that ninth game, we won it
in Chicago, Jack Kramer hit a damn ball over that 402-foot sign in left-center
field. Jack Kramer was a strange guy, a fine guy and a good-looking guy. He
called his mama every night in New Orleans.

"At home Kramer and I roomed together at the Melbourne Hotel on the
corner of Grand and Olive, and we kept it all year long. He'd call his mother
down in New Orleans every night. He had been married to Dotty Dotson, a
prominent singer in Del Courtney's band, and they were split.

"He was a guy who loved his clothes. Shit, he changed clothes two, three
times a day. The other guys got on him all the time, called him a 'fruit basket.'
I told them, 'You'll find out if you mess with him.' He'd knock you on your
ass. You might think he was a fruitcake, but he was just the opposite. And he
talked like Bobo, with a hoarse voice. He talked funny. But he was a handsome
guy. And that Dotty Dotson was beautiful.

JACK KRAMER
(Courtesy Brace Photo)

LUKE SEWELL
(Courtesy Brace Photo)

"After he retired, he worked for a milk company down in New Orleans. He was a great advertiser for milk. He said, 'I sell the greatest food in the world: milk.' "

After winning nine in a row, the team lost ten of its next fifteen and slipped to third behind the Yankees and Senators. Quickly though, the Browns righted themselves. On June 6, 1944, D-Day, as millions of American troops were storming the beaches of Normandy, the Browns were in first place, with the Yankees right behind them.

DON GUTTERIDGE: "There'd be times when the club would have a little slump for a week or two. Luke Sewell would call a little meeting and say, 'Don't get excited. We're going to come out of this thing. We're going to win.' And all year long he'd do the same thing. Sewell was a fabulous guy. He changed the Browns from nonwinners to winners. He did a magnificent job with a bunch of ballplayers no one else could win with.

"And he only had Denny Galehouse to pitch on Sundays. Denny was doing war work over in Ohio, and he'd pitch, and as soon as the game was over, he'd get back on the train to Ohio. Denny talked to me one time. He said, 'I'd just like to stay here all year long. This is awful tough on me.' I encouraged him to stay, and he went to the draft board and asked, 'How long before I get drafted?' And they told him, and he decided he would quit his job and play every day with us, because he figured we were going to be a pennant winner.

"That was the middle of the summer, and he said, 'I'm going to take a chance. If you want me, call me, I'll just go.' And luckily the war was winding down. It was real gutsy. He was willing to give up everything in order to help us win the pennant.''

DENNY GALEHOUSE: "When I started that '44 season, I stayed in that war plant, and on Saturday night I'd get on a train and go to wherever the club was and pitch the first game on Sunday, then leave and go back home and be at that war plant on Monday morning. For almost half a year I did this, and finally it got to where I couldn't keep my physical condition up with the rest of the guys playing all the time, so when it looked like we had a good chance to win the pennant, I went to my draft board, which was in Sarasota, Florida, and asked them, 'If I quit the war job and go into baseball full-time, would I last through the Series, through the end of October?' And they said, 'Yes. You won't be taken before the first of the year.' So I said, 'Okay, that's what I'm going to do.'

"So I went back and I won quite a few games the second half. My record that year was 9-10. I won most of those after I joined full-time and got back into shape.

"We led Boston at the All-Star break.''

DON GUTTERIDGE: "George McQuinn and Vern Stephens batted third and fourth in the American League All-Star lineup in '44. George was very quiet. When he came to spring training he said hello, and when he left in the fall he said goodbye. When he did talk, it was kind of a dry humor. If you told him a joke, he'd kind of grin. But if you hit the ball in his direction, he came up with it. He helped me, because I was a little bit wild at second base. He would catch balls and make outs that no other first baseman made.

"He was also a good steady hitter. Every day he got a hit. I liked George. We got along real good.''

DENNY GALEHOUSE: "In August I remember shutting out the Yankees, 3–0. It was 0–0 through nine, and then through ten. And we scored three in the eleventh, and I got them out in the bottom of the inning.

"But I didn't mind pitching in Yankee Stadium. I could keep most of the hitters from pulling the ball down the short porches. I made them hit to the long part of the field, from right-center over to left-center. For that reason, I had fairly good luck against the Yankees.''

DON GUTTERIDGE: "In early September, the Red Sox lost several key players to the armed services. It would come out in the paper that so-and-so was leaving. It was one of those things that was happening. We'd say, 'That's going to hurt them,' and it would give us a little more impetus. 'They're gone now. We're going to win.'

ELLIS CLARY: "Going into September, we were trailing the Tigers and the Yankees for the pennant. I remember one game where we were trailing, 2–0, to the A's in the ninth inning. Bobo had started, and late in the game they brought in Jesse Flores, and somebody hit a ball into left-center that Bobby Estalella could not catch. I had played with Bobby in Cuba and Charlotte and Washington. A white Cuban. He should have caught that ball, but he didn't catch it. Thirty years later, I ran into Jesse Flores at a motel where I was staying in Orlando, and he told me that Estalella should have caught the damn ball. Yeah, he ought to have caught it, but if you win the pennant a lot of those things happen in your favor. They have to.

"With five games left, we were tied with the Tigers. We're playing the Red Sox in St. Louis, and it's raining. DeWitt has to decide whether to play, and we do, and we lose. Pinky Woods beat us, 4 to 1. It wasn't just raining. It was a storm. And we played anyhow."

DENNY GALEHOUSE: "We felt really down. Yeah. After leading all that time and to have that happen, to have Detroit take the lead. And Detroit was playing Washington, a team that never won, and we had to play four against the Yankees. It was a dismal-looking situation."

DON GUTTERIDGE: "Few people realize that the race was so close that if the Yankees had won those ball games, they would have won the pennant instead of us. But there was no doubt about it. We were going to win."

ELLIS CLARY: "And so we had to win the last four games against the Yankees, and that ain't easy to do. It rained Thursday, and we played a doubleheader on Friday. Jack Kramer won the first one, and then Nelson Potter, who was a hell of a pitcher, shut them out, 1–0. [The doubleheader in St. Louis drew only 6,172 fans, who held out little hope.]

"On Saturday [before a crowd of 12,982] Denny Galehouse won, 2–0, and Mike Kreevich saved it with a catch behind his head. I don't know how he caught it. Nobody but him would have caught that ball. Willie Mays wouldn't have got it.

"Johnny Lindell hit a line drive at him that broke like a curveball. A foul ball will do that sometimes. He was running after it in dead center field, looking over his right shoulder, and the ball broke back, and he stuck his glove behind his head, and he caught it without looking at it. I don't know how he did it. But he did.

"They put up Paul Waner to pinch-hit with the bases loaded. Paul Waner was my all-time, all-time, all-time hero when I was a young'un. In my book no one else played the game like Paul Waner. I said to myself, 'Jesus Christ Almighty, here's my all-time man walking up there to pinch-hit. He's gonna knock me out of the World Series. This is terrible.' It was the only time in my life I've ever pulled against him. And he hit a line drive at Don Gutteridge that ended that. He hit that ball, and Gutteridge jumped up and caught it.''

DON GUTTERIDGE: "Paul Waner pinch-hit, and there was a man on second base, and he hit it over my head, kind of a looper. I went back and caught the ball backhanded with my back to the infield. I made one hell of a play, if I may say that myself. And that was the third out of the inning. Two or three years later, I was in Florida, and Paul Waner said, 'Don, I'll tell you something. You caught the last ball I ever hit in the major leagues.' Isn't that something?''

DENNY GALEHOUSE: "I had pretty good luck against New York. I always did. In fact, if we could go back over and if I could eliminate one outfielder [He wouldn't say who], he cost me three games, not all in one year. It was late in the game and I was leading three times, and a line drive was hit at him, and the first time he came charging in, and it went over his head. The next time he laid back, and it hit in front of him and skipped by him, and the third time he charged in again and did the same thing.''

ELLIS CLARY: "The last day of the season we were tied with the Tigers. It boiled down to one game. They flipped a coin to see where we'd play if the season ended in a tie. We lost the coin toss, and as a result, we all had to pack our bags in the morning before the last game and take them to the ballpark. In the event we lost we were going to Dee-troit for a one-game playoff.

"The Tigers were playing the Washington Senators, and someone called Dutch Leonard of the Senators on the phone and said he wanted him to lose the game to the Tigers. And Dutch Leonard, shit, he wouldn't do that for a billion dollars, and he beat them with that knuckleball.

"Meanwhile, we faced the Yankees. Mel Queen started for them—his son pitched for Cincinnati. Sig Jakucki pitched for us. See, we had used up them four, and Saturday night we met at the Melbourne Hotel. Luke Sewell come over there and was talking to Zack Taylor, the pitching coach. 'Are we going to pitch one of these guys out of turn or pitch Jakucki?' And one of them, I don't remember if it was Luke or Zack, he said, 'Goddamn it, pitch Jakucki. He's due up. Pitch him. And if they start hitting him, we can always take him out. But start him.''

DENNY GALEHOUSE: "Luke went to Jakucki because it was a matter of arm weariness. A bunch of us got with Jakucki, and we said, 'This is an important game you're going to pitch tomorrow. Would you please take care of yourself tonight? And we'll see what happens tomorrow.''

DON GUTTERIDGE: "Jakucki promised to go home and not have anything to drink that night. Our coach, Zack Taylor, was going to watch him, check on him. Well, he didn't, and when he came to the park the next day, he smelled of liquor, and Sewell got on him. 'I thought you said you were going to keep clean and would not drink.' Jakucki said, 'I told you I would not drink last night. I had a drink this morning.' Well, he wasn't drunk, but he did have something to drink.''

DENNY GALEHOUSE: ''The next morning he came out, and he had been all right. I didn't see this, but prior to the warmup someone gave him one shot. Then he went out and warmed up and pitched, and he pitched very well. That one drink was enough to kind of loosen him up.''

DON GUTTERIDGE: ''He could throw hard, and he could throw strikes, and he just started throwing and daring them to hit it, and he pitched a good, good ball game. He surely did.''

DENNY GALEHOUSE: ''For that last game, 35,000 people showed up. They turned away an additional 15,000. We were kind of wondering where those people had been all season long. It was the first time in years, maybe the only time [It *was* the only time], the Browns filled their stadium. All the seats were sold. It was standing room only. People were all over the place. They were around the back of the seats, back all the way around.''

ELLIS CLARY: ''We got behind 2 to 0, and in the fourth inning Mike Kreevich singled, and Chet Laabs got up with a runner on, and he hit that scoreboard and tied it 2 to 2.

DON GUTTERIDGE: ''The score was still tied when they put it up on the scoreboard that the Tigers had lost. When we saw them we whooped and hollered. We said, 'Now we got 'em.' ''

ELLIS CLARY: ''The next time Laabs came up it was still 2 to 2, and Kreevich again singled and Chet hit it again.

''Chet was another strange, quiet guy. He never said nothing, and he couldn't get a damn sign for some damn reason. If he was on first base and you give him a steal or hit and run or whatever, he wasn't paying no attention.

''But he could hit a ball an awfully long ways. He wasn't very tall, but he had arms like Popeye. How he hit a ball as far as he could, ain't nobody ever figured it out. It was magical.

''In that last game, he hit that scoreboard twice in St. Louis. You say, 'He can't do it.' That scoreboard is six dollars and a quarter in a cab. It's in the back of the left-center field bleachers. And geez, he hit that thing twice in one game. You wouldn't believe it. I don't know how he did it.

''Then in the bottom of the eighth, Vern Stephens hit one over the right field fence out onto Grand Avenue to give us a 5–2 lead.''

DON GUTTERIDGE: ''With two outs in the ninth and a runner on, Oscar Grimes came up and hit a ball foul. It would have been a double or a triple. Then he popped up to George McQuinn behind first base. I went over behind George, and I said, 'Squeeze it. Squeeze it. Squeeze it, George.' So George squeezed it, and we won the ball game.''

ELLIS CLARY: "Oscar Grimes ended the game by hitting a foul ball that George McQuinn caught, and he fell into our dugout.

"All hell broke loose."

DON GUTTERIDGE: "The fans jumped out of the stands as soon as he caught the ball. I looked up, and the fans were all over the place. Fact of the matter, we had to fight our way to get to the dugout. They were trying to get our caps, and they were pulling on my shirt. I was right there beside George, and we started running for the dugout, which was on the third base line. We had to go clear over there.

"The fans just wanted to pat us on the back. Nothing malicious. They were just so tickled, so glad. It was very, very friendly."

DENNY GALEHOUSE: "When we won, everyone practically mobbed Jakucki. I sat on my stool after the game, thinking, 'This is why I quit my job.' I had thought we had a chance. And we won."

DON GUTTERIDGE: "By the time I got to the clubhouse, it was full of people. It seemed like it was jammed full, and everybody was hollering and yelling, and there were some champagne bottles, like there always is. I don't know where they came from."

ELLIS CLARY: "There's a picture we made in the clubhouse that's been in all these magazines, and I'm in it—I'm between Jakucki and Don Barnes, the owner, and Vern Stephens, and Al Hollingsworth. I looked at that picture the other day, and I said, 'You know, everybody in that picture is dead except me and the batboy, Junior Scanlon.' Everyone in that picture is gone. There are only six of us left: me and Don Gutteridge, Frank Mancuso, Red Hayworth, Galehouse, and Floyd Baker, and Floyd won't come to our fan club meetings. I go. As long as they pay the freight, I'll go anywhere."

DON GUTTERIDGE: "I'll tell you one thing: I don't know if anybody can really express how you really feel. It's such an elated feeling, and you're so tickled. We had fought all year long. It started in spring training, and you say you're going to win it, and this is the pinnacle of your hopes. Everybody was elated and pounding each other on the back and tickled to know we were going to be in the World Series.

"You know, when I was with the Cardinals, I thought sure one year we were going to win the pennant, because they were such a good ballclub continually. They were always in contention, every year. Then I came over to the Browns and won a pennant to play *against* the Cardinals. It was really something."

CHAPTER 37

IN THE SERIES

S<small>T</small>. Louis was always known for being "first in shoes, first in booze, and last in the American League." That the Browns were able to win the 1944 pennant—regardless of the circumstances—shocked the baseball world.

For only the third—and last—time in baseball history, the World Series was played in one ballpark. For this one year, the city of St. Louis was the baseball capital of the world as the 89-65 Browns (the lowest winning percentage in American League history) met the 105-49 Cardinals (the first team ever to win 100 games three years in a row). The biggest problem caused by the two St. Louis teams winning was that because of wartime restrictions the Browns' manager, Luke Sewell, had been sharing an apartment in the Lindell Towers with the Cards' manager, Billy Southworth. Somebody would have to move out.

Luke Sewell wanted to invite his mother to stay with him during the Series. Sewell told his mom, "Now, you come on up. I want you to see this. You'll probably never see us again in another World Series." The problem was solved when another resident of the building, scheduled to be out of town the week of the Series, invited Southworth to use his apartment.

ELLIS CLARY: "More of the fans were rooting for us, because the Cardinals were supposed to kill us. You know who was on the Cardinal team then? Mort Cooper, Walker Cooper, Whitey Kurowski, Marty Marion, Stan Musial, Johnny Hopp, Danny Litwhiler, Max Lanier, and Harry Brecheen. What a team! I'd like to take my chances with that team today."

DENNY GALEHOUSE: "I was in the shower after I shut out the Yankees on Saturday. I was always a heavy sweater, and I waited until I quit sweating to take the shower, and Luke Sewell was in there, and he said, 'If we get in it, you're starting the opener. But don't say anything to anybody at all.' Which I didn't. They kept trying to figure out who was going to start. His reasoning was that I had pitched better consistently than anybody else."

ELLIS CLARY: "We were kind of surprised that Sewell started Galehouse. We had a saying: 'If you get Nelson Potter two runs in the first inning, we can get up and go home.' There are a million pitchers who can pitch when they're behind, but damn few who can pitch when they're ahead. Anyway, we figured if we could get two in the first inning for Potter, we'd win that one. And then Jack Kramer was a hell of a pitcher. Paul Richards thought ol' Kramer should have been the greatest pitcher who ever pitched until then. And then you had

Bob Muncrief. I had sort of a strange feeling: 'Why did he pick Galehouse?' But he did.

"But Galehouse hogtied them. We won the opener, 2–1. Gene Moore hit a single, and McQuinn hit a home run to beat Mort Cooper. Those were the only two hits we got. Moore hit a line shot to right field for a single, and McQuinn came up and hit the second pitch up over that roof in right field. And Galehouse beat them."

DENNY GALEHOUSE: "The one run was in the ninth inning when we had a 2–0 lead. Marty Marion, the first up in the ninth inning, hit a double. I said, 'We can't pay any attention to him.' The next batter hit a ground ball to second base, and Marion moved to third. The next hitter hit a fly ball, and he scored.

"I have two out and nobody on, and the next guy hit a fly ball to Kreevich, and the game was over. We only got two hits: a single and a home run. We didn't score many runs."

ELLIS CLARY: "Nelson Potter faced Max Lanier in the second game. There has never been a better competitor than Potter. That son of a bitch would battle you. Course, he threw them damn screwballs, spitballs, and other damn things. You can't hit a good screwball if you throw strikes. And he was one of the first ones throwing it back then.

"We had them 2–1, and we could have won, but Potter picked up a bunt and threw it out into Grand Avenue. And we figured that was the turning point of the whole Series.

"And then in the eleventh that dang guy Blix Donnelly forced our runner out at third. He turned and threw in the same motion and nailed him coming into third.

"But they had a great team. They had the best team, but they couldn't match our four pitchers, even with Mort Cooper.

"We figured that cost us, but who the hell knows? It would have been great for St. Louis if we'd a beaten them."

DENNY GALEHOUSE: "The game never should have gone eleven innings, if Potter hadn't made a double error on a bunt. The bunt was in order, he bobbled the ball, and then threw it away at first base, so the runner went from first to third, and that got them the run that tied the score. It was 2–2 at the end of nine, and we would have won 2–1.

"That play by Blix Donnelly in the eleventh was one of the best plays I ever saw made. He turned and threw, and I often wondered if he ever saw third base when he threw. The throw was right on the bag, and McQuinn slid into the ball."

DON GUTTERIDGE: "McQuinn was on second base, and Mark Christman laid down a bunt. Blix Donnelly was pitching, and he fielded the bunt and just blindly threw to third base, and luckily Kurowski caught the ball right on the base, and McQuinn slid right into it. If the ball had been waist-high or it could very well have been wild, 'cause he didn't know where he was throwing it. It could have gone down left field, and everyone would have been safe. That was a big, big play. It turned out to be the turning point of the whole World Series.

"The Cards then scored in the eleventh off Bob Muncrief. Ken O'Dea, who was an extra catcher, singled to score the winning run. We were very disappointed not to win that game, because if we had won it, that would have put us up two games to none, and we'd have really had a chance then. 'Cause we came back and won the third game. We'd have been 3 and 0. Once you go 3 and 0, you figure you're going to win one more."

Jack Kramer won Game 3 by the score of 6–2, striking out 10. Both Card runs were unearned. It was the last World Series game ever won by a member of the St. Louis Browns.

DON GUTTERIDGE: "We faced Harry Brecheen in Game 4, and he was very crafty. He didn't throw the ball hard, but he had very good control, and he threw a lot of breaking balls. [Jakucki gave up a home run in the first inning to Stan Musial and lost, 5–1.]

"In the last three games, we scored two runs. We just didn't score, and you can't win if you don't score."

DENNY GALEHOUSE: "In the fifth game, I struck out 10 batters, and Mort Cooper struck out 12, and we set a record for two pitchers that still stands. There's only one Series game in which the pitchers struck out more, and that was Koufax and about four Yankees [in 1963]. They struck out 25, and we struck out 22."

DON GUTTERIDGE: "I'll tell you the reason for it. Mort Cooper was a good pitcher, but there also was a big crowd. They never used to have anybody sit in the center field bleachers. They wired it off, but at the World Series they opened it up, and it was a sunny day, and everybody in the stands had on white shirts, and you couldn't see the ball coming out of those shirts. The background was terrible. Against Cooper you couldn't see the ball. That's why there were so many strikeouts. We couldn't hardly see the ball."

DENNY GALEHOUSE: "I lost the game, 2–0, on home runs by [Ray] Sanders and [Danny] Litwhiler. I got the count to 3-0 on Sanders. I was trying to pitch everybody inside, and I had to make the ball a little bit better to him, and I got two strikes on him, and then finally I got the ball that he hit inside, but he hit a home run up on the roof. It wasn't hit that great, but it was on the roof, so it was a home run. And Litwhiler I was still trying to pitch tight, but I got it a little out away from him."

DON GUTTERIDGE: "Nelson Potter started against Max Lanier in Game 6. We scored first on a triple by Chet Laabs and McQuinn's single. Then in the fourth inning Walker Cooper walked and Sanders singled him to third. Kurowski then hit a grounder to Vern at short, and I came across the bag, and Stephens was slow—he fumbled the ball just a little bit, didn't field it cleanly—and he threw to me, and in my momentum I was off the bag. George Pipgras was the umpire, and he said I went off the bag. Maybe I did. Because I know I was in motion, and he was late getting it to me. I knew I had to get off the base and get the ball to first base.

"But it was very unusual. Normally on that play, play after play after play where the second baseman's not on the base when he gets the ball, the umpire calls the runner out. That's the usual thing. And I thought the same thing should have happened then. But it didn't, and I got blamed. They gave Vern an error on the play. And then the next two batters, Verban and Lanier, their weakest hitters, singled in the winning runs. That proved we weren't supposed to win it.''

DENNY GALEHOUSE: "Max Lanier won Game 6 for the Cards. Luke told me before that game, 'If we go to seven, you're it.' I said, 'Well.' That would have been with one day's rest. But it didn't turn out.''

ELLIS CLARY: "With our pitching, we were a pretty good match for them. They didn't go out there and take batting practice off our guys. I tell ya, it would have been great for baseball and the city of St. Louis if we had won.

"We always figured we should have won the thing.''

DON GUTTERIDGE: "After we lost that final game, we were back in the club-house and we were very sad, because we really had a chance to win and the Browns had never won a World Series. We were very much down. The owner, Don Barnes, came in. He said, 'Don't worry. You did a great job.' He talked to us. He said, 'I'll tell you what. We're going to have a party tonight anyway, just as if we had won. We're very proud of you. You did a good job for us.'

"He invited us over to the Chase Hotel that night. He said, 'The food and the drinks are on me. Stay as long as you want to.' They had a buffet. We ate, and most of them drank until they went home.

"At the party we kind of went over things a thousand times. But the funny thing was Jakucki wasn't there to start with. He came in a little bit later, and when he came in he had dollar bills stuck in his shirt, in his button-holes, his sleeves, on his ear. He must have had twenty or thirty dollar bills stuck all around. He said, 'Now I'm in the money.' [The Browns' losing World Series share was $2,744. The players had to take 10 percent of that in war bonds.] And he was as drunk as the Lord. I don't know where he got that idea, but Jakucki had ideas like that. We all laughed at him, of course.

"To go on with the story a little bit, they found him about two days later over in Illinois laying in the gutter. He didn't have a penny on him. He went over there and got drunk, and I guess somebody lifted all his money. He was broke and dirty, and then somebody recognized him and cleaned him up and sent him home.''

CHAPTER 38

THE PETE GRAY ERA

WHENEVER the St. Louis Browns are discussed, one event and five names always are mentioned. The event is the 1944 World Series, and the five names are George Sisler, rated as the Browns' greatest player; Pete Gray, who had one arm; Eddie Gaedel, a midget; Satchel Paige, the legendary Negro Leagues pitcher; and Bill Veeck, the flamboyant promoter who was responsible for bringing Paige and Gaedel to the big leagues and in the end who was responsible for the Browns leaving St. Louis.

Gray, whose given name was Wyshner, but who changed it when he started playing semipro ball, hails from the small town of Nanticoke, which is seven or eight miles from Scranton and Wilkes-Barre in north-central Pennsylvania. After a season in Memphis in which he hit .333, drove in 60 runs, and stole 68 bases to tie the Southern League record, Browns owner Richard Muckerman bought him for $20,000 in 1945.

He was thirty years old when he was added to the Browns' roster in 1945 by the new owner, who despaired over the team's attendance, which was poor even while the Browns were winning a pennant. Muckerman decided to promote Gray, who was missing his right arm, into a gate attraction. That he was able to perform at all in the field and at bat in the big leagues with but one arm was an incredible feat. Over the years, when reporters periodically tried to interview Gray, he ducked them. He did not have a telephone in his home. To reach him, you had to call Vedor's Bar. Usually if you reached him, he opted not to talk about his baseball career. Usually, not always. Tony Salin, a longtime friend who loves chronicling tales of old ballplayers, was able to convince Gray to recount his life with him. The normally close-mouthed Gray, who was seventy-seven when he was interviewed, recalled the events leading up to his playing with the Browns in 1945.

PETE GRAY: "I was six or seven years old when a huckster come into town. He was selling potatoes and apples, and he said he'd give me a quarter if I'd go house to house and tell them about the potatoes and apples. After he was done, he was leaving town, and I was on the running board, and he said, 'Jump off.' And I slipped—in those days trucks had wooden spokes, and my arm caught in the spokes.

"He picked me up and brought me home and set me on the porch. A lady was walking by and she saw I was bleeding and so she called a doctor, and they come over for me and took me to the hospital. Well, they cut my arm off that night. I stayed in the hospital for ten to fifteen days.

"Growing up in Nanticoke, we had a baseball team on our street, and I

PETE GRAY
(Drawing by Ron Stark)

was better than any of them. We played other streets. I knew I was pretty good and later on I went to Hot Springs, Arkansas, to a baseball school. Ray Doan owned the school, and he called all over the country to get me on a Class D club, and they thought there was something wrong with him, you know. They thought he was crazy. He tried, anyhow, and he kept me there for ten days, paid my expenses and everything, and then I came home. He said he couldn't do nothing for me.

"Then in 1938 I was playing for a team in Pennsylvania four days a week, and there was a player by the name of Skelton. He went to Three Rivers, Canada, and they wanted an outfielder up there. So he called me up and told me to meet the manager in Montreal at the train station. But Skelton didn't tell them that I had one arm. And I didn't know that.

"At the train station there was a fellow walking with a suitcase and he had a bat on the side of the suitcase. The manager went up to him and said, "Gray," but the guy thought he said, "Say," or something, and they shook hands. So the manager thought that guy was me, and he said, 'Well, we've got to catch the train.' So we're on the train, and he was talking about baseball to that guy. We found out later that he was a softball player.

"A little before Three Rivers that guy got up to get off the train, and the manager says, 'No, you're not getting off here. We're playing tonight in Three Rivers.' He said, 'No, I'm playing here.' And the manager looked at me and he says, 'What's your name?' I said, 'Gray.' Well, he says, 'What's the matter with your arm?'

" 'I don't have any.'

" 'Jesus,' he said, 'Say that again. What's your name?'

" 'Gray.'

"He said, 'What are you coming here for?'

" 'To play ball.'

" 'Who sent you here?'

" 'A guy by the name of Skelton.'

" 'Oh,' he says. 'I'm in trouble.'

"The next stop was Three Rivers, and we got off and the owners were there, you know, the directors, and one of them came up to me, and he said, 'You're a ballplayer? With one arm?'

"I said, 'Yeah.'

"Well, anyhow, when we came to the ballpark, they wouldn't give me a suit or nothing. But the game started, and the first guy for Quebec came up and hit a home run. And that's how that ball game went. In the middle of the game, one of the directors told me to put a uniform on. So the clubhouse boy gave me a uniform, and I put it on.

"Well, anyhow, they used all the batters and the pitcher was the last hitter, with two out and the bases loaded, in the last inning. So the manager says to me, 'Gray, go up there and hit.' The batter had one strike on him before the manager put me in. So I come out of the dugout swinging two bats around. And you could have heard a pin drop.

"Well, anyhow, I got a base hit, and we won the ballgame. And the

people started throwing change on the field. They gave me a check for over
$500. So that was something. It was like a guy wrote a book or something.

"After that I played with the Bushwicks and Bay Parkways in New York."

Playing at such a lofty level with only one arm, Pete was such a curiosity
that the July 29, 1940, issue of *Newsweek* had a picture of him in his Bay
Parkway uniform. The short article mentioned that: "Pete Gray . . . now plays
center field for the Bay Parkways, a semipro team in Brooklyn, not because
of his box office value as a curiosity but because he is really an asset. Up to
last week he had accepted 34 chances without an error and, as leadoff man in
the lineup, he was batting a lofty .449.''

PETE GRAY: "When Three Rivers got in Organized Baseball in 1942, they
knew what I could do, so they sent me a contract. From there they sold me
to Toronto, on the 'look basis.' We were supposed to play the Philadelphia
Athletics in an exhibition game. I got sick and couldn't go, and they released
me. I always had trouble with owners—contracts, you know. Maybe they
thought I was a bad guy. I don't know.

"Well, the papers picked it up. It went all over the country that I was
released by Toronto. Mickey O'Neil, my manager from Three Rivers, was in
Memphis at that time, and he went in and talked with Doc Prothro, the manager
and part-owner of the Memphis club. And Mickey O'Neil told him, 'Get that
guy.' Prothro told Mickey, 'You must be going nuts or something.' But anyway, in about four days he sent me a check and he told me to come out to
Memphis. That was in 1943. I was there 1943 and '44. I had a good year in
'44. I was voted the Most Valuable Player in the Southern Association. [Gray
hit .333 in 1944 and tied a league record with 68 stolen bases.]

"I was a pretty good hitter. And I was a good bunter, too. Center field
was my position. I could cover a lot of ground in the outfield. And if I touched
the ball, I caught it. I had a pretty good arm—up until 1942, when I broke
my collarbone. That sort of held me back a little. I could still throw, but not
like I used to.

"In 1944 Doc Prothro told me I was going to go to the big leagues the
next year. He didn't know if it would be with the Giants or the St. Louis
Browns. He thought it would be the Browns, because Memphis had a working
agreement with them.

"I was thirty when I reached the majors in '45. I'm a little older than
some of the books say. My manager said I should say I was a little younger.
I was born in 1915. I'm seventy-seven now. I knew I wouldn't be up there
too long. When I got there, I was too old: thirty years old. I was hitting the
ball good, but my average wasn't too good. They couldn't strike me out, you
know. I only struck out 11 times in 77 games. They started me off in left
field, and after a while they put me in center field. I played center field all
my life.''

Pete Gray had one magnificent afternoon on May 21, 1945, in a doubleheader against the New York Yankees. Before 20,507, one of the largest

crowds ever to see a game in Sportsman's Park, Gray had three hits, drove in two runs, and robbed Frankie Crosetti with a running catch in a 10–1 victory. Then in the second game Gray caught seven fly balls, including two near the fence on Johnny Lindell and Oscar Grimes, and a running knee-high grab of a Bud Metheny fly ball. His hit also drove in the tying run in a 5–2 victory.

But Gray's heroics were short-lived. The opposing outfielders saw he had little power and began playing him very shallow. Balls that had dropped in early in the year became easy outs. His RBI production dropped to virtually zero. In the meantime, Gray's teammates began to resent the fact that he was taking up a spot in the field that could have better been filled by a more talented two-armed player (although less attractive to the fans). When the shy Gray retreated into his shell, the abuse toward him only increased. His teammates recalled the effect he had on what had been a unified ballclub. To the fans, Gray was a curiosity. To the players, he was more of a distraction.

DON GUTTERIDGE: "Pete thinks the world is against him. He also got the idea the Browns were exploiting him, 'cause he only had one arm. He wanted to be known as a ballplayer who could compete with the rest of us. He didn't want everyone to think we were just letting him play because he had one arm. He wanted to make his own record.

"And he was a loner. When the ball game was over, you wouldn't see him again until the next day. Most of us went out together, ate together, went to the show together, or at least socialized a little bit. Not Pete.

"There was some resentment against Pete from some pretty good outfielders. They would say to other members of the team, 'If only I had been in there . . .' See, Pete couldn't drive in many runs because they played so close. They thought they could have driven in runs at different times to help us win ball games. 'Hey, we could win if Kreevich was out there.' Or Byrnes or Moore, instead of Pete Gray."

ELLIS CLARY: "I went by to see Pete a couple years ago in Nanticoke, Pennsylvania. I was scouting the Scranton team, Philadelphia's Triple A team, and I looked at the map and I knew he was from Nanticoke. It's fifteen miles between Scranton and Wilkes-Barre, and Nanticoke is about halfway. I drove over there and I asked somebody, 'You ever heard of Pete Gray?' 'Yeah, I know where Pete lives.' Anyway, I went over to see him. He lives in a big white two-story house. I knocked on the door, and he pushed the screen open and pointed at me and said, 'You're Clary.' I said, 'Hell, I know that.' I hadn't seen that son of a bitch in fifty years. He was doing all right. This was five years ago. I said, 'Pete, how old are you now?' He said, 'I'm seventy-seven and a half.' I never had anybody say 'and a half' before. He said, 'I couldn't play in the big leagues now, could I?'

"I said, 'The hell you couldn't. You would be making ten million a year.' And the only bad game he ever had was the first Sunday in New York that filled up the Yankee Stadium, 60,000 to see him play, and it was the only bad game I ever saw him have.

"He could outrun a scalded dog, you know."

*   *   *

If Clary felt kindly toward Gray, who usually kept to himself while on the Browns, he was in the minority. The drinkers on the team—Jakucki, Shirley, and Kreevich—made the life of the physically challenged rookie outfielder miserable. Others who correctly sensed that Gray was on the team primarily as a gate attraction saw he wasn't as talented as the veteran outfielders and resented his presence as well. Ellis Clary remembered the disharmony on the team created by the vitriol against Gray. Though Clary was sympathetic toward Gray, Clary also knew that removing Gray from the mix would have returned the team to normalcy and improved it. When that didn't happen, it was inevitable that either Gray or Sig Jakucki, his chief tormentor, would have to go. When it was Jakucki, the Browns lost a valuable, though disreputable, member.

In 77 games Gray finished the season with a .218 batting average, no home runs, and but 13 RBIs. Muckerman may have made some money showcasing Gray, but Jakucki's loss kept the Browns from a second straight pennant that might have given the team legitimacy and saved it from oblivion.

ELLIS CLARY: "If you were an outfielder, and you're setting on the bench with a one-armed man out in the field, you know you're going to be resentful. Jack Kramer could talk like the guy who does Bugs Bunny, and he could do it better than the guy [Mel Blanc] could. And he would sit there on the bench, and it would be quiet, and Jack would say the way Bugs does: 'Eh, don't look now, Doc, but there's a one-armed man out there in center field.' And everybody would crack up. And every now and then, when it was quiet, he would come up with: 'Eh, don't look now, but there's a one-armed man out there in center field.' Every time he'd do that, I'd die laughing.

"You gonna sit Mike Kreevich down and let Pete play center field? See, we had some pretty good outfielders, had Kreevich and Gene Moore and Chet Laabs, and Mike Chartak, and somebody had to sit down and let him play.

"The pitchers didn't want Gray out there either. Nobody did. He was strictly for show, to draw some fans, 'cause he put 60,000 in the ballpark that first Sunday in New York. They didn't come out to watch the Browns. But he drew half of them, I imagine.

"Goddamn, DeWitt [really Muckerman] brought him in there, and you got to put him out there to let the people see him. Sewell was between a rock and a hard place. I remember Bobo Newsom was pitching for the A's back then. He had been with everybody. Bobo was a fanatic about picking up trash on the mound. He'd pick up rocks, anything that was out there and clean up. He was a landscape man. We knew that, and Bobo was pitching, and Gene Moore and Milt Byrnes were playing alongside Pete that day, and they got a piece of paper and tore it into a zillion pieces, and every time they came out of the outfield and crossed the mound to the dugout, they would drop that paper all over the mound. And Bobo'd have to come out there and clean it up.

"So now the first time we played when Bobo was pitching, we prayed that Pete Gray leading off could get a hit off Bobo. We wanted to serenade Bobo. We just prayed Pete would get a hit to lead off the game, and he did. He hit a line drive to center field. In the dugout, we all jumped up and yelled at Bobo. We yelled, 'Bobo, you arc just right for a one-armed man!' And he blew his stack. He walked over in front of our dugout and cussed everybody out.

"I'm so glad I got over there with them bastards. Nobody else had a collection of goats like we did.

"People would flock out there to see a one-armed man play in the big leagues, and that's what I told Pete. And Pete could hit a fastball. Hank Borowy was a Yankee ace back then. Hal Newhouser was over at Detroit. And Hal would grit his teeth when he would see him walk up there. He would try to throw one by him, and he couldn't do it. But Pete couldn't hit a change. That was his weakness. He could not hit an off-speed pitch. But Hank and Hal would throw fastballs, and the harder they threw it, the harder he'd hit it.

"But Pete was an ornery bastard. See, if you felt sorry for him, he could detect it, and he resented that. He was a Polack hard-headed bastard, you know, and he didn't want nobody feeling sorry for him.

"We'd travel on the train, and he'd get on, and when them wheels started rolling, he'd go to sleep. He'd doze off, and they'd hotfoot that son of a bitch. They'd watch him like a hawk, and he wore them black-and-white two-toned shoes, which were very popular back then. He dressed up all the time, wore a bow tie, a coat, or a suit. And he'd go to sleep on that train, and they'd hotfoot that son of a bitch, and everybody would die laughing. And his feet looked like he stomped out a forest fire. His shoes were all smoked up.

"Them guys would think up shit to pull all the time. And they would agitate Pete Gray. All the time. They called him a 'Kildee with one wing shot off.' Somebody hung that on him. And they tortured him, teased him all the damn time.

"We stopped in Toledo one time on an off day and played an exhibition game. Toledo was our Triple A team. And we were down at that old station, where there were four or five tracks, not a terminal like in a lot of towns, just had a stop there. We got there after the game and were waiting on the train to come by to go to Detroit, which wasn't but fifty miles, and it was the middle of the summer, blazing hot, and somebody had turned over a barrel of fish there a day or two before and spilled them all over the place. You could smell them in the next town. And one of them bastards went over there, and got one of them small fish, and another one got old Pete around the neck, tussling with him, and one of them slipped one of them damn fish in his left coat pocket. See, Pete carried his cigarettes and matches in his left coat pocket. And they slipped that fish in there, that stinking thing, and the minute he went to get him a cigarette and run his hand in there and come up with that dead fish, and he just knew Jakucki did it.

"Jakucki was standing over there grinning, laughing at him, and he run at him and tried to hit him in the face and hit him in the chest. If Sig had been a lesser man, Pete'd a-flattened him. Jakucki was a bull, you know. And they had a little scuffle there. But everybody got a big laugh out of him putting that fish in his pocket.

"Every day you could write a book on what they would do to that damn guy. Pete had about four agitators: Jakucki and Tex Shirley, and Nelson Potter picked on him, but in a good-natured way.

"One time we left St. Louis on the train going on a road trip starting in Cleveland. The day before was an off day. Luke flew home to be with his family in Akron, going to meet us at the ballpark the next day. If the manager ever leaves for a day, the shit hits the fan every time.

"Well, we got on that train, and everyone flocked into the club car. We got in there, and they started drinking that beer, and got to fooling around, and got into a scuffle there, and Babe Martin had to separate Tex Shirley, Jakucki, and Pete Gray. I was setting there with them. I don't remember who was in the scuffle.

"They got about half-drunk, and they about got into a damn free-for-all, and Babe Martin—he could pick up a boxcar, you know—he separated them, and it was a mess. It was terrible. And there were other people in the club car besides the players, and it wasn't very pretty. Course, Fred Hofmann and Zack Taylor, the coaches, were in there, and they saw it, so they told Luke when we got there. He called a meeting the next day. Luke took off his coat and rolled up his damn sleeves. He was ready to fight. And Jakucki was the head honcho who started all that shit. If it hadn't been for Babe Martin, somebody might have gotten hurt. He got in and separated them.

"They were in the habit of calling Pete a 'bush bastard' and all this and the other. And Luke rolled up his sleeve, and boy, he was furious. He said, 'It's a goddamn disgrace to put on an exhibition like what happened on that train yesterday. I heard all about it.' He said, 'It's a disgrace to baseball, to the city of St. Louis, the St. Louis Browns, and everybody connected with baseball.' And he said, 'The biggest bush bastard I have ever seen in my life is Jack Jakucki.' Jakucki was sitting on the floor almost behind Luke. He just knew Jakucki would get up and tear into him when he said it, when Luke turned and said 'The biggest bush bastard I ever saw was Jack Jakucki.' But Jakucki broke out and went to laughing. Instead of fighting him, it tickled the hell out of him. He laughed like hell sitting on the damn floor.

"Nothing come of it, but it was terrible. A terrible exhibition. And it all started with them picking at Pete Gray. It was all in fun, but it wasn't much fun for Pete Gray.

"They wanted to make a movie about Pete Gray, and he would not go. They were going to offer him a $15,000 binder just to come out to Hollywood. The hard-headed son of a bitch wouldn't do it. Bill DeWitt and Sewell told him, 'Man, go out there.' 'No, I ain't. Hell, no.' He wouldn't. He was as butt-headed as a goat, you know.

"They even had a kid who was going to play Pete Gray as a little boy when he lost his arm. Believe it or not, did you ever hear what the kid's name was? His last name was G-a-r-y. And the kid had his arm missing, the same arm, at the same place, just above the elbow. They even brought the kid over to meet Gray. He was like four years old. He was going to play him. They thought they could talk Pete into it. Come over there, and there was that youngun,' and his last name was Gary instead of Gray, and he was going to play him in the movie when he lost his arm. And that hard-headed . . . I liked Pete Gray.

"One night me and a couple of the guys were standing outside that Melbourne Hotel, and they had a big formal dance that night. A Cadillac pulled up while we were standing there at the door, and the big dance was starting, and a lady was all dressed up and her husband was in a tuxedo, and they got out of the car, and they were elderly people, and the lady spied Pete Gray standing there, and walked up to him. She was just as nice as she could be, and she said, 'Aren't you Pete Gray, the ballplayer?' That knuckleheaded bastard put his arm around her neck and said, 'No, I'm Pete Gray, the great lover.' Liked to scare the old lady to death.

"And another night we were standing out there, me and him and Frank Mancuso, all standing out there on the corner of the Melbourne, and here comes a drunk down the street, and back then they wore them hard straw hats with the flat top, hard, with the crinkly edges. This guy walked up to us, and he had a pretty good load on, and he was all dressed up with one of them hats on there, and he said something to Pete Gray, and ol' Pete just reached up and took that hat off his head, and run his damn hand right through the roof of that hat, knocked the top off, and put it back on the guy's head and jammed it down over his ears to where he couldn't get it off. If the guy hadn't been drunk, he might have torn his ears off. But that tickled the hell out of me. Jammed that hat back on his head. Pete thought it was funny. Yeah. He laughed like hell.

"We would have won the pennant again if it hadn't been for Pete Gray. He broke up the damn team over there. We would have won it again. Finally Luke had to kick Sig off just before the season ended. He didn't have to get rid of Pete, but he caused a lot of damn turmoil. Pete was the reason we didn't win it again.

"The coming of Gray ultimately was the end for Jakucki for all the shit he pulled. One night we met down at the train station. We were fixing to go somewhere. The whole team was already down there, and Luke was late getting down there.

"Luke had been withholding some of Jakucki's check every month, so he'd have enough money to go home. You got paid every two weeks. Sig would spend every damn nickel he made every payday. He'd blow it all. He'd be broke before the next payday. Jakucki had a wife, a nice wife.

"Anyway, Luke was withholding money for his own good, so he could get back to Texas, and Jakucki was pissed off about it. Jakucki got down there way ahead of Luke, and he was drunk, and he had a fifth of liquor in his right hip pocket sloshing back there, and he was already gassed up, and he was telling Boots Hofmann and Zack Taylor, the coaches, 'I'm going to whip his damn ass. I'm going to beat the shit out of Luke Sewell when he gets here.'

"The train was fixing to leave. And Boots Hofmann and Zack Taylor said, 'Jack, get the hell out of here. Don't let Luke see you.' Cause he was already on the fringe of getting kicked off the team for all that shit he pulled on Gray. They said, 'Don't let him see you. Go get on the train. Get in your compartment. Or go home.' Jakucki was in no condition to go nowhere.

"Jakucki said, 'No.' Now he was going to whip their ass. Luke had to get on the train and get in his compartment and lock the damn door. Because Jakucki said he was going to kill him. Charlie DeWitt, our traveling secretary, was the one who called the police. You see, when you leave St. Louis, you stop first at Del Mar. Charlie told the cops that the train would stop there, so they could come and get him off the train. When the train stopped at Del Mar station, the cops were already there waiting. They went on the train and took him out. That wound him up with the Browns.

"He never played for them [or in the major leagues] again. He came to Chicago the next day. They think he rode a freight train up there. Luke said, 'That's it. You're gone.' This was about a month before the season was over.

"Frank Mancuso, who was our catcher, doesn't like me to tell this story, but Jakucki lived in Galveston. Frank was on the council in Houston for twenty-five years. Frank said it was years after they had played together, and about midnight one night Jakucki called him. Jakucki said, 'I'm at the bus station. I'm out of money. I'm going somewhere, and I ain't got no money. Can you let me have a few bucks so I can get where I'm going?' Frank said he got up out of bed and dressed and went down to the bus station, and took him fifty dollars to get him wherever he was going. Frank said before long he called him again at midnight, said he was going back the other way, and he needed more money, and Frank took him some more.

"We had a twenty-year reunion, and Jakucki showed up. He was in great spirits and laughing, just like everybody else. It's a wonder somebody hadn't killed him. He abused himself every night. He just lived from day to day.

"If it hadn't been for those two incidents, we'd a won the pennant in '45. Hell, with them four pitchers, you had to go like hell to beat one of them. But just Pete Gray's presence screwed up the whole fucking deal. We had a pretty good thing going in '44. We had momentum and had a good team, four star pitchers and enough players to win the damn thing for two or three years if they had kept them all together.

"Well, the owner thought Pete could draw fans, and it worked, but we didn't win."

The last hurrah for the Browns came in September of 1945. Despite the loss of Jakucki, who had won 12 games at the time he was released, the team was in third place and closing on the Detroit Tigers and Washington Senators.

DON GUTTERIDGE: "In late September, the Tigers came to town with two games left in the season. We had to win both games to tie them for the pennant. It rained for three days, and then we played them in a doubleheader. Nelson Potter faced Virgil Trucks. It was still pouring rain."

ELLIS CLARY: "We were leading in the ninth when Hank Greenberg hit a home run off Potter with the bases loaded in St. Louis. It was pouring down rain, and he hit that thing plumb over that hot dog stand in left field. You got to go like hell to drive one through there. To hit it over the back of the left field bleachers, you gotta power it, and it was pouring down rain, and Hank Greenberg hit it, and that won it for them that year.''

Don Gutteridge: "He hit the ball to left field, and we thought the ball was foul, but the umpire called it fair. All hell broke loose. We had a big argument. Everybody out in left field, the fans, were pointing. Everybody thought it was foul, but if you look in the book now, it's fair! We resented that very much, because we wanted to beat them. We held a lot of bitterness at the end of the season. But it was nothing compared to what happened afterward. Don Barnes had sold the team to Richard Muckerman, who spent a lot of money to fix the ballpark, not to buy players, and when the team went broke, he began selling off players, including Vern Stephens and Jack Kramer to Boston. And here we had a chance to have been a dynasty, to win two pennants in a row, and if we had done that, everyone would have taken notice, but instead they went broke, and they sold players, and that was it.

"They tried to get the people to come out, but people still didn't believe in us, and we didn't draw near the crowd that the Cardinals drew. That's how you get money: People pay to see you play. Plus the fact that we still did not have a radio network that paid off for us. The Cardinals had all that sewn up. The fans heard about the Cardinals on the radio and they came to see you.

"We finished seventh in 1946, and at the end of the year I went to Toledo to manage, and in the meantime almost everybody came back from overseas. When Bobby Doerr broke his finger, the Red Sox needed an experienced second baseman until his finger got well, and they bought me. That's how lucky I was: I was on another pennant winner. And because I was playing at the end of 1946, I was eligible for my pension, so I became a ten-year man from the start, five with the Cardinals and four with the Browns. That was the luckiest thing that ever happened to me. I thank the Lord every morning for that.''

Denny Galehouse: "After having won it in '44 and almost winning it in '45, in '46 we fell way down. It showed that things were different. A lot of the top players came back from the war, and it was too tough for us. The Red Sox would come to town, and they'd beat the heck out of everybody. I hadn't been used much, and we were behind about 15 to 2, and I pitched the ninth inning, and Joe Cronin was coaching third base at the time, and he's walking with his head down, and he said, 'I may have been a bastard, but I never did that to you.' And I said, 'I haven't been pitching much, and I need to get some work.' I didn't badmouth anybody, and it wasn't long before I was back with the Red Sox. And after I went back over there, Cronin asked me about Stephens and Kramer, and he traded for them as well. The Browns had to sell ballplayers to survive. They were never in contention ever again.''

CHAPTER 39

DOWN AND DOWN

In 1947 Richard Muckerman bought Sportsman's Park from the Ball estate for $500,000. The park was badly run down, with a leaky roof, broken chairs, and dilapidated clubhouses. He spent $750,000, just about everything he had, fixing up the ballpark. But despite the fix-up, the Browns again drew flies. Only 320,000 fans, an average of 4,000 a game, came to see the last-place Browns.

Muckerman, who had had such grand plans when he bought the team, began to see the graffiti on the wall. Creditors pressed him. He held a fire sale. On Muckerman's orders, Bill DeWitt sold Vern Stephens and Jack Kramer, two of his stars, to the Red Sox for $310,000. The next day he sold Ellis Kinder and Billy Hitchcock to Boston for $65,000. The group would lead the Sox to two pennants.

More bodies were sold during his three-year reign. Infielder Gerry Priddy was sold to Detroit for $125,000. Al Zarilla went to the Red Sox for $125,000. Pitcher Sam Zoldak was shipped to Cleveland for $100,000. Fred Sanford became a Yankee at a $100,000 price tag; third baseman Bob Dillinger and outfielder Paul Lehner became A's for $100,000; pitcher Bob Muncrief and outfielder Walter Judnich went to Cleveland for $60,000; infielder Johnny Berardino to Cleveland for $50,000; outfielder Jeff Heath to the Boston Braves for $25,000. In addition, the ownership sold the Toledo ballpark and the franchise to Detroit for $200,000.

In 1948 Zack Taylor replaced Herold "Muddy" Ruel as manager and led the team to sixth. After selling almost $1 million worth of talented ballplayers, the Browns actually gained two rungs in the standings!

During the winter of 1948–1949, Muckerman threw in the towel. He had inquiries from the cities of Los Angeles, Milwaukee, and Dallas, but on February 2, 1949, he virtually gave the team to his friends and fellow stockholders, the DeWitts, Bill and Charlie, two men who passionately loved the Browns. They acquired the team for $300,000 in notes. Club stock was put up as collateral.

Bill DeWitt began his baseball career in 1916 in the Browns concession stands when he was sixteen. Branch Rickey was business manager of the Browns then, and he asked the head of concessions to pick out a bright, hard worker for an office boy. Bill was chosen. At Rickey's request, Bill studied typing and shorthand, and when he was seventeen Rickey made him team secretary. When he was eighteen, Rickey persuaded him to go to high school at night and study English. He took four years of English in one year. Then he went to St. Louis University and finished four years in finance and commerce in three years.

Bill then studied law for two years. He and Rickey were going to set up a law firm together if Rickey ever left baseball. He never did.

Charlie, meanwhile, went to night school and worked at the ballpark. His first job was as a scout. He received $300 for each prospect he signed. After discovering Al Smith and Emmett Mueller, Charlie went to work for an oil company. A friend asked him to suggest prospective clients for his insurance business. Charlie himself sold them the policies, and he made a small fortune in the insurance business.

When Rickey moved to the Cardinals, Bill DeWitt moved with him. He became a vice president at age twenty-three, and in 1936 he helped round up a group of men, led by Donald Barnes, to buy the Browns from the Phil Ball estate. Working for Barnes, DeWitt made seventeen deals between 1946 and 1948 that netted the Browns almost $1 million in cash and players.

"We were continually forced to sell someone to keep going," said Charlie, "but we'd rather sacrifice a high-priced man to get two or three young guys that are good and may become stars themselves. We think we get more for our dough with six or seven cheaper guys who have strong possibilities than with a $40,000 guy. We just have to limit ourselves to our incomes."

When the DeWitts bought the Browns in the winter of 1949, Charlie DeWitt told reporters that the team was in the same spot that the Cardinals had been in when Branch Rickey took over that team. DeWitt recalled that it took Rickey eight years to pull the Cardinals out of their hole. He felt confident he could do the same. But the times were different, and DeWitt was not the innovator Rickey had been. No one was.

The DeWitts, low on cash, could not bid for prospects, and with most of their top players dealt away, the Browns were now in serious trouble. The few loyal fans became disillusioned after Muckerman began selling off his players, and many of them stopped coming to games. As fewer fans came, the team became even more shaky financially.

Eddie Pellagrini had the misfortune to have played on the end-of-the-line Browns in 1948 and 1949. The Browns were 59-94 in '48 and 53-101 in '49 under manager Zack Taylor. Pellagrini had played with the '46 American League champion Boston Red Sox and again in '47, and he was crushed when on November 17, 1947, he, Roy Partee, Jim Wilson, Al Widmar, Pete Laydon, Joe Ostrowski, and $310,000 were sent to the Browns for Vern Stephens and Jack Kramer. When Pellagrini's great play beat the Red Sox and forced them into a one-game playoff in '48, the proud infielder was ecstatic.

EDDIE PELLAGRINI: "I liked Boston. Detroit was after me, and I thought I was going to Detroit. If I didn't play in Boston, I'd have liked to have played in Detroit. St. Louis always was so awful hot. That's the thing I really didn't like: the heat. I'm a skinny little guy. And the ballpark was just fair. You had to be a pretty good player to play shortstop in that ballpark. The field was used by two teams, and the field never had time to revive. But the people in

St. Louis were wonderful. I loved the people. Just being in the town and meeting those Westerners, they were such nice people.

"Say you broke down late at night in your car. In St. Louis about four or five people would stop and try to help you. Back East, they are always a little leery. In St. Louis it was: 'Can I help you?' Very nice. I loved the people. I really did. I loved the town. I liked the food. I liked everything about it but the heat. The owners, the DeWitts, were very good, and everybody was nice. But the weather, Jesus. I was so tired all the time. The hot weather settled in and never left. It even got warm at night. There wasn't air-conditioning. I was playing in a city series against the Cardinals, and Stan Musial was playing first base that day, and we were talking while they changed pitchers. I said, 'Boy, Stan, how can you play all those years in that heat?' He said, 'It's pretty tough. Those night games kill you. By the time you go to the ballpark, you're really tired.' He said, 'If I played back East, I'd hit a little more.' Most ballplayers could say that. It was really hot there. That's the only part about it that was bad. Baseball is baseball. We had a pretty good ballclub. We had Bob Dillinger, Gerry Priddy, myself, and the first baseman was Jack Graham. We had that kid Garver pitching, and a few other guys.

"We had Les Moss, a wonderful kid, and Whitey Platt and Paul Lehner and Al Zarilla, who was great. Jesus, the day they sold him to the Red Sox we were at the hotel, and he said, 'You ain't gonna believe this, but I just got sold to the Red Sox.' I said, 'What are you complaining about? That's a great place to play, and Fenway Park is a good place for a left-handed hitter.'

"He was telling me that when they told him he was sold, he acted like he didn't want to go. He said, 'Do I have to go?' They said, 'Yeah.' He said, 'Gee, you know, I grew up in this organization.' He acted like he hated to leave. They said, 'I knew you'd take it that way. We hated to sell you, but we had to.' He told me that after he left the meeting he started dancing. He was so happy to be sold to a contender. Al was a great guy. We had some good kids on that team.

"The DeWitts were nice guys, but they never had any money. They had to make that big sale: Vern Stephens and Jack Kramer for a group of us. Roy Partee had been my roommate on the Red Sox. He didn't want to leave the Red Sox either, but you didn't have a say. You went where they sent you. You wanted to squawk, but the best thing was to keep your mouth shut.

"Zack Taylor was our manager. He would have been a great coach. He was a very loyal man, worked hard. Zack didn't get on you. He'd say, 'Hit the cut-off man.' He didn't give a shit if you threw the guy out, as long as you looked good hitting the cut-off man. My philosophy is to get the ball in as fast as possible, so you have a chance to get the guy out going home. But all Zack cared about was that the ballclub looked good! He was that kind of guy: 'Let's look good.' He wanted to win, of course.

"Here's the thing: The easiest clubs to play for are winning ballclubs. They say there is pressure. When you're on a good ballclub, the pressure is on the other team, not on you. A winner is a winner. From the day I had started playing baseball until I went with the Browns, I had never played on a losing ballclub. It was a different kind of atmosphere.

"When you're with a winner, you expect to win every day. When I was with the Browns, it was tough to win. Most of our players knew they weren't equipped. They'd bring young guys up a little before they were ready. You have to believe you can win. You can bullshit yourself. On the Browns, we could say we were going to win, but it didn't mean we were going to do it.

"Things always seemed to work against us. We lost some games in the last inning. We played the Yankees in Yankee Stadium, and Bobby Brown hit a foul ball, and they called it a home run. I said, 'Bobby, every time I see a foul ball, I think of you.' He'd say, 'It was fair.' It was fair because they were playing against the poor Browns. We never got those calls. It was foul, but it was fair. Understand?

"One thing I noticed about a champion in any sport, people kind of gravitate toward them, even the players they are playing against. When we played the Yankees, our players were always kissing their ass. I don't believe in that. I never saw a better baseball player than Joe DiMaggio, but I never kissed his ass. It looked like some of our guys were happy if they said hello to him. 'Hey, I'm in the big leagues, too.' I figure we got to beat these guys. The Yankees had nice guys: Rizzuto was a nice kid, and Billy Johnson was nice. Keller, Henrich, they were all nice. But they won. Those sons a bitches would hold you and hold you and hold you, and it would be 2 to 2 in the ninth, in the tenth, they'd hold you, and then someone would boot one or our pitcher would walk someone, and they'd win the ball game. That was a champion.

"We had on our team a first baseman by the name of [Jack] Graham. He hit 24 home runs, and he was back in Triple A the next year! Who the hell knows why. He was a pretty good hitter. He was in the big leagues. He was a hot shit, though, opinionated. He'd say to Taylor, 'What are you moaning about now, Zack?' He was a good guy. I had more fun in St. Louis than I had anywhere else. We couldn't wait to get on the road, where it would be cooler. We didn't have a bad ballclub. But you need to have thumpers in your lineup, got to have a Ted Williams, and we didn't have that. One year Dick Kokos hit 23 home runs. Kokos was about five-eight, a strong little guy, but of course in St. Louis you could piss over that right field wall. Not knocking anybody, but that was a good place for a left-handed hitter. But like Graham, in no time Kokos was back in the minors. I never understood that. And there was another kid with a funny name who played first base, Hank Arft, a good player but not a 25 home run hitter, and you have to have a couple of those. You need the home run hitters. The Browns didn't get lucky enough.

"We needed more pitching. We had Cliff Fannin, Fred Sanford, Ned Garver. Fannin had stuff and so did Sanford. We had that Al Zoldak. He couldn't break a pane of glass, but he'd get you out. Garver was a good pitcher. He got the ball over, didn't walk too many guys, kept the ball down, knew how to pitch for a kid.

"I can remember when I played for Scranton in the Eastern League, we outdrew the Boston Braves and the Browns. That's what they told us. I can understand why the people didn't come out. It was so hot. I remember Jack Burns, who played with the Browns in the '30s, told me they used to put their

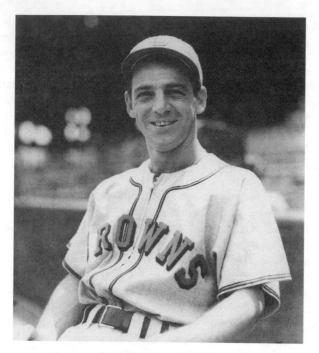

EDDIE PELLAGRINI
(Courtesy Brace Photo)

feet in a bucket of water, it was so hot. That's what he said. St. Louis was a tough place to play.

"In 1948 we made two triple plays in one week. We were playing in Fenway Park, and someone hit the ball, and I caught it and started a triple play. Then the same week we went to Washington, and a guy named Bill Kennedy was pitching. Tom McBride, who had played for the Red Sox, was the hitter for Washington. He hit a ball that hit Kennedy's shoe. The ball flew up to me to right at shortstop. I caught it, flipped to Dillinger, and I said, 'Throw it to first.' Another triple play.

"When you get sold from one club to another, you get pissed off. 'The sons a bitches. I'll show you.' I made a play in the ninth that almost cost the Red Sox the pennant. Birdie Tebbetts hit a ball, and I made a great catch. If that ball would have gone through, they would have won the game and wouldn't have had to play in the playoff of 1948. And then I made a play against Cleveland, and if they'd a won that game, the Indians would have won it without a playoff.

"That's when they tied and had that playoff in Fenway Park. All you could hear was from Tebbetts: 'You dago little bastard, you.' Terms of endearment. And I felt really good. 'Sons a bitches, I told you you shouldn't have sold me!' "

*   *   *

After the 1949 season, Pellagrini spent a year in the minors and then played two seasons in Philadelphia. He then got to experience life with two of the legendary former St. Louis Cardinals: Rogers Hornsby and Branch Rickey. In 1952 he was dealt to Cincinnati, where he got to experience the managerial quirkiness of Hornsby. He didn't last the season after he told Hornsby he thought Ted Williams was a better hitter than he was. His final years were with Rickey in Pittsburgh.

EDDIE PELLAGRINI: "I played with the mighty Hornsby. He liked me a little bit because I had a little balls. I made a play one day, and he said, 'Jesus I never saw that before.' I said, 'You stick around, and I'll show you a few more.' No one talked to him like that. I think he kind of liked it.

"Nobody liked him. He wasn't a fellow who would say, 'Good morning, Pelli. How you feeling today, kid?' I'll never forget, he used to stand in the clubhouse and grease his behind. You could see him do it. He should have gone to a private place to do it. And one day we put some hot linament in the tube. He put that on, and he didn't even flinch. He wouldn't give you the satisfaction of letting you know it was burning him.

"Another time we were talking about hitting. When you talk about the greatest hitter who ever lived, you have to talk about that guy. Christ, he hit .358 lifetime. But I said to him, 'I know a better hitter than you, skip.' He looked at me with those eyes—it looked like an animal's eyes, like a tiger looking at you, and maybe that's why he could hit. He looked at me quizzically and asked, 'Who?' I said, 'Ted Williams is a better hitter than you.' Well, the son of a bitch never played me much after that. I went and looked at Hornsby's record, and he saw he had five years where he hit over .400. Unbelievable. That's hard to do. And one year he hit 40 home runs. He was a second baseman who hit .358 lifetime! I told you, in baseball you have to keep your mouth shut, but that was hard for me to do at times.

"After Cincinnati, I went to Pittsburgh. Mr. Rickey called me up. You'd think I was Joe DiMaggio. He said, 'I want you to come in tomorrow, but I don't want you to tell anyone you're coming.' I said, 'I can't tomorrow. In a couple of days.' I sat opposite him in his office, and he was talking with that cigar, and he said, 'Do you think you can give me a couple of years like you did with the Phillies?' I said, 'Oh yeah, easy, Mr. Rickey. I can do that.' He said, 'We have a bunch of young kids. We got Vic Janowicz and the O'Brien twins, and I'd like them to be around you. Your reputation is great.' I said, 'I can help them.' He said, 'I'd like you to live in the same hotel with them. Would you mind?' I said, 'Not at all, but I'd like to play.' He said, 'Oh, yes, you'll play. Don't worry.'

"We agreed on the money, and I said, 'There is only one thing, Mr. Rickey. I have to have a two-year no-cut contract.' This was the Pirates. He said, 'What?' He said, 'What if I want you to go down to the minors to help the manager coach third base?' I said, 'No. Two years, no-cut. Otherwise I'm not going to sign.' I was very nice. He hurrumphed. He had a secretary named Robinson. He called him in and dictated the terms. Robinson used to hang around at the restaurant we ate in, and he said about me, 'That son of a bitch got a two-year, no-cut contract. Stan Musial never even got one of those!'

"One day Branch Rickey told me, 'I'd like you to manage in my organization. You remind me a lot of Leo Durocher.'

"Leo Durocher was the best manager I ever saw in the big leagues. I'll tell you why. Leo knew how to make a change. If a batter doubled, he would put in a pinch runner who he knew would score on a base hit. Look at Leo's lineups. He used a lot of players in a ball game. That impressed me. I learned very early that you have to play your hand. You can't rely on what the scouts say. You do things to win ball games according to the ability of your players. And that's where Durocher stood out.

"I said to Rickey, 'I'm a better guy than Leo.' He said, 'I know you are. I know you don't drink and run around.' I said, 'That's right, I'm a better guy, but he's a good manager.' I said, 'Mr. Rickey, you flatter me.'

"And I stayed there for the two years and I quit, because my wife was going to release me if I didn't. We had five kids. The wives really deserve a medal."

CHAPTER 40

BILL VEECK AND THE MIDGET

On July 5, 1951, the DeWitt brothers sold the Browns to Bill Veeck, the son of William Veeck, who had been the general manager of the Chicago Cubs under owner William Wrigley, Phil's dad. When William Veeck died, his son Bill was hoping that Wrigley would hire him to run the Cubs, but Bill was too much of a loose cannon for Wrigley, and so Veeck had to set off on his own. After first buying a minor league team in Milwaukee with former Cub star Charlie Grimm and then selling it for a substantial profit, Veeck in 1946 bought the Cleveland Indians. After winning the 1948 pennant, Veeck then sold the team, and in 1951 Veeck used his profits from the sale to buy the Browns. Veeck never had the money to make the Browns into a winner, but under Veeck's aegis, the St. Louis American League team would make headlines for its wacky promotions and for two of the most fascinating characters ever to play the game: Satchel Paige and Eddie Gaedel.

When Veeck purchased the Browns, the sardonic John Lardner wrote: "Many critics were surprised to know that the Browns could be bought because they didn't know the Browns were owned."

Veeck told the DeWitts he would pay stockholders $7 a share. According to Veeck, the stock was worth $3 a share. But to finalize the sale, Veeck said he would have to own at least 75 percent of the stock. The DeWitts owned 56 percent. He would have to purchase the other 19 percent from the 1,400 stockholders.

Veeck's intention was to buy the Browns, promote like crazy, and run the St. Louis Cardinals out of town. The Cards were owned by a man named Fred Saigh, who was wealthy but not rich. Veeck figured he could take him.

The most influential radio personality in St. Louis at that time was an acerbic young man by the name of Harry Caray, who worked for Saigh as a Cardinal broadcaster. On his nightly sports talk show, Caray would advise stockholders not to sell to Veeck, who he labled a "con man." Veeck, nonetheless, succeeded in buying 80 percent of the stock. For revenge, Veeck decided to pay back Caray's boss by taunting him in print whenever he could. Since the Cards were renting the ballpark from the Browns, Veeck barred Saigh from using their special box when the Cards were playing. He plastered the park with pictures of old Browns. Saigh, a real estate developer, responded by printing on his scorecard: THE ST. LOUIS CARDINALS, A DIGNIFIED ST. LOUIS INSTITUTION.

When Bill Veeck took over the team in July of 1951, the Browns were twenty-three and a half games out of first place. To convince the fans of St. Louis that his ownership would not be more of the same-old, on August 19, 1951, Bill Veeck orchestrated the most famous promotion in the history of the game of baseball.

It was the fiftieth anniversary of the American League, and Veeck decided he would throw a party for the fans who came that day and also for the Falstaff Brewery, the team's sponsor. Veeck told the executives of Falstaff that he was going to do something memorable, but he wouldn't tell them what he was planning.

All his life Veeck had contemplated using a midget in a big league baseball game. The idea came from New York Giants manager John McGraw, who often visited Veeck's dad at home when he was a kid. McGraw had as a good-luck charm a very short man by the name of Eddie Morrow. After a few drinks, McGraw would swear that one day he would send Morrow up to bat.

BILL VEECK: "All kids are tickled by the incongruous. The picture of McGraw's gnome coming to bat had made such a vivid impression on me that it was there, ready for the plucking, when I needed it."

Browns manager Zack Taylor, who had caught for McGraw in 1927, heard his manager discuss his notion of using a midget at bat. Taylor was under the impression that he was the one who told Veeck about McGraw's midget, though Veeck certainly had been aware of it independently.

ZACK TAYLOR: "When I was with the Giants, we used to sit around the hotel lobby nights listening to the boss. John McGraw never forgot a pitch of any game the Giants ever played under him. And he always was scheming up new ways to win. One time he came up with the idea that it might not be bad to carry a little fellow around and send him up to bat to get a base on balls if the score was tied in the ninth.

"Of course, nobody ever did it. But I never forgot what McGraw said. So when Veeck suggested hiring a little fellow, I told him what McGraw had said years before. Veeck got on the phone to Chicago right away and checked up to find there wasn't any rule against it.''

Veeck called Cleveland booking agent Marty Caine and asked for a midget who was "somewhat athletic and game for anything." Veeck told four other people: his wife, PR man Bob Fishel, traveling secretary Bill Durney, and manager Zack Taylor.

The name of the midget was Eddie Gaedel, who knew almost nothing about baseball. Gaedel was three feet seven inches and weighed 65 pounds. Veeck instructed Gaedel to go up to the plate and crouch. Veeck measured his strike zone at one and a half inches. Veeck ordered Gaedel not to swing at the ball under pain of death. Gaedel wasn't very happy about that.

Veeck told him, "Eddie, I'm going to be up on the roof with a high-powered rifle, watching every move you make. If you so much as look as if you're going to swing, I'm going to shoot you dead.''

Veeck took the uniform of Bill DeWitt, Jr., the nine-year-old son of Bill DeWitt, Sr., who had sold the team to Veeck. Bill DeWitt, Jr., who currently is the chairman of the board and general partner of the Cardinals, recalled his role in the affair.

BILL DeWITT JR.: "My father and his brother had owned the club prior to selling it to Bill Veeck. Each year, when they ordered uniforms, they would get me one, and I'd go out on the field and play catch with the players and shag flies. So I had an official uniform from the factory. It was a little different from what it is today, when they sell official uniforms in gift shops. Back then the club had them, but really, nobody else did. And so my father came to me one day, and he said, 'Bill is going to have a midget come to the plate and pinch-hit in a game, and we don't have a uniform to fit him, cause he's kind of small, and your uniform is a pretty close fit, so we need to borrow it.' So I said, 'Great.'

"I had number 6 on my uniform on the back. Bobby Dillinger, who played third base, wore number 6. I don't know if it was necessarily for him, but they took the 6 off and put a ⅛ on it.''

On August 19, "⅛ Eddie Gaedel" was listed in the scorecard. The salary for his one at-bat would be $100. Veeck took out $1 million in insurance on his life, in case he was skulled by a pitched ball.

That evening Veeck and his wife were in their apartment with Bob Broeg, a reporter for the *St. Louis Post-Dispatch*. Veeck waited until the paper went to bed to tell Broeg of his intentions.

BOB BROEG: "He said, 'Are you going to press?' I looked at my watch, and it was about midnight, and I said, 'Yeah, why?' And then he told me what was going to happen.

"I said, 'You mean to tell me you thought I would spoil it?' He said, 'I didn't think so, but . . .' I said, 'I'm glad you told me.' He said, 'Why?' I said, 'You don't think you're going to have a photographer out there for eighteen innings on a Sunday evening for your clowns playing Detroit, do you?' Until 1954, photographers were allowed on the field, just like gloves and the horizontal batrack, and so I told our photographer, Jack January, when it was going to happen, and Jack got out and kneeled on the on-deck circle. That's why you have that beautiful picture. You couldn't have gotten that from any other angle if a photographer hadn't been there. If he hadn't told me about it, it would have been a disaster, because there never would have been a picture.''

Veeck had Gaedel sign a league contract and mailed it in to the league office the day before the game. The morning of the game Veeck wired the league office that the Browns were activating Eddie Gaedel.

On the day paid attendance to the doubleheader against the Detroit Tigers was 18,000. Since it was also the fiftieth anniversary of the American League and Falstaff birthday day, every fan was given a slice of birthday cake, a box of ice cream, and a tiny can of beer as they entered the park. No one understood that there was a tie-in between the small can of beer and what they were about to witness. And no one seemed to notice the listing in the scorecard: ''⅛ Gaedel.''

Despite a first-game loss to the Tigers, the Browns' fans were in an up mood. Between games, Veeck put on his birthday celebration. Bob Broeg recalled the madness that followed.

BOB BROEG: ''Bob Fishel, who was Bill's PR man, surreptitiously signed this kid for a hundred bucks. They flew him in, and between games they had a little show on the field. Max Patkin was putting on a show at first base. At second base they had a trampolinist, Bill Keough, who I had grown up with and played soccer, and at third base they had Satchel Paige, Al Widner, Johnny Berardino, and Ed Redys, who had a little band. And all of a sudden they wheeled in from the wagon gate a big papier-mâché cake, a giant cake, and all of a sudden this little character pops out of it wearing a Browns uniform.''

Right before Gaedel was to go inside the cake, however, he lost his nerve when the 18,000 cheering fans spooked him. But Bill Durney, the 250–pound traveling secretary, wasn't about to allow a midget to spoil Veeck's promotion. Durney told him, ''There are 18,000 people in this park and there's one I know I can lick. You dead or alive, you're going in there.''

The frightened Gaedel tried to tell Durney that he couldn't go on because his elf shoes were hurting his feet. Durney picked him up and dropped him into the cake, sat him down, and covered the top with tissue paper. The cake was rolled to the middle of the field.

The PA announcer intoned: ''As a special birthday present to manager Zack Taylor, the management is presenting him with a brand-new Brownie.'' On cue, Gaedel jumped out of the cake. A few fans clapped. Most didn't know what to make of it. No one realized what Veeck intended to do with him.

The executives of the beer company, disappointed that his big surprise was a midget popping out of a cake, were angry with Veeck. Veeck had told them his stunt would make national headlines. This was a minor blip on the radar screen at best.

BOB BROEG: "When Gaedel popped out of the cake and ran off the field, everybody thought that was real cute.

"Well, now Veeck had gone up to the rooftop to orchestrate the show. He had told him, 'I was an expert rifleman in the Marines, and I have a rifle up there. When you get in that ball game today, if you swing that bat, I'll shoot you dead.' So the kid went into the Cardinal clubhouse, which was empty, and they dressed him. Zack Taylor, the manager, came in. The kid's little shoelaces were undone, so Zack put him on his lap, tied his shoestring, and said, 'I don't think they will throw at you.' Gaedel said, 'What?' Zack said, 'I don't think they will throw at you.' The kid jumped off his lap and headed for the door.

"And standing in the doorway was Durney, who stood there with his arms folded and said, 'Where are you going, boy?' Gaedel said, 'I'm getting out of here.' Durney said, 'The hell you are. You know what Veeck told you. That man is on the roof. He will shoot you dead.' "

Zack Taylor recounted what happened in the first inning of the second game.

ZACK TAYLOR: "We got Detroit out in their half of the first inning. Frank Saucier was our leadoff man, but I sent up the midget to hit for him.

"You should have heard [Tigers manager] Red Rolfe moan. He hit the ceiling. Ed Hurley, the umpire, came rushing up to me, yelling, 'What's going on here?' I played it nice and calm, like I had been sending up them little fellows every day. Veeck had told me there might be trouble, so I was prepared. 'What do you mean?' I said to Hurley. 'We just signed up a new player and here is the contract.' I reached in my back pocket and showed him the papers, legal as could be. They had to let him hit. I've got a big picture of it hanging in my house."

BOB SWIFT: "I was catching. Bob Cain was our pitcher. He wanted to throw underhanded, but I told him he couldn't because the fellow had signed a legitimate contract and he had to pitch legal. I was going to catch lying down with one hand propped under my chin, but I decided the thing had gone far enough.

"I wish Hal Newhouser or Dizzy Trout or one of those fastball pitchers had been in there. They would have breezed a couple past him.

"Cain couldn't get the ball over. He threw four pitches and walked him. They put in a runner, but that was that. Turned out it didn't make any difference in the outcome of the game, but it sure created quite a stir."

BOB BROEG: "Gaedel ran down to first base, and I think the sheer joy of getting there without getting clobbered overwhelmed him, because when Jim Delsing came down to pinch-run for him, Gaedel patronizingly patted Delsing on the fanny and ran off.

"I was like a salivating monkey. I asked Bob Fishel when Gaedel was leaving. He said, 'Shortly.' I said, 'Well, get him up here.'

The owner of the St. Louis Browns, Bill Veeck, sent in Eddie Gaedel, a 3-foot, 7-inch stuntman, to pinch-hit in a game against Detroit at Sportsman's Park, in St. Louis, on August 19, 1951. Gaedel walked on four pitches.
(Courtesy AP Photo)

"So he came up to the press box a little later, and I can see him now, wearing the Brown slacks with a yellow sport shirt open, with a light tan jacket. A cute little guy. He came down to where I was sitting. I picked him up and sat him on the ledge so I could talk with him and watch the game. He gave me some canned remarks about now he knows how Babe Ruth felt. I said, 'Bananas. You know what you are now?' 'What?' I said, 'Damm it, you are what all of us dream of being, an ex-big league ballplayer.' And his chest puffed up, and he took off and left."

Bill Miller, a lifelong Browns fan, had an ideal vantage point for the game. Miller recalled his emotions upon seeing a midget go up to the plate.

BILL MILLER: "I was in a first-row box when the midget came up in August of '51. I got the best view of that. When I saw him, I thought immediately, 'This doesn't count. This is kind of a stunt.' And then he stood up there at the plate, and I thought, 'This doesn't count. They're just horsing around.' Well, what happened next, the umpire stopped the game and motioned for Zack Taylor to come out. Taylor handed him a piece of paper, which it turned out later was his contract. I saw the umpire laugh, and then they proceeded. Bob Cain, who was pitching, didn't know what to do. You could see he was saying, 'What am I supposed to do now?' And Red Rolfe was over in the Detroit dugout with his foot on the step with his cap off, scratching his head. He was thinking, 'What is that crazy Veeck up to now?' But I just laughed it off, thinking, 'This doesn't count. They're just fooling around.'

"And we didn't see the significance of it until a few days later. But that was his masterpiece, I suppose."

After the game, 9-year-old Bill DeWitt, Jr., had his uniform returned to him. It became one of his most valuable possessions.

BILL DEWITT, JR.: "They gave it back to me, and I wore it, always kept it, and when Bill Veeck went into the Hall of Fame, the head of the Hall called me and said, 'I heard you might have that uniform? Is that true?' I said, 'Yeah.' He said, 'We need something for Bill's display.' I said, 'I'll loan it to you.' So it went on loan for the induction ceremony, and they thought it was such an appealing item for people who visited there that I've kept it on loan ever since. It still has the ⅛ on it."

The next day American League president Will Harridge ruled that all player contracts had to be approved by the league. He also disqualified Gaedel from future play. Gaedel, prompted by Veeck, made a speech charging Harridge with ruining his career.

Gaedel took advantage of his celebrity. He earned $17,000 from appearing on several television programs, including the Ed Sullivan and Bing Crosby shows. But in early September there was a small item in the paper, datelined Cincinnati. Eddie Gaedel was arrested at two in the morning for getting drunk and abusing a police officer. He was on a street corner screaming obscenities and trying to convince the officer he was a big league ballplayer.

A decade later, in April of 1961, Veeck was owner of the Chicago White Sox when fans complained about vendors blocking their view, so he hired Gaedel again plus seven other midgets to sell peanuts and soda in front of the box seat sections. By then, Gaedel was suffering from high blood pressure and an enlarged heart. He had been falling frequently and was in bad shape.

BOB BROEG: "Ten years later, almost to the day, Eddie Gaedel was mugged either in a bar or outside near where he lived with his mother in Chicago. He crept home, opened the door, crawled upstairs, and died in bed. The Cook County coroner's jury ruled it was a heart attack, not a homicide.

"The only baseball person who went to his funeral was Bob Cain. Some years later, I called Cain over in Cleveland, where he was a longtime sales ambassador for Kraft Foods, and I said, 'Bob, I often wondered why you went to his funeral.' He said, 'I'm kind of a religious guy, but to tell you the truth, I was a goodwill speaker, and guess what my best story was all these years?' "

Eddie's mother, Helen Gaedel, was swindled out of Eddie's bat and Browns pants by a man masquerading as a representative of Baseball's Hall of Fame. The curators at the Hall say that beside Bill DeWitt's jersey, the only remnant of that historic day is the famous photograph, made possible by Bob Broeg's foresight, showing Gaedel crouching with his little bat at home plate with catcher Bob Swift on his knees, waiting for a pitch. That, and a rare tribute.

When he died, Gaedel's obituary was placed on page A-1 of many of the major dailies, an honor accorded only the crème de la crème of professional athletes.

CHAPTER 41

GRANDSTAND MANAGER'S NIGHT

SIX days after Eddie Gaedel's brush with immortality, Bill Veeck staged another night for which he has become infamous: Grandstand Manager's Night against the Philadelphia Athletics at Sportsman's Park. Veeck decided he would give the fans in the stands the opportunity to make the manager's decisions. He hired the A's owner and manager, the legendary Connie Mack, to sit with them while they decided. SHOULD THE BROWNS BUNT? Zack Taylor held up a sign asking the question. In the stands were dozens of fans with flip cards. On one side was YES on the other NO. The fans then voted, and the players would do as the fans demanded. SHOULD THE BROWNS HIT-AND-RUN? TAKE OUT THE PITCHER? STEAL? On this night, the fans made all the decisions.

In a season in which the Browns would win only 52 games, 20 of them by pitcher Ned Garver, on this evening the Browns beat the A's by the score of 5–3.

Garver was on the mound that evening. He, for one, greatly enjoyed Veeck and the excitement he created.

NED GARVER: I was born in Ney, Ohio, Christmas Day, 1925. I can't say I've lived there my whole life. Not yet, anyway. My father was a farmer. I went to work real early working on the railroad as a section hand, and I'd come home in the middle of the afternoon and haul manure, bale hay, and milk cows. You'd walk behind horses and plow, then work up the ground and plant the seeds.

"In those days, you had to raise everything. You didn't buy anything. You grew hay for your animals. You had to have grain to feed those things, so you raised oats and wheat and corn and hay. You had your own milk and chickens. Just about when I was ready to leave the farm, soybeans came along.

"I have two older brothers, and my dad would let us play ball when we got the work done. On the way back to the field, we'd play catch, and we'd play catch on the way back to the house. At the back end of our farm we had a little ditch, and we'd cut white-ash saplings from that ditch, and a man uptown would make us something that looked like a baseball bat on his lathe.

We bought gloves from Sears and Roebuck. We didn't have much money. After the cover of the baseball was knocked off, you'd wrap it with black friction tape, and then you put that in the hog chop—the ground-up grain— and take the stickiness off of it. You could play with a ball like that for a long time.

"Back in those days, you didn't have the opportunity to do so many things. You didn't go to the lake or have a boat. We played baseball. Every community had its own team. I played with guys who were older, so when I got to play on the town team in the summertime, I was playing against guys who were pretty darn good. That was real good training. We didn't have football in high school, so we played baseball in the spring and in the fall. We went to the state championships. I got beat by Leavittsburg in the final game, 3–2, when I was a senior. This pitcher, Eddie Yuhas, who played with the Cardinals, had already been signed.

"I played in the federation league for a Fort Wayne, Indiana, team called City Lite. We went to Youngstown to play in the national championship, and I pitched and played left field. After we got eliminated, my manager announced that I had had four different offers. Different scouts had come to him and offered me a job.

"I signed with the Browns because he was a bird dog for the Browns. In the fall of 1943, I went up to Detroit and enlisted in the Navy Air Corps, but they didn't call me until October. I was training to be an officer in the Navy, but then I got a medical discharge the next spring, early in 1944. If you can imagine it, I had flat feet. So I came home, and I went over to my manager and I said, 'Okay, you said I had offers. I'd like to go try it.' He said, 'Okay, I'll get you a job.' He really wanted me to stay and play another year with him, but I said no.

"Since he had an attachment to the Browns, he got me a contract that called for me to get paid $100 a month. I went to spring training with the Toledo team at Cape Girardeau, the same place where the Browns trained. They stayed in a hotel across the street. We trained in the same facility. They'd show up at the workouts in the morning, and some days there'd be a ruckus, and they'd be all beat up. Sometimes they'd fight among themselves.

"Sig Jakucki was on the Browns team. I later played on the same team with Jakucki down in San Antone. He was tough, boy. He had a bad drinking habit. He would fight at the drop of a hat.

"He and I were pretty good friends at San Antone. We lived in the same hotel. I didn't go the places he went. Our manager in San Antone was Jimmy Adair, and before the season started he announced, 'We have two sets of rules: one set of rules for Jakucki and one set for everybody else.' So the only time Jack came to the ballpark was when they put it in the paper that he was scheduled to pitch. So then he'd come to the ballpark. Other times he'd come, and he'd have a girl on each arm, and he'd be drunk. He'd always come to the games I was pitching to see me. He somehow liked me, and he'd tell me sometimes, 'I don't know why anybody abuses himself like I do.' He'd have an awful hangover the next day and feel terrible. He was a real character, but that son of a gun had a rubber arm. But sometimes he'd be out on that mound,

NED GARVER
(Courtesy Brace Photo)

and Christ, he'd be drunk. He couldn't get the ball over the plate. He'd have trouble getting down off the mound and getting back on it. And so finally they'd have to take him out.

"Adair put up with him because that son of a gun could really pitch. He beat the Yankees on the last day of the season to win the pennant for the '44 Browns, and I want to tell you something, there wasn't anything he was afraid of. I mean, no matter what the circumstances, there wasn't no game too big for him. If he'd been a guy who'd taken care of himself, it's hard to say what the guy might have been able to do. He abused himself terribly and still was able to be reasonably successful.

"I spent four seasons in the minor leagues, one at Newark, one at Toledo, and two in the Texas League after it reopened. That had been closed up for the war. I went to San Antonio and played there for two years.

"I came up to the Browns in '48. They kept selling players and bringing up prospects. Just before I got there, they got rid of a lot of people—Denny Galehouse, Jack Kramer, Nelson Potter, Junior Stephens—buddy, if those guys had stayed there, we could have held our own. But they didn't draw enough people, so they sold players. They got rid of Gerry Priddy and Al Zarilla and Bob Dillinger, Les Moss, Sherm Lollar—guys who could really play. Judas Priest Almighty, those guys could play. But you can't get rid of people for money and expect to do well. Cripes, the Yankees would bring in Gil McDougald one year and Bob Grim another year and build, by Jove. We got rid of players. They didn't trade them and get somebody in return. They would get minor leaguers. That's all some of them were—they weren't no good. They couldn't help you win in the major leagues. Sometimes they'd be on our roster.

"Cripes, I won 17 games at San Antone, and so I was able to pitch. I could play. I got up there, and they didn't have enough pitchers the second year I was there, so I pitched Opening Day. The first four years I was there, I pitched 1,077 innings! I got to play. And by Jove, that's worth a lot. But it wasn't until I got to Detroit that I found out there was quite a bit of difference between how the ballclubs operated. In St. Louis you had to carry your own bag and had to do stuff players on other teams didn't have to do. Detroit operated like a big league ball team.

"In 1949 we had two rookies: Roy Sievers and Sherm Lollar. Sievers was Rookie of the Year in '49. I want to tell you, he was majestic. He looked about like DiMaggio standing up there. He'd just hold that bat. He hit .306 his first season, but then they thought he ought to pull the ball more and the next spring they tried to make a pull hitter out of him. That was a bad move. He got out of the gate poorly.

"Zack Taylor, our manager, was not going to go against management. Taylor was a friend of the DeWitts, and he was not going to be expensive, and they had Bootnose Hofmann as a coach, so if the management said, 'In our ballpark he's hitting a lot of balls in right- and left-center and if he'd have pulled those balls, they'd have been home runs.' Well, that's what they worked out, and it turned out to be a mistake.

"Lollar was the smartest catcher I ever saw. Lollar could help you win ball games, and he did help you win ball games. He caught every pitcher a different way. In other words, some catchers are going to call their game— they don't even know who's pitching. They just put something down automatic. I'd be in games when I'd never shake Lollar off at all. I can remember he helped me win my 20th game because he came out to the mound.

"I was staggering along—they had already scored several runs, and he said, 'You've got a good sinker. For a while here, let's waste everything else, and we'll just make them hit the sinker. Waste the breaking ball. Waste the change-up. Waste everything else and make them hit the sinker.'

"That gave me courage. I didn't know I had anything that good. But he said I did. I went at it, and about three or four innings later, one time through the batting order, he said, 'Let's go back and pitch like you normally do.' And we won. I hit a home run with the score tied to put us ahead, and we stayed there. It was the only home run I hit all year. That was right out of Hollywood.

"In those years, when I was pitching against the Yankees, I had to face DiMaggio, Berra, Rizzuto, Raschi, Reynolds, all those guys. I was mighty pleased and proud to play against them. I loved to pitch against those guys. Like Ted Williams, Judas Priest, I never wanted to walk Williams. They tell you, 'Don't give him anything good to hit. Don't walk Dominick [DiMaggio] or Pesky. But if you walk Williams, that's good, because you just held him to one base.' Judas Priest Almighty, I got to pitch against the best people in the world. And if you get them out, that's fine. You get to match strategies, try this, try that. I went into Boston one day. I was sitting in the dugout and looked at the lineup card. The Red Sox had a team batting average of .311, and our guys were hitting .217. And I led our team in hitting. In 1951 I hit sixth in our lineup. Because I hit .305.

"In '51 I started out winning some games. When we had won 24 games, I had won 12 of them. Somebody from Austin, Texas, sent me a sports page where they listed the standings in the American League, and they had 'Ned Garver' instead of 'St. Louis Browns.' And then Casey Stengel let me start the All-Star Game. The rest of the season things went about the same as they had in '50 when I was second in the league in earned run average and only won 13 games. In '50 I went out there the last nineteen times and I wasn't knocked out of the box. I completed 22 games but only won 13. So in '51, after I had 12 wins, we didn't score any runs for me. I had to win the last four games of the season, my last four starts in a row, to get 20 wins. The odds against that were pretty high.

"But I never felt sorry for myself. There was a lot of talk about my getting traded. You see a lot of stuff written and you can't help see it. The general manager of the Yankees later told me, 'We came *this* close to getting you.' But I didn't worry about that. I had enough to worry about just trying to do my job. My dad and my high school coach had taught me that my job was to make as few mistakes as possible, and if I took care of my job, that's all I could do. If the shortstop made an error, that's okay. I had no control over that. I could learn and be a little better the next time. That was a plenty big enough job.

"Bill Veeck bought the team in the summer of 1951, and I'll tell you, that was the difference between day and night. As long as you played for Bill Veeck, he made you feel like you were ten feet tall. I went one stretch with the Browns in '52 where we went 57 innings in a row while I was pitching and never scored a run. I got beat, 1–0, in ten innings in Cleveland and came back home and the next time pitched against Mel Parnell, and he beat me, 1 to 0, and I only gave two hits. Faye Throneberry hit a home run in that game. Bill Veeck sent down a dozen open-neck shirts like the kind he wore for each loss. What he was saying was: 'I know you pitched well. Keep your chin up and do your job, and I appreciate it.' I still have a half dozen of those shirts at home. I gave a bunch of them to my brothers. He gave me a hundred and some shirts in the years I was there.

"At times we were on the road, and we had a private dining car on the train, and he'd come in there and pick up the tab for everybody. Steak for everybody!

"One time we beat Cleveland three out of four the tail end of the year. He sent us all down to Hally Brothers for a gift certificate. One day when I was in Washington, Satchel Paige pitched nine innings in a seventeen-inning game, and he sent him down to buy a $100 suit. And if you were ever up to the office and he'd be in there, he'd holler at you, 'Come on in.' The door would be open. He'd have his leg up on the desk, putting ashes in that hole in his wooden leg. He'd visit with you. He'd sometimes come down and throw batting practice to us pitchers. Yeah, he did, with a wooden leg.

"I'll tell you something, boy, he had more promotional ideas in a day than most of those people have in a lifetime. He would be setting in the bleachers or in the grandstand with those people, and he'd ask them. People would say, 'We need another water fountain along the left field line under the stands,' and he'd put one in. He'd go to speak at any club, to any group that would have him. If they didn't have an advance sale, he'd say, 'Anybody whose name starts between A and F, you get in free.' Well, who knows what their name was? He let them in because he might sell them a hot dog. He didn't come out and threaten people like today's owners do and say, 'If two million of you don't come, we're going to move to Charlotte.' He tried to go out and manufacture interest so people would want to come to his ball games. And he was always trying to improve his ballclub.

"He did some of the most wonderful things. One time there was a lot of talk about their trading me, so he said, 'After the game, you come up to the press box.' So after the game, I rode the elevator up there. Of course, he told all the newspaper people I was going to be there and he was going to have an announcement. I got up there, and he announced to them that I was going to pitch the next day! Heh-heh-heh. But Judas Priest Almighty, the year I was there, three things happened that only happened once in the history of baseball: one was the midget, one was Grandstand Manager's Night, and one was winning 20 for a team that had lost 102.

"I pitched the first game of the doubleheader before they brought in Gaedel. Jim Delsing was our center fielder, but our manager Zack Taylor used another player, Frank Saucier. We went out into the field and got the Tigers out, and he had Frank Saucier hitting first. Instead of Frank Saucier, here came the midget going up there. We didn't know anything about it. I'm telling you, Veeck did a whale of a job not passing that information along to us. That was a complete surprise. He's got his signed contract in his pocket, and he hands it to Hurley, and they have to let him hit.

"I loved the idea of the midget. At the time if Bill Veeck had said, 'Run through this door,' we'd a tried it. Veeck never made a farce of the game. He had Max Patkin as coach. Max entertained people all over the world. That's what Bill was trying to do. We were in the entertainment business. But he never made a farce. There were times when a guy hit a home run on the first pitch I threw in a ball game, so I was behind, 1 to 0. All Eddie Gaedel did was walk. Now if he'd a used him with the bases loaded in the ninth inning and the score tied, it might have been a different story. He used him in an absolutely perfect way. That happened in 1951, and here it is 1998, and every time I go to speak to any group, they ask me about the midget. Now think of that. By Jove, people remember it for who knows how long. It's been fifty years.

"Lord, I'm just tickled to death that I got to play under Bill Veeck. Remember Grandstand Manager's Night? They got to vote on the starting pitcher, and they voted that I was to be the pitcher. I was a popular guy in St. Louis then. And geez, we were playing the Philadelphia ballclub, and they had scored two or three runs and had men on first and third, but they wouldn't let anyone warm up! Taylor put up a sign: 'Warm up a pitcher?' They voted it down. 'No.'

"The next thing they did was vote to play the infield in. Sherm Lollar came out to the mound and said, 'We don't dare play the infield in. We got to play back and try for a double play.' So we just stalled around there until Zack Taylor took another vote, and this time they voted the infield back, and I got a sinker to Pete Suder, and he hit a grounder, and we did make a double play. That's about all they got. I beat them, 5 to 3.

"When Veeck told the players about Grandstand Manager's Night, we thought that was fine. I never heard a dissenting attitude in all that time Veeck was there. If he said, 'We're going to have Grandstand Manager's Night,' that was fine with everybody on the team. I didn't hear anybody grumble, and if they did, they better not grumble to me, because I was in love with it.

"I just enjoyed the moment. I was glad to be part of that. I thought, 'It's going to be interesting, no matter what.' "

Bill Miller was one of the fans who held up the placards that night.

BILL MILLER: "I was there. The Browns won that game, 5–3. We were handed placards that one side said 'No' in green and the other side said 'Yes' in red. And some of Veeck's office staff sat in front of us in the box and held up these plays. Well, we only did it a few times. Hank Arft got on, and then they put up the sign 'Steal?' Well, then we all voted 'Yes,' and he was out by twenty feet. Because it wasn't difficult for Connie Mack to see what we were voting on. But it was fun. The games were really fun. They really were."

CHAPTER 42

ROGERS'S SHORT STAY

IN an attempt to lure fans away from his crosstown rivals, Browns owner Bill Veeck decided he would hire for his team as many ex-Cardinals as he could muster. At the end of the 1951 season, rumors were rampant that Cardinal owner Fred Saigh was going to hire Rogers Hornsby as his manager. Hornsby arguably was the best player in Cardinal history. Over a twenty-three-year career, including twelve with the Cardinals, he had hit .358, second only to Ty Cobb. He was a living legend. In addition, there were stories that Saigh was hiring him in the face of a lifetime ban handed down during the administration of Kenesaw Mountain Landis. In actuality, Landis had done no such thing, but the idea that Hornsby was being kept from managing the Cards enraged the national citizenry, much as the lifetime ban of Pete Rose angers many baseball fans today. Veeck, who had his fingers firmly on the public's pulse, decided he didn't want Hornsby working for the competition. He signed the great hitter to a three-year contract.

Two months later, just before Christmas of '51, Saigh fired Marty Marion as manager. Veeck knew Marion was going to be fired. After all, Hornsby was the one who supposedly had been tabbed to replace him. When Marion was fired, Veeck hired him, too, paying the former star shortstop $35,000— $10,000 more than he ever made with the Cardinals.

Then Falstaff beer, the sponsor of the Browns, hired Dizzy Dean to announce the Browns games. No former player was more popular in St. Louis than Dizzy Dean. Moreover, 20th Century-Fox was making a movie of his life called *The Pride of St. Louis*. Veeck knew that Dean would help him in his war with the Cardinals.

Veeck didn't stop there. Whenever the Cardinals placed a player on the waiver wire for the purpose of sending him to the minors, Veeck claimed him. Saigh wanted to make pitcher Harry Brecheen a coach so that he could make room on the Cards roster for a younger player. Saigh offered Brecheen $10,000 to remain as coach. Upon the urging of Marion, his former teammate, Brecheen accepted Veeck's offer to play for the Browns.

In 1952 the Browns' attendance rose 300,000 to 518,796 fans, second most only to the champion 1944 season. At the same time, Cardinals attendance dropped 300,000. Veeck clearly was winning his mano-à-mano against Fred Saigh and the Cardinals. He was sure that before long he would survive and the Cards would have to move out of town.

When Bill Veeck hired Rogers Hornsby as his manager, his mother sent him a telegram that read: WHAT MAKES YOU THINK YOU'RE SMARTER THAN YOUR DADDY WAS?'' Hornsby had managed GM William Veeck's Chicago Cubs team from the end of 1930 through 1932, but Hornsby's gambling addiction had a hold on him, and at the time William Veeck fired Hornsby, he owed money to many if not most of his players.

Hornsby last managed in the majors in 1937, when he was let go by the Browns. Veeck was sure that Hornsby would be so grateful to have a job that he would be pliable and a team player. Instead, Hornsby would last exactly two months as Browns manager.

One of the last disagreements between Hornsby and his players revolved around infielder Bobby Young, who lived in Baltimore. His wife was having a difficult pregnancy, and Bobby wanted to leave the team in Washington, where the Browns were playing, to visit his wife. Hornsby refused to let him go. Young grabbed a bat and waited for Hornsby. Traveling secretary Bill Durney stopped him.

Veeck said to Hornsby, "What's the matter with you? Young is worried sick about his wife. Let him go home."

Replied Hornsby, "All players are alike to me. I can't have two sets of rules."

Veeck told Hornsby he was giving Young permission to go home to see his wife. Veeck really wanted Hornsby to quit, but he uncharacteristically caved.

Veeck was going to fire him in New York, but the team won a couple of games. He canceled his flight to New York and booked a new one to Boston, where he fired him, much to the delight of the players. Ned Garver presented Veeck with a two-foot-tall trophy that read: TO BILL VEECK, FOR THE GREATEST

PLAY SINCE THE EMANCIPATION PROCLAMATION, JUNE 10, 1952. FROM THE PLAYERS
OF THE ST. LOUIS BROWNS.

Marty Marion and Ned Garver remember the short, frustrating managerial
stint of one of the strangest, most difficult men ever to manager a major league
baseball team.

MARTY MARION: ''I was hired as player-coach for good old Rogers. Rogers
wasn't a bad guy. He was the kind of person who had no patience at all with
the young ballplayer. He thought everybody should be as good as he was. And
nobody was. And Rogers was kind of an independent cuss. He would sit down
and just be by himself. He never seemed to have any friends to talk to.

"Everybody hated Rog. You talk about a manager who wasn't in time
with his players, that was Mr. Hornsby. Nobody would listen to him. He didn't
say anything. One time he was a great manager with the Cardinals, won the
pennant in '26. But he was peculiar. The players didn't like his attitude. He
was very strict, very critical. Wouldn't talk to you. He had no communication
skills. He was a sullen type of person. He would not have been my choice for
having a good manager if you want good relations with your players. He had
a great name, though.''

NED GARVER: "Rogers wasn't mean. Poor old Rogers just didn't have any
personality whatsoever. He wouldn't talk to you, wouldn't say hello to you.
He wouldn't come out to the mound to take you out of the ball game. If he
wanted to take you out, he'd just stand up in the dugout and wave the guy in
from the bullpen and wave you off.

"When you pitched batting practice, he wouldn't let you put screens up.
Every team when they went to take batting practice and infield practice, the
pitcher had a net in front of him, the first baseman had a net in front of him.
But he wouldn't let us have that. I don't know why. He just didn't want it.

"In those days, we'd throw batting practice. I was throwing batting practice, and he was just to the right of home plate, and he was hitting ground
balls to the third baseman and the shortstop, and boy, I threw a ball in there,
and about the same time he hit that son of a bitch right between my legs. And
from then on, boy, I just watched. If he was just tossing the ball up ready to
hit it, I would just pump again and wait until the ball was past me. That
was ridiculous.

"Hank Arft, our first baseman, got hit in the head with a line drive off
the bat while he hit ground balls and the infielders were throwing to first.
Hank went to catch a ball and about that time a batter hit a line drive. Another
time in New York, Gordon Goldsberry got hit with a line drive right in the
back. He started limping toward right field, and Hornsby hollered out to him,
'If you're scared, go take your uniform off.'

"We went to Phoenix to play the Giants in spring training, and I didn't
pitch that day. We dressed in the hotel. Cliff Fannin pitched, and about the
fifth inning he walked the pitcher. We took a bus after the game back to the
hotel. I was riding up the elevator in our uniform to the rooms to change

clothes, and Rogers said to me, 'You never should have walked that pitcher.'
It wasn't even me.

"He didn't want any coaches. He told Bill Veeck, 'I don't want anybody
as coaches.' Bill said, 'You gotta have some.' Hornsby said, 'Well, you pick
'em.' And he didn't go eat with his coaches.

"We'd be on the road, and Hornsby had us go out to the ballpark before
the other team did. We'd be sitting on the bench, and we were supposed to
watch those guys take batting practice and then decide how to pitch them!
Lord have mercy! So we'd be out there setting while the other pitchers were
taking batting practice, and then he'd come up with something like, 'Mickey
Vernon is a better high-ball hitter, so you have to pitch him low.' Well, Mickey
Vernon was a better low-ball hitter. We'd play in the league for years. He
never asked anybody. And he told our catcher Clint Courtney—he got rid of
Sherm Lollar—'Just put the target in the middle of the plate.' That made it
tough for me. So you're working against one another. How can you pitch to
guys you've pitched to for years, and you know that isn't the best way to
pitch to them, and he's saying, 'That's the way you have to do it.' He's
making it tough because he won't let the catcher give you a target. I never
had an argument with him. My job was a player, and whoever the manager
was, that's who you had. But he was bad—and not because he was mean. He
deserved to be gone. They gave the job to Marty.''

Ned Garver was traded to the Detroit Tigers on August 14, 1952. He left
with few regrets.

NED GARVER: ''I had been in the Browns' organization all that time, and they
just get rid of ya? That gives you a negative feeling, but I got over it pretty
quick. When you played for Bill Veeck, you knew you might be traded tomorrow. He'd always called me his 'team.' When I appeared in *The Saturday
Evening Post,* he had that bound in leather and he put: 'To my team.' Once
he gave me a leather traveling case and he had 'the team' engraved on it. So
he called me 'the team.' But he said, 'I'll trade my team for anybody else's
team.' That was his way.

"St. Louis was a nice place. It had everything I needed. There were plenty
of good places to eat, and the entertainment was everything I cared to go to.
In some places, you were all right if you were winning and no good if you
were losing, but in St. Louis, they didn't take you apart if you hadn't won.
Anyway, it was hard to win if they didn't get you any runs. They'd write:
'Garver hasn't won since April 23.' But when you go over six straight games
and never get a run, you're not going to win. All you can do is tie somebody.

"There were lots of times I sat in my locker after the game was over,
and I knew I had pitched better than the other guy. But I didn't brood about
it or feel bad. I had a wonderful life. When the game was over, we didn't
hash that over, didn't get nasty. We just had a good time.

"The year I won 20 games and the team lost 102, that's the only time
that ever happened. One year Steve Carlton won 27, but the team didn't lose
100. A couple years ago the postal department authorized a postmark saying

mine was the greatest season ever pitched because it was the only time it happened.

"You know I get more mail now than I did thirty years ago. The present-day player is tough about signing, and a lot of people say the fifties were the best years in baseball and they try to accumulate items from those people, and the people who played then are kind of cordial. They are willing to visit and give them some memory."

CHAPTER 43

CHARACTERS

IN 1944 Bill Veeck wanted to buy the Philadelphia Phillies. For a while, it looked like he would get the team, too. But then Veeck made the worst tactical mistake of his career, one that would cost him not only the Phillies franchise but later on his Browns franchise as well. He told National League president Ford Frick of his secret plan: to stock the Phils with the finest stars then playing in the Negro Leagues. Veeck had every confidence that a team with Satchel Paige, Josh Gibson, Judy Johnson, Ray Dandridge, Cool Papa Bell, and Buck Leonard would defeat any of the other National League ballclubs.

Had it been a year later, Veeck might well have succeeded in his grand plan. But for Veeck, it was very bad timing. Frick, when he found out about Veeck's plan, told Commissioner Landis, and before Veeck knew about it, the Phillies were sold to William Cox for less money than Veeck had offered.

A year later, Branch Rickey would sign Jackie Robinson and make history by sending him to Montreal and in 1947 to Brooklyn. Rickey was able to do that because the commissioner was Happy Chandler, not Kenesaw Mountain Landis, who had died in 1945 after years of doing everything in his power to keep white and black ballplayers apart.

When the vote came to replace Happy Chandler as commissioner in 1951, Veeck—who despised Frick for blowing the whistle on his deal to buy the Phillies—voted against Frick, who eventually won the election. In the end Veeck joined his brethren and voted for Frick, but Frick never forgave Veeck for voting against him in the beginning.

When Veeck bought the Cleveland Indians in June of 1946, he quickly became the first American League owner to sign black players. He signed Larry Doby, who in 1947 became the first Afro-American to play in the American League, and he also signed Satchel Paige, rated as the greatest Negro League pitcher and perhaps the greatest pitcher—period—of his time. With Cleveland, Paige helped lead the Indians to the 1948 world championship. When Veeck sold the Indians after the '49 season, manager Lou Boudreau released Paige. When the Giants offered Paige a contract in '50, Veeck told him he'd have another team soon and to keep barnstorming with the Chicago

American Giants. While waiting for Veeck, Paige also turned down the Boston Braves.

After Veeck purchased the Browns in 1951, Paige returned to the majors eight days after his forty-fifth birthday. By this time, the tall right-hander no longer had the unhittable blazing speed of his youth. The legendary pitcher became a crowd-pleasing entertainer. When he wasn't pitching, he'd sit in a rocking chair in the bullpen. When he was on the mound, all eyes were on him. Like Pete Gray and Eddie Gaedel, Satchel Paige was both a curiosity and an attraction. On August 6, 1952, for instance, Paige pitched twelve innings in defeating Virgil Trucks and the Detroit Tigers, 1–0. Wrote Dent McSkimming in the *St. Louis Post-Dispatch,* "His name will go down with such other local pitching immortals as Rube Waddell, Grover Alexander, and Dizzy Dean."

Paige pitched with guile because the blazing speed was gone. Wrote McSkimming, "Never was Paige more tantalizing with his mixture of windups and pitches. At one moment he toed the right end of the pitching slab, then, for another pitch, he was at the left end; then in the middle. This time he pitched from the stretch; now he whirled his arm twice in a full windup; sometimes just once.

SATCHEL PAIGE
(Courtesy Brace Photo)

"His slow ball, particularly the ones he fed to an overeager giant, Walt Dropo, seemed to hang in the air, as though manipulated by wires." McSkimming reported that "Old Burr Head" (Paige's nickname for Veeck) was so thrilled, he bought Paige a new suit of clothes. Paige reported he won the game because manager Marty Marion told the team it would have to practice the next morning if it lost. Paige said he wanted to go fishing, so he made sure the Browns would win.

Marty Marion didn't find Paige as amusing as Veeck and the writers. Marion chose to use Paige mostly in relief, and through the summer of 1952 Paige complained about how much he badly wanted to start despite bragging that he was the greatest relief pitcher in baseball. Said Paige, "You can't do no winning in relief . . . at least not that many."

Manager Marion found Paige's independence difficult to accept. Because Satch had complete autonomy, thanks to owner Bill Veeck, he could pretty much come and go as he pleased. Marion recalled how hard it was for him to put up with having Satch on his squad during his two seasons with the Browns. Marion made it clear that Paige wasn't the only Brownie who presented problems.

MARTY MARION: "I managed Satchel Paige. Oh Lord. You can have Satchel. You can have him. You know why? *He* ran the club, not me! Everything Satchel wanted, Veeck would do. Veeck loved Satchel. Oh God!

"What did he do? He almost got us killed. We didn't have enough baseballs even to take batting practice. Bill was trying to get money everywhere he could, so he scheduled an exhibition game in Providence, Rhode Island.

"We were on our way to play Boston the next day, had an off day, and lo and behold, we had a good crowd, a sellout, in Providence. During the regular games, nobody cared whether he pitched or not because he wasn't that good—he didn't have good stuff—but in his heyday he was great, or at least they tell me he was. And they had advertised he was going to pitch. Satch was a showman, you know. He packed them in. There must have been 15,000 people there at the ballpark, and about the third inning the sportswriters started coming down from the press box. They asked, 'Marty, where is Satchel Paige?' I didn't even know he wasn't there. I said, 'If you find him, I'll pitch him.' Anyway, turns out Satchel skipped the game. He went straight on into Boston.

"Bill Durney, our traveling secretary, came and said, 'Everyone wants their money back. They are ready to lynch us.' I said, 'Well, Bill, you get the money and you get out of here.' And they *were* threatening to lynch us. It was a bad situation.

"The next morning we went to the Kenmore Hotel in Boston. I walked in from the train, and there's Satchel, sitting in the lobby. I said, 'Satchel, you almost got us lynched. They wanted their money back.' Satch said, 'Oh pooh.' He didn't have an excuse or nothing. He wasn't sick. I said, 'That will cost you $5,000. I'm calling Veeck right now.' Bill Durney said to me, 'Hell, Veeck ain't gonna take his money.' And he didn't.

"But that was ol' Satchel.

"One day when I was the manager we were having our clubhouse meeting, and ol' Sugar Cain said, 'Marty, why is it that you make all us white boys do all these things, and you don't ever make Satchel run?' I said, 'I guess you got me there, because, number one, Satchel can't run, and number two, when you get [to be] sixty-five years of age, you can do that.' But Satchel wouldn't do nothing. You couldn't tell him nothing. He'd sit in his big rocking chair down in the bullpen. Oh, he was a character.

"Funny thing about him, though. He didn't mind a white guy getting a hit off of him, but if a black player got a hit off of him, he really didn't like that at all. He wanted to be the king of the black people. And boy, he was king. Everybody looked up to Satchel.

"But he was a bad guy to have on a club. He'd keep everybody up all night on the train, telling all these stories, and everybody'd listen. I used to like to listen to him, too.

"He was a pretty black person, and when he'd get through taking a shower, he'd pour this talcum powder all over him. After he got through doing that, he was whiter than I am. And then he'd put this snake oil on him and rub his arm. What a character! He was good copy, but bad for the manager.

"Satchel would no more pay attention to me than the man in the moon. He knew Veeck wasn't going to take any money from him. That's the only way you can get back at them, take their dough.

"Even so, I loved Veeck. Bill lived high on the hog, and I'm a very conservative person. Other than that, you couldn't help but love Veeck. He paid you well. It was hard working for him under those circumstances because he would sell players and wouldn't even ask me. And when I'd mention trying to get a player, he'd say, 'Marty, we don't have any money.' But Veeck was good to work for. Everybody loved Bill. He was popular with the players. Until he traded them.

"You'd never know what was going to happen with the Browns. It was almost like being on a roller coaster. First of all, we didn't have any players. We had no money. I can't vouch for that. They say we didn't. I'm sure that was the case. And when you're in a financial position where you have to sell players to operate, that ain't gonna be a good year.

"We had Vic Wertz, but some of the players were on the downhill. I had some Browns. I remember the scrap Clint Courtney got into at second base with Billy Martin and the Yankees. They were squaring off, and Courtney came in, and his glasses were about half knocked off, and he had torn his uniform. A typical baseball fight.

"Another one who was a character who I had on the Browns was [Alva] "Bobo" Holloman. The first start he ever made in the majors, he pitched a no-hitter. And he was gone in a couple months.

"We had an exhibition game in Fort Wayne, Indiana, and we all went out to play golf. Bobo had his wife carrying his bags for him on the golf course! And he was perspiring, just wringing wet.

"Bobo wasn't a drinker. He was very superstitious and he had to do everything a certain way. He was just kind of a boastful guy. He thought he was good, and he really wasn't. But he pitched that no-hitter. How he did it, I don't know, but he did. It was a cold night, and he pitched a heck of a game.

"You know, you can tell stories just about everybody in baseball. Everybody has something going on. When you have 25 players together, and they are all prima donnas and everybody makes a fuss over them, you get a lot of good stories."

BOB BROEG: "There were a lot of good stories about Satchel Paige when he was with the Browns. There was a late-night departure out of Washington for St. Louis, and the Browns and Senators were playing this long extra-inning game. Bill Durney, the traveling secretary, came down and leaned over the railing and said to Marty Marion, our manager, 'Unless we get this over soon, we're going to blow that train.' And Paige said, 'What did you say?' Durney repeated, 'We're going to miss that train.'

"The game went into the seventeenth inning, and Paige pinch-hit a single to get the run across, and in the last inning he struck out the side on ten pitches. He came in, and they hurried to the train, and Paige was grumbling on the way there. Marion said, 'What are you unhappy about?' He said, 'That umpire, damn it, he missed one pitch.'

"Bob Bowman, the veteran trainer, said that when Satch got aboard a train late at night, even though the Pullman galley was closed, they would open it for him. If they had some catfish aboard, they'd prepare it for him. Bowman said Satch sat up most of the night in a roomette typing, answering letters, and he would sleep in the daytime until they got back to St. Louis.

"A writer I brought aboard as a sportswriter with the *Post-Dispatch,* Dave Lipman, wrote *Maybe I'll Pitch Forever* with Satch. When they made the book into a movie with Billy Dee Williams playing the role of Satch, Dave gave his share of the receipts to Satch, which was nice."

CHAPTER 44

MEMORIES OF SATCH

SATCHEL Paige, arguably the best of the many great players to perform in the Negro Leagues, will always be a minor figure in the context of the civil rights movement in that it was Jackie Robinson, not he, who was the first Afro-American to break the color line and play major league baseball. From the day Robinson stepped onto the Ebbets Field grass in April of 1947 to the day Paige died in 1982, the famed pitcher deeply felt the slight.

Branch Rickey skipped over Paige because the Dodger president knew Paige had a reputation for not always being reliable, and was concerned that at the age of forty-one—or maybe even a couple years older—the showman pitcher was over the hill. Rickey had wanted a college-educated man with character who could excel but make no waves, so he chose Robinson and then anointed Don Newcombe and Roy Campanella to be his pioneers. Paige had to wait another year for another showman, Bill Veeck, to get his chance to perform in the majors with the Cleveland Indians.

Paige, who was born in 1906, began pitching professionally in 1924, when he was eighteen, and he pitched and won perhaps as many as 600 ball games over thirty-seven years—in the Negro Leagues, in Caribbean leagues, barnstorming against teams of all-white major leaguers, finally in the major leagues, and then in the minors—until he finally hung up his spikes at the age of sixty-one after an exhibition appearance with the Atlanta Braves in 1967.

Paige lived in Kansas City, and in 1957 he began writing his memoirs with David Lipman. Lipman befriended the great pitcher and remembers him with fondness.

DAVID LIPMAN: "Satchel was born in 1906. His mother, on occasion, said, 'He was actually born in 1904.' She had it in her Bible. But nobody ever saw that Bible, not even Satchel. I pinned down his birthday reasonably well: July 7, 1906. Given everything, that seems to be a reasonably acceptable date.

"Leroy Page, P-a-g-e, was born in Mobile, Alabama, on that day. Satchel's family name had been Page. As he put it, they later added the 'i' to make it a little more high-toned.

"I'm not sure I ever asked him how many games he won or if he had an answer. It would be hard to say, partly because of the way records were kept and the way they used him. Early on, and we could document this, his first year pitching in Mobile in 1924, he won 30 games and lost 1. One. And winning 25, 30 games a year a year was not unusual for him. Satchel had an extraordinary fastball, and the extraordinary ability to pitch day after day. It got so he was such an attraction in the Negro Leagues that they almost stopped using him as a starting pitcher, and he'd pitch two or three innings every day so he could pitch in the next town.

"As a relief pitcher with Cleveland in 1948, he was 6-1 with 14 saves, and when you think about it, that's a rather impressive relief pitcher's record. I'd say whether you're talking about Walter Johnson or [Joe] 'Iron Man' McGinnity, Satchel would have equalled either one of them. In fact, he did talk about pitching both ends of a doubleheader, pitching two complete games.

"Satch had parallel careers. There was Negro League baseball—and his barnstorming activities. When you look at his career, he pitched almost year around. After the Negro League season was over, he would go to Cuba or the Dominican Republic or to the islands, and during the winter months while it was still warm in the United States he would tour, play against the major leaguers, then he'd go off to the islands, then he'd go to Mexico. There was a period of time he'd pitch in North Dakota or the north-central part of the United States, where there were several leagues, and he would pitch there. So he pitched and traveled almost year round.

"He certainly achieved reasonable fame with the Monarchs, but the Negro Leagues in those days, if you looked for coverage during that period, it was rather minimal. As a result, that didn't give him quite the visibility he achieved by barnstorming, especially against the great white major leaguers. He would play against Bob Feller and outpitch Feller. He would pitch against Babe Ruth and survive very well. He did extremely well, and of course, he pitched throughout the Caribbean and achieved fame there. In a way, it was as the showman that he really achieved such high fame.

"When he was with the Kansas City Monarchs, Satchel was *the* star of the league, although Josh Gibson was the other one. Cool Papa Bell was a very glamorous figure. Cool Papa Bell was in a way the Stan Musial to Satchel Paige and Josh Gibson, the Walter Johnson and Babe Ruth. Those two were the premier attractions and the premier success stories in the Negro Leagues, and the ones who would draw the biggest crowds on the barnstorming tours.

"Satch always liked to tell one story, that he and Josh had an ongoing debate as who was the greatest baseball player: Was Satchel the better pitcher or Josh the better hitter? So one game—and it may have been in the Negro League World Series, but maybe I'm glamorizing too much, but it was a Negro League game—Josh would have been the fourth man up. Satchel walked the bases full intentionally to pitch to Josh, and he struck him out with three sidearm fastballs down on the knees.

"I've run into others who authenticated that he would have his outfielders sit down while he was pitching against a minor league team or another Negro League team, or sometimes in an exhibition game, and still get the out.

"Satch, a great anecdote teller, remembered the Negro Leagues with fondness. He viewed it without any bitterness that I could tell. In fact, I was always stunned at his lack of bitterness about being segregated, about being pinned into the Negro Leagues, not being able to play in white man's baseball. He made it sound like an exciting and very rewarding life. And Satchel was a practical man. I think he realized he was doing quite well from a public standpoint. He had high public visibility, and he was making a damn good living.

"In fact, I remember one time when I asked him whether he was resentful about being forced to play only in the Negro Leagues, missing the opportunity to play major league baseball, he said, 'You gotta remember this—at a time Stan Musial [just breaking into the major leagues] was making $5,000 a year and Enos Slaughter was making $3,500, I was making $25,000.' He added, 'Now, I managed to spend most of it . . .' He was a high liver.

"Satchel felt the one value of being in the major leagues, was that it gave him the opportunity to build up the statistical evidence that would support his greatness. Although *The Saturday Evening Post* and other publications of that era were writing features about him, praising him to the sky, referring to him as 'The Greatest Pitcher in Baseball' with regularity, the documentation was not really there. It was hidden off in this corner called Negro League baseball, or barnstorming. He often was viewed as a man with tremendous ability, but not necessarily as someone of the same quality as players in the major leagues. Were any of the Harlem Globetrotters ever considered the equals of the George Mikans, the Bob Kurlands, the white players in the NBA? They probably should have been, and as I recall they beat the NBA champions in a tournament one year, and this is what Satchel demonstrated in his barnstorming. But you're not seeing those major league averages every day. If you're not the Most Valuable Player or the earned run average leader or strikeout leader, you're not remembered in the same light as someone who has had statistics to support them.

"If there was a touch of bitterness, it was that Satchel felt he deserved the opportunity to be the first African American in major league baseball. There was a little resentment, not toward Jackie or even Branch Rickey, with whom he seemed to have gotten along quite well, but just that he wasn't honored as the first one. He thought he deserved that. He made a little to-do about it, just as he offered such little fuss when he was first proposed for induction into the Hall of Fame. They were going to create a segregated Negro wing, and it was only the public uproar afterward that forced major league baseball, with its unbelievable instincts for self-destruction, to change its approach. Yet, he voiced almost nothing but gratitude for being considered for the Negro wing. He was very pleased when they did induct him into the regular Hall of Fame, but before that, when it appeared he would be in this segregated area of baseball, he didn't fuss very much.

"Satchel had a lot of friends in the entertainment business. Especially in his younger days, he was very much a fixture in the black-white nightclub circuit. He'd go to the Apollo. He was comfortable in Hollywood. And he was comfortable in athletics.

"I will say this: He took reasonably good care of his body, although he was not averse to a drink, but I never felt he abused alcohol. We would meet at the neighborhood bar near Brooklyn Avenue, which was not far from his home and where the old minor league ballpark used to be in Kansas City. Satch would sip his drink, Old Charter, a bourbon, but he never overdid it. There was a graciousness about him. I won't say he was one of the most punctual or reliable people, yet I cannot recall any real difficulties having him honor our appointments.

"Satch had amazing control. I talked to people who saw this: He could put virtually every pitch right over the plate into the catcher's mitt. It's hard to say what he would have done if he had come into major league baseball as a young man. When you think about it, he was outstanding when he first entered major league baseball. He pitched Cleveland into the World Series, and he always did a fascinating job in St. Louis, although he probably attracted more people who came to see him in his rocking chair than to see him pitch.

"Again, his skill was to throw the ball with great speed, and to throw it accurately, a unique talent, but beyond that he did have a flair for showmanship.

"I never saw Satchel in a game, but I can personally attest to his accuracy. After we agreed to move ahead with the autobiography, I was at Satchel's house at 2626 East 28th Street in Kansas City, a lovely three-story redbrick home, and we were in the living room chatting, and I said to Satchel, 'You know, I used to play a little baseball. I never was very good. But I could play. Do you have a baseball and a couple of gloves around? I'd love to go out and catch you for a little while.'

"Satchel, who was very thin, lanky, an interesting presence, leaned forward and said, 'Boy, you sure you want to do that?' And I said, 'Yes.' So he went upstairs and in just a few minutes he came down with a catcher's mitt, a fielder's glove, and a baseball. We walked out in the backyard, and he paced off the distance to the pitching mound, and I would bet my bottom dollar if I had a tape measure, it was sixty feet and five or six inches. I don't think he missed by an inch.

"He got out there and turned around and said, 'Boy,' and I was always amused by the way he used the term 'boy,' 'Boy, you sure you want to do this?' I said, 'Yes.' So I crouched down in a catcher's crouch, held up the catcher's mitt, doubled up my fist behind the mitt, the way I had been taught as a kid, and said, 'Let it go.'

"Satch took a small windup, just pumped once, and threw the ball, and that was the last thing I remembered until I came to and realized my chest was aching like a son of a bitch. I never saw the ball. I never saw a ball move that fast in my life. And thank God for his accuracy. Seriously. The ball hit my glove, and that absorbed most of the shock, and it bounced off it and crashed against my chest. I had a nice little bruise, but I survived. If he hadn't hit the glove, it would have killed me! I laugh at it now.

"We played catch in a more leisurely fashion after that. He moved with a grace and rhythm. Even then, he struck me as being a marvelous athlete.

"He only had arm trouble, as I recall him telling me, once, and he had this strange concoction, which he called 'Snake Oil'—I don't know what the hell it was—that he would rub on it, but he was a man who believed in staying very limber, the antithesis of the weightlifters of today, so he had this very fluid motion which enabled him at the age of sixty-one to pitch in a spring exhibition game for Atlanta, when Bartholomew brought him back so he could complete his requirements for his major league pension, because without that pension he would have been left penniless. That would have been the final tragedy for someone with such tremendous athletic ability, who had been deprived of the opportunity to play major league ball. Once that racial barrier was removed, not to qualify for the pension would have been a tragedy.

"My experiences were based on our visits together, interviews, conversations, and I come away with this memory of a thoughtful person, very low-key, a little morose, a little dour in his demeanor, but full of fun, someone who enjoyed fun.

"He was not a clown. He could play the entertainer. I'd call him an entertainer, not a clown. He certainly was no buffoon. I spent a lot of time researching, going through *The Sporting News* files here in St. Louis, the *Post-Dispatch,* the *Globe-Democrat,* the *Star-Times* in Kansas City, the Kansas City papers, and papers from Mobile and other places he lived. Once an image or character was established, there was a constant repetition of that. A writer would pick up a clip and see 'Satchel is called a clown,' and he'd call him a clown. Over the years after he reached a certain position of prominence, the questions directed to him by sportswriters tended to elicit the responses they were looking for, and he knew how to play the publicity game. He looked for those opportunities. He wasn't a Step 'n' Fetchit, but that's how he was pictured. When he was interviewed with care, there was always a more serious tone to the article, and his quotes ceased to be created in the mind's eye of the author and reflected what Satchel was really saying. He was thoughtful with a clever turn of phrase.

"Satchel struck me as dour to droll in his speaking manner. He was not as funny as everyone pictured him. He was almost morose. It was almost as if the young man had settled down and grown up. I kept feeling I was seeing a more serious Satchel than the playboy. His marriage to Lahoma was a definite plus. She ran a pretty tight ship. She was just a wonderful woman.

"He would often say something that might have been thoughtful, but it would provoke a chuckle. 'Don't look back, someone might be gaining on you.' Which in a way he said, but frankly his eight rules of living were really crafted by a sportswriter. Satchel always referred to him as 'a sportswriter in the East.' The statements themselves were vintage Satchel. I'm sure one time he said, 'Don't eat fried food.' The crux of those eight rules were articulated. But the organization of the eight rules was the world of the sportswriter. The beef was fashioned, sliced and diced by Satchel. I wouldn't deprive him of the credit for those rules. He just never put those eight down himself.

"It's been almost forty years since I wrote that damn book. I'm one of those who don't look back, either. I've never reread it. But I have this cherished memory."

CHAPTER 45

SAYONARA, BROWNS

BILL Veeck fought the Cardinals for the hearts and minds of the fans of St. Louis throughout the 1952 season, and it appeared that he was winning the battle until he learned during December of 1952 that the war had been lost when Cards owner Fred Saigh turned down an offer from a Milwaukee syndicate and two from Houston groups and announced the sale of the team to the hometown Anheuser-Busch Brewing Company, one of the largest breweries in the world.

Veeck, who thought he could run Saigh out of town, instead found himself on the run. No amount of clever promotion could overcome August Busch's millions. The Browns owner knew he had lost "The Battle for St. Louis," and when he went to the baseball winter meetings, he informed the other owners that if the deal went through, he wanted to move. Veeck didn't think the other owners could stop him. Nor did he think they would.

But the liberal Veeck had made enemies among some of the conservative owners. In addition to making an enemy for life in Commissioner Ford Frick, he also alienated Del Webb and George Weiss, co-owner and general manager, respectively, of the New York Yankees. Veeck continually and publicly accused the Yankees of being cheap, and once when Joe DiMaggio was holding out for more money, at a baseball dinner told the audience: "If the Yankees

BILL VEECK
(Courtesy Brace Photo)

don't want to pay him what he's worth, well, I'll take him and pay him $200,000." Weiss, who Veeck described as "a fugitive from the human race," stormed off the dais.

At the winter meetings in 1952, Del Webb convened a meeting of the other owners. Veeck, not seeing the blind side coming, declined to attend. Though the 1953 schedule had already been made and distributed, at that dinner they voted not to schedule any of the lucrative night games with the Browns.

The Browns were dependent on road receipts, and his only chance of drawing decently was at night. He was a dead man in St. Louis, and he knew it. Veeck appealed to Frick, who ruled it was none of his business.

Veeck decided to move to Milwaukee, where the county was building a stadium. His timing, however, was awful. A close friend, Oscar Salinger, had just sold the Milwaukee franchise to Lou Perini, the owner of the Boston Braves. Veeck now had to buy territorial rights from Perini, who himself had his eyes on Milwaukee. Veeck put a great deal of pressure on Perini to sell him those rights, offering him $750,000. He even offered to buy the rights to Toledo, so Perini could play there if he decided to move. To get Veeck to back off, Perini asked Commissioner Frick to silence the pushy Browns owner.

Spring training began. Veeck was in a bind. He needed to move or face playing an entire lame-duck season in St. Louis before fans who were aware of his intentions to leave them behind.

At a league meeting in March, Veeck pleaded with Perini to give up the territory or move there. Perini finally decided to leave Boston for greener pastures in urban Wisconsin, and he received the hearty approval of the other owners. Veeck was running out of maneuvering room.

BOB BROEG: "Bill was one of the most engaging guys I was ever around. I spent a lot of time during the winter [drinking] with him in his apartment at the ballpark. I found out the only way with him, even though he didn't like it, was to come as close as possible to staying even, which you're never going to do around him. But as far as an avid interest in books, in the theater, especially musical comedy, and charades. . . . I don't think any woman could ever enact *Birth of a Nation* with the same affection he gave it.

"I liked Bill Veeck very much. I didn't like the conclusion. Nobody liked that. I understood it, though. When the brewery bought the Cardinals, Bill knew he couldn't lick the brewery, and so he prepared to move the Browns to Milwaukee. The only problem was that the Boston Braves' attendance had dropped to about 280,000 in attendance from 1.4 million four years earlier, and the Braves' owner, Lou Perini, had territorial rights to Milwaukee because his farm club was there. I remember it was on my birthday in 1953 when it was announced that the Braves were moving to Milwaukee. It was the first move of a major league franchise since, oddly enough, Milwaukee moved to St. Louis and became the Browns in 1902."

Veeck needed an escape, and he chose Baltimore, which was the only other major American city without a major league franchise that was building a stadium. He could have gone to Los Angeles, but the dimensions of the Coliseum seemed too crazy for baseball. All the while the other owners were telling Veeck that he was free to move anywhere he wished. They told him he had the votes. Veeck arranged for the National Brewing Company in Baltimore to be the team's sponsor were he to come to Baltimore.

At a meeting at the Tampa Terrace Hotel, Veeck told the other owners of his desire to move to Baltimore. He asked for a vote, and he was turned down, six to two. Frick told Veeck, "It's too close to the start of the season. And there are contracts involved with television and radio people and concessionaires." A month earlier, Perini had been free to make such a move. Because it was Veeck, however, it was no go. Veeck knew he was being kept in St. Louis as a personal punishment. Veeck was told a special committee was being set up to study whether Baltimore would make a suitable host for a major league team. Veeck was gullible enough to believe the other owners when they told him he could move at the end of the season.

After the meeting, said Veeck, he felt the urge to jump out the window of a tall building. Three weeks remained before the start of the '53 season.

MARTY MARION: "Bill called me on the phone in San Bernardino, California, during spring training of '53, when the Cards were sold to Anheuser-Busch. He said, 'That's the end of it for us in St. Louis. We can't buck Anheuser-Busch.' And that year was just a wasted year. He knew that, too."

Everyone knew Veeck was in St. Louis against his will. The reporters kept asking him whether he intended to keep the team there. Veeck, too honest for his own good, said he would make every effort to move.

To keep the team going in '53, Veeck had to sell his stars. He sold Virgil Trucks to the White Sox for $95,000. During this time, he was offered the contract of a young Kansas City Monarch shortstop with a powerful swing by the name of Ernie Banks. With the coming of Jackie Robinson to the big leagues and the host of Negro League stars who came to the majors after him, the Negro Leagues were failing. Bill Baird, the owner of the Kansas City Monarchs, was hard pressed for money, and offered his star to Veeck for $31,500. Veeck, who didn't have the money, asked Baird if he would please send Banks to the National League. Veeck phoned Jimmy Gallagher, the general manager of the Cubs, and told him to grab the future Hall of Famer. Phil Wrigley's chewing gum money landed him "Mr. Cub." Banks would star in Chicago for nineteen seasons.

By the end of spring in 1953, the warmth for the Browns fled. So did the fans. Attendance dropped from the 518,000 of '52 to only 297,000 in '53. The team finished last. Veeck, so long the cheerleader, stopped trying to promote. He had no money left. Pitcher Max Lanier had been a mainstay of the Cards' pitching staff when he was traded to the Giants in '52. After a desultory season, the Giants released him in '53. Bill Veeck, always on the lookout for a former Cardinal, signed the thirty-eight-year-old Lanier, who finished out his major league career with Bill Veeck's hapless Browns.

MAX LANIER: "When I joined the Browns, Veeck had twenty-five players on his roster, and that's all he was allowed. He had to get rid of one before he could sign me. I was with them two weeks before he could sign me. He said, 'Go with us on the road. I'll start your salary, but you can't sign a contract.'

"Marty Marion managed the club. He just didn't have a good club at all. Vic Wertz was playing the outfield. Billy Hunter was a good shortstop. The rest of them, like me, were about through.

"I remember we lost six or seven in a row. We were in Cleveland. Veeck said, 'After the ball game, I want everybody to come up to the aviation room. We're going to have a party.'

"We lost, and we had dinner up there. He said, 'I don't want anybody to leave until I tell him he can leave.' It was one in the morning, and he had his peg leg off, and he was shaking it at everybody. He was shooting champagne at everybody. Vic Wertz and I had a bottle of champagne, and we poured it down his back. And he hauled off and threw one bottle against a picture in the aviation room. I think the party cost him $1,800. He wanted to loosen everyone up. We went out and next day and got beat again!

"Satch Paige was on our team. A lot of times he wouldn't come to the ballpark in St. Louis until the fourth or fifth inning. He said, 'I know I ain't gonna pitch until the end.' It wasn't an excuse. He got by with murder. Marty would fine him, but Veeck wouldn't take his money.

"I liked Satch. He was a lot of fun. He still had a good fastball. His curveball didn't break that much, but he could pinpoint it. I never will forget, [in 1965] I went to Atlanta when my son Harold was with San Francisco, and Satch was with Atlanta working out. I said, 'Hey, Satch, how you doing?' He said, 'Max, I'm just out here killing grass.'

"Don Larsen was on our team. We were in Cleveland, and it was twelve o'clock at night. He was sitting in the lobby. Marty told him, 'You're supposed to be in your room at twelve o'clock.' He just broke every rule in the book.

"We also had Bob Turley. He had a good fastball. So did Virgil Trucks, but Veeck had to sell him. We just didn't have the cash. As long as he had it, though, he didn't mind spending it. I remember we were in Washington, and Dick Kokos hit a home run in the tenth inning. He came in the next day, and he had him a dozen sports shirts in his locker. He done that all the time.

"When the Browns released me, he said, 'Max, we just don't have the money any longer.' I said, 'I've enjoyed it while I was here.' "

Lanier wasn't around for the finale, and neither were the fans. A sparse crowd of 3,174 attended. The Browns lost, 2–1, in twelve innings. During the extra frames, ump Art Passarella called for more new balls, but there were none left. He had to used scuffed ones to finish the game.

MARTY MARION: "The last game of the season we played the White Sox in an extra-inning game. At the end of the game we didn't have enough new balls to play with. It was kind of a disastrous year. You weren't winning. You had no support. Hell, it was just horrible. And there was nothing you could do about it. Not a thing you could do about it.

"All I can remember, after the game all the kids came around the clubhouse, and everybody was throwing uniforms away, giving them to all the kids. We threw them from the clubhouse window. All the kids were outside. I wish I had kept mine."

The Browns were moribund, and everyone knew it. Marty Marion jumped ship before it sank, taking the first solid offer to come his way.

MARTY MARION: "I got a call right away from Frank Lane out of Chicago. He wanted me to come up and work for him, which I accepted gladly. Frank was very blunt. He called and said, 'Nellie Fox doesn't know how to make a double play. Would you mind coming up here and teaching him?' I said I'd try.

"Then when Paul Richards left as manager, they gave me the job. I enjoyed Chicago. They had a pretty good ballclub. We almost won the pennant in '55. If my ace pitcher, Dick Donovan, hadn't come up with appendicitis right at the end of the year, we'd have won it."

To keep from going under, Bill Veeck sold Sportsman's Park for $1.1 million to August Busch. It wasn't smart business, but he had no choice. He was defaulting on the mortgage, and he didn't have the money to fix up the place. The Browns had no income from television and none from radio. He also sold his beloved ranch in Arizona. His one remaining hope was being allowed to move to Baltimore.

When the other American League owners met in New York in September of 1953 and voted on whether Veeck could move his team, he needed six of the eight votes to move. When New York, Boston, Philadelphia, and Cleveland voted against him, he found himself two votes short of what he needed.

Yankee co-owner Dan Topping told Elliott Stein, one of Veeck's major stockholders, "We're going to keep you in St. Louis and bankrupt you. Then we'll decide where the franchise will go."

The other Yankee co-owner, Del Webb, said he had friends who wanted to move the Browns to Los Angeles, and when that question was put up for a vote, it was passed unanimously. Webb, a wealthy contractor with powerful L.A. and Las Vegas connections, held a check for $1 million signed by mogul Howard Hughes.

For twenty-four hours, Veeck contemplated going to L.A. The specter of having to play in the oddly shaped Coliseum haunted him. In the end, he decided to let a third party buy the Browns and move the team to Baltimore.

At a meeting of the owners on September 29, 1953, he made a farewell speech. He told them: "I am selling against my own desires. Obviously, though, you want to get rid of me. All right, you have succeeded. I have my partners to consider. It has been my understanding that Baltimore is acceptable without me and that these people are acceptable to you. You have kept Baltimore hung up from the beginning of this season to the end. I suggest that you vote them in without any more delay."

The vote in favor was unanimous.

MARTY MARION: "I suppose the St. Louis Browns fans thought maybe Veeck was the reason they lost the Browns. I'm sure Veeck wasn't very popular here—he didn't win any beauty contests—after the team left."

Veeck sold his 79 percent interest in the Browns for $2,475,000 and left baseball, bitter that the other owners hated him badly enough to force him out of the game he loved. Veeck didn't return to the game for six years. In his first year back with the Chicago White Sox in 1959, he won the American League pennant, no solace at all for Browns fans.

BILL MILLER: "In 1937, when Don Barnes and Bill DeWitt took over the club, they floated some public stock to get some support in St. Louis. It was very modest by today's standards, of course. My uncle bought twenty shares at $5 a share.

"My dad and I took him to the All-Star Game in 1940, the first time the game was held in St. Louis, and that was in July within three days of my birthday, and my uncle gave me the stock. So I became a stockholder.

"I was born in 1925, so I would have been twenty-eight in 1953, when we heard that Veeck was going to move the team to Baltimore.

"We cheered the Browns and really enjoyed them. I must admit, they were not one of the contenders, so when they did win, it was especially enjoyable. In 1951, Ned Garver inevitably would start the first game of a home doubleheader—and of course, that was the year he won 20 games and also hit

.306—and if Garver would win that first game, then the rest of the day you didn't care what happened. It was a thrill to see them, even though you knew they were overpowered to a great degree, especially when they played the Yankees or the Red Sox. But we got a kick out of that.

"And when we learned they were leaving, that was very dispairing. As a matter of fact, I went to the last stockholders' meeting with Veeck. And I must admit, I have never been to any meeting in which personal insults flew back and forth as a matter of conversation. The session was very tense.

"There was a group of maybe twenty-five of us in his office, and I remember my cousin, who was with me, he said, 'This is as if you came into St. Louis and stole the Chase Hotel and the Park Plaza.' And then Veeck answered something to the effect of: 'We're doing what's best for the team.' He never told us he was going to be selling the team, which only happened a few days later.

"Though nothing was said publicly, the league told Veeck, 'The team doesn't move until you get out.' I tell you who I think was responsible: Will Harridge, the president of the American League, because he canceled the midget's contract the very day after he made his famous appearance, and I think he felt that Grandstand Manager's Night was making too much of a plaything out of the game. I understand after that night Veeck got a very, very stiff letter from Harridge. So what happened was, one of the conditions to the Browns' moving—they wanted the team to move, of course—but they also told Veeck to take a walk.

"And when we found out the Browns were leaving, it was depressing, really. You knew you were really going to lose something. One [thing lost] would be keeping in touch with the American League, which we couldn't do anymore. And we were resentful against Veeck because when he came in to buy the team in 1951, he said over the radio, 'The Browns will stay in St. Louis as long as the Yankees are in New York.'

"We talked about that as we stood outside his office. He had really broken his promise.

"There is no doubt who the villain of the whole thing was. And yet when I look back on it now, I was glad when Veeck was voted into the Hall of Fame, because he introduced the fun side of the game."

THE CARDINALS

CHAPTER 46

ESCAPE TO MEXICO

THE Cardinals weren't hurt badly by World War II until it was just about over. There were enough complaints about coddled ballplayers safely at home while American boys were dying overseas that as a PR move the armed services revised its policy: If you could play ball, you could be drafted. Many of the players competed for a service ball team rather than fight Germans or Japanese, but that didn't seem to upset anyone. After Germany surrendered on May 8 and Japan gave up unconditionally on August 6, the issue became moot, but not before the Cardinals lost a group of their starters.

In late January of 1945, Stan Musial was drafted into the armed forces and joined the Navy. He was assigned to Special Servies and assigned to Pearl Harbor in Hawaii, where he was given ship repair duty. He played baseball every afternoon in an eight-team league.

STAN MUSIAL: "We played about four times a week. About that time, there were at least 100,000 men coming through Honolulu every day. We had a stadium that sat about 10,000, and sailors and Army personnel would come to the games for relaxation and recreation. That was the good thing about the Navy. They let us play ball. Every team had five or six big league ballplayers. They had a lot of them: Ted Williams, Billy Herman, Bob Scheffing. We even had an All-Star Game between the American and National leagues. It was a good experience because it allowed us to keep our hands in. That was a great break for a lot of us. Bob Feller was on an aircraft carrier for three years. He didn't have an opportunity to play, and when he came back it was tough for him to jump back into professional play. For us, it worked out fine."

Danny Litwhiler was drafted and missed the '45 season. Litwhiler played only some softball on his base.

DANNY LITWHILER: "I was in charge of basic training at Fort Lewis, Washington. They didn't have any recreation for basic training, and while I was there I got some guys together and we started playing softball. The commanding officer of Fort Lewis happened to be riding around, and he saw us playing. He asked me to set up recreation for the whole 10,000 troops. I said, 'Ten thousand troops? I have to have help and equipment.' The executive officer said, 'He can't do that, because he's only a private.' He said, 'Hell, get him an officer.' So they assigned an officer to me, and we set up a Special Services branch for recreation. We started on softball, touch football, and basketball leagues, put cards in the rec rooms, and put on shows. Doc Severinsen came through as an eighteen-year-old kid, and I got him assigned to the orchestra, and we put on terrific shows.''

Max Lanier had a similar experience.

MAX LANIER: "I was drafted in 1945, and I don't know why. I was at Fort Bragg in Special Services to begin with, and then I went into field artillery. Colonel Johnson was a great baseball fan. He was in charge of Special Services, and he said, 'Max, I don't know why they sent you down here. By the time you get your training over, this war is going to be over with.' And it was.

"I played in an Army tournament up in Greensboro, North Carolina. I won two games, but we lost it. Rudd, the other pitcher, got beat. I played right field.

"I hurt myself in Fort Bragg. The major league All-Stars were coming down there, and Colonel Johnson wanted to see me pitch. I said, 'Shucks, I haven't had a ball in my hand in three weeks.' I pitched one inning and hurt my elbow.''

The spring training of 1945 was held in Cairo, Illinois, but the Cards had to move to Sportsman's Park when the Mississippi and Ohio rivers flooded, putting the Cairo fields underwater. Pitcher Mort Cooper held out, and shortly after the season started, Sam Breadon traded him to the Boston Braves for Charles "Red" Barrett and $60,000.

One new arrival was a skinny, freckle-faced kid just off a farm in southern Illinois, not far from St. Louis. His name was Albert "Red" Schoendienst, and when he joined the Cards in 1945, the twenty-two–year-old looked so young that the clubhouse guards at Wrigley Field and Ebbets Field turned him away because they didn't believe at first that he could possibly be old enough to be a major league ballplayer. Schoendienst was a quiet kid who kept to himself, but his demeanor masked a toughness, smarts, and a zest for the game that would keep him in a major league uniform for more than fifty years. As much a symbol of the Cardinals as his teammate, roommate, and close friend, Stan Musial, Schoendienst has been the embodiment of the old-fashioned, small-town values of fair play and decency that have marked the team's image since Branch Rickey created it in the 1920s. Musial played for the Cards for twenty-two years and was general manager for two seasons. Schoendienst played second base for the Cards for fourteen of nineteen seasons and served as St. Louis's manager for twelve full seasons and parts of two others. Musial was elected into the Hall of Fame in 1969, Red in 1989.

Musial and Schoendienst, both products of the Rickey farm system, have been living symbols of what America's heartland is all about: hard workers who earn every penny of their pay without fanfare or ceremony. They are self-effacing, considerate of their teammates and fans, and modest to a fault. Unchanged by fame, they seem simple, yet are extraordinary men.

Red grew up on a farm in Germantown, Illinois, a town of less than 1,000 residents about forty miles from St. Louis. His father was a coal miner, electrician, carpenter, and a state prison guard. Red learned responsibility and discipline early. When he was caught skipping school, his father would hang him up on a hook on the side of the house and let him dangle there for a while.

As a boy, Red fished and played baseball when he wasn't going to school or doing the many chores on the farm. (One of nine children, Red was the last of four boys to play professionally. Three brothers played in the minors.) When Red was sixteen, he quit school and left the farm to join the Civilian Conservation Corp, a New Deal government program designed to put people to work building public projects.

The CCC was like the Army, without the fighting. Though most of those who tried out for the CCC camp baseball team were in their twenties and Red was only sixteen, he made the team at shortstop.

His career almost ended before it began when a nail flew into his eye while he was building fences. Red pleaded with the doctors not to take out the eye, and though he suffered from double vision for a while, the eye was saved and he was able to continue playing.

When he was nineteen, Red and his friend attended a Cardinal tryout camp. Neither had a car, and they hitchhiked on a dairy truck the forty miles to the tryout. Red had fifty cents in his pocket. He was surprised to find that almost 400 kids were trying out. Two kids trying out that week were Lawrence "Yogi" Berra and Joe Garagiola.

Red and his friend were asked to return the next day. His friend stayed with a relative, but Red was too proud to ask if he could stay there, too. With little money to spend, he had no idea where he was going to spend the night. After getting kicked out of Union Station, he slept in the park across the street until it began raining. He then spent his last fifteen cents on a room in a "fleabag" hotel.

Red worked out for a week. The Cardinals gave him a quarter a day so he could eat. At the end of the week, Red was disappointed when no contract was tendered, but soon after he returned home, he was offered a chance to play for the Cards for $75 a month. Red was ecstatic.

Red's stay in the minors was uncharacteristically short. In 1942 he began his career with Union City of the Kitty League, Class D. After six days, the entire league shut down, and he was transferred to a team in Albany, Georgia, where he played shortstop. He was twenty when he began his second season in Lynchburg, Class B, then quickly was promoted to Rochester in Triple A, where he led the International League with a .337 average, the youngest player to lead the league in batting since "Wee Willie" Keeler in 1892.

After spending the winter working for the highway department in Illinois, Red returned to Rochester for the 1944 season. He would have gone to the Cardinals, but Branch Rickey knew he was going to be drafted and decided to keep him in the minors until he returned from the service.

Red was based at Pine Camp, New York, where the Italian prisoners of war were housed. He played a lot of baseball. After injuring his shoulder, he was discharged, giving him enough time to rest his body before spring training in 1945.

When Red arrived in camp, he saw that he wasn't going to get to play shortstop, his regular position, because Marty Marion was there. With Musial

RED SCHOENDIENST
(Drawing by Ron Stark)

and Litwhiler in the service, manager Billy Southworth decided that the youngster would play left field, where he played admirably. Red led the league with 26 stolen bases.

Even without most of their stars, the Cardinals in '45 almost won their fourth straight pennant. After a 2-3 start with the Boston Braves, Barrett won 21 more games for the Cardinals, as Marty Marion, George "Whitey" Kurowski, Schoendienst, and outfielder Elvin "Buster" Adams led the team to within three games of the Chicago Cubs. With six games to go, the Cardinals trailed by only one and a half games but could not catch up.

MARTY MARION: "We should have won that year. I don't know what happened: We didn't play very good. We did lose a few players: Enos, Harry Walker, Danny, Stan, Max. I know we had a better ballclub than the Cubs did, and they beat us. We just didn't have the desire, I guess."

By the time the Cardinals reconvened for spring training in 1946, almost every one of the 384 ballplayers in the service returned. The Cardinals had so many players that Sam Breadon sold what he considered to be his excess. The Cooper brothers had nettled Breadon with their salary demands. The year before he had gotten rid of Mort. In January of 1946, he sold Walker Cooper, arguably the best catcher in the game, to the New York Giants for $175,000. With his starting outfield coming back, he knew he could afford to sell Johnny Hopp and Ray Sanders to the Braves for $40,000, and he peddled Jimmy Brown, Al Jurisich, and ex-Pirate Johnny Wyrostek to other teams.

Upon their return from the service, some of the former Cardinals discovered that the magic was gone. Pitching sensation Johnny Grodzicki, for instance, had been shot in the thigh by the Nazis, and he found he couldn't field his position well enough to continue. Pitcher Johnny Beazley's arm was too sore for him to go on. Terry Moore was discharged from the Army with a knee injury and was never the same, and Howie Krist, who had been 37-9 from 1937 through 1943, discovered his fastball was gone. After an 0-2 start, he was dropped, never to return.

Another loss was that of manager Billy Southworth. The Boston Braves had been purchased by three men in the construction industry, and led by Lou Perini, Boston's ownership, called the "Three Steamshovels," set a course to bring them a pennant. (Which the Braves attained in 1948.) Their first move was to offer Southworth a lot more money than Breadon was paying him. When Breadon didn't match it, Southworth headed for Beantown. Breadon replaced him with Eddie Dyer, who had left the Cardinals in 1944 as director of the club's Double A farm teams to go into the oil business. Stan Musial recalled the turmoil of 1946, how the manager moved him to first base, and how the loss of Walker Cooper, more than anyone, affected the team.

STAN MUSIAL: "I was surprised that Southworth went to Boston, but so many things happened after the war. You're coming back, getting to spring training. All of our veterans came back. Enos Slaughter, Terry Moore, and I were to be our outfield.

"What happened: Dick Sisler was our first baseman, and he was having problems. He had a great minor league record, but he had trouble hitting the high fastball. Ray Sanders had been the same way. He had a great minor league record. They traded Johnny Mize [in '42] because of Sanders. Well, Sanders had problems with the high fastball. He'd either strike out or pop 'em up. So they traded him to Boston. Billy Southworth took all those guys, Ray, and Danny [Litwhiler] and Johnny Hopp.

"Eddie Dyer asked me to play first base until Sisler got squared away. You know, I stayed there [on and off for] ten years! I didn't like first base. It was work. At first base you work. But I stayed there ten years, believe it or not.

"When Breadon traded Mize [after '41] and Walker Cooper [after '45], that upset the balance of the ballclub. When we lost Cooper, the other teams started throwing a lot of left-handers against us, saving them for Slaughter and me. Cooper and Kurowski were our right-handed power. Joe Garagiola came in there, and he was a left-handed hitter, and Del Rice caught some, but Cooper was a power hitter, and so we lost some power. That upset the balance of our team. That hurt us."

According to Marty Marion, the trade of Walker Cooper to the Giants may have had as much to do with a disagreement between Cooper and new manager Eddie Dyer back in the minors as the $175,000 that owner Sam Breadon made from the sale. Either way, Marty Marion didn't think very much of the deal.

MARTY MARION: "The story goes back in the minor leagues, where Walker Cooper and Dyer did not get along together. Walker never did like Dyer, and that had something to do with it. And the money had a lot to do with it.

"Dyer always regretted that. He said, 'Everybody blames me for getting rid of Walker, because we had some words when we were in the minor leagues together, and Walker never did like me for that.' But Dyer swore, 'I never did do anything to Walker that would hurt him the way that would happen personally.' But that was a big rumor here in town. It was a fact that they did have words in the minor leagues and that they didn't like each other. But Dyer didn't think that was the reason he was sold to Boston. It was $175,000 for Walker Cooper, which was a lot even back in those days when money was pretty important. But Walker was a hell of a ballplayer, and to give up Walker Cooper for $175,000 seems like you're crazy. But that's what happened. Nobody asked me. 'Cause Walker was one of the mainstays on our team.

"Ken O'Dea was supposed to replace him, but he got hurt, and Joe Garagiola and Del Rice were not Walker Coopers. No. Walker was one of the mainstays, I guarantee you.

"I understood why Breadon traded Ray Sanders and Johnny Hopp. That was a calculated risk, because Dick Sisler was a rising young star. They thought he was going to be a lot better than he turned out to be. And Southworth took Ray Sanders to Boston. Ray got his arm broken when Erv Dusak hit him at first base, running past. Sanders tagged him and broke his arm, and that was the end of Ray.

"When he was with us, we used to call Ray 'Dead Body.' He was a big, tall, skinny guy. He was the laziest man I ever saw in my life. The first day in spring training he was sitting next to me. He said, 'Marty, I wish the season was over!'

"Ray was touted. A St. Louis boy. He had good talent, but he was lazy. He was supposed to be better than he turned out to be. Another guy who was lazy was ol' Frank Crespi. God, we used to have to wake him up off the rubbing table every day. 'Game's starting. Let's go, Frank.' He'd be sleeping on the table. Some people have desire, and some don't. Now once they got on the field, they played ball. But their off-duty habits were something else."

If the departure of Walker Cooper and Billy Southworth weren't enough, the Cardinals lost three of their members to a most unlikely source: a new professional league begun in Mexico by seven brothers by the name of Pasqual.

When the Cards traveled to New York to play the Giants, the Pasqual brothers contacted Stan Musial about playing in Mexico.

But Musial, a humble man, cared more about playing for the Cardinals than he did the money.

STAN MUSIAL: "Jorge Pasqual had Mickey Owen with him, and Mickey was trying to get me to go to Mexico. They offered me something like $125,000 for five years, and my salary was only $13,500. He had five $10,000 cashier's checks if I agreed to go.

"I had always wanted to be a big league ballplayer. No matter what those guys said, I wasn't going. I told Mickey Owen, 'Don't bother me.' After they left, they kept calling me from Mexico City. I never had any desire to leave the Cardinals.

"Baseball back then wasn't like it is today. Our game has changed. It's strictly a business now. With free agency, a player takes the best offer. In a way, it's the American system to go where you can make the most money. You can't blame the ballplayers, because the owners have the money available to them.

"Back in my day, we didn't think about money as such. We enjoyed playing the game. We loved baseball. Money was kind of secondary, really. I didn't think about anybody else but the Cardinals. And, of course, as a boy I loved the Pirates, too."

MARTY MARION: "See, I never did have the good fortune to turn down $100,000. Pasqual never contacted me or a lot of other ballplayers, but he did contact Stan, and the smartest thing Stan ever did was to turn him down."

Musial's salary was $13,500 while most of the other players were still making $6,000 a season. Breadon's penury embittered many of them. When the Pasqual brothers offered several of the Cardinals an alternative, they jumped at it, as much to earn bigger salaries as to get back at Breadon.

The first to accept Pasqual's windfall were Fred Martin, a pitcher, and second baseman Lou Klein, who had lost his starting job to Red Schoendienst. They were solid pros, but neither was an impact player. When Max Lanier, the team's ace pitcher who began the 1946 season with a 6-0 record, jumped to Pasqual's Mexican League, the Cards suffered a serious blow.

STAN MUSIAL: "Max was one of our mainstay pitchers. Lou Klein was our second baseman, and Freddie was a good spot starter and relief pitcher. So we lost a lot when they left."

Max left in the middle of the night.

RED SCHOENDIENST: "I was rooming with Max, and I knew something was going on because he kept acting a little jumpy. Lanier never actually told me he was leaving, but he left me a note in our hotel room one night. 'I'm leaving and keep hitting line drives. Hope to play against you.' "

According to Max Lanier, Breadon's stinginess was the primary reason he felt he had no other choice but to play in Mexico.

MAX LANIER: "I had won 17 games for the Cardinals in '44, and I was 2-2 before going in the service in '45. I was down in St. Pete in '46, and Breadon wanted to give me a $500 raise. Eddie Dyer was the manager, and Eddie said, 'Come to my office. I have another phone here. I want you to listen to what I have to say to Sam Breadon.' Eddie called him in St. Louis. He said, 'Mr. Breadon, this guy is worth more money than what you're offering him.' Breadon said, 'I'll give him $500 more. He can take it or leave it.' So I took it. I couldn't afford to go home.

"With Breadon it was always 'Take it or leave it.' They know darn well you're not going to go home because you can't afford to go home, 'cause I was just getting out of the service.

"The Pasqual brothers came to see Fred Martin and Lou Klein first, and then they looked at my record. I was 6-0 at the time. I never asked them, but I'm sure Lou and Fred said they ought to ask me. I was close to Lou and Fred. I was pretty close to most of them. They said, 'Bernardo Pasqual wants to talk to you.'

"We were staying at the Knickerbocker Hotel in New York. I went over to the Commodore Hotel, and Pasqual offered me so much money. I said, 'Let me think about it.' I went back to the hotel. Fred and Lou begged me to come with them. 'Go with me.' I finally decided to go.

"They gave me a $30,000 bonus, and a contract for $20,000 a year for five years. I never saw that money. My salary was cut the first year. I lost the $30,000 in the restaurant business. Max Lanier's Diamond Club in St. Petersburg. The worst thing I ever done. I thought I knew my partner. I used to eat in his place all the time, and he wanted to open up another restaurant, so I put up my part of the money. We made money in the wintertime, when I was around, and then in the summertime I'd go away, and he'd steal me blind.

"Before I went to Mexico, I won 6 ball games and completed them. Somebody said to me, 'You almost cost us the pennant.' Because the Cards ended up tying the Dodgers and had to play in a playoff. I said, 'Listen, if I'd a lost one of those six games, you'd a never been in it.' I said, 'Give me a little credit at least. I won six games for you before I left.'

"The railroad was on strike, and Fred and I went from New York to Baltimore by bus. I had a big radio, and we put our bonus money inside the radio and took it on the bus. We kept looking at that radio all the time, seeing if it was still there. Then we got a plane from there to Chicago. When we couldn't get a plane to St. Louis, we took a taxi all the way from Chicago. It cost four hundred and some dollars. Pasqual paid for it.

"When we got to St. Louis, I bought a Chrysler Windsor. It was hard to get cars then, but a friend got it for me.

"On the way to Mexico, we stopped in Laredo, Texas. I got a call from George Weiss, the general manager of the Yankees. He said, 'I tried to get you from the Cardinals to come and play with the Yankees.' He said, 'Sam Breadon says you'll play for him or you won't play for anybody.' That's the way it was.

"We went to the Mexican side that night, stayed at the Laredo Hotel, and the next day we drove on to Mexico City. I'll tell you, it was rough going around those mountains. It was dangerous. You'd find cars on the wrong side of the road.

"When we were playing, a lot of times we took a bus. Sometimes we'd fly in these two-motored planes. We went to Tampico once, and halfway we stopped and picked up someone in a cow pasture. Imagine that. You'd take off and see the leaves on the trees bending over the pressure of the plane.

"As for the quality of the baseball, Monterrey was a good town to play in. Mexico City was okay. We drew well in Monterrey and Mexico City. The rest of it was terrible. In Tampico they had a railroad track than ran through the center field. They had to open up the gates for the train to come through! In the middle of the ball game! That's the truth. The outfielders had to contend with a railroad track between them and the infielders. Pueblo was just as bad. They had goats come on the field and eat the grass before the game started! We stayed at a hotel that didn't have no screens in it. Those mosquitos, I'll tell you!

"The food was brutal. I was sick half the time. The first time I ate bacon and eggs for breakfast, I didn't know what I was eating. In Pueblo the altitude was such that you'd eat, and the food wouldn't digest as quick. You'd be ready to eat again. I think that's what made you sick a lot. Finally I found an American restaurant in Mexico City, and I ate there quite a bit. I never got sick after that.

"The reason the Pasquals got us down there, his brother-in-law was running for President of Mexico, and he knew all the people loved baseball. And the league helped get him elected, and after he won, that's when they cut our salary in half. I will never forget, our clubhouse was very small—we had three showers—and I was taking a shower when the clubhouse boy told me, 'The election was yesterday, and I voted seven times!'

"I played for Vera Cruz but played all our games except for one in the park the Mexico City Reds played in. I pitched against the Havana Reds a lot. They had Ray Dandridge. He was a hell of a shortstop. They had a good ballclub.

"The first game I pitched, Jorge Pasqual, who owned our team, said to me, 'I know you're not used to this altitude. I'll let you work out and run a lot the first week.' The second day I was there, Jorge was sitting in the stands. Someone had brought him food on a silver tray. The bases were loaded. Nobody was out. He came down and said to me, 'Warm up. I'm going to hold up the game to let you warm up.'

"I went in and threw ten pitches and struck out the side. You know what Jorge said? He said, 'Max, I won that game.'

I played in Cuba after the end of the Mexican League season. I was playing with Almandaras, and Lou Klein and Fred Martin were with the Havana Reds. They had a two-game lead with three games to play. Adolpho Luque was our manager. I pitched the first game and beat them, 3–1. We also won the second. We needed to win all three. So Adolpho Luque came to me and said, 'Max, we'll give you $500 to pitch if you win it.' This was on one day's rest. I said, 'No, win or lose.' He said okay.

"I had them shut out until the ninth inning. We beat them 9 to 2. I never will forget, we were in the clubhouse celebrating with Luque and all the players. Somebody knocked on the door. Luque said, 'Maxie, they want you outside.' I went out, and one man handed me a $100 bill. And they kept doing that. I didn't even count it. I put the bills in my pocket. I had seventeen $100 bills in my pocket! When I left the clubhouse, here came the fans. I thought they were going to take every piece of clothing off of me.

"We only played in that Mexican League that one season. Pasqual came over and asked me to come back. I said, 'No, I ain't coming back. You cut my salary in half. It's supposed to be a five-year contract.' He said, 'We can't pay that.' I said, 'Forget about it.' I didn't go back."

Using history as hindsight, Lanier and the other men who jumped to Mexico turned out to have made a serious mistake. They may have received bonus checks and promises of hefty salary raises in multiyear contracts, but the Mexican League lasted only through the '46 season, and so much of the promised money never materialized. The jumpers, moreover, were suspended from being able to play major league baseball for five years. And the baseball owners punished them further by making them ineligible for their pensions, ensuring that many of them, including Max Lanier, would live out their old age under dire financial circumstances.

MAX LANIER: "One night in '47, Fred and I got in my car at midnight, and we drove all night back to the border without telling them we were leaving.

"When we got home, there was no use calling the Cardinals. We were suspended. I was banned from baseball for five years. I started calling the other players who had been in Mexico: Sal Maglie, the pitcher with the Giants, he lived in Fort Worth; George Hausmann, the second baseman; Danny

Gardella; Lou Klein; Fred Martin; Roy Zimmerman, a first baseman who belonged to the Giants and who was in Triple A most of the time; Red Hayworth, a catcher; Jim Steiner, another catcher. I organized a barnstorming team.

"We had a good ballclub. We started out in Monroe, Louisiana. We beat them in a close game, and they wanted us to come back a week later, and we beat them worse than we beat them the first time. We ended up playing 80 ball games and won them all. We beat this meat packing company in Kansas City, 1–0. We played a colored team out of Chicago, and we beat them bad. They thought they were going to run all over us. We had a pretty good ballclub. We played all over the Midwest, in Nebraska; Iowa; Monroe, Louisiana; Missouri; Iron Mountain, Michigan. We went on a bus, had a trailer and everything.

"I'll tell you what happened. We were booked solid for a while until Happy Chandler stopped us. He sent telegrams to these college kids and said, 'If you play against them, you will be ineligible.' I told everybody, 'Ain't nobody ineligible unless they sign a professional contract. Don't let anybody tell you otherwise.' But all at once we couldn't get a ball game. We couldn't play in any professional ballpark. They wouldn't let us.

"We thought we were going to get Abe Saperstein to promote us, but Happy Chandler must have got ahold of him, because all of a sudden he said, 'We just can't do it now.'

"In 1949 I played semipro ball up in Drummondville, Canada. They paid me as much as the Cardinals paid me when I left, plus they gave me a place to live. Sal Maglie, Danny Gardella, and myself were on the same club. Red Hayworth played for Sherbrooke. A lot of players who went to Mexico played in that league. We drew 6,000 or 7,000 every time we played. Tickets were $2 or $2.50. They treated us great up there. They had good food. We enjoyed it up there.

"On the last day of June 1949, Fred Saigh, the new owner of the Cardinals, called me and said, 'Max, you've been reinstated. How about coming back?' I said, 'How much?' He said, 'The same thing you got.' I said, 'Mr. Saigh, that's what I left for. I weren't making no money.' I said, 'I'm making more money here, counting free board and room.' He said, 'Well, you done an injustice when you left.' I said, 'Mr. Saigh, you didn't even own the ballclub then. You have no right to say that.' Those were the very words I told him.

"He said, 'You be here by the Fourth of July, and I'll give you $1,000 expenses and double your salary for the rest of the year.' I said, 'I'll be there.' I was there by July 2. And because I went to Mexico, I never did get a pension. Fred Saigh told me over the phone, 'I'll get your pension started from 1938.' And I believed him. When I got back, I found out it was not true. They never did give me a pension. They passed a rule that if you weren't on a major league roster at the end of '46 or the beginning of '47, you weren't eligible for a pension. I played fourteen years in the big leagues, and I've had to live out my retirement years on Social Security. It's barely enough to cover my medical bills.

"In '49, they asked me to contribute to the pension, but I got no credit for the years I had put in and I knew I wasn't going to pitch five more years, and that's what you needed then. What was the use of signing? Bud Selig promised to get me my pension, but I have never heard a word from him. I am still waiting.''

CHAPTER 47

SLAUGHTER'S MAD DASH

DESPITE the departure of Lou Klein, Fred Martin, and Max Lanier to Mexico in the spring of 1946, the Cardinals didn't fold. One of the reasons was the outstanding play of second baseman Red Schoendienst, who made the All-Star team, shortstop Marty Marion, who led the league in putouts and assists; the hitting of Enos Slaughter (.300, 18 homers, 130 RBIs), Whitey Kurowski (.301, 14 homers, 89 RBIs), and Stan Musial (.365, 16 homers, 103 RBIs); and the pitching of Howie Pollet, a 21-game winner, and two 15-game winners, Harry Brecheen and Murry Dickson.

Marion remembered the upset felt on the team when the trio left for Mexico. But he also recalled that most of them accepted Sam Breadon's cheapness as a fact of life.

MARTY MARION: "There was a lot of dissention on the club about Lou, Fred, and Max going to Mexico. Players were upset about this guy going, that guy going. The dissention wasn't over the low salaries, because we were used to that. That was nothing new. Everybody knew the Cardinals were a cheap club. You have to remember, back in those days it was an honor to be in the big leagues, and you didn't want to do anything to rock the boat. Most guys would have played for small amounts. We always called Mr. Rickey 'cheap' and Mr. Breadon 'cheap.' And they were cheap. We didn't see much of their money. But if you argued too much, you'd be back in Rochester again.

"Max had won 6 games when he left for Mexico. Max didn't say a word in the clubhouse to anyone about nothing. I never did talk to Max or Martin or Lou about it. But after they left, the dissention didn't last too long. In '46 we had a rookie manager, Eddie Dyer, and we went on to win the pennant.

"Dyer had been in the minor leagues managing for a while. He was a baseball man. He was a company man. He worked for the Cardinals, and you knew that. There was nothing fishy about him. He was very serious. He knew baseball. No question about that. He was more or less like Southworth: He tried to keep you happy. I always liked Dyer, and he always liked me.

"Dyer was Howie Pollet's mentor. When they were together in Houston, Dyer took Howie and raised him like a son. The year before when we played Houston in an exhibition, Dyer said, 'Boy, you guys got to see this Pollet. He can pitch.' We pooh-poohed him. But Pollet's ball really moved. It had something on it. He was a good pitcher.

"Howie was another of my roommates. He was a good Catholic boy who went to church like he was committed. He would go to bed every night with his arms folded across his chest, and he would wake up the same way. I never saw him turn over. He was the calmest person I ever saw. Howard Pollet, a good ol' boy. And Dyer loved him."

According to Marion, the Cardinals were successful even though the team was split into the group that drank and played cards and the rest who didn't, including Marion. The cardplaying clique had once been the domain of the Cooper brothers. Even after they were traded away, the division continued.

MARTY MARION: "We had cliques on the club. One group was the boys who drank a lot of beer and loved to play cards. Oh, my gosh. The guys who didn't play, me and Harry Walker and Pollet and Brecheen and those kind of guys, they called us 'the college kids,' although none of us probably went to college. But we were the 'nice' kids. We weren't the rough boys. Stan was kind of on our side. They had enough rounders. But practically the whole pitching staff, Mort, Beazley, and Lanier, they all loved to play cards, and they'd always have a card game going. When you went back to the hotel, they all went to the card games, and we all went to the movies.

"I would sit and watch them play a lot of times. Finally they had to stop. Mr. Dyer had to put a ban on cardplaying. Well, when you play cards, the loser is always the guy who can't afford to lose. And they were getting complaints from the wives at home, that they were losing money, so they must have been playing for pretty good stakes. I never gambled in my life, so I never played cards. But they used to play cards in the clubhouse all the time. They played pinochle before the games. Finally Dyer had to stop them from playing cards in the clubhouse.

"We called them 'the mean bunch.' They were a little bit more aggressive than we were. Kurowski loved the play cards and drink beer. Ol' George could drink beer. We definitely had two different types of people on that team, but when we got on the baseball field, it was a different thing. We had the will to win and the desire to do so, and we did. We had the ability, too. The writers talk about this team not getting together, the players not liking each other. Well, that's all a lot of baloney. We never had that problem."

In June of 1946, the Cards left St. Louis for a fifteen-game road trip. After winning five of seven, the team headed for Brooklyn. In three games Stan Musial went 8-for-12. Whenever Musial would come to bat, the Brooklyn fans would start a chant. Up in the press box, reporter Bob Broeg wondered what the fans were saying. That evening he asked traveling secretary Leo Ward about it.

BOB BROEG: "Leo and I were having dinner. I said, 'What in the hell were those people chanting?' He said, 'They were saying, "Here comes the man." '

I said, 'Do you mean, "Here comes *that* man?" ' 'No. No. Here comes *the* man." '

"So I recounted what I had heard in my overnight. 'Stan the Man Musial." I was a little surprised at how quickly it stuck. You didn't have to be a brain surgeon to figure that 'Stan the Man' was pretty good. And over the years he's been very proud of it.

In mid-July the Dodgers came to St. Louis for a four-game series. In the first game, Musial stole home and singled to start the winning rally; in the second game, he tripled and scored the tying run and then homered in the ninth to win it, 2–1; in game three he had four hits—two singles, a triple and a home run. On July 16, Erv Dusak's grand slam completed the sweep. A few days later, the Cards beat the Phils and took over first place.

At the end of the season the Cards won twenty-three of their last thirty-one games, but it was enough to only tie the Dodgers.

Mort Cooper, the former Cardinal ace, helped the Cards greatly when he pitched the Boston Braves to a last-day win over Brooklyn to force a three-game playoff. Danny Litwhiler, who played with Cooper on Billy Southworth's Braves ballclub in '46, recalled his role in the events leading to Cooper's crucial victory.

DANNY LITWHILER: "Mort was a great pitcher. He pitched with sore arms. When he was with the Cards, after the game his arm would swell up, and Doc Weaver, the trainer, would hang it up by a strap, and he'd milk his arm, stick it in ice.

"Mort had pitched for us in Boston, and we were going into Brooklyn, and Brooklyn had to beat us to win the pennant. And Southworth didn't know who he was going to pitch. I asked Mort, 'Couldn't you pitch?' He had just pitched two days before. Mort said, 'Hell, yes. I have no place to go. I can pitch.' He really wanted to beat Leo and the Dodgers.

"I caught Billy going out on the subway, and I rode with him, and I said, 'Why don't you pitch Mort?' 'Oh no, he can't pitch. He just pitched two days ago.' I said, 'He won't have to pitch anymore after that. And he'd like to pitch. I know he'd like to pitch. He told me he wants to pitch the game. Why don't you just pitch him as long as you can?'

"So Mort pitched and won the ball game, and the Cardinals tied for the pennant."

Though the Cards had finished in a tie with the Dodgers for the 1946 pennant, observers blamed Sam Breadon for turning a sure winner into a horse race.

BOB BROEG: "On the closing day of the season, Biggie Garagnani and Henry Ruggieri, friends of Stan and catcher Joe Garagiola, threw a party for the team. Sam Breadon and a lot of the Cards players attended.

"J. Roy Stockton, the chief chronicler of the Gashouse Gang, a brilliant writer who wrote more *Saturday Evening Post* pieces than anybody trying to crack that market, had a few martinis.''

Stockton, acting as toastmaster, told the crowd that it would be appropriate to stand for ten seconds of silence in tribute to "the man who made the close race possible." All eyes turned on Breadon.

He mentioned Breadon's trades of Walker Cooper, Johnny Hopp, Emil Verban, and the three players who jumped to the Mexican League and suggested that if some of these men hadn't been lost to the team the Cards would have won in a runaway.

"All the glorious excitement would have been missed," Stockton said sarcastically. Then he added, "I hope Sam hasn't cut the baloney too fine."

BOB BROEG: "Which Sam had, for Christ's sake. We were a heavily favored team, and the season came down to a tie. Sam had miscalculated. Rickey was gone, and he just kept unloading. He made what I called 'The Cape Cod Cardinals.' Two years later, the Boston Braves won the pennant, largely with acquisitions from the Cardinals.

"Everybody was furious at Roy. Harry Caray was one of them. But that didn't bother Stockton. He could have knocked Caray on his ass.''

After Stockton sat down, Caray was invited to go up to the dais. He talked about how lucky the Cardinal players were, how being a Cardinal almost guaranteed each player a World Series check. Caray recalled how Sam Breadon had sent checks to Grover Cleveland Alexander long after the alcoholic pitcher had outlived any usefulness. Caray said that if any ballplayer ever had personal problems, Breadon was always there to help out.

After Caray was finished, Stockton glared at him. Breadon came over, shook Caray's hand, and told him, "Young man, that was awfully nice of you. I will never forget it."

BOB BROEG: "Harry Caray was a company man. He always knew when a Breadon or a Busch was in charge. But Caray could be very tough on anybody who didn't sign the checks."

The next spring Sam Breadon expanded his radio broadcasts to include road games. He had to choose between the team of Dizzy Dean, sponsored by Falstaff Beer, vs. the team of Harry Caray and Gabby Street, sponsored by Greisedieck Bros. Beer. Dizzy Dean had the bigger name and Falstaff had the bigger budget, but Breadon chose to go with Caray.

When Breadon told Caray of his decision, Caray was flabbergasted. Before he left the meeting, Breadon told him, "Young man, a few months ago at that testimonial dinner, I told you that I would never forget what you did. Well, consider this proof of that."

As a result, Harry Caray became "The Voice of the Cardinals" and would go on to broadcast Cardinal games for the next forty years.

*   *   *

The Cards had to get past the Brooklyn Dodgers in a best two-out-of-three series to reach the World Series.

Leo Durocher, the manager of the Dodgers, won the coin flip. Durocher, making a disastrous call, chose to play the first game in St. Louis and the next two at home in Ebbets Field. Leo didn't anticipate how tired the long train trip from Brooklyn to St. Louis would leave his players.

MARTY MARION: "Leo was a gambler and he took the best odds. You get to play two games at home against one. That's why he made the decision. Everybody knows that. But he had to travel. A long way to play the first game, and all the way back to play the second. We beat 'em both games. Howie Pollet won the first one. We beat Ralph Branca, 4 to 2.

"What I remember about that game was Leo Durocher. He was standing along third base, and he said, 'Kurowski, Marion, Schoendienst, and Musial. You couldn't get a pint of blood out of your whole infield.' We were all skinny, you know. [Could Durocher have been commenting on the icewater in their collective veins?]

"I used to love ol' Leo. I used to argue with him all the time. 'Come on, Leo. Do something.' He was fun. He was a showman. He had Laraine Day for a wife. Ol' Leo did all right.

"We won the first game, and the star was Joe Garagiola. Joe was a lot better ballplayer than he gives himself credit for. He makes fun of himself, but it really wasn't true. Joe wasn't a bad hitter, not at all. And he wasn't a bad catcher. He didn't have a great arm, but other than that, he was a good ballplayer.

"We returned to Brooklyn after winning the first game, and Murray Dickson beat them by 8–4.

"Naturally, we never even got to play them in a third one."

WHITEY KUROWSKI
(Courtesy Brace Photo)

The first game of the 1946 World Series was at Sportsman's Park. The Cards lost a heartbreaker in extra innings on a long home run by Rudy York. In this game, manager Eddie Dyer employed the "Boudreau Shift" on Ted Williams. Third baseman Whitey Kurowski left his position and moved to the right side of the diamond.

MARTY MARION: "I stayed at shortstop. Kurowski moved over to the right side. He and Schoendienst were over there. Ted didn't try to hit the ball my way. Bunting was against his code. He wanted to challenge everybody, try to hit the ball through there.

"Ted and I played in the All-Star Game that was held at Fenway Park that year. He hit two home runs, and the American League beat us pretty bad [12–0]. I'm playing shortstop, and he's coming around second base, and he gives me a wink and in that froggy voice says, 'Kid, don't you wish you could hit like that!' I just looked at him as he ran by. I was speechless."

The Cardinals won the second game, 3–0, behind a six-hitter by Harry Brecheen.

MARTY MARION: "Ted didn't do a thing in the World Series. Brecheen crowded him with the ball the whole time. He didn't do a thing."

With the games tied at one apiece, the Series moved on to Boston for three more games. The final two, if it went that long, were scheduled for St. Louis.

MARTY MARION: "We figured if we could win one game in Boston, we could beat them in St. Louis."

In the third game, Boston's "Boo" Ferriss himself pitched a shutout, and Rudy York hit a three-run home run off Murray Dickson in a 4–0 victory. In this game, Ted Williams finally gave in and bunted the ball.

MARTY MARION: "He bunted one time. That was against his code. And the next day there were big headlines: 'Williams Bunts Safely!'"

The Cards won Game 4 by the score of 12–3. Joe Garagiola, Enos Slaughter, and Whitey Kurowski each had four hits as the Cards tied a one-game Series record with 20 base hits.

The Red Sox took a 3–2 lead in games with a 6–3 win in Game 5. Howie Pollet didn't get out of the first inning. It would remain to be seen whether the Cards could win the two remaining games as Marion had anticipated.

Harry Brecheen won Game 6 to tie the Series at three apiece when he defeated the Red Sox, 4–1. Game 7 would prove to be one of the most memorable in World Series history.

With the score tied at 3–3 and nobody out in the eighth inning, Enos Slaughter came to bat. Slaughter had been hit on the

JOE GARAGIOLA
(Courtesy Brace Photo)

right elbow by a pitch in Game 5, and was thought to be out for the rest of the Series. Doc Weaver, however, worked on the elbow all day and night, allowing Slaughter to start the seventh game. Leading off in the eighth inning, the peppery Cardinal outfielder lined a single to center field off reliever Bob Klinger.

The next two batters were retired easily. With Slaughter still on first base, the Cardinals' Harry Walker then blooped a hit to shallow left-center. The fleet Slaughter, running even before the crack of the bat, flew around second, headed for third, ran through coach Mike Gonzalez's stop sign, and hustled his way home as he somehow scored to give the Cardinals a lead they never relinquished. It's not every day that a runner scores from first on what should have been ruled a single to left-center. (After the throw home, Walker went to second and was inexplicably credited with a double by the official scorer.) It was the singular play of Slaughter's distinguished nineteen-year career.

MARTY MARION: "It wasn't an exciting play when it happened. Enos was on first, and Harry Walker hit the ball into short left-center. Leon Culberson was out there [Dom DiMaggio was the regular centerfielder, but he pulled a muscle on a hit that tied the game in the top of the eighth], and he got the ball back to Johnny Pesky, the shortstop, who was on the edge of the grass. Enos was coming around third base. Mike Gonzalez was our coach, and he had an accent, and he was hollering, 'No no no.' Enos says, 'I thought he said, "Go go go." ' Anyway, Pesky hesitated—he dropped his arm and turned around to throw and had to double pump—and there was no contest. I could see right quick he didn't have a chance to throw Enos out at home. I didn't even have to tell him to slide. Roy Partee, the catcher, was way up the line as he slid across home plate.

"In the defense of Pesky, nobody told him where to throw the ball. His back was to the infield, and nobody was telling him what to do, which is a cardinal sin. The second baseman should be hollering 'Home, home, home.' I can't blame Pesky at all.

"And every time I see Harry, I say, 'Harry, nobody even says you hit the ball!' He got no credit for it at all.

"Later Enos said, 'I was going all the way.' I don't know whether he was or not. You never know what's in Enos's mind. He's a character. What did he say?"

ENOS SLAUGHTER: "A lot of people have asked me on that play, Was it the biggest thrill of my baseball career? To me it was just a routine play as far as baseball is concerned. I scored from first. They gave Harry Walker a double, but ordinarily it should have been a single.

"I was stealing. A 3-2 pitch, two men out. I was running on the play when Harry hit this little looping ball into left-center, and as I rounded second, I said to myself, 'I can score.'

"The reason I kept running was, in an earlier ball game, the fifth game, a game we got beat, Mike Gonzalez, the third base coach, had stopped me too quick on a relay throw, and that's when they juggled the ball. I could have walked home. But I had stopped. To me, when you stop running on a play, the best thing to do is stay at that bag. And we didn't score in that game, and we got beat.

"I went to Eddie Dyer. He said, 'From now on, if you think you have a legitimate chance to score, I'll take the blame.' Well, this play came up. I was the winning run. And I knew Dominick DiMaggio had been taken out of the ball game. And he had a great arm. When he was taken out, and Leon Culberson replaced him, I knew Culberson didn't have a great arm, and I said to myself when I rounded second, 'I can score and score easy.'

"Culberson threw the ball in to Johnny Pesky. In baseball, word of mouth is important. Bobby Doerr was the second baseman, Pinky Higgins the third baseman, and they made Johnny Pesky the goat. Well, his back was to the infield when he took the relay throw.

"If either Doerr or Higgins had hollered 'Home with the ball,' Pesky could have been wheeling, and I think he could have maybe thrown me out by eight or ten feet. But no one said a word, and he turned toward second. When he turned back to me coming home, it was too late. He threw the ball, and Roy Partee took a couple steps in front of the plate, and I slid across easy. Like I said, it was a routine play as far as I'm concerned."

CHAPTER 48

FALLOUT FROM THE FIRST

As one indication just how low Sam Breadon's salaries were compared to some of the better-drawing teams, the Cardinals owner offered Stan Musial a salary of $21,000 for the 1947 season at a time when Joe DiMaggio of the New York Yankees, Ted Williams of the Boston Red Sox, and Bob Feller of the Cleveland Indians each were earning between $40,000 and $50,000. Musial asked for $35,000, a reasonable request, considering that in 1946 he hit .365 and won the National League's Most Valuable Player Award.

After the defection of Lanier, Klein, and Martin the year before, Breadon feared that the Pasqual brothers might lure some of his other players, and he gave $5,000 raises to Musial, Enos Slaughter, and Terry Moore to keep them from jumping to Mexico. Musial wanted the $5,000 added to his $21,000 base to mark the starting point of his negotiation for the '47 season. With the Mexican League no longer a threat, Breadon played hardball and insisted the $5,000 payment had been a bonus and only a one-shot deal. His salary, Breadon insisted, was not $26,000, but still $21,000. What Musial had going for him in his negotiation was public sympathy. The talented batsman had become one of the most popular players ever to wear the Redbird insignia, and it was bad PR not to pay his star a competitive wage.

At the winter baseball dinner in late January of 1947, Breadon increased his offer to $24,000, then to $27,000. Musial continued to hold out. Bolstered by a plea of fairness from manager Eddie Dyer, Musial was able to up his salary to $31,000, way short of what the other stars of the period were making, but more reasonable than before.

In addition to having to pay higher salaries than he wished, in the spring of 1947, Sam Breadon was facing one of his most serious crises of confidence. When his world champions started the 1947 season 2-11, he became concerned about the team's financial health. A worrier during the best of times, Breadon became downright panicky over the team's dismal start.

His former executive, Branch Rickey, moreover, created a firestorm around the league when he announced that he intended to promote from the International League a black player by the name of Jackie Robinson to play for the Brooklyn Dodgers. Like every other owner, in a secret meeting designed to stop Rickey from foisting Robinson on the rest of the league, Breadon had voted against Robinson's eligibility. But Rickey, who was feeling the pressure to back off even from his immediately family, had seen the spectacular play of Robinson during his season at Montreal in '46, and he was determined to bring him up to the Dodgers. Making the move possible in the face of unanimous bitter opposition was support from a most unlikely ally: Commissioner Happy Chandler. The former governor and senator of Kentucky, a son of Dixie if there ever was one, assured Rickey he would approve Robinson's contract and fight the fight along with him. Whether the other team owners wanted Robinson or not, like a runaway freight train the hulking black infielder was heading their way.

At this time, the entire United States lived under a system designed to keep blacks out of sight and out of mind in white communities. Even in the North, blacks were kept out of public accommodations, such as hotels and restaurants. When Jesse Owens returned from the 1936 Olympics after winning four gold medals, he was not allowed to stay at the Plaza Hotel in New York. With blacks excluded from most communities and relagated to designated neighborhoods, whites and blacks went to school separately.

Southern blacks had it worse. Led by Bible Belt ministers who justified segregation through the Scriptures, passionate white supremacists passed rigid laws to prevent blacks from entering white society. Blacks by law could not drink from the same water fountains as whites and could not urinate in the same restrooms. Blacks by law were not allowed to perform on ball fields with whites. If Negro players were as good as the major leaguers, the color barrier, which had held since before the turn of the century, made sure that no one would ever find out. Judge Landis, who ruled baseball from 1920 until his death in 1945, chastised anyone who dared voice his opinion that Negro League players could play in the major leagues. Leo Durocher, for one, said publicly that a number of Negro League players could play in the major leagues, and he received a tongue-lashing from Landis for his remarks. Later the steel-eyed Landis barred major league barnstormers from playing Negro League teams to make sure the color line held. Besides his famed ruling that banned for life eight Black Sox players equally without regard to any evidence of fault or complicity, his spirited defense of racism has been the esteemed judge's lasting legacy.

When he was running the Cardinals, Branch Rickey had never even considered signing a player from the Negro Leagues. The atmosphere prohibited such a move. Even had Rickey wanted to do so, Landis would not have allowed him to do it, and the powers that be in St. Louis, a distinctly Southern city, surely would have stopped him as well.

At the time Rickey arrived in Brooklyn, World War II was under way, and from the time it ended in 1945, there was great pressure on society to change its restrictive racial policies. Blacks had fought and died for their country, and left-wing political activists argued that they should be able to enjoy liberties won through their sacrifices. Pickets surrounded Ebbets Field, calling for an end to segregation in baseball.

Branch Rickey, a pioneer when it came to the game but an executive known best for his chain gang and his low salaries, was the last person anyone would have chosen to shake up the game, never mind the society. But Rickey decided the time was at hand to end what he saw as years of terrible social injustice. In the spring of 1947, he brought a black man to Brooklyn to perform as an equal on the same playing fields as white men! It was a move that shocked the country, especially in the cities in the South like St. Louis. Would any of the white citizens of St. Louis boycott the games because a black man was on the field? Sam Breadon wondered about that. According to Bob Broeg, who wrote for the *St. Louis Post-Dispatch* and covered the Cardinals at the time, Breadon's musings about such a boycott set off a chain of events which, he says, has falsely branded the Cardinals as the most racist of teams. No, says Broeg, the players weren't happy that Robinson was coming into baseball, but neither were whites on any other team, but when a New York reporter wrote that the Cardinals intended to go on strike, everyone believed the story.

The problem, says Broeg, was that the story was based on Breadon's paranoid musings and wasn't true. Broeg, Stan Musial, and Marty Marion explained what they saw and experienced during that tense period when Jackie Robinson broke baseball's color barrier. All deny categorically that the Cardinals ever threatened to go on strike against Robinson. If you look at the time line, what they say seems to add up. Particularly telling is that the story broke after the Cardinals played three games against Brooklyn during which there were no incidents of any kind. Something else comes into play. As a journalist, you get to know your subjects. I spent many hours with Bob Broeg, Stan Musial, and Marty Marion. They all spoke honestly, about themselves and their teammates, covering a range of topics. I am convinced they were being truthful about this subject as well.

Until there is proof to the contrary, my unshakable conclusion is that the Cardinals have been falsely accused. I hope this sets the record straight.

BOB BROEG: ''There was no threat to strike against Robinson. There was talk on *all* clubs, but the Cardinals had no plans to strike. I know, because I was with them.

''The story that the Cardinals were going to strike came from Sam Breadon's fears. Breadon had led the world championship Cardinals of '46, had his biggest attendance ever, went over a million for the first time, but for the first time, too, he was faced with considerable salary increases. In Breadon's mind's eye, when a player got around $15,000, he became nervous in the service. For years the only players he paid more than that were Rogers Hornsby and Frankie Frisch, and Grover Alexander carrying over. One of the things that created a screw-up, returning servicemen were supposed to get the top salaries they were making before they went into the service. Terry Moore was $13,500, and Marty Marion did real well, and the Coopers did real well, and Marion sweet-talked him finally into going up to $15,000. He was preparing to do the same for the Coopers, he said, but they found out about it and lashed out at him, and of course he angrily traded Mort, and then he sold Walker, which was a grievous blow, a faux pas to take away that hard-hitting good defensive catcher.

"So when they got off as world champions in '47, losing eleven of the first thirteen games, Breadon really panicked. It was a two-team town, and also the Cardinals were not as big a draw, partly because of the other club, and one night Breadon was drinking with Dr. Robert F. Hyland, who Judge Landis called 'The Surgeon General of baseball.' Doc Hyland was a great baseball fan, and a knowledgeable guy, and Breadon was moaning and groaning about the ballclub. Breadon said, 'Jeez, I'm worried about this black guy. They're going to strike. Things like that are distracting.'

"About this time, Rud Rennie [of the *New York Herald Tribune*] came into town with the Yankees, and all the New York writers really loved Breadon because he was one of their own. Sam threw his best parties in the summer whenever the New York club was in town. He never lost his accent. In fact, when he was club owner and Frisch was manager, if you heard them in conversation or on the radio, both of them referred to the Cardinals as the 'Cah-dinals.' So one of the first things Rud said to Doc Hyland was, 'Bob, how's Sam?'

"Dr. Hyland said, 'Don't ask.'

" 'What do you mean?'

" 'Oh shit, you know the club is going bad.'

" 'I know that,' said Rennie.

Dr. Hyland said, 'He's afraid the club is going to strike against the black player.'

"Now Rennie, not willing to hurt his relations with Hyland or Breadon, told that to his editor, Stanley Woodward, and Woodward got ahold of Ford Frick.

"I remember very well we were in New York. It was the third day of the series with the Dodgers. The Cardinals' losing streak had ended at Boston. On a Saturday afternoon, Breadon dealt Harry Walker and a pitcher named Freddy Schmidt to the Phillies for Ron Northey to get more power. On Sunday at Boston, Northey, joining them, hit a home run to win the game and break the nine-game losing streak. They go into Brooklyn, and in those days whenever the Cardinals needed to get well, all they had to do was play Brooklyn. They lost the first game, but they won the next two. They were playing against Robinson. Nothing happened.

"After the last game, I went to bed a little earlier than usual, because the next day we had a train trip to Pittsburgh. They didn't travel much in the daytime. I was in bed, and Arch Murray of the *New York Post* called me. He said, 'You seen the late *Herald Tribune*?' I said, 'No. Damn it, I just got to bed.' He said, 'In the late *Tribune* . . .' and he told me the story about the Cardinals going on strike.

"I got up and got a *Tribune,* and I awakened Terry Moore at two in the morning. He was the captain. I said, 'If I'm awake, you got to be awake.' I told him about the strike story, and he said, 'That's ridiculous. For Christ's sake we know we'd have to forfeit our games if we didn't play.'

"As part of that story, Stan Musial hadn't played that day. He was sick. The next morning up in his hotel room he was lying in the bed naked as they were deciding what should be done. The hotel doctor said he needed an appendectomy and wanted to do it in New York, and Musial didn't want it done in New York, and Dyer said, 'I can't take you on the train to Pittsburgh, pal, because if that thing bursts, you'll be in real trouble.'

"Finally they agreed to fly him to St. Louis, and they talked to Dr. Hyland, and Del Wilber went along as his caddie, and I mention that only because it links in later.

"They fly to St. Louis, and we go on to Pittsburgh, but the strike story has broken that morning—after they played the three games. Frick, on the supposition, said they'd get suspended for that, which was obvious.

"So that strike story, to this day, lingers.

"In the meanwhile, the Dodgers shortly thereafter came to St. Louis for the first time, and I was sitting on the Cardinal bench with Eddie Dyer, and Robinson felt comfortable enough to come through the Cardinals' clubhouse, instead of, as some players did, clippity-clopping with their spiked shoes on the cement floor, which was a little awkward going around. It was much easier and shorter to come through our dugout and go across the field, and Robinson stepped into the dugout, and he started to walk through, and Dyer said, 'Iliya, pal,' and he turned and said, 'Hi, Eddie.' I teased Dyer. I said, 'Aha, consorting with the enemy, huh?' He said, 'Consorting with the enemy, hell. This guy is like Frank Frisch. He's a great all-around athlete, and if you get him mad, like Frisch, he'll beat your brains in himself. I've told my guys, "Take it easy on him." ' Naturally, with Frisch as my favorite player, I always remembered that. And it was true."

STAN MUSIAL: "The story came out that we might strike against the Dodgers and Robinson, but none of that was true. We never had a meeting or talked about anything of that nature. We never considered it, talked about it, or had any ideas about it.

"We had a lot of Southern ballplayers on that club, but I can't remember anyone saying anything about not playing. There might have been grumbling, but we never had a meeting or anything of that nature. You can talk to any of the ballplayers who were there, and they will tell you the same thing: We never had any discussion of this nature."

MARTY MARION: "The press made such a big deal out of Jackie Robinson coming to the big leagues, but it was no surprise. He was playing in Montreal for a year, so everybody knew he was coming to the big leagues, because he was that kind of ballplayer.

"They kept talking about the Cardinals going on strike. I never heard such a stupid thing in my life. Nobody is their right mind would do a thing like that. There was never any meeting that we talked of striking. Striking? Sure, we didn't like Jackie Robinson. We didn't like anybody. That had nothing to do with Jackie Robinson being black."

RED SCHOENDIENST: "Some players on some teams didn't like the fact Robinson and Branch Rickey had integrated the major leagues, but I think those guys were in the minority. There were always rumors that players on the Cardinals were going to go on strike and not play against Robinson, but nobody ever said anything to me about it, and I never saw any incidents that I thought were direct attempts to injure or harm Robinson."

The national press really did a hatchet job on the Cardinals. As part of the bogus strike story, *Collier's* magazine in August of '47 alleged that Stan Musial, the righteous Northerner, got so upset with Enos Slaughter, the unyielding Southerner, that they got into a vicious fight, and that was the reason Musial didn't play against Robinson that May series. The story was written from innuendo and untruths. There was not a scintilla of evidence that it ever happened. Musial was in the hospital suffering from appendicitis at the time. Visitors swear there wasn't a scratch on him.

MARTY MARION: "There was a story that Stan and Enos got in a fight. Oh God. I never saw that, either. I heard that story, too. Why do things get started like this?"

STAN MUSIAL: "The rumors were that Slaughter and I got into a fight. How those rumors ever got started were amazing. It was in New York, so evidently it was a New York writer.

"I had an appendicitis attack in New York at that time. I was in my hotel room, and they called the doctors, and I forget who I was rooming with, but they sent Del Wilber to escort me to St. Louis. I wanted to see Dr. Hyland, our physician, and have him give me an opinion rather than a doctor in New York.

"As I look back on it, I wish I had had my appendix out in New York right then and there, because I was tired all that season. When I got back, they said they could give me medicine and control this appendicitis, but I was tired all year. I got it out in October, and the next year I came back strong, had the best year I ever had."

Bob Broeg confirmed that Musial missed the game because he had been in the hospital suffering from appendicitis, not because he had had a fight with a teammate, a story which Broeg attributed to the vindictiveness of a spurned magazine reporter.

BOB BROEG: "Kyle Crichton wrote a piece for *Collier's* magazine in August of '47 debunking Musial. When Stan was in the hospital in May, Crichton had tried to get an interview with him. Stan, bedridden, was forced to push him off, and he got angry, so he lashed out. He wrote in the article, 'When they said he was out of the lineup, the truth is that Slaughter beat the hell out of him.' Two or three of us newspapermen had seen his body upstairs, and there wasn't a mark on it.

"Kyle Crichton was a good writer. I helped him as a kid a few years previously, when he did a story on Paul Christman for *Collier's*. I didn't know he was that venomous, but he was way off base.''

Nevertheless, the rumors of strife on the Cardinals when Robinson came into major league baseball have never died. In his autobiography written in 1992, Hank Aaron dredged them up.

HANK AARON: "I understand he [Stan Musial] was one of the few Cardinals who refused to go along when they were talking about boycotting Jackie Robinson in 1947, and he got into an argument with his teammates over it.''

The third incident that helped make more plausible the other two was an incident on August 20 at Ebbets Field involving Robinson and Enos Slaughter. In the seventh inning, Slaughter hit a ground ball to second base and as he crossed first base he spiked the back of Robinson's right leg. The injury was minor, but the question has always been whether Slaughter did it purposely in an effort to injure Robinson. Ralph Branca, the Dodger pitcher that day, accused Slaughter of doing just that. Because he came from North Carolina and played aggressively, in the minds of the Dodger fans, Slaughter was found guilty. That spiking for many years kept him out of the Hall of Fame.

Slaughter has always denied malacious intent. Bob Broeg and his teammates convincingly back him up.

BOB BROEG: "The other thing that lingers, unfairly, is the extent to which Enos Slaughter later cut Robinson. He cut him, but it was so minor that I hardly even remember it, and Enos didn't remember it, but in the Ken Burns series, he had David McCullough saying words obviously written by Burns or someone else: 'Slaughter leaped and deliberately slashed his thigh.' You use the word deliberately, and you better be able to show that in court. To this day, Slaughter can't get ahold of Burns. Burns won't talk with him.

"Now, as I said, Slaughter didn't deny having cut him, but the year before, in '46, Slaughter had put Eddie Stanky in the hospital, sliding hard into him, and Stanky always claimed that Enos did that deliberately. A few years later, when Monte Irvin was trying to play first base for the Giants, Enos grounded down the line, and Monte's foot was on the bag, and Enos stepped on it, and he turned around and wheeled, and Enos said, 'Goddamn it, Monte, watch your foot. They're still on my ass for that Robinson thing.' So I asked Monte, and he said, 'That's exactly what he said to me.' Monte said, 'He's all right. He plays in my golf tournament.'

"Slaughter created a problem in '49. On Labor Day, he slid real hard into Danny Murtaugh. They almost had a fight, and the last week of the season when they were playing Pittsburgh, I was having dinner with Bill Meyer in Pittsburgh, a rainout. Meyer, I guess, because the Cardinals were a white team and the Dodgers weren't, but maybe for other reasons—maybe he didn't like Rickey. He said, 'I sure hope your club wins. But I don't think they will. Slaughter awakened our club Labor Day, and beside, I think your team is tired,' and of course, he was right. So Slaughter's aggressiveness boomeranged at times, too.''

MARTY MARION: ''Enos stepped on him one time at first base. I don't remember that even. I don't think Enos did anything. I don't remember any Cardinal player doing anything that he wouldn't have done against a white person. Just because he was black, they made a big deal out of it. Never in my life. . . . I never heard Enos say he did anything wrong. I have no idea why Enos got blamed for that.''

STAN MUSIAL: ''In 1998 I went to a conference on Jackie Robinson in Brooklyn, and the people in New York still believe that Enos tried to purposely hurt Jackie. They went after Enos. They still had that feeling. I could sense it. But there's nothing to it. That play when he spiked Robinson at first was a close play, and he stepped on his foot. I don't know of any professional ballplayer who would deliberately hurt another professional ballplayer. The same thing happened in 1950 with Joe Garagiola, who tripped over Robinson at first base and broke his shoulder.

   ''We had our battles with the Dodgers because we were rivals. They were either first or we were winning. They'd hit us, and we'd hit them. We'd knock them down, and they'd knock us down. It was part of the game, and after the game was over, the next day we went out and did the same thing.''

DANNY LITWHILER: ''I remember when Jackie Robinson came, he was complaining that everybody was throwing at him. They asked, 'Anybody in particular?' He said, 'Mort Cooper.' The New York writers were trying to get an argument going. We came in to play them, and they asked Mort, 'Jackie Robinson says you throw at him a lot.' He said, 'Certainly, I throw at him. I throw at the white guys, but they don't say anything about it.' He did. Mort threw at anybody who was going to hurt him, and that was the same with the Brooklyn club. The Dodgers would ride you a lot. From the bench, they would ride you. They'd throw at you, too.''

MARTY MARION: ''Most things that happen in baseball you never hear about, like cliques on the club. One bunch plays cards, the other goes to the movies. The writers say, 'That's dissention.' Big deal. But I can't think of anything in baseball that has so many false remarks than the Jackie Robinson story. 'Cause I have never seen one Cardinal player, Terry Moore, Harry Walker, any of them, do anything bad to Robinson. Sure, they didn't like him. They didn't like anybody. It had nothing to do with him being black. Everybody made it sound like it was because he was black. But that wasn't the case at all. By the way, Mr. Jackie Robinson was a fierce competitor, too. He would step on you if you got in his way. Oh yes. So many of those stories are so false, but it got a lot of publicity. He packed them in the ballpark. When he got in the league, you could hardly get in the ballpark for the blacks showing up. You never saw so many black people in your life. He drew them in Sure, he did. Today, you know, blacks don't go to ball games. They don't support the clubs. Not at all.

"Now I can remember when you talk about being from down South, I didn't get to go to many ball games when I was in Atlanta, Georgia. We had a team called the Atlanta Crackers. They had a special bleachers for just blacks, and they were great ball fans. But there were only a couple hundred of them there. And that was a special thing for them. And then they had another section where all the gamblers sat. All they did was gamble, bet on the game. So I was used to the black stands.

"But you can go to a ball game right now, and you won't see 1 percent of the crowd black. But Jackie brought them in. Jackie was a big story in baseball, and he's done a hell of a lot for the black player. The reason whites resented him, they were going to lose their jobs. You know, blacks are good athletes. The whites didn't want to lose their jobs. They had a a white fraternity. A lot of blacks could have played ball. And who got in trouble by saying black men can't swim? Ol' Al Campanis with the Dodgers. A simple thing like that got him kicked out.

"Jackie was a challenge to play against. When he hit a ground ball to you, he'd hit it hard. And I picked him off second base one time, like I did Joe Gordon in the World Series. I had the honor of picking the famous Jackie off second base. And he just dusted himself off and walked off like everybody else does. But he was always jumping up and down. He was aggravating. He really was. He kind of got on your nerves. But he was a good ballplayer, no question about that.''

BOB BROEG: "To get back to Breadon, Breadon created this problem himself with that anxiety, and of course, it turned out the Cardinals, after that bad start, had a long winning streak around midseason. They had the U.S. Open in St. Louis, and with the streetcar strike and the U.S. Open, the Cardinals swept four from the Dodgers, and made a race out of it. Although the Dodgers won it, Breadon drew about a million and a quarter, the most he ever drew. But he hung the rap on those guys inadvertently.

"To this day, everybody still talks about the anti-Robinson feeling on the Cardinals, and it's a shame, because I was with them, and I know, as Ford Frick says in his autobiography on page 273, in trying to knock that thing down, he said, 'The St. Louis club accepted Robinson better than most others,' and that's the truth.''

In 1947 Jackie Robinson by himself began to change the balance of power in the National League. Branch Rickey's Cardinals dynasty was at an end, and now Branch Rickey's Dodger dynasty was just beginning. Rickey brought up Negro Leaguers Roy Campanella [in '48] and Don Newcombe [in '49] to Brooklyn, which proceeded to win the National League pennant in '49, '52,

'53, '55, and '56. The Giants, another team featuring former Negro League stars Willie Mays, Henry Thompson, and Monte Irvin, won pennants in 1951 and 1954. An all-white Philadelphia Phillies team won in 1950. The Cardinals, who were slow to sign black players, would not win another pennant until 1964, when a group of talented young blacks—Bob Gibson, Bill White, Curt Flood, and Lou Brock—helped lead the Cards to a World Series victory over the New York Yankees.

STAN MUSIAL: "We finished second in '47, '48, and '49. We weren't far behind, but the Dodgers signed Robinson, Campanella, and Newcombe, three of the best black ballplayers at the time, and that made the difference as far as winning the pennant. If the Dodgers hadn't signed them . . ."

CHAPTER 49

THE SAIGH ERA

JUST before Thanksgiving of 1947, Sam Breadon stunned St. Louis by selling the Cardinals and twenty minor league affiliates to the partnership of two local investors, businessman Fred Saigh and Robert Hannegan, for $3.75 million. Breadon, at the age of seventy, felt ill, and he wanted to choose the new owners, rather than leave that decision to his heirs. He told Saigh he would sell him the team if he could get Breadon's friend, Hannegan, to go in with him.

BOB BROEG: "He wasn't feeling well. He felt the inroads of cancer. At this juncture, he and his wife had a very flimsy marriage, and he didn't want a woman to inherit the club. He had acquired the club from Helene Hathaway Robison Britton back in 1916, who had inherited it after the death of her father and uncle. He also knew there had been a problem with the New York Yankees when Jake Ruppert willed everything to his mistress, and they had to sell the Yankees to meet the inheritance tax, enabling MacPhail, Dan Topping, and Del Webb to get the club cheaply.

"Breadon had about $1 million in profits and $1.1 million in a building fund. And Uncle Sam said, 'Either build the new stadium or declare it out.' And Sam owned 78 percent of the stock.

"Fred Saigh was talking to him about capital gains and about people interested in buying the team, and that's why Saigh brought in Bob Hannegan, who Breadon really loved. Hannegan was Postmaster General at the time. Saigh arranged for Hannegan and himself to own the club. Saigh owned the primary stock, but the idea was for Hannegan to be the president.

"Saigh didn't know it, but Hannegan was dying also. I went to see Breadon in '49, and his neck was real small. He had a cancerous-disc death look going, and he was kind of angry when Hannegan sold out to Saigh after only one year.

"Fred had to explain to him, 'Sam, I gotta do this.' "

Until he bought the Cardinals, Fred Saigh had been an obscure criminal lawyer and a real estate investor. In 1946 he first came into public view when he was a principal in the purchase of two large downtown St. Louis commerical high-rises worth more than $10 million.

When I went to visit him at his Clayton, Missouri, office in the fall of 1997, Fred Saigh was ninety-two years old. Except for some deafness, which made it hard for him to converse on the telephone, the former Cardinal owner was sharp of mind, eloquent, and wistful about his Cardinals days. He owned the Cardinals from 1947 through 1953, when he voluntarily sold the team after he pleaded guilty to income tax evasion. The six years owning the Cards was a joyous period in his life.

When I arrived Saigh was at his desk, studying the Stock Market ticker on his computer. A millionaire many times over, Saigh had made a great deal of money in the market. On the car radio on the way to his office, I had heard that the market had dropped an alarming 500 points that day, one of the worst in history. When I arrived around three-thirty Central Standard time, the market had closed in New York. Saigh welcomed me and never once mentioned what surely had been for him a disastrous and costly day. During my visit, he showed no emotional strain from the steep decline. Perhaps he was confident his stocks would rebound, as they soon did. Everyone else I talked to with investments that day seemed petrified. The man, even in his nineties, seemed to have steel nerves.

FRED SAIGH: "I was born in 1905, and I grew up in Kiwanee, Illinois, about 200 miles from St. Louis. I never played baseball as a boy, but I was very interested in it. Actually, I was a Cubs fan. In those days, you didn't have television or radio, but they posted information on what was going on at the newspaper. We used to go down there and watch what was happening.

"I remember the Black Sox scandal, the men involved, and the trial. They were kicked out of baseball, of course. We had family grocery stores in Illinois. In those days, they had mixed stores, with dry goods on one side and groceries on another and meat on the next. All the stores were that way. In the early 1920s, we sold the stores. My mother had a brother near here, so we decided to come here. I saw Babe Ruth many times here in St. Louis.

"I went to Bradley University, and then I went to work for a lawyer by the name of Sigmund Bass. I studied with him for quite a while before I took the examination. I didn't try many things except divorces and preliminary things. He was a terrific trial lawyer, and I was a young man starting out.

"In the '30s, I went into business. We sold machinery. For instance, we sold the machinery to make caffeine for the Coca-Cola people. I was one of the partners founding a company to make cigarette-vending machines. I sold out, and at the time I started my own company, the war came along. We couldn't get material. I had to abandon it. The people who took the company over from me went into bankruptcy because they couldn't get the material either.

"The first big deal was the purchase of the Railway Exchange Building. The second one was the purchase of the Syndicate Trust Building.

"I first became involved with Mr. Breadon when I went to see him because one of my tenants wanted to build a warehouse. I understood that he had exactly what they wanted, because of the transportation facilities at Soto and Grand. Mr. Breadon owned that property. He was going to build a new ballpark there, but then he got sick. It wasn't known to many people.

"He said he wasn't interested in selling the property, and I started out the door after a few words, and when I got to the door he said, 'Close the door and come back.' He said, 'I notice you're about the only one involved in a large transaction. Would you be interested in the Cardinals?' I said, 'Of course.' He said, 'Do you know that much about baseball?' I said, 'Not in a business way. As a fan I do, because I go to the Cardinals games.'

"He said, 'I understand Bob Hannegan understands a good deal of baseball. If you approach him as a partner, we'll feel more comforable having somebody to run it.' Mr. Breadon was an awfully wonderful gentleman.

"Bob had been a friend of mine for years. He was Postmaster General at the time, and I went to Washington to see Bob. I told him about the deal, and he acquiesced because he wanted to quit anyway. He got 49 percent, and I got 51 percent, but I gave him the authority as CEO. He operated the Cardinals for a little under a year.

"I bought the Cardinals for $3.75 million. I don't discuss that very much, but it's sort of public. The deal involved some assumption of debt. Mr. Breadon gave me the statements of several years, and I saw exactly the condition the team was in. I had a terrific adviser at that time, George Simpkins, and I discussed it with him, and we found a way to buy it. Mr. Breadon and I remained friends until the day he died. He sat in my box when he could come. He was comfortable with the deal, and we never had a word of questioning anything.

"When I first took over, I looked over everything. It was a very well operated club and so were its subsidiaries. They had good managers and good financial men. Actually, there was enough cash in the company that we could use part of it to buy it. It was a great deal.

"Mr. Hannegan ran the operation of the club, and I ran the financial end.

"One of the first people who contacted me after I bought the team was Branch Rickey. I think Branch Rickey was one of the greatest baseball men around. Some people have the idea that he talked to me about bringing Jackie Robinson into baseball, but Robinson actually was in baseball a couple years before I took over. But Rickey did talk to me about wanting to put a black man on the Cardinals, and I'm fairly sure the black man he wanted me to take was Joe Black.

"I said, 'I think we'll be ready for him pretty soon.' But my business came from the South, and I wanted to explore how much effect it would have. One time we took pictures in our park of the cars in the parking lot, and we had people from forty-six states, most of them beside the scattered ones were from Arkansas on down. We had about $300,000 of business from Texas. One of the reasons was that I had Houston, a Double A club, as a farm team.

"Another time Rickey came to see me, wanting to buy a pitcher I had by the name of Pollet. Pollet won 20 games in 1949. Rickey wanted to buy him for $480,000, which was a lot of money at that time. I turned him down because I said I couldn't face the public if I sold Pollet. Well, he won 14 games in '50, and the next year he won 6 games! That's baseball!

"Another time Rickey took me to lunch. He had an idea he wanted to sell his part of the Dodgers and wanted my opinion as to how much I thought it would be worth. I gave him an idea, compared to the worth of my ballclub at the time. About a year later, he sold it.

"After about a year, Bob Hannegan sold out his interest to me. We had an agreement that if he wanted to sell, I had first chance, and if I wanted to sell, he had first chance. He wasn't well. He had had heart trouble for a long time, and he wanted to get his family financially better set than they had been.

"My general manager was Walsingham, Mr. Breadon's nephew. He always wondered why his uncle didn't give him the ballclub. Evidentally, he didn't have enough confidence in him. Bing Devine was in charge of PR. We needed a general manager at Rochester, and Devine took over there and did a very good job. One day he called me and said he wanted to hire Jack Buck as an announcer. I told him, 'Go ahead.'

"The Cardinals announcer was Harry Caray. I fired him about three times. Harry was a great second-guesser, and our manager, Eddie Dyer, would come to me and threaten, 'Either Caray or me!' So I'd fire Caray for a day or two, and they'd kiss and make up, and we'd hire him back. Dyer was touchy about second guessing. The players didn't like it, either. Very few baseball players have a good word for Harry. And I don't think many of the Cubs, either. But he draws people in, business in.

"Greisedieck Beer had hired him, not me, and they paid me for his broadcasting, and even though I would fire him, it was up to them, really. I'd talk to Dyer for a long time, told him not to pay any attention to it. You've heard Harry, haven't you? Couldn't you feel when he was second-guessing?

"I think I became a pretty good baseball man. I don't care who, Walter O'Malley or any of them, they have to depend on experts. I had very excellent scouts, had a good undermanagement. I think we did pretty well. For my part running the club, I think I did a good job."

When Saigh and Hannegan bought the Cardinals in November of 1947, Saigh was unknown. Marty Marion remembered when the new owners first came onto the scene.

MARTY MARION: "I knew who Hannegan was, but I never heard of Saigh. I think Mr. Saigh kind of put the deal together. I remember the first year they owned the ballclub; I got a letter from Hannegan about my contract. He wrote me a nice, long letter. He said, 'We don't dicker. We tell you what we're going to pay you. That's the way we do it in Washington.' And he sent me some ridiculous offer. I just wrote him back a letter with my famous words: 'I ain't gonna play for that.'

"Finally he said, 'We can't do things here like we did in Washington, can we?' "

One of Bob Hannegan and Fred Saigh's first acts as Cardinals owners was to raise Stan Musial's salary. They called Musial in and Hannegan offered him a contract for the 1948 season calling for a $45,000 salary plus $5,000 for every 100,000 fans the team drew over 900,000. Musial countered and received a contract calling for a salary of $50,000 a year and an additional $5,000 if the team passed 900,000 in admissions. Musial should have accepted Hannegan's offer. The team drew 1.4 million fans. Stan would have made $70,000. At that salary, he would have been well worth it. In 1948, a year in which the Cards finished second behind Billy Southworth's Boston Braves, Musial led the league with 230 hits and a .376 batting average, led the league with 131 RBIs and 135 runs scored, led the league in doubles (46) and triples (18), and he finished second in home runs with 39 to Johnny Mize and Ralph Kiner, who hit 40. As a result, he missed winning the prestigious Triple Crown.

STAN MUSIAL: "In '48 I came within one home run of the Triple Crown. I had one home run rained out, actually, and Red Schoendienst reminded me that I hit another ball in Shibe Park in Philadelphia that hit the speakers of the PA system above the fence, and Frank Dascoli called it a two-base hit. Red said it should have been a home run, or else I'd have led the league in everything."

In 1949 the Giants' Danny Gardella and several of the men barred from playing after going to Mexico sued major league baseball. In the suit they challenged the legality of the reserve clause, allowing a team to retain the rights to a player indefinitely. He also asked for compensatory damanges.

The case, filed in New York State, began with a dismissal. The judge refused to overide an illogical (even absurd) ruling in a case brought by the Federal League and decided in the U.S. Supreme Court by Oliver Wendell Holmes, who in 1922 declared that baseball was exempt from antitrust laws because it was not involved in interstate commerce. As a result, Baseball was allowed to do whatever it wanted to do to its players, including blackballing them. In an appeal to the federal court, Gardella's attorney, Fred Johnson, argued that the addition of radio and television had made the game national in scope and thus laid the groundwork for a reversal of the Federal League ruling.

On February 10, 1949, it was announced that by a two-to-one vote, the appeals court would hear the case before a jury. Here was a real challenge to the reserve clause.

But Happy Chandler was working on the other former exiles against Gardella. He suggested to Lanier, Martin, and Mickey Owen that if Gardella dropped his suit, he would drop the lifetime ban and immediately allow them back into the major leagues. The case was scheduled to go to trial in November of 1949.

In the spring of 1949, Gardella, Lanier, and Martin tried to get a judge to order baseball to take them back, but their order was denied. Then on June 5, 1949, Happy Chandler announced an amnesty for all Mexican League jumpers. Max Lanier, Lou Klein, and Fred Martin returned to the Cardinals, where they helped bring the team to within one game of the 1949 pennant.

Gardella's lawyer recommended that he accept an out-of-court settlement. There were good reasons for him to do so. Gardella had made money in Mexico and Canada, but he really wasn't good enough to earn a spot on the Giants. And pursuing the case was costly, and he didn't have much money.

Happy Chandler wanted to settle the case as well. He did not want to risk a decision that just might overturn the Holmes decision and make every player a free agent. Chandler figured it would be easier and cheaper to pay Gardella off. Which is exactly what he did, arranging with Saigh for Gardella to get a tryout with the Cardinals in '50 and paying Gardella more than $60,000, half of which went to his lawyer.

But not all the baseball owners were happy with Chandler's decision. Some, like Fred Saigh, who didn't want to pay Gardella a red cent, insisted on a complete victory. And as a result, it was Saigh, along with Yankees co-owner Del Webb, who was largely responsible for Chandler's ouster as commissioner in 1951.

FRED SAIGH: "I was sitting in the [St. Louis] ballpark watching a ball game when I got a message that Commissioner Chandler wanted to see me in New York. I took a plane and met him around midnight. He wanted me to settle the Mexican cases for him. There were six of them, including Maglie, the great pitcher who stayed in New York; Martin; Lanier. The screwball Gardella, he was a Giant. Chandler said, 'Let's settle. I don't want it to go to trial. It's bad for baseball.' I saw this weak-kneed man.

"On Sunday night, I went to the Sherry-Netherland Hotel. His assistant was lying on the bed, and he said, 'We can't try this thing.' So I called the lawyer for the players, went over, and in a couple of hours I settled it. I told Baseball the amount, and they agreed to it.

"I insist to this day if that case was tried, athletics—all of them—would be in a different situation. Because we had a good atmosphere for a trial.

"I lost all respect for Chandler. I thought he was a weak sister. He would listen to the last guy who he was talking to. O'Malley had a big influence over him. O'Malley wasn't against him. O'Malley came to me in the washroom when we were voting [on whether to renew Chandler's contract.] He said, 'Do you think they have to votes to get rid of him?' I said, 'I think we have.' He said, 'Then I won't vote against him for political reasons.'

"I told Del of the situation and we cooperated in getting Chandler out. I was for the National League, and he was for the American League. But I think I instituted it."

In 1949 the Cardinals benefited greatly from the return of Max Lanier and Fred Martin to the team.

MAX LANIER: "I pitched my first game back in St. Louis against the Dodgers. Newcombe was the pitcher, and I beat him, 1–0. They'd say to me, 'You can't pitch this guy high,' and I would pitch Campanella and Hodges up there, and I was striking them out. I didn't have any trouble with them.

"I enjoyed pitching for Eddie Dyer. When he came to the club in '46, he had said to me, 'Max, you've been here longer than I have. You pitch your own ball game. I ain't telling you how to pitch.' Eddie was a pitcher himself. That's one of the reasons I liked Eddie Dyer a lot.''

The Cardinals had a one and a half game lead over the Brooklyn Dodgers with five games remaining at the end of the 1949 season. The Cards had to play the sixth-place Pittsburgh Pirates twice, and the last-place Cubs three times. With only four games left in the season, Enos Slaughter threw a ball in to Red Schoendienst at second, and it skipped off his thumb, breaking it. His loss proved to be a hardship the Cards couldn't overcome.

The Cards needed to win and the Dodgers to lose for the season to end in a tie. After defeating the Cubs, 13–5, on the final day, the Cards players sat in the clubhouse listening to the end of the Dodger–Philly game. The Dodgers had led 5–0, but then the Phils came back to tie the game at 7–7. When Duke Snider singled to win the game, 9–7 in the tenth inning, and Jackie Robinson made a spectacular catch to save it, Fred Saigh resignedly had to return $1.5 million in World Series orders.

The Cardinals dropped to fifth place in 1950 when first Musial and then catcher Joe Garagiola were injured. Stan hurt his knee rounding first on loose dirt. Garagiola was run over at home plate by a charging Jackie Robinson. His career would never be the same. By early September, the Cards trailed the "Whiz Kid" Philadelphia Phillies by fourteen games. Rather than be fired, Eddie Dyer resigned at the end of the '50 season. Fred Saigh replaced him with Marty Marion, who in '51 finished third behind New York and Brooklyn before he too was fired.

FRED SAIGH: "Marty was awfully nice, but for instance, once when I wanted to make a trade, I couldn't find him. It developed he was at the movies."

MARTY MARION: "Fred said he fired me because I would never visit him up in his front office. I guess I was guilty of that. I thought I'd just run the team. And I would always go home. I'd never go up to the office. And I should have."

Saigh hired one of Leo Durocher's pupils, Eddie Stanky, to manage the team. In addition to his managerial duties, "The Brat," as he was called, also filled in some in the infield. In the spring of 1952, Saigh wanted to make certain that his hitting star, Stan Musial, was happy.

Musial had become a hitting machine on almost the same level as former

Cardinal legend Rogers Hornsby. In '48 Musial had had a near Triple Crown season; in '49 his numbers were .338, 36 homers, 123 RBIs; in '50 he finished .346, 28, and 109, and in '51 he led the league with a .355 average, 124 runs scored, and 12 triples.

When Musial came to spring training in the spring of '52, Saigh put a blank contract down in front of him and told Stan to fill in any amount he felt was fair. The transaction said a great deal about both Musial and Saigh. When Musial wrote in a figure, Saigh was pleased for his star player.

STAN MUSIAL: "I was surprised when he did it. I put in $85,000. I jumped from $50,000 to that number. I had some good years then, especially in '48 and '50. I was winning batting titles in '50 and '51 and '52. And the range of salaries, the top guys, Feller and Williams, were making eighty, eighty-five, ninety. I was being fair. I thought I was in that range."

FRED SAIGH: "I felt Stan was a good, honest guy. We let him know how much the Cardinals were making, and he settled down a good figure. I added that if he did more, he'd get an extra amount, which he did.

"With the figures floating around today, that would be foolhardy. One time not long ago I asked Stanley how much he would be worth now if he was playing. His wife piped in, 'Maybe ten or fifteen million a year.' And she's not too far away. He'd be worth it. If he was a young man coming up today, he'd be worth a hell of a lot of money. So would Red Schoendienst, and Slaughter, and Marty. A couple shortstops the Cards have had since can't hold a glove to Marty. I contend now that they are not playing the baseball that we played in my era."

Fred Saigh loved owning the Cardinals. He loved being able to say that he signed the paychecks for Stan Musial and Red Schoendienst, men who have remained his close friends to this day. But after Saigh's world came crashing to the ground in the spring of 1952, when he was sentenced to fifteen months in a Federal security prison on charges he evaded paying income tax, he no longer could hold his head high, and he decided it would be in the best interest of baseball and of the Cardinals if he sold the team, rather than own it under the cloud of his conviction. In February of 1953, Saigh put the Cardinals up for sale. After receiving solid offers from Milwaukee and Houston, he chose to sell the team to the Anheuser-Busch Brewing Company for around three quarters of a million dollars less than the outside groups were willing to pay. Saigh, who loved his city, thought it more important the Cardinals remain in St. Louis than he make the extra money.

It was because of Fred Saigh that St. Louis fans got to see Bob Gibson, Tim McCarver, Lou Brock, Ozzie Smith, and Mark McGwire. If Saigh had been like Walter O'Malley, Horace Stoneham, Lou Perini, or Arnold Johnson, St. Louis may well be an American League city today, with the Browns the city's darlings and not the Cardinals. If justice were to be served, the Cardinals should erect a statue of Saigh the same way they put up one for Stan Musial.

Had it been any other owner, the rest of Musial's career might well have been played in either Milwaukee or Houston.

The great irony of the story was that when Saigh sold to Anheuser-Busch, he, more than anyone, including Gussie Busch, realized how much the deal would benefit the beer company, and he bought a substantial block of Anheuser-Busch stock. That investment over the years would make Fred Saigh one of the richest men in St. Louis history.

More than forty years after he decided to do the honorable thing and sell the team, Fred Saigh, at the age of ninety-two, found his eyes welling up when he told the story of his divestiture. As a result of a double cross by the judge after a promise made to him in the highest offices of the land that if he pled nolo contendere to the tax charges he would receive no jail time, he ended up going to jail for an unspecified crime not satisfactorily explained to him to this day. He has not gotten over the shame of it, despite the salve of earning hundreds of millions of dollars in the Stock Market. For Fred Saigh held his reputation to be more important than all the money in the world. And it was his reputation that was taken from him.

FRED SAIGH: "I'll tell you what happened. One afternoon an agent by the name of Charles Shrimpfevver, who couldn't have had a two-by-two [for a brain], came to see me. He said, 'We'd like to look at your books and those of the club.' I said, 'You're welcome to it.' He sat there, and I talked to him about the Cardinals, and he kept saying, 'Why couldn't it happen to me? Why couldn't it happen to me?' All afternoon. I didn't feel anything was wrong. I never knew anything was wrong. And then his superior came in. He said, 'We have some figures. We'd like to take them up with you.' I said, 'Go ahead.' He listed a few things. I never did know exactly what it was. I don't to this day.

"Someone had a dagger out for me. I don't know who. I don't. Or they wanted window dressing for a senile judge. Ron Harper was my judge, a young judge, but Harper kissed the ass of his superior—Moore was his name— all the time, a senior judge who was senile.

"The figures they had were preposterous. [In one newspaper account, it said the government was looking into $49,000 in unpaid taxes.] See, [law partner] Bass was always spending more than he made. He had a farm. We would keep exchanging money back and forth. When I had it, I gave it to him. When he had it, he gave it to me. Well, they counted all that as income. I had one woman, Mrs. Shaddock, I got $28,000 for. It was in my account. She said, 'I don't want to take it, because if you give it to me, I'll spend it. Give me so much every month.' Which I did. But they counted that as income. I never knew what else. I just had to assume that they took my bank account and added it up.

"And Breadon accepted a $350,000 loan in the Cardinal purchase as part payment, which we paid off the following year. I made the loan to pay it off. And they counted that as income, too.

"At the time I was indicted, the brother of Cardinal Glenn on St. Louis was indicted, because they found $22 million in his box. The president of Union Electric also was indicted. It was a horrible atmosphere. Finnegan was the prosecuting attorney. If I had been in New York, they would have laughed at him.

"It's hard for you to visualize what was going on in St. Louis at the time. This originated in Washington, probably when Bob Hannegan was with the Internal Revenue Department. He was head of the IRS, and he may have made some enemies there. Our representative at the time made the statement that they started in on Hannegan and then doubled on me. I don't know. I want to be careful with what I say.

"I had an understanding through a great source that I would be fined $15,000 if I pleaded nolo contendere. A lot of people take that as a plea of guilty, but it was a measure given by the founders of the Constitution when there is an area in doubt. We don't consider it that way anymore. A top politician in high places [he led me to believe it was President Truman] told me over the phone that if I pleaded nolo contendere I would be fined $15,000 and receive no jail time. So I did. And [Harper] sentenced me to fifteen months. There was nothing I could do about it. He wouldn't let me change my plea or appeal. They just needed a victim, and they got one. President Truman was furious. He told me he had been double-crossed by Harper.

"[In 1997] they held hearings in Congress about abuse of power in the IRS, and I was going to testify. I wrote something up, but then I decided against it. I don't want to make enemies with the IRS. Those days are over.

"I went to Terre Haute, Indiana, for fifteen months. It wasn't a tough prison. They put me in charge of the legal files. They wanted to thin them, and I did that.

"I was so disgusted, so horrified that after having such a good name in the community that they would do this to me. I just gave up.

"I told Frick I didn't want to embarrass baseball. I said, 'There is nothing you can do to get me out. I just don't want to embarrass baseball.' Like with Steinbrenner of the Yankees. They slapped him on the wrist for something a hell of a lot more serious than what I did.

"When I made it known I wanted to sell the team, I got an offer from Milwaukee and two from the Houston area. Nobody from St. Louis. Finally, Jim Hickock, who was president of First National Bank, and Dave Calhoun, who was president of St. Louis Union Trust, went to Gussie Busch and really had to twist his arm. They bring out that he was a savior, but that was bullshit. The ego of some people is hard to understand. He did not volunteer. No. Hickock and Calhoun went to him and told him Anheuser-Busch should take over the team. They explained to Gussie that it would be a good thing for the city and a good thing for the brewery. We had a couple of meetings. They had to do a good deal of arm twisting. I could have made between $700,000 and $750,000 more. But I wanted to leave the team in the city. The public had been good to me, and I would have felt I would have let them down otherwise. It mattered because I would have had to answer to this fan or that fan: 'Why did you do it?' My reputation was important. I had the public in my mitt. I'll never forget the first year I had the team, after the final game I had the organist play 'Auld Lang Syne,' and tears were in some people's eyes.

"After I sold the team to Anheuser-Busch, Busch and I never got along after that, for some reason. I don't know what to call it: ego or comparison. I don't know, but we didn't get along. They withheld $1 million. When I wanted to buy my car, which was in the Cardinals' name, a company car, they wouldn't let me do it. I said, 'I'll give you full price.' 'No, we want it.' I don't know why. They penny-pinched a dime. I finally just swept it aside. Ego. Gussie for a long time never let it be known that Anheuser-Busch owned the team, not him. It was always Gussie.

"And after I sold the team, I didn't want to go to the damn stadium [Busch Stadium], the new one or the old one, but I would go Brooklyn or the Giants or Chicago. I saw about a half a dozen games in Brooklyn, maybe the same at the Giants before they moved.

"I'll tell you why I bought Anheuser-Busch stock when I sold them the Cardinals. It's a matter of history. Schlitz, the leading beer company in this country, had Cub television and radio, and they lost it. Within two years, you never heard anything of Schlitz. When Anheuser-Busch took over the Cardinals, they were third behind Schlitz and Miller. And I knew it. And I knew baseball was going to make Anheuser-Busch. So that's why I bought the stock."

BOB BROEG: "His buying Anheuser-Busch stock was not part of the sale. But at the time of the sale, Saigh told Jim Hickock he wanted to buy stock. Hickock asked him how many shares. 'Oh, about 25,000 shares.' Shortly thereafter, a woman who had 28,000 shares died, and he said, 'That's all right. Get that.' So he bought those 28,000 shares, and he never bought another share. Before the last division at one juncture he had 1,089,000 shares. The last was a double. If I'm not mistaken, he put in the equivalent of $6 million and earned $60 million. I recently asked him about it. He said, 'I got rid of some, so it's not as dramatic an increase as you might think.' "

CHAPTER 50

GUSSIE

GUSSIE Busch, who took over the presidency of the Anheuser-Busch Brewing Company when his brother Adolphus died in 1949, was a larger-than-life fixture on the St. Louis landscape for more than seventy years. He was immensely wealthy. In 1947 his $132,222–a-year salary made him the highest-paid executive in the city. The value of his stock and real estate holdings was valued in the many millions of dollars.

His 281-acre palatial home, called Grant's Farm, once the homestead of the former general and President, had been built by his grandfather. Gussie, who loved to hunt and fish, surrounded this Gothic mansion with a zoo and a hunting preserve on which herds of wild animals roamed.

Busch, a sybarite, threw the wildest and showiest parties in town. He could be seen wearing a Tyrolean costume or lederhosen while turning a pig on a spit during a party for his closest 200 friends. And always he would serve huge vats of beer, Budweiser beer. He would never drink beer made by a competitor, and you better not either.

He was larger than life. In their book *Under the Influence*, Peter Hernan and Terry Ganey described Gussie Busch as a man whose daughter once toasted him as "the greatest stud of them all." Cardinals broadcaster Harry Caray, who was one of Busch's favorites for many years, greatly enjoyed his boss's company.

HARRY CARAY: "Gussie Busch was my kind of guy, what I call a booze-and-broads man. He liked to have a drink, appreciate the qualities of a beautiful woman, tell a few stories, and play a few hands of cards. No pretense. No bull. For all his money and prominence—which [was] considerable, Gussie has always been a basic, down-to-earth person."

He was also "tyrannical, profane, prolific, shrewd, a vindictive bully, a brawler, a hard drinker, a superb rider, a teller of tall tales, one of the giants of the profession. He changed the history of brewing."

Gussie Busch was the great-grandson of Adolphus Busch, cofounder along with Eberhard Anheuser in 1865 of the landmark St. Louis firm. Adolphus, the son of a Bavarian innkeeper and land baron, had emigrated to America in 1848 to escape the Prussian invasion and had settled in St. Louis, which was virtually a German colony and where his older brother, John, had established a brewery. St. Louis not only had an excellent water supply for beer, but it also had caves in which to store and age the beer at temperatures below 50 degrees.

When Adolphus came to the city, he began selling brewing supplies. One of his customers was Anheuser, who had acquired a beer plant called the Bavarian Brewery. Anheuser was struggling at the time they met. Adolphus began dating Eberhard's daughter, Lilly, and three days after Lincoln was inaugurated in March of 1861, they were married. Adolphus was twenty-two, Lilly sixteen.

In 1865 the twenty-six–year-old Adolphus bought half interest in the Bavarian Brewery from Anheuser's partner William D'Oench. That year the brewery turned out 4,000 barrels a year. By the end of the century, it would become a million barrels a year.

Anheuser made beer inferior to that of competitors, but the company did well because Adolphus was a dedicated supersalesman. He knew all the tricks, ruses, and illegalities of beer salesmanship, including bribes to tavern owners to sell his beer exclusively and sending agents to taverns to buy beer on the house. Sales of St. Louis Lager Beer soared.

As immigrants flooded into St. Louis, they provided cheap labor and thirsty customers for their product. As new railroads were built and Indians were tamed in the West, markets expanded in all directions.

Adolphus continued traveling back to Germany in an attempt to learn the secrets of brewing a better beer. In 1862 he learned of the discoveries of Louis Pasteur and began pasteurizing his beer four years before Pasteur published his book on the process.

Pasteurization revolutionized the beer business because it meant that beer could be bottled and preserved for longer periods without deterioration. A brewery could ship its beer long distances and it would still be fresh. By 1877 St. Louis Lager Beer could be purchased in saloons and restaurants all over the world.

In 1879 the name of the firm was changed to Anheuser-Busch Brewing Association, and the Anheuser-Busch brewery became a major showplace in St. Louis. Six guides gave tours. Adolphus had 3,500 employees in the main brewery, 1,500 others in the forty-two branches.

Adolphus Busch died on May 2, 1880, after developing a throat tumor. His stock was left to his children. August Anheuser Busch, who was fifteen at the time his father died, would over the years buy up as many shares as he could and push the Anheusers out of the company.

It was August who began selling Budweiser-brand beer, made with its special process. The famed beer was first discovered by a man named Carl Conrad, who ran across it in Busweis, Germany, while traveling with a friend. The beer was aged by a special Pilsener process, using special artesian well water drawn through sandstone rock. It was laced with specially selected malt, at the right moment spiced with a special hop, and aged in the cool rocky cellars, waiting for carbonation to produce a frothy head and pale color all Bud aficionados have come to recognize.

Carl Conrad first registered the Budweiser name in the United States. Under contract, Anheuser-Busch began producing the brand under the name Conrad's Budweiser Beer. When Conrad went bankrupt in 1882, he had a debt of $300,000, including $94,000 owed to the Anheuser-Busch Brewing Association. In exchange for the rights to the name and the formula, August Busch gave Conrad a lifetime job.

Between 1870 and 1900, the population of the United States swelled from 39 million to 76 million, and many of those immigrants were German. August Busch became fabulously wealthy when many of those millions of newcomers enjoyed his beer.

August began building lavish estates around the country. He built them in St. Louis; Pasadena, California; Cooperstown, New York; and in Bad Schwalbach, Germany.

The estate in St. Louis was called One Busch Place. It was on the brewery property, and it had antiques, expensive paintings, a wine cellar, and a stable of thirty horses with drivers and stablemen. When the train pulled in at One Busch Place, a cannon at the brewery would fire to salute August Busch's arrival.

August would spend summers in Pasadena, where he hosted industrialists Andrew Carnegie and J. P. Morgan and the banker Russell Sage. He spent early summer in Cooperstown, the center for the finest hops in America, and in the fall traveled to his 1,200–acre estate in Germany, where the Kaiser would visit him.

August's most bitter fight began in 1890 when a woman named Carrie Nation burst into a saloon in Medicine Hat, Kansas, and started chopping it up with an axe. In conjunction with the Christian fundamentalist movement, Nation and other women prohibitionists equated beer drinking with sin and vowed to eradicate it.

Because August Busch's Germanic presence and wealth alienated many Americans, he became for many the symbol of the beer empires and became a prime target of the prohibitionists. Busch, who despised organized religion and resented those who spearheaded the prohibitionist movement, fought back with equal viciousness. Busch told his friend Charles Nagel, at one time the Secretary of Commerce and Industry under William Howard Taft, "A great many people are religious or select a certain creed not because they believe in it but because it pays them better. . . . Many Americans put up their religious flag to promote their business and social standing. Religion proper is a secondary matter."

He added, "Another bad trait in the American's character is hypocrisy. He recommends and speaks for prohibition and downs the manufacturers of all liquor while, at the same time he drinks like a fish and becomes as drunk as a fool."

At the turn of the century, beer sales to German and Irish immigrants grew even more dramatically, and as a result the prohibition movement became an antiforeigner crusade as well. When women gained the right to vote in 1920, the movement grew stronger.

Busch had significant political clout and used it. He tried to keep President McKinley from supporting the prohibitionists, and he courted both Theodore Roosevelt and William Howard Taft, frequent visitors to his homes in St. Louis and Pasadena. But he could not find a national figure to speak out against prohibition. Teddy Roosevelt avoided the issue. In 1908 Busch supported Taft against William Jennings Bryan, a religious zealot who went so far as to compare saloons to slaughterhouses.

In 1910 Taft betrayed Busch when he made a speech advocating total abstinence. Wrote Busch to the President, "Let every man do as he pleases. No one on earth has the right to mix up with the personal freedom of another."

In 1911 August and Lilly celebrated their fiftieth anniversary in style. August gave each of his six children a mansion as a present. He gave Lilly a $200,000 gold tiara. He spent a fortune entertaining in a very public way.

August wanted to give his eldest son, August A., his home at One Busch Plaza, but August A. said he wanted to build his own home instead and he built the castle on Grant's Farm. August paid for it all.

To the temperance people, such displays of wealth earned from the sale of "the devil's brew" were galling and offensive.

Prohibition forces, meanwhile, were gaining in Congress. In 1911 Teddy Roosevelt mounted a third-party campaign to unseat Taft. The result was the election of Woodrow Wilson, whom Augustus (wrongly) suspected of being a prohibitionist. August's last hurrah came in 1913, when he got Taft to veto the Webb–Kenyon Bill that would have outlawed the transportation of alcohol into dry states. On October 13, 1913, August Busch died in his sleep. His estate was divided into eight shares. August A. got two, Lilly one, and each of his five daughters one. August A. received control of the brewery, a railroad, a diesel engine company, and bottling companies.

When World War I broke out, August A. and his wife were summering in Germany. Early in the war, the Busches supported the Kaiser. But when a U-boat sank the *Luisitania* in 1915 and 128 Americans died, anti-German fever broke out. Canadians and Americans began boycotting the German-labeled Busch beer.

By 1917 the Busches were forced to cut all ties to Germany. To prove his patriotism, August A. offered to build submarine engines for the U.S. military. When war was declared on Germany on April 6, 1917, August A. wrote to President Wilson, pledging loyalty to the United States. But with the start of the war, the prohibitionists now had the argument of wartime rationing to say it was wasteful of natural resources to produce alcoholic beverages. In September of 1917, a law was passed outlawing the production of distilled liquors. Beer production was cut 30 percent and eliminated altogether by the fall of 1918. By 1918 the plants had to close altogether because of wartime restrictions.

August A. did everything he could to combat whispers by a prohibitionist minister he was secretly supporting the Kaiser. He even took the double eagle off the Budweiser label. The attacks continued relentlessly. He was pilloried for buying German war bonds, even though they had been bought two years before America went to war and the sale had been sanctioned by the U.S. government. When it turned out the money was used to buy a paper dedicated to German propaganda, the whole affair was very embarrassing to the Busches and the entire beer industry.

In January of 1920, prohibition was passed. The vote was quick. President Wilson vetoed it, but he was overridden. Wilson lashed out at the hypocrites, but to no avail.

August A. Busch didn't know what to do. He was fifty-five, Prohibition was upon the land, and he was in big trouble.

August A. tried selling alternate products. He produced a soft drink called Bevo, another called Kicko, and a third called Buschtee in a lime-green bottle aimed at women. There was Caffo, a coffee-flavored beverage. All failed to catch on.

Budweiser continued as a near-beer. Imbibers, however, preferred Al Capone's hard stuff: rotgut booze, bathtub gin, and moonshine.

August A. had five children: Adolphus, Augustus, and three daughters. Adolphus, although shy and reserved, was a playboy. He had a lot of girlfriends in the theater crowd. He married Florence Parker, a divorcée ten years older than he. She was 31, a mother of three, and the marriage was made for scandal. Each had a drinking problem, and they would fight. When they divorced in 1930, the papers had a field day. Two months later, Adolphus married another divorcée, Catherine Bower, from a wealthy Texas family.

When August A. needed important work done, he didn't send Adolphus but rather his second son, Augustus, known as Gussie, who was proving himself a dedicated, inventive beer man. Gussie, a fearless man with a bad temper, was used to getting his way.

August A. determined that if Anheuser-Busch couldn't sell beer during Prohibition, it could keep afloat by selling the products that were needed to make it. To survive, August A. determined that Anheuser-Busch would have to get in bed with the one man powerful enough to continue to make beer: the gangster Al Capone, who controlled half a dozen breweries in Chicago. August A. sent Gussie to meet with Capone in Miami, where the mob boss lived at Palm Island. Capone offered a deal: Don't ask questions, and I'll guarantee sales for your yeast and sugar products. Gussie took the deal. During Prohibition, Busch sold malt syrup, which made a superior home brew, to Capone.

Gussie Busch once confided, "We ended up as the biggest bootlegging supply house in the United States. Every goddamn thing you could think of. Oh, the malt syrup cookies! You could no more eat the malt syrup cookies. They were so bitter. . . . It damn near broke Daddy's heart."

They also began selling yeast in 1927. Succeeding against the Fleishmann monopoly may have been August A.'s greatest achievement. The yeast and syrup business accounted for a third of the company's sales.

According to Gussie's daughter, Lotsie, "Daddy made the brewery a fortune."

As an aside, the deal also enabled Gussie to buy his booze from Capone, whose bootleggers delivered to his house.

Prohibition continued under Calvin Coolidge and Herbert Hoover, but the fervor was beginning to wane and the opposition was beginning to grow. When Al Smith ran against Hoover on an end-Prohibition ticket in 1928, anti-Catholic sentiment, not prohibitionist feeling, defeated him. When Hoover threw out the first ball in Washington for the 1928 baseball season, fans shouted, "Beer, beer, we want beer."

The Stock Market crashed in 1929. In May of 1931, August A. suggested that allowing the sale of beer would be a quick way to alleviate the doldrums of the Depression. He claimed it would put 1.1 million Americans to work, that it would create a large market for grain, it would increase business for the railroads, and the government would save the $50 million spent annually to police Prohibition. It would, moreover, add $550 million in tax money it had lost by outlawing the sale of beer.

By 1932, Prohibition was on the way out as Franklin Roosevelt campaigned for repeal. Hoover pledged to continue it, but Roosevelt swamped him in the election. Nine days after his election, Roosevelt recommended the return of beer.

Anheuser-Busch spent $7 million renovating the plant. Gussie was in charge of the renovation. August A. was sixty-seven and in failing health as his heart problems became more severe.

In 1932 Charles Nagel suggested to the board of Anheuser-Busch that the company buy six high-stepping Clydesdale horses to pull a red-and-yellow beer wagon for advertising purposes. Gussie went to the Kansas City stockyards and bought sixteen of them, and at the cost of $10,000 he built the beer wagon.

Two days before beer was declared legal again, the thirty-four–year-old Gussie hitched up two teams of Clydesdales and paraded them in front of his father. The demonstration brought tears to the eyes of the old man.

Prohibition ended on April 7, 1933. The celebration was greater than that for Charles Lindbergh or for the armistice of the Great War. The CBS radio network nationally broadcasted the ceremonies at the Anheuser-Busch plant in St. Louis, where a band played "Happy Days Are Here Again," and at the Pabst and Schlitz plants in Chicago and Milwaukee.

There had been 1,392 breweries in operation in 1914. At Prohibition's end, there were only 164. Under August A. Busch, Anheuser-Busch had survived.

When Anheuser-Busch began selling Budweiser again, many customers complained about the taste. After thirteen years of drinking sweet concoctions of bootleg liquor and soda, the public wasn't used to it. But August A. refused to emend the formula. He knew it was right and that the public would return. He even foresaw that the sales of Budweiser would one day outstrip the company's ability to make it. He predicted that one day someone would want to make it faster, but warned against it.

"That we will never do," August A. proclaimed. Gussie never forgot the moment.

In February of 1934, August A. Busch suffered from terrible chest pains. He had trouble breathing and collapsed on his bed. He awoke at five in the morning, clutching his chest. After writing a message—GOODBYE, PRECIOUS MAMA AND ADORABLE CHILDREN—August A. Busch took a police special from the nightstand and shot himself in the left temple. He died immediately.

At the time Adolphus III, Gussie's older brother, was forty-two, and Gussie was a couple years younger. The voting power of August A.'s stock was left to Adolphus III. Gussie had been an important force working with his father, but he would have to wait his turn before taking over the company.

During World War II, Gussie, sensitive to his German heritage, made certain everyone knew where his loyalties lay. He headed the St. Louis Brewers' Victory Committee, checking for enemy aliens, sponsoring blackout drills, heading defense bond sales and Red Cross war relief drives.

Forty-three years old when he joined the Army, he went to Washington, where he used his position to sell beer in Army camps in the South after Congress in 1941 killed bills prohibiting the sale of beer to servicemen. By 1944, 16.4 percent of Anheuser-Busch's output was to servicemen.

Gussie spent much of his military life chasing women. He once reminisced about himself and a friend, "Jack Pickens was in the service with me. We used to smell powder together—that is, women's face powder."

He and his second wife, Elizabeth, who had been the wife of a good friend when they first met, fought bitterly. They had married in 1933, but it was not a happy marriage. She drank heavily. He stayed away from home and played around. By 1939, the marriage was in trouble. The joke was that during the war Gussie did his fighting at home. Sometime between 1943 and 1945, they separated.

When older brother Adolphus died on August 29, 1946, Pabst was the number-one brewery, outselling Anheuser-Busch for the first time since the end of Prohibition. In 1947, in fact, Anheuser-Busch ranked fourth, and in 1953 it ranked second.

Gussie Busch's purchase of the St. Louis Cardinals that year would change all that. As Fred Saigh brilliantly anticipated, Anheuser-Busch, led by Gussie Busch, through its affiliation and identification with the St. Louis Cardinals, would go through a period of growth unparalleled in its history as the popularity of its Budweiser beer skyrocketed.

The decision to buy the Cardinals had been a beer decision, not a baseball one. At the press conference announcing the purchase of the team by Anheuser-Busch, Busch told reporters, "I am going at this from the sports angle and not as a sales weapon for Budweiser beer." He also said he wasn't bothered that a rival beer company, Greisedieck Bros., was sponsoring the team. This was public relations drivel to make it appear he had bought the team in the spirit of civic pride. Nothing could have been further from the truth, which was that Gussie Busch, who had never been a baseball fan, thought the game "dull." As he described it, "There's a lot of standing around."

When Mr. Busch spoke before the Anheuser-Busch board of directors he revealed his real motives. He predicted to his directors, "Development of the Cardinals will have untold value for our company. This is one of the finest moves in the history of Anheuser-Busch."

The first time Gussie Busch toured Sportsman's Park, he was appalled at how small and decrepit it seemed. He demanded that the landlord, Bill Veeck, fix it up. "I'm ashamed to bring my friends out here," said Busch. When Veeck said he had no money to do anything, Busch bought the ballpark from Veeck and cleaned it up himself. More importantly, buying the park also enabled him to control the advertising inside Sportsman's Park. According to Bob Broeg, one of his first orders was to remove all ads from the walls of the stadium. As the crass Busch put it, "Get that crap off the walls."

Busch, ever the pitchman, at first thought it "natural" to rename the park Budweiser Stadium, a naming which met with dismay and derision from Protestant church groups. At first Busch refused to back down, but when someone asked how he would feel if the Cubs renamed their park Juicy Fruit Stadium or Doublemint Stadium, Busch admitted his mistake and the next day switched to Busch Memorial Stadium in honor of his father, grandfather, and late brother.

As owner of both the brewery and the ballpark, Gussie could make sure there was an incessant drumbeat of Budweiser advertising and promotion at Cardinals games.

Gussie took down all other advertising and devoted all the ad spaces at Busch Stadium to selling his beer. During every game, he made sure the catchy Budweiser theme song was played. On special days, he trotted out the Clydesdales and the colorful beer wagon and had it ridden around the park. Starting in 1954, he also made sure that radio personality Harry Caray—a dedicated Budweiser consumer and the finest pitchman of beer in the history of the business ("Buy Bud, the King of Beers.") and the game—let everyone within earshot know that Budweiser was the breakfast, lunch, and dinner of champions. And within four years of buying the team, Anheuser-Busch became the number-one brewery in America. And it hasn't lost its crown yet.

As a beer baron, Gussie Busch had no equal. Busch was an expert, perhaps a genius, when it came to brewing and selling beer. He led Anheuser-Busch autocratically and by fiat. His decisions, though frequently off the cuff, usually were sound if not farsighted.

But if St. Louis fans felt Gussie Busch's confidence that he could do for the Cardinal ballclub what he knew he could do for the beer company, for many years they would be disappointed. When Gussie Busch used those same dictatorial powers to run the St. Louis Cardinals, often his moves proved disastrous. Like many baseball owners, Busch was convinced that because he could successfully run one business he could also run a baseball team.

For the first years of his ownership, Gussie Busch took a hands-on approach to running a business he knew absolutely nothing about. Usually he would allow the men he appointed to do his job. But in baseball "usually" is often far too little. During the early years of his reign, he would personally order untalented players to be bought, make a disastrous hiring of a general manager after listening to a so-called expert who had caught his ear, and hired one manager who broke the spirit of the team because he liked the way he had behaved when he was traded as a player. And too often, after hiring the right people, in a fit of impatience he would fire them when things weren't going well.

Not until he hired a talented general manager, Bing Devine, did the Cardinals win a pennant—after eleven years of ownership. But even with that pennant on the horizon, Gussie Busch's impatience would hurt the team when he prematurely and unwisely fired Devine, prompting Devine's close friend and hand-picked manager, Johnny Keane, to quit the Cardinals after winning the first Card pennant in eighteen years and a World Series. Worse, after letting Devine assemble the right pieces to mold a winning ballclub, Gussie Busch submarined those efforts by ordering certain players traded because of personal pique directly at those players. Some of those moves, like Gussie's imperious banishment of future Hall of Fame pitcher Steve Carlton and the trading away of pitcher Jerry Reuss because of his facial hair, would hurt the Cardinals for decades.

It would take Gussie Busch almost thirty years before he would trust someone enough to let him handle the hiring and trading of players without interference. Until then, Cardinal fans would have to be satisfied with enjoying short stretches of greatness while enduring long periods of suffering and frustration. Meanwhile, if they needed to drown their sorrows, Cards fans knew they could always count on the great taste of Budweiser.

CHAPTER 51

EARLY INTEGRATION

AFTER Gussie Busch bought the Cardinals, he called in manager Eddie Stanky for a meeting with the board of directors. Busch, who figured it would be a simple task to go out and buy a championship, said to Stanky, "Tell us what you need, and we'll get it for you."

Busch asked Stanky what he needed. Stanky said a hard-hitting first baseman would be nice. "Who's the best first baseman in baseball?" Busch asked. Stanky said probably Gil Hodges of the Dodgers. "Get him," Busch said. "What will it cost us?" Stanky said that it would be in excess of $100,000.

John Wilson, the executive vice president of Anheuser-Busch and the man who pushed Busch to buy the team, was at the meeting. Said Wilson, "We all fell on the floor. It was our first experience with the costs of baseball. That was modest against salaries of today and costs of the future, but it stopped us. Gussie asked Stanky, "What else does Mr. Hodges do besides play first base for $100,000?" Stanky explained his talents but also added he was probably unavailable. "The Dodgers liked him, too," understated Wilson.

When Busch offered New York Giants' owner Horace Stoneham $1 million for Willie Mays, Busch was astounded when he was turned down. He tried buying Ernie Banks from the Cubs, but that didn't get him anywhere, either.

Busch then ordered the Cards organization to "go out and find our own players." Led by Mr. Busch himself, initial efforts proved less than spectacular. Al Fleishman, Busch's right-hand man, recalled the details.

AL FLEISHMAN: "We bought three players for $100,000 apiece. One of them was Memo Luna from Mexico. They were so happy, celebrating that he had been purchased by the St. Louis Cardinals that he pitched a doubleheader that night in Mexico, and he never pitched a whole game after that.

"The second player was [good field, no-hit minor league shortstop] Alex Grammas [acquired in a trade with the Cincinnati Reds], and we bought a third player, Tom Alston, a Negro first baseman from the San Diego Padres [then a Triple A team in the Pacific Coast League].

"Mr. Busch visited with the San Diego Padres in Los Angeles. We were looking for a first baseman, and they had a first baseman, and they sold a first baseman to him. Mr. Busch had no reservation about black players. Mr. Busch felt that baseball was an American game, and that he didn't know any reason why there should be any restrictions anymore."

The Cardinals finally were going to break their own color barrier, six years after Jackie Robinson, but Gussie Busch wasn't the careful calculator that

Branch Rickey had been with the Dodgers. Instead, he was desperate to find talent, and he didn't have the patience or the knowledge to scout and sign players. Nevertheless, he scouted and signed Alston.

Alston's numbers weren't bad. He hit .297, with 23 home runs and 101 RBIs for San Diego in 1953. He arrived for spring training in 1954 with a sore back and high expectations. Said manager Eddie Stanky, "I think we have a real player in this colored boy." Early in the season, Alston hit two home runs on consecutive days, but by July was exiled to Rochester. He played twenty-five games over the next three years, then was gone.

RED SCHOENDIENST: "Mr. Busch knew the Cardinals needed to have black players, and some scout had recommended Alston, but he just didn't have the experience he needed to play at the major league level. He was a good guy, and he worked hard and tried to learn everything possible, but the ability just wasn't there."

BING DEVINE: "Tom Alston was acquired before I had anything to do with it. On Mr. Busch's direction, the Cardinals had to begin to add black players, and Alston, to my knowledge, was the first. To show they were going about the same direction, they acquired a player from Mexico by the name of Memo Luna.

"Tom Alston didn't work out. He had a lot of problems, most of which I can't be specific about, except to say he was troubled. I was never sure whether the pressure of being the first black player and having something written about him may have been troubling him; in other words, he may have thought he had to meet certain standards and play a certain way, and it put pressure on him and got to him.

"Some time after he quit playing, he was accused in a church burning, an arson case in Carolina. I don't know what happened to him. My best word, to go back to what I said previously, was 'troubled.' "

BOB BROEG: "The man was, I'm sure, mentally disturbed, and it had a physical effect. In other words, it was as if the bat was swinging him, rather than him swinging the bat. He was lanky and lean, and he could run like hell, a hell of a fielder. If he could have hit at all, he would have made it, but he just wasn't ready.

"Fred Hutchinson was managing the club around '56 or '57, and Busch would badger him about giving Alston another chance, so belatedly in spring training he assigned Alston to go over to Vero Beach by bus for a trip, and Tom forgot to bring his baseball pants. Well, he couldn't play, because he was so much taller than anyone else. When Hutch got back, he explained to Busch what happened. Busch said something, and Hutch said, 'Mr. Busch, if you want a clown, why don't you get Emmett Kelly?' "

Tom Alston was the lone black on the Cardinals in 1954 until pitcher Brooks Lawrence was promoted from Columbus in the American Association in June of that year. Lawrence, unlike Alston, was an immediate sensation.

When he first came up, manager Eddie Stanky pitched him, it seemed, almost every day, either as a starter or in relief. He finished the season with a 15-6 record and a 3.74 ERA. But Lawrence was given little emotional support. A college attendee, Lawrence was very intelligent and well read. He particularly enjoyed reading the novels of Ernest Hemingway. "I got the reputation that I could read a line or two," he said. He became friends with author James T. Farrell, who once knew the Black Sox players and wrote a book about them as well as his most famous tome, *Studs Lonigan*. Farrell was so taken with Lawrence's breadth of knowledge that he brought him to the New York headquarters of "The $64,000 Question" to be a contestant. At the audition Lawrence was asked to recite "Captain, My Captain" by James Whitcomb Riley. He did. They gave him a list of questions to study, but when his February appearance date came, Lawrence decided it would be best to report to spring training instead.

A thinker, Lawrence felt things deeply. He had suffered the slings and arrows of racial prejudice all his life and had learned the best way to get along was to stay out of everyone's way. As a result, because he played ball in a social climate that called for him to be invisible in a white world, he spent much of his time on the road by himself.

Lawrence once told a white sportswriter, "Being a Negro is an interesting life. Every morning I wake up with a challenge staring me in the face."

BROOKS LAWRENCE: "I grew up in Springfield, Ohio. I wasn't allowed to play high school ball. I had to play around town in the sandlot league. At the time, 1942, 1943, the black kids could play basketball, football, and track, but we weren't allowed to play baseball. The baseball coach, Russell Paul, didn't want us to play.

"There were a bunch of us black kids around town who used to laugh at the white kids playing ball. We said we could beat them. And we kept that up, kept that up, until the coach demanded that we come out and beat his club or shut up. So we went out there, and I pitched, and we beat them.

"This was my senior year. The season was over, and the state track meet was coming up. I was on the track team. I was doing the running broad jump— the long jump now—and I was going to the state meet. I wasn't allowed to participate in two sports, and Russell Paul said if the baseball team got to the second game of the state tournament, he wanted me to pitch. Therefore, technically, I was on the ballclub. I got to take my picture with the baseball team. But the team lost, and I didn't get to pitch."

In high school Lawrence took a course in foundry work. The assumption was that he, like many of his classmates white and black, would go to work there. During his junior and senior years at Springfield South High School, he would work one month in the foundry and spend the next one at school. When he graduated in 1943, he went into the Army. "It was the only place you could go," says Lawrence. For basic training, he was sent to Biloxi, Mississippi. "What was it like?" he asks. "Like you think it was. We weren't even allowed to go downtown and stand on the corner."

BROOKS LAWRENCE
(Courtesy Brace Photo)

The black soldiers could not go to the white sections of town. They could shop if they needed to buy something, but they could not eat in the restaurants, which were reserved for whites.

Lawrence joined the Army engineers. He was sent to Guam, where he drove a road grater.

BROOKS LAWRENCE: "We were completely segregated. You had a black Army, and you had a white Army, and never the twain shall meet, except when we played ball. That was one thing that wasn't segregated. It was everybody against everybody else. I pitched for my company."

Lawrence's outfit, based on the upper end of Guam, was building North Field, the airstrip from which the *Enola Gay* left to drop the first atomic bomb on Hiroshima on August 6, 1945. In September Lawrence left the Army and returned home to work in the foundry. Playing baseball for a living was not something he thought much about. He had a wife and a child to support. It was only after Jackie Robinson signed with the Dodgers in 1946 and after several years of backbreaking foundry work that he entertained thoughts of playing baseball for pay.

BROOKS LAWRENCE: "Working in the foundry was always tough. We were pouring shoots every afternoon. We were building engine blocks for battleships. Each day we had to go into an area like a Quonset hut after the mold was complete, and you had to clean all off all the dirt. They'd roll this huge motor in there, and you would take a helmet and put it over your head, and you'd blow all the dirt off the motor. And nobody could stay in there too long because you were bound to get dirt in your lungs.

"When Jackie Robinson signed, I followed him. Not closely, because in a small town like Springfield they didn't follow much of anything. But it had an impact because we were wildly excited about the fact that a black man was going to play baseball. But I was still working in the foundry, so I ain't got too much time to worry about that, because I have a wife and son to bring up.

"I had dreams like everybody else. But dreaming about playing major league baseball wasn't in the forefront. But then some strange things happened: I got tired of working at the foundry. I thought, 'There has to be something better in life than this.'

"I was eligible for the G.I. Bill of Rights, so I went to my track coach in high school and asked him if he could get me into Miami [of Ohio] University. He did, and that was in '48, when the Jackie Robinson thing was going really strong. And I got to thinking, 'If he can do it, I can do it.' After two years at Miami, I signed with the Cleveland Indians."

Brooks Lawrence believes he is the only black player to have been a member of teams at every level of the minor leagues, going from D ball all the way to Triple A. It was a five-year journey to the major leagues.

BROOKS LAWRENCE: "I began in 1949 in Zanesville, Ohio, in the Ohio–Indiana League. I was the only black person in the league. It wasn't that hard on me, because you don't have a very big audience. Not that many people cared about it. The towns were all small. You would hear things, but no one tried to do anything to you or make it tough for you. As a matter of fact, when we played in Springfield, which was in the league, our players would come over to my mother's house to eat.

"I wasn't impacted that much by color because I had gone to an integrated high school. I spent all my time growing up on white teams. You learn real quick what you can do under the circumstances. I found it easiest to stay by myself."

Lawrence played for various teams in the Northeast, including Harrisburg, Wilkes-Barre, and Reading in Pennsylvania, Pittsfield, Massachusetts, and Portsmouth, Virginia. At Portsmouth his intention was to finish out the season and quit. He had given himself five years, and his time was up. He was at his parents' home mulling whether to go back to the foundry, work with his father in construction, or get a job at the post office when he received the phone call that changed his life.

BROOKS LAWRENCE: "My mom said, 'Brooksie, there's a phone call for you. I don't know what the man is talking about.' He was the owner of the Caguas–

Guayama team in the Puerto Rican winter league. Mickey Owen had been managing Norfolk in the Piedmont League, and he saw me pitch, and he asked the Caguas owner to bring me down there. Later on I heard that the owner said to Mickey, 'No Class B pitcher can win in this league.' But Mickey said he thought I could. So I went down there and won 13 games. On that team we had Bob Buhl, Ray Crone, Rance Pless, Dale Long, Hank Aaron, Felix Mantilla, and Jim Rivera. Mostly Braves. That was the Braves connection down there. Henry had gone down there to learn how to play right field.

"In that particular year, we won everything."

Lawrence was signed to a contract with independent Oklahoma City in Double A in the Texas League. Owen warned the Reds that if Lawrence wasn't brought to the majors, he would be drafted by another team. When the Reds didn't buy him, he was drafted by the Columbus Redbirds in the American Association. His manager was Johnny Keane.

BROOKS LAWRENCE: "Columbus was only thirty-five miles from Springfield. It was wonderful. I could come back and forth home. I didn't have to ride all those buses anymore. The farther you went up, the better it got. But the situation as far as the players were concerned, it got a little more testy in a lot of places. Owen Friend hit a ball to the first baseman, and I went over to cover first, and he intentionally spiked me in the leg. He stepped on the back of my heel.

"My roommate was Bill Greason. Again, there were only one or two (blacks) on a ballclub, and generally one good one. Greason is now a minister in Birmingham, Alabama. They called him up to St. Louis before they called me. St. Louis was taking any good pitchers they could find. He went up there and stayed a week at the most, maybe ten days. They hit him like he stole something, they beat on the ball so bad. So they sent him back and took me and a (white) pitcher from Cincinnati named Ralph Beard. He didn't last either. They didn't play fair with him. We joined the Cardinals on June 23 or 24, and when we got there it was raining. When we stepped off the plane, Eddie Stanky told me, 'You're pitching today.' That day it rained. I pitched the next day, the last game of the series against the Pirates, and I won. Ralph was going to pitch the next day, the first game against Cincinnati. Can you imagine the trauma of pitching the first game in the major leagues in your hometown? And against a ballclub that could hit the daylights out of the ball like the Reds? Well, that's what they did. And it made it tough on him. He never won a game.

"I don't think my year in '54 has ever been matched. I was 15-6 with the Cardinals after being 6-4 with Columbus. I was 21-10. But nobody talks about it. In the first thirty days, I pitched in nine ball games. I won seven and lost two. Then there were times I pitched three and four days in a row, starting and relieving.

"I don't want to say anything negative about Eddie Stanky, but Bob Broeg once asked him, 'Aren't you afraid that you'll hurt a pitcher using him like that?' And Stanky reportedly replied to him, 'I didn't know you could hurt one of them.' If I told you how I was used, no one would believe me. I might start today and pitch in relief tomorrow and go nine the next day. That happened. Sure did. But Stanky was still better than the turkey who followed him [manager Harry Walker].

"My roommate was Tom Alston. I roomed with him as soon as I got there. We lived together in St. Louis. We stayed with a lady there, Mrs. Green. We never went more than five blocks from the house. We never went across. We almost never went downtown. So Tom never had any problems as far as being black was concerned.

"Tom had a weakness as a hitter. And any time you have one weakness, you have two. And they found that out. He couldn't handle a ball close to him. But he could murder the pitch outside. But after they pitch you inside long enough and back you off the plate, then the outside becomes your weakness. So between the two of them, he got in a lot of trouble.

"Tom had the problem that because the Cards paid so much money for him, he thought he had to live up to the price. When he couldn't, it broke him. I worried him to death. In rooming with Tom, I would wake up some nights and hear him praying. He'd be saying, 'I can hit. I *know* I can hit.' And he'd go out the next day and wouldn't hit anything. That has to get through to you. And when they found Tom after he burned those churches, he was saying the same prayer.

"He had to go out there and face Robin Roberts, who was throwing that fastball in on his hands, in on his hands, in on his hands, back him up six or eight inches, and then wear out the outside part of the plate. And everybody got to doing it. And that's when they brought up Joe Cunningham."

Life for the early black players was solitary. After the game was over, Lawrence went his way and the white players went theirs. With his family back in Springfield, Lawrence spent most of his private time alone. No one considered the toll it would take.

BROOKS LAWRENCE: "I was not friends with anyone on the club. Some of the pitchers were older. There was Alpha Brazle [forty], Gerry Staley [thirty-three], Stu Miller [twenty-six], Hal White [thirty-five], and Vic Raschi [thirty-five]. Harvey Haddix was there. He and I grew up in the same town. He was a nice guy. He grew up on the farm. Harvey was a farmer. Anyway you looked at him, he was a farmer.

"Harry Caray was the broadcaster. I don't remember speaking to Harry one time the whole time I was out there. I don't know whether Caray cared too much for blacks, but he was in the press box and I was on the field, and seems to me, East is East and West is West and never the twain shall meet. I know Harry changed after a period of time, as did a lot of other people. Even Harry Walker changed, 'cause now him and Bill White go fishing together in Florida.

"The whole time I lived in St. Louis, I didn't go downtown more than twice. There wasn't anything downtown for me. They wouldn't let me in the restaurants, wouldn't let me in any of those public places. As matter of fact, at the end of the '54 season Harry Walker invited me to the team party at the Chase Hotel on Kings Highway. Only thing was, I knew I couldn't go.

"I had tried to go before. Nat Cole, a jazz musician who I knew real well, came to town, and he was working at the Chase. I would leave him tickets for the ball game, and I asked him if I could come out there to watch him sing. He said, 'Sure.'

"I asked Jack Buck to see if I could go out there and get a table and sit back in the corner and watch Nat Cole. I said I wouldn't get in anybody's way, infringe on anybody's rights. What kind of answer did you think I got? A resounding no.

"Matter of fact, when the Cardinals got on the train to leave St. Louis, I'd have to sit in the colored waiting room. They knew we were ballplayers. The whole Cardinal team was in there. The people knew Stan Musial, Red Schoendienst, and some of the others. They knew who we were. We were waiting on a private car.

"One day they let me sit over there with the [white] guys, waiting on the train, and I'm sitting there with pitching coach Bill Posedel, and Bill ordered a beer and a Coke. The waitress said, 'I can serve you, but I can't serve him.' Bill said, 'That's all right. Just give me a beer and a Coke.' So she brought him that, and he gave the Coke to me. And that's the way that worked.

"Strange as it may sound, that was the only incident I ever had in St. Louis. I never was in any place to be causing an incident."

Going into the 1955 season, Brooks Lawrence was supposed to be an ace of the staff, along with Harvey Haddix. But events conspired to reduce his productivity drastically. The worst catastrophe was the onset of ulcers. Making matters worse was the hiring by St. Louis of Rochester manager Harry Walker of Pascagoula, Mississippi.

BROOKS LAWRENCE: "During the summer of '54, I had some bad stomachaches, but I didn't know what they were. In the winter of '54, I had a bleeding ulcer. I passed out, lost a lot of blood. I guess I had been worrying a lot and didn't have any ability to release it. That's what the doctor told me. An hour later, they wouldn't have had to bring me to the hospital. They could have taken me to the undertaker. I had a bad one. Could have been the tension from pitching in the major leagues. Probably had a great deal to do with it. But when I returned for spring training in '55, I didn't have any strength. My wife gave me the last quart of blood I got. I would tease her. I'd say, 'I haven't been right since.'

"Stanky was fired early in '55, and he was replaced by Harry Walker, who didn't like black shoes and didn't like blacks. Walker didn't make any bones about it. I had read what he and his brother Dixie and Bobby Bragan said when Jackie Robinson came up. It wasn't any secret how he felt, so I just decided to stay out of his way, because I was the ONLY black on the team at that time.

"I could tell how he felt by the things he did to me. Just little things. He tried to change the way I pitched. And the final thing occurred in September of '55. Harry needed thirty days on a major league roster to become a vested member of the pension plan, and he had to send one player out. So he sent me to Oakland in the Pacific Coast League.''

Feeling less alienated at Oakland, Lawrence regained his strength and finished the season 5-1. St. Louis should have brought him back, but because there was no serious attempt to stock the team with black players, Lawrence was allowed to be discarded. When he was traded to Cincinnati, he was welcomed by a group of black players, including Frank Robinson, George Crowe, Pat Scantlebury, Bob Thurman, and Joe Black. Lawrence won his first 13 decisions in a row on the way to a stellar 19-10 season. The Reds missed winning the pennant by two games to Brooklyn in '56 while the Cards finished a distant fourth.

Lawrence won 16 in 1957, and after suffering from arm miseries retired at the end of the 1960 season. After opening a bowling alley, Lawrence worked in the front office of the Cincinnati Reds for ten years. He was then contacted by Wilmington (Ohio) College to coach the baseball team. After ''winning everything,'' Lawrence is now retired back in his hometown of Springfield. He runs a golf tournament for B.A.T. to benefit indigent retired major league ballplayers.

CHAPTER 52

DER BINGLE

WHEN Gussie Busch's initial efforts to run the Cardinals resulted in a lot of wasted money and effort, he decided he'd better put someone else in charge of the team. Gussie asked whether any of his Anheuser-Busch executives knew anything about baseball. Richard Meyer, a top executive of the brewery, volunteered that he had played first base when he was a Lutheran seminary student. ''Okay,'' said Gussie, ''you're appointed.''

Meyer was now in charge—except during those times when Gussie Busch lost patience, went over his head, and unilaterally decided to act.

Among the executives brought to the St. Louis front office by Meyer was Bing Devine, a mild-mannered, savvy baseball operative whom Meyer brought up from Rochester after a successful six-year tour running the Cards' top Triple A franchise. According to Devine, Meyer had hand-picked him to take over the team's general manager's job when in the winter of 1954 Busch, without telling Meyer, hired Frank Lane, who had just left the Chicago White Sox, to be the team's general manager.

BING DEVINE: ''When Anheuser-Busch bought the ballclub, Mr. Busch and a couple of bankers and the board of directors discussed who they wanted to run the ballclub. Mr. Busch said, 'Dick Meyer played baseball with Concordia Seminary. Let him do it.' In fact, Dick Meyer probably could have gone on to become a minor league ballplayer, but his father wouldn't let him sign professionally. Which didn't bother Dick. The Anheuser-Busch people said, 'Dick Meyer is a good man. We know him. Let's make him the general manager.' And Dick was general manager for nine or ten months, even though he didn't want to be general manager.

"Dick didn't like being out in the public eye. He wanted to do his job and live with his family and not have people call him at all hours questioning him or criticizing him about player deals. So Dick never had the desire to do that, so the first thing he did was look for was someone to take over, and he became impressed with me at Rochester. The Cardinals brought me back to St. Louis after the '55 season, and as Dick told me later, primarily to be the general manager so he could return to the brewery, and as he put it, 'return to my normal life.'

"In the interim, Mr. Busch got some recommendations from outsiders, friends, big investors. A friend of his, a big Anheuser-Busch investor from Chicago, told him, 'You need to get a general manager who is experienced. Frank Lane is out of favor in Chicago. He wants to move. You ought to hire Frank Lane.'

"So it was, 'Well, gee, so-and-so told me I ought to hire Frank Lane. Let's go hire Frank Lane.' That's the way these things worked. And so the Cardinals hired Frank Lane and left me hanging, working here in St. Louis to make the transition to general manager. Dick said to me, 'If you don't mind, I'm going to talk to Frank Lane about keeping you here in some capacity. But I'd like to have you stay. I'm sorry this happened. I couldn't control it.'

"Dick Meyer and Al Fleishman, who ran his public relations firm, had a lot of imput with Mr. Busch, but that didn't mean they could always get him to listen to them or to get him to change his mind. But if anyone had a chance to make Mr. Busch sit and think about something, it was Dick Meyer and Al Fleishman.

"At any rate, Dick Meyer talked with Frank Lane, and Lane had no objections to my staying. Lane didn't bring a lot of people with him. When he came in, it was: 'Here I am.' And he didn't want to be bothered with anything except running the club on the field—handling the manager and the players. And so as far as Lane was concerned, anyone else could do anything he wanted, as long as he did his job, and as long as he didn't interfere with him. And I fit that completely. I had a pretty good feel for that kind of thing early. So I said, 'Fine.'

"One of the first things Mr. Busch wanted to do was get rid of all their properties, so they put me in charge of selling the Rochester property. Busch didn't want to own minor league properties. He didn't want to have to worry about the properties spread out all over the country. He wanted locally operated teams. All he was interested in was player development. And he was right. In my case, I knew Rochester, had been there, and I was asked to find a buyer and work out a deal. They were in the transition from owning minor league teams to letting the minor league team be owned by the local people and just be operated from the standpoint of player development. Busch sold the teams from a distraction and financial standpoint. He knew he could make money with a big league club, but he didn't see any future to making money with a minor league club. And this was because in the mid-fifties television was siphoning off attention in the minor leagues. People could sit home and watch television instead of going to the ballpark.

"As for Frank Lane, he never asked me anything. He would talk about what he intended to do, so I knew what he was thinking. I don't think he wanted my advice. And I liked Frank Lane. I learned from him that if you make a bad deal, don't let it stop you from making another deal. Go out and make another one in a hurry.

"Frank *loved* to make player deals. They called him 'Trader Lane,' and that was his life. Some of his trades were nuts, and some were good. Frank wasn't remorseful about a deal if it didn't pan out. He was satisfied as long as he got attention out of it. He would have traded Musial. He *liked* the thought of trading Musial. But Mr. Busch stopped him. Al Fleishman had a hand in that. Mr. Busch wanted to have some control over what went on. If you wanted to make a player deal, Mr. Busch wanted you to talk to him first. Frank didn't like that. Frank's philosophy was: 'You want me to operate the club? Okay, I'm going to operate it, but don't try to tell me what to do.' After a couple of years, Frank began to find out with Mr. Busch it never worked like that.

"One of the deals that Frank made early was trading Bill Virdon to Pittsburgh for Bobby Del Greco and Dick Littlefield. That made no sense at all. [Virdon was voted the Rookie of the Year in the National League in 1955.] But Frank worked to convince everyone that Virdon had bad eyesight, that his sight was going bad so that 'he won't be able to play much longer.' He was selling the deal. Frank was a salesman. I never became a salesman. If I liked the deal, I gave you all the facts.

"Dick Meyer and I were at the ballpark, sitting with Lane one night. After the game, Frank and Dick were in deep conversation about the deal that Frank wanted to make. I dragged along, listening. If Dick had asked me anything, I would have told him, but Dick would not have asked me in front of Frank Lane. He valued my advice, but he was smart enough not to say to Bing Devine, 'What do you think of Frank's deal?'

"The worst way in which you could become an enemy of Frank Lane was to try and talk him out of a deal, even if you had a good reason to do it.

"Dick said to Frank, 'If you want to make a deal, okay. We hired you to run the club.' Dick was that kind of guy. Dick said, 'However, Mr. Busch does not like to hear about these deals after the fact. I'd like to go back and talk to Mr. Busch in the morning, and I'll call you back after I see him and in all probability Mr. Busch will say, "Okay, if he wants to make it, let him make it." '

"At seven in the morning, the phone rang in my house. I picked up the phone, and it was Dick Meyer. Dick said, 'Tell me something. You heard the conversation I had with Frank Lane last night. What was the last thing I said to him?'

"I repeated what Dick had told him. Dick said, 'Well, you'd better turn on the radio because the deal has gone down.'

"Frank did that sort of thing, and Dick didn't like it because it put him on the spot. Mr. Busch for sure didn't like it, and that's when Frank began to discover that this was not going to work. So over a period of time he was phased out and he went to Cleveland. And they quickly made me the general manager."

In the three years under Frank Lane, the Cardinals improved from sixth place in 1954 to second place in 1957. But the relationship between Mr. Busch and "Trader" Lane worsened as his stewardship went on, and the relationship reached a breaking point in 1957 when Lane insisted on trading Ken Boyer, a young third baseman who in his second season in 1956 hit .306 and hit 26 home runs, and Harvey Haddix for longtime Philadelphia icon Richie Ashburn and another player. When Busch vehemently objected to the trade, Frank Lane upped and quit to take over as general manager of the Cleveland Indians. A patient Bing Devine was named to replace him.

Bing Devine was born in 1917 in Overland, Missouri, a suburb of St. Louis. He played baseball at Washington University and was invited by the Cardinals to work out at the ballpark. In addition to his studies, Devine wrote a sports column for a county newspaper, the *Watchman Advocate*, in Clayton, Missouri. When Ed Staples, the Cards' publicity director, asked him if he would like to work for the Cards as a part-time publicity man, he jumped at the offer. The pay was meager, but it was a chance for Devine to be around the ballpark.

In 1940 Devine, who had played college ball, sometimes would pitch batting practice. In those days, there were no protective screens. He would stand in the middle of the diamond, throwing to the likes of Johnny Mize and Joe Medwick. Pitching to Medwick in particular was hazardous duty.

BING DEVINE: "I think back now, 'You got to be crazy.' There were a bunch of guys who could hit the ball hard enough to hurt you, but Joe Medwick was the only one who looked upon you as an adversary. Medwick liked to hit balls at batting practice pitchers. And particularly at me. He liked me less than other batting practice pitchers because I worked for the front office, and Joe Medwick was one of the early enemies of the front office.

"A couple of times he met me at the door going in and out of the clubhouse and said, 'What are you doing here today?' I told him, 'Pitching batting practice.' He said, 'You better look out. I'll get you.' A couple of times he didn't even take his turn at bat when I pitched. But he never did fulfill his threat to hit me.

"One of the jobs I had to do in the morning was collect all the telegrams and put the standings of the minor league clubs on the board. And in those days, the Cardinals had thirty-three minor league clubs. They didn't use the phone line like they do now. Everybody sent a Western Union wire with the result of the game, the standings, games behind, games ahead, and I would change the standings every day on the board.''

Bing Devine began his Cardinal executive career in 1941 with Class D Johnson City as the team's business manager. The war was brewing, and he was told that if the team lost an infielder and didn't send a replacement, he should suit up as a player. Devine had a high draft number, and after his second baseman was drafted, he played the position the second half of the year.

In 1942 the Cards sent him to Fresno, Class C, and when the league folded halfway through the season because of the war and the blackout, he went to Decatur, Illinois. In '43 he ended up in the service as a Navy officer but spent the war at Kanaoa Bay in Hawaii, across the island from Pearl Harbor, servicing aircraft.

He returned to the Cardinals organization after a year and a half, going to Columbus, Georgia, a Class A team. Then he was recalled to St. Louis to be director of public relations, just in time to witness the sale of the team by Sam Breadon to Fred Saigh and Robert Hannegan. Devine was dispatched to run the Rochester team. Devine was impressed with both Hannegan and Saigh.

BING DEVINE: "I got to know Robert Hannegan. He was not well. He showed some real compassion for people like me, lower executives. Both he and Saigh were patient with me. None of this was as sophisticated as it is now. I went through a training period where Hannegan would bring me in, and I'd sit with him and I'd talk about my job and how I was doing. He'd give me suggestions. They had different personalities, but both were very nice to me, very kind, very understanding and patient.

GUSSIE BUSCH
(Courtesy The Sporting News)

BING DEVINE
(*Courtesy* The Sporting News)

"I spent six years at Rochester from 1949 through 1955. We liked it there, despite the winters. We were in six straight playoffs. The Cardinals in those days had two Triple A clubs, Rochester and Columbus, and a Double A club, Houston, that we really treated like a Triple A club. But Rochester was given the better ballplayers, so we had clubs that were in the playoffs every year."

In agreement with Gussie Busch, in one of his first acts as GM, Devine, the architect of three Cardinal pennant-winning teams, rescinded the deal for third baseman Kenny Boyer, who would go on to a stellar fifteen-year career, eleven with the Cards.

BING DEVINE: "Frank was going to trade Ken Boyer for Richie Ashburn and another player. I canceled the deal. I called John Quinn and said, 'Let's forget it. We're not going to make that deal.' I liked Boyer. I had come to know him, liked him, and that was a deal I didn't like. So my first move was not to make a deal that Frank had set up to make."

Devine's second move demonstrated that he was willing to sign and trade for the best possible player regardless of color.

He brought to the Cardinals one of the finest ballplayers ever to wear the Redbird on his chest, a youngster by the name of Curt Flood. In December of 1957, Devine traded pitchers Willard Schmidt, Ted Wieand, and Marty Kutyna to the Cincinnati Reds for Flood and outfielder Joe Taylor. Flood would not star for the team until 1961, but he would become a fixture in the Card outfield for a decade.

BING DEVINE: "The only guy besides Frank Lane who would try to force you into making a deal was Gabe Paul. Gabe Paul would sit there and say to you, 'Let me tell you why you should make this deal.' We'd get all through, and I'd say, 'Gabe, you're probably right, but why are you making the deal?' I'd tell him, 'It's good for you, but I don't think it's good for me.' He'd say, 'No, but let me tell you why you should make it . . .'

"Nevertheless, the very first deal I made, for Curt Flood, was with Gabe. Curt didn't fit his club. Maybe Gabe didn't anticipate he'd be that good a ballplayer. Curt played third base on the minor league level for Cincinnati, while we ended up playing him in the outfield.

"I was sitting in Colorado Springs in the hotel with Dick Meyer and Fred Hutchinson at a meeting with Gabe Paul and Birdie Tebbetts of Cincinnati. That was my first major league deal. Pretty interesting that the first deal of any consequence would be for Curt Flood, with all the things that went on with Flood after that. He had a lot of distractions in his personal life, but he was a heck of a ballplayer. I often wondered with all the things he had going on personally how he could come out and play a ball game. But he could put it all aside and play the game and you'd never know anything was going on otherwise."

His second outstanding trade occurred on March 25, 1959, when Devine traded pitcher "Sad Sam" Jones and outfielder Ray Jablonski for San Francsico Giant first baseman Bill White and pitcher Don Choate. Like Boyer and Flood, Bill White, who later would become the president of the National League, would become a Cardinal legend.

BING DEVINE: "I always had the theory, especially in the days before free agency, that any time you could trade a frontline pitcher or a pitcher who was beginning to advance in age for an everyday ballplayer, you do it. A pitcher will appear in 30, 40 ball games. Any everyday ballplayer will appear in 150 games a year. If I thought the deal was helpful to the team and the talents were there on both sides, I went ahead and made the deal. That was my theory. That was behind the Ernie Broglio for Lou Brock deal [June 15, 1964].

"Sam Jones was a talent—an overwhelming pitcher at his best, an interesting character in his own right. He was completely uneducated—he had trouble doing more than writing his name. But he was a nice man. He had a family back in West Virginia. But his lack of education made it hard for him in society.

"One day he said to me, 'I never go home before I sign a contract for the next year.' On account of his not having any money at the end of the season.

"The season ended, and he came in and wanted to sign a contract. I said, 'I haven't even talked to the people I have to talk to. I haven't even set up my figures for next year.'

"He said, 'I can't go home until I sign a contract.' I said, 'I don't know what we're going to do about it.' He said, 'I'm going to stay here,' meaning my office. I said, 'Well, you can't stay in the office. I have to work.'

"He said, 'I'll go walk around the ballpark, and I'll come back.' I don't remember the details of how I did it, but I went to Dick Meyer. I said, 'Here's a worthwhile figure. Let's sign Sam Jones and get him out of my hair and send him home and keep him reasonably happy.' So we did.

"Then in March of 1959, I was in St. Petersburg, thinking we needed to make a deal. We needed an outfielder, and our intention was to make Bill White, who played first base for the Giants, into an outfielder.

"I sent Eddie Stanky out to watch the Giants in spring training. Eddie Stanky was working for me as a special assignment scout. He had managed the club and gotten fired previously. I called Stanky in Arizona from the beach at St. Petersburg. My wife and I had gone to dinner, but the time difference led me to have to make the call from a beach phone while the family was eating. I called and said, 'We're talking about a deal of Sam Jones for Bill White.' And Eddie gave me all the reasons why we should make the deal. That helps you make a deal."

Bing Devine will always be remembered for the trade he refused to make (Ken Boyer) and the three trades he did make for three potential Hall of Famers, Curt Flood, Bill White, and Lou Brock (in 1964). It's a remarkable list few general managers can match.

These acquisitions ultimately would help bring the Cardinals three National League pennants.

Ironically, Devine would be canned by the mercurial Gussie Busch just two months before his wheeling and dealing would finally bear fruit.

CHAPTER 53

THE PROFESSOR

Six months after pitcher Jim Brosnan put down every penny he and his wife had to buy a home outside of Chicago, he was traded to the Cardinals for Alvin Dark. He had been the Cubs' starting pitcher on Opening Day of 1958 because Bob Rush came down with pneumonia and two others were doing a six-month stint in the service. Brosnan defeated the Cardinals, 3–2, striking out Stan Musial twice on curveballs.

He was making $15,000 because Cubs owner P. K. Wrigley, another of baseball's more quirky owners, unilaterally decided that every starting pitcher should make that amount. When Brosnan arrived in St. Louis after the May 20, 1958, trade, Card GM Bing Devine was surprised and stuck—because he had seen his original contract calling for a $8,500 salary and hadn't known about the revised one. The trade didn't look quite as good to Devine at $15,000 a year.

Once Brosnan arrived in St. Louis, his manager, Fred Hutchinson, decided he would be best used as a relief pitcher. In that role, Brosnan would perform with distinction, amassing 52 saves over the next five seasons. With St. Louis, Brosnan also began a second career—as a tell-it-like-it-is journalist.

Since the earliest athletes hurled spears in Greece in the Olympic Games, the clubhouse credo was: What you see here, stays here. The athlete's code of silence was as unbreached as the Mafia's or the police's blue wall of silence. Ballplayers had written autobiographies after finishing their careers, but no player had ever published a journal while still an active player. Jim Brosnan became the first modern-day baseball player to break the code, first in *The Long Season*, then, after being traded to the Reds, in *The Pennant Race*, describing the details of Cincy's 1961 National League championship.

When Brosnan arrived in St. Louis from Chicago in 1958, what he noticed most about the Cardinals was how close-knit the organization was compared to that of the Cubs. He noted how well everyone, including the black players, seemed to get along in segregated St. Louis. He was touched by the generosity of Stan Musial and Red Schoendienst. When Cards manager Freddie Hutchinson made Brosnan a reliever, his career took off. The two men, the professorial Brosnan and the gruff Hutchinson, had deep respect for each other. When Hutchinson was fired as Cards manager at the end of the 1958 season, he moved on to Cincinnati. Brosnan lost his status under new manager Solly Hemus, who the players roundly despised. Shortly afterward, Brosnan was traded over to the Reds to join Hutch.

JIM BROSNAN: "Those Busch people ran things very well in the beer business, and so the baseball business ought to have been run at least as well. Gussie had a good organization because he was an organization man.

"I don't credit Gussie with much. As far as I was concerned, Bing [Devine] ran that team. He was a soft-spoken, quiet guy. He wasn't the Frank Lane type. He was more like the Cubs general manager, John Holland, only brighter.

"The St. Louis Cardinal organization was a family organization. Everybody grew up in it. Everybody knew each other, both on and off the field. The Cubs never had that when I was there. The Cubs were a motley crew.

"When I got to the Cards, I learned you ate dinner with the guys. The Cardinals didn't have loners or cliques. Everybody was supposed to get along well with each other. Bill White was able to get along with anybody. St. Louis was a Southern place. I lived in the Chase Park Plaza, where blacks were allowed if they were serving meals, but you didn't see any blacks on the streets or in the apartments. As black as Bill was, he could pass as white.

JIM BROSNAN
(Courtesy Brace Photo)

White was white—if he wanted to be. He was a very bright man who knew
how to get along. He didn't make any deal out of being blackballed by certain
restaurants or yelled at by the rednecks in the bleachers, which I'm sure he
was. Sam Jones could care less, one way or the other. Curt Flood was young,
really kind of feeling his way. I didn't know whether he would ever hit, but
he was a superb center fielder, and on that basis he was very welcome by all
the pitchers.

"Stan Musial had a superstar's ego when it came to what he did, how he
played the game. He had an arrogance about playing the game, about baseball
and everything that had to do with it. He'd say to Joe Cunningham, 'Why
didn't you take the pitch to left field? Because you can do that. It was a pitch
you can hit, but you didn't do that. Why not?' In that sense, he was a teaching
leader—if he wanted to. He didn't always do it, but when he did, it was:
'Yes, sir. You're right, sir.'

"You never questioned what Stan said about what opposing pitchers were
throwing and why, because that was something he knew better than anybody
else. For one thing, he had the experience. He had swung many more times
against all these pitchers than anybody else on the club.

"I once ran into Stan and Red Schoendienst in a little restaurant in New
York, their favorite place. They asked me how I came to be there, and I said,

'I wanted some chicken.' It was advertised somewhere, and I had seen it, and it wasn't too far from the hotel. I could walk there, so that's where I went. Stan and Red were eating with a Hollywood actor—he became the star of a detective show on television—I had just come in, and they introduced me to him. They left, and he came over and sat down, and we talked. I thought, 'That was a real nice thing that Stan and Red did.' The two of them had passed along this TV star to me. It was the kind of thing you did if you were a Cardinal. You were introduced to the friends of players as if you were likely to be a friend of theirs, because you were a Cardinal.

"I had a different take on Stan when he sat down next to me one day and started talking about his problems buying Liberty Bank. He was just talking, airing himself. He certainly wasn't asking my advice. Should he put $100,000 into the bank, or not? But he chose me to be his sounding board. On Opening Day, I had struck him out twice on curveballs, and two months later, he was treating me as a member of the Cardinal organization. I could not have had more respect for a player.

"And I recall something else he did: Not long after I joined the team, Stan came and asked me how the Cubs pitchers had been pitching him. I said, 'I can remember how I pitched you.' Because that's all I was interested in. How the others pitched him didn't make any difference to me, because they had different stuff. But Stan wanted to know. You don't get to his level without having that curious mind and a willingness to ask anybody for any kind of help you can get—if you think they have something. I don't know that I gave him anything useful. He had already proved to me that he knew how to hit me!

"I never had a feeling that Stan flaunted his money. He didn't overdress. He was no Beau Brummel. He dressed well, but didn't flaunt anything. He and Schoendienst together were a couple of good guys who obviously deserved all they got. They didn't lord over anyone. They weren't bigger tippers in the clubhouse or dress differently. I remember the stories they would tell about the kind of money they made playing D ball or C ball or B ball coming up through the organization, playing for nothing.

"The hitting star of the team was Ken Boyer. Ken was aloof. I think he was very shy. I really do. He and Larry Jackson and Hal Smith were very close. That's all he needed: two friends. Not that he would be unfriendly to anybody else. I don't think he needed any more, 'cause it was tough for him to make the effort to be a friend with anybody.

"If Boyer wasn't the captain, he should have been, and I think he was. I can't think of anybody else on that team who would have been. Although he was shy off the field, shy in conversations, Ken had the poise of a leader in the infield. Musial was playing first base, but Musial wouldn't come over to a pitcher and say, 'You gotta do this,' or 'You should do that.' 'You can get this guy out with this.' Boyer would do that. If we weren't getting a guy out, he might say, 'Let's try this.' He would remember you weren't getting a guy out with a certain pitch, and he'd say, 'Let's try something else.' It means a lot to a pitcher to hear from a guy who seemed to know exactly what he was talking about. Ken had been through it, and although he might be pointing out something you might not want to hear, you knew damn well you should hear it. So you better try something else. That's the kind of leader he was. He said the right thing with a few words.

"At bat he drove in a lot of runs, many of them in the clutch. He'd go to right field when he had to, although he was a much better pull hitter. He liked to pull. In the field, I can't think of a play he couldn't make.

"Our shortstop and second baseman were Don Blasingame and Eddie Kasko, who were quality guys, but not great players. Kasko was the next level below Roy McMillan, same type. Both 'Blaze' and Eddie knew exactly where to be. If I was in the stretch position, I'd look over to see where Kasko was, to certify what pitch I had decided to throw and where I was going to throw it, because that's where he was going to go. Both of them were like that.

"Vinegar Bend Mizell was a religious fanatic who I thought might be a preacher when he got out of baseball. He was a bright guy, articulate, with plenty of dialect. He could have gone anywhere to start a congregation because of who he was, and he could charm them. That's the way I thought of him. He hung out with Hal Smith, who was also very religious.

"Our manager was Fred Hutchinson. Hutch said a good manager is one who can get a group of men who can get along well together to play the game well together. He had a lot of that but not enough talent. The club didn't hit well, even with Boyer hitting what he was hitting. We just didn't score runs. During one streak, we went forty-two innings without scoring a run.

"Hutch was hunting for someone to become the relief pitcher. Larry Jackson wanted to start. So did Billy Muffett. He used both of them a few times. I was a starter when I came over. In the middle of the season, Hutch made up his mind that I should be a relief pitcher.

"We had a one or two-run lead against the Phils in Philadelphia, and they had runners on first and second and nobody out to start the eighth inning. He put me in to save the game. So I struck out the first batter, Ted Kazanski, on four pitches, and Carl Sawatski fouled off two pitches up and in. I threw him a sinker down and away, and he hit a two-hopper to shortstop, a double play, and we were out of the inning.

"I walked into the dugout, and Hutch said, 'That's the way you do it.' Now I didn't know that's the way I was going to be doing it from then on, but the next day we had an off day—in Philadelphia they had a curfew on Sunday—and he called me up to his room. He had a bottle of Scotch and a bottle of bourbon, unopened—I guess he didn't know my preference, and I have none—but actually, we never did get around to drinking anything. He told me that when I started games, I would get through the first three innings with no problems at all, but in the sixth and seventh innings I'd make a mistake, think too much, throw the wrong pitch, and 'We can't afford that because we can't score.' His exact words were, 'We can't score for shit.' He thought it would be good for me and good for the team.

"The phone rang and it was Walker Cooper calling from somewhere. They talked for a half hour, and he got off the phone and said, 'Well, that's what I want you to do.' I said, 'You're the boss, Hutch.' Hutch was not only your father but your patron. He had gotten me over to St. Louis. Except for

Bob Scheffing with the Cubs, Hutch was the first real veteran baseball man who was convinced I could pitch in the big leagues.

"And that was it. As far as I know, he drank the Scotch and bourbon all by himself. I never had a drink. I suppose he was going to offer me a drink if I was going to make an argument with him. His plan was to seduce me with alcohol. Or maybe he had a sportswriter coming in right after that! The fact of the matter is, from then on I was a closer.

"Hutch was fired in mid-September of '58. We all felt sorry for Stan Hack when Gussie fired Hutch. Hack didn't want to be the manager. P. K. Wrigley had made Stan the manager when he didn't want to be the manager in Chicago, and here was Gussie Busch making him the manager when he doesn't want to be the manager in St. Louis. Stan loved being a coach, because he really didn't like the responsibility of manager. He didn't like chewing out people. He wanted to be the nice guy he always was. He had just gotten remarried, and he was happy with his new wife, and all of a sudden he has to go through the same shit he went through as Cub manager. He knew what kind of ballclub he had. It was a sixth-place ballclub.

"The man who took Hutch's place as manager was Solly Hemus. Solly was easily despised. I thought he could have been a very good manager because of his knowledge, but he simply did not know how to handle different types of people. Going back to what Hutch said, it has always been the manager's job to find people who will understand what he has to say and are coachable, are manageable, and get along with each other. Solly didn't have that.

"Solly had Harry Walker and Johnny Keane as coaches. I had a feeling that they had sharp knives hidden on their persons, that they would be glad to stick it in each other's backs. Keane and Walker knew Hemus was going to fail, and both of them wanted the job. With that sort of discord, muted or in the background, I know I was unhappy. There wasn't much smiling going on. We weren't winning, either. We weren't playing good baseball at all. The guys had seen similar things in the minors. All Cardinal teams didn't win, though they were all learning the same way. And they had had bad managers in the minors as well as good ones. You want to play for a good manager, not a bad one. All families have problems. Some get out of it without being damaged. They didn't get out of it until Solly was fired and went to the Mets.

"In May of 1959, I was traded from the Cards to the Reds while I was eating dinner at Stan and Biggie's restaurant. The reason the trade was made was that Hutch was with the Reds, and he knew he was going to be replacing Mayo Smith. Gabe Paul asked him whether there was anything he could do for Hutch. Hutch probably knew I wasn't getting along very well with Solly, 'cause Hutch had his sources.

"Solly was fired by the Cards the next year, and I remember I was with the Reds, and he was coaching third base for the Mets. It was 1962, their first year, and they were a terrible ballclub. I came in to relieve and save a game, and at the end of the inning I was walking off the mound, and Solly started to yell at me from third base. I thought he'd stop and stick his face in my face, but he didn't, he just kept going by, still yelling in the other direction. Hutch was laughing when he heard what Solly was saying. What Solly said was: 'You were horseshit then, you're horseshit now, and you'll always be horseshit.' Which I could echo. So far as both of us were concerned, it was the right expression for each other.''

After the 1958 season, the Cardinals were invited by Japanese promoter Ysetsuo Higa to travel for six weeks to Hawaii, Guam, the Philippines, Japan, Okinawa, and Korea. They won all the games but one, and during the trip Brosnan and teammates Bill Wight and Phil Paine were offered the fabulous sum of $50,000 to play in Japan the following year, an offer Brosnan turned down because his family had had a tough time whenever he played in Puerto Rico or the Dominican Republic, and he was not about to move to Japan, an entirely different culture, just for money, even though the pay was more than three times his $15,000 salary.

Brosnan had written a book review of Mark Harris's *Bang the Drum Slowly* for the magazine *Etcetera,* and then wrote a couple pieces for *Sports Illustrated,* including one on being traded to the Cardinals and another entitled "Me and Hutch." Bob Creamer at *S. I.* hired him to write an article about the trip to Japan, and when Bob Broeg of the *St. Louis Post-Dispatch* learned of it, he offered Brosnan $100 an article for a series of stories about the trip. Brosnan made $1,100 from the *Post-Dispatch.*

Though Brosnan's article for *S. I.* "didn't come up to the magazine's standards," according to Brosnan, he did receive a free half-hour seminar from Bob Creamer on how to write a magazine piece. During the conversation, Creamer told him, "I know a guy down at Harper & Row who's a big baseball fan. I'll call him up. Why don't you go talk to him? Maybe you can do a book for him."

Creamer contacted publisher Evan Thomas and after a short meeting, Brosnan had a contract to write a book about the 1959 season. He received no advance. As Brosnan explained it, "They took me right off the street and shucked my jeans." What he came away with was a promise; an editor, Buzz Wyeth; and lunch. The result, however, was a revelation.

Brosnan's first book, *The Long Season,* published in 1960, was the grand-daddy of all modern baseball books. It gave readers—for the first time—a player's-eye view of what it was like to be a major leaguer. Successive books like *Ball Four* by Jim Bouton and *The Bronx Zoo* by Sparky Lyle may have been more bawdy and provocative, but what made Brosnan's book the classic that it has become was the combination of the personal diary form and the straightforwardness of the events and anecdotes described in the book. When it came out it was a smash, and Brosnan, like Bouton and Lyle after him, was feared and shunned by some players and most front-office types for his writing skills and descriptive powers. Brosnan's flippant yet serious attitude was that he was writing the truth, so what was the harm? He was too naïve to have appreciated the value of propaganda. Behind the uniform lurked a journalist, not an ad man.

JIM BROSNAN: "Nobody knew I was going to write a book, which was something I wanted to do from the time I was eight. When I started to learn how to read, I always wanted to see my name on a book in the library. And here was a shot at it. I had a chance. Even Evan Thomas was enthusiastic, not greatly, but he had liked the two pieces I had done.

"I was told that the only player to write a journal before me was John Montgomery Ward, who wrote one during the Players' League of 1890. I've never seen it, but I think it was Jerome Holtzman who told me about it. Maybe it's in the Hall of Fame.

"I had experience enough to know I could probably do it. The pieces had turned out all right, kind of funny, but personal, especially the 'Me and Hutch' piece. When I wrote the two pieces, catcher Hobie Landrith didn't like it because I wrote that Hobie had his choice of bats that were too long, too short, or ones that had holes in them. Hobie didn't care much for that, but I was much taller and stronger than he was, and he was a nonaggressive guy anyway.

"I had no understanding of what I was doing. All I wanted was to go into the library and see that my book was there. That was the spur, the goad that kept me going at the beginning. Well, enough people liked it that it was on the bestseller list a couple weeks. There have been four hardcovers and four paperback editions. It's available still, and my guess is it has sold three quarter of a million to a million copies altogether. I can go to damn near every library, and if I want to be an egomaniac, if I don't find it I can say, 'Why *isn't* it there?'

"When *The Long Season* came out, certain writers and broadcasters gave it positive reviews. Red Smith wrote a beautiful little column on me. Rex Stout, of all people—he invented Nero Wolfe—gave it a good review. I had just finished a book Peter DeVries wrote about how his daughter died of leukemia, a beautifully written piece, and I wrote to him, and he wrote me a note back and said, 'I read your book and liked it, too.'

"I was with Cincinnnati when the book came out. Most of the book was about my long season with the Cardinals, and so the reaction came from the Cardinals, as it should have.

"I was writing about things I shouldn't have written about: the pomposity of the organization, and my slant on guys like Solly Hemus, who was just a rookie manager; Harry Walker, a fixture for a long time; and Johnny Keane, who was a coach under Hemus. I should never have been hitting on those people, quoting them as I did when they sounded like assholes, because you didn't do that. You weren't an organization man if you did that.

"In general and sometimes in specific terms, everyone said what they were supposed to say in the Cardinal organization who was not pleased. Two players who expressed their displeasure were Ken Boyer and Larry Jackson. Boyer and I had hung out together. Boyer said I was not a good enough pitcher to write a book like that. Which has always stuck in my mind. And Jackson, who was off-and-on my roommate, wouldn't talk to me for a while until he came over to the Cubs and admitted: 'I thought some of it was pretty funny.' And that was as much praise as I could get out of a ballplayer. Joe Garagiola just leaped all over the book. He said, 'This is the worst thing that could have happened to the Cardinals,' and said I had no business doing it because I had not been with the Cardinals long enough! Joe and I long since patched that up. Not that he apologized for ripping my ass. He later saw other books as being a hell of a lot worse, including *Ball Four*. The other reaction came from my Cincinnati teammates. Their immediate reaction was: 'Put this in your book.' Or 'I got something for your next book,' most of which was not usable. They told me stuff that both of us knew was not going in a book. I'd have a little laugh and off I'd go. Marshall Bridges was always giving me stories. He wanted me to recount his adventures off the field. He always wanted me to put in the book the length of his penis, because he said it was the largest in the major leagues, and he would bet anybody. Poor Marshall got shot in the ass by the husband of some woman he was knocking up. Marshall was fun.

''It's probable that my writing helped end my baseball career. I don't know for sure. There was a paragraph in the standard baseball contract everybody signs that the ballclub had the right to review the publication of material the club deems harmful to the club. Which gave them the right of censorship.

''The man who wrote *The Last Angry Man*, not Graham Greene, another writer named Green [Gerald], was a producer at CBS. He had had this notion of putting a remote mike on New York Giant linebacker Sam Huff to describe what happens in an exhibition game. Green thought it would work in baseball if he could find someone articulate enough who wanted to do it. So he said to me, 'We'll give you four grand.' Four grand was exactly the amount I was arguing over in contract talks with Bill DeWitt, the Reds general manager. I had had a 4-4 record, and he wanted to cut me four thousand bucks, which was as much as he could cut me.

''When Green called him and said, 'I'll tell you what we are going to do,' I guess it ruffled DeWitt's feathers. What were they going to do with his property, and I was his property. So DeWitt said straight out, 'We have the right to look at the finished product and agree or not agree to allow it to air.' Green said, 'John F. Kennedy does not have that right.' That didn't sit too well with DeWitt, either. Anyway, the show went down the drain, along with my four grand. I was looking forward to it. DeWitt and I were quits, and I was gone by mid-May when he traded me to the White Sox.

''When I reported to the White Sox, I landed in Kansas City from Cincinnati, and the general manager, Ed Short, who was just that, short, very short—he had a very short speech for me. He said, 'You can't write here, either.' So there I was, facing the possibility of not having an avocation, and I didn't give a goddamn. I didn't care much for the American League, and they didn't care much for me, either, the way they hit line drives. I wrote a couple of pieces for *Atlantic Monthly*, but it came down to the same thing: 'We get to see what you write, and if we don't like it, we have the right under your contract to prevent you from publishing.' And I said, 'The hell with you. That's my business on the outside.'

''I told that to Brent Musberger, who was the darling of the Chicago *Daily News* at the time, and he decided he'd start a feud. He'd go to Short with things, and he'd come back to me with what Short said, and I'd open my mouth, and pretty soon it was done. Short sent me a release—postage due.

Which allowed me to write a piece for *Sports Illustrated* in which I described it exactly: I had gotten 'Short shrift.' Hell, that was an extra twelve hundred bucks. I don't know what ever happened to Ed Short. He probably shrunk.''

When Brosnan was released, he immediately contacted the ACLU to present his case. *The Sporting News*, which initially had championed the pitcher's right to free speech, grumbled about "outside agitators" intruding into the game.

John E. Coons, chairman of the Illinois branch of the ACLU, in a letter accused Arthur Allyn, the owner of the White Sox, of censorship. Allyn contemptuously threw Coons's letter in the trash can. *The Sporting News* applauded Allyn for doing so. Brosnan's career, meanwhile, was over, the victim of a blackball.

This was 1964. John Kennedy was dead and so was Camelot. Under the surface, the underpinning of the status quo was slowly giving way. Bob Dylan was singing his anthem, "The times, they are a changin'." Vietnam and civil rights and the players' union would not be far behind. Jim Brosnan would become the Rosa Parks of the players' union.

CHAPTER 54

CIVIL UNREST

BING Devine was acutely aware of Gussie Busch's lack of patience and what disaster could befall the team when that patience ran out. He was aware, moreover, that Busch wanted to make manager Freddie Hutchinson the scapegoat for the poor performance of the team in 1958. Devine pleaded with Dick Meyer, Busch's right-hand man whom Devine categorized as "one of the finest men I've ever known," to exert his influence on his boss, but once Busch made up his mind to act, Meyer was no more able to change the baron's mind as anyone else. And so, as general manager Bing Devine looked on helplessly, on September 17, 1958, Gussie Busch fired Freddie Hutchinson and for the last two weeks of the season had Stan Hack man the position. Busch then hired Solly Hemus to manage the Cardinals in 1959, even though the former Cards infielder had never before managed. The appointment of Hemus by Busch turned out to be unfortunate. There would be widespread dissension and unhappiness during Hemus's tenure. Devine could only sit back helplessly and watch.

BING DEVINE: "Dick Meyer called me and said, 'I'll give you a few days to write up all your thoughts about Fred Hutchinson. I know you like him and want to keep him, even though you didn't hire him. Prepare something, set up a meeting, and come down to the brewery and give Mr. Busch all the reasons why we should keep Fred Hutchinson.'

"So I did that. We met at Grant's Farm. I went with my prepared text, with all my points, to make sure I didn't overlook anything. I read through them and answered a few questions.

"Mr. Busch looked at Dick and said, 'Now that was a fine presentation. I'm very impressed with that. Dick, do you want to tell him or should I?' Dick said, 'Well, you go ahead and tell him.' Mr Busch said, 'I'd like to have you hire Solly Hemus.'

"He had been impressed with Solly Hemus. When Solly was traded by Frank Lane from the Cardinals to Philadelphia, he had written Mr. Busch a nice letter that said, 'Dear Mr. Busch, I really enjoyed playing in the Cardinal organization. You have a fine, first-class organization. I'm sorry to leave, and if I ever come back it would fulfill all my expectations. I would be gratified if I could come back.' And Mr. Busch was impressed. He knew Solly was a hell-bent-for-leather, fiery ballplayer with limited talent, and he had made up his mind to hire Solly Hemus. So we hired Solly Hemus.''

Hemus was determined to run things his way. One of his decisions concerned how much and where to play Stan Musial. Though Musial had hit .337 with 17 homers and 62 RBIs at the age of 37 in 1958, Hemus insisted that Musial ride the bench or retire. At the same time, he had to know that if he benched Musial and the team didn't do well, Gussie Busch, who loved Stan, would be offended. Give Hemus credit: he stuck his neck way out.

The rookie manager started the 1959 season with Joe Cunningham on first base and Stan in the outfield, but soon benched Musial and used him in a secondary role, playing Bill White and Gino Cimoli in his place. The next year White played first base and Musial was benched in favor of thirty-three-year-old journeyman outfielder Bob Nieman. There were talks of Musial going over to the Pirates, but Pittsburgh GM Joe Brown would not give up a young player for him. When Nieman was injured in late June, Musial returned to the lineup. He finished the 1960 season productively with 17 homers and 63 RBIs. By the end of 1960 Busch was ready to fire Hemus. During the following off-season the Cards owner called Stan Musial to his home for a meeting to discuss Hemus's future. He wanted to know from Stan whether or not he should fire Hemus. Musial, one of the classiest individuals ever to don a baseball uniform, told Busch that Hemus, his nemesis, deserved another chance.

STAN MUSIAL: "He was a young manager. He didn't have managerial experience anywhere, and Solly figured I was getting older, so he took me out quite a bit.

"After the '60 season, Busch wanted to know what my plans were. He called me out to Grant's Farm and we had a discussion about Hemus and what I thought of him as a manager. I said, 'I think Solly deserves a little more chance of being the Cardinal manager.' As I look back, I probably could have ended Solly's career at that time. He was thinking of firing him, but I gave Solly a vote of confidence. I thought maybe Solly'd let me play the next year.

But I didn't play much. So he let him manage the next year, and about halfway into the season they got rid of him.''

Among some players, Hemus seemed fair and competent. Carl Warwick, who was traded from the Los Angeles Dodgers to the Cards early in 1961, enjoyed playing for the Cardinal manager. He thought Hemus did the best he could under the circumstances and if there was any dissention on the club, then he—for one—didn't see it.

CARL WARWICK: "I didn't have any problems at all. He and Bing made the trade for me, and I felt very comfortable with him. They traded Daryl Spencer for myself and Bob Lillis. I guess they figured they could get a younger player and someone to back up the infield. They had a pretty good outfield at the time. They had Curt Flood and Charlie James, and Stan was still playing. I had no problems with Solly at all. I read there was a problem between Solly and Bob Gibson, but I never did really see that. It seemed to me Solly was pretty fair. Now he benched Musial, which made everybody mad in St. Louis. But there comes a time when somebody has to do that. The Cardinals were trying to find a way to replace Stan. With Flood in center, the Cards moved me to right, and that was fine with the short fence out there.''

At the time Hemus began managing in 1959, Bing Devine, per Gussie Busch's dictates, was actively desegregating the Cardinal ballclub. Devine had assembled some of the finest black talent in the land, including pitcher Bob Gibson, outfielder Curt Flood, and first baseman Bill White: three fiercely proud, highly intelligent men who would go on to become not only great players but loud voices in the movement for players' rights. But since they were starting out in 1959 they didn't dare complain about their treatment—on or off the field—and it was only years later, after garnering fame and recognition for their All Star play, that the complaints by White, Flood, and Gibson about their racist treatment by society and gripes about their manager by Flood and Gibson surfaced. Had Flood and Gibson flourished under Hemus, chances are he would not have been fired two and a half years after taking over the job.

Nineteen fifty-nine was a full half-decade before the landmark Civil Rights Act of 1964. It was an era when blacks still were supposed to be invisible or servile on the streets of Southern cities, such as St. Louis. Jackie Robinson had led the line of black players into the major leagues, but their professional status could not protect these men from hurtful racial attitudes that had become ingrained in the society since long before the Civil War.

Hemus, like so many white men of that transitional period, was not able to change his attitudes fast enough in an America that was moving almost overnight from a segregated society to one that required cooperation and mutual trust between whites and blacks for maximum productivity. A manager who didn't use his black players to ultimate advantage not only hurt the team but hurt himself. In St. Louis, Hemus would treat Gibson and Flood badly, finding fault with their play while favoring less talented white players. As a result, the black players silently raged. At the same time, Hemus created some discord when he limited the playing time of Stan Musial. Hemus's reign would be marked by lackluster play and a great deal of bitterness.

While Bill White expressed no qualms about Hemus—"I don't think he didn't make me feel welcome. I played from the time I got there. I was a guy who hit home runs for him."—Tim McCarver noted how badly Hemus underestimated Bob Gibson's talent.

TIM MCCARVER: "He said Gibby'd never make it as a big league pitcher. 'Hell,' he'd mumble, 'the guy throws everything the same speed.' Maybe he did, but that speed was about a thousand miles an hour, and it nearly tore up my hand every time I caught him. He had to be the hardest pitcher I ever caught, with that fastball moving and sailing away like a belligerent butterfly."

Curt Flood and Bob Gibson recalled how negatively they viewed their experiences under Hemus.

CURT FLOOD: "Under Solly Hemus nothing worked out fine. He was manager during 1959, 1960, and half of 1961. It was common knowledge that he had obtained the job by writing a humble but hopeful letter to Mr. Busch. I have not seen the letter, but Solly once wrote one to me and I have seen his style. Shades of Horatio Alger. Busch loved the letter.

"Talk about disasters. Hemus did not share the rather widely held belief that I played center field approximately as well as Willie Mays. He sat me on the bench, preferring to use men such as Gino Cimoli, Don Taussig, Don Landrum, and even poor Bill White, who was unquestionably the best first baseman in the league but was its most miscast outfielder. Hemus acted as if I smelled bad. He avoided my presence, and when he could not do that, he avoided my eyes.

"I tried to believe that my chance would come. All that came were insomnia and chronic indigestion. When I got into the lineup, I was uneasy. Getting hits or making spectacular plays helped not a bit. I was an outcast. And I did not know why.

"My roommate, Bob Gibson, was just as badly off. He could throw as hard any man alive. He was such a fine athlete that he had moved from the Harlem Globetrotters basketball team to the Cardinals' highest minor league farm club in 1957. It seemed obvious that 'Hoot' only needed work to become one of baseball's leading pitchers. Hemus did not see it that way. During 1959 and 1960, he shunted Gibson back and forth between St. Louis and the minors. He never used him if someone else was available.

" 'A hell of a way to treat a nice, clean-cut colored kid from Omaha,' 'Hoot' would say from his bed.

" 'What about me? What about a nice, clean-cut little colored kid from Oakland?'

" 'Don't change the subject.'

"One afternoon [shortstop Julio] Gotay made a brilliant play. Later Hemus saw Bob Gibson and said, 'Wow, Julio, you did great out there today.' "

BOB GIBSON: "Hemus must have been the only manager ever to have a problem handling Stan the Man, who didn't hit well that year—in part because Hemus had him and our other power hitter, Ken Boyer, bunting and hitting behind the runner, a strategy best restricted to utility infielders like Hemus—and found himself on the bench, of all places. Then Hemus moved him from left field to first base, which sent Bill White to the outfield, where he floundered. Under better circumstances, White might have gotten some help in the outfield from Curt Flood, who was the best center fielder I ever saw, but Flood was in no position to help anybody after Hemus told him he'd never make it as a big leaguer and replaced him with Gino Cimoli.

"Hemus's treatment of black players was the result of one of the following, and I won't try to speculate which: Either he disliked us deeply or he genuinely believed that the way to motivate us was with insults. The result was the same, regardless. He would goad us, ridicule us, bench us—anything he could think of to make us feel inept. He told me, like he told Flood, that I would never make it in the majors and went so far as to suggest that I take a shot at basketball instead. He was apparently convinced that I didn't have a thought in my head when I was on the mound, and he was not in the least reluctant to insult my intelligence."

During a game against Pittsburgh, Hemus, the only playing manager in the majors, sent himself in as a pinch hitter against Bennie Daniels, who was black. Daniels knocked him down with the first pitch. On the second, Hemus swung and sent the bat flying toward the pitcher. The next pitch hit Hemus in the back. When Hemus related in a team meeting how he had called Daniels a "black son of a bitch," the black players on the Cardinals shook their heads.

CURT FLOOD: "Gibson, White, Crowe, and I sat with our jaws open, eyeing each other. We had been wondering how the manager really felt about us, and now we knew. 'Black sons a bitches.' Any one of us could have chewed Hemus up and spit him out, but we said not a mumbling word. No white player looked at us or mentioned the meeting afterward. We talked it over among ourselves many times and agreed that the Daniels incident had been the last straw for Hemus. The meeting had been his way of revealing the principles for which he stood—the great beliefs that prompted him to bench a good center fielder, ignore a good pitcher, and play a good first baseman out of position.

"Until then, we had detested Hemus for not using his best lineup. Now we hated him for himself. We became more discerning in our evaluations of baseball's employment policies. We became connoisseurs of the Good of the Game, noting how unconcernedly the owners sabotaged the sport by hiring incompetent or prejudiced or just plain stupid managers. And we saw more clearly than before that black players of less than star quality tended to disappear from the scene in a few years, whereas mediocre whites hung on long enough to qualify for pensions. In baseball, as elsewhere, the black had to be better than the white of equal experience, or he would be shown the door."

*   *   *

The indignities heaped on the black players on the Cardinals were not limited to their treatment by the manager. As the 1950s were coming to a close, there was a stirring in the land for better treatment for its black citizens. Bob Gibson, who grew up in Omaha, could not believe the indignities he had to suffer when he traveled from Omaha to St. Petersburg, Florida, for spring training in 1958.

The Cardinals played at Al Lang Stadium, and the players were supposed to be staying at the Bainbridge Hotel. When Gibson arrived in town, the Bainbridge Hotel clerk made it clear that Gibson was not wanted. The clerk gave the cabbie an address. Gibson got back into the cab and was taken to the south side of town to a private home, where he roomed with Curt Flood, "Sad Sam" Jones, and a few other black players. Gibson was disappointed.

"So this," Gibson said to himself, "is the major leagues."

Bill White has never forgiven the city of St. Petersburg for its racist past. When asked to discuss how blacks were treated in the early 1960s, his tone grew sharp, his words clipped. When asked how he felt about being excluded from the team's hotel and having to room with a black family in St. Petersburg,

BILL WHITE
(Courtesy Brace Photo)

he replied, "The negative things you tend to put out of your mind." I asked him whether he was forced to stay by himself much of the time. He said, "Yeah." Then he paused. "The place was segregated," he said. "*Highly* segregated." Then he was silent on the subject for the moment.

Treatment of blacks in St. Petersburg was little different from the way they were treated in most of the rest of the country at the time. In 1960 Bob Gibson was told he was welcome at a new hotel in St. Pete. He invited his wife and daughter to drive with him from Omaha to vacation in sunny Florida. The trip, he admitted later, was a mistake.

BOB GIBSON: "Everything in between [Omaha and St. Petersburg] was disgusting and degrading. We could not eat, because most of the restaurants would not serve us. We could not stop for the night when we were tired, because most of the motels would not accommodate us."

Curt Flood had had similar experiences during spring training. Flood, who was from Oakland in relatively tolerant California, had begun his career with the Cincinnati Reds in 1956. He was eighteen years old when he flew to Tampa, Florida, and experienced the Jim Crow South for the very first time in his life. These experiences scarred him for life.

CURT FLOOD: "As I floated toward the baggage claim area, I saw the drinking fountains. One was labeled 'White,' and the other 'Colored.' For a wild instant, I wondered whether the signs meant club soda and Coke. The truth struck, like a door slammed in my face. I had heard of such drinking fountains and here they were. Thank goodness I was just passing through on my way to the Floridian and baseball."

But when Flood arrived at the Floridian, he learned he could not stay there with his white teammates. He was taken to Ma Felder's, where the black players lived.

CURT FLOOD: "I was at Ma Felder's because white law, white custom, and white sensibility required me to remain offstage until wanted. I was a good athlete and might have an opportunity to show it, but this incidental skill did not redeem me socially. Officially—and for the duration—I was a nigger."

He was shipped to the team's minor league center in Douglas, Georgia. He began his career at High Point–Thomasville, North Carolina, Class B, where he led the Carolina State League in hitting with a .340 average.

CURT FLOOD: "I was ready for High Point–Thomasville, but the two peckerwood communities were not ready for me."

A fan and his four sons sat in a front row box and began yelling "Black bastard!" at him. He was the target of racial epithets, home or away. His teammates seemed offended by his presence and didn't speak to him off the field. He got no help from manager Bert Haas. Flood could not eat with his teammates. He was barred from the rest rooms. He was on his own.

CURT FLOOD: "What had started as a chance to test my baseball ability in a professional setting had become an obligation to measure myself as a man. As such, it was a matter of life and death. These brutes were trying to destroy me. If they could make me collapse and quit, it would verify their preconceptions. And it would wreck my life.

"My teammates despised and rejected me as subhuman. I gladly would have sent them all to hell. More than once during that horrible season, I was tempted to strike out so that our cracker pitcher would lose another game. More than once, I almost threw the ball away or dropped a fly for the same vengeful purpose.

"If I did not sabotage the team (and I never did), it was only because I had been playing baseball too long and too well to discredit myself. And I was too black. Pride was my resource. I solved my problem by playing my guts out."

After tearing up the Carolina State League, Flood joined the Cincinnati Reds at the end of the 1956 season.

Flood expressed his wish not to return to High Point. In 1957 he was sent farther south to Savannah, Georgia, Class A, where the city was undergoing great tension over school desegregation. Again, he was alone. The only other nonwhite player on the team was Leo Cardenas, who spoke little English and spent his off-hours in the Spanish community. Flood was forced to eat meals at the bus station, because after games he was barred from entering restaurants with his white teammates.

Again, he was called to Cincinnati at the end of the season. He went to Venezuela to learn how to play second base. Immediately he contracted dysentery, and he was not well enough to play second. The Venezuelan club owner fired Flood. And then Gabe Paul traded him to the St. Louis Cardinals. One unstated reason: The Reds would have fielded an all-black outfield of Robinson, Pinson, and Flood.

Reds general manager Gabe Paul had refused to raise his salary from $4,000. When the Cards sent him a contract for $5,000 a year, Flood's spirits soared.

When Flood reported to the Cards in the spring of 1958, the racial climate in St. Petersburg was no better than it was on the other side of Tampa Bay. He and the other black players felt the cold slap of rejection from the local populace.

It would be another year before the municipal swimming facilities, closed in 1956 after a desegregation order, would be reopened for all. Lunch counter sit-ins in St. Pete began in 1960. In January of 1961, seventeen businesses, including Webb City, the city's largest drug store/general store, ended their discriminatory policies.

There was progress, but the resistance to change was great.

Each year the St. Petersburg Yacht Club hosted a "Salute to Baseball" breakfast for the Cardinals team sponsored by the local chamber of commerce. The greenest of the white players were invited. The team's black players— Bill White, Curt Flood, George Crowe, Frank Barnes, Marshall Bridges, and Bob Gibson—did not get invitations.

White was articulate, educated, and unused to such treatment. In the spring of 1961, White did something unheard of at the time. He spoke out. He expressed the pain he felt from being so obviously discriminated against to Joe Reichler of the Associated Press news service. White told Reichler, "I think about this every minute of the day. I think I am a gentleman and can conduct myself properly." He told the *Pittsburgh Courier*, "This thing keeps gnawing at my heart. When will we be made to feel like humans?"

BOB GIBSON: "[White] had been raised in a basically white community in Ohio, was college-educated, and by nature took shit from nobody. He was polite, dignified, and unyielding on this point, having been hardened by playing minor league ball in Danville, North Carolina, where he sometimes carried a bat in order to get through the hostile crowds that stood between him and the team bus. Local people threw stones at the bus as it drove off."

When I interviewed Bill White about the snub by the St. Petersburg chamber of commerce, it was clear to me that though the incident took place over forty years earlier, the hurt and anger remained. Perhaps that explained his actions when as National League president he stopped cold the transfer of the San Francisco Giants to St. Petersburg in 1994. In his voice, I could hear that he had yet to get over his bitter feelings toward the city, where I now live.

BILL WHITE: "The St. Pete Yacht Club had always invited the white players and not the blacks from the time the team had black players. But that was a pimple among all the things we had to go through in Florida and the South at the time.

"One of our doctor friends had a yacht, and we were talking one night, and he mentioned that he couldn't dock his yacht at the St. Petersburg Yacht Club, although that club, from what I understood, was leased for a dollar a year from the city of St. Petersburg, where that doctor was paying taxes. So that's a little bit of the background.

"So as far as the breakfast was concerned, first of all, I certainly didn't want to go. Going to a breakfast where you had to get up at seven o'clock in the morning didn't really appeal to us. We didn't want to go to the goddamn breakfast. But in speaking up, it was a chance to put a spotlight on some of the things that were going on down there, and it worked."

When Bill White told AP correspondent Joe Reichler about the slight, Reichler wrote an account that was printed across the country, including the black paper in St. Louis, which called for a boycott of Anheuser-Busch. When the news became public, black players on other teams began to complain about the racism, and the pressure increased to end it for the ballplayers.

When Gussie Busch threatened to move the Cardinals out of Florida if conditions didn't change, desegregation came quickly to St. Petersburg.

AL FLEISHMAN: "Mr. Busch simply told the St. Petersburg Baseball Committee that if they didn't have all the players together, he was not going to go back to St. Petersburg.

"They said, 'Don't worry about that,' and the next thing we knew, they bought two motels, and we took them over for spring training. All the Cardinals stayed there, Stan Musial as well as Tom Alston."

BILL WHITE: "I like to say they segregated all of us. Bing Devine and Al Fleishman were responsible for that: two good men."

BING DEVINE: "Al and Dick Meyer worked together to help [a St. Petersburg businessman] buy the two motels adjacent to each other, where they could put the whole baseball team in one of them. I was in on that. I recognized they were right and we should do it.

"At the time, it was a remarkable thing to do. I don't remember any hue and cry in St. Petersburg about it, but when you did it, you were shaking the dice."

BILL DAVENPORT [St. Petersburg chamber of commerce]: "At the time, St. Petersburg was typical of any Southern town. Our facilities were still pretty much segregated, and as a result, there were some serious problems on the team. The black players didn't like what was going on, and I don't blame them. Bill White—I got to be careful here—Bill White was pretty militant about it, and I don't blame Bill White. He was a star. Everyone cheered him when he hit a home run, but nobody wanted him to live in their house. And that's not right.

"There was an organization known as the Bat Boys. We were a goodwill ambassador team for the Cardinals. We had annual parties in St. Pete during spring training. Mr. Busch's birthday was during spring training, and we had a big birthday bash for him every year. We looked after the Cardinal executives and their people when they were here: the manager, the coaches, the traveling secretary, and, of course, Gussie Busch, who was a hell of a nice guy, very outspoken. He called a spade a shovel if he had to. But a very honest and straightforward guy.

"Gussie Busch was a throwback to feudal times. He was a baron, and he ran the place like a baron. He loved to party, and I was at some of those parties, and they were fun. We went on a trip to St. Louis every year, and as a result, we were close to the Busch family.

"And so the word trickled down to some of us who were close to the Cardinals that there has to be a way to accommodate *all* the ballplayers in the same facility or we're going to have to look elsewhere. And we didn't want the Cardinals to look elsewhere. They'd been training here forever, and they were our friends, and we were all Cardinal fans, and we didn't want that to happen.

"At a lunch one Saturday, I was sitting with Rolly Greene and Jack Lake of the *St. Pete Times*, and we got talking about this problem, and we said, 'We just have to do something about it.'

"We left lunch and called on John Mercer Brown, who ran the Swanee Hotel. 'Mercer was the chairman of the Committee of One Hundred. We said, 'Mercer, you're in the hotel business. You're the head of the Committee of One Hundred. What are we going to do?'

"Well, the long and short of it was, he called a fellow by the name of William Mills, Sr., and he got Jim Walter involved. Walter owned two motels at U.S. 19 and the Skyway Bridge. Jim said, 'I'll make it available.' And that was the first integrated facility that the Cardinals ever had. And after that, it never was a problem.

"I do a lot of zoning work, and there's a zoning phrase called NIMBY (Not In My Backyard). That's the way people felt. There was that attitude in general, but after Jim Walter said, 'We'll do it,' there was no opposition. Everyone was in favor of the Cardinals staying put. And through Brown and Mills and Walter, it just happened."

The new arrangement, with whites and blacks living together and swimming in the same pool and eating meals together, shattered every racist convention in the South. But instead of crosses being burned, the motels attracted a lot of business from the curious who wanted to stay with the major leaguers. The arrangement also had a positive affect on the players. Unlike on many ballclubs, the white and black Cardinal players, living under the same roof, got to know each other and became friends.

BOB GIBSON: "Several of the white players had traditionally stayed with their families in beachfront cottages during spring training, but when Musial and Boyer gave up their private accommodations to move in with the rest of the team—blacks included—the Cardinals had successfully broken down the local custom. The Cardinal motel became a tourist attraction. People would drive by to see the white and black families swimming together or holding one of our famous team barbecues, with Howie Pollet making the salad and Boyer, Larry Jackson, and Harry Walker grilling up the steaks and hamburgers.

"The camaraderie on the Cardinals was practically revolutionary in the way it cut across racial lines."

Segregation in Florida for major league ballplayers ended within a few short years. No longer would team owners tolerate racism. When the Soreno Hotel refused to allow Elston Howard and other black players on the New York Yankees to stay, the team moved from St. Pete across the state to Fort Lauderdale.

In the glare of national publicity, the black players on the Cardinals found they could eat in restaurants and nightclubs as well. The same was not always true for the black citizens who weren't baseball players.

Curt Flood, a deep thinker and a philosopher, was quick to see irony in situations. He would sit in a nightclub and stand for applause whenever he would be introduced and notice that all the busboys in the room were black.

"Were we becoming establishment blacks?" he would ask himself.

Even after he became a famous ballplayer, Curt Flood continued to be stung by slights, large and small. One night in St. Louis, he was denied service when he sought to bring a date to the immensely popular Stan and Biggie's Restaurant. The "Stan" in the restaurant title was Stan Musial.

CURT FLOOD: "One night I decided to make a big impression on a girl by taking her to a famous restaurant.

"The maître d' stopped me at the door.

" 'Can I help you?' he asked, as if wondering why I was stupid enough to make a delivery at that hour of the night—and through the front entrance to boot.

" 'I want a table for two,' I said.

" 'I'm sorry,' he answered without sorrow. 'We don't serve you here.'

"Thank God I had the poise not to identify myself as Curt Flood, baseball star. The bastard might have given me a table.

CURT FLOOD
(Courtesy Brace Photo)

"The next day in the Cardinal clubhouse I went to Stan Musial, one of the proprietors of the famous restaurant.

" 'Stan, what kind of eating place are you running there?'

"He looked at me. 'What do you mean?'

"They stopped me at the door. I tried to take a girl to dinner last night and they wouldn't let me in.'

"Musial turned livid. He said he'd look into it. I never raised the topic with him again, nor did he with me.

"When I returned to the restaurant a few years later, St. Louis was no longer so blatant a Jim Crow town. This time the man at the door nearly piddled with joy. It was 'Mr. Flood this' and 'Mr. Flood that' and 'Please let me kiss your fanny, Mr. Flood.' I accepted the adulation with practiced grace, as if it were my due. I assume that I would have been treated courteously, even if I had been a menial on his night out.

"Times had changed."

CHAPTER 55

THE RETURN OF MR. RICKEY

THE Cardinals finished in seventh place in 1959, jumped to third in 1960, nine games behind the Bill Mazeroski–Roberto Clemente Pirates, and in July of 1961, with the team floundering and dispirited, Bing Devine decided it was time to make a managerial change.

BING DEVINE: "I liked Solly. The only thing was that Solly was his own worst enemy. Solly came in convinced that the way to run this thing was: 'Here's the way it works.' He tried to overpower everybody, including the players. It just didn't work that way. He didn't have any background. Solly and Stan didn't get along so well. I don't know that they saw eye to eye or fit too well. Hemus was kind of an overwhelming personality. You had to know Hemus to like him.

"Solly and I became very close, and when I had to fire him, I finally went to Mr. Busch and said, 'This isn't working. I have to fire Solly Hemus.' And I'll say this for Mr. Busch. He said, 'If you think so, go ahead. Who would you hire?' Finally I was getting my chance to hire a manager. I said, 'Johnny Keane.' Johnny is on my list of the top ten people I ever knew.

"The club was on the West Coast when I finally convinced Mr. Busch it was time to make a move. I went out to the West Coast and fired Hemus and hired Keane, who was a coach.

"When Johnny Keane managed for me at Rochester, we never finished out of the playoffs. After the third year there in '51, I thought we needed a change of personality to keep the fans interested, so we made a change within the organization and Harry Walker came in, while Johnny went to Omaha.

"Keane was a man for all seasons. He was the opposite of Hemus. He knew how to adjust himself to handle situations and different people in different ways—and not only ballplayers but ownership and management. He came up through the organization as a manager. He learned all that as he came along. He had it by nature, but he learned it too by experience.

"When Johnny took over, he did all the right things. No matter what the status between Musial and Hemus, Johnny did what was right to adjust it."

When Johnny Keane assumed the reins in the middle of 1961, he was not expected to be a tough disciplinarian. But Keane displayed his toughness very quickly and established his authority.

TIM MCCARVER: "It had often been written that Solly went too far toward being one of the boys. So Keane felt he had to be a bit tougher when he stepped in.

"At the age of nineteen, I was not about to test Keane, even if he was generally known as a docile man. But there was a guy on the club who did test him. That was pitcher Mickey McDermott, a southpaw who had had some success previously with the Red Sox [Yankees, Tigers, A's] and Senators, where his press clips suggested he was slightly addled. A garrulous thirty-three-year-old, Mickey was a nightclub crooner in the off-season and one season had hit .301 for the Red Sox. Such credentials enabled him to walk around saying, 'I can pitch, hit, and sing.'

"After his first few days as Cards manager, Keane called us together for a team meeting. We had no idea what was up. What took place was a painful scene that none of us had anticipated.

"Pointing to McDermott, Keane said, 'We checked your room four nights in a row, and you weren't there.' They also checked his room during the day—he was never there. As a matter of fact, no one had any idea where he stayed. 'We gave you cab fare and we gave you a job. You came to spring training and you were broke. I will not have guys like you tear down the tradition of the organization.'

"Nobody uttered a word. You could hear a pin drop. The clubhouse was as quiet as an ancient church. In a hoarse voice, McDermott finally spoke up. 'John, if you feel that way, maybe I oughta take my uniform off,' he half-whispered.

"'That's exactly what you'll do. Here's your pink slip,' answered Keane, and he pulled the paper out of his pocket. Most players, almost to a man, are released quietly, normally in the manager's office. But Keane wanted this made public. He was making a statement.

"Johnny Keane's decisive action had quite an impact. At least it did on me. The general reaction was that he'd been fair and just."

Another of Johnny Keane's early moves was to let an aging Stan Musial know that he was wanted and valued. As a result, Stan Musial flourished. In

May of 1962, he singled off L.A. Dodger reliever Ron Perranoski for hit number 3,431, breaking Honus Wagner's record for most hits by a National Leaguer. When Don Landrum trotted out to take Stan's place, the usually undemonstrative Musial was shouting at the top of his lungs, "I got it. I got it!" It was the one record he had really wanted. On July 7 and 8, 1962, he hit four consecutive home runs, only the twelfth major leaguer to ever do so. And in September he made hit 3,516, passing Tris Speaker to become number two on the hit list behind Ty Cobb and his record of 4,191.

In 1963, his skills eroded by time, Musial connected for his 1,356th extra base hit, passing Babe Ruth for that record. He completed his career with 1,951 RBIs, at the time fourth only behind Cobb, Lou Gehrig, and Ruth.

Tim McCarver was one young teammate who appreciated what Musial had meant to the ballclub.

TIM MCCARVER: "The impact of a man like Musial on a bunch of ballplayers can't ever be exaggerated. Year in and year out, it was more than his seven batting titles that made an impression on his teammates. Those who spent time around him recognized that he was a person of good character and decency. He tried to lead by example. He wasn't much of a talker, a special pleader, or a clubhouse lawyer. He was just a good man.

"Sometimes the respect for and feeling about Stan reached such proportions that his teammates actually felt that with Stan around, nothing bad could happen to them. I'm referring here especially to the possible dangers inherent in travel, by both air and bus. With Stan onboard, everybody felt we'd make it to the next destination. With Stan on the plane, nothing could possibly happen to the craft or to us."

Carl Warwick, who had idolized Musial as a boy, saw his dignity and greatly admired him as a teammate. Warwick also discovered that "the Man" was not above playing a practical joke on a rookie.

CARL WARWICK: "Stan always seemed kind of bashful. He would never come at you and say, 'I'm the best left-handed hitter in baseball.' He was a gentleman through and through.

"My first year we were sitting in the Commodore Hotel in New York one night. It was my first road trip, and I hadn't as yet built any friendships, when he and Red came through. 'We're going to dinner,' Stan said. 'Why don't you come with us?' I said okay.

"We walked outside, and there was a limousine to pick us up, and we went to Toots Shor's restaurant. Toots Shor came over and sat down. A couple of Hollywood celebrities came over to talk to Stan. Also, Ed Mosler, the head of the safe company, was with us.

"Back then we got $10 a day meal money, and I gave half of that to my wife. I looked at the menu, and a meal cost $15.

"We ate, and the bill came, and Stan looked at me and said, 'Your part is $50.' I only had about $100 in my pocket, and I figured after I paid my share, I would have to eat the next days on $5 a day. I reached into my pocket to pull out the money, and Stan said, 'Gotcha. I'm just kidding. I sign. We don't pay here.' I thought, 'Whew.' Stan put it on me pretty good that night. Scared me to death. He really got me.

"Stan is a fine person."

HARRY CARAY: "Just outside the ballpark, in the players' parking lot, there would always be a group of kids—100 of them, maybe 200—waiting for autographs. At the end of one of those marathon dog-day doubleheaders, other ballplayers might duck the crowd. And who could blame them, really?

"But when Musial came out, it was different. When the kids saw him coming, they would all gather around his car. (His Cadillac was always parked in the same spot, just across from the press entrance to the ballpark.) They would part and let him reach the door to his car. Once he was there, he would turn around, lean against the car, and stand there and sign autographs for as long as it took to satisfy everyone. Forty-five minues, an hour, it didn't matter. Stan would not flinch. He would not complain. He would always have a smile or a kind word. He even carried pictures of himself to give away. He figured it was just as much a part of his job as hitting home runs or making great catches. And he was right, of course. I think it's a shame that more athletes haven't developed Musial's sense of and flair for public relations."

Stan Musial wasn't the only one to benefit from the stewardship of Johnny Keane. Bob Gibson had been 2-6 under Solly Hemus in '61. The night Johnny Keane took over, he handed his big pitcher the baseball and told Gibson that he had confidence in him. Gibson, who won the game, finished the season 11–6 under Keane to complete a 13-12 season. A decade of greatness would follow, and Gibson would be elected into the Hall of Fame in 1981.

That first day Keane also told Curt Flood, "You're the center fielder, Curt." Hemus had been reluctant to play Flood until Gussie Busch stepped in and ordered him to play him. Keane, who realized Flood was as good a center fielder as there was in the game, had no such reservations.

Keane also decided that Bill White would be his first baseman. In that first game under Keane, played over the Independence Day holiday, White hit three home runs. Under Johnny Keane there would be no more discrimination, overt or otherwise. When he freed Gibson, Flood, and White to reach their potential, the stock in the Cardinals rose dramatically.

It would be a few more rocky years before these men would combine to win a pennant.

After being on the job only two years, Bing Devine got to experience firsthand the mercurial nature of his owner, Gussie Busch, whose philosophy was to keep switching general managers and managers until he could find a winning combination. But because musical chairs in baseball usually results in chaos, Busch was his own worst enemy.

When the Cards didn't win a pennant in either 1960 or 1961, Gussie Busch's lack of patience made Bing Devine and Johnny Keane likely candidates to go out through the revolving door.

One reason Busch lacked confidence in Devine was that his general manager didn't smoke, drink, or run around with young girls like he did. During the summer of 1962, Mr. Busch considered firing him at a time when Devine was in the middle of his first vacation in years. For a time, Devine feared that he wouldn't survive the trip.

BING DEVINE: "I was the general manager and learning on the job, really, even though I had worked at the minor league level. I was learning to live with all these personalities: Gussie Busch, Dick Meyer, who was no problem; managers; players—personalities and egos.

"In July of 1962, the club was going badly when I went on a trip. I had never taken a vacation in the summertime. But my wife and I wanted to go back and visit our Rochester roots, so we made a plan to make a trip through Rochester and visit there and go on to New York and pick up the Cardinals. It was one of the few vacation trips I made with my family in the summertime, before or after.

"I went to Busch Stadium, watched part of the game, came home, picked up my wife, and left with our young children. We stayed overnight in Springfield, Illinois, and left late in the day.

"We had played a bad ball game Sunday, and I was in a miserable mood. The next day we were traveling somewhere on the road when I saw a headline in the paper.

"[Sportswriter] Jack Herman had visited Mr. Busch out at Grant's Farm, as Jack was wont to do at times he thought appropriate when he thought he might have an especially good story, and he asked Mr. Busch what he thought about the ballclub, knowing he was going to get: 'Lousy club. Can't play for anything.' Jack asked him what he thought of the manager. 'The manager is obviously not doing very well.' 'What about the general manager?' 'Well, we might have to take a look at him, too.'

"I called in to the office, and I was told, 'You better call Dick Meyer.' Dick gave me this picture of what was going on, talked about the story in the paper, of what Mr. Busch had said. I asked him, 'Do you want me to come back to St. Louis? You want me to turn around?' He said, 'No, go on and make your trip. I'll handle it to the best of my ability. If I think you need to come home, if it's reached a crisis point, I'll call you.' So I made my trip, which didn't make it as the greatest trip in the world.

"By the time we got back, we set up a meeting and sat down and talked about the club and where we were going and managed to get through a difficult time."

In 1962 the San Francisco Giants and the L.A. Dodgers both won over 100 games, and the Cards finished sixth. By 1963, Gussie Busch had owned the Cardinals for a full decade, with no hint of a pennant in sight. He sought opinions from the members of his legion of cronies as to what he should do to improve the team. One drinking buddy, Robert Cobb, the owner of the Brown Derby restaurant in Hollywood and the Hollywood Stars baseball team, had been a close friend of Branch Rickey's. At one time, the Stars had been a minor league farm club of Rickey's Brooklyn Dodgers. Cobb suggested that Mr. Busch hire Rickey as his general manager. Rickey was a name, and no one had been more successful. His last general manager's job, running the Pittsburgh Pirates, had come to an end. Cobb told Mr. Busch, "The best brain in baseball is sitting in Pittsburgh doing nothing."

Busch didn't fire Devine. Instead, in 1963 he hired a legend of a man to watch over him. At the age of eighty-one, Branch Rickey was hired to be a "senior consultant" to the team he had first helped run back in 1917. Mr. Busch was expecting a miracle worker who could finally bring his team a pennant. What he didn't realize was that he didn't need Rickey, that he already had an outstanding executive who could handle the job: Bing Devine. If Busch hadn't sent a strong enough message before, the hiring of Rickey put Devine on notice that unless the Cards won, and soon, his days running the team were numbered.

BING DEVINE: "I realized quickly when Mr. Rickey was hired that it was a move made by Mr. Busch. Richard Meyer, who was at one time the president of the brewery, was very close to me and the main reason I had been brought in, and he would lead me along by briefing me on what Mr. Busch was thinking. There were some things that Mr. Meyer and Al Fleishman could control, but there were some things that they couldn't. And this was one they couldn't. Mr. Busch could make a quick decision. Al Fleishman, the public relations man, was one of the closest people to him, and Al Fleishman used to say, 'The old man,' meaning Mr. Busch, 'flies by the seat of his pants.' Mr. Busch had made up his mind with some advice from outsiders, which wasn't unusual, that he bring in someone with a name and a baseball background. Rickey was hired and came in. He occupied Mr. Busch's office at the old Sportsman's Park/Busch Stadium office, and you have to understand I had been a young fellow when Mr. Rickey was there originally. At that time, I was little more than a runner around the ballpark. And now I'm the general manager.

"One day Mr. Rickey called me down to his office, and he said, 'I need a ride home today.' He was staying with his daughter out in Ladue, Missouri, and I had a home within a mile of where she lived, and he knew that. He said, 'My chauffeur is tied up. He can't pick me up. Can you drive me home?' So I said yes, and when we got in the car, we started talking, and he said some things that led me to say, 'Mr. Rickey, why don't you tell me the truth of why you feel you're here?' He said, 'Well, Mr. Busch brought me in, has some confidence in me, wants me to run the club where we can succeed and win the pennant and the World Series. I'm really here to run the club.' He asked me, 'Are you and I going to have trouble?'

"I said, 'Mr. Rickey, you and I already have trouble.'

"From then, he knew where I stood, and I knew where he stood. And trouble came only if one of us overstepped the bounds, where I pushed it too far and he went to Busch or he pushed me too far and I made some kind of silly mistake like threatening to resign. I tried to make it work, knowing there were some things Mr. Busch wanted to do. I don't think Mr. Rickey and I fought. At my age and his position, with what he had done, you have to figure out a way not to fight with somebody like that. And I figured a way around it.

"When we wanted to make a player deal while Mr. Rickey was here, I would gather a group of baseball people around like Harry Walker and Johnny Keane, and my people would come in, and we'd have a meeting and discuss the baseball picture, and they'd know in advance who and what we were talking about. We would get a unanimous opinion from the baseball group what we should do, and Mr. Rickey would go to Mr. Busch and say, 'They want to make such-and-such a deal, go ahead and make it. I approve it. I think it will be good.' "

When Devine determined that Julio Gotay was not an everyday shortstop, during the winter of '62, he told Rickey that he wanted to trade the youngster along with pitcher Don Cardwell to the Pittsburgh Pirates for Diomenes Olivo and Dick Groat, the sure-handed, seasoned veteran. Rickey, to Devine's dismay, was against making the trade.

BING DEVINE: "He wouldn't approve the Dick Groat deal, because we were going to put Julio Gotay, a young player, in the deal. He told me, 'I'm not going to approve the Groat deal. The reason I'm not is, I don't believe in dealing young ballplayers for older ballplayers. I always got the young player in my deals.' You have to realize that times had changed, just as they've changed now from when I was running the club.

"We were at the instructional league, and I set up a meeting during a game in St. Petersburg at the old Al Lang Field. I had gathered a circle of my baseball people, and we brought up the Groat deal, and Mr. Rickey said, 'I don't like the deal. I'm not going to approve it.' And he looked around at me and the baseball people, and he said, 'You've loaded this meeting, haven't you?' And I said, 'I've loaded it with people working for me. They are baseball people, and they all agree we should make the deal.' He said, 'I'll tell you what I'm going to do. I'm going to go to Mr. Busch and tell him, 'If they want to make the deal, they should go ahead and make the deal. Because you should judge a general manager on what he wants to do and what he does, and not what you tell him to do. If you say go ahead and make the deal, then they will make the deal, but understand it's not with my approval, but my acceptance.'

"Well, we made the deal. You can pick out two or three key players we acquired, but I don't think we would have won that pennant [in 1964] without a player like Dick Groat."

Groat solidified what was fast becoming the finest infield in the league. In the All-Star Game in 1963, the entire starting infield consisted of St. Louis Cardinals: Bill White, Julian Javier, Dick Groat, and Ken Boyer. It was the first time this happened in the history of the All-Star Game.

Nineteen sixty-three also marked the emergence of a young catcher by the name of Tim McCarver. Loquacious and arrogant, he was a contradiction in so many ways. Though a Southerner from Memphis, his baseball heroes were black men: Hank Aaron and Monte Irvin. His father was a policeman, but many of his friends had had run-ins with the law. He had been a great high school football player, but he wanted to play a sport professionally without having to go to college first, and so he went into baseball.

Sixteen teams had wanted to sign him. After he was scouted by Yankee Hall of Famer Bill Dickey, New York offered him a $50,000 signing bonus. The Giants upped it to $58,000. The Yankees went to $60,000, and then St. Louis bid $75,000. Dickey had promised to call McCarver with a final offer but never did, and the Cards told him to "Take it or leave it," so in June of 1959, he signed with St. Louis. He gave $15,000 of the money to his parents to pay off their mortgage. He bought them a new car. He invested in AT&T stock. Only seventeen years old, he gave up his paper route.

TIM McCARVER
(Courtesy Brace Photo)

He got his first taste of the big leagues at the age of nineteen. When a St. Louis newspaperman compared him to the Gashouse Gang catcher Bill De-Lancey, he wasn't flattered. Instead, McCarver, who after his playing career would be revered by many for his outspoken nature and his keen insights and opinions as the premier TV baseball commentator of his day, bristled at what he considered to be St. Louis's choking provincialism. Unlike others who found the comparisons flattering, McCarver rebelled at having to live with the pressure of being compared to a Cardinal legend who had died young. He wanted to be appreciated for himself.

TIM McCARVER: "The brewery does a remarkable job of instilling a tradition into the Cardinal players without alienating them, without commercializing them. It does as good a job as they do in their subliminal advertising. The same thing with the players. It's not brainwashing, but you're constantly reminded of the people who played before you.

"I remember in '63 I went to Pittsburgh and hit 3-for-4, hit the ball really well, and a big article came out in the newspapers comparing me with Bill DeLancey. I was twenty-one years old, a nice, polite kid from Memphis, Tennessee, and people were asking me questions about Bill DeLancey. 'What do I think?' I didn't want to be nasty, but I had never even heard of Bill DeLancey. I was trying to be as straightforward as I could, but I had never even heard of this guy.

"One of the bad things about the Cardinal tradition was the provincialism there in St. Louis that as far as the press was concerned was a lot more unfair than the Eastern press. Everyone says the Eastern press is a lot tougher. I disagree with that. Because provincialism is a lot more difficult to deal with than a press that may be tougher but is more objective, and I'm talking about New York, Philadelphia, Boston. St. Louis is more provincial than any of them. And that provincialism, like the obligations of the family, is much more difficult for the athlete to deal with. Wherever there's an obligation, there is less desire to do it, because you feel you have to do it.

"In St. Louis, they feel obligated to direct your career. In the East, they give you a chance to prove yourself right or wrong. They don't feel like they own you. In St. Louis, inevitably you have to be compared to somebody, which is the dumbest thing in baseball.

"The scouts will say, 'Doesn't he remind you of a young Roberto Clemente?' 'Doesn't he remind you of a young Jim Bunning?' No. He doesn't. He reminds me of himself.

"The newspapers had a lot to do with it, but certainly the organization. And just an awful lot of tradition there."

When McCarver became the Cardinals' regular catcher in 1963 at the age of twenty-two, the comparisons didn't stop, but before McCarver's twenty-one-year career was over, he would surpass DeLancey and take his place as the standard against which all future Cardinal backstops would be measured.

Pitcher Nelson Briles recalled what made McCarver such a leader.

NELSON BRILES: "Timmy, behind the plate, was the captain. I have never pitched to a catcher who could call a better game, strategize behind the plate, know what was going on. He was a fiery competitor as well. He was really into the game. He paid attention to game situations, paid attention to the way the hitters were hitting, paid attention to their stance and if they had changed. And watched what was going on.

"And if you shook him off, he was in your face, wanting to know why. 'What's your reason for doing that? I'll tell you why I called for my sign: Two pitches from now, I want you to do this.'

"Maybe he was not the best defensive catcher, but he battled for you. He was in the game and would constantly be there to kick you in the pants or to lift your spirits.

"And Timmy was a fine offensive catcher. He could run above average, had occasional power, and he hit in the clutch.

"Timmy wanted to be involved in everything. We used to scream at him that he was camp coordinator. 'What are you going to do? Take over as camp coordinator?' This was the way we got on each other all the time."

Yet despite the improvement in the Cardinals in 1963, they could not derail Koufax, Drysdale, and the L.A. Dodgers. The Cards made a late run for the pennant, winning nineteen of twenty games to close the gap to one game in mid-September, but when Bob Gibson broke his leg while taking batting practice with two weeks to go in the season, the task became too difficult without him.

The Cards won 93 games and finished second, six games out. The late run saved Devine's job. While Bob Gibson won 18, Sandy Koufax had one of the greatest seasons in National League history. He finished the year 25-5, including 5 big wins over St. Louis. His ERA was 1.88. Koufax's year was the difference.

To win the pennant, the Cards would have to find a way to neutralize Koufax. To Bing Devine's credit, he would go out and find just the player who could do that.

CHAPTER 56

1964

DESPITE the team's strengths, Bing Devine still had a few holes to fill. He had youngster Charlie James in left, and during the winter he traded with Houston for right fielder Carl Warwick, who had been a starter for the expansion Colt 45s.

Warwick had played for the Cardinals in 1961, but was traded to Houston early the next year. He was traded back to the Cardinals for the start of the 1964 season. "I guess I was on a two-year loan program," says Warwick. On hearing of the trade back to St. Louis, Warwick expressed unhappiness at leaving his Texas roots. "Course," says Warwick, "it turned out I couldn't have been in a better place at a better time."

Johnny Keane started the 1964 season with Curt Flood in center and Warwick in right. The right fielder recalls what it was like playing with his distinguished teammates, Curt Flood, Ken Boyer, and Bob Gibson.

CARL WARWICK: "Curt wasn't a big person. When he was in center and I was in right, we had the smallest outfield in baseball. I thought Curt Flood was a fine guy. He was as fair as anyone I've ever seen. The whole time I played with Curt, he never caused a problem. I heard fewer complaints from him than anybody. He was quiet. He played as hard as anybody did. He was a good team person and didn't seem to have any jealousies or chips on his shoulder or anything. He was a very talented person, very creative artistically, and he was pretty creative on the ball field too.

"He had good ideas about where to play the batters. He directed the outfield, and a lot of times when someone who we thought might be hitting to right-center came to bat, if a lefthander was pitching he'd walk over between innings and say, 'I really think we need to shade him more to the left.'

"That was in the days we had charts that showed where the opposition hit the ball. Harry Walker first started keeping the charts we had on the hitters. He'd say, 'This guy hits most of his ground balls between short and third, hits all his fly balls to right-center.' But those charts didn't differentiate between right-handers and left-handers. Curt kept saying, 'I don't think you can say that the batter will hit the ball the same place when Curt Simmons is pitching and when Ray Sadecki is pitching.' Curt would say, 'Let's shade him a little more toward the line.'

"I never would question him at all, because he was pretty much on target. And he went back on the ball as well as anyone. He didn't do anything fancy. He was not a showboat. He had a knack of being at the right place at the right time.

Our third baseman was Ken Boyer, who was one of the finest guys I ever played with. As long as he was playing, you didn't have to worry about third base. He was a big guy, and you couldn't believe the way he could move around. He made some plays! He would throw out runners on his knees. He and his brother Clete were as good as we've ever seen. You'd think Clete was faster and had better range, but you'd look at Kenny, and you would notice that you didn't see many balls getting by him, either.

"If anyone could lead a ballclub and never say a word, Kenny could do it. He was the kind of guy, when he said, 'I have an idea,' everyone stopped to listen.

"Late in the season and in the World Series, Kenny played with a pulled muscle. They were giving him shots of novocaine back behind the dugout, and I don't think anybody knew. He never once let on there was something wrong with him. He was just a manager's player.

"Bob Gibson was the kind of pitcher, you give him the ball, and he'll give you everything he can. Once he started throwing good, he never let up, and Bob knew not many hitters were going to hit his fastball. I played with Koufax and Drysdale, but if I had any game I had to win, I'd want Bob Gibson pitching. Bob was *the* Cardinal pitcher. Yet I'm not too sure Bob got the credit in the press that he should have gotten.

"I can remember when I was playing for Houston, we went into St. Louis to play. The visiting team had to walk through the Cardinal dugout in the old ballpark to get to its dugout, and one night we went in there for a three-game series, and I went 4-for-4 off Bob and hit a home run off a slider. The next day I walked in, and I said, 'Hey, Bob.' He said, 'Next time you're never going to see anything but a fastball, and one of them is going to be inside.' Then he said, 'Go away. Get out of here.' He was laughing, but I knew he meant it.

"Whatever Bob did was very positive for the ballclub. He was very vocal. He had his say in the locker room, on the bus, the airplane. He was a very positive force. As Bob went, we went. In the last days of the '64 season, Bob never once said 'I can't pitch today.' He gained the respect of the whole team.

"We struggled at the start of the 1964 season. And then Bing made the trade for Lou Brock, that just put the whole thing together.''

Devine got Brock, then a young outfielder with the Cubs, in June of 1964, just before the trading deadline. The Cubs were giving up on Brock despite his obvious talent, and the player they wanted in return was Ernie Broglio, who had won 21 games in 1960 and 18 in 1963. The trade would prove to be the best of a brilliant string of deals. After Broglio went to the Cubs, he won a total of 7 games in three years, and by the end of 1966, he was out of the game, while Brock over a nineteen-year career would hit .293, score 1,610 runs, and steal 938 bases, the most in his time and now second to only Rickey Henderson.

BING DEVINE: "The club was going badly, so you're looking for things to do. It's important to change the chemistry. That doesn't mean you make a bad deal. But that's the ideal time to make a change.

"The trading deadline was June 15, which you no longer have. In the off-season, I had talked with John Holland, the general manager of the Cubs about Brock, who was an interesting talent. But he still really hadn't produced much. And he didn't fit too well in an outfield in Wrigley Field, which could always be difficult to play—he wasn't the best outfielder.

"So somewhere between the tenth and fifteenth of June, I was traveling with the team on a Western trip. The club was going bad, and I felt I belonged with it. We played an afternoon game in Dodger Stadium, and we played very badly, and after the game, as was my custom, as I waited for the club to travel by charter to Houston, I went in and started making some phone calls. One of them was to John Holland.

"I said, 'We got beat again. We're going badly. I guess we're going to have to make a deal. Can you talk about Brock?' He said, 'It's interesting you called, because we've reached the point you have where we need to make a move. And yeah, we're willing to trade Brock.'

"I said, 'Okay, for whom?' He said, 'You gave me a list of pitchers several weeks ago. One of them on there was Broglio. We'd be interested in Broglio for Brock.'

"We both agreed we had to have some tag-ins to the deal. He said, 'If we get rid of an outfielder, we're going to have to get an outfielder.' I said, 'I'll need a pitcher,' and so we put together the deal.

"I remember this distinctly: I left the phone booth and went out and waited outside the clubhouse, got on the plane, and we took off. I was sitting in the front end of the plane with Johnny Keane. I said to Keane, 'Let me talk to you about something.' I said, 'Looks like we could make a deal where the key players are Brock and Broglio.' He looked at me and said, 'What are we waiting for?'

"You can't get a better answer than that. When a manager I trust says that, that helped solidify my thinking. That tells you he doesn't have any reservations, to go ahead and make the deal. So we did."

At the time of the trade, the Cardinal players felt disgruntled about losing their veteran moundsman. Broglio had won 18 games in 1963. The kid from the Cubs was very, very raw.

BILL WHITE: "None of us liked the deal. We lie and say we did, but we didn't like that deal. In my opinion, Lou had a lot of talent, but he didn't know anything about baseball. He might steal a base if you were up ten runs or down ten runs. But somehow, when he came to us, he turned everything

LOU BROCK
(Drawing by Ron Stark)

around. Somehow Johnny Keane put very few restrictions on him. Lou Brock
is now in the Hall of Fame. And we could not have won in '64 without him.''

Lou Brock hit .348 the rest of the year, with 33 stolen bases.

CARL WARWICK: ''You knew Lou had power and you knew he had speed.
But the Cubs had been trying to get him to get on base for [Ron] Santo and
[Ernie] Banks, and he did a lot of drag bunting, and the Cubs didn't have that
good a ballclub, so when he got on base, he didn't steal a lot.
    ''When he got to St. Louis, Johnny Keane said, 'You're the left fielder. You
play the best you can play. When you get on base, run any time you want to run,
and just get up and hit and do what you want to do. You're not going to be bunting. You're going to be swinging the bat.' And that's what Lou Brock needed.
There is nothing more gratifying in baseball or in the corporate world, either, to
have someone come up and say, 'Look, this is your job. You got it. And you're
going to play until you prove to us you can't play.' A player needs to have that,
and when Lou got that, see what happened. Lou Brock found out he could steal
bases, and then he began to work on his technique, took base stealing very seriously. He was on a ballclub where we had enough hitters, and Curt could run. All
of a sudden he did his own deal and made himself into a ballplayer.
    ''And listen, Lou found out he had a lot more power than anybody ever
thought. He hit one over the center field fence in St. Louis—the only one who
hit one close to that was Orlando Cepeda. Boy, Lou was a valuable asset to
the ballclub. And he worked on his outfielding skills, too. He worked hard.
He seemed to get into a work pattern that was unbelievable. He was always
taking fly balls, and he felt comfortable and secure, and security gives you
confidence, and that helped him a whole lot. Gosh, what a ballplayer!''

BOB GIBSON: ''Presto. We were transformed.
    ''None of us could believe this Brock fellow when he put on the Cardinal
uniform. In batting practice, he hit balls as far as White and Boyer, and on
the bases, he was mind-boggling. When Keane and his coaches were able to
convince Brock that his speed would take him and the team much farther than
his power, he condensed his game and as a result refined it, much as Flood
had done a couple years before.''

On July 9, the Cards were in sixth place, eleven games behind the Phils,
who appeared to be running away with the pennant. At the All-Star break, the
Cards were two games under .500 at 39-41. Gibson was 5-6. The team appeared to be floundering. Ken Boyer was playing well, but he was a prime
target for announcer Harry Caray, who criticized him viciously. One time
Caray intoned, ''Here's the pitch to Boyer . . . and I'll be back with the
wrapup after this message.'' Since the fans tended to take everything Caray
said as gospel, Boyer was booed soundly in St. Louis.

BOB GIBSON: ''When they started to announce his name, I'd yell, loud enough
for him to hear, 'One . . . two . . . three . . .' Then the boos would come,
and Kenny would just turn around and laugh at me.''

As a measure of his toughness, Ken Boyer, an outstanding performer for a decade in St. Louis, would drive in 119 runs and be named the league's Most Valuable Player by the end of the '64 season.

Timing is everything, and for Gussie Busch, Bing Devine, and Johnny Keane, events occurred in 1964 that created one of the strangest scenarios ever to play out on a baseball team. The first scene of the drama behind the drama occurred in the Cardinal clubhouse, where manager Johnny Keane and short-stop Dick Groat were feuding.

BOB GIBSON: "At the start of the season, Keane had given Groat the go-ahead to use the hit-and-run whenever he chose. But it wasn't working out very well, and after a screwed-up game in Los Angeles when Groat tried the hit-and-run three times and it backfired each time, Keane revoked the privileges. Groat rebelled, and the two of them stopped talking. The tension divided the club for a while.

"I'm sure Groat didn't intend to undermine the ballclub in his dispute with Keane, but it was working that way and Keane knew it. Just after the All-Star Game, Keane called a team meeting in the clubhouse at Shea Stadium and let it all out. He said, 'You guys might get me fired, goddamn it, but if you do, you can bet your asses that I'm taking some of you bastards with me!' He let it be understood in no uncertain terms what he thought about players second-guessing him and grumbling behind his back."

CARL WARWICK: "Johnny was not a yeller. He could pretty well let you know how he felt in a few words. He was pretty blunt. He called a meeting and said, 'It's time for us to stop all this stuff.' Because some of it was leaking into the press.

"I don't think he was really pointing out one person. Johnny would never point out a person in a meeting like that. If he had a problem, he'd do it in his office. I think he was saying, 'If the shoe fits, wear it. Let's *all* stop this. Let's don't have these whispering sessions.' And, of course, everybody was kind of down during these times. We had a good ballclub and we looked like we ought to be winning.

"We won a couple of ball games in the late innings, and then we went to New York, and Dick apologized to the players and the coaches, and after that the whole team kind of melded together. That's where we really kind of kicked it off.

"I remember I was sitting on the bench, and Howard Cosell was sitting there. Howard was talking to me, and I told him, 'Yeah, we had a meeting, and everything is fine.' Dick walked into the clubhouse, and Howard said to Dick, 'May I interview you for a minute?' Dick said, 'Yes—if you will not mention the meeting. Let's talk about the season but not the meeting.' And Howard Cosell agreed.

"Howard talked to Dick for five or six minutes and was about to finish, and he said, 'Dick, by the way, can you give us any information about what you said in the meeting today?'

"Dick's face got red. That was Howard Cosell. It really made Dick mad, and it was unfair for him to do that after he told Dick he wasn't going to do it. But Dick said, 'Yes, we had a meeting and we got a lot of things straightened out.' "

BOB GIBSON: "When Keane was finished, the air had been cleared. Afterward, Groat went up to him, apologized, and confessed that he had been one of the chief offenders of what Keane had been talking about. Those two were finally on the same page, and with that, the ballclub caught fire."

Meanwhile, Branch Rickey was working on Gussie Busch to get rid of Bing Devine and Johnny Keane. He wanted to replace Devine with Denver's Bob Howsam. Rickey had insinuated himself with Busch by explaining how he could put together a ballclub that would play better and cost less.

During the summer, a series of events that began with Keane's explosive team meeting caused Busch to distrust Devine and Keane further.

As events would have it, one of Dick Groat's best friends was Eddie Mathews, the star third baseman for the Milwaukee Braves. Mathews, it turned out, was dating Elizabeth Busch, Gussie's lovely daughter. When Groat told Mathews about the brouhaha at the team meeting, Mathews in turn made mention of it to Elizabeth, who in turn mentioned it to Gussie Busch. It was like a bad game of telephone.

When Gussie Busch finally learned of the incident several weeks after it actually occurred, he asked Devine and Keane whether there was trouble on the ballclub. The two unequivocally declared that there was not. They made no mention of the Keane–Groat blowup, because in their minds the situation was in the past and everything was going smoothly.

But Busch, who might have been seen as being more than a tad paranoid had he not been so wealthy and powerful, felt angered and embarrassed over having learned of the incident not from his baseball people, but from his daughter, and rather than analyze the situation objectively, he took out his feelings of humiliation for not being properly informed on Bing Devine.

Though Devine had been named Major League Executive of the Year in 1963, Busch had not been impressed with Devine's trades, nor with the players in the minors. Ironically, during the period when Branch Rickey and Devine worked together, the perceptive "Old Man" realized that Devine well knew what he was doing.

When Busch brought up the idea of firing Devine in July of 1964, Rickey pleaded with Busch to let the GM finish out the season. Busch agreed, but two weeks later, with the team nine games out of first and his patience spent, he fired him anyway. Player development director Eddie Stanky also was fired, as was business manager Art Routzong.

BING DEVINE: "I was fired on August 18, 1964. Dick Meyer was in the hospital at the time. He had an indication of heart trouble and an ulcer.

"When Dick found out he couldn't control Mr. Busch to stop him from firing me, he told Mr. Busch, 'I want to be there when you fire Bing Devine.'

Mr. Busch said, 'You're in the hospital. We can't do that.' He said, 'Yeah, we can. Bring him down to the hospital. We'll do it there.' So Mr. Busch, and Dick Meyer and Al Fleishman and I were there, and he did it there.

"Johnny Keane and I had been very close in the minor and major leagues. Our families were close. And Keane talked to me about his disappointment of seeing that happen to me."

The newspapers wrongly blamed Rickey for the firing of Bing Devine and the departure of John Keane. An angry Bob Broeg, accusing him of having stabbed Devine in the back, labeled him "Branch Richelieu." When the proud Rickey defended himself in the press, he placed the blame squarely where it belonged: in the lap of Gussie Busch. Rickey's candor would signal the end of his final stay with the Cardinals.

Shortly before Devine was fired, Gussie Busch and Caray were drinking at the Chase–Park Plaza Hotel, when, according to Harry Caray, Busch turned to him and said, "How about you becoming my general manager?"

"You've got to be kidding," said Caray.

"Hey," said Busch, "you've been in baseball all your life. You know a lot about the players, the teams. Why couldn't you be my general manager?"

"No," said Caray. "First of all, I'd have to take a cut in pay, and second of all, I'd wind up getting fired." Caray told him, "You ought to get yourself a real good, solid baseball man, so you don't have to even think about your baseball operation."

"Who do you think I should get?" Busch asked.

"Bill Veeck," said Caray.

"You know," said Busch, "it might not be such a bad idea at that. Do you know how to get hold of him?"

When Veeck said he would take the job only if he could acquire a controlling interest of the stock in the team, the discussions ended.

When Busch also informed Branch Rickey of his intention to fire Devine, the beer baron asked Rickey to take the job. Rickey didn't want it either. He told Busch, "I'm eighty-three, and there is no way I can be general manager. Bing Devine is a great general manager, Gussie. Keep him." Busch again asked Rickey to take the job. "No way," said Rickey. "I'm too old."

At Rickey's suggestion, Busch hired Bob Howsam to replace Devine. Howsam and Rickey had worked together to start a third major league, the Continental League, which died stillborn when major league baseball expanded to New York and Houston in 1962. Rickey looked forward to working with him.

But upon taking over as Cardinal general manager, Howsam was ordered by a Machiavellian Gussie Busch to fire his benefactor, Branch Rickey. Howsam knew it would bring a glorious career to an end. Such an order seemed cruel, both to Howsam and Rickey.

In their last conversation, the tormented Howsam said, "Mr. Rickey, I feel so bad about this that I want to hand in my resignation. I'd like to leave and . . ."

"Nonsense, Robert," said Rickey, "if you did that, you'd accomplish nothing. You just go ahead with your job and develop a winning team. I believe in you."

Howsam himself only lasted a couple years as Cardinal general manager. Like Rickey, Howsam worked hard to keep the player payroll down, and he would be bitterly resented by the players. Bing Devine, despite having been fired in midseason, would be voted Major League Executive of the Year at the end of the 1964 season. Devine, respected by all the players, was conscientious and decent. When the players learned that Devine had been fired, they vowed to do well for Devine.

BOB GIBSON: "I felt bad when Bing Devine left. I thought he was probably the best general manager in either league as far as his treatment of players was concerned. I couldn't imagine one being any better. Bing was really for the ballplayer. Most general managers are organization men, but Devine was pretty close to us.

"Howsam, on the other hand, was a difficult man to understand. He tried to run a baseball club the way you would run an elementary school classroom. He would send memorandums down to the clubhouse that a player was slouching too much on the bench or wearing his pants too low. Howsam was nice as an individual, but some of his ideas on running a baseball team were strange."

CARL WARWICK: "I think Gussie Busch made the biggest mistake of his career in baseball by firing Bing Devine and bringing in Bob Howsam. When they fired Bing, everybody was mad, very upset. I don't know of any player on that ballclub who had had an argument with Bing Devine. He's a nice guy and straightforward. If he tells you he's going to do something, he'll do it. It was unusual for Howsam to do that. After all we did in '64, Howsam sent me a contract with a $1,500 cut. And I found out all the other guys got contracts with cuts. I have no respect for Bob Howsam."

The Cards were nine games behind the Philadelphia Phillies at the time Devine was fired. With nineteen games left in the season, they were eleven games back. The Cincinnati Reds also were challenging to make it a fight. No one could have imagined that the Cardinals even had a chance for the pennant.

In mid-August of 1964, Busch came within a phone call of replacing Keane with Leo Durocher, who had managed for Rickey in Brooklyn. Durocher was a coach with the Dodgers, who were in town. The intrigue began when Harry Caray struck up a conversation with Durocher around the batting cage and invited him to be a guest on his pregame show. Durocher hesitated, but Caray told him he still had a lot of fans in St. Louis—Durocher, after all, had been the shortstop on the 1934 Gashouse Gang team. Durocher agreed to go on.

During the conversation on the air, Caray asked Durocher how he could be satisfied coaching. "You're a number-one man," said Caray. "You should be managing a major league club."

Durocher explained that he was ready to manage again, that he had fulfilled his obligation to Walter Alston, his manager in L.A., and said Durocher, "If somebody came to me and asked me to manage a team with some talent on it—a team like the Cardinals here—well, I'd jump at it in a minute. Because a club like the Cardinals should be winning."

Gussie Busch, meanwhile, was listening to the conversation on the radio, and before the game started, Caray received a call from Busch ordering Caray to drive Durocher out to Grant's Farm for a meeting the next morning.

At nine the next day, Caray, on Busch's direct order, picked up Durocher and brought him to see Busch. According to Caray, he was very uncomfortable being with the two of them because of his fondness for Johnny Keane. Caray was present to hear Busch offer Durocher the job—"if we make a change."

Before he would hire Durocher, though, Busch decided he had to get Dodger owner Walter O'Malley's permission first. Durocher worked for O'Malley, but the other consideration was that Budweiser was sold exclusively at Chavez Ravine, where the Dodgers played. Busch didn't want to anger O'Malley.

Walter O'Malley was on safari in Africa and could not be reached. Gussie was forced to wait. Had O'Malley been accessible, the likelihood would have been that Durocher would have gotten Keane's job. The whispers of Johnny Keane's demise were growing louder. Keane learned of the meeting between Busch and Durocher. He picked up the phone and called Bill Bergesch, GM Ralph Houk's assistant with the New York Yankees. Bergesch had been the GM at Omaha when Keane was managing there. The two were close friends.

The surge of the Cardinals in 1964 corresponded with the emergence of Bob Gibson as an elite, Hall of Fame–quality pitcher. It started on August 24 at Busch Stadium, when he struck out 12 while shutting out the Pirates. The win brought his record to 11-10. He then pitched 5 complete games in a row, averaging a run a game against.

In yet another important move before he was fired, Bing Devine brought outfielder Mike Shannon up from the minors. Shannon was an excellent right fielder with a gun for an arm, and during the last part of the year hit 9 home runs and drove in 43 runs. Though Shannon took Carl Warwick's spot, Warwick had the good grace to appreciate the fine job done by his successor.

CARL WARWICK: "Mike never got the credit he deserves. If you look at the other players on the club, Bill White, Ken Boyer, McCarver, Ray Sadecki won 20 games, Gibson, Flood, Brock. There are just so many guys who can get publicity. And I don't think Mike got what he deserved in the last part of 1964. He ran the bases, had a great arm. He was raw-boned and tough, and he turned into a great all-around ballplayer.

"And Barney Schultz came along and pitched well, and no one ever talks about Mike Cuellar. He came into the first ball game he pitched and won a big game, throwing that screwball, and they couldn't even touch it."

When the Cards left New York on September 23, they were five games behind the Philadelphia Phillies. The next opponent was Pittsburgh, which boasted one of the finest pitching staffs in the league.

CARL WARWICK: "We then went on and beat the Pirates in Pittsburgh five straight, and you're talking about Vernon Law, Bob Friend, and Bob Veale. The adrenaline was flowing, and all of a sudden you're saying, 'We're not out of this thing,' and then you look at the scoreboard, and Cincinnati is winning one and losing one, and Philadelphia is losing."

The Cards hosted the Phils for three games and won them all. Bob Gibson outpitched Chris Short in the opener, and then Ray Sadecki and Curt Simmons each pitched masterfully as the Cardinals took the lead for the pennant. The collapse of the Phillies in '64 would go down in history as one of the worst foldaroos in major league history.

BILL WHITE: "First of all, the Phillies were playing out of their skull. Gene Mauch did a good job managing them. He was playing guys out of position. Infielder Cookie Rojas played center field once in a while. Ruben Amaro played all over the place. And they all played well. And at some point the bubble burst.

"If you look at the stats, even when they were playing well, we won most of the games against them. We always played well against them, and we were fortunate to get them in our place with about a week left and won all three games."

With three games left against the Mets, the standings looked like this:

Cardinals	92-67
Cincinnati	92-68
Philadelphia	90-70
San Francisco	90-70

The first Met game pitted Bob Gibson against Al Jackson, a little lefty with poise and control. Jackson won the game, 1–0, allowing just five hits, while the Phils defeated the Reds, 4–3. The Cardinal clubhouse was filled with gloom. St. Louis and Cincinnati were in a tie, with the Phils one game back. Gibson was inconsolable.

BOB GIBSON: "I have never known a loss that was harder to take than that one against the Mets that Friday night."

On Saturday the Reds and Phils weren't scheduled. When the Mets beat the Cards again, this time by 15–5, the Cards and Phils were tied going into the final game. At game's end, the Cards were feeling very low.

CARL WARWICK: "Everybody had his head down. It was quiet in the clubhouse, very somber. You could hear shoes being thrown into the locker, a glove thrown in. Then Johnny Keane walked in and closed the door. Johnny doesn't give pep talks. His pep talk is no louder than his mad talks. He just said, 'Guys, let me tell you something. If you want to pout about this and if you want to keep your heads down and just call this a season, that's fine. I can't do anything about it because I can't play for you.' But he said, 'I want to tell you something. We have come from eleven games back. No one thought we could. We've been given every chance that could be given to an athletic team. The rest of the season is in the past. It's over with. We have [one game] left to be in the World Series. Which would you rather do: Be in the World Series or go home? If you want to go home, pack your gear. If not, let's go out there and win, and we won't have to worry about packing.'

"Kenny Boyer spoke up. He said, 'I'd rather play in the World Series. And Gibson too. Gibby said, 'We'll get them tomorrow.'

"When we left, the pressure seemed to be off the next day."

The final game matched Curt Simmons against the Mets' Galen Cisco.

BILL WHITE: "Cisco was a right-hander, and it was tough for a right-hander to beat the Cardinals, especially in the old Busch Stadium."

Bob Gibson began the game in the bullpen. The Mets led, 3–2, in the fourth, when Keane brought Gibby into the game. The big right-hander got out of the inning, and when the Cards scored three in the fifth, St. Louis had the lead. Gibson allowed but one run while the Cards batters padded the margin of victory to 11–4 going into the ninth. The scoreboard, meanwhile, showed that the Reds were clobbering the Phutile Phillies, who would lose, 10–0.

When reliever Barney Schultz, Bing Devine's last acquisition before he was fired, induced Ed Kranepool to pop out to catcher Tim McCarver, the Cards were the improbable National League champions. It was Gussie Busch's first pennant and the Cards' first since 1946.

CARL WARWICK: "I just kept thinking, 'Is it luck? Is it fate? Did the Lord just want me to be on the St. Louis Cardinals in 1964?' I had only been playing in the majors since 1961, and the sad part, Stan Musial had played seventeen years since playing in his last World Series, and in my mind I thought about all the players who had never been in a World Series, like Ernie Banks. And here I am, going to the World Series.

"You dream this as a kid, all your life. Well, here you are, and I thought, We had been eleven games down. We're not supposed to be here.'

"Over the years, I see Jim Bunning and the other Phillies, and they say to me, 'How in the world did you win it?' I'd say, 'We won, and you lost.' And it was the greatest thing I ever felt. At that point it didn't make any difference whether we won or lost the World Series. We were *in* the World Series."

CHAPTER 57

GASHOUSE GANG REDUX

WHEN the 1964 World Series opened in Yankee Stadium in New York, Carl Warwick made a beeline to center field to view the marble monuments dedicated to Babe Ruth, Lou Gehrig, and their manager, Miller Huggins.

CARL WARWICK: "I was floating. That was the first time I had ever been to Yankee Stadium. When you stepped into Yankee Stadium, you were on sacred ground. I wanted to go to first base, because I knew Gehrig had played there. It was quite a thrill. They will never take away those memories.

"During batting practice, I could see the press talking to the guys, Whitey Ford, Mantle, and Maris. I thought Maris was one of the greatest, just a gentleman through and through. He was my unsung hero. You were in awe of those pinstripes.

"Of course, we came from St. Louis, where the ballpark held 33,000, and here we were in a park that sat 60,000. The noise was quite a bit, and the other thing I couldn't wait to see was the shadow I had heard about all my life. And it came. I can tell you it was really dark at home plate when Bob Gibson was pitching."

The Cardinals, however, weren't very impressed with the Yankee team, despite the big names, many of whom were at the far side of their careers.

BILL WHITE: "We trained together in St. Petersburg, and we always beat them—we played hard in spring training and they just went down to get in shape. They had an older ballclub. Yogi [Berra] did a great job bringing them a pennant. We were not in awe of them."

The Cards' Ray Sadecki faced a subpar Whitey Ford in the opening game. Ford, nursing an arm injury that threatened to end his career, led, 4–2, after five innings. In the sixth, Ken Boyer singled against Ford and took second on a passed ball. After Bill White struck out, Mike Shannon measured a slider that didn't break much and sent it on a line 500 feet to deep center field. The score now was tied.

Tim McCarver then doubled, and Al Downing replaced Ford. Manager Keane sent Carl Warwick to the plate to pinch-hit for Sadecki. Two weeks earlier, Warwick had been struck just above the eye during practice by pitcher Ron Taylor, who was hitting fungoes, and suffered a broken bone. Doctors cleared him for the Series. When Warwick singled, McCarver scored. The Cards led and weren't to be headed.

CARL WARWICK: "I had taken a little bit of batting practice. Johnny Keane came down before the game and asked me, 'Can you hit?' I said, 'When I left the hospital, they said I could do what I needed to do.' He told me he was going to use me as a pinch hitter. Against Downing, I got the first pitch. I drove in the go-ahead run. Julian Javier ran for me. That was a pretty good thrill.''

Mel Stottlemyre led Bob Gibson, 4–2, going into the ninth inning of the second game, and then the Yankees scored four more runs against the Cards' bullpen to even the Series. In Game 3 the Yankees' Jim Bouton and Curt Simmons waged a pitching duel. The score was tied, 1–1, through eight innings.

CARL WARWICK: "Bouton certainly didn't overpower anyone, but he knew how to pitch. The hat coming off his head when he threw was a distraction to the hitters. Also, we had not seen him before. In fact, no one on our club had seen him. And Curt pitched a very good ball game that day.''

In the ninth inning of that game, Mickey Mantle led off against Barney Schultz, who had been almost invincible after coming to the Cards in midseason. The Cards' knuckleballer threw one to the switch-hitting Mantle that neither fluttered nor darted. Mantle, batting left handed, had been told by the Yankee scouts that Schultz's first pitch often was thrown harder than usual so the pitcher could start off with a strike. Mantle golfed a titanic blast into the third deck in right field, his seventeenth World Series home run, a record. The Yankees won the game, 2–1, and led in games, 2–1.

TIM McCARVER: "What was poor Barney Schultz doing all this time? Was he screaming at my bad call? Was he bitching about what a lousy catcher I was? Was he blaming me for calling for his knuckler? Nope. Not Barney.
" 'That's the way it goes,' said Barney, shrugging his shoulders. 'We'll get 'em the next time.' ''

CARL WARWICK: "I was sitting next to Bob Uecker, and I heard him say, 'Uh-oh.' The ball never did knuckle. It kind of stayed right where it was. It had a big ol' 'Hit Me' sign on it.
"Everybody walked into the clubhouse, and we felt, 'Okay, now it's 2 to 1, but Bob's going to pitch, so we're still okay. We just wanted to play. We came to play, and I'm not too sure the Yankees didn't underestimate us a little bit.''

The Yankees took a 3–0 lead in Game 4. Ray Sadecki did not finish the first inning after allowing two quick runs. The reliever was Roger Craig, another Bing Devine acquisition. Devine had felt he needed a swingman who could start and relieve, and he determined that Craig, who had lost 24 and 22 games in his last two seasons with the woeful Mets, was that pitcher. Craig pitched a shutout (with the help of Barney Schultz) during the stretch run and, coming into this game, felt confident. He gave up a base hit to Elston Howard, allowing the Yankees a third run, but he was sharp. The Yankees would not have an easy time against him.

The Cards, meanwhile, had made only one hit off Al Downing in five innings. In the sixth, Carl Warwick pinch-hit for Craig.

CARL WARWICK: "I started that inning off. Until then we had only three hits. I singled, my third pinch hit in a row, tying a World Series record, and then Curt Flood singled to right, and I went to second, and then after Brock flew out, Groat hit a ground ball, and they had a screwup at second base. I was running, so I didn't see it, but Vern Benson, the third base coach, told me that Bobby Richardson got ready to throw it to shortstop Phil Linz, bobbled it, and Linz had gotten across the bag when he finally threw it. Flood slid in and beat it when Linz couldn't get hold of the ball. The bases were loaded.

"Downing was pitching, and Ken Boyer hit a change-up into the seats for a grand slam home run. That made it 4 to 3."

Ron Taylor came in and pitched four shutout innings. For eight and two-thirds innnings, Craig and Taylor allowed just two hits. Thanks to them—and Kenny Boyer—the Series was tied at 2-2.

Bob Gibson was overpowering in Game 5, leading the Yankees, 2–0, with two out in the ninth, when Tom Tresh hit a two-run home run.

CARL WARWICK: "You were playing the Yankees. Everyone was kind of quiet, but you still had to think, 'Shoot, we have a good chance, too.' This was what's amazing: We never thought we couldn't beat them. Especially after the first day. When Tim McCarver homered in the tenth to win it, we were really on a high.

"We lost Game 6 to Jim Bouton. Johnny Keane gave me a chance to pinch-hit in that ball game and I popped it up, and we lost. After the game, Johnny's comment to the players was: 'Here we are. We're looking at the same situation we were in the last day of the season. Now it's a one-game Series.'

"Bob Gibson volunteered to pitch on two days' rest, and he was ready for the task. You can't do it the way the Phils did that year, pitching Bunning and Short every two days. But Gibson was young and a lot stronger than people gave him credit. Like I always say, 'If you need to get to a higher level, Bob can do it.' And Bob did more than what anybody expected. And Ken Boyer, too. We did everything no one expected the Cardinals to do."

In the seventh game, the Cards led, 7–3, going into the ninth, when first Clete Boyer and then Phil Linz, two of the light-hitting Yankees, hit home runs to close the gap. There were two outs. Gibson was tired.

CARL WARWICK: "First thing we're thinking, 'Don't walk anyone and let someone else hit one.' I don't think Johnny had any thoughts about taking him out. No. None. I don't think he would have done that. Bob didn't even look flustered to us. He just reared back, and you knew he was throwing just as hard as he could throw. With a two-run lead, you have to leave him in there.''

Gibson was really struggling. Bobby Richardson, a pesky hitter, was up. Two-time American League MVP Roger Maris, the tying run, was on deck. Johnny Keane came out to the mound to talk with Gibson and catcher Tim McCarver. Said Keane, ''Well, pal, it's yours to win or lose.'' He returned to the dugout.

Bob Gibson: ''The hitter was Bobby Richardson, who was hitting pretty good all Series, especially against me. I was pitching him wrong. The scouting reports had instructed us to pitch him away, and he kept wearing me out by hitting the ball back through the middle. McCarver had a suggestion.

'' 'He's been hitting the ball away pretty good,' Tim said. 'Let's try something different. Let's come in on him.'

''By this time, I had lost all faith in scouting reports and I was willing to try something different, so I quickly agreed.

'' 'Yeah,' I said, 'that's a pretty good idea. We'll come in on him.'

''I threw him a fastball in tight, and he hit it off his fists and popped it up on the right side of the infield.

'' 'Don't let it hit you in the coconut, Max,' Groat shouted.

''And Dal Maxvill didn't. He squeezed that ball and everybody went wild. We were world champions.''

Carl Warwick recalled the pandemonium in Busch Stadium that followed.

Carl Warwick: ''We won, and it's hard to describe what happened then. Everybody was everywhere. People were on the field. They finally brought the wives into the locker room to get them away from the crowds. It was just like a dream come true. You look back and say, 'Unbelievable.'

''We won it, and everyone wanted to know how. 'Are you sure you won it?' That's the way it was after it was all over, it seemed like. You can imagine what they would have said in the press had we lost the Series: 'There was no doubt the Cards were going to lose.'

''I was at a function with Mickey Mantle, and they introduced me as one of the key players in the '64 World Series, and Mantle said, 'How were you a key player?' I said, 'If you had gotten me out two out of three times I hit, you probably would have won both those games.' He said, 'Maybe you're right about that.' That was the Yankee way. They didn't think they were ever going to lose.''

The Cards had repeated their crazy Gashouse Gang season of 1934, coming from behind, fighting adversity from within and without the organization, winning the pennant by a hair and becoming champions of the world. The 1934 Gashouse Gang had been personified by Dizzy Dean, the '64 Gang by Bob Gibson. Both were supremely talented, powerful personalities, and stubborn.

Dean would go on to become an announcer and a beloved cult figure. Gibson, proud, in-your-face, and prone to snapping whenever he felt put-upon by the public, thus reenforcing his mean-guy image, would become the Cards' unapproachable hero.

After the game, reporters flocking into the Cards' clubhouse asked Johnny Keane why he had opted to stay with Gibson and not bring in a reliever. Keane's asnwer has become part of Bob Gibson's legacy. Keane told reporters, ''I made a commitment to his heart.''

BOB GIBSON: ''It is probably the nicest thing that can be said about an athlete and I will always remember it. I will also remember what John said to me after the game. We had come into the clubhouse before any of the reporters or television people entered and John came to me and threw his arms around me and hugged me.

'' 'You're on your way, Hoot,' he said. 'Nothing can stop you now.' ''

What Gibson didn't realize was that Keane was saying goodbye.

Gussie Busch didn't know it, but when he fired Bing Devine, he was also saying sayonara to Johnny Keane. When Gussie Busch called a press conference the day after the Series, it was to announce that Keane would return as manager.

But unknown to Busch, when the New York Yankees were on the verge of losing the pennant in September, general manager Ralph Houk decided to fire his manager, Yogi Berra, and after talks between Keane and his assistant, Bill Bergesch, Houk asked Keane to take Berra's place. Keane signed a contract with New York on September 28, before the Series, to manage the Yankees in 1965.

JOHNNY KEANE
(Courtesy Brace Photo)

The day after the Cardinals won, Gussie called a press conference to announce a long-term contract for Johnny Keane. He finally had realized that Keane had done an amazing job to bring his team a pennant, and he was offering Keane a multiyear contract extension. Gussie Busch, a man used to getting his way, had no idea he was about to be sandbagged.

Keane walked into Busch's office fifteen minutes after the press conference was to begin.

''Come on. They're waiting for us and we're late,'' said Busch.

Keane handed Busch a letter. Instead of reading it, he put it in his pocket.

''I think you'd better read that before we go in there,'' said Keane.

"Let's go. Let's go. I'll read it later."

"I think you'd better take a look," said Keane.

"Let me see that letter," said Dick Meyer. Busch handed it to Meyer, who read it and turned white.

"We can't go in there," said Meyer.

"Why not?" said Busch.

"He's not going to manage," said Meyer. "He's resigning."

Shouted Busch to Keane, "You can't do that. We've got a press conference in there."

"I'm sorry, Mr. Busch," said Keane quietly. "I've made other plans."

When reporters asked Keane what he intended to do, he announced that he was going fishing. The story would change the next day.

CARL WARWICK: "My wife and I were on the airplane, flying home [to Dallas] with Howie Pollet and his wife and Johnny Keane's daughter and her husband. We landed, and when we got to the airport, we found out Johnny had resigned from the Cardinals. Nobody knew he was going to do that. Howie Pollet, our pitching coach, was one of his best friends, and he didn't know it. So that was a complete surprise.

"Yes, Johnny took Bing's firing very personally. He was not going to be able to get along with Bob Howsam after that."

The next day Johnny Keane flew to New York City and to the surprise of Cardinal fans and consternation of Yankee fans, it was announced that the unknown Keane had signed to manage the Yankees.

BILL WHITE: "I think John was one of the better managers I played for. I know he was the best *man* I played for. I liked him, but you cannot have emotions when you play baseball. We used to drive home together after Cardinal games.

"John had to take care of himself. You can't blame him [for taking another job], because during the season evidently Busch had talked to Leo Durocher. We felt John had been screwed. If we hadn't won, Johnny would have been fired.

"The deal with the Yankees was made earlier in the season. There was some kind of agreement, either verbal or written. John knew he was going to manage the Yankees, because Mayo Smith, who scouted for the Yankees, was with us about every day, and what was strange, he was scouting for the Yankees. So I think Yogi had been fired, and Johnny had known that he would manage the Yankees."

The stunning move turned out to be a wrong one on Keane's part. The Yankees were old, and their farm system was empty because owners Dan Topping and Del Webb had stopped spending money on prospects several years earlier to maximize their profits in anticipation of the sale of the team. The decline and fall of the Yankees would coincide with the arrival of Johnny Keane, and the decent Johnny Keane would become the scapegoat. The Yankees would finish sixth in 1965, their lowest finish since 1925. After a 4-16 start in 1966, Yankee general manager Ralph Houk would fire and replace him. On January 6, 1967, Johnny Keane would die of a heart attack.

Harry Caray, for one, was convinced that the Yankees didn't want to hire Keane once Berra won the '64 pennant and that Keane really didn't want to go to New York after the Cards won their pennant. But because Johnny Keane was a man of his word, because he'd made a deal, said Caray, he would never back out of it.

Bing Devine would always rue that his close friend John Keane didn't advise him of his plans before jumping ship and signing with New York.

BING DEVINE: "Johnny Keane never did tell me what was going to happen to him. There was some talk that Durocher had come in and interviewed with Mr. Busch. I didn't know that, but I heard it. Mr. Busch was getting ready to sign Johnny to a new contract. He didn't tell me he wasn't going to take it, because if he had told me, I would have tried to talk him out of it. Johnny Keane belonged in the St. Louis environment. I really think I would have been smart enough to say, 'Don't do that—for me. Take care of yourself. Get the best contract you can, sign it, and stay here.' Johnny didn't do that. And it was a mistake. Among other things, the Yankees was a dying organization, and New York was a completely different environment. Johnny Keane was great at handling almost every situation. I couldn't picture him handling New York.

"He never did ask me. He didn't even tell his wife. And he was as close to his wife as you can get. He wouldn't do a lot of other things without talking to her first. He did not tell her because he figured she might try to talk him out of it."

CHAPTER 58

THE PASSING OF A LEGEND

WITH the departure of Johnny Keane to the Yankees, Gussie Busch was left with beer on his face. His manager had shown him up by going to a press conference called to announce his new contract only to see him walk away. What could Busch do to make things right with the fans?

His answer, a brilliant stroke, was to bring back two of the most popular Cardinals in team history: Stan Musial and Red Schoendienst. Musial was appointed to the front office as a vice president, his duties unclear, and Schoendienst was named manager, even though in his heart of hearts he much preferred to coach than to manage. The two were so universally beloved that very quickly Johnny Keane and Bing Devine were forgotten, and Gussie Busch just as quickly was forgiven. The moves could be criticized, but only gently.

CURT FLOOD: "Stan's administrative gifts were not exactly apparent while he was knocking the shit out of the ball. But no matter. He was 'Stan the Man,' and Busch could bolster him with whatever assistant was needed. For field manager, he chose Red Schoendienst, another popular player. Red was and is immensely personable. He led the Cardinals to the 1967 and 1968 pennants by the simple expedient of letting the players play. When he was required to think two or three moves ahead, as in choosing pinch hitters or replacing pitchers, he accepted advice readily. And it was given matter-of-factly, with every consideration for Red's position."

CARL WARWICK: "There was no lingering resentment over Johnny Keane's leaving because Red was so popular with everybody on the ballclub. If they'd have gone out and hired someone from outside who no one knew, they might have felt that way, but with Red there, you couldn't help but love Red. You knew he was going to be on your side all the time. Red did so much for me. He helped me with my mental attitude for pinch-hitting. Red was available to help anybody any time. Having Red as the manager was almost like having an extra player. I don't think there was any resentment at all anywhere. You kind of felt, 'Well, Johnny didn't want to stay.' The players made the transition."

Johnny Keane had always said that to win the pennant, the Cards had to defeat Koufax. In 1965 Lou Brock set out to do that personally. That year Koufax shut out the Cards in their first three meetings. In the next game, Brock bunted for a base hit, stole a base, and scored. The Cardinals wondered what Koufax would do. They didn't have to wait long.

The next time up, Koufax hit Brock with a pitch and broke his shoulder. With Brock out, Koufax and Drysdale went on to win 49 games between them that year. The Dodgers went on to win the pennant.

The injury to Brock was one in a series of calamities as the Cards finished at 80-81 in 1965.

BILL WHITE: "Everybody got hurt. I got hurt. Flood led the team in runs batted in [with 83]. I drove in 70-something runs [73], and Boyer was down in RBIS [75]. Things just didn't jell for us.

"And even if we had been in pretty good shape, it would have been hard to overcome Koufax and Drysdale. The National League has always been competitive. It's never been dominated by one team during my time."

Another reason for the fall of the Cards, says Carl Warwick, was the resentment the players felt toward their new general manager, Bob Howsam.

CARL WARWICK: "After the '64 World Series, they were talking in the papers about it being Howsam's team, and I know that irritated every player on the ballclub. He may have been the general manager, but it was Bing Devine's team. He put it together. Bing made the trade for Lou Brock, and after that you didn't need to make more trades.

"And with Howsam, we got isolated from the front office. There was never a closeness that I could see like what we had with Bing, who was always in the clubhouse doing things. Howsam was there trying to save money. I know a lot of players were very upset with what they finally signed their contracts for. That shouldn't have anything to do with your playing, but sometimes it works on your mental attitude."

In 1966 Howsam would cut the payroll by trading away the team's top three wage earners: Ken Boyer, Dick Groat, and Bill White.

BILL WHITE: "I think Howsam wanted to put his own stamp on the club. He said that we were getting old. In fact, I had a problem with him because he leaked it to the press that I was older than whatever I was supposed to be. That disturbed me, and I went in, and we had a nice talk about it. I said, 'When you trade people, you should say good things about them and let them go.' Though publicly I called him a liar.

"I don't know if I would have wanted to play for Howsam. And he probably didn't want me playing for him, either. So it was mutual."

It was a hardship for Bill White to leave St. Louis. He had begun a career in radio with KMOX. His home and family were there. His kids were in school. When he arrived in Philadelphia, he became a television sportscaster durring the off-season. In time he would go on to New York, where he would team with Phil Rizzuto on Yankee broadcasts. From there, the courtly respected White would go on to become president of the National League.

Also dealt to the Phils in the Bill White trade was reserve catcher Bob Uecker, who liked to use his mimicry skills to imitate and make fun of favorite targets, such as Harry Caray, much to the glee of his teammates.

NELSON BRILES: " 'Ueck' had a very dry wit. He'd say things and not crack a smile. In those days, he was great at imitating Harry Caray. 'Goooood evening, everybody . . .' And he had it down to a science. Harry was always on Ken Boyer's back. At the end of one game, the tying and winning runs were on second and third, and Harry was describing the action. And Boyer was at bat. And so Harry described it, 'Boyer with a chance to win the game, and here's the pitch to Boyer. Here's Jack with the wrapup.' And so Uecker would bring that up all the time on the team bus. And, of course, we would all laugh at it while Harry did a slow burn.

" 'Ueck' would do things, and the team was the right atmosphere for it, because we always needled each other all the time anyway, and so that really created an audience for Uecker. On the team bus going to or from the ballpark or to and from the airport, he would read excerpts from a book and paraphrase it, and we would laugh. He would have a captive audience for forty-five minutes to an hour.

"And an interesting phenomenon was that arguably the best pitcher in the mid-1960s was Sandy Koufax, and Uecker could hit Koufax! It didn't matter what he threw, he could rip him. 'Ueck' would always have some words: 'This over-the-hill left-hander can't get me out. Bring the heat.' Going to the park, he'd say, 'That left-hander is going to catch his lunch today. Tell him to bring that 98-mile-an-hour fastball and that curveball to "Big Ueck." ' And he was not a bad defensive catcher. I liked throwing to him. He was very self-effacing about it, but he was a good defensive catcher. Of course, you knew he wasn't going to start because Tim McCarver had established himself, so Bob was going to be a part-time platoon player."

In addition to Harry Caray, another favorite target of Uecker's was Bob Howsam, who he imitated with deadly, hilarious accuracy. Howsam, of course, knew of the mimicry and like Caray resented it. When it came time to deal Bill White to the Phils, Howsam refused to okay the trade unless Philadelphia accepted Uecker as well. For Howsam, it was addition by subtraction.

Through his reign as general manager, the players resented Rickey's man, Howsam, who would quit the Cards after the 1966 season to become GM of the Cincinnati Reds. To his credit, Howsam would become known as the man who built the "Big Red Machine" of the 1970s. But in St. Louis Howsam would be remembered by the Cardinal players more for his cheapness, annoying memos, and his prissiness than for his front office abilities.

Meanwhile, Branch Rickey, the man largely responsible for both Howsam's hiring and the chaos that marked the 1964 season, suffered his sixth heart attack and was hospitalized in the fall of 1965.

When the day came for the eighty-four-year-old Rickey to be inducted into the Missouri Hall of Fame, against medical advice he checked out of a St. Louis hospital in order to attend the Missouri–Oklahoma football game and to make his acceptance speech at the banquet that night. Rickey, a sick man for several years, promised to go back to the hospital after the ceremonies.

His wife Jane didn't want him to go, but he wasn't the sort of person to pass up an opportunity to entertain or be lionized before a packed house. He described his philosophy of living by often telling a story about how his father approached things late in his life.

"My father was eighty-six when he died," said Rickey. "As an old man, he was still planting peach and apple trees on our farm near Portsmouth, Ohio. When I asked who would take in the fruit, he said, 'That's not important. I just want to live every day as if I were going to live forever.' "

Rickey sat outside in the cold in a late November afternoon cheering as Missouri beat Oklahoma that day. He then rode to the Daniel Boone Hotel in Columbia, Missouri, to speak and receive his award. Bob Broeg, recalled the events leading up to Branch Rickey's final performance.

BOB BROEG: "I was one of the people behind the Missouri Hall of Fame, which was more a state of mind than anything else. In '65 we had an affair after a Missouri home football game. The inductees were Rickey, George Sisler, and the late Taylor Spink, a pretty appealing group, because these men made their mark here.

"Rickey was ill in the hospital, and I figured we were going to have to put up with people being disappointed. But Mr. Rickey insisted on coming, I thought, rather stupidly, because it was a cold day in late November. Missouri is not usually that cold, but it was cold that day, and Missouri beat Oklahoma, 30–0. Dan Devine's team was headed for the Sugar Bowl. Rickey watched the whole game, and after the game, when there was about an hour's rest back at the hotel, he kind of held court. He missed his chance to rest.

"I had to write my story about the football game, and so I got to the dinner a little late. By the time I arrived, everyone was seated, and Rickey was at the head table. I walked up to thank him for coming, and at that juncture he probably wasn't too happy with me, because I had chided him for his activities leading to Bing Devine's problems. I had called him 'Branch Richelieu.' He said to me, 'You didn't think I was coming?' I said, 'No, I didn't think you were coming, Mr. Rickey. Your health is more important.'

"Rickey was the third and featured speaker. Johnson Spink represented Taylor, and then Sisler spoke, and then Rickey got up and said, 'I want to talk to you about three degrees of courage,' and he talked about physical courage, telling about the time Jim Bottomley, with a badly strawberried thigh, slid across home plate and ripped his thigh open to win a game. You could have heard a pin drop while he was speaking. Then he gave an anecdote for mental courage, and then the third degree was spiritual courage. There's a biblical story about the tailor and the flies, a little story he told, but in the midst of telling the story, he suddenly straightened up, took one step back, and said, 'I don't think I can continue.' And he dropped. It was a dramatic way to go out.

"Everyone froze for a while. The fire department was right across the street. They came with their resuscitator, and Doc Nigro was there to help. Dr. Dominick N. Nigro was a great sports buff. He was the person Knute Rockne had dropped off and visited with in Kansas City. Doc put Rockne on the plane, and after he took off, Rockne crashed.

"Rickey lived almost a month, but never regained consciousness. He died the way he lived, with the audience in the palm of his hand."

Branch Rickey died at Boone County Hospital in Columbia on December 9, 1965. His wife Jane and his daughter, Mrs. Stephen Adams, Jr., were at his side in the intensive care ward of the hospital.

Rickey had been in baseball sixty-years, beginning in 1905. Few could remember when he wasn't involved in the game. His influence was so great that only Alexander Cartwright, the man who drew up the original baseball rules in 1845, could be said to have had a greater impact. Rickey had given jobs to many of baseball's top executives: Warren Giles, Bill DeWitt, Sr., Larry MacPhail, Roy Hamey, Gabe Paul, Bing Devine, and George Trautman. His genius for developing players had been unmatched. He had come up with the Knothole Gang idea. He also had been responsible for expansion. His Continental League forced major league baseball to expand to New York and Houston in 1962. He had popularized spring training, and not incidentally, his teams often were winners.

From 1926 through 1957, thirty-two seasons, his teams in St. Louis and

BRANCH RICKEY
Drawing by Ron Stark

Brooklyn won fifteen pennants. The team he put together in Pittsburgh went on to win the pennant in 1960.

In addition to the above, Rickey became a national figure when he stuck out his neck and broke the color barrier with Jackie Robinson in 1947. One could argue for Branch Rickey's place in American history as well as baseball's.

When Rickey died, Bob Broeg put his career in perspective.

BOB BROEG: "Branch Rickey was responsible for every St. Louis–developed star since Rogers Hornsby and before Ken Boyer. Every standout player up from the ranks from Jesse Haines in 1920 through Red Schoendienst in 1945 was bought, signed, scouted, or approved by the game's foremost visionary.

"Rickey and revolution have been synonymous in baseball. He wasn't a dealer in superficial revisions. He went to the root. His thinking was generally about three laps ahead of the field. His conceptions brought about deep institutional changes. They were incorporated into the structure of baseball and became the building blocks of the future.

"If he had been younger, he would have been precisely the kind of man baseball should have elected as its commissioner, but would have been odds-on to ignore."

CHAPTER 59

ROGER AND "CHA-CHA"

ON May 12, 1966, the Cards moved out of creaky Sportsman's Park/Busch Stadium and into a brand-new modern facility downtown. For the fans, the new stadium meant saying goodbye to a small intimate ballpark with few amenities but great sight lines and saying hello to a gleaming metal bowl carpeted with artificial turf and with twice the seating for fans of both the baseball and football Cardinals. To pitcher Nelson Briles, the change reflected a whole new era for the game of baseball.

NELSON BRILES: "The old field wasn't a stadium; it was a ballpark. You had that feel, the old smell of the ballpark. For me, you could smell the popcorn, the hot dogs, and, of course, the beer in the cement, in the girders, in the seats. That was really a major league baseball park to me.

"It was a friendly park if you could make the hitters hit straightaway. It was a little more generous in left field, and right field was a short porch, so you really had to work on the left-handed hitters an awful lot. And, of course, the club houses were not air-conditioned. I can remember very distinctly, the way you cooled off, back behind the dugout there was a little room, and a huge fan and a block of ice. The fan blew across the ice! That was how you tried to keep cool in those hot summer months in St. Louis.

"And when we moved to the new Busch Stadium, at the time it seemed like the Taj Mahal. It brought us into the state of the art. We even had air-conditioning in the clubhouses. And that was a treat in St. Louis. That air-conditioning came down the tunnel leading to the dugout, and in those hot summer months, you could sneak in the tunnel and get a little break.

"But moving over there, it was the transition from the ballpark—small, close to the fans, electric atmosphere—to a big stadium, which was a compromise for everybody, because you are removed from the field, and you lose that intimacy and the closeness to the action, and you also lost a good angle of view. And as a result, the fans suffered a little bit.

"And to me it was also the introduction into how important marketing was going to become. It began the end of the age of innocence for baseball where it was just a game, where you opened the gates and the fans came and you played for the pride of the game and the win. And that was the real focus, balls and strikes, home runs, outs, base hits. Once marketing became a more integral part of the total operation, there was a focus on promotions. In the past, you didn't see too much of that because the older opinion seemed to be that it was too gimmicky. Promotions made too much a circus of the game. Back then we were there for the pure baseball people. Today you can't survive with just the purists. Today you must market to the masses. That started in the mid-sixties and began to evolve. You began with Hat Day, Bat Day, Ball Day. Then we had pregame entertainment, game entertainmnent, and post-game entertainment.

"When we moved to the new stadium, I found that it was a pitcher-friendly park, especially at night. If you were a pitcher who could make the hitters hit the ball from left-center to right-center, it was spacious. The ball didn't seem to travel quite as well."

In 1966 the Cardinals finished sixth. Having traded Bill White and Ken Boyer, the team began the season with no power whatsoever. The Cards monotonously would lose one low-scoring game after another. Nelson Briles, who finished with a 4-15 record that year, had a stellar 3.21 ERA. He never got any runs with which to work.

NELSON BRILES: "What happened to our club in '66 was that we literally did not make up for the loss of Boyer and White offensively. That was an awful lot of RBIs that you sent away and did not get the same type of production in return. As a result, we did suffer. We didn't score a lot of runs. And defensively, we weren't as good a ballclub. Charlie Smith replaced Boyer at third.

"And it wasn't until May that we got Orlando Cepeda to play first base."

In early May, Bob Howsam traded left-handed starter Ray Sadecki to the San Francisco Giants for slugger Orlando Cepeda. This trade appeared to be a gamble. Cepeda had been disabled for most of the 1965 season with bad knees. By the time he returned to active duty for the Giants in '66, Willie McCovey had taken over for him at first base, and Cepeda was too crippled to play in the outfield. Another mark against him was that Giants manager Herman Franks and he didn't get along. "Cha-Cha" Cepeda's Latin nature clashed with Franks's nose-to-the-grindstone style of play. The Cards were desperate for a power hitter in their new stadium. Howsam accepted the risk. Quickly, Cepeda became an indispensable cog in the Cardinal machine.

ORLANDO CEPEDA
(Courtesy Brace Photo)

NELSON BRILES: "Orlando plugged the hole at first, but it took him a while to get untracked. He had an MVP season in '67, but in '66 that team wasn't together yet. That year I was pitching in relief, especially in the second half of the season. It was one of those years when it doesn't matter very much what you do, [bad] things are just going to happen.

"For instance, I was pitching a game in Philadelphia. It was the bottom of the ninth, the bases were loaded, and hitter hit a pop-up to Julian Javier, who never missed one. But he missed this one, and all the runs scored, and we lost. So they were unearned runs, because he was given an error, but it was still a loss. Those types of things seemed to plague me the second half of the '66 season. That's why I had a very good ERA, but a lousy won-lost record."

And so Cepeda, "the Baby Bull," helped—but not enough. At the end of the 1966 season, general manager Bob Howsam apparently no longer wanted to work under Gussie Busch. When asked why he came to Cincinnati, he told reporters, "Here I have complete charge."

When Howsam departed, he was replaced as general manager by the ever-congenial Stan Musial. Critics wondered whether Stan was qualified for so important a position, but in December of 1966, he showed a Midas touch when he pulled the trigger in a deal for Roger Maris, the reserved and moody slugger who had beaten Babe Ruth's single-season record with 61 home runs in 1961 and had suffered greatly for having done so, in part because he had hit only .269, in part because the Mickey Mantle fans resented that he had done it and not Mickey, and in part because the Ruth fans were equally resentful.

Like Cepeda, Maris had become unpopular in his hometown, despite winning back-to-back American League Most Valuable Player awards in 1960 and 1961, a year in which he not only hit the 61 homers but led the league in RBIs with 142 and tied Mickey Mantle in runs scored with 132. The next season naturally was a disappointment, though he did manage 33 homers and 100 RBIs. In '63 he was injured and had a subpar season.

After a decent season in 1964, the final year of the Yankee dynasty, in May of 1965, Maris broke his left hand sliding into home plate. Though the Yankees had X-rayed it several times and had found it broken, they chose not to tell Roger because they needed his celebrity on the field to draw fans to a team that was slowly rotting away from the inside. The Yankees kept him playing, despite the bad hand, and that year he hit .239 and was booed unmercifully.

In July of 1966, Maris, disgusted with his own performance, informed the Yankees he intended to retire at the end of the season. General manager Ralph Houk asked him to wait until spring training of the following year before making it official. Maris, a team player, agreed. Houk's trade of Maris to the Cardinals for third baseman Charlie Smith in the spring of '67 was yet another deceit on the part of the Yankees to Maris. They knew his intention was to retire. They traded him anyway. It saddened Maris that the Yankees would treat him so shabbily.

ROGER MARIS: "I went home after the [1966] season ended. [President] Lee MacPhail called me up one day and asked me if I had changed my mind. I said, 'No. I haven't.' But just detecting the way he was talking, I thought he had something in mind, and I said, 'Lee, if you have any intentions of trading me, let me know now, and I'll announce my retirement.' He said, 'No, we have no intentions of trading you.' I said, 'Then let's just do it the way Ralph wanted to do it, wait till spring training, but I'm still not going to play.' And he said, 'Okay.' And a few days later, I was traded. So I personally thought that they could have respected me a little bit by letting me retire if I wanted to retire in-

ROGER MARIS
(Courtesy Brace Photo)

stead of doing things the way they did them. If I wanted to retire, I think I should have had that much courtesy from the ballclub. But when this came up the way it did, I had voiced to only a couple of people that I was retiring, and the writers would have made me look bad again. They'd say, 'Well, he's not going to play because he was traded away from the Yankees.' They would have jumped on me like it was a big news story. So I finally agreed to go ahead and play the year."

Stan Musial knew there was some risk in trading for Maris, clearly damaged goods, but though the blond bomber may have lost much of his power after breaking his hand, he was a solid pro and still one of the great fielders of his era. Maris had a strong arm, had speed, and he brought experience and presence to the Cardinal team. He had played in five World Series with the Yankees, and he would play in two more with the Cardinals. Maris, a private man, was often surly toward reporters, and in general did not warm up to the fans, but on the field he was a star who won wherever he played. When he arrived in St. Louis, he joined Lou Brock and Curt Flood to complete one of the more memorable outfields in Cardinal history.

NELSON BRILES: "What made pitching for the Cardinals very special was that we had some great outfielders behind us. You had Curt Flood, who, in my opinion, nobody was better playing center field during his time than Curt Flood. You had Lou Brock, who could outrun the ball, outrun some of his mistakes. And in '67 and '68 you had Roger Maris, who was known for the home runs, but was an outstanding defensive player. The combination of the new ballpark and that outfield was the greatest incentive to throw strikes. As a matter of fact, Curt Flood told the pitchers, 'I don't want to tell you what you should do, but you guys got to be the dumbest guys going if you don't make them hit the ball in the air.' He said, 'If it has a hump in it, I'll catch it. Just make them put a hump in it.' And he wasn't lying. Boy, he caught a lot of my mistakes. Thank goodness for that.

"Being in the National League, a lot of us didn't get to see Roger play on an everyday basis. All of us were very aware of the trouble he had had in New York. And what we came to realize was that Roger was not a person who would seek the limelight. That was very unimportant to him. What was important was to be the best baseball player he could be. Also, he loved his family. That too was more important than the limelight, and he shunned it. In New York there had been the attitude: 'We'll make you what we want you to be.' And Roger didn't like that, and that set up an adversarial relationship.

"When we got Roger, we didn't know what to expect. Except that as soon as we got to spring training and watched him go about his work, you said, 'Oh my, look at this.' He said when he broke his hand at Yankee Stadium, he never had quite the same strength in his left hand, and that's why he lost a lot of power. But you could see that sweet swing, and he started to sting the ball a little bit. Then you watched him do his outfield work. You watched his arm, and you could see that sneaky speed. He may not have been known for it, but Roger was an above-average runner. And a great base runner. Coming out of that spring training the thing that impressed me most about Roger was how fundamentally sound he was offensively and defensively."

The addition of Roger Maris was the last major piece of the Cardinal pennant puzzle. Nelson Briles recalled how the addition of the two castoffs seemed to make the team come alive in '67.

NELSON BRILES: "We had gotten Cepeda, who was our number-four hitter and an outstanding defensive first baseman, and now you add Maris to the outfield, a left-handed hitter that we needed, a third-spot hitter we needed, a defensively sound ballplayer who was not prone to make mistakes, and that's three and four, offense, defense, attitude, all of it really molded together. Cepeda and Maris were good fits on our club because we were pretty loose, except when we got on the field. And when we crossed that white line, we were really junkyard dogs. We came after you. We played the game *hard* every day. That seemed to strike a melodious chord with both of them.

"When Cepeda came to St. Louis, his personality just seemed to blossom. There was a good comfort zone for him. I liked him very much. He had the nickname 'Cha-Cha,' and we really liked that. After the games in '67, we would come back to the clubhouse and have a players' meeting—you knew you really have things rocking when the players have a clubhouse meeting after the game—we would go through the hero of the game ceremony, and Orlando would get up on a trunk, and we'd say, 'Who was the hero of the game? Was it Heinie Manush?' And everybody would yell, 'Nooooo.' 'Was it Toulouse Lautrec?' 'Noooooooo.' 'Was it Julian Javier?' And everyone would say, 'Yeeesssss.' We'd laugh and go on, and that was the year Orlando nicknamed us, 'El Birdos.'

"And that atmosphere worked very well for Roger. He didn't have to carry anything. He could be the role player. He could sit back and play the game he loved and wanted to play. No New York people were living with him on a moment-to-moment basis. And when you combined that with the players already in place—Tim McCarver, Dal Maxvill, Javier, Mike Shannon, Lou, Curt—and our pitching—Bob Gibson, Steve Carlton, Ray Washburn, myself, Larry Jaster—the timing seemed to be absolutely perfect, with an integration of young players with veterans, an excellent combination."

To make way for Maris to play right field, Red Schoendienst asked Mike Shannon to move to third base. It was not a position Shannon played naturally, but he agreed to do it for the sake of the team. Like Pepper Martin of the Gashouse Gang before him, a star outfielder expediently moved to third base, Shannon gamely played a lot of ground balls off his chest, and his ability to make the switch was a large factor in the team's success.

NELSON BRILES: "When they made the trade for Roger, they asked Mike if he would move to third base, and, of course, with Mike and his attitude, his answer was: 'I'll play anywhere.' Red Schoendienst was the one who thought Mike could do it, because he was a fine athlete, had a strong arm. We'd say to Mike, 'You don't really have to catch the ball. It's the hot corner. Just knock it down and throw him out.'

"Mike was up for the challenge because he knew he wasn't going to play much with Roger in right field, and third was the best chance for him to play. He worked his fanny off all winter, practicing at third, and then all spring. Mike went to spring training early with the pitchers and catchers. I can't tell you how many hundreds upon hundreds of ground balls he took. You'd see him day after day, and in the beginning he did take a lot of balls off his chest. But he had good hands, and by the end of the spring training, he was more than adequate, and it kept his right-handed bat in the lineup.

"Mike had some pop and fit right in, so when you add Maris and Cepeda and then Shannon's willingness to convert to third base and doing more than an adequate job there with his bat in the lineup, all of a sudden you turn a sixth-place team into a real contender coming out of spring training.''

The Cardinals were securely in first place right after the All-Star break, when on July 15 Roberto Clemente of the Pirates lined a ball off Bob Gibson's leg. In great pain, Gibson pitched to the next batter, then collapsed. X rays revealed that he had pitched to that batter with a broken leg. His teammates would never forget how tough a competitor and a man Gibby was.

NELSON BRILES: ''Clemente used a forty-ounce bat, a club. You never wanted to get a pitch down and over the plate to him because it came right back up the middle and hard. Clemente hit the ball hard. He hit that ball at Gibson about six inches high, just a rocket.

''Gibson tried to pitch to the next batter, and he fell down on the mound. The speculation was that if he hadn't thrown to the next hitter, maybe it would not have been broken, only cracked. But you don't know.

''They took him out, and when we came into the locker room after the game, Gibby was already back from the hospital with a cast up to his knee. And we were fighting for a pennant, were right in it, and you could feel the mood of the clubhouse quiet down, and, of course, the press jumped all over that.''

Nelson Briles took Gibson's spot in the rotation and pitched surprisingly well. From 4-15 in '66, the plucky right-hander in '67 reversed his record to 14-5 with a 2.43 ERA. Briles's turnaround helped keep the Cardinals in first place during the six weeks Gibson was healing.

NELSON BRILES: ''What helped me, I went to winter ball after the '66 season and started every fourth day for Ponce in Puerto Rico. I came back to St. Louis and was back in the bullpen until Gibson's leg was broken by a line drive off the bat of Clemente. I was inserted into his starting position—and there was a *little bit* of skepticism. 'How is this runny-nosed kid from Northern California going to replace Bob Gibson?'

''Earlier when Ray Washburn took a line drive off his thumb and broke it, the press was saying, 'Now's the opportunity to put Briles in the starting rotation.' But Red said, 'No. We have four other starters. We need him in the bullpen. We're going to leave him there.'

''Well after Gibson was felled by the line drive, they asked, 'Who is going to take his place?' They didn't want to bring up an inexperienced player from the minor leagues, being we were in a pennant race. And so it was decided I would now start in his place.

''The writers were saying, 'This is it for the Cardinals. The leader is gone.' They were starting this kid who was not successful as a starter in '66.

''In my first game, I pitched very well. Hank Aaron beat me with a home run, 3–2, on a Sunday afternoon. Henry was a tough out. Like most superstars, he could beat you many ways. He could beat you with the long ball, and in the sixties he wasn't pulling the ball as much. He was still spraying the ball around, so you couldn't pitch to him one way. You had to mix them up and move them around. And I got a fastball down and over the plate, and he was right on it, hit it out of the ballpark.

"Of course, everybody was saying, 'That would have been Gibson's start. We lost, and it doesn't bode well.'

"And then, fortunately, I went on to win 9 in a row during the season and 1 in the postseason, and completely turned around that thought process. Not only was it 9 in a row for me, but it was in Gibson's position. Rather that looking at it as, 'Boy, there's a lot of pressure on me. I'm trying to fill his shoes,' I had a positive approach to things. I go back to this continually when I speak: You always have to be ready to walk through a door of opportunity, because it might only open one time for you, and if you're not ready to take advantage of that, that might be the only opportunity you ever get.

"And fortunately I was ready, and I made the most of my opportunity and went from there on to the rest of my career. And that also labeled me as a guy who was not afraid of pressure, of not being afraid to pitch in big games, and that stayed with me the rest of my career."

In addition to Briles, youngsters Steve Carlton and Dick Hughes pitched well. The three were a combined 19-6 while Gibby was mending. Hughes, a character, liked to focus with the scope of his hunting rifle on pedestrians from the window of his hotel room. Carlton, a tall, talented southpaw, began his career ruing his every outing.

CURT FLOOD: "Steve Carlton was always certain that each inning would be his last. 'I haven't got it,' he would moan to me on the bench while our side was at bat. 'I'm shot. I'll never make it. They better take me out.'

"I used to give him the old Knute Rockne. 'Goddamnit, Carlton, you gotta hang in there. You're all we've got. Now get your ass in gear and earn your money.' And he would drag his miserable self to the mound and throw the best left-handed stuff since Koufax, dying with every pitch."

In 1967 Carlton came into his own. Nelson Briles, his roommate on the road, saw his obvious talent.

NELSON BRILES: "He was a high-strung guy but also a fierce competitor. The attitude of the pitching staff rubbed off on him as well. It's what all the young pitchers took away from pitching in St. Louis. The team was competitive, and that had to rub off on you. Steve didn't develop the slider until his last year in St. Louis [1971]. He was a fastball, curveball pitcher and didn't enjoy the success he was to have until he added that Sparky Lyle–type power slider, and shoot, he won four Cy Youngs after that."

As a result of the solidification of the pitching staff, the Cardinals clung to the top spot while Gibson recuperated. When the big right-hander returned on September 7 to pitch against the New York Mets, the Cards were a solid ten games in front. His return gave the entire team a boost. His ferocity and will to win imbued the rest of the pitching staff, which turned up the heat a notch or two.

NELSON BRILES: "Gibson came back in September and won three in a row. Watching him helped me become better. He had a fire in his belly when he went to the mound. His approach to the game rubbed off on me, helped me to focus a little better. I've always been very competitive, but I really saw in action what it meant to have the eye of the tiger.

"You see in him a quiet confidence. You see in him his approach to every hitter. He didn't concede any at-bat to a hitter, much like Pete Rose never conceded any at-bat to a pitcher. It was that focus, confidence, and the ability to get the job done every pitch, every time. And also what I learned from Bob Gibson, he refused to accept excuses. There is a difference between a reason and an excuse. He didn't want to hear the excuses. Didn't want to hear it. If a pitcher said, 'They didn't get me any runs. If I'd have been pitching yesterday, I would have won the game,' he would say, 'If you're only going to get three runs, then only give up two. If they aren't scoring for you, don't give up the first run. Because you might lose.' He always had a positive approach. His glass was *always* half-full, and that rubbed off and helped me. It wasn't as though he put his arm around me and said, 'Hey, kid.' It wasn't that at all. It was daily observation. He never slacked in his work. He was a *very* hard worker, as were almost all the guys on that team.

"Other teams might have had more talent, position for position, but I don't think there was a team at that period of time who got more out of their talent or players who worked better together. It was a team of twenty-five junkyard dogs going about their business. They'd find a way to win.

"And from my perspective, Red was the best manager for that ballclub, because he was dealing with veterans. He was dealing with players who had won a Series in '64, and so they knew what winning was all about. They guys had five, six years of major league experience and so what Red did, what was so important, he stayed out of the way. These are guys who can play every day. He didn't have to make a lot of lineup changes on a daily basis. And so he allowed the players to play the game the way they liked to play. He let Brock and Flood do their game. Curt would take pitches deep into the count to let Brock steal, and they had their own hit-and-run. They had their own defensive things that they did. Same thing all the way through the lineup. And that was a huge plus. And Red didn't seem to be one to panic. He liked to emphasize, 'Work hard and play hard. You have to enjoy the game, enjoy the challenge.' He allowed the players to kind of manage themselves, and that's what made Red so special."

The Cards finished the 1967 season with 101 wins, ten and a half games ahead of the Giants. Orlando Cepeda, the Giants' castoff, hit .325 with 25 homers and led the league with 111 RBIs. Cha-Cha was named MVP in the National League.

CURT FLOOD: "Cepeda had been traded to us with a reputation as a trouble-maker. He had been indispensable to our 1967 championship, when he batted in 111 runs and also supplied a personal exuberance that we had lacked. He was our cheerleader, our glue."

Another player who had an important role in the Cardinals' winning the pennant in 1967 was relief pitcher Joe Hoerner, who saved 15 games. Hoerner was a free spirit with a heart problem. He was unpredictable and wild. A bar hopper, Hoerner rarely pitched on Sundays because he had the habit of staying out all Saturday night.

NELSON BRILES: "Joe epitomized the journeyman ballplayer. He had been in the Houston organization, and at the end of spring training in '66, he was given a chance because Hal Woodeshick was hurt, so they needed to bring north with us a left-handed relief pitcher. He was given an opportunity, and he became a tough left-handed pitcher for us.

"He was a unique character in that if he threw the ball overhand, it bothered his heart. He would have to take medicine all the time. As long as he threw sidearm and took his medicine, he was fine. As a matter of fact, in one game, Joe came in in relief on a hot Sunday afternoon, and he was warming up and it seemed like he was having a hard time breathing. He threw some pitches to the first hitter, who got a base hit, and he was having a hard time. So Red finally went out and said, 'Joe, what's the matter?' He said, 'Red, I'm having trouble. I forgot to take my pills.'

"Joe was also a fun-loving guy. We were in Atlanta, Fulton County Stadium, and after the game, we were waiting on the bus driver, who didn't show up. Atlanta Fulton County Stadium had an inner concourse, and the bus had pulled in there. Very difficult turns to get in and to get out. Joe became impatient, and he said, 'I can drive one of these things. I drove a tractor on the farm.' We were all laughing. Most of us didn't even know how to start it. Joe started it up.

"He said, 'As long as we have it started, we might as well get under way.' Of course, about ten guys bailed off the bus right there. I was up front, and he said, 'Nellie, I'm just going to take it up here a few feet just to play.' And when he got going, he said, 'Why don't I take it around once?' And so we started to go around once, and we came to the exit, and Joe said, 'I can make it. I can make it!'

"Professional drivers had trouble with this, and I'll be a son of a gun if he didn't wheel the thing right through the exit! Didn't stop, nothing, made the turn, and now we were out of the stadium and heading down the street to the hotel! Oh yeah!

"We were going the back way and were coming to an overpass. We looked at the clearance and the height of the bus, and we said, 'Joe, stop. It won't fit.' Joe said, 'If you get up enough speed, it will fit anywhere.' And he floored it.

"We went under, didn't hit it, and I don't know how. So then he pulled into the Marriott. He cut it a little too short, and he parked the bus on top of the 'Marriott' sign that was in the flowerbed. And then we scattered!

"That was Joe Hoerner, a fun-loving guy. But during his time, he was one of the best from the left side. I once went up to Willie Stargell and I asked him, 'Toughest short reliever ever?' He said, 'Joe Hoerner. I never got a hit off him. I hated to face him.' "

What made the team special was the team's makeup during a period of great civil unrest in America. The team was interracial, led by black stars like Curt Flood, Bob Gibson, and Lou Brock, white ones such as Tim McCarver, Mike Shannon, and Roger Maris, and a Latin star, Cepeda. America couldn't help but notice that the obvious camaraderie among the players contributed greatly to their success.

CURT FLOOD: "The Cardinals of 1967 and 1968 must have been the most remarkable team in the history of baseball. I speak now of the team's social achievements, without which its pitching, batting, and fielding would have been less triumphant than they were. The men of that team were as close to being free of racist poison as a diverse group of twentieth-century Americans could possibly be. Few of them had been that way when they came to the Cardinals. But they changed.

"The initiative in building that spirit came from black members of the team. Especially Bob Gibson.

"It began where motivation always begins in baseball. We wanted to win championships so that we could make more money. And we blacks wanted life to be more pleasant, championships or not. The process took five or six years. It began with Gibson and me deliberately kicking over traditional barriers to establish communication with the palefaces.

" 'How about coming out for a drink after the game?' Hoot would ask a player who had never gone to a bar with a black man in his life. He was turned down more than once. So was I. But the spirit was infectious. After breaking bread and pouring a few with us, the others felt better about themselves and us. Actual friendships developed. Tim McCarver was a rugged white kid from Tennessee and we were black, black cats. The gulf was wide and deep. It did not belong there, yet there it was. We bridged it. We simply insisted on knowing him and on being known in return. The strangeness vanished. Friendship was more natural and normal than camping on opposite sides of a divide which none of us had created and from which none of us could benefit.

"Friendship was better for the team. It brought that World Series look closer. It was a more potent force than the locker room pranks and other forms of on-the-job congeniality, which had previously been the limits of baseball togetherness. We knew each other's families. Those of us with a taste for the joys of the night swapped booze and chicks from one end of the country to the other.

"It was baseball on a new level. On that team, we cared about each other and shared with each other, and face it, inspired each other. As friends, we had become solicitous of each other's ailments and eccentricities, proud of each other's strengths. We had achieved a closeness impossible by other means.

"And we did it by ourselves.

"There we were, including the volatile Cepeda, the impossible Maris, and the impenetrable Gibson—three celebrated noncandidates for togetherness. There we were—Latins, blacks, liberal whites, and redeemed peckerwoods—the best team in the game and the most exultant. A beautiful little foretaste of what life will be like when Americans finally unshackle themselves."

NELSON BRILES: "We were very much aware how free from 'racist poison' we were. Coming from a small town in Northern California, I really wasn't exposed to racism. And when they would tell me that they hadn't been able to stay at the same team hotel in spring training, I was flabbergasted. That wasn't so when I joined the club. That was back in '62, and when they started telling me stories, I said, 'Aw, you're just making that up.' And they'd say, 'No.' But I can tell you with all honestly that the statement made by Curt Flood is absolutely correct. We went out together as a team. We played hard together on the field as a team. We won as a team, lost as a team, and it was nothing to see white and black and Latin players out together afterward.

"And back in '67, that was rare. How about this situation? We were going to Boston for the 1967 World Series, and Boston was the favorite, the 'Impossible Dream' team. They had the American League Triple Crown winner, Carl Yastrzemski, and 22-game winner Jim Lonborg. All of New England was going nuts, because they hadn't won since before Washington was President. And there was all this electric atmosphere.

"Gibson, Brock, Flood, myself, and others were jazz enthusiasts, and we would go to jazz clubs on the road together. Well, Gibson, Flood, and Brock came to me and said, 'Nellie, do you and your wife want to go to a party tonight? It's being hosted by Bill Russell's wife. Cannonball Adderley [a big saxophonist of the day] and his brother, Nat Adderley, are going to play a bit.' He said, 'We're going to have a little soul food, and it's going to be a nice social evening.' I didn't hesitate. 'Absolutely,'' I said.

"When we got there and walked in the door, I was the only white guy in the whole place. Just me. Wayne Embry, the Celtic basketball player, was there with his wife, and K. C. Jones and Bill Russell and their wives, and I never had such a good time in my life. We shared baseball and music and the food, we'd had some champagne and wine, and as we were getting ready to leave around ten o'clock at night, Wayne Embry and K. C. Jones said to Gibson, Flood, Brock, and me, 'The only reason we got you guys here is that we just wanted to fill you full of champagne and wine so we can kick your fanny tomorrow.'

"Well, Gibson went out and struck out 10, hit a home run, and after the game, they both came down to the sidelines, and we said, 'How about another party tonight?'

"They said, 'Oh no, that's mother's milk to you guys.' "

CHAPTER 60

WORLD CHAMPIONS

GOING into the final day of the 1967 season, the Detroit Tigers, Boston Red Sox, and Minnesota Twins fought for the American League pennant. Boston's Jim Lonborg, a workhorse all season long, faced Dean Chance of the Minnesota Twins. Chance, a sinkerballer, seemed to dominate the Sox.

Chance led, 2–0, going into the sixth inning, but Carl Yastrzemski, who had been superhuman the final month of the season, singled with the bases loaded and Chance was done. After an error and two wild pitches, the Sox had the victory. When Detroit lost to the California Angels, the Red Sox were league champions.

After the pennant-clinching game, Boston manager Dick Williams told Yastrzemski, who finished the year with 10 hits in his last 13 at bats, "I've never seen a perfect player, but you were one for us. I never saw a player have a season like that."

The Red Sox had completed their "Impossible Dream," their first pennant since 1946, when they were beaten by the Cardinals in the World Series.

Nelson Briles recalled the madhouse that bubbled around Fenway Park as the Series was about to get started. What impressed him most were how many reporters and TV newsmen were covering the game.

NELSON BRILES: "The day before the first game in Boston, I walked out of the tunnel coming into the dugout and looked out on the field while Boston was taking batting practice, and I saw 2,000 to 3,000 media on the field at one time. It blew me away. Everybody wanted a piece of you. And they were very competitive. Everybody wanted their angle, their story. I just . . . it was almost overwhelming. But thank goodness, I was on a team that had been there before, and so after that, Tim McCarver and Curt Flood and Lou Brock and Mike Shannon and those guys said, 'Here's what's happening. And this is what they are going to try to do,' and it settled things down. That helped a lot.

"A little story about workout day: It was just about our turn to go out and take batting practice. Boston hit first, and they came off the playing field, and Gibby was hitting with the starting lineup, and Gibby was the first guy in the cage so he could get his swings out of the way. And being the outstanding athlete he was, he hit a couple on the screen. He was chirping a little bit. He said, 'A right-handed batter should pay to play in this ballpark. You don't have to be anything special to hit here.' And Yaz chipped in, 'Well, what if you were a left-handed hitter in this ballpark? This is what Ted Williams had to face. This is what I have had to face, that deep right-center field.' Well,

Gibby turned around on the other side, and he hit one out! He said, 'Any questions?' He turned and walked away. True story.''

Bob Gibson pitched against Jose Santiago in the opener. Santiago allowed two runs, Gibson one. Gibson struck out 10 and allowed but 6 hits. Santiago walked Curt Flood in the 7th, and with two outs, Julian Javier doubled into the left field corner for the game winner.

Lonborg evened the Series at one game apiece when he pitched a 5–0 shutout in the second game. When the teams moved to St. Louis, Red Schoendienst tapped Nelson Briles to pitch. He faced Red Sox right-hander Gary Bell.

NELSON BRILES: "All my family had come in from California. We didn't make any money in those days. I was making $7,000, and so when my family came in—they didn't have any money—they stayed with us, and I slept on the floor. I'm starting a World Series game, the first one in my life, and I'm sleeping on the floor in the living room so my mother could have a bed.

"Anyway, it rained during batting practice the day of the game. I was walking down the right field line to warm up in the bullpen, and Casey Stengel was sitting down there in the stands, and Casey said, 'You're representing the National League, kid. You can do it. Give it all you got.' I said, 'Thanks, Case.'

"I warmed up. Everything was fine. A few butterflies but not bad. I came back into the dugout, ready, they introduced everybody, we went out. I warmed up. Everything was fine. They played the National Anthem. Everything was fine. I looked in to get the sign, and everything was fine. The umpire said, 'Play ball.' And all of a sudden somebody opened up a syringe of adrenaline. I have never in my life had such an adrenaline rush like that. And it was uncontrollable. I mean, my heart was going 10,000 beats a second! I was known as a pretty poised player, someone who was pretty much in control of my emotions. I thought, What's going on here? I don't understand this. I'm prepared. I'm ready.'

"I backed off the mound, and I got back on, threw the first pitch, and I bounced it in front of home plate. Then I tried to throw a curveball, and I bounced that. I thought, 'Man, I got to get control.' So I backed off, took a deep breath, and then threw the first strike, and once that was done, that was all over. That's something you never forget.

"In the first game, Gibson struck out 10. Lou Brock stole bases, had a lot of base hits. Flood had a good game. In the second game, Jim Lonborg knocked three or four of our guys down, hit a couple guys. Our pitcher did not retaliate. Yaz had a big game, hit two home runs, and they beat us.

"It was coming to the third game, and nobody said a word to me. Nothing. So I went out to the mound, and the first out was made by Jose Tartabull, and the ball came around the field, and Mike Shannon, who had a strong arm, was over at third base, and he took the ball and tried to throw it through my chest. He was saying, 'What the hell is going on? Isn't anybody going to protect us?' That's the message that came with that throw.

"The next guy up, the same thing, a ground ball out, around the infield over to Shannon, and now he tried to throw it harder. And I caught it. Same message.

"Next hitter up was Yastrzemski. I hit him in the knee. And from that point on, we had a Series. All the junk was out of the way. There were no more knockdowns, no more nonsense. And I think at that moment I gained the respect of the ballclub. I threw a complete game [5–2] victory.

"Of course, I was fined, and everybody was yelling at me. The next morning in the clubhouse, 100 telegrams from New Englanders stacked in my locker three feet high saying: 'If you ever come up here, we're going to kill ya.' 'My son will burn your baseball cards. He will never speak your name again.' All kinds of stuff.

"I said to my teammates, 'Look at this stuff.' Of course, the ones that were threatening I had to turn over. We had to call in the FBI. I said, 'I guess I upset some people.' But understandably. Yaz was their darling. This was their 'Impossible Dream' team. And they were ardent, deep-rooted baseball fans. They are the purists. And so you can understand all of those things.''

Said an angry Dick Williams after the game about Briles' attack on Yastrzemski, "The St. Louis Cardinals are as bush as the name of the beer company that owns them.''

Bob Gibson further angered the Red Sox fans when he shut out Boston, 6–0, in Game 4. Briles recalled his mastery.

NELSON BRILES: "I recall most the surgical precision he had. Gibby was not only a hard thrower, he moved the ball around. He backed hitters off the plate. He could be intimidating.

"He didn't throw at that many guys, but he would back you off the plate, which was only good if you had command of your pitches within the strike zone.

"And you talk about having focus and concentration, deepness of thought, shutting everything out. Well, for those three games that he pitched, every one seemed like a duplicate of the previous one. Total focus, total command. He had his 'A' game, with everything together. His pitch selection was good, and he was able to make his pitches. Just the whole thought process and physical execution were together at one time. And when you see an athlete do that, sometimes it's just for one moment or one game. When you see that mastery, that's special. When you see that, that's a special moment.''

The Cardinals were just one game away from winning the Series. In Game 5, Jim Lonborg showed his top form, defeating the Cardinals, 3–1, on a three-hitter. Schoendienst started Dick Hughes in Game 6.

NELSON BRILES: "Dick Hughes had a big year for us. He had pitched Game 2, and we needed him to come back in Game 6, but he didn't fare well. The Sox scored three runs off him in the fourth inning to take the lead, and after Ron Willis retired the side, I came in to start the fifth to not really a standing ovation in Boston.

"The fence in the outfield bullpen was hanging ten deep. Oh, as soon as I got up in the bullpen and took my jacket off, the Boston fans started talking about my upbringing and motherhood and fatherhood and just absolutely everything.

"Under a lot of circumstances, that can be very intimidating. But I seemed to feed off that, and the worst they got, the more competitive I got, and I just used that and came into a game in a crucial situation and was able to do well. Red pinch-hit for me, and we went on to lose that game. But when I came into that ballpark, oh my. And like an idiot, sometimes you do things you can't explain. They sent out the golf cart with the baseball hat on it. I sent it back. I was walking! In front of all 38,000 of them. 'Come and get me!' I was feeding on it. Looking back, you think, 'How stupid can you be?' But by the same token it was fueling my emotions. But that doesn't do you any good if you're not able to concentrate and focus on the job at hand and keep control of your emotions and thought processes."

After an 8–4 Red Sox victory in Game 6, the country's eyes were turned to Fenway Park for the final contest of the '67 Series. Schoendienst started Bob Gibson on three days' rest. Dick Williams decided to go with his best, Jim Lonborg, on two days' rest.

NELSON BRILES: "We were staying at the Sheraton out in Quincy. It had been closed, but we ended up having to stay there. That was because the Red Sox had won the pennant on the last day, and our traveling secretary was trying to make reservations in all the cities, and we were late getting to Boston, because for a while it didn't look like they were going to win. And so the only place we could get was this closed Sheraton way out in Quincy.

They opened it for us, and the rooms were musty and there was no food service. We said, 'This is a New England plot.'

"Before the seventh game of the World Series, we were on the team bus going to the ballpark, and we were complaining about breakfast, and all of a sudden Gibby said, 'I haven't eaten any breakfast yet.' I thought, 'We're going to the World Series, Game 7, and you haven't eaten breakfast?' We said, 'We can't have this,' and we stopped the bus in the neighborhood, and somebody ran into this greasy spoon—this was a Sunday—and came out with a fried ham and egg sandwich. And in those years you still cooked with Crisco, and the grease was dripping in the brown bag. And that's what Gibby pitched on. But again, no excuses, no reasons, nothing. That's what it is, let's deal with it, let's go do it. That's the way the day started out, with our pitcher eating a greasy ham and egg sandwich.

"Then going into the game, I remember watching him work. You don't want to make glaring mistakes, but I was struck by how aggressive he was and in total command he was, and then, to top it off, not only was he a great pitcher, but he was an outstanding athlete, and in the fifth inning he hit a long home run."

Despite pitching that day with a toothache, Gibson was sharp and Lonborg hittable. Gibson's 380-foot blast off a hanging slider by Lonborg gave the

Cardinals a 4–0 lead en route to a 7–2 win. Bob Gibson recalled the ninth inning of the final game with pride.

BOB GIBSON: "There was so little left of my fastball that I was mostly throwing sliders. Yaz, who still wouldn't quit, caught one of them for a single, and then [Hawk] Harrelson pulled a hard grounder to Maxvill, who threw to Javier, who threw to Cepeda for possibly the fastest double play I'd ever seen them pull off. I had the pleasure of striking out [George] Scott to end the Series with a three-hitter."

Gibson's three victories in the 1967 World Series catapulted him to national prominence. Before the Series, Gibson had been a St. Louis phenomenon. By winning three games in the Series and joining such legends as Christy Mathewson, Charles 'Babe' Adams, Jack Coombs, "Smoky Joe" Wood, Urban "Red" Faber, Stan Coveleski, Harry Brecheen, and Lew Burdette, the big Cardinal right-hander ensured himself a secure place in baseball history.

NELSON BRILES: "In '64, Gibby won two games in the Series. He wasn't really the focus that year. Ken Boyer was the big man. Boyer was MVP, and Bill White and Flood and Brock also were the story then, as Gibby was just beginning to make a name for himself.

"Sixty-seven was his stage. Like the '71 World Series was Roberto Clemente's stage. He had the worldwide opportunity to display all he was and all that he had. In '67, that's exactly what it was for Bob Gibson. And he certainly did not disappoint."

Briles recalled the crush and the celebration in the Cardinal locker room after the final game of the Series, as he looked back with nostalgia on one of the great Cardinal teams in history.

NELSON BRILES: "It's very small, and it was not only our people but the media, the owners—everybody in the world you could cram in there. There was no room to move. One thing that impressed me: When you work for Anheuser-Busch, everything is first-class, top drawer, so when we came in the clubhouse, there were washtubs and washtubs and washtubs full of the best champagne you could buy. There was all you could want and more. And we were there for four hours. We were there and celebrated the victory in a true first-class manner. We sent champagne outside to the wives.

"You realize you are world champions, that you've won the World Series, but the importance of that doesn't really sink in until you've had a chance to think about it over the winter. And you hear people talk about it and how special it is, and how few people are able to enjoy that as a player. And what a special relationship the players on that team and the fans had, and the character of the club, the camaraderie of that club, the blended talent, is something that a lot of teams never capture.

"And the luster of that memory continues to grow, and it was something in your life that can never be taken away. You were on a team that was so special for that frozen moment in time."

CHAPTER 61

THE INTIMIDATOR

IN 1968 Gussie Busch did something he didn't do very often. He publicly admitted he had made a mistake. When Stan Musial decided he no longer wanted to be general manager after one very successful season, in 1968 Busch rehired Bing Devine, whose firing in August of 1964 had led to the embarrassing resignation of Johnny Keane. Devine would run the Cardinals until Mr. Busch would again lose his patience, firing him again in 1978.

BING DEVINE: "I was in New York with the Mets from 1965 through 1968. The last thing I did with the Mets was sign Gil Hodges as the manager.

"When I moved to New York, my wife Mary said to me, 'I can see you're going to be moving around a lot. You go ahead and work, and I'll stay here in St. Louis and keep the children in school and give them stability. And you come visit me when you can, and I'll come visit you when I can.' We lived that way for three years. In the wintertime, I commuted to St. Louis three nights a week. In the summer, I was traveling with the club or with the minor league teams.

"I liked the Mets and liked working with them, and Joan Payson was the nicest person in the world to work for. I got along with Donald Grant, thought he was great, easy to work for, even though a lot of people didn't like him. You had to do some talking with him, but he listened to reason.

"I came back to the Cardinals because we had the family and house here. I was originally a St. Louis man. The truth was, although I did a pretty good job in New York—a lot of that '69 team was my players—I might have been the right person at the right time for St. Louis. It seemed the right thing to do at the time.

"After the one year, Musial didn't want to work. Like everything else he ever did, he did his job well. He spent a lot of time on the phone with me in New York, saying, 'I got a deal I can make. What do you think from my standpoint?' So Stan won the pennant, he won the World Series, and it was time for him to get out and do something else. Stan never made any bad decisions. Stan is one of a kind. What you see is what you get. He's a nice man in every respect, as he was as a ballplayer.

"Dick Meyer apparently convinced Mr. Busch to bring me back. Mr. Busch said to Dick, 'Stan is leaving. What are we going to do?' And Dick Meyer took the opportunity to say, 'I think Bing Devine can be brought back,' and as Dick told me the story, Mr. Busch said to him, 'Why would he come back? He's in New York. He's doing fine there.' And Dick said, 'His family is here. I have a feeling he'd be willing to come back.' So Mr. Busch said, 'Go ahead and contact him and see what you can do.'

"I don't really have any sense whether Mr. Busch regretted having fired me. Mr. Busch did things at the spur of the moment that struck him as right, and most of the things he did were right, even though he may have gotten advice from an outsider or someone who wasn't even working for him. But when you think about it, somehow he made everything work. He was a tough man, but beneath that exterior he was a nice man. My wife will tell you that. She loved him.''

Devine also became available because he no longer could abide the meddling of New York Mets president M. Donald Grant. Many baseball organizations have amateurs who meddle, laymen who think they know the game, even though they have had no training. Grant was such a man. He was a successful stockbroker by trade, but he thought he knew baseball talent, and he had his pets. Whitey Herzog, who was working for Grant, recalled the events that helped Devine decide to return to St. Louis.

WHITEY HERZOG: "In the winter of 1967–68, we went down to Mexico for the winter meetings and had a deal all set with the White Sox. We were going to give them Don Shaw and outfielder Tommy Davis for Tommy Agee, a young outfielder everyone in the Mets' organization was hot for. Gil Hodges wanted him. Bing, Bob Scheffing, and I all wanted him, and we had the deal set. But Bing said we'd have to wait until [Mets president M. Donald] Grant flew in to approve it.

"The deal leaked to the papers, and when Grant hit town, he was furious. 'How could you think about trading my Donnie Shaw?' he asked.

"And he killed the deal. We eventually got Agee anyway, but Grant's decision cost us a good man—Bing Devine. 'I don't really believe they need a general manager around here,' he told me.

"And he went back to the Cardinals.''

The year 1968 was a very traumatic one for the country. In April, the Reverend Martin Luther King, Jr., was murdered in Memphis. The season opener was scheduled for the day he was to be buried. When the Cardinals asked the black players whether they would be willing to play, they said no. The front office postponed the game.

The next month Robert Kennedy, campaigning for President, was assassinated in Los Angeles. During the speech prior to his murder on June 4, the night he triumphed in the California primary, Kennedy paid tribute to Dodger pitcher Don Drysdale, who pitched his sixth consecutive shutout and set a major league record for consecutive shutout innings with 58⅔.

The deaths of King and Kennedy infuriated blacks (and many whites) across America. One who seethed with anger over the plight of black America was Cards pitcher Bob Gibson, who seemed to wear a perpetual scowl on and off the field. But Gibson, who had strong opinions on race or politics, never expressed them in public. Once when he was asked by a TV reporter about a civil rights demonstration, he replied, "I don't give a fuck. I have a ball game to pitch"

The reason Gibson rarely opened up to the media was that he was a complex man who believed that the less people knew about him—especially the hitters—the better off he would be. He wanted to be a total mystery. He didn't want the opposition to know about his family, his religion, his hobbies, his feelings—nothing, because he believed that the more they came to learn about his habits and peccadiloes, the easier it would be for them to guess what he was going to throw on the mound. As a result, he never talked to players on other teams. And he would never apologize for hitting a batter.

Gibson was fanatical about being mysterious. He refused to allow anyone to clock the speed of his pitches. He refused to talk with the team psychologist. During spring training, he asked Red Schoendienst to pitch him exclusively against American League teams. When he played in an All-Star Game, he would leave the ballpark immediately after coming off the field so as not to make any friends among opponents. Late in his career, he could be cruel to young players. It was important to him that no batter think he was a nice guy.

Gibson needn't have worried. Gibson was so intimidating that his catcher, Tim McCarver, was reluctant to go out to the mound to talk to him. There were times when manager Johnny Keane would order him out there. McCarver knew he'd get a roasting. Gibson would growl, "Now what in *hell* are you doing here? Keep your ass away from me while I'm working. I like to work fast, and I don't need any help from you. Just put those goddamn fingers down as fast as you can. If I don't like it, I'll just shake you off."

Another time Gibson told him, "Get back there where you belong. The only thing you know about pitching is that it's hard to hit."

And yet, the fearsome Gibson would become upset whenever commentators referred to him as "the world's meanest ballplayer." Gibson felt that because he pitched during the height of racial unrest in the late sixties, when frustrated blacks burned cities and expressed their anger at white society and clenched their fists in defiance of Jim Crow, that both the public and opposing batters saw him as a Black Panther in a baseball uniform, that because he was black he was seen as being meaner than white pitchers like Don Drysdale and Stan Williams.

Said Gibson, "As a result, I was more threatening to them—more intimidating and unsettling and menacing—than white pitchers whose stuff and pitching patterns might strongly resemble mine."

Despite how the press or the fans might have felt about his menacing persona, what everyone began to notice was that Bob Gibson, who began the '68 season 3-5 despite a 1.32 ERA, was pitching just as well as the heralded Drysdale. He had lost one game, 1–0, to Drysdale and was beaten, 1–0, by Philadelphia when Philly first baseman Bill White singled in a run in the tenth.

Gibson's teammates, who admired the big pitcher for his combativeness, noted his pleas and entreaties when he didn't get enough support.

CURT FLOOD: "During the game itself, he was at us constantly. 'Get me some runs, you miserable bastards,' he would mutter in the dugout. And as the game proceeded, he'd begin moaning, 'I'm just a poor, clean-cut colored kid. Can't you help me out with just one run? One run! Is that too much for you mothers to do?'"

Gibson shut out Houston, then the Braves, then pitched a third shutout, a four-hitter with 13 strikeouts against the Reds. His ERA fell to 1.29. Gibson then shut out Fergie Jenkins and the Cubs, 1–0. On June 26, Gibson's shutout streak reached 5 complete games with a four-hitter against the Pirates. He had 47 consecutive scoreless innings and was closing in on Drysdale's record of 58⅔ set only three weeks earlier.

Gibson's next opponent was the great Drysdale himself at Chavez Ravine. Another shutout would leave Gibby just three innings shy of the record.

In the first inning, the Dodgers' Len Gabrielson singled, and Tom Hall hit a grounder that Julian Javier booted, sending the runner to third. A pitch to the next hitter sailed high but could have been handled by reserve catcher Johnny Edwards. When the ball got away from Edwards, Gabrielson scored.

Had the Dodger official scorer properly ruled the play a passed ball, the run would have been unearned, and Gibson's streak would have continued. But the game was in Los Angeles, and it was ruled a wild pitch, ending Gibson's chance to catch the Dodger pitching ace.

BOB GIBSON
(Courtesy Brace Photo)

The Cards won the game, 5–1. It was victory number 135 for Gibson, moving him ahead of Dizzy Dean into second spot in career Cardinal wins. (Jesse Haines had the most with 210.) His next start was against Juan Marichal and the San Francisco Giants. In his own mind, his streak was still intact. He needed 3 more innings to break the record. He loaded the bases in the first inning with nobody out, then struck out Willie Mays, Willie McCovey, and Jim Ray Hart. Gibson shut out the Giants, 3–0. His ERA was down to 1.06.

In his first start after the All-Star Game, Gibson went 6 more scoreless innings against Houston before Rusty Staub singled and scored on a double by Dennis Menke. His scoreless streak should have been 71 scoreless innings. But he was robbed in L.A.

His catcher, Tim McCarver, recalled what made Bob Gibson so dominant that year.

TIM MCCARVER: "He always had great stuff: an exploding fastball and a sweeping slider. Your stuff is God-given. But it's corraling it that makes the difference. It seemed that everything came together as far as his control was concerned. He could put a ball in a space of about four inches on the outside part of the plate and at the knees to a right-hander, and when a left-hander came up, he would raise it six inches and put it right on the hands. His control was almost perfect. He rarely came inside to right-handers, and occasionally he'd go away to left-handers.

"He could put the ball about four inches on the outside part of the plate with his fastball or slider, and he could also throw a riding fastball any time you wanted it. It sailed, almost like a natural slider. It was his best pitch. It stayed on the inside part of the plate to left-handers and the outside part of the plate to right-handers. Plus, he was so consistent with that pitch that umpires started giving him pitches just off the plate. They were almost unreachable by right-handed hitters."

The fans poured into whatever ballpark Gibson was appearing. By July, the strongest Cardinal team in history had virtually clinched the pennant with a 49-15 record. They led the league by fourteen and a half games. Bob Gibson's ERA was down to 0.96. No one in the history of the game had been better.

When he beat the Mets, 7–1, it concluded one of the most amazing pitching streaks in the history of the game. Over 96 innings Bob Gibson had allowed just two earned runs! His ERA during that eight-week stretch was 0.19!

By the end of August, his record was 19-8. His ERA was 0.99. Ten of those wins were shutouts.

Gibson won his 20th in Cincinnati when Julian Javier homered in the tenth inning to give the Cards a 1–0 victory. The next time out it took a no-hitter by Gaylord Perry of the Giants to beat him, 1–0. When the Cards' Ray Washburn pitched a no-hitter the next night, it marked the only time no-hitters were pitched back-to-back.

When the Dodgers beat Gibson, 3–2, in his second to last start, his ERA stood at 1.16. In his final start against Houston, he pitched a masterful six-hitter and gave up zero runs. Bob Gibson's 1968 record was 22-9 with an era of 1.12. His 13 shutouts were second-most in one season in major league history behind Grover Cleveland Alexander's 16. He completed 28 of 34 starts in compiling one of the greatest seasons ever pitched in the big leagues.

NELSON BRILES: "Gibby dominated the whole year in '68. I remember pitching a shutout against the Pirates the last game of a homestand, and we went to Pittsburgh, and Gibson came back after that to shut the Pirates out, 1–0. He pitched 13 shutouts that year! Thirteen! With 28 complete games! It was just mastery.

"He was injury-free and just pitched phenomenal baseball. Of course, I had my biggest year in the majors [19-11, 2.81 ERA], though it paled in comparison to his. It was so incredible. He just dominated the whole year. Incredible."

Despite all his success pitching for the Cardinals, Bob Gibson never became the St. Louis icon that Dizzy Dean became thirty years before. Dean had been difficult with the press, but he always maintained a homespun image of being a country boy from the sticks who didn't mean it when he screwed up and did mean it when he took on the city slickers and won. His reward was a long second career working in radio and television.

Gibson's image was that of an angry black man scowling from atop a pitching rubber before throwing what might be a hard strike on the outside corner, or a brushback, or a nasty, hard-breaking curve, or a batter's worst nightmare—a knockdown pitch. He was sharp with the press, and he often barked at fans who became too pushy. A Hall of Famer [1981], he is approached often for autographs, but always gingerly. He was respected but difficult to love. His reputation for being a hard man has never left him.

NELSON BRILES: "His relationship with the press was adversarial at best. He tended to be short with people, but when you look at his background and what a lot of black ballplayers had to go through for a long period of time, and then to be criticized and questioned, well, that wore thin. But he just used all that to fuel himself.

"If personal attention came Gibson's way, okay. But if it didn't, it was no big deal. He wasn't one who sought out or reveled in the limelight. He was very much the professional player, and what he liked doing most was competing. I think in his mind he felt he had a lot to prove.

"They talked about how mean he was on the mound. I'll tell you what, in my recollection of our conversations, he liked to talk about hitting guys, but he was more efficient than that. He did knock guys down. He did move them back. We all did. But he enjoys a reputation of being mean on the mound and hitting a lot of guys, when in truth he didn't want to put guys on. He wanted to make them earn their way on. But that was his reputation more than being an outstanding pitcher. Rather than look at how dominating he was, they played up the angle of how mean he was."

Gibson never was satisfied, no matter how well he pitched. He was hard on people, but hardest on himself. Only someone with his perfectionist nature could downplay a season in which he produced a 1.12 ERA, fourth best in major league history behind Emil "Dutch" Leonard, 1.01 in 1914; Mordecai "Three Finger" Brown, 1.04 in 1906, and Walter Johnson, 1.09 in 1913.

BOB GIBSON: "The 1.12 is the number that seems to have impressed a lot of people over the years, but at the time I wasn't that impressed myself. It seemed to me that, for all the great players around, nobody really hit that year. There were only five guys in the National League who averaged .300 or better [Pete Rose, Matty Alou, Felipe Alou, Alex Johnson, and Curt Flood]. Several pitchers had ERAs under 2.00, and two won more games than I did—Marichal, with 26, and [Denny] McLain, whose final tally of 31 remains the most since Lefty Grove in 1931. As the first 30-game winner since Dizzy Dean in 1934, McLain received much more attention than I did during the season."

Perhaps, but Gibson nevertheless was voted the Most Valuable Player in the National League in 1968 as the Cardinals waltzed to the pennant by nine games over the San Francisco Giants. It's rare for a pitcher to be named MVP, but Bob Gibson beat out Pete Rose for the award as four of the top seven vote getters—Gibson, Flood, Brock, and Shannon—were St. Louis Cardinals.

The Cardinals faced the Detroit Tigers in the 1968 Series. The buzz was over the matchup of Bob Gibson vs. Denny McLain, whose 31-6 record and 1.96 ERA led the American League. McLain was as charismatic and as unconventional a character as Gibson wasn't. McLain even played the organ in a rock band.

A major story line concerned Tiger manager Mayo Smith's gutsy move of shifting outfielder Mickey Stanley to shortstop to replace light-hitting Ray Oyler so Al Kaline, who had played sixteen years and had never played in a World Series, could start in right field. The versatile Stanley had played only nine games at short during the regular season, one at second, and fifteen at first. Most of the season, he played the outfield.

The Series began smoothly for the Cardinals as Bob Gibson pitched what may arguably have been the finest World Series game ever pitched. In the first inning, Gibby struck out Dick McAuliffe and Al Kaline, in the second, Norm Cash, Willie Horton, and Jim Northrup, and in the third, Bill Freehan and McLain.

After striking out Northrup and Freehan in the seventh and pinch hitter Eddie Mathews in the eighth, Gibson had 14, one short of Sandy Koufax's record of 15, set against the Yankees in 1963.

In the ninth, neither Gibson nor catcher Tim McCarver were aware that Gibson was close to the record. After a leadoff single by Mickey Stanley, Kaline struck out for number 15. With the St. Louis crowd cheering noisily, the scoreboard noted that Gibson was one away from a new Series record.

McCarver tried to tell Gibson by pointing at the scoreboard. Gibson just wanted the ball. "Come on, come on, let's go," he said.

Then he saw the announcement and tipped his cap. Gibson quickly returned to work. He struck out Cash on a curve and caught Willie Horton looking on a breaking ball on the inside corner. Gibson had struck out 17 in a 4–0 Cardinal victory.

Mike Shannon would say about Gibson's performance, "It was like pitching against Little Leaguers."

Mickey Lolich showed his poise and skill in winning Game 2 by the score of 8–1 against Nelson Briles. Lolich allowed six singles and hit a home run.

TIM MCCARVER: "This guy could pitch. He was really impressive. Against a lefty batter, he ran the ball in on you and ran the breaking ball away, and anybody who could do that consistently, could work both sides of the plate, can be a very effective pitcher, and that's what Mickey did."

In Game 3, Ray Washburn won, 7–3, after Tim McCarver hit a three-run homer. The Cards seemed to have the Series wrapped up when Bob Gibson came back and defeated McLain, 10–1, in Game 4 on a wet and rainy day.

Gibson struck out 10 to earn his seventh straight Series win, a record that still stands. The goat for Detroit was McLain, who had tendinitis and was suffering.

TIM MCCARVER: "His stuff was terrible. When you crank it up that many times over a seven-month period, you wear down. There's no question that he was hurting during the Series."

With a 3-1 lead in games, the Cards needed just one more win for the championship. The last time a National League team had won back-to-back world championships was back in 1921 and 1922 when John McGraw and the New York Giants accomplished the feat.

The Cards began strong in Game 5 with a three-run first against Mickey Lolich. In the fifth, the Cards threatened to knock the Tiger lefty out of the game when Lou Brock doubled and raced for home on Julian Javier's single. When catcher Bill Freehan went to block the plate, Brock decided that instead of sliding into Freehan, he would try to go around him. Willie Horton fired in from left field, Freehan made the tag, and the upright Brock was called out.

Had Brock scored, the Cards lead would have been up by two runs, and manager Mayo Smith would have been forced to pinch-hit for Mickey Lolich in the seventh. Instead, Lolich batted with one out and hit a bloop for a single. It was at that point that Red Schoendienst took out Nelson Briles and brought in Joe Hoerner.

TIM MCCARVER: "In defense of Lou, Lou said if he had slid, Freehan would have knocked him off the plate, and I agree with that, even though Lou was a guy who slid hard. Sometimes you can reach the plate faster if you don't slide. Lou has been the anti-Christ in the deal for too long a period of time. I know exactly what Lou was talking about, because Freehan was all over the plate. Horton made the throw of his life, and Freehan blocked the plate as well as you can block it."

NELSON BRILES: "When Brock didn't slide at home and knock Lolich out of the game, I don't know if that was a turning point or not, but they seized the opportunity, and we never won another ball game.

"I was the pitcher that day, and one of my great disappointments was being removed from that game at that time, because I thought I was throwing well. I was removed from the game and we gave up six consecutive hits, therefore the lead, and we never won again.

"I wanted to say something to Red. Absolutely I did. But in those days, you didn't show anybody up. It was said quietly, under your breath, but once he made the move, you're gone.

"So he made the move, and I was upset. Matter of fact, I wanted to say something to him in the dugout. The competitive juices were flowing. But rather than doing it in the dugout, where the cameras could catch me, I went into the tunnel going back to the clubhouse and waited to ask Red to come in.

"Our first base coach, Dick Sisler, stuttered, which made our situation unique because it takes him a while to tell the runner to 'Ge-ge-ge-ge-get back,' and W-w-w-w-w-watch out.' But we won with him at first base.

"Anyway, he came down to the tunnel, and in his way he said, 'N-N-N-N-Nellie, j-j j-just don't do anything to hurrrrrrrrt yourself.' And I said, 'Dick, get lost. I'm trying to be mad here.' He just deflated everything, and I turned around, went back into the clubhouse, put on a dry shirt, came out, and rooted like hell.''

Denny McLain, armed with a cortisone shot, went up against Ray Washburn in Game 6 and won, 13–1. Jim Northrup hit a grand slam home run as the Tigers scored ten runs in the third inning. The Cardinal advantage had vanished.

Game 7 would be in the hands of Bob Gibson. Mickey Lolich took the mound for the Tigers on two days' rest. When Gibson struck out 5 in the first three innings, he set a new record of 31 strikeouts in a Series. For six innings, Gibson and Lolich didn't allow a run. Gibson retired twenty of the first twenty-one batters.

NELSON BRILES: "Bob was pitching a great ball game, as was Lolich. We didn't rough up Mickey at all the whole Series. He pitched fantastically. I pitched against him twice, and he certainly didn't give us much to hit at all. You talk about great pitching performances. Even though it's not publicized, you have to look at Lolich's performances on short rest in the World Series as one of those special things that happened in Detroit history. But they [the games] were tooth and nail.''

In the seventh with two outs, Norm Cash singled, then Willie Horton bounced a single to left. Jim Northrup was the batter. He hit the first pitch hard to center.

NELSON BRILES: "It was a 0–0 game, and everything was on the line, riding with every pitch. And then Northrup hit a line drive, and in the daytime in St. Louis, it's sometimes a little hard to see. Curt Flood broke with the ball and saw that it wasn't going to be a sinking line drive, tried to recover, slipped, the ball went over his head, two runs scored, and that was it.

"And of course, Flood was criticized for misjudging a fly ball that he never misjudges, but in baseball they always tell you that the hardest ball to judge is a line drive right at you. And when he did recognize it and tried to recover, he slipped and just wasn't able to quite get back to it. Had he not slipped, he would have caught the ball.''

TIM MCCARVER: "The playing conditions that day were very bad in the outfield. Curt broke in initially to his right and one or two steps in and then he got stuck in the mud. When he got stuck, his quickness wasn't there, and Northrup's ball, which was well hit, got past him.''

Northrup's hit went for a triple, and when Bill Freehan doubled, the Tigers were ahead 3–0. Schoendienst stayed with Gibson in the ninth, and after the

Tigers scored a fourth run, Mike Shannon hit a solo home run in the bottom of the inning to make the score 4–1, but it was too little and very late. The Tigers had won the 1968 World Series.

NELSON BRILES: "We had the Series in our hands and just didn't close the deal. Pure and simple. We both played well. We pitched well, battled back and forth, and to the Tigers' credit, when they were given an opening, they took advantage."

TIM McCARVER: "You have to give them credit. It's only seven games, and we dominated them in our three wins. Then they came back, and you tip your hat to them."

In the dugout after the game, Curt Flood went over to Bob Gibson to apologize.
"It's all my fault," said Flood.
Said Gibson, who never took out his frustrations on his teammates, "It's nobody's fault."

The next day Bob Burnes expressed his frustration over the Cards' not winning the World Series when he wrote a column accusing the players of caring more about dressing well than about winning. Some players reacted with anger. Pitcher Nelson Briles was more analytical about it.

NELSON BRILES: "We were, for our day, a little flashy. We would wear bright sport coats. But really, how much are you going to do making $10,000 a year? But again, that was the mantle you have to wear when you don't win, when expectations are extremely high. So those shots are going to be taken, and of course it wasn't but a couple years later that the whole team was just about dismantled."

CHAPTER 62

GUSSIE VS. THE PLAYERS

AMERICA was in an upheaval over the Vietnam War in 1969. It was the year of Woodstock, of Flower Power and hippies, and of Black Panthers and fiery rhetoric. There were several deep schisms in the country as distrust mounted between rich and poor, corporation and worker, establishment and student, old and young. At the same time, the divide between longtime Cardinal owner Gussie Busch and his ballplayers had been growing ever since a labor lawyer by the name of Marvin Miller had become head of the Players' Association in December of 1966 and had begun having his way with the owners.

Miller had negotiated the first Basic Agreement in February of 1968. For the first time, the players had a say in how the basic contract would be drawn. A formal grievance procedure was worked out. The minimum salary was raised from $7,000 to $10,000. Moreover, the owners and players agreed to study the reserve clause, which held a player in perpetual bondage to his team, though the owners insisted that the players would never break free of its terms.

Right before spring training was supposed to begin in 1969, the Players' Association asked the owners to increase health care, life insurance, and pension benefits. The owners refused. Management was furious the players had turned down their final offer. In response, the players refused to sign their individual contracts, threatening the start of spring training.

When Interim Commissioner Bowie Kuhn intervened, the owners backed down, a strike was averted, and Miller and the players got their way. By the summer, he would be given an eight-year contract. Kuhn would never again have such a high approval rating.

In 1969 baseball made its most dramatic structural change since the establishment of the American and National leagues. The game expanded, adding teams in Montreal, San Diego, Seattle and Kansas City. Baseball's decision makers decreed that that two twelve-team leagues would be too unwieldy, and with an eye toward giving more teams an opportunity to make the playoffs, each league was split into two six-team divisions, and a playoff tier of five-game League Championship Series in each league was added, with the winners going to the World Series.

The question then arose: How much of the television windfall emanating from those games should go to the players and how much to the team owners?

The acrimony over this issue added to the tension. When the owners tried to sever the longtime link between the pension fund and the TV and radio income, the players accused them of wanting to keep the money for themselves.

The players may have had logic and right on their side, but they did not have the press or the public. The outcry rose that the players were being greedy, that they were making more than enough money. The players were mystified by the reaction.

BOB GIBSON: "It was curious to me and the other players that there didn't seem to be much parallel sentiment concerning the greed of the owners, despite the fact that they had just signed a new television contract that raised their network revenues from half a million dollars to seventeen million. At the same time, the owners were attempting to reduce the players' percentage of the TV money."

Gibson made his case on "The Tonight Show." Gussie Busch was furious, and his relationship with his star pitcher became strained.

Meanwhile, as players from all teams fought for a larger share of the pie, individual Cardinal players were demanding to be rewarded for bringing two straight pennants to St. Louis.

CURT FLOOD: "The leading members of the Cardinals added insult to injury. They demanded substantial salary increases. I, for one, did not sign my contract until March 3—having been an official holdout for two brave days. I had rejected a $77,500 offer.

"[Gussie] had a fit. Profanity rattled the windows and turned the air blue. Labor annoyances were not what he had envisioned when he took up baseball. They could not be classified as a wholesome sport. They were no fun at all. They boded ill for the future of the game. What would become of the fans? The fans? Mr. Busch decided to attack us on behalf of the fans. Accordingly, Mr. Busch staged a happening. He ordered all the Cardinals to a special meeting on March 22 at St. Petersburg, our Florida training base. He summoned the corporate directors of his beer and baseball enterprises. He whistled up the gentlemen of the press. When all had assembled, he addressed himself to the players.

"He questioned the integrity of our attitudes. He raised doubts as to the single-mindedness of our professional efforts. He accused us of upstaging and occasionally manhandling our devoted fans. He deplored methods of our Association. He warned that failure to mend our ways would ruin St. Louis baseball. He depicted us as a rabble of ingrates headed for a fall. Having humiliated us to the best of his ability, he exhorted us to go forth and win another pennant.

"The speech demoralized the 1969 Cardinals. The employer had put us in our place. Despite two successive pennants, we were still livestock. Proud of ourselves and our skills, we had assumed that the feeling permeated the front office as well. In fact, we had heard with some amusement that Busch himself was not above taking credit for certain of our achievements. But now it was over.

"After we had finished, Busch asked if there were any questions. We had none. He had been telling us to behave or get out. I feared that if I so much as hinted at the truth about that meeting, I would be gone from the team in a week. I was sick with shame and so was everyone else on the Cardinals, except Busch and his claque.

"We remained keen about each other as athletes and men, but the opposing team was no longer our chief adversary, nor was the next game the most important problem in our lives. Each of us was miserably aware that the ax was over our skulls, by proclamation of Mr. Busch. We no longer believed that we worked for the best organization in baseball, a relative accolade that the Cardinal management had earned by leaving its players pretty much to their own devices, paying them comparatively well, and transporting them in comfort. Far from applauding what we had built for ourselves and our employer, the front office appreciated it not at all. Indeed, the front office was prepared to destroy what we had built. It was hell-bent on reinstating conventional relations, which find the players in a constant state of terrified insecurity.

"And so we began behaving like conventional baseball players. During 1969, I protested more vigorously than usual and even broke into print a few times. This did not endear me to management. Especially not at $90,000 a year."

NELSON BRILES: "[Busch's talk] was disappointing, especially when you're a competitive person and you have been successful. You don't know who has been feeding who information, so you don't know the people who had Mr. Busch's ear. I did know that the years I played there I was treated fairly, and you have to accept criticism along with the applause. And sometimes you just have to grin and bear it, but I do think the strike threat of '69 made a turn for the worse in relationships between the players and management. And it wasn't long after [Busch's tirade] that Cepeda was traded, and they started to break up the ballclub.''

CURT FLOOD: "A few days later, the front office underlined the message and completed the havoc by trading away our most popular player, Orlando Cepeda. He had symbolized the joyful togetherness of the champion Cardinals. In return for 'Cha-Cha,' the Atlanta Braves sent us Joe Torre, a congenial man and an excellent player. But the glue was gone. We finished fourth in the National League's Eastern Division, thirteen games behind the upstart Mets. The great Cardinals were all washed up.''

NELSON BRILES: "St. Louis was never an organization that stayed pat a long time—if you look at their history. So that wasn't anything out of the ordinary, but the Cepeda trade was a shock because, again, that signals to the players that they are probably going to start breaking up this club. It happened in spring training. Remember the camaraderie I was talking about? It started to chip away at that, even though Joe Torre was a great guy, a great player, and blended in extremely well. But the composition of what we had was changed.

"Sometimes you don't realize as a player, and as management, how special it is when you get a unique blend of players together on a team that are not only talented but are dedicated to one another and have that spirit and devotion to one another, and when you get that, you want to ride that as long as you possibly can, and once you start to chip away at that, it's hard to get that back.''

The year 1969 marked the end of the domination by pitchers. In 1968 the National League ERA had been 2.99. In the American League, it had been 2.98. While Cincinnati hit .273, the next two teams, Atlanta and Pittsburgh, were at .252. The championship Cards as a team hit only .249. The league average was .243.

Only five National League hitters, including Curt Flood at .301, had hit over .300 that year.

It was even worse in the American League. Oakland, the top AL team, hit .240. The American League batting average was .230. Carl Yastrzemski, the AL batting leader, hit just .301. The powers that be decided to lower the mound, increase the strike zone, and boost offense. In 1969 the National League batting average jumped to .250. The AL rose to .246. Pitchers would never be as dominating in baseball again. Many pitchers, including Nelson Briles, were hurt by the changes.

NELSON BRILES: "In 1968 a lot of pitchers had great years. Cleveland had a staff of three or four pitchers who had their biggest years: Sam McDowell and

Luis Tiant had ERAs under 2.00, and so did Denny McLain [Tommy John, and Dave McNally]. A lot of pitchers had ERAs under 3.00, myself included.

"I think it was one of those anomalies, and in my opinion baseball over-reacted, panicked, because they never panic when there is too much hitting or too many runs scored. But they certainly do complain and react quickly when there are not enough runs scored and the pitchers are having good years.

"So baseball panicked after '68, lowered the mound, narrowed the strike zone, did a lot of things that hurt me. I had an overhand curveball, and lowering the mound really hurt me. I ended up having to go to a slider. I never had that same curveball again. So I had to make adjustments."

Briles compiled a 15-13 record in '69. It would be his last solid season in St. Louis.

The year 1969 was not a productive one for Curt Flood. It began with a deep gash in his right thigh, an injury resulting from an accidental spiking by the Mets' Bud Harrelson at second base during spring training. Flood received stitches and a tetanus shot, and he spent a sleepless night. He fell asleep in the morning hours and slept through the team's promotional banquet, angering Gussie Busch and the front office.

CURT FLOOD: "No offense is less forgivable than that. For my arrogant and thoughtless failure to awaken in time, drag my torn self to the banquet, and pay tribute to season-ticket holders galore, I was fined $250. I protested angrily. I protested more things than one during that horrible season. Each complaint became another nail in my coffin. I was not speaking well of the boss. At $90,000 a year, I no longer looked so good in a hotel lobby. My days were numbered."

During the summer, when the Cards still had a shot at winning the pennant, Flood and the other veterans became enraged when manager Red Schoendienst began playing two rookies, Joe Hague, who batted third and played first, and Ted Simmons, who batted fifth and caught. With Hague in the lineup [he batted 17 for 100], opposing pitchers didn't give Brock or Flood decent pitches to hit. Flood suspected that the Cardinal front office was behind the moves and grumbled that it was sabotaging the team's effort to win the pennant. Flood went to Red Schoendienst and demanded that if he insisted on playing the two rookies, at least he should put them lower in the batting order. When the unconfrontational Red readily went along, Flood knew his suspicions had been correct that Red had been acting on orders. He made his anger known by going public.

CURT FLOOD: "I knew in my bones that the experiment had been suggested by the front office, and now the feeling was confirmed. Angrier than before, I confided to Jack Herman, a reporter for the *Globe-Democrat*, that the top management had tossed in the towel for 1969. I went on at some length.

" 'The next day he published my views, attributing them to an unnamed veteran. Bing Devine, our general manager, responded with a crusher. 'The only reason the regulars are complaining,' he said, 'is that they are afraid of losing their jobs.' "

It was then that Flood knew he would be traded. On October 8, three days before he was to fly to Copenhagen, Denmark, he received a call from the assistant general manager telling him he had been traded to the Phils. He, Tim McCarver, Joe Hoerner, and Byron Browne were traded for Dick Allen, Cookie Rojas, and Jerry Johnson. After twelve years with the Cards, it was "See ya!" and Curt Flood took it personally. Flood, only thirty-one, called Bing Devine and said he would retire. He also told reporters he would retire. But no one believed him.

When Flood wrote a letter to Commissioner Bowie Kuhn declaring himself a free agent in December, attention was paid. The departures of Cepeda and Flood marked the beginning of the end of the Cardinal dynasty of the 1960s.

TIM MCCARVER: "To this day I'll always think that the trade contributed largely to the disintegration of the Cards in the seventies, but that's baseball. With the exception of Brock and Gibson, they totally dismantled that club over the space of two and a half years. We all wished we could have stayed with the Cards. We thought we could win. But it wasn't to be. If you go around in life looking for fairness and trying to analyze whether people are getting what they deserve, you're wasting your time. Fairness, to be blunt about it, simply doesn't exist in this world, and I don't say this with any residual bitterness."

BOB GIBSON: "I loved the Cardinals, was proud to be one, and recognized that Curt Flood and Tim McCarver were two of the biggest reasons why. With them gone, being a Cardinal would never mean quite the same thing."

NELSON BRILES: "First Cepeda, then it was Flood. The dominoes had started to fall, and you have now literally pulled apart that special atmosphere, uniqueness, camaraderie we had enjoyed for that three or four years.

"Maybe it was because the players had banded together. That could very well be. In those days, it was uncharted waters. Nobody had a history to react to, and so it was just going on an awful lot of emotion, and it did change the climate of player-management relationship and set the stage for the introduction of the agent, which totally changed the negotiations between the player and front office forever.

"And it took a while for that organization to win again."

After Curt Flood left for Copenhagen, Denmark, a city he loved for its beauty and tranquillity, he chose to sue baseball on constitutional grounds, giving the courts the chance to do away with the reserve clause. Flood wanted to leave his mark.

Marvin Miller contacted constitutional law scholar Arthur Goldberg to represent Flood. The former Supreme Court justice may well have been the most famous lawyer in the world. Flood wrote a letter to every ballclub saying he was available to sign with any major league club. Goldberg asked for an injunction under the Sherman and Clayton antitrust laws to void the trade, to have Flood declared a free agent, and most importantly, to end the bondage of the reserve clause. In the support of Flood, Jackie Robinson commented, "All he is asking for is the right to negotiate."

Paul Porter of the prestigious Washington, D.C., law firm of Arnold and Porter represented the owners. Porter rejected all chances to settle the suit.

Flood received a tall pile of racist hate mail. Said Flood, "I am pleased that God made my skin black, but I wish He had made it thicker."

One of Curt Flood's bitterest disappointments was that he took a beating in the press. One reporter said that a victory for Flood would mean "the collapse of our national pastime." He shouldn't have been surprised. Newspaper reporters had sided with the owners since John Montgomery Ward tried to break Albert Spalding's $2,000 minimum salary by starting the Players' League in 1890.

CURT FLOOD: "Comparatively few newspaper, radio, and television journalists seemed able to understand what I was doing. A player's contention that he was trying to serve a human cause was somehow unbelievable. For them, the only plausible explanation was derangement. Or perhaps I was a dupe of Marvin Miller. And, in any case, I would surely show up in time for spring training. I began to wonder if the whole goddamned country wasn't infected with moral corruption."

Robert Lipsyte of *The New York Times* was one of a handful of reporters who understood what Flood was trying to do. Most did not.

CURT FLOOD: "Nothing I said in interviews got through to these people. The guys evidently felt that responsibility to principle was the hallucination of a nut."

Judge Irving Ben Cooper of the Federal Court for the Southern District of New York ruled in February 1970 that the issue of the reserve clause had to be decided by a full-dress trial. The decision made it impossible for Flood to play in 1970.

Robert Short, the owner of the Washington Senators, traded with Philadelphia for the right to talk to Flood about playing in 1971. Goldberg told Flood that having sat out in 1970 and having lost his $100,000 salary was enough to ensure that the case would not be deemed moot if he returned to play. Flood asked Short for a contract without the reserve clause. Bowie Kuhn said he would not sign one without the clause. And so the contract had a clause saying that his playing would not prejudice his lawsuit. Flood signed to play with Washington in 1971, but his skills had faded from the inactivity and he couldn't go on.

TIM McCARVER: "Flood suffered two losses in the lower courts and a 5–3 setback before the U.S. Supreme Court, but there's no doubt in my mind that

Curt's action got the ball rolling toward freeing players from the shackles of the ninety-year clause that could tie them to a team against their wills. Those million-dollar contracts of today exist in large part thanks to Curt Flood. But how the battle cost him. After missing the 1970 season, he played about a month and a half in 1971 for Bob Short's Washington Senators. Then he more or less faded away into baseball oblivion.''

After he lost his suit, the proud and sensitive Flood disappeared from public view. He moved from Copenhagen to Barcelona and then to the island of Majorca, where he owned an inn. He then moved to the tiny country of Andorra, high in the Pyrenées Mountains between France and Spain. He returned to the United States and in 1989 was named commissioner of the ill-fated Senior Professional Baseball League. The league, for retired major league baseball players thirty-five years of age or older, received no support from major league baseball and folded after a season and a half. That Flood had been commissioner certainly did not help the league's relations with baseball's top brass.

Curt Flood would be vilified and smeared by those who opposed him—owners, reporters, and fans who bucked change—but he refused to back down or take a cash settlement to stop the lawsuit the way Danny Gardella did after he had sued baseball in the late 1940s.

Because Flood ultimately lost in a close decision in the U.S. Supreme Court, the Flood case did not end the reserve system, but the scorn and criticism of the blatantly unfair system that resulted from an airing of the case would lead to its demise. In May of 1970, a second Basic Agreement provided that agents could represent players. The minimum salary was raised to $12,000 in 1970 and $15,000 by 1972. Most importantly, an outside arbitrator was assigned to hear baseball's grievances. Lewis Gill, then Garbriel Alexander, then Peter Seitz were named to the post. It was Seitz who in November of 1975 ruled that when Andy Messersmith and Dave McNally played an entire year without a contract, that at the end of the period they were free agents, that the reserve clause did not mean forever.

By the end of 1976, most major league veterans would have the economic freedom Curt Flood had been seeking.

In baseball history, Curt Flood would go down as a man whose adherence to principle advanced the economic cause of all ballplayers. It was his brave stand that led to freedom of movement and to the big salaries of today. The players owe Flood a great deal of gratitude.

MARVIN MILLER: "I liked Curt very much. Before this whole thing started, I did not know him very well. I would talk with him in spring training meetings, and he always was a very interested member of the team when we'd visit and talk about the current issues. He would always make time at the end of the meeting to talk about problems. He would stop in the office when the team came to New York, and we got to know each other.

"When the case started, I would not have said I knew him well. But as things progressed, I certainly did get to know him. He was a very shy man, even though many people didn't seem to have that perception of him. It took him a long time to warm up to people. I think he was suspicious of people, but he was a very gentle man.

"I was close to Curt while he was undergoing his trial by fire and the period after that as well.

"I think what most people may not realize is that although he didn't foresee it as a losing task in the beginning, Dick Moss and I spent many, many hours with him, simply to make sure he did understand that while it was a good cause, we were pretty confident we would lose. Just to say that doesn't give you a good picture of how much we drilled it into him. Because one of the things that was always important to me was not to have a player stick out his neck without understanding the consequences. I thought the consequences would be very grave, indeed, because I thought he was underestimating the long memories of the owners, including the institutional memory of 'Don't reward your enemies.'

"So I tried for weeks and weeks to really make sure he understood that there was very little they wouldn't do if they thought it necessary, because this was an important issue to them. I said such things as: 'I don't want to know any details, but if there are things you would rather not see in the newspapers about your life, stop and think, because I wouldn't put anything past them.' And as an example, and I will tell you because he wrote about it later in his book, he told me at the time, 'My brother is in jail for drugs.' I said, 'Okay, expect to see it in the public press.'

"And they did that. That was just one small example.

"I didn't want to dissuade him, but I did want to make certain that he understood everything I knew about what could happen here.

"In terms of his principles, let me just tell you, at one point I told him, 'As much as I think this is a difficult case and we're going to probably lose,' for all kinds of reasons, including the Supreme Court doesn't like to reverse itself, and the fact that courts have always backed the owners, and that the Supreme Court on questions of property rights vs. individual rights almost certainly come down on the side of property rights. I said, 'If by some miracle we were to win this case, I don't think you would win, because I don't think they would apply any damages retroactively.' Because that would mean that the court was penalizing the owners for living and practicing in a way that the court said was legal. And so I could see, if the miraculous happened and we won the case, they would simply say, 'This is prospective. And you don't win any damages.'

"And he went ahead anyway, because he was a very principled man. You could not shake him. He would say to me, 'I just think this is right. I'm disappointed that you tell me there is no way I can win this individually, but I still think it has to be done.' I really don't think the full flavor of that has ever been realized. He understood *every* part of this.

"As you know, we unfortunately were quite accurate in our predictions. It was close, but we did not win the case, even though some people think we did.

"Nevertheless, I do think that it raised the consciousness of a lot of people about what was going on. And when I say a lot of people, I mean some part of the press, some part of the public, but most important, the players. I think that they got into the Flood thing reluctantly. The people making the decision—the player reps, the executive board—they understood, but I think if you had taken a vote among the rank and file, it would have been close as to whether we should invest the money and time supporting him. But I think as the case went on, it proved to be a great educational tool. So that was a plus.

"Also the Flood case had a strong impact on the union getting arbitration, which led to the Messersmith case and the end of the reserve clause.

"When the Flood case was filed, this was the winter of '69, and we were in negotiations on a new Basic Agreement. We had negotiated the first one in '68, a two-year agreement, and it was due to expire at the end of '69, and one of the issues that I was pressing very vigorously was to have impartial arbitration of grievances. To that time, whether there had been informal grievance procedures, as there were before the union, or a formal one after the union, the commissioner was still the arbitrator. And as long as the commissioner was the arbitrator, there was, of course, no point to even think about a Messersmith–type case where you would bring up the question: 'What did the contract really mean with respect to the reserve clause?' In those negotiations, we kept pressing for impartial arbitration at the end of the grievance procedure. And somewhat to my amazement, in the spring of 1970, when we came to an agreement on the new Basic Agreement, they agreed to it. And they did so because of the pending Flood case.

"One of the defenses baseball had always used in antitrust cases, or anything closely resembling them, was the argument that baseball was different, that it didn't need government regulation—which antitrust law meant to them—that baseball was a fully developed, self-governing instrument with a commissioner of baseball given full authority to dispense justice, et cetera, et cetera, et cetera. And therefore, there was absolutely no need to be concerned about the things that antitrust law was meant to correct.

"And if you look at the court records, you will see that courts bought this argument time after time. They bought this not just in cases involving players, but regarding the movement of teams—the movement of the Milwaukee team to Atlanta, for instance—and all kinds of cases where owners then and later objected to discipline imposed by a commissioner—courts always upheld this notion of the impartiality of the commissioner.

"Now, as we got into the Flood case, which was pending during the 1970 negotiations, I know from various things said to me later that the owners' attorneys were concerned they were going to go into court and make that defense on a really serious issue—the reserve clause—and for the first time there was going to be a body of people—namely in the form of the Players' Union—that was going to say, 'You're full of crap. The Emperor has no clothes.'

"There had never been anybody to say that to a judge before. And the owners' attorneys knew damn well we were going to go in there and say, 'What kind of self-governing mechanism are they talking about? The commissioner of baseball is an employee of the owners. He's recruited by the owners. He's fired by the owners. The authority he has is given to him by the owners. He's paid by the owners. If they don't like any decision he makes, they fire him.' They *knew* we were going to say that.

"And I believe it was the most important element in their lawyers saying, 'Look, if we're going to make this argument that we don't need antitrust law, we've got to at least be able to say we have impartial arbitration of what the contracts mean, what the major league rules mean.' And so the Flood case, in its own way, was a powerful instrument in our getting impartial arbitration, and our getting impartial arbitration, of course, made the Messersmith case possible, and made the ultimate decision in the Messersmith case possible.''

CHAPTER 63

GUSSIE'S PIQUE

ON October 9, 1969, Harry Caray, who had been broadcasting Cardinal games since 1945 and who had been Gussie Busch's faithful beer promoter and team cheerleader since Busch bought the team in 1953, abruptly disappeared from St. Louis to become play-by-play broadcaster for Oakland. The dismissal shocked St. Louis, especially after all Gussie Busch had done for Caray the year before.

In November of 1968, Caray had been run over by a car in rainswept downtown St. Louis across the street from the Chase–Plaza Hotel. He suffered a broken nose, shoulder separation, and multiple fractures of both legs below the knees. There had been some whispers that perhaps someone was out to get him, that it had not been an accident. But that was because Harry loved his booze and his broads, played around in the open, and didn't care who knew it. When Harry told everyone the driver had been a Vietnam vet who had gotten engaged that afternoon and must not have been paying attention to the road, the rumors subsided.

When in December he was well enough to leave the hospital, Gussie Busch provided Caray with the use of his winter quarters in Pass-a-Grille, near St. Pete Beach. Busch arranged for a private plane to fly him there, and he paid for a twenty-four-hour-a-day nurse to watch over him. Gussie Busch loved Harry Caray like a brother.

But Harry was harboring a secret, and while he was in the hospital recuperating from his injuries, detectives were unearthing clues that would reveal it and lead to his dismissal.

ANONYMOUS FRIEND OF HARRY CARAY: "While Harry was still convalescing, some members of the Busch family began to notice there were a lot of telephone charges on the bill linking Harry's room to one of the Busch residences.

This rang a bell, and after some checking around, some following by a detective of Harry, it was discovered that Caray was apparently having an affair with the wife of young August Busch [III], Gussie's son. Naturally, this isn't the greatest way to keep your job—breaking up the marriage of your boss's son—and as it got more involved, it wasn't long before the situation became impossible. Why the hell else would Harry have been fired? He was tremendously popular, the greatest salesman Anheuser-Busch ever had.''

When asked about his affair, Caray would only say, "I never raped anyone in my life."

One of the more cryptic comments that appeared after Harry's departure: "Broadcaster who antagonize wrong woman commit Harry Caray."

Harry Caray would spend an unhappy year with Charlie Finley in Oakland and then return to his Midwestern roots, broadcasting for the Chicago White Sox until 1982, when after a rift with owners Eddie Einhorn and Jerry Reinsdorf, he jumped crosstown to the Chicago Cubs to become the most popular and beloved personality in "the Second City" before his death on February 18, 1998.

Regardless of the reason for it, the departure of Harry Caray from St. Louis would leave a huge hole in the hearts of Cardinal fans. They would miss him terribly.

GARY MORMINO: "I was born on the Illinois side of St. Louis, which was certainly Cardinal territory. For me, it is difficult to separate my earliest consciousness from Harry Caray. I was literally weaned on the radio. We were living in the country at the time, on a farm, and I remember having a radio propped against the window, learning the game. I can remember him talking in '54 or '55 about this young Brooklyn pitcher. 'If he could ever get control, he would be a great pitcher.' Of course it was Sandy Koufax, who had won one game at the time.

"Most people don't realize it, but Harry was Italian-American. In fact, his real name was Enrico Caribina. Enrico is Italian for Harry. He took the name of Harry Caray, a great screen character actor in the forties. He always said there was a prejudice against Italian-Americans. I once heard Harry talking about when Joe Garagiola first broke in, that many of the executives would mock Garagiola, calling him 'the dumb dago.' Harry would kind of chuckle, 'cause most people didn't associate him with being Italian. But he grew up in St. Louis on the Near North Side, in a tough area called Little Italy.

"Harry had a classic working-class St. Louis accent. In fact, my father had a tonal quality very similar to Harry's, as well as to Yogi Berra, who also has a pronounced St. Louis accent. I have a phonograph record. It's the best of Harry and Jack Buck during the 1967 season, the highlights of that season. What struck me listening to that record was how precise his language was. He didn't slur his words like he did at the end of his career when he was eighty, years ago. He was just at the top of his game at the time.

"Harry could be caustic when criticizing the Cardinals. There was always a running debate whether Harry was too tough on Ken Boyer. And yet I can't imagine anyone being a homer like Harry was. The term you often hear is 'a fan's fan.' Harry could also idolize, as he did Stan Musial, and Caray obviously adored Bob Gibson, one of the great warriors of baseball history.

"And I can remember when Harry left the Cardinals. The delicious rumor on the street was that he was carrying on an affair with Augie Busch's wife, and it was crushing when he left. Harry had always been there for you, and at that time it just seemed unconscionable that a team could dismiss a loyalist like Harry. It was devastating. Again, a delicious irony that Harry would come back, but sad most people now associate him with the Cubs. What a second career!

"To me, Harry was the best—without a doubt. The question is: Who is in second place?"

BILL JAMES: "I love Harry Caray. You have to understand what Harry Caray was to the Midwest in my childhood. In the years when baseball stopped at the Mississippi, KMOX radio built a network of stations across the Midwest and into the Far West that brought major league baseball into every little burg across the landscape. Harry's remarkable talents and enthusiasm were the spearhead of their efforts and forged a link between the Cardinals and the Midwest that remains to this day; even now, some of my neighbors are Cardinal fans.

"A Harry-Caray-for-the-Hall-of-Fame debate is in progress. To us, to hear New Yorkers or Californians suggest that Harry Caray might not be worthy of the honors given to Mel Allen or Vince Scully is (a) almost comically ignorant, sort of like hearing a Midwesterner suggest that the Statue of Liberty was never of any national significance and should be turned into scrap metal, and (b) personally offensive. That Harry should have to wait in line behind these wonderful men but comparatively insignificant figures is, beyond any question, an egregious example of the regional bias of the nation's media.

"But besides that, the man is really good. His unflagging enthusiasm, his love of the game, and his intense focus and involvement in every detail of the contest make every inning enjoyable, no matter what the score or the pace of the game. His humor, his affection for language, and his vibrant images are the tools of a craftsman."

Concluded James: "To Harry Caray, the greatest sports broadcaster who ever lived. This Bud's for you."

Cardinal fans were fortunate in that after the banishment of Harry Caray, he was replaced as "Voice of the Cardinals" by a deep-voiced mellifluous announcer by the name of Jack Buck, who combined an unerring eye, a sharp tongue, and a keen wit to entertain millions of Midwesterner baseball fans for another twenty-five years.

Buck was born in Holyoke, Massachusetts, one of seven children. His father was an accountant for the Erie Railroad. His father had to move to Cleveland when the company moved its headquarters there. Two years later, the rest of the family joined him. Jack was fifteen. Not long afterward his dad died, the victim of uremic poisoning.

After graduating from high school, Jack Buck worked as a porter, cook, and baker on a Great Lakes steamer. He was drafted into the Army in June of 1943, and in March of 1945, he was part of the 9th Infantry Division responsible for taking the bridge at Remagen. It had been wired for demolition by the Germans, who didn't want the Allies crossing the Rhine River to come after them. Buck and the other men crawled across the bridge on their hands and knees. A week later, he was struck by shrapnel in the left leg and arm, the shrapnel just missing a hand grenade hanging on his chest. He won a Purple Heart. When the war in Europe ended on May 8, he was in Paris in the middle of the celebration.

After coming home, on a whim he attended Ohio State University, majored in radio speech, and graduated in three years. "As a kid, I wanted to be a radio announcer," said Buck.

At night he hosted a sports talk show on WCOL in Columbus. He also did play-by-play of the OSU basketball games. When his professor told him he ought to find something else to do for a living, Buck confidently brushed off the criticism.

In 1950 Buck won the audition to broadcast the ball games of the Columbus Redbirds in the American Association. Three years later he became "the Voice of the Rochester Red Wings," the Cards' other Triple A team, when their announcer told a dirty joke and was fired on the spot by GM Bing Devine.

After just one year at Rochester, he moved to the big booth at Busch Stadium, where in the spring of 1954, he joined the team of Harry Caray, Milo Hamilton, and Gus Mancuso on KMOX and its reach into fourteen states, including Oklahoma, Arkansas, Tennessee, Mississippi, and Alabama.

When Joe Garagiola, Caray's personal pick, replaced Hamilton, Buck became odd man out. He was fired in 1959, though the Cardinals retained his services as a public speaker. Robert "Buddy" Blattner was hired to replace him. Caray fared worse with Blattner than he had with Buck, who all the while remained in St. Louis, working for KMOX on the radio and ruling the rubber chicken circuit. One year he made 385 appearances boosting the Cardinals.

It wasn't long before both of Caray's partners became sick of having to take a backseat to him. Blattner left for the minor league Angels in California and Garagiola joined NBC for "The Game of the Week" and "The Today Show." Caray always resented having given Garagiola his start, but never being given credit for it by his protégé. The two never again spoke.

Beginning in 1961, the mild-mannered Jack Buck became Caray's second banana and was content to do so.

When Caray was abruptly fired in 1969, Jack Buck suddenly became "the Voice of the Cardinals," a position he held until his retirement in 1998.

JERRY LANSCHE: "Caray and Buck was the greatest broadcasting team of all time—without question. Jack Buck and Harry Caray were so perfect for each other that they were almost symbiotic. Caray was rah-rah, and Jack was more serious. But if you were a Cardinal fan, Harry Caray just monopolized your interest.

"Harry'd do the first three innings, and Jack did the next three, and Harry finished up. But those first three innings with Harry were draining. Harry was such a good broadcaster that you were in the game every inch of the way. You felt like you were there. And when Jack came along in the fourth inning, he was more of a professional broadcaster, and Jack almost was a relief to listen to. He was more low-key than Harry, and then after you got through his three innings, Harry was brought in for the conclusion.

"Once Caray left, Jack assumed the lead role. He became the one you looked forward to listening to. He became more of a rah-rah guy, but he was always the consummate professional. Jack knew when to talk, and he knew when to shut up. If there was something going on that was especially exciting, if someone had hit a home run, for instance, Jack knew he didn't have to fill the air with the sound of his voice. Jack would just let you listen to the crowd. Jack would let you hear the crack of the bat on the ball. And a lot of broadcasters don't do that. Jack would say, 'He winds. Here's the pitch,' and there would always be a pause. Where a lot of other broadcasters keep on talking.

"Jack also was a better interviewer than Harry. Jack had once worked with Jonathan Winters [in Rochester], and one night Winters came into the booth, and he was playing the role of Whip Willis, a Ring Lardner–type pitcher with not very much upstairs. He told Jack it was his night off, that he was going to pitch the next day, and Buck interviewed him while he stayed in character. And I tell you, it was one of the funniest conversations I ever heard. It was wonderful.

"Jack would end his broadcasts by saying, 'Thanks for your time, this time, until next time.' His two most famous calls came in 1985 in the playoffs against the Dodgers. The first came when Ozzie Smith hit a home run to right field to end the game. Buck said, 'Go crazy, folks. Go crazy.' It was a wonderful call.

"The other one, which I thought was better, was the home run that Jack Clark hit. The Dodgers still had an inning to bat, but Jack got wrapped up in it, and for Jack it became a game ender. He said, 'There's a long fly to left field. . . . and that may be a World Series home run!' He was trying to get them into the World Series, even though they still had an inning to go. But it was a great call nonetheless.

"I remember at the time my son was two years old, and I was playing hooky from work. I had my boy at home, and he was sound asleep, and Clark hit that ball, and I had the volume as low as I could to hear Jack's broadcast, and I was going through the pantomime of celebration, trying not to waken my son. It's a memory I will carry with me the rest of my life.

"Jack has aged, but he's still the best there is. Jack doesn't forget anything, and he doesn't make mistakes. I have to say, Harry Caray notwithstanding, Jack Buck is the greatest broadcaster of all time.

"I've heard most of them. In St. Louis on a clear evening, I could hear Bob Price or Ernie Harwell. Not taking anything away from those guys, they are no Buck and they are no Caray. There are only two broadcasters in the last forty-five years—that covers my age span—who stand in the pantheon, and that's Harry Caray and Jack Buck. These two guys were the very best there ever was.''

In 1970 Harry Caray was gone and so were the team's pennant chances. Despite a 23-7 record compiled by Bob Gibson, the Cardinals sunk below .500. Joe Torre, who drove in 100 runs, was the hitting star, along with Dick Allen, who hit 34 home runs and drove in 101 runs. Allen, one of the first of the eccentric prima donna players, hated to practice. He often kept to himself. Allen also found himself playing a strange position after a mysterious kidney ailment to Mike Shannon forced Red Schoendienst to move Allen from first to third base, a position he did not like to play.

And yet, out on the field, he was heroic and masterful. In 1970 he was voted the league All-Star first baseman over Orlando Cepeda, Willie McCovey, and Ernie Banks.

After the Cards started badly in 1970, the team began to bond, and by the second week in August was only nine and half games out of first when Allen tore a hamstring sliding into second base.

Allen had lived the season without controversy. He had kept his nose clean, but after the injury, he insisted on getting his treatment in Philadelphia. The Cards wanted him to recuperate in St. Louis. Allen, who lived in a hotel room, insisted on going home.

After his injury, he appeared in only one game, the last ever to be played at Connie Mack Stadium. Though his leg throbbed, he wanted to play. In the eighth inning, facing Rick Wise, on the second pitch he hit a fastball into the left field seats.

Allen had felt he had had an excellent season, despite the injury. But two weeks after the season, he was traded to the L.A. Dodgers for infielder Ted Sizemore and minor league catcher Bob Stinson. He was labeled a malcontent.

Bing Devine had engineered the trade for Dick Allen. He discussed why he made it and why it wasn't as successful as he hoped it would be.

BING DEVINE: ''That trade never did work very well. But I guess it didn't work very well for Philadelphia, either. But we felt we needed a power hitter for the ballpark. Busch Stadium is a *big* ballpark. We had never come up with a power hitter, and for a lot of reasons Dick Allen was available, and we decided to take a chance. I remember we had a meeting where we had all our scouting people together, and we got reports on who was available, and the one name that kept coming up was Dick Allen.

''Red Schoendienst was the manager of the club, and after the meeting I said to Red, 'It looks like the one guy we can get who has some power, which would change the picture of the club, would be Dick Allen, and I think we ought to make a pitch for him.' He said, 'Go ahead. I'm not going to stop you. The only thing I want to tell you: Dick Allen may need special handling, and I don't plan to handle him specially. I'll let Dick Allen do his thing his way,' and Red turned out to be right. That's the right way to handle Dick

Allen. He said, 'If you want to make the deal, go ahead, but understand I'm not going to try to make over Dick Allen.'

"I liked Dick Allen. He did what we wanted him to. I remember after we traded Dick Allen to the Dodgers, the Dodgers came into St. Louis, and Dick saw me in the lobby of the ballpark and he got me aside and said, 'You made a deal for me once, got me here, and then you traded me away, and now the Dodgers are talking about trading me again. What happened?' I said, 'I can't tell you. You might take a look at what you're doing to make people feel that way.' And the Dodgers did trade him.''

Allen was traded to the Dodgers at the end of the 1970 season. In 1971 the Cardinals' star player was a tall left-hander by the name of Steve Carlton, who had burst onto the scene in 1969 with a 19-strikeout performance against the New York Mets.

Carlton was not your normal guy. Communicating with him was not always easy. On the mound, he would tune out all distractions. Off the mound, he did the same. If he considered you the distraction, he'd direct at you an icy stare. Teammates considered him to be a recluse. He hated to sign autographs. He refused to talk to reporters for long stretches at a time. He was devoted to the martial arts. He studied Far Eastern religions. He was a wine connoisseur. He pissed people off with his standoffishness and arrogance.

STEVE CARLTON
(Courtesy Brace Photo)

Carlton was also the finest left-handed pitcher of his generation. In a career that would last twenty-four years, he would win 329 games, ninth all-time, with an ERA of 3.22. His 4,136 strikeouts were second all-time only to Nolan Ryan. Unfortunately, most of his career was not spent in St. Louis but rather in Philadelphia.

In 1971 he had forged a 20-9 record and was demanding a raise of $10,000 more than what Gussie Busch wanted to pay him for the '72 season.

President Richard Nixon had ordered wage and price controls for the country at that time, and Busch informed Carlton it was his patriotic duty to honor the President's request to a salary ceiling.

Carlton held his ground. The pitcher, who could be churlish when unhappy, angered Gussie Busch so badly that as spring training approached, Busch finally ordered general manager Bing Devine to trade him. Devine well knew what a great pitcher Carlton promised to be, but he was boxed in because Busch would not bend on the question of giving Carlton the extra $10,000, and neither would Carlton.

BING DEVINE: "We hadn't been able to sign Carlton. There was no free agency, so he didn't have the freedom to say, 'Sign me or else.' He was being very difficult to sign for the ridiculous amount of $10,000 between what he wanted and what we'd give him. Many times Mr. Busch gave me a little leeway in the budget, but in the case of Carlton, Mr. Busch developed the feeling that Carlton was a 'smart-aleck' young guy, 'and I'm not used to having young smart-alecks tell me what to do.'

"Frequently Mr. Busch and I would have conversations where he'd say, 'Have you got Carlton signed yet? If you haven't got him signed, figure out what you're going to do with him.'

"I was hoping we could get through this and not have it develop into a major issue. Finally I began talking to clubs, saying, 'If we can't sign Carlton, maybe we'll have to trade him.' And one of the people I talked to was John Quinn of Philadelphia. John Quinn said, 'I think we'd be interested in Carlton.' And we talked about the people who could be in the deal and talked about it like the way we had talked about Brock over a period of weeks.

"Often I would get early-morning phone calls. I do get up early. I don't always leave the house early. One morning the phone rang. It was Dick Meyer. This time he said, 'What have you done about Steve Carlton?' I said, 'What do you mean?' Dick said, 'Do you have a trade you can make for him, something you want to talk to us about?' I said, 'Yeah, I think I could probably make a deal with the Phillies. Why?' He said, 'Because my ulcer is acting up, and I don't like having people [Mr. Busch] affect my health and how I feel.' He said, 'Mr. Busch comes in every morning and says, "Have you gotten Carlton signed? If you don't have him signed, do you have him traded? If you don't have him traded, why not?" So Dick said, 'I'm tired of putting up with that and having my ulcer act up, so my best suggestion to you is that you do me a favor and trade him today.'

"I said, 'You mean today, period?' He said, 'Yeah, today, but I'll give you a little leeway. But I think we ought to get the deal made so I can tell Mr. Busch, 'It's done.' And that was it. I traded him to the Phils for Rick Wise.

"Three, four years later, after Carlton had established himself as a Hall of Fame pitcher, I remember talking to Dick Meyer kind of facetiously one day. I said, 'What do you think would have happened if I would have really bowed my neck and made it a major issue with Mr. Busch about Carlton?' He said, 'I'm going to tell you something. You'd have been gone first—and Steve Carlton right behind you.'

"I thought that probably was true.

"Rick Wise was a reasonably good acquisition for Carlton at the time he was acquired, but obviously over a period of time, history will tell you it was a bad deal. Same thing with Jerry Reuss for Scipio Spinks."

Jerry Reuss was another supremely talented pitcher. His transgression was growing a beard. Gussie Busch demanded that Reuss cut it off. The big right-hander refused. On April 15, 1972, Busch had Bing Devine trade him.

BING DEVINE: "This was a deal I had to make, because Mr. Busch said, 'Jerry Reuss is growing facial hair,' and he didn't like facial hair on ballplayers, or executives, either. 'Let's get rid of Reuss.' Because he was growing a beard. I didn't have any ultimatum handed down, but I knew he wanted to trade him. We didn't have him signed. We made a deal with Houston, and we got Scipio Spinks.

"Spinks had the appearance of becoming a pretty good pitcher. But he slid into the plate one day and injured himself and never became a success at it at all."

The trades of "Lefty" Carlton and Jerry Reuss may have cost the Cardinals at least four division championships. As a result of withholding the $10,000 that Carlton had wanted, Gussie Busch probably lost many millions of dollars from lost attendance and World Series revenues.

Carlton would go on to pitch fifteen seasons with Philadelphia. He would win 241 games with the Phillies, leading the league in wins four times. His 27-10 record with a 1.97 ERA in 1972 was made on a team that won only 59 games.

After winning 22 games with the Cards in his three seasons, Reuss would go on to win 198 games for a series of teams in a career that would last until 1990. He would pitch in five League Championship Series, two with the Pirates and three with the Dodgers.

If Gussie Busch was unhappy with the attitude of his players before, the player strike in the spring of 1972 infuriated him. It was the first industrywide work stoppage in the history of the game. The issue was a cost-of-living increase to the players' medical benefits and pension fund. The owners, as always, refused to consider it. In March the players voted to strike.

Said Gussie Busch, "Let them strike."

The strike began on April 1. Eighty-six games were canceled before the owners finally gave in.

BING DEVINE: "Mr. Busch was angry. He felt he had been good to the ball-players, within his framework, and he couldn't understand why all of them would go on strike and the Cardinal players would go along with it, even though he was smart enough to recognize that, unions being what they are, everybody is supposed to go along with the majority. He recognized that, but he did take exception to it. He thought in some way it was a personal insult."

In 1972 the Cardinals finished fourth in the National League East, twenty-one and a half games behind the Pittsburgh Pirates. The next year the Cards, led by the best pitching staff in the league, had a five-game lead over the Chicago Cubs in August. It was then that Bob Gibson suffered a torn cartilage in his knee. Lefty pitcher Rich Folkers took his spot in the rotation. Folkers did a creditable job, but with the soul of the team on the mend, the Cardinals folded badly, losing 29 of their last 47 games.

With two days left, the Cards were two games behind the New York Mets. Gibson returned and beat Carlton, 5–1, but when the Mets beat the Cubs, the pennant was theirs. The Cards finished the 1973 season 81-81, only one and a half games behind Yogi Berra's "Miracle Mets."

Rich Folkers was drafted and signed by the New York Mets in June of 1967. He rose to Triple A, then tore a muscle in his back in spring training in 1970. He pitched poorly because his back ached the whole season. In the fall of 1971, he was traded to the Cardinals, where Arkansas manager Fred Koenig taught him how to throw the screwball.

When Bob Gibson hurt himself in '73, Folkers got his first start with the Cards. His opponent was Steve Carlton.

RICH FOLKERS: "Bob Gibson broke a leg bone in New York, so I went into his spot in the rotation, and my first start was against Philadelphia down in Philadelphia. I was leading the game, 2–1, going into the seventh inning, and Joe Torre was playing third, and a ground ball on the AstroTurf hit a seam and caromed off, and a run scored, tied it up, and they took me out. I didn't get a decision.

"But I pitched well, especially against Carlton, because if you give up two runs against him, usually you lose. I stayed in the rotation until Bob Gibson came back at the end of the season.

"Our manager was Red Schoendienst. He was a very calm, a low-key individual. Not a lot of hype. He let you play the game, let you do your own thing, didn't get too involved in giving you too many things to do, so instead of thinking about all these other things, you could think about the game.

"To me, he was a very good manager. I always said, 'If you can't play for Red, you can't play for anybody.' He made it comfortable.

"We didn't have a lot of hitting, and that was our downfall. Rick Wise was on the club, and he ended up 16-12, and he lost eight games by one run. We'd get beat 2–1, 3–2, 1–0, 2–0, 3–1, a lot of games. If we just had a little bit of offense, some key hits, we'd have done real well. In '73 we finished a game and a half out and the next year a game and a half out. We came down to the last day with the Mets one year and the Pirates the other. And both won it on the last day.

"Joe Torre was our star. He was the head of that club. [In 1971 Torre hit .363 and won his MVP.]

"Joe, to me, was a great guy. He worked with everybody, got them focused, just like a team leader is supposed to. He didn't let them stray. If you needed a slap on the back, he'd do that. If you needed a kick in the butt, he'd kick you in the butt. Which is what you were supposed to do. He was a big help to Red. We called him 'Assistant Coach.'

"Before he came to St. Louis, he had been a catcher with Atlanta. He was a little overweight, and we'd pitch him in tight pretty good. He lost the weight, and his hands got quicker. He had a short stroke, a nice line drive type hitter. He hit the ball to all fields. He didn't run the greatest, but not too many first basemen do.

"Ted Sizemore, our second baseman, was probably the best number-two hitter I saw in my career. He hit 0-2 more than any hitter I ever saw, because with Lou Brock getting on base, he took and took and took, waiting for Lou to steal bases. And without a good number-two hitter, you're not going to steal a lot of bases. 'Cause he's always fouling pitches off, not giving you a chance to steal a base. Sizemore would still hit .270 and do that almost always with two strikes on him, which I thought was incredible. I thought he was outstanding, though Ted never got the credit. These are the behind-the-scene things. You might say, 'This guy only hit .260 in the big leagues?' Yeah, but consider some of the things he did: Every time there was a man on second, he got the ground ball to move him to third, or he took strikes so Brock could steal. That's why you can't say: 'You have to hit .300 to be a great player.' There is a little more to it than that.

"That whole group of Cardinals was pretty close. We did a lot of things together. Going out to a pizza place, we might have twelve guys. It was a pretty tight club. Other clubs I've been on, each of them go their own way, a couple hang out. None were as close as that club was. It was Ted Simmons, Lou Brock, Bake McBride, Bernie Carbo, Reggie Smith. We'd go out.

"In '73 Timmy McCarver returned to the Cards. He caught a little bit, played a little first base, and pinch hit.

"Timmy talked quite a bit, if you know Timmy. He was another good influence on the young ballplayers. He'd been around, knew the game, how it was played, how it should be played. So with Torre and McCarver there, we had two guys who did it on the field also. So it was good to be around those guys.

"Bob Gibson was the ace of the pitching staff. He was kind of all to himself. I remember one time myself and Alan Foster went out to eat in Pittsburgh, and Gibson was there, and he motioned us over: 'Come, sit here.' So we sat, and it wasn't five minutes when he said, 'Oh no, here we go again.' He had just gotten his meal, started to eat, when people started coming over for autographs, and he could not stand that.

"His feeling was, 'Here I am, in the middle of the meal. At least wait until I am done.' Which is right. Sometimes the fans go overboard. Get the autographs at the ballpark. Later he ended up refusing to sign autographs. He got tired of it. 'Cause a kid would get an autograph, take it to a dealer, and then he would sell it. Sometimes the same kid would come to you five or six times getting autographs, and then he'd go over to somebody else and give it to him, and the guy'd give him five bucks, and he'd sell it. That's why a lot of guys don't sign autographs.

"Gibby wanted his privacy. I don't blame him. There are times I will do things for the public and times, hey, let me have my own little space. I don't want to be a twenty-four-hour public figure. You see that with movie stars. They like to have some time when they're not having their picture taken or put in the tabloids. It's a little worse now than it was back then.

"I remember the day Gibby got hurt. We were in Shea Stadium, and a ball got knocked back at him and hit him in the shin area, and it cracked a bone. They didn't think he was going to come back all year. He came back in September, which was unbelievable, and he went back into the rotation, and he pitched fairly well. And he wasn't young. He was thirty-four or thirty-five.

"I took his spot. I didn't feel any pressure. I was one of the guys who could start, so that's what happened. 'Cause I had started throughout my whole minor league career. I didn't pitch in relief until I was called up by the Mets. And I had no clue how to warm up or anything. You have to learn by trial and error and watch other people. I was always a starter, so I never thought much about: 'How do you warm up in relief?' You'd think it would be the same way, but it's not. It's completely different. I learned to warm up correctly, not to overthrow, not get too warm too quick. You have to get ready, then slow it down a little bit so you don't waste it all in the bullpen. They might set you down and get you up the next inning or two hitters later. It's a yo-yo, and if that yo-yo is up and down too many times, you lose it out in the bullpen, and you get in the game and you don't have anything left.

"It's different when you're starting. When you start, you're not afraid to make a mistake. You can be a little bit more aggressive, 'cause if you give up a run here or there, you're still in the game, whereas as a reliever, you have to come in and you got to get that first guy. It's important out of the bullpen to get that first guy out, set the tone. You're only going to be in there maybe one hitter, or two innings, depending on whether you're a setup guy or a closer. So, to me, it's a different ball game.

"Not many guys can start, go in the bullpen for a day or two, and then come back five days later and start again. I tried it with San Diego when I was traded over there—I'd start one game, pitch seven innings one day, then two days later pitch in relief. I wasn't the biggest guy in the world. I weighed about 172 pounds. That would take wear and tear out of you. I finally told them, 'Either relieve me or start me.' And I always liked starting better than relieving.

"In our bullpen we had Al Hrabosky, 'the Mad Hungarian.' Before the first pitch, he'd stomp around the mound. He started that in St. Louis. He was struggling early in the season, and he tried to get something going. I don't know if it just happened, or whether he said to himself, 'I got to do this back of the mound, be aggressive and go after them,' but that day he ended up pitching well, and it went from there. Later he added the Fu Manchu. Anything that gets you ready to pitch, that motivates you, where you get to that higher level, you do it. And he started pitching great. Al threw hard and a little bit erratic, which is good at times, because that hitter won't set in on you. He had a little breaking ball, worked on the forkball, and ended up having some very good years.

"Of course, it was all an act. Al and I had played together in Little Rock one year. He was really pretty quiet, a homebody. He was not a wild guy. Nor was he mad, but anything to make you better on the playing field. 'I got to get you out somehow as a pitcher.' If that's what was going to do it, then you do it.

"After starting out 0-11, we had a lead in August then lost it. We started losing, but nobody panicked. The mood stayed pretty consistent. Guys went out there every day and just played their game. We did have some good veteran players, so you watched them, and you'd say, 'Shoot, they're doing it, so we can do it.'

"But the thing was, the reason we lost 2–1, 3–2, we just didn't have quite enough offense for a duration of a season. Put us in a short series, with our pitching and defense, well, we might win a 2–1 game. Which we did. But we still lost too many of 2–1, 3–2 games. That was our downfall. We just didn't have that one extra hitter we needed to drive in runs.

"Our offense was Lou Brock getting a base hit, stealing second, and Ted Simmons knocking him in. Joe Torre struggled a little bit that year.

"We were very disappointed to have lost to the Mets that year, especially with the Mets going on to beat Cincinnati, which had a very good club, and if it wasn't for a couple errors in one game, they would have beaten Oakland for the world championship. So there was a club with little better than a .500 record, but with their pitching staff and good defense, like we had, in a short series you never know what might have happened. That could have been us.

"The next season we added Reggie Smith [in a trade with Boston] and Bake McBride to give us more speed. We had a lot of speed on the club.

"Reggie Smith was a good guy. During the three years I was with the Cardinals, there wasn't anybody who was disliked. Each had his own disposition but went about doing his own thing his own way. All of them were good guys who worked hard together. When Reggie was in the lineup, he did real well, but he had a couple of nagging injuries: his leg, then his hand. Bernie Carbo went in for him and had some good playing time.

"But once again we were lacking that one extra hitter, and we didn't have a year when everything went right. When you play 162 games, you have to have things go right, have to keep away from injury. Everybody has got to stay healthy, and you have to have two or three guys who do better than their average, have to have that one year where instead of knocking in 50, they knock in 85. That's how you win championships. And when you get to a short series, anything can happen. That's when you rely on the pitching, good defense, and get some timely hitting. And we didn't get that.

"That year Bob Gibson struck out batter number 3,000. I pitched in relief that game. Against Cincinnati, he struck out Cesar Geronimo.

"I really admired him, especially after coming back and pitching the way he did after suffering a broken leg. Every time we went out there he gave 150 percent, and man, he was nails. Bob was a *very* aggressive pitcher.

"To watch him pitch out there, Gibson was so businesslike and so mean out there, and people perceived that as being him. And it wasn't him. That's the game. A lot of times you see guys on TV—pro wrestlers doing what they do, and off the field or off the mat when you meet them, they are a different person. A lot of guys you wouldn't even recognize if they walked the street. You think that's how he is in real life because that's how he acts on the mound, or on the mat, or on the basketball court. But no, that's not true.

"In 1974 we were battling the Pirates for the division title. Their pitching was good but not outstanding. They had a very explosive hitting team. They had Willie Stargell, Al Oliver, Rennie Stennett, Richie Hebner, Bob Robinson, Richie Zisk, Dave Parker, and Manny Sanguillen behind the plate. There were no easy outs on that club, where against some teams you could pitch around one or two guys and then face three or four weak hitters in a row. Not with that club. You had to try to keep it in the ballpark. And they were a comeback team. They won a lot of games late. Because of the bats. The Pirates were a very tough club.

"Pittsburgh was a club I did fairly well against. Why, I don't know. Their top power was left-handed: Stargell, Hebner, Parker, and Al Oliver. You can cut that down a little throwing from the left side.

"That last series was up in Montreal. Red said, 'Just go out there and do your job, boys.' That's the way Red was. Nothing out of the ordinary. No big speech.

"We lost the second-to-last day of the season when late in the game Al Hrabosky was on the mound, Joe Torre was playing third, and McCarver was catching. There was a pop-up, and somehow nobody called it. The ball landed fair. It was one of those freak things. We ended up getting beat that game.

"On the last day, the Pirates lost. A win would have put us in a tie. We would have had to go to Pittsburgh for a playoff game. We were talking about: 'Who are we going to start?'

"We were in Montreal. It was 36 degress, slight sleet, cold and windy. We had those big hearts in the dugout to stay warm. Gibson was pitching in the eighth inning with a 2–1 lead, and Mike Jorgensen was up. There was a man on first, and Hrabosky was up in the bullpen.

"Red stuck with Gibson. He was the main man. You're going to go with your best. You can look back and say, 'Gee, he should have taken him out,' but he was winning the game, 2–1. They only had four hits off him. He was pitching good.

"But the wind was blowing out, and he got a pitch up that Jorgensen normally didn't hit. Mike was a low-ball hitter, and Gibby threw a pitch high and in, and Mike turned on it a little bit, got it up, and it went out. And we ended up getting beat that game. There went that year.

"It was one of those games, but you can't go back and say, 'Well, this game lost it for us.' When you play 162 games, that's only a part of the puzzle. There were other games during the season that we should have won.

"We packed our gear and went home.

"That's baseball, the only game where you have to get the last out. No time is going to run out on you, like the other sports. In baseball there is no time limit. You can't have the clock run out and say, 'Geez, it's the sixth inning and we've played three hours, sorry, the game's over, we win, 2–1. Bases loaded, no outs. Bye. See ya. You can't walk off the field. You have to play until that last out.''

Bob Gibson should have retired at the end of '74, but his marriage had broken up and he needed baseball one final season. Around the All-Star break, he was sent to the bullpen. In one game in early September, journeyman first baseman Pete LaCock hit a grand slam off him. Gibson felt humiliated. He knew he was through.

When Red Schoendienst came out to get the ball, Gibson handed it to him, walked off the mound, and he never pitched again. With thirteen road games left in the 1975 season, Bob Gibson left the Cardinals, ending a brilliant seventeen-year career.

In 1981 he became the sixth pitcher to be voted into the Hall of Fame in his first year of eligibility. The others were: Walter Johnson, Christy Mathewson, Bob Feller, Warren Spahn, and Sandy Koufax. In his acceptance speech on the steps of Cooperstown, Bob Gibson thanked everyone who helped him in his career. In typical Gibson fashion, he failed to mention Cardinals headman Gussie Busch, who was offended and never did forgive his star pitcher for the oversight. The Budweiser franchise that Gibson—the best pitcher Gussie Busch ever had—always dreamed about never materialized.

CHAPTER 64

ENTER WHITEY

At the end of the 1976 season, the impatience of seventy-five-year-old Gussie Busch began to grow. Without a pennant since 1968, he determined that Red Schoendienst, a personal friend and a hunting companion, was too soft on his players, and as a replacement he hired Vern Rapp, a minor league manager with a schoolmarm reputation for being a strict martinet. Rapp had rules against being overweight, against drinking in the hotel bar on the road, and taking a cue from Gussie Busch, he banned beards and mustaches. He wanted his players to look like Marines rather than hippies. He ordered Ted Simmons to lose weight and demanded that Al Hrabosky cut his Fu Manchu and long hair. During spring training, Hrabosky refused. In late May, Rapp suspended his relief star for two games for not attending a meeting, the subject of which was to be the length of his hair.

Then on July 14, 1977, Rapp held a team meeting, during which, after demanding some players shave more closely, he then suggested that some of the players were not earning their pay.

The players were ready to mutiny.

KEITH HERNANDEZ: "Vern Rapp in St. Louis held some destructive ass-kickings. He picked up the habit managing in Triple A in the Cincinnati organization, the most conservative in baseball, and he brought it over to the Cards in 1977. Both he and his meetings were intensely disliked. I wouldn't say we had a negative attitude; rather, we didn't have the positive attitude of 'Let's play for this guy.' Rapp lasted a year and a half."

Rapp was sarcastic and ornery to the end. His last act was to call St. Louis hero Ted Simmons "a loser." Simmons's crime: turning up the stereo in the clubhouse too loud.

Three weeks into the 1978 season, Bing Devine recommended to Busch that Rapp be fired. Ken Boyer, strong but silent like Red Schoendienst, was named manager. Though Boyer's record wasn't much better than Rapp's, one important move he made was to install Keith Hernandez as the regular first baseman.

When 1979 began, the impatient and moody Hernandez was worried. When he hit .232 in April, he felt his career was on the line. Boyer took Hernandez aside and told him, "Look, you're my third hitter every game this year. Don't worry about it. You're the man."

Hernandez would go on to hit .344 and win the batting title and be named the National League's MVP. Boyer had probably saved his career.

Boyer, however, was not good enough to save Bing Devine's career. In 1978, ten years after Devine had returned to St. Louis for his second stint as general manager and ten years since the last Cardinal pennant, Gussie Busch fired him and in one of life's great ironies, replaced him with a man whom Devine had been helping find work in baseball. Devine was dumbfounded when he learned that the person his friend would be replacing would be himself.

BING DEVINE: "Mr. Busch had a very close personal adviser by the name of Lou Sussman, who had a great influence on Mr. Busch, and Lou helped Mr. Busch make a change. I'm not being critical of Lou Sussman. He was doing his job. He did it the way he thought he should do it. That's the way it happened.

"Mr. Busch finally said to Mr. Sussman, 'Okay, we'll get rid of him. Who do we get?' And Lou Sussman said, 'John Claiborne is out there somewhere working at another job. He isn't in baseball. I think we can get him.'

"When they hired John Claiborne to replace me, he was working in another business somewhere in New England. [John Claiborne is now the head of the New England Sports Network, which is owned by the Bruins and Red Sox.] At the time, John was talking to me about how to help him get back in baseball.

"In the course of all this, Lou Sussman called John and said, 'Mr. Busch wants to talk to you about becoming the team's general manager.' They talked and negotiated a deal, and then Lou Sussman said, 'I know you're close to Bing Devine. Don't you dare tell him this is done. We want to announce it on our time.' And John Claiborne didn't tell me.

"Later, after it was all over, John came out to my house with his wife and with tears in his eyes said, 'I never can get over the fact that I didn't have the courage to tell you while I was talking to you about helping me get a job that I was hired to replace you, and I apologize.'

"I said, 'Forget it. It's not going to change anything. It's water over the dam. Let's forget about it.' "

That was Bing Devine, decent to the end. Devine had been able to blunt and counteract the negative moves of Gussie Busch as well as anyone. His replacement, John Claiborne, lacked experience, both in handling Busch and in trading with the other sharks. By the late 1970s, the Cardinals were moribund and without flair. Keith Hernandez flashed leather at first base, and Ted Simmons, who averaged .301 between 1971 and 1980 and whose 2,530 total bases during that period was third best behind only Pete Rose and Steve Garvey, became a fan idol. Lou Brock was another player who could still thrill the Cardinal fans, and he would retire after the 1979 season with 3,023 hits, only the fourteenth player to reach the hallowed 3,000 mark. Equally remarkable, during his nineteen-year career he stole 938 bases, leading the National League in steals eight seasons. In 1985 he would be elected into the Baseball Hall of Fame.

WHITEY HERZOG
(Courtesy Brace Photo)

By the spring of 1980, Gussie Busch became fed up with the performance of his team under manager Boyer. John Claiborne suggested that the Cards hire as a consultant Dorrel Norman Elvert "Whitey" Herzog, who was available because he had managed the Kansas City Royals to three straight divisional titles in '76, '77, and '78, but each time the team had lost to the Yankees in the play-offs. After a couple of nasty confrontations between Herzog and owner Ewing Kauffman in 1979, the pharmaceutical magnate fired him at the end of the season.

When Claiborne contacted Herzog, Whitey freely gave his opinion about some of the Cards players but turned down the consulting job. Three weeks later, Gussie Busch's lawyer, Lou Sussman, called Herzog to offer him the managing position. When a one-year contract was offered, Herzog told Busch he wasn't interested under those terms. He had managed in Kansas City under one-year contracts, he told Busch, and he would not do it again. "I want some hammer," said Herzog. After Busch and Sussman conferred, Busch said, "You're right. I'll give you a three-year contract."

When Herzog came to St. Louis, he was immediately taken with the way the eighty-one-year-old Busch did business. Busch didn't confer with committees, didn't waffle when a decision was needed, didn't try to play it safe. Thought Herzog, "I wondered where he's been all my life."

Busch later would express the same feelings about Herzog. "He's the guy I've been looking for for twenty-nine years," said Busch. "He's not only a great manager but a helluva guy. He and I talk the same language."

That they did. Among their common bonds were their German ancestry and a shared love of beer. Whitey Herzog was born in 1931 in New Athens (pronounced *Ay*-thens), Illinois, a German town forty miles from St. Louis. His father worked for the Mound City Brewing Company. As a boy, Herzog worked for a funeral home, digging graves, and also worked in the brewery, doing cleanup work. Herzog grew up drinking beer. "Hell," said Herzog, "we were Germans, or at least not very far removed. Beer was part of our food."

*   *   *

Herzog had been a utility player during an unremarkable eight-year major league career. He came up as a center fielder with the New York Yankees. In spring training in 1956, Yankee manager Casey Stengel told him, "You're a pretty good ballplayer, but you're not as good as the feller I got." That feller, Mickey Mantle, would go on to win the Triple Crown that year. Herzog was traded to the Washington Senators for pitcher Mickey McDermott.

Manager Chuck Dressen loved him, but when he hit only .245, the next year he was replaced in center field by Albie Pearson. Harry Craft, his former minor league manager in the Yankee chain, brought him to the Kansas City A's, where he platooned with Bob Cerv. In 1961 Trader Lane shipped him to Baltimore, where he was an outfielder under manager Paul Richards. His last stop was Detroit, where he spent most of his year on the bench. After the 1963 season, he retired.

Next came the climb up the scout/coach/managerial ladder. He scouted and coach for Kansas City owner Charles Finley, then went to the New York Mets as third base coach.

When Bing Devine went to the Mets, Devine hired him as his right-hand man. When general manager Johnny Murphy died in January of 1969, Herzog was named head of player development, and the two helped build the 1973 championship Mets team while Herzog spent seven frustrating years watching Mets president M. Donald Grant trade away his best prospects (Nolan Ryan, Amos Otis, Kenny Singleton, Tim Foli, and Mike Jorgensen.) Herzog should have been named manager after Gil Hodges died in April of 1972, but Grant preferred Yogi Berra, so Whitey left the Mets and in 1973 began his managerial career in Texas, one of the worst-run teams in baseball history at the time. He spent a frustrating year because his general manager, Joe Burke, wouldn't make the moves Herzog wanted to make. When Billy Martin became available in September, Burke replaced Herzog.

He worked in 1974 as coach for Gene Autry's California Angels under manager Bobby Winkles, even managing four games as interim manager before Dick Williams took over.

In 1975 Herzog was hired to manage the Kansas City Royals after Jack McKeon was fired. His general manager was again Joe Burke, and again they didn't get along, but his personnel included George Brett, Amos Otis, Hal McRae, and Darrell Porter.

Herzog, who had great skill at talent evaluation, discovered that working for a general manager with whom he wasn't on the same page made his life as manager too difficult. After years of fighting with Ewing Kauffman and Joe Burke and then getting the boot at Kansas City, Herzog determined that in order to succeed at turning the Cardinals around, he needed to be GM as well as manager. It didn't take very long before Gussie Busch agreed to give him that authority.

Early on, Herzog bluntly told Busch, "I'm shocked at what I see on the field. If I had known it was this bad, maybe I wouldn't have come." The equally blunt Busch was bowled over by Whitey's refreshing honesty.

During the summer of 1980, Busch fired John Claiborne as GM. Announced Busch, "What I want is somebody who can make this team a winner again." Herzog was the one he wanted for the job.

GUSSIE BUSCH: "I wanted him to do something about it. He said he would have to make some deals, to get rid of some players, come up with some others. I told him he'd have a clear hand if he became general manager."

Herzog took the GM job on the condition that he could continue to hold both jobs or could go back to being only the manager when the time was right to do so.

"Great," said Busch.

Herzog decided that the team desperately needed two essentials: speed and a solid bullpen. During the summer of 1980 Herzog managed for 73 games, then decided he needed more distance in order to evaluate his players more objectively. On August 30 he turned the team over to Red Schoendienst and moved upstairs to the general manager's office.

WHITEY HERZOG: "I've never seen such a bunch of misfits. Nobody would run out a ball. Nobody in the bullpen wanted the ball. We had guys on drugs—and another guy who sneaked off into the tunnel between innings so he could take a hit of vodka.

"A couple of weeks after I took over, Gussie called me up to his office in the stadium and growled, 'Well, what have I got?'

" 'Well, Chief,' I said, 'You've got a bunch of prima donnas, overpaid SOBs who ain't ever going to win a goddamned thing. You've got a bunch of mean people, some sorry human beings. It's the first time I've ever been scared to walk through my own clubhouse. We've got drug problems, we've got ego problems, and we ain't ever going anywhere.'

" 'You really think it's that bad?' Gussie said.

" 'I know so. We ain't going to win with this sorry bunch. We've got to do some housecleaning.'

" 'Well,' said Gussie, 'Keep me posted.' "

Herzog's problem was that getting in touch with the busy beer baron wasn't that simple. He asked Bing Devine, who suggested he call up and say he was coming up for a few beers. Herzog would do that around lunchtime, and he and Busch would talk. Whitey might bring a fresh fish or some cheese, and they'd sit around, play gin, and drink beer. It was that direct access, says Herzog, that was critical to the team's success in 1981 and 1982.

After turning the team over to Red Schoendienst for the rest of the 1980 season, Herzog began to study the minor league talent. Herzog drew up a master plan. Busch Stadium, a large park, demanded a team featuring pitching, speed, and defense. He judged that most of the prospects were either too old or not far enough along. He promoted Tommy Herr, John Stuper, and Andy Rincon to the Cards and rejected the rest.

Had the Cards not switched from Boyer to Herzog, the young Herr, who would go on to a fine thirteen-year career, nine with the Cards, may well have played his career elsewhere.

TOMMY HERR: "I came up in 1979 in the September call-up, and one of the things that struck me about that team was that there seemed to be a lot of rebels there, a lot of guys who had their own agenda and didn't have a lot of respect for authority. Ken wasn't real vocal. He was more of a stoic guy, but that type of manager needs players who have their own disciplinary values and can police themselves. That group of Cardinal players didn't have that.

"In 1980 the Cards fired Boyer and hired Whitey, and I felt that it was going to help me, because I didn't feel that Ken Boyer liked me or was in my corner. In fact, he had said some things to me that indicated that he didn't like my whole act. He felt I was lazy and wasn't a hard worker. Basically, that's what he said. I felt very offended by that at the time. Here I was, just the twenty-fourth or twenty-fifth man on the roster, and he had a lot of other guys causing problems, and he chose to pick on me. I felt like he would have been better served to go after some of the big guys. I felt like I didn't know if I was going to get a real chance as long as Ken Boyer was there unless I could change his attitude about me. So that's when we were going through that process, when he got fired and Whitey came in in the middle of the season.

"He took over at the All-Star break, and one of Whitey's first moves was to send me to Triple A. Whitey called me into his office and said, 'Look, it's not doing you any good to be up here and not playing. You need to be playing every day, so we can see what you can do.' So I went down to Springfield and played the rest of the season, had a very good year, and then he called me back to the big leagues, and I had a very good September, and that winter Whitey made some big deals and gave me the second base job based on what I had done the second half of that season.

"Whitey was a straight shooter. He was a no-nonsense kind of guy. He let you know where you stood. If you played hard for him, he was going to be in your corner. His style of managing and what he liked in a ballplayer was conducive to my game, because he liked speed and defense, and offense created by aggressive baserunning, and that really fit my style of play. I knew if I could show him anything, that I might be the kind of player he would like."

His first priority was to bring in a good defensive catcher and a stopper.

He met with the top brass at Anheuser-Busch and told them exactly what he intended to do. He told them he wanted to do it fast and under budget. The one restriction the brewery nabobs placed on him was that if Herzog signed a high-priced player, he had to let one go at the same time. Herzog hired Joe McDonald, who had been the general manager of the Mets, to be his assistant.

He started making inquiries at the playoffs and the World Series. Joe McDonald worked the phones as well. They agreed to trade any player except shortstop Garry Templeton.

In October Herzog and Busch agreed that he would manage the team in 1981.

"All of a sudden I was a one-man band," said Herzog.

He began by trading catcher Terry Kennedy to San Diego for relief pitcher Rollie Fingers, catcher Gene Tenace, lefty pitcher Bob Shirley, and a rookie catcher named Bob Geren. Herzog still coveted another reliever, Bruce Sutter, who had led the National League in saves the past two years with the Cubs.

Herzog figured that if he could get Sutter, he could trade Fingers for a different need. Herzog traded first base prospect Leon Durham, outfielder Ty Waller, and infielder Ken Reitz to Chicago for Sutter.

In November catcher Darrell Porter filed for free agency. An important cog in Herzog's Kansas City division champions, Porter had had an outstanding season for Kansas City in 1979, batting .291 and driving in 112 runs and earning recognition as the American League's All-Star catcher. But then he became caught up in the cocaine epidemic and scandal that raged through baseball during that time. During spring training of 1980, he checked himself into a drug and alcohol rehabilitation center, one of the first athletes to admit his drug dependency. When he returned, he played poorly, hitting only .249. When his contract ran out at the end of the 1980 season, he became a free agent.

Porter was on a cruise ship on his honeymoon during the winter of 1980 when he received a call from his agent. Whitey Herzog, his former manager with the Royals, wanted him to play for him in St. Louis. Porter came running.

DARRELL PORTER: "When I left spring training and went away for drug rehab, nobody was coming out and admitting it. In fact, I believe I was the first player who ever admitted he had a drug problem. Don Newcombe, an old pitcher, had come to spring training and he talked to us about what alcohol had done to him, and I was sitting there, listening to him, and it was like he was talking to me. He gave us ten questions, and he said, 'If you can answer three of them yes, you've got a problem. And I answered them *all* yes. I knew I had a problem, and to tell you the truth, when you're that messed up, you know your life is miserable, and I just wanted to do something about it. I didn't want to live that kind of life. So I admitted I had a drug problem and went away. And then I came back, and I got off to a great start in '80, but I ended up having the worst season I had in years. The routines I used to go through every day just changed. I no longer went to the bars. Life had become so different. Everything.

"I was a free agent, and the one thing you want to do when you're a free agent is have a good year, and mine was terrible! And to top it off, I was an admitted drug addict. So I was thinking, 'Who's going to call me?' Well, not very many people did, but Whitey did. He told me, 'Darrell, I don't care what you've done. I don't care anything about the past. I don't care about the drugs. I don't care about anything like that. I know your heart. I know what kind of ballplayer you are. And I want you to come to St. Louis and play for me, and,' he told me, 'I really believe if you do, that it will give me the opportunity to make some other moves, and I really believe if I can do that, I can put together a championship team.'

"And so it didn't take much for him to convince me, because of my faith in Whitey."

For Herzog, getting Darrell Porter was the key. Under Herzog's system, his players had to be tough and they had to be unselfish. They had to be willing to give themselves up by moving a runner from first to second on a ground ball to the right side with less than two out. They had to be willing to sacrifice for the good of the team. Darrell Porter, in addition to being a fine defensive catcher, had always done as he was asked, and it was Porter who became one of the backbones of Herzog's division champion Kansas City teams.

When Porter's signing, Herzog decided to move the Cards' hard-hitting, but subpar-fielding catcher Ted Simmons to first and to play Keith Hernandez in left field.

When Ted Simmons's agent called Herzog to tell him his client would not be happy playing first base, Herzog decided it best to trade him. He packaged Simmons, pitcher Pete Vuckovich, and Rollie Fingers and traded them to Milwaukee. In exchange he received Sixto Lezcano to play the outfield, Lary Sorensen, a righty pitcher, lefty starter Dave LaPoint, and David Green, the prospect he wanted to replace Durham. On paper, the deal looked better than it turned out. Green was a bust, and Lezcano and Sorensen didn't do much for the Cards.

But the trade of the popular Simmons put everyone on the team on notice that Whitey Herzog was top dog, that it would be his way or the highway.

BILL JAMES: "Suppose that you are the new manager of an office, or a loading dock, or the new plant manager in a factory, and things aren't running worth a hoot, and people are bitching and moaning a lot instead of working together, and you approach your highest-paid employee, who is also the most popular, visible man in the organization, and who is also a friend of your boss, and you tell him that you're going to assign him some different duties. And he tells you to stick it. What are you going to do?

"De facto authority, that is the message. You either get rid of that son of a bitch, or you accept the fact that he is running the show and you are not. If Whitey Herzog didn't have the guts to run Ted Simmons out of St. Louis, he might as well have quit on the spot. Because if he didn't, from that moment on he was not the man-a-ger of anything."

Herzog's three transactions got everyone's attention. The headlines trumpeted: "WHITEY SHUFFLES THE CARDS."

WHITEY HERZOG: "By God, the Cardinals were ready. They hadn't won a damned thing since 1968, so I figured,'What the hell? We might as well shake things up and see what happens.' "

*   *   *

Herzog was roasted by the fans for trading Simmons, who had become a St. Louis institution. He was on the board of the museum and involved in charities. In his place came Darrell Porter, an admitted drug addict.

DARRELL PORTER: "From day one, a few of the Cardinal fans (it seemed like the whole stadium) took an instant dislike to me. And they showed it every chance they got.

"Having people like me has always been important to me—probably too important. Consequently, this vendetta by the St. Louis fans really hurt me. Things got worse and worse, and gradually it affected my game to the point that I hated coming to the stadium.

"Enduring the spite—the hatred—of that handful of St. Louis fans was one of the hardest things I have ever done. It was almost harder than kicking the beer and drugs."

In June of 1981, Herzog traded infielder Tony Scott for Joaquin Andujar, the temperamental pitcher from the Dominican Republic. Andujar was a gamble because of his sometimes strange and emotional behavior. He might run the bases wearing his warm-up jacket on the arm he didn't pitch with. He might shower in his uniform. On the mound after a strikeout, he might blow on his finger like it was a six-shooter. Sometimes on the mound, his anger would flash out of control.

Andujar began in the Cincinnati organization, where Sparky Anderson sent him to the minors. During the winter league, he was coached by Hub Kittle, and it was Kittle who convinced Houston GM Tal Smith to acquire him. In five years with the Astros, Andujar averaged only 8 wins a season, despite great stuff and an impressive earned run average. When Kittle moved to St. Louis, Kittle convinced Herzog to get the pitcher who dubbed himself "One Tough Dominican."

The Cardinals in 1981 won more games than any other team in the division, but 1981 would be a year like no other. After a fifty-two-day midseason layoff brought on by a strike by the Players' Association, Commissioner Bowie Kuhn ordered the season split into two halves—pre-strike and post-strike—a popular format in the minor leagues. The winner of the first half was to play the winner of the second half for the right to go to the World Series.

The Cards finished second in both halves. They had a higher combined winning percentage (59-43) than anyone but finished a game and a half behind the Phils in the first half, and half a game behind the Expos in the second half. For the Cardinal fans, what happened to the Cards in '81 was disgraceful. To the players, life goes on.

DARRELL PORTER: "We won more games than anybody in our division that year and didn't even go to the playoffs. We were disappointed, but that was just the way it worked out. it was just a part of the game. We didn't dwell on it or anything; we were just coming into our own. St. Louis hadn't done anything for how many years at that point? [Thirteen.]"

TOMMY HERR: "The strike was very frustrating for me as a young player, because I was so excited about being in the big leagues and getting a chance to play every day. Our team was playing very well at that point. We were neck and neck with the Phillies when the strike occurred, so it was frustrating. I wasn't really plugged into the union affairs and really wasn't sure what the issues were. They tried to educate the young guys as well as they could. Basically the young players just go along with what's recommended by the older guys. You don't make any waves.

"At the end of the season, we had the best overall record and didn't make it to the playoffs. A lot was made of that in St. Louis. I think it was rather obvious once they decided to divide the season into two halves, with the Phillies already assured of a playoff berth based on the first half, that they played the second half differently. They could afford to rest guys and look at people because they were already in. I think there is some value to the fact that we won the most games, but I don't really put a whole lot of stock in it. We used it as a motivational tool for the following year. We felt like we could play with anybody in our division based on what we had done in '81, and we needed to continue that."

One disappointment for Herzog during the 1981 season was the play of star shortstop Garry Templeton. Herzog began to lose confidence in Templeton, who infuriated Herzog when he kept complaining about being too tired to play day games that followed night games. Herzog didn't want to hear it, and before a Ladies' Day game in St. Louis, he told Templeton he had to play, like it or not.

WHITEY HERZOG: "So Tempy goes out and loafs his way through the first four or five innings. Everyone in the park could see what he was up to, and the fans were booing the shit out of him. I don't blame them; if I'd paid good money to see a professional ballplayer put out, I'd have been booing too. So Templeton comes off the field after one inning, stops in front of the pitcher's mound, grabs his crotch, and gives the fans the finger.

"When he got to the dugout, I reached out and pulled him down the steps, and if the other players hadn't come between us, I guess we'd have had a pretty good fight right then and there. I've never been so mad at a player."

Herzog suspended him, and he spent three weeks in a hospital for drug rehab. The press release tried to mask the trouble by saying he was getting treatment for a "chemical imbalance." When Templeton came back, he asked to be traded. Herzog was happy to oblige.

Herzog almost acquired Ivan de Jesus of Chicago for Templeton, but Cub GM Dallas Green was wary and instead traded Ivan de Jesus to Philadelphia for Larry Bowa and a kid named Ryne Sandberg. Detroit said no to a Templeton–Alan Trammell deal. The Angels refused to give up Rick Burleson, and initially the Padres' Ozzie Smith seemed out of the question because San Diego's GM Jack McKeon had expressed his undying admiration for the slick-fielding, light-hitting shortstop—until Ozzie's agent angered McKeon during the winter. Suddenly McKeon was ready to deal: Smith for Templeton, even up. Herzog wanted the deal badly. When he learned that Ozzie had a no-trade clause, Herzog flew out to San Diego to try to convince Smith and his agent to come to St. Louis. He offered Ozzie a one-year contract, arguing that if he wasn't happy at the end of the year, he could become a free agent and sign wherever he wished.

Ozzie accepted the trade. It was one of the landmark deals in the history of the Cardinal franchise.

Since his rookie year in 1978, the acrobatic Smith had become the standard by which all shortstops were judged. He won his first Gold Glove Award after two years and would go on to win the award every year until his retirement in 1996.

Before the start of an inning, Smith would race out onto the field, and without using his hands, do a forward somersault, tumbling and landing on his feet with the grace of a ballet dancer. Each time the crowd would roar in amazement.

In San Diego Ozzie had become a local celebrity. With the Cardinals, "the Wizard of Oz" thrust himself onto the national stage. Tommy Herr was in his second full season with the Cards when Ozzie joined him to become one of the finest double play combinations in baseball.

TOMMY HERR: "Ozzie had made his mark in San Diego on the West Coast, playing on teams that weren't very good, so unless you were a Padre fan, you really didn't know a whole lot about Ozzie. Obviously, he made the highlight films with some of his great plays he made. He came over to St. Louis with the reputation of being purely a defensive player and an offensive liability.

"The first few days of spring training we didn't talk much. We got our work in. He'd take ground balls and feed them to me, and I'd feed them to him. We would talk on the field as to where we liked to receive the ball on the double play. Gradually our relationship grew. The thing that impressed me most about Ozzie was his willingness to work very hard both at his defensive game and his offensive game. His work ethic was his number-one asset, because he did a lot with the physical tools that he had. He wasn't as big and as strong as some guys, but he got a lot out of his body because of his work ethic."

DARRELL PORTER: "It's difficult to say how much a defensive player means to a team, but if you had seen the plays that Ozzie made, he had to have accounted for at least one run every two games. He was just great. It got to the point where Ozzie made so many great plays that when somebody would rip one up the middle, and Ozzie would dive, stretch totally out, and the ball would hit the end of his glove and bounce off, you'd be setting there thinking, 'Come on, Oz. You have to make that play, man.' It was unfair, but that was the way it was with Ozzie.

"He meant everything. He wasn't just the leader in the way he played. He was a leader in the clubhouse. He was a guy who demanded other people do their best, that they play for the team. He made you go out and play your

OZZIE SMITH
(Drawing by Ron Stark)

hardest and try to win. Ozzie was a very vocal guy. He was a leader that way. He was a very integral part of that championship team.''

WHITEY HERZOG: ''I knew when we got him that he was good, but watching him every day I've found out just how good he is. Of all the shortstops I've seen, and I've seen some good ones—guys like Marty Marion, Mark Belanger, and Luis Aparicio—Ozzie (was) the best. I've never seen anyone do the things on a baseball field that he can do.''

In October of 1981, Herzog made a little-noticed deal with the New York Yankees when the Cardinals traded for a minor league outfielder by the name of Willie McGee, a roadrunner who would become a Cardinal star for most of the next two decades. In exchange he sent the Yankees a pitcher by the name of Bob Sykes, who never pitched an inning for New York, and ''future considerations.''

McGee had hit .322 for Nashville in the Yankee farm system, but when the Yankees signed Dave Winfield, they had to drop a player from their forty-man roster, and McGee was named, making him available in the winter draft.

The Cards had a low draft pick, and so Herzog had Joe McDonald call Bill Bergesch, the Yankees GM, for a trade. The Yankees, unenthusiastic about McGee, asked for Sykes and a player or two to be named later. When McGee hit .296, stole 24 bases, drove in 56 runs, and wowed everyone in center, the Cards sent the Yankees two fine prospects, Stan Javier and Bobby Meacham. (Cardinal fans chortle that St. Louis had swindled George Steinbrenner, but that was an exaggeration. Javier and Meacham were blue chip prospects, but like most Yankee minor leaguers never fully succeeded because few rookies ever made it under the crushing pressures of having to play for George Steinbrenner in New York.)

The final deal Herzog made to form the nucleus of the 1982 Cardinals team was trade Silvio Martinez and Lary Sorensen, two pitchers he felt dispensable, to the Philadelphia Phillies for the lightning-fast Lonnie Smith.

DARRELL PORTER: ''We called Lonnie 'Skates.' He would go out in the outfield, and they'd hit him a fly ball, and he'd fall right on his face. The guy would literally fall right on his face.

''He was not a great defensive ballplayer. But the really weird thing about Lonnie was that he did make some great plays in the outfield. It was one of those things, you kind of held your breath when the ball went out there. He might fall on his face, or he might make a great play.

''Offensively, he was definitely a catalyst.''

WHITEY HERZOG: ''All Lonnie did for us in 1982 was hit .307, lead the league in runs scored [120] and steals [68], and finish second in the Most Valuable Player voting. All we gave up for him was two guys who didn't figure to pitch much for us anyway.''

*   *   *

In eighteen months, Herzog had cleaned house. Bob Forsch was the only starting pitcher left. He had acquired speed, relief pitching, and the catching the team needed.

In February of 1982, Herzog quit as general manager. He was tired of having to deal with agents, weary of being tied to his desk when he knew he should be out fishing. He picked his friend Joe McDonald to replace him. At the time, Gussie Busch gave him a two-year contract extension and gave him a $75,000 a year raise.

Going into the 1982 season, fifteen of the twenty-five players on the Cardinal roster were Herzog acquirees. Though no longer the general manager, manager Whitey Herzog was ready for the season to begin.

CHAPTER 65

DARRELL'S REDEMPTION

WHEN the 1982 season began, Whitey Herzog had on his team several players who had acquired bad reputations with other teams. Although Joaquin Andujar, a talented pitcher who had been obtained from the Houston Astros in June of 1981, had tremendous "stuff," his quick temper and argumentative ways had alienated Astro manager Bill Virdon, who was glad to be rid of his quirkiness. Who needed a pitcher who showered in his uniform?

Herzog was a manager who could look the other way when a player was flaky, kooky, or different. Whitey didn't care about Andujar's uniqueness. He wanted his arm.

DARRELL PORTER: "He was the best pitcher I've ever caught, and I'm telling you, I played on a lot of great teams. Whitey was real unique in that he really went after guys who could pitch. Joaquin was one of those guys. We always had those pitching staffs where I'm sure guys would come to the plate and they'd get four good rips at the ball and never make solid contact, and I'm sure they'd go back to the dugout, thinking, 'Man, I can't believe I missed that pitch.' But that had everything to do with our pitcher's location, the way we pitched guys.

"Joaquin was the greatest, the kindest-hearted guy you could ever run around with. He was just the greatest, but when Joaquin walked into the clubhouse on the day he was pitching, everybody was his enemy. He would slam the door. He would curse everybody when he walked by them. I think that's why people didn't like him, why he got a bad reputation, because they couldn't let Andujar be what he was. And on a normal day, he was great, but on game day, you always knew when Joaquin was pitching, because you'd be setting there getting dressed, and all of a sudden the door would slam, and he'd come across the room, cursing, '*RRRRRrrrrr*, let me alone.' He was like a jerk. But we understood that. And Whitey understood that. So you just let him be that way. That was just the way he was.

"Hey, this guy threw over ninety miles an hour, in the ninety-five mile an hour range, and he had movement on his fastball. He had three pitches, and he could throw them for strikes in any situation. Even if it was three balls and no strikes, he could throw his slider for a strike. That's what made Joaquin so good. Everybody thought he was wild, but I think he was wild intentionally. Because he had great control. He had absolutely great control.

"He and I had a great relationship. He bought me a cedar Bible holder and inscribed it, 'To Darrell Porter, my friend.' I knew him, loved him, and I think we complemented each other. I allowed him to be what he was, and he responded, and he was a great pitcher. The best I have ever caught."

Another player with a checkered past was outfielder George Hendrick, one of the first of the modern ballplayers to refuse to talk to the media. To the public, Hendrick seemed like a surly and arrogant athlete. To his Cardinal teammates, George Hendrick was a player who hit in the clutch and drove in a lot of important runs.

DARRELL PORTER: "George was a much better guy than people ever thought. He may have done some things when he was younger that gave him a bad reputation. One of the bad raps he got, because he was so tall and lanky and he moved so smoothly, it was one of those deals where if you watched him, it almost looked like he wasn't trying. People may not have thought he tried, but he *did*. I'm tell you, for those years I was with him, he was Mr. Clutch. He drove in lots of big, big runs, and he made some great plays in the outfield and made them look easy. And he had a great arm, and he threw a lot of guys out.

"But to me, George was a great guy. I liked George a lot. And to me, he was an important player."

The third enigmatic player featured on the Cardinals was Darrell Porter himself. Herzog loved him for his fiery nature, his toughness, his leadership, his ability to handle pitchers, and his skill at throwing base runners out.

Porter was such a competitor that he considered the players on the opposing team "the enemy." During batting practice, he never talked to the players from the other team. His attitude was: "I don't want anything to do with those guys. I'll kick their rear ends."

When Herzog asked Porter about his drug problem, Porter told him that he had straightened himself out. Whitey, who admired Porter's character, took him at his word.

It was this trust, this type of attitude toward a player, that earned Herzog an acolyte in Porter.

DARRELL PORTER: "Whitey thinks about things most managers don't think about. Whitey thinks way beyond what most people think. Most managers say, 'Get a hit. Score a run. Make a pitch.' But Whitey thinks about how guys run the bases. Should they take an extra base? He thinks about all the little things, like a guy hitting a ground ball to the right side to move the runner over. He's made an out, it doesn't look like anything, but to Whitey, that's important, because now he's got a guy in scoring position.

"And Whitey always thought way in advance. I can remember so many times when I'd come to Whitey after a game and say, 'Rat, why in the heck did you do this in the second inning?' And he'd always say, 'You know, Darrell, I knew if I did that in the second inning, that when we got to the seventh or eighth inning, I'd be set up in a situation where a certain thing would happen. And it would give our ballclub an opportunity to do something that would help us.'

"He was always *way* in advance, *way* ahead in the game, and he *always* had a reason for doing what he was going to do. I mean, he was one of a kind. I think he is a genius.

"Whitey's the greatest. He's the guy responsible for getting me to Kansas City, and when I was down, he instilled a lot of confidence in me. He proved to me he knew what he was doing when we were together in Kansas City. I just trusted him. I believed in him.

"Whitey is a baseball kind of guy. He's a throwback to playing the game the way it's supposed to be played, pitching guys strategically, playing defenses, bunting, sacrificing yourself. Whitey instills in his players that this is a team game. I was only a .247 hitter in my career, but Whitey made me feel like I was a *great* .247 hitter, and what I mean by that, there were so many times Whitey would say to me, 'Darrell, even though you made an out, it helps our team,' because what I would do in situations, I'd try to pull the ball to the right side, get a ground ball where runners could advance. And Whitey recognized those things. And so Whitey would say to me, 'You're important to this team. Even though you went 0 for 4, you moved three runners over tonight. We scored two of those guys.'

"He was so unique about how he could put a team together. He just knew a guy's strengths and weaknesses and he really exploited their strengths. He never put people in situations where they were likely to fail. He was great in that way."

In April of 1982, the Cards had a 12-game winning streak, and moved into first place. David Green, on whom Whitey had figured big things, hurt himself in mid-May. To replace him, Whitey brought up Willie McGee, the minor leaguer he had gotten out of the New York Yankee chain. McGee was very quiet off the field, but on it he played an inspired center field, stole bases regularly, and hit close to .300.

DARRELL PORTER: "When Willie came up, he was so quiet and so humble. He didn't make any impact in the clubhouse. He did that on the field. Willie is just one of the neatest, most unique people I've ever been around. He meant a lot to that ballclub. He drove in a lot of runs [56] that year, and he ended up having a great career."

*   *   *

Like Darrell Porter, Willie McGee quickly developed a deep appreciation for Whitey Herzog.

WILLIE McGEE: "He managed the game, not the players. He just let us go out there and play. Once the game started, you didn't know he was there. It was the only time in my career when I felt I was just out there, playing Little League. He let us play our game.

"Most impressive, I would watch Whitey in the dugout, and he would be looking in the other dugout. He was watching the game develop. He managed the game. He had coaches to teach us, to prepare us, to prep us, to make sure we were ready to play.

"We were a bunch of professionals. We had a lot of respect for each other. We worked hard and went about our business. I think Whitey liked attitude. When he went and got a player, he'd make sure the player was about what *he* was about. That made a big difference in his team. That's why he won a lot of games and a lot of pennants."

Toward the end of June, the Cards fell out of first place by percentage points when Steve Carlton of the Phils defeated them, 1–0. Third-place Montreal was only half a game back. The team then struggled through the summer. After the 12-game winning streak in April, the Cards played at only a 46-44 clip. Everyone seemed pessimistic, including Herzog, until a game against the San Francisco Giants on August 23 in Busch Stadium. In the twelfth inning, substitute catcher Glenn Brummer was on third base with the score tied, 4–4. Brummer was not particularly fast, but like most of Whitey's players, he was cagey and daring, and with a left-hander on the mound and two outs, on his own he took off for home as the hurler went into his windup. When the umpire called him safe, the Cards were winners. It was a play that inspired the entire ball team as the Cards maintained a slim lead.

DARRELL PORTER: "I was so stunned when he did it. There were two outs with a left-hander pitching, and he was in his stretch, and he stole home! It was a great play. I'm sure he went on his own. Glenn was that kind of guy."

TOMMY HERR: "Gary Lavelle was the Giant pitcher. Lavelle was a guy, even in the stretch when he began his delivery home, had a very high leg kick and a slow delivery to the plate.

"The odd thing about the play was that there were two outs and two strikes on the hitter. If the pitcher just throws a strike, the batter is out, and the run doesn't score. So in that sense it was kind of a silly time for Brummer to do that. You don't try to steal home when there are two strikes on the hitter. But that's what made the play so nostalgic, because Brummer's nickname was 'Farm Boy.' He liked to play up the image he was just a dumb kid off the farm. He was a hard-nosed player, and he was going to run over you if you got in his way. So this play kind of fit into that image of Brummer.

"And what made it so special was that we were in a heated pennant race, it was late in the year, and that one particular play won a big game for us.

To have him contribute in that way was a real lift for the whole team, because for us to win, we really needed a lot of guys to contribute.''

DARRELL PORTER: ''And that was just the sort of thing to turn a team around. It's like a batting slump. When you go into a batting slump, you can't hit anything. You'll be up there hitting line drives, and they'll go right at guys, right at 'em, and it's like, 'Good night, what's happening?' And then all of a sudden you'll break your bat right in two, hit a flare over the first baseman's head, and you'll get a double, and it turns the whole thing around. Same sort of thing with Brummer's play.''

TOMMY HERR: ''Oftentimes, certain plays or certain big hits do seem to ignite a team and give you a burst of adrenaline that can propel you through the next few days. During the dog days, you need those type of things to get you going again, because physically you're so tired that you need something to spark you mentally or emotionally to get you through the tiredness.''

By early September, the Cards opened a small lead behind Joaquin Andujar and a rookie pitcher by the name of John Stuper. One of Stuper's greatest contributions to the morale of the ballclub was the show he and utility infielder Mike Ramsey would put on for the whole team called the ''The John Cosell Show.'' In their skit, Stuper was the interviewer, à la Howard Cosell, and Mike Ramsey was always his ''special guest.'' The two, plus occasional appearances by Jeff Lahti, Dave LaPoint, and Glenn Brummer, would make fun of the stupid questions asked by reporters.

JOHN STUPER: ''Mike, you're now a world champion, and being basically the joke you are, how do you feel knowing that there are many, many players in this league who are much better than you are and who have never been a world champion?''

MIKE RAMSEY: ''Well, John, it's great to fool so many people into believing you make a contribution to the team.''

JOHN STUPER: ''Mike, is it true that you lost fifty pounds during the season and that Dave LaPoint found them? I'm talking about LaPoint, a man who has no ability to do anything whatsoever except throw a change of pace.''

JOHN STUPER: ''Glenn, is it true your catcher's glove is made by Everlast?''

GLENN BRUMMER: ''No, Black and Decker.''

The Cards defeated the Mets on September 18 to complete a five-game sweep of their New York rivals, and then the next night when Joaquin Andujar, who would compile a 15-10 record with a 2.47 ERA, beat the Phils, 4–1, the race was all but over. The Cards then won eight in a row to edge Pete Rose and the Philadelphia Phillies by three full games.

The opponent in the National League Championship Series was Atlanta, led by Phil Niekro, a forty-three-year-old knuckleballer with a 17-4 record and an elastic arm. In the first game, Niekro had a 1–0 lead over Joaquin Andujar and the Cards when with one out in the fifth inning, the skies opened up. After a delay of two hours and twenty-nine minutes, umpire Billy Williams called the game off and ordered it replayed from the beginning. Had the Braves gotten just two more outs, they would have been declared the winners.

DARRELL PORTER: "That was definitely a great advantage for us. They only had two outs to go before it would have been an official game. And it was also an advantage because of Niekro. He was forty-something or sixty-eight or however old he was, and he was having a great year—knuckleball pitchers are never easy to hit. And even if we had come back to play, Niekro probably wouldn't have been able to come back because of his age. That was a big key, and if you went and talked to the Braves' players, they would say that's what cost them the pennant."

The next night Bob Forsch pitched a three-hit shutout in a 7–0 win over the Braves. Darrell Porter had two hits and a walk.

DARRELL PORTER: "Forshie never had the greatest stuff, but he was one of the greatest competitors you could ever find. He was so intense, and he was very smart. He knew how to pitch. He was not afraid to pitch inside, and he was not afraid to throw the breaking ball, and he was not afraid of any hitter. Didn't matter who came to the plate; he wasn't afraid of him. I loved to catch him, because it was like a day at the beach. Whatever I called, he threw and at the spot I asked for it. And when I wanted him to brush somebody back, he brushed 'em back. He was such a competitor. He was not about to let anybody beat him. That's what made Bobby so good."

In Game 2, St. Louis opened the scoring with a run in the first inning, but Atlanta came back with two runs in third inning and tallied again in the fifth against John Stuper to take a 3–1 lead. The Cards closed to within one run in the sixth on a double by Keith Hernandez and a single by Porter, who was on a hot streak. In the eighth, the Cards tied the score on a walk to Porter (he had two hits and two walks in the game), a single by George Hendrick, and Willie McGee's chopper over the mound. It was a typical Whitey Herzog run, manufactured and ugly, but a run nevertheless.

The fourth and winning run came in the bottom of the ninth on another Herzog concoction when David Green opened the inning with a single off Gene Garber, moved to second on Tommy Herr's sacrifice bunt, and scored on Ken Oberkfell's single.

DARRELL PORTER: "You have to understand Whitey's mentality: that's the way all his teams play the game. And I'm not so sure how he got us all to do it. It's just we trusted him, so we did it. I think he had a unique way of finding people who would do that. And also, Whitey was such a great guy. He is such a people kind of person that people want to do things for him. When he asked you to do something, you just *want* to. Because he made all the players feel special. It's not hard to keep a star player happy. You play him every day, put him in the lineup. He's happy. But it's those guys sitting on the bench who only get to play once a week who need special handling. I'll tell you what: Whitey is the only manager I was ever around that when you walked by him, he had something to say to you. No matter whether you were Ozzie Smith or Glenn Brummer, he had something to say to you, and it was personable. He made you feel like he really cared for you.''

After the game, 53,000 Cardinal fans paraded around downtown St. Louis, celebrating. The next day the teams traveled to Atlanta for Game 3. Joaquin Andujar started for the Cardinals. In the top of the second inning, the Cards scored four runs off Rick Camp to take a 4–0 lead. In the bottom of the inning Chris Chambliss lined a ball off Andujar's shinbone, but Andujar remained in the game. He left after six and two-thirds and was credited with the 4–2 win after Bruce Sutter set down seven straight Braves to end the game.

DARRELL PORTER: "My personal opinion is Joaquin just had a very low tolerance for pain. I mean, after he got hit, I was sitting there, laughing. I was thinking, 'This can't hurt that bad. I'm a catcher. I'm beat up all the time. Baseballs are hit off me all the time.' And so we were disappointed that Joaquin had to come out of the game.

"Bruce then came in and threw his nasty forkball and got everyone out. Sutter was very easy to catch. His arm motion was so good that it looked like he was going to throw the ball ninety-five miles an hour, and it came up there at eighty-two, but the unique thing was that right at the end it would just fall off the table.

"It would be hard to say there was a catalyst on Whitey Herzog's team, because Whitey's teams were the most rounded teams you could find. He had guys who could do everything. But the fact of the matter is, if you don't have a closer like Bruce Sutter, you're not going to win. We proved that in Kansas City for several years, trying to beat the Yankees. We never had anybody who could close the games, and we kept getting beat, until we got Dan Quisenberry, and then we finally beat them.

"So Sutter was very key."

Porter had a single and walked twice in a 6–2 victory and was named the MVP of the LCS.

DARRELL PORTER: "All of a sudden the booing turned to cheering in St. Louis, even from those hard-nosed fans. I was feeling so good about things, it was hard not to forgive them.

"You know, it was a hard year, just a very tough year for me, but in the end it made it all worthwhile."

WHITEY HERZOG: "Everybody talked about how we rolled over the Braves, but they don't know how close that series really was."

Winning the 1982 National League pennant was a tour de force by Whitey Herzog, a rebuilding/managing job for the history books. Herzog had been in baseball for thirty-three years, and he was making his first trip to the World Series. The opposition was the Milwaukee Brewers, led by manager Harvey Kuenn. In contrast to the speedy, manufacture-a-run Cards, the Brewers were a home-run-hitting club led by Paul Molitor, Robin Yount, Gorman Thomas, Cecil Cooper, and ex-Card hero Ted Simmons.

Herzog had promised Brewer GM Harry Dalton he'd help win him a pennant with the trade of Ted Simmons, and he was right about that too. For the first time in baseball history, you could say that one man had a hand in the winning of both pennants.

The first game was forgettable, as the Cards got pounded at home, 10–0. Ted Simmons hit a home run, and Paul Molitor became the first player in World Series history to have five hits in a game.

Don Sutton started out Game 2 pitching well for the Brewers, but in the sixth, Darrell Porter doubled to drive in two runs to tie the score at 4–4.

In the eighth, Keith Hernandez walked and was forced at second by George Hendrick. Porter, still hot in the postseason, singled. Brewers manager Harvey Kuenn pulled reliever Bob McClure and replaced him with Pete Ladd.

Lonnie Smith walked on a 3-2 pitch. All the Brewers, including Ladd, were sure the pitch was a strike. Smith said he was surprised when home plate umpire Tom Haller called it a ball. He said he suspected it was a strike but couldn't get at it. "It was a fastball up and away, and I had no chance of hitting it," he said.

The walk to Smith loaded the bases. Steve Braun, Whitey Herzog's pinch hitter extraordinaire, then batted for David Green, and he walked on four pitches to bring in the winning run.

Sutter, who had come into the game in the seventh, shut out the Brewers the rest of the way.

DARRELL PORTER: "Steve Braun was the perfect example of what I was talking about. When he walked with the bases loaded to bring in the winning run, that was his job. That's what he got paid for. And he knew it when he walked up there. He used to tell me, 'I just want to get on base. I want to get on base one time this week.'

"Braunie was a great pinch hitter, but if you looked at his stats, they weren't that great. But as a pinch hitter he got on base a lot, and Whitey knew that he could work that pitcher to death until he got a walk.

"See, other managers don't think about those kinds of things. Whitey did. And so Braunie knew after talking to Whitey that if he could get on base once every two or three times he went in to pinch-hit, he was successful; that it didn't have to be a hit.

"And that's one of the reasons Whitey had such a good rapport with his players. He was able to get them to do those kind of things, because he made them understand those things were important.''

In the first inning of Game 3, rookie Willie McGee made a spectacular catch of Paul Molitor's drive to deep center. In the fifth, he hit a home run with two men on base against Pete Vuckovich to break a scoreless tie. In the seventh, he hit another home run, deep into the right field seats. In the ninth, he made a truly spectacular play, leaping up against the wall in front of the left-center field seats and stretching just over the top of the fence to make the catch, robbing Gorman Thomas of a home run.

Joaquin Andujar was given credit for the 6–2 win, even though he had to leave the game in the seventh inning after Ted Simmons struck him below the right knee with a line drive. Andujar crumpled to the ground. Catcher Darrell Porter just shook his head. It was the second time in the postseason that a line drive took the big pitcher out of a ball game.

DARRELL PORTER: ''I must have been thinking, 'Aw, good night. He's gone. If it touched him, he's leaving the game. But that's okay, really okay.' That's one of the reasons we were able to be a winning team: We let people be what they were. And that's why Whitey did very well: He allowed his players to be who they were. He allowed them to play the game the way they could be successful. You have to realize that some people can handle pain, and some can't. Some managers would have gone out and said to Joaquin, 'You big wimp. Get some guts and get up and let's go. Put this thing away.' Not Whitey. He accepted Joaquin the way he was.''

Leading 2–1 in games, the Cards had a 5–1 lead going into the seventh inning. The players were beginning to envision a world championship. To start the seventh inning, pitcher Dave LaPoint ran to cover first base on a ground ball to first baseman Keith Hernandez. When LaPoint dropped the relay, batter Ben Oglivie was safe, and Hernandez was charged with an error. Milwaukee then scored six unearned runs as the Brewers won the game, 7–5.

''It was a nightmare,'' said Whitey Herzog.

DARRELL PORTER: ''When LaPoint dropped the ball, I just knew, 'Oh, my gosh, we had this game won,' and this simple play we practiced all the time flawlessly. It's hard for some teams to pull off a fundamental play like that, but for us it was commonplace. And when it happened, it was like, 'Oh, my gosh.' When something like that happens, there's a sense that good things are not going to happen. And they didn't.''

It was Hernandez's second error of the Series. After the game, he walked around the clubhouse with ten plastic forks taped to his fingers.

KEITH HERNANDEZ: ''The guys got on me about my fielding. Asked me if gold (four Gold Gloves) had turned to steel. I would have wondered what was going on if they hadn't needled me.''

After Robin Yount's four hits led Milwaukee to a 6–4 win in Game 5, giving the Brewers a 3–2 lead in games, Whitey Herzog decided to start rookie John Stuper. Catcher Darrell Porter wondered what his manager was doing, starting such a raw rookie in such an important game. Another loss, and the Series would be over.

DARRELL PORTER: "I remember thinking, 'Whitey, what are you doing here?' This was a young kid, and we had to win this game. This was a *big* game. 'This is it. And we're starting Stuper?' My first thought was, 'Oh, my gosh.' But that's the way Whitey was. He took his players, and he put the guys out there who he thought could do it. And he put faith in guys, and the guys responded.

"Stuper didn't have a lot. He was a fastball pitcher, had a little breaking ball, but not much. But he went out there and battled them and won the game."

Stuper, who was called up from the minors in May after starting the season 7-1 at Louisville, finished the season for the Cards with a 9-7 record. In this game, Stuper didn't pitch like a rookie, though. He threw a four-hit complete game in a 13–1 Cardinals victory.

Darrell Porter hit a home run in the fourth inning to make the score 4–0. Keith Hernandez had four RBIs, including a two-run homer in the fifth.

DARRELL PORTER: Keith was a very clutch hitter, a very important hitter in our lineup. He was a great defensive player as well. I loved him. He was a fun guy. He always had something funny to say, and he was a good guy to have around. He had some problems. He was so much different than I am morally and all kinds of things like that, but I'll tell you, I loved Keith Hernandez. I loved him as a player, and I loved him as a person."

The final game of the Series, played in St. Louis in 44-degree weather, was the perfect example of what became known as "Whiteyball." Bench players did their job, and Whitey's rehab projects, George Hendrick and Darrell Porter, did theirs as well. Keith Hernandez, who led the Cards with eight RBIs in the World Series, also had a key hit.

The Brewers led, 3–1, in the sixth against Joaquin Andujar, but in the seventh, with one out, Ozzie Smith singled against starter Pete Vuckovich and Lonnie Smith doubled. Manager Harvey Kuenn took out Vuckovich and brought in lefty Bob McClure. Gene Tenace, pinch-hitting for Oberkfell, walked. Mike Ramsey pinch-ran for Tenace.

On his twenty-ninth birthday, Keith Hernandez batted. Hernandez had started the Series by going 0 for 15 in the first four games. He told reporters, "There is nothing to worry about. I am hitting the ball hard."

The tension was heavy, but Hernandez, always a clutch hitter, responded well in key situations. On 3-1, McClure threw an inside fastball, and Hernandez singled to center field, driving in the two Smiths to tie the score. The noise in packed Busch Stadium was deafening.

George Hendrick then singled in Ramsey to put the Cardinals ahead to stay.

In the top of the eighth, Herzog took out Andujar and brought in Bruce Sutter, who retired all three batters.

In the bottom of the eighth, Lonnie Smith doubled again, Hernandez walked, and with two outs Darrell Porter came to bat and singled off lefty Mike Caldwell, scoring Lonnie Smith. When Steve Braun singled, the Cards were ahead, 6–3.

The first batter in the ninth to face Sutter was Ted Simmons, who grounded back to the pitcher. Ben Oglivie then grounded to Tommy Herr at second. Gorman Thomas ran the count full, then fouled off two pitches, both split-fingered fastballs. Porter signaled for a fastball, and Thomas swung and missed. The Cards were World Champions.

Sutter faced the last six batters without one ball leaving the infield. Many thought he should have beeen MVP. He had 2 saves and 1 win in four appearances. But Darrell Porter won the award.

DARRELL PORTER: "I was surprised and very elated and happy. I didn't have a very good year at all, and all of a sudden in the postseason I just got hot. Really, in the World Series there were several players who could have been the MVP. My personal opinion is, the Lord was just being faithful to me, and I think he just gave it to me. That's kind of the way I feel about it.

"Considering how low I had fallen the year before, this was definitely a highlight of my career. It means a lot to me. And I was very happy that I got that."

The next day 200,000 fans jammed streets and sidewalks to celebrate the city's first world championship since 1967. High school marching bands, papier-mâché floats, politicians, red crepe, confetti.

DARRELL PORTER
(Courtesy Brace Photo)

WHITEY HERZOG: "There were a lot of people around baseball—writers mostly—who just couldn't believe the Cardinals were world champions. They said we didn't fit the mold, whatever that was, because Hendrick was the only guy in the lineup who could hit the ball out of the park with any regularity. They weren't too impressed with our pitching, either, so they wrote us off as a fluke. They seemed to think there was something wrong with the way we played baseball, with speed and defense and line drive hitters. They called it 'Whiteyball' and said it couldn't last."

DARRELL PORTER: "I'll tell you, when you look all around on that team, we just had guys who did their jobs. As an example, Tommy Herr, our second baseman, wasn't flamboyant at all, but he just got the job done and he knew the game. And all those guys were really concerned about winning. That was the deal. Play the game and do what you have to do to win the game— whatever that is. And I don't think that happened very much then with teams, and I don't think it happens very much at all now. I don't think players have that kind of attitude. Players are so into personal stats, and I don't think they are into the team aspect of it, and that's what made us strong.

"When you look at our team, nobody put fear in anybody at all. They would come into our place, and we would sweep them, and they would go away, thinking, 'How did that happen?' But it just kept happening. And they would feel very comfortable with us sweeping them, because we didn't dominate people. Nobody was afraid of us. They didn't even know they had been dominated until they got beat three times in a row and left. They didn't think they got dominated, but they did.

"I can remember the celebration after we won the World Series. My gosh, it was incredible. One of my favorite pictures is of me standing up in the back of a car, waving to all the people. There are people everywhere, and it was an incredible time. I played on great teams in Kansas City, but there is nothing like being a St. Louis Cardinal. I am so proud to have worn the Cardinal uniform. I just can't believe I got to do it. When you think of all the championships they've won, and they've won more than any team except the New York Yankees, to have been a part of that, of the winning tradition . . . I just love the Cardinals, love the Cardinal fans. These people just appreciate baseball. It's important to them, and they know the game very well. And they love their Cardinals."

TOMMY HERR: "The Cardinal fans are lifelong fans. St. Louis baseball is a cultural and regional phenomenon in the Midwest. The love for the Cardinals isn't just in the city of St. Louis. It's all over. I think to have all that culminate in a World Series championship and a parade, you could really sense the love and the enthusiasm for the Cardinals."

CHAPTER 66

A PENNANT SURPRISE

IN 1982 the Cards won 92 regular season games. In 1983 the Cards finished four games under .500. The reason: lousy pitching (Andujar was 6-16 and Bob Forsch won only 10), a silent offense (the team's 83 home runs all season was worst in the National League) and drug use, an epidemic that was sweeping all of major league baseball.

WHITEY HERZOG: "What I didn't count on was how quickly things can go sour on you in this game. Over the next two years, a lot of very sour, very strange things began happening to the St. Louis Cardinals."

The team was in first place in early June, but the pitching was poor, and Herzog was particularly unhappy with the way certain players were performing. The player who galled Herzog most was Keith Hernandez. His offensive production was way down, but what bugged Herzog most was his attitude. As far as Herzog was concerned, Hernandez was dogging it. He almost seemed not to care sometimes.

Herzog had two basic rules—be on time and hustle—and Hernandez was breaking both of them.

TOMMY HERR: "I have no idea what sort of words were exchanged personally between them. Whitey doesn't have a lot of rules, but one rule he makes very clear. He wants guys to hustle. He wants you to run hard until you're out. I think Keith got into a phase in his career and his personal life that detracted from the effort he was putting forth on the baseball field. He wasn't playing as hard as Whitey wanted him to. When that happens, you're going to have problems with Whitey. One thing kind of led to another, until the point where Whitey felt that Keith was expendable."

Herzog talked Gussie Busch into trading Hernandez just before the June 15 trading deadline in 1983.

WHITEY HERZOG: "I told Gussie that I thought we'd have trouble signing Keith the next year anyway. His contract was up for renewal, and he was on the verge of becoming a five-and-ten man in the big leagues, which would severely limit what we could do with him.

"I told Gussie that my reading of the market indicated that Hernandez would demand about $1.5 million a year and that I didn't want to pay him that much money and put up with his horseshit attitude."

"Trade the son of a bitch," Gussie growled.

Gary Froid, who was a member of the Bat Boys of St. Petersburg, recalls standing in Gussie Busch's swimming pool as Busch told him of his intention of unloading Hernandez.

GARY FROID: "Every year we would go to St. Louis at least once or twice as the guests of Mr. Busch. Fifteen to twenty of us went, and we always went out to Grant's Farm. He had an open bar, including a beer keg, but most of the talking was done in his kitchen.

"This particular afternoon we went down to his swimming pool and bathhouse, and it was so hot that nobody was in the pool except me. I just wanted to swim awhile, when down the hill came Mr. Busch and Frank Jackson, his personal valet, driver, the man who took care of him all the years. Mr. Busch got in the pool, and he started to complain about how cold it was. He had a prostate problem, and he really liked to have it warm, and he was complaining to Frank.

"He stayed in, and there were just the two of us, and that was the day it came out in the papers that Keith Hernandez had been traded. Everyone was speculating on why the Cardinals had traded him. So here I was with the one guy who knew, and I said, 'Mr. Busch, what's the scoop on Hernandez?' He said in his raspy, crackly voice, 'That son of a bitch wanted a million and a half dollars, so we got rid of him.' I got the real story just by being in the guy's swimming pool."

According to Herzog, the Cards traded Hernandez to the only team interested in him. The New York Mets traded pitchers Neil Allen and Rick Ownbey for Hernandez. Neither succeeded with the Cards.

WHITEY HERZOG: "People always say it's the worst deal I've ever made, but I don't believe that. You can't always justify a deal strictly by the talent involved. Getting rid of Hernandez was addition by subtraction. I really feel that if we had kept him, his attitude and his bullshit would have ruined our ballclub. I know he never would have been as good for us as he has been with the Mets. Ballplayers are like Missouri mules—sometimes you have to hit them on the head with a two-by-four to get their attention."

The fans, as they had been when Herzog unloaded Ted Simmons, were furious.

WHITEY HERZOG: "I tried not to pay much attention to what the fans were saying. If I didn't want to be second-guessed, I'd have to get a new job. I had enough to worry about with the way we were playing after the trade."

Hernandez's teammates also were nonplussed.

TOMMY HERR: "Keith was such a talented guy. He was a fun guy in the clubhouse, so sure his getting traded was upsetting. You lose a teammate and a friend and a guy you've gone to battle with, it's hard to lose a guy like that."

Even without Hernandez, the Cards were only a half game out of first the day after Labor Day in early September. But on a five-city, thirteen-game road trip, after beating the Cubs two of three, the Cards lost all but one of the remaining dozen games. The Phils beat them six straight times in September, and they finished fourth in the NL East, eleven games behind the Phillies.

DARRELL PORTER: "One of the hardest things for a professional athlete to deal with is to come back and repeat, and the reason is that when you look at all the teams, in reality there is not a lot of difference between them. Every team is capable of winning, but it's the team that really desires it, that really wants it the most and has the right attitude that's going to go out and do it. And after you win, it's real hard to stay hungry. You just don't have the same intensity, and you lose the edge, and once you lose that, you can't compete at that level. And I think that's what happened.''

In 1984 the team stopped hitting altogether. George Hendrick was not productive. Said Herzog, "He'd gotten his life turned around after kicking his drug habit, but in the process, he'd lost his aggressiveness." Andy Van Slyke didn't hit well. Lonnie Smith only hit .250. And Darrell Porter didn't hit. After David Green's mother died, he became an alcoholic and never did reach his potential.

TOMMY HERR: "Baseball is funny. It's a team game, but it's made up of individual performances. Each at-bat is one individual against another individual, so you're wrapped up in what you're doing as an individual, but also in what the team is doing. Usually the teams that are successful are ones that can get more guys focused on team-type things and not to worry so much about individual-type things, and in 1984 I'm not so sure we were able to do that. We had a lot of individual turmoil. A lot of guys were going through personal problems that I really don't want to get into. I don't know specifics of things, but drugs were involved, and the problems of the league in the early '80s have been well documented. We had some guys who were part of that.

"The individual problems detracted from how the team did. Myself personally, I was going through injury problems at the time. I had three knee operations in a ten-month span from the end of '82 until the end of '83, so the '84 season for me was a season when I was trying to show not only myself but the Cardinals that I was healthy again.''

Joaquin Andujar was one of the few bright spots that year. He won 20 games.

JOAQUIN ANDUJAR: "These people, the Cardinals, they treat me like a human being. They talk nice to me, my manager and everybody else, and when I go out there to pitch, I would die for them.''

Stopper Bruce Sutter also was outstanding. Sutter saved 45 games and had an ERA of 1.54. Another bright spot was the emergence of Terry Pendleton, a fine defensive third baseman.

Still, the Cards in 1984 finished 84-78, twelve and a half games behind the Cubs. Afterward, Herzog's first order of business as he looked toward the 1985 season was re-signing Sutter, who had won 26 games and saved 127 games in his four years as a Card. Bruce had won or saved 46 percent of all Cardinal victories.

WHITEY HERZOG: "If you don't have outstanding relief pitching, you might as well piss on the fire and call in the dogs." Added Whitey, "My whole team was the preliminary act to Bruce Sutter's showstopper, and the whole world knew it.

"Well, maybe not the whole world. The Cardinals front office didn't seem to have caught on entirely, which brings up another problem we were having in 1984.''

Sometime after Herzog took over, Gussie Busch, whose advanced age and declining health made it harder and harder for him to run the brewery and the ballclub by himself, agreed to share his decision making with Fred Kuhlmann and Lou Sussman, two Anheuser–Busch majordomos. The three formed the executive committee to run the ballclub. Herzog, who had rebuilt the team, felt it to be a slap in the face. The biggest problem was that when Herzog wanted to meet with the committee, they were spread to the ends of the earth. Another problem was that Lou Sussman and Fred Kuhlman weren't as fond of Herzog as Gussie Busch was. When Bruce Sutter filed for free agency, Whitey could not get Sussman and Kuhlman to rubber-stamp his desire to retain Sutter. When Sussman made Sutter angry in the negotiations, Sutter jumped ship to Atlanta.

TOMMY HERR: ''Bruce wanted to stay in St. Louis. I don't think the money was that big of a deal. It became more of a personality conflict—Lou Sussman was handling the negotiations for the Cardinals. At some point, Lou rubbed Bruce the wrong way, and Bruce just said, 'The heck with it. I'm going somewhere else.' Bruce did it just to spite Lou. And that was unfortunate, because we felt Bruce was just such a weapon for us. We knew if we led a game going into the eighth inning, we were going to win the game. That's a great weapon to have and a great way to approach the games. It puts a lot of pressure on your opponent, because they understand they have to beat you in seven innings instead of nine innings.''

Herzog received another jolt when his friend and assistant general manager, Joe McDonald, was forced to resign at the end of the year. McDonald was fired by Gussie Busch, who had warned him, ''I don't want any surprises. Make sure I get information before it's in the papers.'' The last general manager to get canned for that infraction had been Bing Devine, when Busch found out about the Johnny Keane–Dick Groat feud. This time McDonald checked outfielder David Green into a drug rehab center without telling Busch. When the story hit the papers, Busch fired him.

As an indication how little Gussie Busch had learned about running a baseball team, the man he wanted to replace McDonald was announcer Jack Buck.

Buck was called to a meeting at KMOX at nine o'clock in the morning. Bob Hyland, who ran KMOX, informed him, ''Lou Sussman is going to be here shortly. He wants you to be the general manager of the Cardinals.''

Buck thought Hyland was joking. He wasn't. He told Hyland, ''I'm not going to be general manager of the Cardinals. In the first place, I don't know enough about it. Secondly, I'm quite content broadcasting. And thirdly, that's the sort of job you get fired from very easily. I'm not at all interested.''

Buck left before Sussman arrived. Hyland delivered Buck's answer. The subject never again came up. Dal Maxvill was named to the job.

*   *   *

With his close friend McDonald fired, Whitey saw that his reign as decision maker was coming to an end. In fact, to observers, Whitey Herzog started the 1985 season as the manager most likely to be fired.

TOMMY HERR: "Whitey wasn't one to keep his feelings hidden. He would voice his displeasure. We were picked to finish last in our division in '85 by just about everybody."

What happened to Whitey Herzog was the capper of an already brilliant career.

WHITEY HERZOG: "(The 1985 Cardinals) may have been the best (team I've ever managed). That was sure the most fun I've had as a manager, the perfect team for the way I like to operate."

TOMMY HERR: "It was kind of a funny year. We opened up the season and lost our first four games, did not look like a very good club, and yet we got it going, and it turned out that club was more resilient than any team I played on with the Cardinals. We bounced back from a bad start and bounced back from losing Bruce and played very, very consistent baseball throughout the rest of the season, put together some very nice winning streaks. I think the quality that team had was just being able to take care of business, day in and day out. We beat teams we were supposed to beat and really beat up on the bad teams. We just held our own against the good teams. That was why we won."

Despite losing Bruce Sutter, the Cards' bullpen wouldn't blow a ninth-inning lead until Game 6 of the World Series.

TOMMY HERR: "Whitey coined the phrase 'bullpen by committee.' The pitchers all kind of bought into that. They realized they each had a role. And Whitey was very, very good at manipulating a pitching staff. He was not afraid to bring in a guy to pitch to one batter and bring in another guy to pitch to the next batter. Those guys in the bullpen always had to stay on their toes. And they did a super job.

"We didn't have a lot of name guys. We had various styles out there that really meshed well together. For example, Rick Horton was very tough on left-handers, because he threw a good slider. He could come in and get left-handers out, throwing a breaking ball. And Ken Dayley was another left-handed pitcher, but he was a power pitcher. He threw ninety-three, ninety-four miles an hour and could overpower both left-handers and right-handers. And Pat Perry, another lefty, his best pitch was his changeup. He was a guy who could come in more in middle relief and hold teams at bay until we could get to the late innings.

"From the right side, Bill Campbell was a junkballer who threw breaking balls, screwballs. Jeff Lahti was the power guy. So we really had a nice complementary bullpen. And then when Todd Worrell came in late in the year, he was the guy who really gave us another stopper again. He was a big power pitcher who threw very hard, who could get you strikeouts when you needed them. So he just made the bullpen even better.''

Dal Maxvill realized that the Cards needed a number-two starter behind Andujar, and he traded George Hendrick to get John Tudor from the Pirates. Tudor started the year 1-9 and then won 20 of his last 21 decisions. He would lead the league in shutouts with 14.

TOMMY HERR: ''Tudor was an unknown quantity. The early part of his career was spent in Boston, and he never really put up great numbers in Boston won-lost-wise, because that's a tough place for a left-hander to pitch, and then in Pittsburgh he was pitching for a bad team, so his record wasn't that great. But when you dissected his statistics and looked at his strikeouts to walk ratio, for example, his ability to pitch inside to right-hand hitters because of his experience at Fenway, I think he was an attractive guy.

''I don't think anyone envisioned what he became with the Cardinals for a couple of years there. He went from being kind of an unknown guy to challenging for the Cy Young Award. He was as good pitcher as there was in the National League for a two-year span there.

''John was kind of a cantankerous guy. He wasn't in a good mood a lot. And yet he had a good sense of humor and was a lot of fun to be around. He didn't give a physical impression of being a tough guy, and yet when he was on the hill, there was nobody who was as mentally tough as he was. John wouldn't back down to any situation.

''He was also a guy who was very concerned about team goals. He was very supportive of other pitchers and other players. When he wasn't pitching, he was the cheerleader type. He was just another important piece of the puzzle.''

The other great trade made by Maxvill was the acquisition of Jack Clark from the San Francisco Giants for David Green, Dave LaPoint, Gary Rajsich, and Jose Uribe.

TOMMY HERR: ''Jack gave us a bona fide thumper in the middle of the lineup, which we had never had. George [Hendrick] was a very good, quality hitter, but he wasn't an intimidator like Jack was. Jack would hit vicious line drive home runs. And Jack had a persona as kind of a mysterious, tough-guy power hitter. He gave our team a mood or a persona that was lacking before. He just gave us a big hammer in the middle of the lineup. It really complemented the parts around him.''

The third new player to come to the 1985 Cardinals was promoted from the minor leagues after Willie McGee and Tito Landrum got hurt. The kid's name was Vince Coleman. He had stolen 100 bases in Triple A, and as soon as he came up, Whitey Herzog put him in the leadoff spot in the batting order, moved Willie McGee to second, batted Tommy Herr third, with Jack Clark fourth. The club, which was scoring runs a good clip before Coleman's arrival, quickly became a run-scoring machine.

TOMMY HERR: "Vince wasn't just a base stealer. He was an unstoppable base stealer. What he gave to our lineup was instant speed, instant run-scoring potential. When he would get on, he would steal second and third before the next hitter was out of the batter's box. He just created such havoc out there, caused such consternation for other teams. Pitchers were so preoccupied with what he was doing, and at first he kind of caught people by surprise. After the first month, when people realized he was for real, they really started to pay attention to him. He not only changed the way pitchers pitched to batters after him, he changed how the infielders played. He really was an offensive force for us.

"The big question was whether he was going to be able to hit enough to stay there, and he did that. He put the ball in play. He got a lot of infield leg hits, and he could bunt very well. He had enough veteran players around him that helped him get through the transition to major league life, and that was helpful as well."

The Cardinals still lacked a lot of power. Even with Jack Clark, the team hit only 87 home runs, the only team beside the Pirates (80) to hit under 100 that year. But in 1985 the Cardinals led the league with 59 triples and its 314 stolen bases led second-place Chicago (182) by a wide margin. The Cards finished second in the league in runs scored with 695. Houston led with 706.

Coleman, the leadoff batter, finished the year with an average of .267, 110 stolen bases, and 107 runs scored. Next up was Willie McGee, who led the league in hitting at .353 and contributed an amazing 82 RBIs. Tommy Herr, batting third, hit .302 and drove in 110 runs, an unheard of feat for a second baseman. Jack Clark drove in whatever Herr didn't.

VINCE COLEMAN
(Courtesy Brace Photo)

TOMMY HERR: "First of all, it starts with Vince and Willie. Vince hit well, and he stole 110 bases. And Willie led the league in hitting and stole 56 bases himself. I was up next, and you're talking about me hitting in a situation where guys were always on base in front of me, and not only that, they got themselves in scoring position.

"If you look at my RBI statistics, I had 26 of my 110 RBIs when I made out, either ground ball outs or fly balls. I was always a guy who moved the runner over. But now with guys on third base all the time, I was able to drive them in with ground ball outs or hit a fly ball and drive them in. So I didn't really change all that much. It's just that I was hitting with guys always on second and third base.

"Jack batted behind me. I was always a hitter who could work the count in my favor, so when I did get favorable counts, I knew that my chances of getting a 3-1 breaking ball were not good because the pitcher didn't want to risk walking me and having Jack hit a three-run homer behind me. So it was an ideal situation for me to hit in, because I was a smart hitter who was hitting with men on base with a great hitter behind me.

"The first half of that season I was extremely hot. I was locked in for about a two-and-a-half-month span. I was leading the league in hitting for a good portion of the first half of the season. I had 63 RBIs by the All-Star break. So it was a dream year for me—and really for the whole lineup. It just seemed that three or four guys had career years that year. Sometimes that's what it takes."

Baseball held its breath in the middle of the 1985 season when the players went out on strike over the issue of salary arbitration. The strike of 1981 had lasted fifty-three days. Fortunately, the negative fallout from that action helped the owners and the players union settle after only two days. Everyone breathed a sigh of relief. Both games were made up, and the two-day vacation was a tonic for a tired team.

On August 23 Joaquin Andujar won his 20th game. He would win only one more the rest of his season—his last as a Cardinal.

TOMMY HERR: "Joaquin was real high-strung, very touchy if you criticized him or joked around with him. But a lot of that was because of the language barrier. He didn't quite understand when you were joking sometimes. He considered himself a macho guy. He was fun, a funny guy, fun to tease. I remember Ozzie would get on him quite a bit.

"What really helped Joaquin, the thing that gets overlooked about those Cardinal teams was the great defensive teams they were. Up the middle we were as good as any team that has ever been put on the field, with Ozzie and myself at short and second and Willie McGee in center. And then Terry Pendleton was a great third baseman, and this was the early part of his career before he won an MVP Award with the Braves. And before him, Ken Oberkfell was a very good third baseman in '82.

"We always played good defense. That often gets overlooked, but that makes pitchers better when they feel they don't have to strike everybody out and you're going to make the plays behind them.

"Joaquin was a power pitcher who relied on a moving fastball that he could throw over the top or sidearm, and he had a very nasty slider, and he had a cockiness about him that he was not going to give in. You have those ingredients in a pitcher, and he's going to be successful.

"Joaquin only won 1 more game after winning his 20th in last August. Two things happened. Twenty games is such a feat for a pitcher, when you get it, you just kind of breath a sigh of relief, and he relaxed a little, took his foot off the accelerator that he had to get him to that point, and when you're at that level, if you lose your edge a little bit, either physically or mentally, it's tough to maintain. I don't know he changed anything other than maybe he just relaxed a little bit.

"The other thing that happened, Jack Clark in late August swung and missed a pitch and pulled a muscle in his side and had to miss the last month of the season with a rib injury.

"At the time, we felt that was a devastating blow, because Jack was having a big year for us. We really, really felt cripped by that.

"In late August Whitey [and Maxvill] swung a deal to get Cesar Cedeno from Cincinnati, and what Cesar did for us has been well documented. He hit over .400 for us, stepped in and gave us another shot in the arm. He had been dead in the water in Cincinnati and was rejuvenated by the trade. He really gave us a boost. I don't think we could have won it without him, because we really would have missed having that power in the middle of the lineup."

Despite the offensive pyrotechnics, the Cards had great difficulty running away from the dogged New York Mets. With six games left in the season, the Cards led by three games as the Mets came to town for a three-game series. The Mets won the first two games to close the gap to one. In the finale, Danny Cox defeated the pesky Mets. Two nights later, John Tudor won his 21st to clinch the pennant.

TOMMY HERR: "We had a three-game lead, and we knew if we could just win one of those games with the Mets, we were going to come out of that series with a two-game lead with three to play. We felt like we just needed to win one. We would have liked to have gotten that out of the way the first two games, but the Mets threw Dwight Gooden and Ron Darling at us, and you knew any time you faced the Mets in a three- or four-game series, you were going to face some really good pitching.

"Gooden had a great year that year [24-4] and Darling was very good [16-6], and in the third game Danny Cox was going for us, and Cox [18-9] was a clutch, big-game pitcher, another guy who was mentally tough. He had good stuff. He would challenge hitters. Danny had a very good slider, a very good change-up, and Danny was the right kind of guy pitching a game like that, because he liked the challenge of the big games. He really came up huge that night."

Facing Mets' rookie Rick Aguilera, Cox and the Cards won, 4–3, despite five hits by the Mets' Keith Hernandez. Jeff Lahti got the final out when he induced Gary Carter to hit a lazy fly ball to left field.

After winning the division, the Cardinals then traveled to Los Angeles to open a best-of-seven LCS against the Dodgers. Fernando Valenzuela and Tom Niedenfuer shut out the Cards in the first game, and Orel Hershiser allowed only two runs in an 8–2 rout. Back in St. Louis, Danny Cox came back to win Game 3, but then before Game 4 one of the strangest events in postseason play occurred, one that almost doomed the Cardinals' chances. As the St.

Louis ground crew was unrolling the tarp that covered the field, somehow Vince Coleman got in the way, and the tarp rolled over his leg, pinning him to the ground. Chaos broke out before anyone could figure out how to extricate the outfielder. The injury caused by the incident kept Coleman out the rest of the postseason.

TOMMY HERR: "I was in the clubhouse when it happened. I remember the hysteria, the confusion. All of a sudden people were screaming and running all over the place, saying that Vince was caught in the tarp and was hurt, so everyone ran out to see what was going on. There was a huge crowd gathered around the area of the tarp where it had rolled up over his leg. They were trying to figure out how to get it off of him. It was so heavy they couldn't. They realized the only way to get it off was to roll it back off, even though he was sure to experience some pain when they rolled the thing off him.

"Then they carted him off the field on a stretcher. No one really knew what the severity was—or if there even was an injury. We knew he probably wasn't going to play that night, but we didn't know that we had seen the last of Vince that year. It turned out to be a devastating thing for us. Our offensive production in the World Series was not there. Not having Vince was something that really hurt us.

"It's something to joke about as you look back on it. 'Remember when the fastest guy in the baseball got run over by the tarp that moves one mile an hour?' The way that thing works, it pops out of the ground, and then it begins rolling very slowly. I think as it popped out, it just got onto Vince's ankle, and he couldn't get away from it. It was just an unfortunate accident."

The Cards still won Game 4 without Coleman in a 12–2 rout behind John Tudor. The series was tied at two games apiece. Then in Game 5, with the score 2–2 in the ninth, light-hitting Ozzie Smith came up. His whole career he had never hit a home run batting left-handed. And this time he was facing Dodger fireballer Tom Niedenfuer, a formidable opponent.

TOMMY HERR: "Fernando started the game for the Dodgers. He had always been very tough on us. Bob Forsch pitched for us. The game was tied going into the late innings, and they brought in their stopper, Niedenfuer. And Ozzie just turned on a fastball. He got the head of his bat out and hit a line drive off one of the cement supports out in right field. At first there was some question whether it would clear the fence or not. The umpire gave the home run signal.

"I just remember the bedlam after that, because it was such a shock to win that game. But Ozzie had a tremendous flair for the moment, and that was another great moment for him and for our team."

Still trailing in games by three to two, in Game 6 Dodger outfielder Mike Marshall homered in the bottom of the eighth to give L.A. a 5–4 lead going into the ninth. To face the Cardinals in the top of the ninth, Dodger manager Tommy Lasorda again brought in the hulking Niedenfuer.

TOMMY HERR: "With one out, McGee singled and stole second, and Ozzie walked. I came up with runners on first and second. The bunt sign was on initially, and I fouled it off, and then topped one down the first base line that they couldn't make the play on anyone but me, so now there were two outs and runners on second and third and Jack Clark was up with an open base.

"You ask me why Lasorda would pitch to Clark, but the last time up Niedenfuer had blown Jack away. He struck him out on three pitches. That factored into it. He figured he got him before and he can get him again. The second thing was the old baseball 'book': You have a right-hander against a right-hander. Andy Van Slyke, a left-hander, was up next, and Lasorda figured if he walked a right-hander to get to a left-hander and if the left-hander would have gotten a hit, everyone would have said, 'Why did you do that?' The other variable was that he had Jerry Reuss warming up in the bullpen. A lot of people said, 'He should have walked Clark and brought in Reuss to face Van Slyke.'

"But those are decisions you must make at the moment as a manager. Lasorda went with his decision, and unfortunately for him, Jack deposited the first pitch into the left field seats!

"When people ask me, 'What was the highlight of your career?' I always say that home run Jack hit off Niedenfuer was it. That was the highlight of my career, because it basically got us into the World Series. It was so dramatic, and I'll always remember the way Jack reacted when he hit it. Instantaneously, you knew it was gone, and he strutted around the bases, and the whole team met him at home plate, and for the people of St. Louis it was like the Kennedy assassination. 'Where were you when Jack hit the home run?' The magnitude of it was just unbelievable. To be a part of that was fantastic.

"We still had to get three outs. Ken Dayley went out and finished the business, so we were in the World Series.

"It was a great trip back to St. Louis after that win. We felt like we had the best team in the National League, and we felt we had proven that, so the World Series was icing on the cake.

"Really, there is more pressure in a League Championship Series than there is in a World Series, because you go through a regular season and win your division, and if you don't win the playoff, you really have nothing to show for your great season. I think it was a collective sigh of relief and euphoria to get into the World Series."

JACK CLARK
(Courtesy Brace Photo)

The opponent in the 1985 World Series was the team from across the state of Missouri, the Kansas City Royals. It was a "Show-Me State" rivalry to end all rivalries. Here was Cards manager Whitey Herzog, fired by Kansas

City not too many years before, coming back to get some measure of revenge on his former employers.

The Cardinals were prohibitive favorites. But when the tarp ran over Vince Coleman, his injuries were serious enough to cause the speedster to miss the entire World Series. Without Coleman, Herzog led off Willie McGee and moved Ozzie Smith into the number-two slot. In seven games, the offense would drive in exactly 13 runs.

TOMMY HERR: "We were set up to have a tough time against Kansas City, because when you're a heavy favorite, it's tougher to win than when you're the underdog. It's easier to motivate an underdog. That, plus we didn't have Vince, and that was a big factor, because our lineup was different without him, no doubt about it. Whitey juggled things around, and we ran into a hot pitching staff. You have to give Kansas City credit. They had some young guns on the mound who got hot at the right time, and they really did a good job pitching to our lineup."

The Cardinals began the Series with two impressive wins. John Tudor outpitched Danny Jackson, 3–1, and then in Game 2, with the Royals leading, 2–0, in the ninth, Terry Pendleton doubled with the bases loaded off Charlie Leibrandt to win the game. Despite the two wins, the Cards were concerned. They weren't hitting.

TOMMY HERR: "We did come out of Kansas City with a 2–0 lead, but they were both games that were real pitchers' duels. We didn't really hit like we were used to hitting, and still we won those games. Going back to St. Louis, we really felt we wanted to end the Series at home. We knew if we could win two out of three at home, it would be over. Bret Saberhagen beat us [6–1] in Game 3. He was pitching against Joaquin, and in that game it seemed that the home plate umpire had two different strike zones. It was almost like nobody wanted us to win this thing in four, that they wanted to stretch it out. So Saberhagen got the benefit of the doubt. Still, he pitched great. Meanwhile, Joaquin is a volatile guy. When he doesn't get some close calls, he can explode. He let his emotions take away from the focus he needed out there. It was a prelude to what happened later in the Series.

"It was the third straight game where we really didn't hit. There was a trend developing."

In Game 4 John Tudor threw a five-hitter against the Royals in a masterful 3–0 victory. The win gave the Cards a seemingly unbeatable 3-1 lead in games.

TOMMY HERR: "The funny thing about that game, Tudor went out there in Game 4 very, very sore-armed. He was at the end of his rope. He gave it everything he had that game and put us up 3-1, and I'm sure he felt he wouldn't have to pitch again, wasn't even sure if he could pitch again.

"Then we went to Game 5, and Danny Jackson beat us 6 to 1. Bob Forsch pitched for us. That sent the Series back to Kansas City, which nobody wanted to do. We were so disappointed that we had to go back there, because anything can happen when you're in the other team's ballpark.''

In Game 6 Danny Cox faced Charlie Liebrandt, and the two pitchers threw goose eggs through seven innings. When Brian Harper drove in a run for the Cards in the eighth, it looked like the Series was theirs. After all, the Cards had not lost a game all season long after going into the ninth inning with the lead. Eighty-eight times Cardinal relievers had held a ninth-inning lead. Back in the Cardinal clubhouse, the champagne was waiting.

TOMMY HERR: ''The bottom of the ninth was such a nightmare. Ken Dayley had finished up in the eighth. Dayley was an extremely hot pitcher. He had blown the Dodgers away to get us into the World Series, got Pedro Guerrero out and Mike Marshall out. He was just hot at the time. But Whitey was afraid of Hal McRae and his ability to pinch-hit, and because of that, he wanted to bring in Todd Worrell, the right hander. And that's not taking anything away from Todd, because he had pitched very well too, but when I look back on it, I always wonder, 'What would have happened if we had just left Kenny in there?' But those are things you tend to second-guess when you cough one up. So I was disappointed when Whitey took Dayley out.

"The inning started with [pinch hitter] Jorge Orta hitting a little topper halfway between the pitcher and first baseman. Jack made the play and tossed to Todd, and Orta was clearly out. I had a perfect view of it. And Denkinger blows the call. That's how the inning started, with an obvious blown call. I went over and got right in Denkinger's face. It was just unbelievable. I could see the guy was out.

"The most important out of an inning is the leadoff out. If we get that out, we win the ball game. I'm convinced of that. Not only don't we get the call, but the emotional upheaval it created—we were just screaming at this guy—it kind of got us off what we needed to do to finish that game out.

"After that, there were a series of things. Steve Balboni hit a pop-up down the first base line that Jack kind of misjudged around the dugout steps. That could have been an out. Then Balboni ends up getting a single.

"We get a mix-up on the catcher getting crossed up, and it was a passed ball, and then [Dane] Iorg hit a jamshot into right to win the game. So it was just one thing after another that happened that inning, all started by the bad call at first base.

"Obviously, we were a devastated team after that. We felt like we had gotten ripped off. And it was just too much to bounce back from. Whitey was incredulous. He was really upset at Denkinger, really fired up. We all kind of felt we had one taken away from us.

"John Tudor started the last game, and he was spent. He really had nothing left. Like I said, I'm sure he didn't figure he'd have to pitch a Game 7 after we were up 3 to 1. He probably went through the same thing Joaquin went through when he won his 20th game. He was thinking, 'It's over for me. Now I can relax.' But it didn't turn out that way.

"I don't like to make excuses. You only hear excuses from the losers. So

I give credit to Kansas City, because they did what they had to do to win that Series. They beat us 11–0 in that last game. They pitched great against us, they scored enough runs, and I give them credit. The bad call hurt us, but the fact remains that they shut us down that Series. We didn't hit, and you have to give them credit for that.

"What people remember most about that last game was what Andujar did when he came in to pitch in the fifth. The Denkinger situation was like a bomb waiting to explode. After he blew the call in Game 6, Whitey made a comment, 'We got him behind the plate tomorrow. What do you think that's going to be like?' That was the history. And Joaquin had come off a game where he felt he had gotten squeezed in his previous outing.

"Now he's out there, and he throws one that's a borderline pitch. He doesn't get the call again, and he just goes off. It was a predictable thing for us if you knew Joaquin."

After Denkinger called the pitch a ball, Joaquin motioned for catcher Darrell Porter to come out to the mound. Denkinger, thinking Joaquin was addressing him, came out to respond. Herzog sprinted from the dugout, yelling for Denkinger to "get his ass back behind the plate."

Said Herzog, "By then, I was fed up." He said to the home plate umpire, "We wouldn't even be here if you hadn't missed the fucking call last night."

Denkinger tossed Herzog out of the game.

Andujar threw a second pitch, his last one as a Cardinal. It was high and inside, and Denkinger called it ball four, loading the bases. Andujar charged the large arbiter, bumped him, and Denkinger threw him out of the game as well.

The Royals won the game 11–0. John Tudor blamed himself for the loss. "I don't know if I can feel worse than this," he said after the game. When Anheuser-Busch ordered Dal Maxvill to trade Andujar, Herzog no longer cared. He had had enough of his antics. During the offseason, Andujar was traded to the Oakland A's.

TOMMY HERR: "It was just a very frustrating sequence of events for our team."

CHAPTER 67

MAGRANE'S YEAR

FOR the first half of the 1986 season, the Cardinals couldn't do anything right. By the All-Star Game, the Cards were far behind the Mets, on their way to becoming the first team to go from 100 wins to 100 losses.

Willie McGee and Tommy Herr really struggled, and McGee lost his aggressiveness in the field. Mike Heath went 4 for 56 during one stretch. Jack Clark didn't drive in runs. Terry Pendleton hit under .200, and Vince Coleman began throwing to the wrong bases and became a defensive liability. Andy Van Slyke stopped hitting entirely. Tommy Herr remembered the frustrations.

TOMMY HERR: "It was almost as if we still hadn't recovered from the World Series. I truly think that's what the problem was. It was such a devastating culmination of the '85 season that it was almost like we couldn't will ourselves to go through that again.

"It was so bad, Whitey was ready to quit. It got so bad, they wouldn't put our batting averages up on the scoreboard. Everybody struggled. As good as we were in '85 to a man, we were that bad to a man in '86. Once we were out of the race, then we did get it going a little bit. We ended up with some guys salvaging a decent year. But it was a frustrating season, no doubt about it."

At the All-Star break, the team, which had been 36-50 the first half of the year, started to jell, and it finished the season a very respectable 43-32. Because the New York Mets won 108 games that year, there was great dissatisfaction at the brewery with the performance of the fourth-place Cards.

In 1987 there was a lot of pressure on Whitey Herzog to get rid of some of the players who hadn't had good seasons in '86. He felt he needed Terry Pendleton and kept him. He held on to both Vince Coleman and Tommy Herr. The one trade GM Dal Maxvill did make came just before the start of the season. He sent Andy Van Slyke, Mike LaValliere, and Mike Dunne to the Pittsburgh Pirates for catcher Tony Pena, whom Herzog had coveted for years.

Another addition to the starting rotation was a young left-hander by the name of Joe Magrane, who scouts saw as the second coming of Steve Carlton. Magrane was six-four and very strong, the kind of anchor around which to build a pitching staff.

Growing up in Morehead, Kentucky, where his father was a professor at Morehead State University, Joe Magrane was a child prodigy. When he was thirteen years old in the seventh grade, he played on the high school varsity baseball team with eighteen-year-olds. Magrane recalled that his teammates had beards and seemed so much older. "I was the only one who was physically afraid of his girlfriend," he said, perhaps in jest.

Even then he had a golden arm. And he had great coaching. Through his high school years, he was able to train with former New York Yankee pitcher Steve Hamilton, the coach of Morehead State College's baseball team. When it came time for Magrane to go to college, Hamilton touted Magrane to his old friend Jerry Kendall, the head coach of the University of Arizona, and on Hamilton's word, Kendall placed a phone call to the admissions department, and within hours the boy was awarded a full scholarship to Arizona.

"It was amazing," says Magrane. "Kendall had never even seen me throw. That was kind of neat."

In his senior year Magrane and his Arizona teammates were eliminated from the College World Series in 1985 after losing their first two games. Greg Swindell of Texas beat him, 2–1.

Magrane had heard from the Kansas City Royals and the Philadelphia Phils and had been told that both intended to draft him in the first round of the June of 1985 amateur draft. He was surprised when he was chosen by the Cardinals.

JOE MAGRANE: "The Cardinals were all the way down at the eighteenth pick, and so as we were driving home from the College World Series in Omaha, we were passing through Kansas City on the way to Kentucky. I picked up the phone and called my sister back in Morehead, and she said, 'Yes, you did get drafted. It wasn't by the Royals. It was by the St. Louis Cardinals.'

"They left a number who to call, and as luck would have it, we were going to be passing through St. Louis within an hour, and they said, 'Come to the ball game.' They told me they had picked me on the eighteenth selection and told us where to go.

"It was amazing how fast it happened, 'cause as soon as my dad dropped me off at the main doors at Busch Stadium, they took me right upstairs. There was a rain delay, and thirty seconds after getting off the elevator, I was doing an interview with Jack Buck and Mike Shannon.

"It was kind of weird. We had been driving all day, listening to the game on the radio, and *bam,* I was right up there. In hindsight, I thought it was the neatest thing that ever happened to me. I was glad to be a member of a team with such great tradition. I always have been very very proud of that."

After signing in June of '85, Magrane spent only a year and a half in the minors. He was sent to Johnson City, Tennessee, a long step down compared to what he had been used to at the University of Arizona.

JOE MAGRANE: "I can remember when I was at Arizona, the players were bitching because we didn't have a direct flight into Omaha, that we had to stop in Kansas City. And then ten days later, I was weaving in and out of Appalachia in a school bus. A school bus!

"Rich Hacker was my manager. He later became the first base coach with the Cardinals and also with the Blue Jays. I can remember my very first pro game: There were a lot of Latinos who had great skills but didn't quite know the game. Pitchers didn't know how to throw out of the stretch. And this guy by the name of Luis Iglesias was in the on deck circle, and it was his turn to hit, and all of a sudden he called timeout, and he ran back into the corner of the dugout, dropped his drawers, took a dump, took a towel off the trainer's bay, wiped his ass, pulled his pants up, ran to the batter's box, swung at the first pitch, and popped out. And he came right back to the dugout and sat down like nothing had ever happened!

"I thought to myself, 'We were in the College World Series on national TV two weeks ago, and I'm seeing this!' Another time I watched a guy steal second, and thinking the ball was foul, jogged back to first, only to have the umpire call him out for making a travesty of the game by running the bases backward. Just goofy stuff.

"I was only there twenty-six days, but it felt like twenty-six years. There used to be one plane that flew overhead in Johnson City every day, and I would think, 'One of these days I'm going to be on that.'

"It seemed like a long time, but I was there for only three starts, and then I went to St. Petersburg and did fine there and finished up the season, and in '86 I started the season in Little Rock under Jimmy Riggleman, who was the Travelers' manager.

"While I was in Little Rock, we used to go out at night to a couple of bars, and I got a chance to see someone who at that time was the governor of Arkansas, Bill Clinton, who was going to the same places we were going. It seemed that everybody knew who he was. He would ask us how we did, what was the score of the game, and was frequently out there.

"And he's President of the United States, and I'm retired in Tampa.

"At Little Rock they divided the season into halves, where the winner of the first half plays the winner of the second half, and right after the second half got started, I was called up to Louisville, and Jim Fregosi was my manager for about forty-eight hours when he took the White Sox job.

"I was two-thirds of an inning from winning the ERA title in Louisville. Things worked out real well. I was called up to the Cardinals in September.

"I came back to the Cards in the spring in '87, my first big league camp. Whitey was one of those guys: 'Let's throw this guy into the fire right away.' So I started the first spring training game against the Mets, and of course I was facing Hernandez, Carter, and Strawberry. In Darryl Strawberry's first at-bat of the entire spring, I was trying to throw the ball through a wall, wasn't even thinking about where it was going, and it got right out of my hand, and he wore number 44 back then, and I hit him right between the blades! The ball dropped right down. He got all geared up to go out there. I thought, 'Now I'm going to have to get ready to fight Straw in my first inning of spring training.'

"At that time in the offseason, Strawberry had been wrestling with his wife a little too much, and right when he was gearing up to come after me, Bob Forsch yelled out of the dugout, 'Your wife paid him to do that!' And Straw kind of looked and trotted down to first. There was all kinds of bench jockeying like that, and nowadays if you do that, the players look at you and wonder, 'What's the matter with this guy? Has he drunk too much coffee?'

"I was thinking everything was going to be great, that I was going to be on the team, and then I was sent down to Louisville for two and a half weeks, so I couldn't get in a full year of service. At the time, they were real hard-line about arbitration and kept guys down to put it off.

"I was called up and made my debut against the New York Mets. I got my first victory in my debut. It was Whitey Herzog's 1,000th win, and it was against the world championship Mets, coming off '86. Quickly I learned there was a real hatred between the Mets and the Cardinals going back to the '85 days. That rivalry was extraspecial. When I wasn't pitching, it was fun to watch Whitey and Davey Johnson of the Mets go at it.

"I had been called up because John Tudor broke his leg when the Mets' Barry Lyons slid into the dugout in Busch to catch a foul pop and slid right into Tudor's leg and broke it. [He was out two and a half months.] After he came back, the guys used to say to Tudor before he would go out for his start—because he hated the statement—and you can see this coming a mile away, 'Good luck today. Break a leg.'

"My manager was Whitey Herzog. As a fan of the game, I had watched him for a long time, all the way back to Kansas City, Texas, the Mets, and all this history. He's been around some great teams and great players. In my view, Whitey was this know-all, tell-all omniscient figure. Everybody on the team had the utmost respect for him. It was: 'Whitey says this. Whitey wants this done.' And because Whitey had so much juice with Gussie Busch, the players knew if something went wrong, you could be on a slow boat to China within hours, so the team completely policed itself.

"It was interesting to see other managers, instead of focusing on trying to put their best foot forward and win the game, were always caught up in managing against him. I saw a lot of managers try to outdo themselves in an effort to manage against him. It was always neat. It happened so often. We'd say, 'There it goes again.' This was back when you carried ten pitchers; they'd try to play the right-left game in the sixth inning.

"Whitey had this innate ability: He was part riverboat gambler, part 'Father O'Leary Herzog.' He could make the number-one guy or the number-twenty-five guy feel like the number-one guy. You don't see that. He was a manager who'd sit down and play cards with the players, but everyone still knew where everybody stood as far as what their roles were. He could make the guy who never played feel just as important. He was so adept at keeping all his guys fresh. Nowadays, reserves won't walk onto the field for two weeks. Whitey made sure he got these guys two or three at-bats a week, and the same thing with the bullpen. He said, 'If I have twenty-five guys, my idea is to use every single one of them.' And they were always getting up in situations where they could succeed.

"As an example of his managerial acumen, he'd go up and tell Johnny Morris three innings in advance: 'Be ready to pinch-hit because I'm going to send this batter up, and they are going to double switch and bring in this pitcher, so you be ready.' He could make things like that happen in a game. So all his pinch hitters were ready. It's the same thing when you're pinch-hitting or relieving, and someone says, 'Go get a bat,' or 'Get up.' There is an immediately adrenaline rush, where your heart beats out of your chest. It takes the experienced player a long time to learn how to channel that and get over that. So everybody was always prepared under him.

"And out of respect, you didn't see any grab-assing during the game. Everybody watched the game and were into the game. And I thought he was great at taking players who had reputations with other teams for being disturbances and making them fit in. The mileage he was able to get out of Pedro Guerrero when he came over after trading John Tudor, and then getting Tudor back, and to step backward, to see how he was able to use role players. He always had these great role players, like Johnny Morris, Curt Ford, Steve Braun, people like that who succeeded under Whitey, who went to other organizations, and the other organizations could not utilize them the way Whitey was able to. As a result, he was adept at getting the most out of every one of the players.

"And when you needed a lift, he wouldn't call you into his office and give you this long half-hour talk; he could speak in a sentence, and it would speak volumes.

"He could Gettysburg Address any of the managers. So many other guys would get happy-go-lucky and want to think that something productive would actually be done in a team meeting. That was the biggest waste of time I'd ever see in my whole life. Because veteran players start talking, and it breaks down into a bullshit session, and half the guys who talk the talk don't walk the walk. It's a load of crap, and everybody ends up losing respect for everyone.

"I only remember one or two meetings that Whitey ever called, and he never allowed any of the players to speak. He'd say a paragraph, and that was all. So by the time the meeting was over, you knew what the purpose of the meeting was, before it broke down into all these soliloquies from anyone who had more than five years of time entered. So I thought he was great like that.

"The team was owned by Anheuser-Busch, so we had our fair share of their products on the plane to the point where we had to move them around to where we could sit down. We'd have cardplaying and during this flight the guys were throwing a lot of paper and beer cans and rolls at one another, and it was one of the rare times when we had to deplane from the rear of the plane, those D. B. Cooper steps, and we went out the plane like that, and Whitey had seen the mess, and he called a meeting. He didn't call it on the team bus, because those were the days when there was only one bus and the reporters were on there, but when everybody got to the park, he held one.

"Whitey always began every meeting with the tag line, 'I'm only going to tell you cocksuckers one thing and right fucking now.' If he had an audience with John Paul II, he'd probably begin it the same way. That was his thesis statement. And he went on to talk about how the plane was trashed, and he said, 'The next time I see that happen, I'm going to take all the fucking booze off the plane.' Not the beer, but the booze. A couple guys were unnerved by that. So we policed ourselves and got it all straightened up."

In 1987 Whitey Herzog did a masterful job of handling the pitching staff. No pitcher won more than 11 games (three did that), and yet the Cards went on to win 95.

JOE MAGRANE: "Here is a perfect example that lends credence to what I was saying about how Whitey utilized every person. Every pitcher was able to take the ball, meaning every one of those ten guys participated. There wasn't anybody who was growing splinters on the bench. A lot of wins came out of the bullpen."

What made the job of any Cardinal pitcher a pleasure was the rock-solid defense behind him. And at first base, Jack Clark drove in the runs.

JOE MAGRANE: "During spring training, Whitey got tired of pinch-running late in the game for Steve Lake or Mike La Valliere, so he decided to trade

La Valliere, Andy Van Slyke, and Mike Dunne for Tony Pena, a trade that was highly criticized.

"Tony came over with that sidesaddle stance he had that flare for, and there were some balls getting by him, and it took him a while to get adjusted, but after a while he was beloved by all of the pitching staff, including myself. I was very hurt after the '89 season when they let him go. He was a guy who wanted to be in every single ball game, take infield every single day. He'd take a foul ball off the nuts or off the throat and shake it off and cuss in Spanish for a couple seconds and get right back down there and be ready to rock and roll. Yeah, so I thought that team was absolutely loaded.

"The reason Whitey was so heavy on left-handed pitching was the combination of Ozzie Smith at short and Terry Pendleton at third. The guy who gets lost in the shuffle around all of that talk about Ozzie is Terry Pendleton at third. This guy was a legitimate Gold Glover. A lot of people don't think this way, but Whitey decided: 'Holy cow, we have one of the best left-side defenses in baseball, why don't we get a lot of left-handed pitchers?'

"Ozzie Smith could make any play from his right to his left. He would always say, 'Whatever you do, make them hit it to me.' He used to bust my ass. He'd say, 'Quit throwing that cut fastball on right handers. Keep sinking the ball down and away. You have your best fielders on the left side of the field.' [Second baseman] Tommy Herr and Ozzie Smith set a record for double plays that year, and the ironic thing about it they didn't really enjoy each other's company that much. In fact, I don't think they spoke the entire year, other than the open-mouth, closed-mouth signals about who was covering the bag. But it goes to show what they were able to accomplish. Who said baseball's a conversational game? I didn't know the specifics of it, but I was certainly glad they were able to put their differences aside and handle it professionally on the field.

"We had Willie McGee in center field, at that time it was 385 to the alleys and 414 to center, and he could cover so much ground I never saw him have to dive. And it was absolutely amazing. I remember Bobo Milliken, who used to pitch for the Brooklyn Dodgers, was one of my pitching instructors in the minor leagues. When I first got to Johnson City, and I thought he was nuts, he said, 'The higher you go in baseball, the easier it is to pitch.' I thought, 'That can't be right.' And Jim Fregosi said something similar to that. He said, 'The higher you go, the easier it is to throw your fastball.' Because the hitters are more selective, and if you can get it to a spot, they are going to give you that. Like George Hendrick said he didn't believe a pitcher could dot the i and cross the t down and away three times in a row, and he said, 'If he did, my hat was tipped, and I was heading back to the dugout.' So anyway, I'm out there where I have this great defense, so why don't I just think, 'Down and away,' and spin a breaking ball with two strikes. And these guys made all the plays, including on AstroTurf. If there was a runner on, I had a high leg kick and have this deceptive move to first base. I said, 'Why waste my time? I'll make a slide step, a quicker move, and just try to get a ground ball.' And all I was thinking was: 'Keep it down,' because my ball had good movement. I usually got to one of the corners. I was able to get ground balls. And those guys were one of the better defenses assembled in a long time, especially after watching a lot of American League baseball now, where it's glorified softball. Put a keg in the dugout, and let's do 'the Earl Weaver three-run homer thing,' and those games aren't decided until the eighth inning in the American league, because that's when the lineup comes around for the last time. It's more pitching and defense in the National League. Obviously, being a pitcher, I have a preference for that style of play, but one isn't any worse than the other. Fans love seeing guys put balls in the seats. They don't expect them to catch them all the time in AL, where it's expected when you're in the NL.''

"We had Jack Clark, and he was the walking, talking E. F. Hutton man. He didn't say much, but he was the leader of that team. I never saw him hit an unimportant home run—and that was really neat to see. Whenever it was needed, he had the innate ability to pop one into the seats. Jack was the main piece of the puzzle, because Ozzie and Vince and Willie ahead of him would go wild, and it seemed he would either strike out, walk—he walked over 100 times that year—or hit one into the seats.

"We began the second half of the season with a ten-and-a-half-game lead. The second half was one foot in the grave and the other on a banana peel. We were just trying to hang on. I don't think we relinquished the lead, but coming into two weeks left, we had a game-and-a-half lead over the Mets and the Expos. The season ended with three games against the Expos and then three against the Mets. We figured the games against the Mets were going to decide it.

"But before the Mets we had the three games with the Expos, including a doubleheader, and I started the first game. It was one of those deals where at five o'clock the place was absolutely jam-packed, and if you've seen a game in St. Louis when things are going good, it's really a great ballpark and a great place to be. I was going up against the Expos, who I had some difficulty with that year, and it was one of those magical days. Steve Lake was catching, and everything he put down was the right pitch, and I was able to execute it, and I pitched a three-hit shutout, and that was just absolutely outstanding.

"And getting back to Whitey, I was a rookie, and I was leading, 1–0, and nowadays when there's three outs to get in a very important game, the reaction is to go right to the closer and not even think about it. I came walking off the field with purpose. I wanted to finish that game. Whitey said, 'How are you?' I said, 'I'm going to finish it.' And he said, 'Go do it.'

"I got them out one, two, three, and he was really great for a young guy, to give you confidence. If he believed in you and knew you were going to compete, he didn't want you looking over your shoulder. He wanted you to finish it yourself. Nowadays, in a lot of situations, pitchers tend to get coddled and held away from adversity. Guys come up from the minor leagues and are pulled in the sixth inning when they have runners on first and third and a one-run lead. Now they get to the point where they have three years into their big league career, and they never have to face any real adversity, and a lot of guys aren't equipped to handle it. Mental toughness is the one skill that is learned. It's not something you're born with. He was very adept at being able to bring out the best in people from that regard.

"And then Greg Mathews came back in the second game—he and I were viewed as the two flaky left-handers with no small thanks to my manager, who helped promote that—he came back and we were leading, 1–0, and he left the bases loaded in the top of the ninth and Todd Worrell came in and struck out the side. The place went absolutely bananas! Up until last year when I was still living in St. Louis, people would come up and say, 'I was there that day.' More people than were actually at the game. So that was really neat, and then the very next day the Mets were in attendance. They were up in a box, and we needed to win this game against the Expos to totally clinch the division and make that three-game Mets series irrelevant, and with the Mets looking on, Danny Cox went out and beat them, 8–2, and all the fans were pointing and screaming epithets at the Mets up in the box, and Keith Hernandez was up there, showing off his Budweiser. It was really neat.

"It was really a magical year, my first year. We were going into the playoffs, and I was thinking, 'We're going to do this every single year.' And we never got back there.

"I wish I had been a little bit more mature to really appreciate what was really going on there. It was really special.''

CHAPTER 68

ONE GAME AWAY

It was Whitey Herzog's third pennant in eight years of managing the Cardinals. The opposition in the NL League Championship Series was Roger Craig's San Francisco Giants, a group of swaggering home run hitters led by Will Clark, Chili Davis, Candy Maldonado, Kevin Mitchell, and Jeffrey Leonard, who angered opponents by flapping his right arm against his side as he ran around the bases after hitting a home run.

The day of the first game pitcher Danny Cox awoke with a stiff neck. Gary Mathews didn't learn he was to start until he got to the ballpark that afternoon. The lefty allowed just four hits in seven and a third innings. He also drove in two runs in the sixth inning with a single.

JOE MAGRANE: "Danny Cox, who had a penchant for winning a lot of big games and who had pitched the pennant clincher, had been scheduled to start the first game of the playoffs. But Coxie showed up with a stiff neck and couldn't go.

"Greg Mathews wasn't scheduled until later in the series, so Greg didn't think he was pitching. He played golf that morning with some buddies, and they were having a couple beers on the course, and the last thing he was thinking about was pitching. And when he came to the park, all of a sudden Whitey said to him, 'You're pitching.' Of course, he almost pissed down his leg, but once he put on his uni, he threw an absolute gem and won the game, which is proof positive that sometimes when you're not thinking about it, it's all right.

"Dave Dravecky shut us out, 5–0, in the second game. We had two hits. Dravecky was absolutely nasty. It seemed like he was breaking a bat an AB [at bat] with that nasty cut fastball. We were hoping we wouldn't have to see him again, because he was really tough.

"I pitched the third game. I opened up in Candlestick. I thought we had lost that game.

"Jeffrey Leonard was coming around to score, and Tony Pena was catching, and the throw came in from Vince [Coleman] in left. Leonard was going to try to run him over. Tony got the ball and just shoved his glove—he basically punched him with two hands right in the face. That was his nicely applied tag.

"I was backing up home plate. Eric Gregg gave this big 'out' sign. A lot of times umpires will meddle in situations like that, and right after he called him out, as I was getting the ball from Tony and walking back to the mound, I heard Gregg say, 'Man, you guys be playing *some* hardball.' It was fun, great stuff.

"I left the game losing, 4–0. Bob Forsch, the wily veteran, came in, and he was going to take control of the situation. Jeffrey Leonard was up. He had hit a home run in each of the first three games.

"With one out with runners on first and third, you would think, 'You don't want to flame him here.' On the first pitch, Leonard had to throw up his hand up to prevent the ball from hitting him in the neck, and knocked him on his ass. He took first, and Forsch threw a double play ball after that, and I thought that changed the entire series right there. And Jim Lindenman came up and hit a home run and we won that game, 6–5.

"It was a really neat time. We had a big rivalry, because we had brawls with the Giants that year, and Roger Craig and Whitey had a rivalry going, and Roger was always, 'Hum, baby,' and 'We're going to kick their ass,' and all that.

"We lost the next two games [4–2 and 6–3], so we were coming back home to St. Louis trailing 3 games to 2, and then John Tudor went out and pitched an absolutely ballsy game, won it 1–0, and then Danny Cox came out smoking. He [with the help of Bob Forsch] also pitched a shutout [in a 6–0 win]. And here's another Whitey Herzog happenstance—Jose Oquendo, of all people, came up and hit a big three-run home run. Whitey just was able to utilize his players like that. That year Jose was our secret weapon. In fact, in one game, he played all nine positions. He filled in for Ozzie at short. He was very underrated. He had one of the strongest arms in the league. He played second. He played right field, for God sakes. He could play anywhere. I remember on a couple of occasions, the turf was fast at Busch and Jose would say to the pitcher, 'If you're not going to get the ball down, I'm going to have to go back to the locker room and put my cup on.' He was so secure in his hands that he would play without a cup!''

It was the Cardinals' fifteenth National League championship. The Giants had hit 205 home runs during the regular season (second best in the league), and 9 in the first five games, and manager Roger Craig had trouble believing his team couldn't score a run in the final two games. Jeffrey Leonard said he thought the Giants were a better team, even though they lost.

The Cardinal response was swift. Said Ozzie Smith, "They're a classless act. Some of the greatest baseball teams in history have been beaten. Those guys came in like they were the greatest thing since cornflakes.''

The Cards were going to Minnesota to play the Twins in the World Series. But they would have to do it without their main spark, Jack Clark, who was out with torn ligaments in his ankle, and Terry Pendleton, out with a rib cage injury. Herzog would need to be—and was—at his best as St. Louis took the Twins to a seven-game Series.

JOE MAGRANE: "Ironically, two years previously I had pitched in the Metrodome for the University of Arizona against the [University of Minnesota] Gophers in a Wheaties College Tournament, and there were only 3,000 people there, and the next time there were 65,000 fans with whistles and anything that wasn't nailed down. I wore earplugs the first game, and it was just unbelievably loud, but I didn't like the feeling with the earplugs because there was an echo, and it made me feel like I was in a phone booth down the street.

"The Twins' record was so horseshit on the road, and so unbelievable at home, we figured that they had to be tipping signs in the scoreboard or something like that. So when Coxie won Game 7 against the Giants, my assignment was to start Game 1, and we were very paranoid they were picking up pitches.

"I have always liked to have it as simple as possible. One's a fastball, two's a curve, three's a change-up. And we were doing something called 'ahead, behind, even,' all these different sequences, and we were changing the indicators every hitter, and definitely every inning. And I just couldn't keep up with it. I was throwing 90 percent fastballs anyway. And things got away from me in the fourth inning.

"I was ahead, 1–0, going into the fourth, and they they hit a bunch of balls in between short and third, and Whitey pulled me out when it was 2–1. It was a blowout game, and we lost, 10–1.

"It was one of those strange years where they won every game at home, and in the second game they clobbered us pretty badly [8–4].

"We then returned to St. Louis. In the third game, the Twins led, 1–0, in the seventh, and Vince Coleman doubled home two runs against [Juan] Berenguer to pull out the 3–1 win.

"Vinny was the igniter. He would chop it on the turf or he'd work a base on balls, and run like crazy. I saw him two or three times score from second on a short-to-first putout. And you could hear the fans coming to a crescendo, 'Holy cow, he's going home,' and it put a lot of pressure on the first baseman to hurry, and he'd make the bad throw, and the thing was, Whitey empowered Willie and Vince. He didn't care if they got thrown out. He'd say, 'That's our game.' It was a bunch of base stealers and Jack Clark. He had told them a couple of times, 'Run until they tag you out.' So their minds were freed for only two things: run like hell and turn left, and run until they tag you out. And they were successful a great deal of the time.

"In the fourth game, Frank Viola was beating us, and then Tom Lawless hit a three-run home run and we scored six runs and won, 7–2. As I've said, Whitey was able to get performance out of people like that.

"Since originally I was from Minnesota, it was kind of weird. After the first game, my parents and I were just looking for a place to eat, and we went to a suburb way outside the city, went to a T.G.I. Friday's, the only place that was open, and there was only one other table there with six people, and I had six people, and it was Frank Viola. We were both at the same place, and he came over and introduced himself to me and my parents and shook their hands, which was really a nice gesture.

"In Game 5 Coxie and Bert Blyleven were having a pitchers' duel, when Curt Ford hit a single with the bases loaded to win the game. Curt was another guy who was a role player with Whitey, a little skinny guy who if he used a black bat, it would be hard to tell the difference between the two. He was real skinny and about as short as the bat he was handling, and he could absolutely hit a fastball all day long. He could pull a bullet. A pitcher would see a guy diminutive in stature up there and try to challenge him, and it never worked. Curt got the big hit, and we won, 3–2.

"We were ahead in games, 3-2, with the last two back in Minnesota, and at that point, it was, 'Holy cow, we can't win in the Metrodome, and they can't win here.' Both teams seemed to be confident of that fact.

"We went up there, and we had John Tudor on the mound for Game 6, and I was thinking, 'Okay,' because John had won a lot of big games. Tommy Herr hit one above the upper deck, and we had a 5–2 lead in the fifth with John Tudor on the mound. So I'm thinking, 'This ring is going to look pretty nice.'

"At that time, before the game, everyone was asking whether there was going to be a Game 7, and who was going to start, and before that game, Whitey told me, 'If there is a Game 7, you're going to start.' I said, 'All right.'

"So Tudor had the lead. Don Baylor came up with runners on first and second. And Baylor cheated. He got way up on the plate, got one of Tudor's change-ups, and he flicked it over the left field fence and tied the game. And of course, the place went apeshit, and the momentum just kind of changed, and they ended up winning that game.

"It was the eighth inning, and it looked like we were going to lose, and just to show you, a lot of managers wouldn't even be thinking about the fact that I'm a rookie, and Whitey said to me, 'Why don't you go upstairs and shower and get out of here, so you don't have to face the media and answered questions like, 'What's it going to be like starting Game 7?' I took his advice and got out of there. [The Cards finally lost Game 6, 11–5.]

"So I was in my hotel room faced with starting Game 7, and at that time a rookie hadn't started Games 1 and 7 since Mel Stottlemyre [in 1964]. I didn't get any sleep at all that night. First of all, there was just no way I could sleep. I was visualizing the ball coming out of my hand, perfectly located. And I was thinking about all those days in the backyard, when it was always Game 7 of the World Series, and now I was going to get the chance to actually do it!

"I thought, 'This could really make my year, my career, my life. And regardless what happens, just the excitement, the fanfare.'

"Ironically, my idol was Steve Carlton growing up, and Jim Palmer and Tim McCarver and Al Michaels were broadcasting the Series, and during that Series, McCarver was nice enough to introduce me to Steve Carlton, who was in his last year. He was on that Twins team, but wasn't on the World Series roster, and we were in St. Louis, and McCarver said, 'Steve's going to be at the Adam's Mark Hotel, having a glass of wine,' and he told me to come over, and I went over and shook his hand, and when you meet your idol, a lot of people are disappointed by that, but I certainly wasn't. I didn't know whether he was going to bite my head off or threaten to break my neck. He had this mystique of not talking to the media, of being a martial arts expert. And he was absolutely great to me.

"So before Game 7, I went to have lunch at some restaurant with my agent, and who walked in but Steve Carlton and his wife, and he walked by and said 'Hi' to me, and I thought, 'That is really neat.'

"And we got to the park at twelve o'clock for an eight o'clock game, and when I got there, everybody was already dressed, ready to rock and roll. I was in my underwear in the training room, and Whitey was in there, and he began everything like I told you, and he said to me, 'Tell you what,' as he was pulling up his pants over his boiler. 'You win this game, you shut them out, and I'll get the old man to get you a Porsche.' He was referring to Gussie Busch.

"I said, 'How about a Beemer?' And Whitey, who couldn't hear all that well, said, 'Huh?' I said, 'How about a Beemer? A BMW.' He said, 'What the hell is that?' I said, 'A BMW 750.' 'You got it.'

"And Johnny Lewis, who was in there with us, looked at me and said, 'Can't beat that.' This was twelve-thirty. 'Let's go.' I had some extra incentive.

"I was single at that time, and before the final game, C. J. Cherrie, our traveling secretary, called a meeting, and you know how the wives are in the postseason when they have their furs and their diamond jewelry. They were taking what they thought was a big role in all of that, trying to get on TV, and the traveling secretary said, 'The wives want to have a parade, whether we win or lose.' I thought, 'This is kind of peculiar to have a meeting about this before Game 7.'

"And then a player, one of the leaders on the team who will remain nameless, said, 'Hey, fuck the wives.' And Cherrie said, 'Okay, the meeting is over.' And that was it, so we could get back to focusing on baseball. I thought, 'That was a great team meeting.'

"I came out to start the ball game, and everything was going great. Every pitch was an absolute adrenaline rush. Every pitch carried more adrenaline than the next, and the secret is: If you're not feeling poised, you must act poised until you start feeling that way again.

"Sometimes there is a lot of playacting going on to keep your emotions where they need to be. So I have a 2–1 lead, and Lee Weyer is at first base, and there is one out, and Greg Gagne hits one of those tweeners. I go over to first base, the throw is behind me, and I have to catch it reaching back. I back into first and kick the bag, clearly—two years previously we had that Don Denkinger play—and clearly Gagne was out, but Lee Weyer called him safe. And of course I didn't bother to argue. We couldn't hear one another anyway. And so then Gagne was on first with one out and Kirby Puckett up in the bottom of the sixth with a 2–1 lead, and Whitey comes out, and it was at that time when Coxie was warming up in the bullpen. He had not pitched out of the bullpen all year. But he had won a lot of games, a clutch pitcher, and he was on his second day, his bullpen day, still very tired from the game where he threw a lot of sliders, and Kirby Puckett was the next hitter, and so the tying run was on first, and Whitey came out, and I said, 'I feel great.' He said, 'I don't give a fuck. I'm not going to let a rookie decide this game with Puckett.' I said, 'I've shoved it up his ass the whole Series.' He said, 'No. Good job.' He called me 'Jody.' I don't know why. He said, 'Good job, Jody.' And I said in naïvety and rookie bravado and stupidity, all wrapped in one, I said, 'If we win this game, do I still get the car?' And he said, '*What?* Get the fuck out of here.'

"Everybody thinks mound conversations are laced with strategy. It's usually a pitcher saying, 'I feel great,' and the manager saying, 'No, you don't.'

"So Coxie comes in and unfortunately hangs a slider on the first pitch, and Puckett hits a double off the wall, and the game is tied, and we ended up losing the game, 4–2.

"The ironic thing about all of that was that Whitey was playing possum the whole time about 'They have all these big boppers.' Terry Pendleton missed most of the Series because he had torn a rib cage muscle, and so did Jack Clark, because he had sprained his ankle ligaments, and Whitey was saying, 'Some of these guys we're sending up there, we have no chance. They have all these big boppers.'

The Game 7 starting lineup was Steve Lake catching, Jim Lindenman at first, Tommy Herr, Ozzie, Tom Lawless at third, Vince, Willie, Jose Oquendo in right, and our DH was Tony Pena. And we almost won the thing. I guess Whitey was playing possum for us to win this game. 'Oh, what a genius.' And I could see what he was doing. But in our meetings he wasn't downplaying us. He was very complimentary. 'Let's kick their ass.' I thought it was kind of funny.

"And looking back in retrospect, John Tudor was the guy who always spoke his mind. We were having our scouting meetings with these guys who had scouted the Twins through the playoffs, all our advance scouts, and before the Series starts, we go over these players, and the number-one guy Puckett, and they say how to pitch to him, and John says, 'That's fucking wrong. That ain't right.' So the scouts were completely wrong about the first three guys in John's mind. The pitchers were certainly more apt to trust John than they were the advance scouts. Basically the first half of the meeting was John 'motherfucking' the scouting reports, and so he basically ran the first part of the meeting about how to throw to certain hitters. We were more apt to listen to him.

"But we ended up losing that Series, and it was really disappointing. We won every game at home, and so did they, and we just happened to be playing the three games in St. Louis, and they had the four in Minnesota.

"But when you go to a seventh game of the World Series, you realize that season is a long time. As we were coming out of the Metrodome, snow was falling, and there were eight inches of snow on the ground. And I thought, 'Man, this is really a long season.' I'll never forget it. I can remember every part of it.''

CHAPTER 69

WHITEY'S LAST STAND

THE 1987 World Series appearance would be Whitey Herzog's last. With the failing health of Gussie Busch, the decision making became more bureaucratic, and after Busch's death in September of 1989, the communication between the brewery and Herzog ceased altogether. The new head, August Busch III, held no love for baseball, and it would be a matter of time before he would push Anheuser-Busch to sell the team. Herzog no longer could stand the inaction and quit midseason in 1990. Joe Magrane recalled the events.

JOE MAGRANE: "In 1988 we fell apart. That's when [free agent] Jack Clark went to the Yankees. Dal Maxvill was the general manager, and there was no love lost for Dal Maxvill among the players at that time. Dal was a very affable guy as a coach, but as general manager he just loved to play hardball, and he did it in the form of threats. We knew how important Jack was to the team, and when the negotiations between Dal and Jack became acrimonious, Jack said, 'Screw it. I'm going to the Yankees.'

"To the team, it was a sucker punch to the stomach, 'cause Jack was a big part of the team. He drove in all the important runs that Ozzie and Vince and Willie would set the table for. And that had a lot to do with our finishing fifth in '88. We just didn't score a lot of runs. That was not a memorable year at all.

"To show you how tough it was in '88, I won the ERA title. The Mets' David Cone was 20-3 with a 2.22, and I had a 2.18. We both won our last starts of the year, and I finished 5-9. We just didn't get runs. That was a big character builder. It was: 'Come on, everybody. Let's score some runs.' But it taught me that it doesn't do any good to grouse about that. It really helped me mature from the standpoint of seeing that every pitch really means something, that you can't go brain dead on the bottom of the order. At that time, I was becoming the number-one starter, but we didn't score a lot of runs. Vince would lead off the game, walk, steal second, and Terry or somebody would hit a fly ball, and he'd score on a shallow fly ball, and I'd go up against Gooden or Hershiser, and Vince'd come in and say, 'There you go. Hold 'em.' All right. We were going up against Carter, Strawberry, Hernandez, and [Kevin] McReynolds and a cast of thousands. So that really taught me to be very precise, that every pitch meant something.

JOE MAGRANE
(Courtesy Brace Photo)

"Nineteen eighty-nine was magical from a standpoint that we were in the pennant race with the Cubs all the way until the last week of the season. Pedro Guerrero, who was one of the best clutch hitters with two strikes that I ever saw, seemed to get every big hit. He especially had the ability to spit on sliders just off the outside corner with two strikes, work the count to 2-2, and they'd come back with the same pitch, and he'd flick it into right field for a single. He had an unbelievable God-given ability to hit with runners in scoring position. Pedro had a fantastic year.

"Jose DeLeon [16-12] had a great year from the pitching perspective, and I had a decent year as well at 18-9. Tony Pena and I really clicked that year. He was great. But the year also was disappointing to me. I had a definite chance to win 20 that year. I had five starts left and didn't get it done. If I could have won three of those starts, I very realistically could have been the Cy Young Award winner. I finished third that year. It just didn't happen, and I was very disappointed.

"We fell out of the race the last week and finished third. Our closer, Todd Worrell, had worn his arm out, and Dan Quisenberry, whom Whitey had managed at Kansas City, took up the slack. Quiz was so good to me. He and I hung out a lot the two years we were together. He was a wonderful guy, never boring; he could speak in riddles to where you would figure it out for yourself about how to do things as opposed to him ordering you to do something. He was a very unique, very gifted man. I miss him a lot.

"And then on September 29, 1989, Gussie Busch died. In hindsight, it meant that the Cardinal organization as we knew it was never going to be the same again. That's when the brewery turned into a roundtable of people making decisions, as opposed to Whitey going to Gussie and saying, 'Let's do this,' or 'Let's go get this guy.' And that was a defining moment that things were never going to be the same in the organization, and Whitey felt that his say had been diluted a lot, and that really frustrated him.

"Toward the end of his life, Gussie was pulling back the reins on his day-to-day involvement. He was leaving that to August Busch III, who made no bones about his dislike for the game. He thought Gussie owning the Cardinals was more upsetting to him than it was positive.

"When Busch III took over, his CEO salary was $3 million, and there were players making more than that, and he became frustrated with the salaries and the players. And he felt much the same way that Jackie Autry felt about Gene owning the club, that it was more bad than what it was worth.

"In 1990 we finished last in our division, and it was absolutely terrible. Whitey was saying that he didn't have the same control over the players, that the players did not police themselves as much as they once had.

"Every Tom, Dick, and Harry was coming into the clubhouse. Certain players were bringing all these people in and they were hanging around, drinking beer. So we had a meeting. Whitey told them, 'This clubhouse is ours. If they aren't your father or your brother, you aren't allowed in the clubhouse.' And right after that meeting was over, here comes a horde of friends of a certain player, and Whitey just tore his ass, and between what was going on with the brewery and between that kind of thing, that frustrated him.

"At that time, a lot of guys were in their free agent years. Whitey wanted to lock up a lot of these guys and put them on multiyear deals. Whitey said, 'Let's give this guy another three years,' but the roundtable of accountants did not want to do that, so Whitey had guys who had wanted to be back, and when they didn't get signed, a lot of guys started playing for themselves, and that was frustrating to Whitey as well."

RED SCHOENDIENST: "There were ten players who were in the final year of their contracts in 1990, and Whitey wanted some decisions made to clear up their status. He thought the players were thinking too much about their own futures instead of the united goal of trying to help the team win. No matter how many times he brought up the subject, nothing changed and no decisions were made."

The team began the season 33-47. During one series in San Francisco, the team played poorly, Some players were acting as though they didn't care, laughing and clowning on the bench. At the same time, Whitey wanted certain players signed, or in the alternative, traded. With the death of Gussie Busch only three months earlier, Whitey was unable to get the front office to act. Frustrated, he quit.

JOE MAGRANE: "We were out in San Diego, and there was a press conference, and Whitey announced he was quitting. He just said, 'Fuck it.' That was the last major league game that he managed. That was a sad day for a lot of us.

"I was sure he was going to come back. He became the general manager with the Angels for a while. He was trying to catch lighting in a bottle with the same type of relationship with Gene Autry as he had had with Gussie Busch. He loved both of those guys very much.

"The writers were wondering, 'Why would Whitey quit?' Because he didn't mention why in his press conference. And so everyone was trying to figure it out. The columnists started pointing fingers as to why. And this one columnist said it was the pitchers against the regular players, the blacks against the whites, and all this bullshit. And it was a very unpleasant situation.

"Red Schoendienst came in and managed the club for two weeks until Dal Maxvill hired Red's successor at that point, and that was Joe Torre. Joe spent the rest of the year observing, and it was an ugly situation. From all that stuff that had happened, people were laying blame why the team was horseshit, and it all fell apart.

"It wasn't the same group that it had been. If the bus would have broken down, there would have been twenty-five cabs, everybody going in their own different direction.

"I came to spring training in '91 and was playing catch, and I had always had a bone spur in the shape of a fishhook inside my left elbow. I always knew that it was there, and it just kept digging and digging with each pitch into the ligament, so I knew that one day I was going to have Tommy John surgery. When I started in 1987, I was making the minimum, which was $62,500. We weren't making a whole lot of money back then, so I was trying to hold on as long as possible. I had been held down for a lot of years by arbitration, and since my career was going to be over, I was trying to make a situation where I'd have something to fall back on. Also the surgery at that time hadn't been that effective. So in the spring of '91, my elbow finally blew, and [Dr.] Frank Jobe fixed it, so I was out all season. And then I started in '92 in extended spring, went up the ladder, and made it back the last month of the season. I came back and got established again.

"I pitched in '93. There was a whole different group. One of the hurdles that Joe Torre had, which was inevitable, is that he and his coaches would try to do things, to make changes, and the players would say, 'Well, Whitey did it this way,' and that was kind of frustrating for Joe, 'cause he was trying to do his own thing. It was still 'The World According to Whitey.'

"I pitched in '93 out of the number-three spot, and I got off to slow start, was going to get released, and then won five games in a row in June, and then lost a couple games and they put me in the bullpen, and since I was going to be a free agent at the end of the year and since they said they did not have interest in me beyond next year, I asked Joe for a trade and he said he had talked to Maxvill, and he said there was no interest.

"Mike Perez was coming off the disabled list, so I asked for my release, and they were kind enough to give that to me, and I went over to Whitey and the Angels. For two months, I pitched real well and ended up getting a contract for the next couple years. I ended up having surgery in the spring of 1994, and had one of those hot and cold years where the arm was good one time and wasn't the next. In hindsight, my better days were behind me. After the surgery, it just didn't get any better after that.

"From that point, it was really frustrating, because I had come up with the Glavines and Madduxes and used to go toe-to-toe with those guys, and a lot of times was successful against them. That's how I looked at it. They were my peer group, and they were still pitching and doing real well.

"I don't waste any time thinking about it or having any regrets how things played out. I knew they could have played out much better, but they didn't.

"The neatest thing about the Cardinals: I realized while I was there that Red Schoendienst knew my name, knew who I was. Stan Musial knew who I was and would call me by name. Bob Gibson and Lou Brock, a great guy, all these guys who come around, and Red would introduce me to them. I thought the Cardinals did a great job holding on to their roots and tradition. I remember sitting at the dais with Red. He introduced me to Warren Spahn. I knew the history of the game, and I could talk about Warren's delivery and how he had that deception with his hand and the batters would have a hard time picking it up. And I said that to him. He wanted to know how I knew that. I told him I had read it in the Dead Sea Scrolls. Talking to Enos 'Country' Slaughter was like sitting and waiting for a bus. I just thought it was real neat to get to see these guys. They were around. The Cards had their numbers retired in our clubhouse. We saw those every single day. You really felt proud to be a Cardinal, all the way back to the days of Harry Caray and Jack Buck and down through the history. I felt very proud to be a part of it."

CHAPTER 70

A NEW REGIME

ON October 14, 1994, Dal Maxvill was fired as general manager and replaced by Walt Jocketty, who had a long career with Oakland and Colorado as assistant GM and was ready to move up to the top job. The manager he wanted was Tony La Russa. Joe Torre was fired after a 20-27 start, and he was replaced by farm director Mike Jorgensen. La Russa was hired on October 23, 1995, after seventeen years in the American League.

La Russa had managed the White Sox from 1979 to 1986, leading Chicago to a first-place Western Division title in 1983. He was named Manager of the Year. After he was fired in Chicago on June 19, 1986, he was hired three weeks later by Oakland.

His A's team won the AL West in 1988, 1989, 1990, and 1992. In 1989 the team swept the Giants in the World Series, the Series that was interrupted by an earthquake.

La Russa, a Tampa native, was a grad of Florida State University Law School. He passed the bar exam in December of 1979, making him the fifth lawyer among major league managers. The other four were John Montgomery Ward, Hughie Jennings, Branch Rickey, and Miller Huggins. All are in the Baseball Hall of Fame.

On March 21, 1996, the Cards were sold by Anheuser-Busch to a group led by William O. DeWitt, Jr., whose father had owned the St. Louis Browns and who later ran the Detroit Tigers and the Cincinnati Reds. He owned a piece of the Texas Rangers, then the Baltimore Orioles, before buying the Cards on March 21, 1996.

BILL DEWITT, JR.: "I got a call from a friend in St. Louis who said he heard the team might be for sale. I talked to another friend, and he made contact with the brewery. A representative from the brewery called me and said, 'Are you serious? I thought you were hooked up with Baltimore.' I said, 'No. I'm on the verge of getting out of that.' So we had a meeting, and I told him of my interest, told him of my background in St. Louis and my father's background with the Cardinals and the Browns.

"I grew up in St. Louis, graduated from high school here. My father sold the team to Bill Veeck, but stayed in St. Louis and continued in baseball in a variety of capacities. In 1960 we moved to Detroit, where he became the president/CEO of the Tigers. He was there about a year and a half and then he heard about the Cincinnati situation. A representative of Powell Crosley called him up and said, 'Would you be interested in coming and running the Reds?' He said he would, and that's when we all moved to Cincinnati. My dad made some great trades that first year in '61, and the Reds won the pennant.

I was at Yale, graduated in '63. I worked for the Reds in the summer. Then I went to graduate school for two years at the Harvard Business School, getting out in '65. And then in 1967 my father sold the Reds to a local group, of which I was one of the members. I was there about a year and a half, and I sold my interest and went off and did other things. George Bush, Jr., and I were business partners. We were in the oil and gas business together. He was working on his father's campaign, and then he and I headed up the group to buy the Rangers. We closed in '88.

"I wanted to get something closer to home, and I was able to negotiate the purchase of the Cardinals. I got a small group of guys who were interested in going in with me to buy it.

"We had an agreement to purchase the team in the winter of '95, so we had a lot of say about what happened between then and when we actually closed, which was in March of 1996. We made a bigger effort to sign free agents, and '96 was a wonderful year. We won the division. This is now our fourth season. Our goal is to go on and win the pennant and the World Series."

In July of 1997, Card GM Walt Jocketty made a trade that would change the history of the game. He sent to the A's three pitching prospects for hulking first baseman Mark McGwire.

The reason McGwire was on the trading block had to do with baseball's two-tiered system of haves and have-nots. Half the teams have large TV, radio, and cable incomes, the other half don't. Half the teams can afford the best players. The other half can't. Oakland, having to share its too-small market with rival San Francisco, perhaps could least afford McGwire's $9 million-a-year contract demands. Oakland's entire salary was budgeted at $18 million.

If McGwire had been a gate attraction, Oakland might have considered it.

But because McGwire was injury-prone, he had not been much of a draw, so the A's were forced to sell him to any team that could afford him.

Jocketty, who had worked in Oakland before coming to St. Louis, loved McGwire's power, as did Tony La Russa, who had been his manager in Oakland. They downplayed his record of injuries, concentrated on his home run potential, and figured the change in scenery would do McGwire a world of good. It was one of the smartest—and most important—calculations in the history of the franchise and the game.

Once he arrived in St. Louis, McGwire became a sensation, both at the plate and at the box office. He was a low-ball hitter entering a low-ball hitter's paradise, the National League, where few pitches above the navel are called strikes. In 1997, after hitting 34 home runs for Oakland, McGwire came to the Cards and hit 24 more.

The next year he and Sammy Sosa had breathtaking seasons as they battled not only to break Roger Maris's hallowed record of 61 home runs in a season, but far eclipsed the mark. McGwire's 70 home runs in the 1998 season set the new standard against which all sluggers now will be measured. With his heroic feat, he became the first hitter in major league baseball to hit 50 home runs three years in a row, staking his claim to be remembered as the greatest power hitter ever to play the game. In 1998 Mark McGwire became the greatest drawing card in the history of baseball—not even Babe Ruth packed 'em in the way McGwire does.

But above all, Mark McGwire will be remembered for his grace under pressure and for his ability to stay humble, to keep his humility, and to give the children of America a role model of whom all can be proud. In an age when far-less-talented professional athletes vainly strut around like cocks of the walk and treat their fans like a necessary evil, Mark McGwire showed a grace under pressure as impressive as any of his 500-foot home run blasts. It had been that way all his life.

On October 1, 1963, exactly two years to the day that Roger Maris broke Babe Ruth's single-season home run record in 1961, Mark McGwire was born, not in a manger, but in a regular hospital like the rest of us. He grew up in Claremont, California, a suburb of L.A. at the foot of the San Gabriel Mountains. He would grow to be as big as those mountains.

His father, John, a dentist, taught his five sons about dedication and overcoming obstacles. In 1944, when he was seven years old, John McGwire had contracted polio. The vaccine would not be perfected for another ten years, and after the disease took its toll, John McGwire wound up with one leg an inch shorter than the other. Despite his handicap, John McGwire became a fine golfer, a long-distance bicyclist, and a college boxer.

Mark McGwire's mother was a nurse who quit her job to raise five massive sons. Mark McGwire topped out at six-foot-five. One of Mark's brothers, Dan McGwire, rose to six-seven and became a pro quarterback with the Seattle Seahawks.

Like Babe Ruth himself, Mark McGwire began his baseball career as a pitcher, although because he suffered a severe muscle pull in his chest, McGwire didn't begin playing baseball at Damien High School in LaVerne,

California, until his junior year. "He was one of the most talented pitchers I ever saw," said his coach, Tom Carroll. McGwire threw over ninety miles an hour. He could also hit. In practice, he once hit a ball over 500 feet, a blow that helped make the teenager a local legend.

During the summer of 1980, Carroll was attending an L.A. Dodger game when he bumped into Marcel Lachemann, the pitching coach at the University of Southern California. Lachemann wanted to know whether Carroll had any good pitchers. Carroll told him about McGwire.

When Lachemann came to watch McGwire play, he was equally impressed with his pitching and his hitting. USC was the only college to offer McGwire a scholarship.

The Montreal Expos, meanwhile, had drafted McGwire as a pitcher in the eighth round of the 1981 draft. When they offered only an $8,500 signing bonus, McGwire chose college over the Expos.

By his sophomore year, McGwire was the ace of the USC staff, which was quite a feat, considering that Randy Johnson was also on the team. McGwire led the pitching staff with a 2.78 ERA. When not pitching, McGwire hit 19 home runs in 190 at-bats.

In 1982 McGwire played summer ball in Alaska with the Anchorage Glacier Pilots. He signed on as a pitcher, but as happens in baseball and in life, circumstances changed his career plans.

Of the three Pilot first basemen, one got a summer job, the second was hurt, and the third signed a pro contract. The position was open, and McGwire was tapped to fill it. During two months of summer ball in 44 games, McGwire batted .403, with 13 home runs and 53 RBIs. The Alaskan experience changed the way McGwire saw himself.

MARK MCGWIRE: "Somewhere along the line up there in Alaska, it hit me. 'You know, I'd rather play every day than every fifth day.' Then I started getting some hits. Ron Vaughn [an assistant coach at USC and at Anchorage], who's one of my biggest mentors as a hitter, pretty much started me and taught me everything I needed to know."

When McGwire returned to USC for his junior year, he told head coach Rod Dedeaux that he wanted to play regularly and not pitch. Dedeaux had seen other high school stars begin at USC as pitchers and become hitters. Dave Kingman and Fred Lynn were two of his stars to make the switch. At first, Dedeaux resisted. But when McGwire started hitting at a pace unknown to college hitters, Dedeaux gave in.

As a junior, McGwire hit 32 home runs to set a new Pac-10 record. In '84 he was *The Sporting News* College Player of the Year and was a member of the U.S. Olympic baseball team.

What was most interesting about McGwire was that though the college sports world saw him as a star, in his own mind, he never saw himself that way. He'd tell himself, 'Anyone can hit a home run with an aluminum bat.' When asked about his honors in the USC media guide, McGwire left the space blank. At home, his pile of trophies were stashed in the back closet.

The night before the 1984 baseball free agent draft, McGwire called the home of Nancy Mazmanian, who was director of Sports Information at USC, and told her that his father and the New York Mets were negotiating a contract. ''I might be the number-one pick in the country,'' McGwire told her. ''Is there somebody I should call to talk about this?''

There wasn't, it turned out. The Mets insisted that McGwire sign a contract before the draft, and Mark wouldn't do it. The next day the Mets took Shawn Abner as the number-one player in the draft. Other players selected before McGwire were infielder Jay Bell, slugger Cory Snyder, and pitcher Bill Swift. McGwire ended up being taken tenth by the Oakland A's.

Sandy Alderson, the A's general manager at the time, recalled the events leading to McGwire's selection.

SANDY ALDERSON: ''When Mark entered the draft out of USC, our scouts saw big-time college power. The question was whether that would be realized at the professional level. At the time, there had been some notable failures of college power hitters [Shawn Abner and Cory Snyder were notable busts], but it was the big-time power everybody saw, and that was a great class of college players that year. So it was a question of who to select among a number of players who were really of top quality.

MARK McGWIRE
(Courtesy Brace Photo)

"The Mets had first pick and wanted to take McGwire. They attempted to make a deal with McGwire before the draft, but Mark refused to sign a contract before the draft. I think it was strictly on the basis of principle. In retrospect, one should not have been surprised that he would have taken that position. He comes from a very principled family.

"I was surprised when Mark was still available at pick number ten. On the other hand, I was fairly new to the baseball business at that time, and there are a couple of things that can happen, and what happened in this case, some clubs had already locked in to other players and made pre-draft deals based on their projection of the way in which the top picks were going to fall. Alternatively, other clubs were put off by the Mets' inability to sign Mark before the draft and may have been concerned about the amount of money that he was demanding. Those were probably the two reasons he fell to ten.

"Also, there are always surprises, even in the top ten picks. And there were surprises that year. There were a number of high school catchers taken: Eric Pappas comes to mind. But when Mark dropped to us, there were still three very highly touted players available: Mark was one, Oddibe McDowell was another, and Shane Mack was a third. We basically decided to go for the power. At that time, we were looking to build a team around power, and I'm not sure exactly why that was, but it had a lot to do with my inexperience in the game and my subscription to the theories of Bill James. He believed that power and on-base percentage were the keys to winning, and Mark had plenty of both. Ultimately, we went for the power."

McGwire played under the cloud of an unhappy marriage. Like his father, Mark was tight-lipped and chose to avoid talking about problems in the marriage rather than confronting them. He was also handsome and young and was a magnet for the girls who flocked around him. His wife Kathy had great difficulty handling Mark's fame. So, apparently, did Mark.

MARK McGWIRE: "I did so much stupid stuff. Kathy and I never talked about things. We still have never talked about why the marriage went bad. I didn't know how to communicate them. I guess I didn't care. I just closed it off."

Kathy had a different explanation.

KATHY McGWIRE: "I think there were too many things calling Mark's name: women, fame, glamour."

During his first season in 1984, McGwire was suffering emotionally off and on the field. In his first season with Modesto, he came to bat 55 times, had 11 hits and only 1 home run. He was doing so badly that he considered quitting.

He didn't quit. After a stellar season at Modesto and fine stints at Huntsville and then Tacoma, Mark was called up to the Oakland A's in September of 1986. GM Sandy Alderson was impressed from the outset.

SANDY ALDERSON: "Mark was a first baseman and a pitcher in college. In terms of his development, I can't even say he didn't come as quickly as we thought. The thing about Mark, in his first month in the big leagues, which was the end of 1986, he hit under .200, but if you extrapolate his RBIs [9] and home runs [3 in 18 games at third base] over a full season, just on that thirty-day look, he would have had an incredible first season. So in spite of the batting average, he had the production, even that first month. Even the year that he hit .201 [1991], he still had good production. Frankly, we made the mistake in '91 of trying to get him to raise his batting average from .270, and of course, in Mark's case, batting average has always been irrelevant. He's now started to hit much better. He's a better hitter than he ever has been. In those days, he had a very high on-base percentage, he was scoring runs, driving them in, and those are the only things you're really concerned about."

When Mark McGwire came up to the majors to stay in 1987, he electrified the Bay Area by hitting 49 home runs and was named Rookie of the Year. He and Jose Canseco teamed up to become the "Bash Brothers."

McGwire might have hit the magical 50 that year, but with one game to go in the season, his wife Kathy went into labor, and he wanted to be with her. His teammates pleaded with him to stay and hit number 50, but Mark wanted to be present for the birth of their baby, Matthew, so he skipped the final day of the season. Ten years later, Matthew would become a prominent figure in McGwire's quest for immortality. Only a few years later, Mark and Kathy would be splitsville.

Mark and Kathy separated for good just as the 1988 World Series against the L.A. Dodgers was getting under way. She retained custody of their son. Troubled over the breakup, McGwire went 1 for 17 against the Dodgers and Oakland lost in five games. With his marriage ended, McGwire was left with guilt and regrets.

In the next two years, his batting average sagged into the .230s. Then in 1991 he hit .201 with only 22 home runs. Once again McGwire was seriously thinking about quitting. At the end of the season, he drove five hours from Oakland to his home in L.A., pondering his future the entire way. When he arrived home, he decided he badly needed psychotherapy. He called a therapist.

MARK MCGWIRE: "I had to face the music. The therapy was exhilarating. I was figuring out who I was. I played the first five, six years on physical ability. Now I'm convinced the mind is 99 percent of the game.

"Therapy brought emotions about me. There's nothing wrong with emotion."

SANDY ALDERSON: "He was having some personal problems while he was with us. I was aware of what was going on. I didn't seek to be a confidant. I did make every effort, as did the rest of the organization and Tony [La Russa], to provide the kind of assistance he needed to get through that. I did not consider it my job as a club executive to be giving him advise in areas where there were others far more expert and professional. My job was to find those other professionals and experts. We had things in place that he was able to take advantage of. Mark had the self-confidence and courage to take advantage of those things.''

In 1992 McGwire rebounded with a solid season: 42 home runs and 104 RBIs, but then he began to suffer from physical woes. Seven times he was on the DL. McGwire's proclivity for ending up on the disabled list was due in large part to serious injuries to his feet, first his left and then right. He also had back problems. He filed for free agency in October of 1992 but re-signed with the A's. In 1993 he played in only 27 games (9 homers, 24 RBIs, .333); in '94 only 47 games (9 homers, 25 RBIs, .252); and in '95 only 104 games (but 39 homers, 90 RBIs, .274.).

While out, McGwire would sit behind home plate during games and study opposing pitchers. Healthy again in 1996, he hit .312 with 52 home runs. In 1997 he was again on his way toward hitting the magic 50 when in July the Oakland A's team owners ordered GM Sandy Alderson to trade him, in order to avoid paying a huge salary the team couldn't afford. Alderson was directed to unload McGwire by the trade deadline, a difficult task, it turned out, because he had been injured so often.

Since joining the A's in 1987, McGwire had missed more than 280 days of work, and fans had become leery of rooting for him, despite the 52 home runs in 1996 and his great start in 1997. When they came to the ballpark to see him, too often his name had not been in the lineup. The A's fans preferred the more entertaining Jose Canseco, who not only hit home runs but also dated Madonna. A's fans turned out in droves to watch Jose.

When Alderson shopped his big slugger, he discovered that only one team, the St. Louis Cardinals, run by former A's exec Walt Jocketty and former A's manager Tony La Russa, had a serious interest in acquiring him. They knew how good he was. And because the Cards were the only ones interested in acquiring him, Jocketty was able to get Big Mac cheap. On July 31, 1997, one of the important days in St. Louis Cardinal history, the Cards traded Blake Stein, T. J. Mathews, and Eric Ludwick, three young pitching prospects, to the A's. Alderson, who is now assistant to Commissioner Bud Selig, knows that for the rest of his life he will be known as the man who traded Mark McGwire. That the economics of the game forced him to trade McGwire has left him wistful.

SANDY ALDERSON: "In '93 and '94 Mark missed a lot of games with injuries. At various times, he had back problems, and he also had some severe foot problems. He had torn fascia in his heels, which cost him a substantial amount of time, actually two years in a row, in both heels. And so when he hit 52 home runs in '96, even though he led the league, unfortunately, he wasn't much of an attraction, and that's because the difference between Mark hitting 45 and 52 is not a great deal, and he was even out from time to time during that season. He didn't miss a lot, but he missed just enough so that the hysteria surrounding the home run chase in '98 never materialized. Because there had been such a long history of injury with Mark, every time he'd sit, if it only turned out to be for two or three days, fans would throw up their hands and say, 'Gee, he's out again. He's not going to be able to hit 60.' So there was always this skepticism on the part of a lot of A's fans that had developed out of his past injuries that he would play a full season. I don't think the fans ever got behind him.

"As a result, we were forced to trade him. The economics were quite simple. Mark was looking for $9 million or $10 million [a year] at that time, and our payroll was 50 percent of that in '96 and didn't figure to go up in '97 or '98. Mark at the same time was not drawing fans the way a player of that cost, at least in our case, would have to in order to offset the additional cost. So it was pretty clear-cut. Nine million was half of about $18 million, which was what we were spending. We still weren't a very good ballclub, and we weren't drawing fans much beyond a million. It was pretty clear he had decided at some point in the season he wanted to be traded to a contender, did not want to stay with a club that did not have a future competitively. One couldn't really argue with that. So it became a matter of trying to move him by the trade deadline, in order to satisfy his desire and also to avoid any further distraction that arose out of his situation.

"In the final analysis, only St. Louis showed interest. The Angels had an opportunity to acquire him. They passed. The Yankees made a cash offer of $1 million at the last moment, which was not satisfactory. And so it was left to St. Louis, and to their credit, they felt if they could get Mark to St. Louis, Tony and his staff, all of whom had formerly been in Oakland, would be able to convince him to stay in St. Louis, because of the kind of baseball town it was and the kind of ownership direction that they had. And they were right about that.

"In the meantime, they also knew there was little or no market for Mark, which sounds like an amazing circumstance, but it's typically true in a midseason trade. Most clubs who are in a pennant drive are looking for pitching. Very seldom to you see top-quality young position players traded. It happens occasionally, but it would have to be a very special need, and I think St. Louis was looking just as much at the long-term as they were for the short-term with Mark. And so ultimately they were able to make the trade because we didn't really have any other viable options.

"In return, we got some prospects. We'll see how they turn out. T. J. Mathews is a solid major league pitcher. But we did get a prospect: Blake Stein. On the other hand, if you were to compare it to similar deals in the same time frame in other years, typically when pitchers are involved in trades, they typically generate more value in a stretch drive kind of trade. Ultimately, the important thing was not what we got back but that we had to let him go in the first place, and that is just a commentary on where baseball economics are today and have been in the last four, five years."

McGwire finished the year by hitting 24 home runs in St. Louis. Along with the 34 he hit in Oakland, his 1997 total was 58 home runs, tying him for third place on the list for most home runs in a season with Hank Greenberg and Jimmie Foxx. There was speculation that McGwire would become a free agent and wouldn't return to St. Louis after the season, but after his young son Matthew visited and approved of Dad's new hometown, McGwire signed a three-year, $28.5-million deal with an $11.5-million option year.

As part of the signing announcement, McGwire said he was donating $1 million each year to help support facilities in St. Louis and Los Angeles that work with abused children. When he broke into tears when making the emotional announcement, he became that rarity in sports—the superhero with a big heart. Everyone, including the top brass of the Cards, greatly appreciates what McGwire has meant to the franchise.

BILL DeWITT, JR.: "It's been unbelievable. Really, it started the day Mark got here. We had been on the road, playing in Philadelphia, and he didn't have a particularly good road trip. He came over and was having a very good year, and then they traded him at the trading deadline, and we were on the road, and he didn't hit any home runs, and yet the first time he came up to bat at home he got a standing ovation. From that point forward, he was just captivated by the town and vice versa.

"I'll remember for the first time the first home run he hit for us. It was a line drive, not his classic towering home run, and he went on a tear and he ended up in '97 with 58 home runs and became the talk of the town. St. Louis is a wonderful baseball town. I don't know of any as good or better, that's for sure.

"Then 1998 was *really* a magical season. It's been quite something ever since Mark arrived. The fans came out in droves. I don't think it necessarily would have happened in other places. When Mark came here, prior to that, St. Louis hadn't been all that good for a while. St. Louis has such a wonderful tradition, with great players and so many Hall of Famers, fifteen pennants, and the second most number of world championships, that they really gravitated to him, knowing this was an epic figure in the history of baseball.

"When Maris was trying to break Babe Ruth's record, the Yankees didn't sell out. And they weren't necessarily rooting for him. There were plenty of people who didn't want him to break it.

"I think *everybody* wanted McGwire to break it."

CHAPTER 71

GOD

FOR fifty years, Cardinal fans have had Stan Musial, the "Grand Old Man" of St. Louis, to look up to as the man who embodied all that was best about St. Louis baseball, and now they also have McGwire, who in 1998 produced the greatest single-season performance in the entire history of this wonderful game.

McGwire opened the 1998 season in dramatic fashion by hitting a grand-slam home run off the Dodgers' Ramon Martinez. When he came into the dugout, he slapped catcher Tom Lampkin so hard on the back that Lampkin had to wear an ice bag to reduce the swelling.

In the second game, the Cards and Dodgers were in extra innings when McGwire came up in the twelfth inning with two men on and hit one into the upper deck. In the third game, against San Diego, he homered, and then the next day he did it again.

Said Lampkin, "It's unbelievable. He has a chance to hit the ball out of the ballpark every time he walks up to the plate."

On April 14 against Arizona, McGwire hit three home runs, the first player ever to perform that feat at the new Busch Stadium. When on May 12 McGwire hit a ball 527 feet off Paul Wagner, the longest ball ever hit at Busch Stadium, Wagner commented, "He has the power of three men. He's a man among boys." After McGwire hit a 545–foot home run off the ST. LOUIS POST-DISPATCH sign at Busch Stadium on May 16, a large Band-Aid was placed over the dent.

On May 19 he had another three-homer day, this time against the Philadelphia Phillies.

He hit 16 home runs in May, finishing the month with a total of 27 home runs. When asked over and over whether he stood a chance to break Roger Maris's record of 61 home runs, McGwire became annoyed. "How can I answer a question if I'm not in that situation yet? There's nothing to talk about." If he had 50 home runs by September 1, he said, he'd address the question.

In Chicago, meanwhile, Cub outfielder Sammy Sosa was also mounting an assault on Maris's record. Between May 22 and June 20, Sammy Sosa hit 21 homers, the most ever in a thirty-game skein. During the month of June, the Dominican native with the ready smile hit 20 home runs, more in a single month than hit by anyone ever—including Babe Ruth, Roger Maris, Willie Mays, who had the National League mark of 17, and Rudy York, who had held the major league mark since he hit 18 home runs in August of 1937. In addition, Sosa broke Hack Wilson's record of 29 RBIs delivered in one month. When he hit home run number 32 on June 25, it was his 19th June round tripper, his 12th homer in thirteen games, his 23rd in his last twenty-six games. Sammy Sosa had transformed himself from sullen underachiever into a national superstar and a challenger to McGwire.

When the Cubs traveled to St. Louis for a head-to-head meeting between McGwire and Sosa, the eyes of the entire nation were on the doings at Busch Stadium. Everyone expected a confrontation. Instead, what the public was treated to was a display of sportsmanship and generosity rarely seen on or off the ball field. Sammy Sosa was first to show his gentle side.

Before the series, Sosa worked to make it clear that he and McGwire were not rivals. In conversation, he would refer to the Cardinal slugger as *"Mi Padre,"* "my father," a term of great respect. He told reporters, "I don't have any kind of jealous feeling toward him. To me, he's the man who's going to break the record." In their face-to-face competition, each homered once in the three games.

Perhaps it was the influence of Sammy Sosa, but by the end of August, Mark McGwire was beginning to relax and enjoy himself too. McGwire began to blow kisses like Sammy. It was a sign of flattery, and McGwire's actions received smiles and applause. When McGwire hit home runs 50 and 51 against the Mets on August 20, he became the first player ever to hit 50 home runs three years straight. The next day Sosa homered—his 49th—in a Cub victory. Two days later, Sammy homered twice—his 50th and 51st—and McGwire hit his 53rd.

By the end of August, McGwire and Sosa each had 55, and it was no longer a question of whether they would break Maris's record, but which one and by how many.

Ken Griffey, Jr., in Seattle, also was challenging for the home run record, as was San Diego's Greg Vaughn. The race to unseat Maris in an attempt to break the most prestigious record on the hallowed books of baseball was the shot in the arm baseball desperately needed in its fight to regain its fandom after the long strike in 1994.

Blared a headline in *The New York Times:* A SPORT IS REBORN. In the final paragraph of his article, journalist George Vecsey credited McGwire.

GEORGE VECSEY: "Tonight, in the shadow of the Gateway Arch, the big man will flex muscles as broad as the river that flows past. Baseball lives."

Another nationally known journalist, Robert Lipsyte, noted that the home run chase not only was bringing baseball back after the disastrous strike in 1994, but also was raising the spirits of Americans across the country feeling low in the midst of the sex scandal surrounding President Clinton.

ROBERT LIPSYTE: "Just when we needed it most, twisted with guilt and self-loathing for wallowing in a sad sex opera, along came baseball opera, outdoors and clean, big boys swinging big bats in public. There was a show somewhere in the country almost every day and night."

On September 1, McGwire hit two home runs—numbers 56 and 57—against the Florida Marlins. Cub fans may have been disappointed, but Mark McGwire's actions and words let everyone know that not only was he not competing with Sosa, he felt a fondness for the Cubs star. In a press conference after the game, he spoke to reporters of his admiration of the year Sosa was having and talked of how envious he was that the Cubs were in the playoff race and not the Cards.

The next day, September 2, Sosa hit his 56th home run to tie Hack Wilson for the most home runs ever hit by a Cub in a season. Along with McGwire, he had become only the third National Leaguer ever to reach such an exalted number. The home run helped the Cubs defeat the Reds, 4–2, and keep Chicago a game ahead of the Mets in the wild card race. That night McGwire hit two gargantuan home runs—his 58th and 59th—against the Marlins at Pro Player Stadium near Miami.

Sosa, though, would not let McGwire pull too far away, and on September

4 he hit number 57 off Jason Schmidt in the first inning before 36,510 Three River Stadium spectators who honored Sammy as he made a run at Maris's record rather than watch hometown kids play football on the opening night of the high school season. Sammy had brought his one-man carnival with him, and during every at bat a continuous popping of flashbulbs lit up the Pennsylvania night like a blanket of gigantic fireflies.

After the game, a 5–2 victory, Sosa bragged about McGwire, predicting that his rival would hit 70 home runs before the end of the season. "Yeah, I'm pulling for Mac," said Sosa. "He's going to do it."

On September 5 Sosa hit his 58th home run, a 418-foot drive off Pirate rookie Sean Lawrence. The 37,711 at the game in Three Rivers Stadium would not stop roaring until Sosa came out of the dugout and tipped his hat.

McGwire, meanwhile, refused to allow Sosa to catch him. In the first inning in a game against Cincinnati, he hit his 60th home run in the first inning.

JACK BUCK (with the call): "This is it! It's a home run. Wake up, Babe Ruth, there's company coming! It's Mark McGwire with number 60!"

McGwire was now tied with the Babe and only one behind Maris. And he still had 21 more games to go.

After the game, McGwire was asked by a reporter what he might say to Ruth or to Maris.

MARK MCGWIRE: "I would ask them if they ever felt the way I'm feeling right now. I'd ask them if the emotions ran through them, the way my emotions are right now. I have this incredible feeling inside. Did they feel this way too?"

When the Cards met the Cubs at Busch Stadium on September 6, the appearance of McGwire and Sosa on the same field marked a milestone. Never had two players with so many home runs been in the same game since Roger Maris and Mickey Mantle played together with the New York Yankees in 1961. That year Maris hit 61 and Mantle 54. At the start of this game, McGwire had 60 and Sosa 58.

Major League Baseball flew Pat Maris and her six grown children to St. Louis, but during the plane ride, Mrs. Maris suffered an irregular heartbeat and was taken to a local hospital. Four of the Maris boys watched as Sammy got two singles and McGwire hit a pitch that went foul by no more than seven feet.

The next day Mrs. Maris and her sons were seated behind the Cardinal dugout for the Labor Day afternoon game, a sellout affair before a national television audience. Like a baseball Woodstock, it was a love-in—to the two competitors, and to baseball and its history. Tony La Russa noted that before the game during batting practice, McGwire seemed at peace with himself, smiling and demonstrating an almost carefree attitude.

When Sosa came to bat in the first inning, the Cardinal fans gave him a long ovation. Not long afterward, McGwire hit the first pitch delivered by Cubs pitcher Mike Morgan into the seats for home run number 61, tying Maris. Sosa watched from his post in right field.

Once he crossed home plate, the Cards' slugger was greeted by his ten-year-old son Matt. McGwire picked up the boy and carried him into the dugout. When he returned to the field, he mouthed the words "Happy Birthday" to his dad, who was in attendance, celebrating his sixty-first birthday. He then pointed skyward in a religious gesture and then went into the dugout to hug manager Tony La Russa and trainer Barry Weinberg, a close friend.

After he returned to the field for a curtain call, he gestured toward the Maris family. He blew a kiss to Roger Maris in heaven and pointed upward.

The scene affected everyone looking on.

When Sosa singled in the eighth inning, the Cub and the big first baseman hugged. Sosa told McGwire, "Don't go too far now. Wait for me." Sosa was stalled at 58.

After the game, Sammy was asked how he could hug someone who played on the other team. Said Sosa, "It doesn't matter if he plays for the Cardinals and I play for Chicago—we still have a relationship as people, as friends." During a joint news conference, Sosa and McGwire sat side by side, sharing a microphone and answering questions. Kids across America saw something very rare in sports, a display of sportsmanship, along with a strong feeling of deep respect between opponents.

McGwire smote the record breaker on September 8. During the morning, McGwire filmed a public service announcement on sexual child abuse. Never before had the topic been airly publicly. That McGwire was the spokesman made it possible.

Once McGwire arrived at the ballpark, he seemed noticeably tense.

TONY LA RUSSA: "I worried when I saw it. I thought, 'This guy wants to do it so bad today, there's no way he can do it.' He wanted to do it for all the reasons: family, St. Louis.

"And the son of a gun did it."

The first pitch thrown by the Cubs Steve Trachsel in the fourth inning was a slider that McGwire hit on a low trajectory toward the left field seats of Busch Stadium. The ball hung to the right of the left field pole and just did clear the railing below the seats. At 341 feet, it was the shortest home run McGwire hit all season long. But home run number 62, his 7th home run in seven games and his 15th in twenty-one games, instantly became one of the most renowned moments in modern baseball history.

MIKE SHANNON (with the call): "A shot into the corner. It might make it. There it is: 62, folks! And we have a new home run champion. A new 'Sultan of Swat.' It's Mark McGwire. He touches them all. Unbelievable!

"I haven't seen anybody like him, and you're never going to see anything like him. In Mark McGwire, what you're talking about is John Wayne, Paul Bunyan, and Superman rolled into one. You're never going to see a show like this."

*   *   *

Succeeding in a relentless quest for immortality, McGwire sprinted to first base, his fist pumping in the air, slowing when he saw the ball clear the fence. He leaped to embrace first base coach Dave McKay, missed first base, then came back, touched the bag, and headed around the bases for his date with destiny.

He saluted the Cubs' bench twice before stepping on home plate. He pointed to heaven and then kissed his son Matt and hugged him twice before he was mobbed by his teammates.

One of those teammates was Tom Lampkin, who—until this home run— had a routine he followed with McGwire after home runs. Big Mac would come into the dugout, and Lampkin would wave him off with a mock-sarcastic "Whatever . . ." This time Lampkin dropped all pretense. He ran out onto the field and was embraced and lifted into the air by McGwire.

During the ten-minute-long celebration, Sammy Sosa came in from right field to the first base line and hugged McGwire. They then exchanged trademarks—Sammy playfully punched Mac in the stomach and McGwire tapped his chest, à la Sammy. The St. Louis crowd of 49,987 roared and roared their thanks for having been privy to the excitement the two men had generated.

McGwire then jogged to the field box near the Cards' dugout, stepped over the wall, and greeted each member of the Maris family. He hugged and embraced the four sons and two daughters of Roger Maris with his Popeye arms, whispering something personal to each of them.

When he returned to the field, he spoke over the loudspeaker. McGwire confided to the throng, "I told them today when I met with Hall of Fame [officials], they pulled out Roger's bat . . . and I touched it. I touched it with my heart."

MARK MCGWIRE (after the game): "The last week and a half my stomach has been turning, my heart has been beating a million miles a minute. I just give thanks to the man upstairs, to Roger Maris, Babe Ruth, and everybody watching up there."

NBC announcer Bob Costas was sitting with Commissioner Bud Selig and Stan Musial at Busch Stadium when McGwire hit number 62.

BOB COSTAS: "If what McGwire accomplished had been about home run hitting prowess alone, it would have been exciting, but nothing more. What made it truly moving and lastingly memorable was McGwire's genuine respect and appreciation for the fact that he is now forever linked with two men he never knew but whose presence he said he felt: Babe Ruth and Roger Maris.

"In a moment unblemished by any of the hype and contrivance that seems to be everywhere these days, McGwire connected the present to the past in a fashion so authentic and dramatic that it raises goosebumps to think of it even now."

Teammate Willie McGee was duly impressed that McGwire was able to sound so many perfect chords.

WILLIE McGEE: "This guy, it's amazing how he hit all those situations. He didn't leave a stone uncovered that day that I saw. He did not leave anything to question that I could see.

"Just like with us. He's been giving us things [signed baseballs and other souvenirs] as we go along. Unbelievable. I looked in my locker today, and there's something else there. Like I said, for him to be able to foresee that, to have that foresight, that's amazing . . .

"With all the distractions and all the concentration that's required, all the media, people don't understand what you go through to achieve it. For him to be able to keep his concentration, keep his focus, keep everybody around him happy, it's amazing, you know?

"It's amazing that one man can overshadow a whole league, can dominate to the point where nothing else matters. It's not Mark's fault. It's just the power of what he's doing, the magnitude of what he's doing."

The next day convivial and modest McGwire spoke to reporters about his race with Sammy Sosa. "Wouldn't it be great," he said, "if we just ended in a tie? I think that would be beautiful."

"Tied at what number?" he was asked.

"Seventy is a good one."

On September 11 Sammy hit number 59 against Milwaukee at Wrigley Field and the next day reached number 60 in a wild 15–12 win over Milwaukee as Sosa drove a Valerio De Los Santos pitch over the back fence and out of Wrigley Field.

On September 13 Sosa mystified the pundits who thought McGwire a lead-pipe cinch to win the home run title when he hit two home runs—his 61st and 62nd home runs—to help defeat the Brewers, 11–10, but also to retie McGwire for the all-time record lead. In the fifth, Sammy hit a 480-foot bomb off Bronswell Patrick over the left field wall and into the street. In the ninth he hit another huge blast off reliever Eric Plunk.

After hitting the second home run, Sosa sat in the dugout, overcome with emotion. Tears mixed with sweat rolled down his face. The unbelieving Cubs fans brought him out for three curtain calls. A six-minute delay followed as the fans chanted his name and threw a cloud of ripped paper onto the field.

McGwire regained the lead on September 15 when he pinch-hit in the ninth inning and homered against the Pirates for his 63rd. Sosa regained his share of the home run title the next day by hitting a game-winning grand slam against San Diego. When McGwire hit homers 64 on September 18 at Milwaukee and number 65 two days later, once again the big Cardinal looked to have the title sewn up, but Sosa, in a remarkable display, on September 23 hit homers 64 and 65 against the Brewers to regain his record share of the homer title.

What made the two home runs by the Cubs star all the more poignant was the effect they had on his homeland, the Dominican Republic, which had been savaged by the merciless Hurricane Georges two days earlier. One hundred and twenty miles an hour winds damaged 80 percent of the residences of

San Pedro de Macoris, Sosa's hometown. The city was virtually destroyed. Said shoeshine boy Papi de la Rosa, a local resident, "Sammy Sosa is our only hope. Sammy will help us. He always does when he comes home."

Across the island, more than 200 lives were lost, electricity was out, and most TV and radio stations were off the air. When the first reports came in that Sammy had once again tied McGwire with his 64th and 65th home runs, unbelieving countrymen accused the Dominican government of making up the story just to improve morale. But after one of the TV stations came back to life and showed clips of Sosa's home runs and the Dominicans finally accepted the story as factual, impromptu celebrations broke out amid the heartbreak and wreckage in the streets of the battered Caribbean country.

The Garague Hotel in Santo Domingo still was flooded and without elevators and electricity, but someone took the time and trouble to slip notes under every guest's door announcing the news. More than 1,000 people filled Mercedes Church in downtown Santo Domingo to say prayers for their hero.

"The nation has come to pray for the boy," said the Reverend Jose Arellano. "He helps us unite."

Sosa, who had despaired over the devastation to his country, told reporters, "I am at the side of all Dominicans, of my people, of my nation in these difficult times. Hopefully, these home runs will bring a little happiness."

Mark McGwire also was feeling the goodwill showered upon him by fans from all over the country. His father had praised him for showing America how a man and his ex-wife could amicably raise a child. Before he was done, McGwire correctly saw that his chase of the home run record was not about how many home runs they hit, but about the impact they were having on the country. Stacks of fan mail flooded in. Their admiration and goodwill was universal.

Dear Mark,

You are a real honest, good person who is responsible for the rebirth of baseball. I am eighty-six years old and have been watching the Cards, Browns, and Chicago Cubs for over seventy years as my favorite teams. But when the million-dollar prima donnas went on strike, I quit watching and going to the games. The league owners should put you on a pedestal. You made a fan out of thousands of people again. You have a love for the game and the fans. I wish we had people like you in Washington, D.C. God bless you and your family and bless Sammy also.

Throughout, Mark McGwire maintained his humility. He was genuinely touched that he was making so many people so happy.

MARK McGWIRE: "Whichever way the season ends, so be it. I'm pretty proud of what I've done. I think a tie would be fantastic, but if I'm ahead or if he's ahead, just look at what we've done. People have been saying for thirty-seven years that this couldn't be done, and yet two guys have done it. What I'll take away from this is the impact I've had on people's lives. It's amazing that a guy who swings a bat can affect the country.''

On Friday, September 26, the second-to-last game of the season, Sosa hit home run number 66 against Houston. The drive was measured at 462 feet and went into the third deck of the Astrodome. Though Mark McGwire had gotten so much of the publicity, here was Sammy Sosa in the lead with only two games remaining in the season.

McGwire, incredibly, tied Sosa forty-five minutes later in a game against the Expos. Teammate John Mabry couldn't believe it.

JOHN MABRY: "It's an amazing thing, to look up and see the flash that Sammy just hit 66, and then Mac hits one too. You wouldn't believe it unless you were here to see it. It's like one of those bad baseball movies that people make.''

On Saturday, September 26, McGwire hit home runs number 67 and 68 against Montreal in St. Louis. Said manager Tony La Russa, "The worst thing you can do is stop being amazed because you start taking it for granted.''

The next day, the final day of the season, Big Mac hit two more, including number 70 in his final at-bat. The three-run blast in the ninth inning off reliever Carl Pavano defeated the Expos, 6–3. As McGwire rounded the bases, each Expo infielder shook his hand.

"I amazed myself that I could stay in the tunnel this long," said McGwire. "It showed I can overcome almost anything with the strength of my mind." Though his words may have sounded bombastic and a tad braggadocious uttered by someone else, no one thought badly of McGwire for saying them. What he said was undeniable. You had to agree with him. To have hit 70 home runs in one season seemed, well, Ruthian.

His ego, on the other hand, is not. Despite his great wealth, McGwire owns one car. He wears one necklace. At home, he often watches the Learning Channel. He has turned down offers for a shoe contract, and he refuses to allow McDonald's to exploit his name. "I don't eat Big Macs," he says. He has said no to the national late-night talk shows and to book deals. His great wish is not to be treated differently because of his celebrity.

MARK MCGWIRE: "I am a normal person who plays sports. I really hope people allow me to be who I am. People have slowly changed around me, wanting to touch me, acting differently. I'm asking that they not look at us differently. Sammy and I go to the grocery story and take care of our children like everyone else.''

This will not be easy as his fame and legend grow. By the end of the 1999 season, McGwire had 522 home runs, only the 16th person to reach that magic number. Should he hit 200 more before he retires, he will stand third behind Hank Aaron (755) and Babe Ruth (714). He is the first to hit 50 home runs in four straight seasons. Of course, he could hit a lot more than 200 before he is through. Seemingly the slugger with the twenty-inch biceps could hit as many as he wants. As McGwire once said, "I'm a perfect example of the person who is normal that can conquer things if they dream and believe in themselves."

All hold him in awe.

DANTE BICHETTE: "He's the kid who, when he played Little League, all the parents called the president of the league and said, 'Get him out of there. I don't want him to hurt my son.' I had my mom call the National League office to see if she could do it for me."

To prove that the 1998 season was no fluke, McGwire in 1999 again struck over 60 home runs in a season. On September 9, he trailed Sammy Sosa by 59 homers to 54, but then Big Mac again demonstrated his superhuman talent, and after striking six home runs in his final seven games, he once again edged out Sosa, this time by 65 to 63. It was his fourth home run title. Over his last four seasons, McGwire has averaged 61 home runs a season!

His 522 home runs lifetime moved him past Ted Williams and Willie McCovey into tenth place, and his election at first base along with Lou Gehrig to the All-Century team has insured McGwire's immortality.

None of the accolades or adulation, however, seems to have changed him. Mark McGwire remains a role model for all who follow the game. Stated McGwire in a line that will always be the measure of the man, "I don't play the game for records. I play the game because I love it."

NOTES

Chapter 1

p. 4 Ben Franklin, who was born in 1760, died in 1790.

p. 5 "It was in the early fifties that Mr. Frain brought the game to St. Louis." *Judge Landis and Twenty-Five Years of Baseball* by J. G. Taylor Spink, page 38.

According to Cliff Kachline, who worked at *The Sporting News* at the time, this book was actually written by Fred Lieb, author of many great team histories. Spink paid Lieb to write it, but he put his own name on the book.

p. 5 In October the White Stockings beat the Empires again, this time by a score of 46–8. *Chicago Tribune,* April 30, May 2, 1870.

p. 6 Cuthbert, known as an innovator, was credited as the first player ever to slide into a base. *The National League* by Ed Fitzgerald, page 7; *Baseball in the Afternoon: Tales from a Bygone Era* by Robert Smith, page 57.

p. 7 The Red Stockings folded before the end of July after a 4-15 start. *Baseball Through the Knothole* by Bill Borst, page 6.

p. 7 . . . 2,000 sought a view from light poles, housetops, and trees. *St. Louis Democrat,* May 7, 1887.

p. 7 ". . . save the terrific 'poulticing' the Browns had administered to the Chicago Whites." *St. Louis Dispatch,* May 7, 1875.

p. 8 "A victim, she, of too much blow." *St. Louis Democrat,* May 8, 1875.

p. 9 . . . the St. Louis team withdrew from the National League. *Commy* by G. W. Alexson, pages 55–56.

For an account of the founding of St. Louis, see *Missouri Bittersweet* by MacKinlay Kantor, *Missouri: Faces and Places* by Wes Lyle and John Hall, and *Undaunted Courage* by Stephen Ambrose.

Chapter 2

p. 10 ". . . and he was only a kid at that." *Commy,* pages 40–41.

p. 10 Shaughnessy wrote down the $50 under "general expenses." Ibid., page 43.

p. 11 . . . the first minor league to complete a season without folding. Ibid., page 50.

p. 12 "The runner knows where he is going . . ." Ibid., page 48.

p. 13 "It was Eddie Cuthbert . . ." *St. Louis Globe-Democrat,* February 7, 1905.

p. 13 . . . where fans could sit and drink beer while watching the game. *The Beer and Whiskey League* by David Nemek, page 29.

p. 13 "I wish to see this beverage become common." *Beer, U.S.A.* by Will Anderson, page 6.

p. 13 Jefferson's beer was well known in Virginia. See *Brewed in America* by Stanley Baron.

p. 14 St. Louis breweries were second only to New York in beer sales. Ibid., page 14.

p. 15 "It has come to solve the liquor problem." Ibid., page 286.

p. 15 . . . Spalding made his players pledge not to drink.
He and his star outfielder, Mike Kelly, were constantly at odds over Kelly's love of liquor. See *Wrigleyville* by the author.

p. 15 Horace Phillips managed the Pittsburgh club of the American Association until July 1889, when he began having delusions that he was a wealthy tycoon. He tried buying different businesses, including several major league teams. On August 1, 1889, he was locked up at his wife's urging in an insane asylum near Merchantville, New Jersey. *The Beer and Whiskey League,* page 93.

p. 16 Each telegram said that the recipient had been the only one not to attend the initial meeting and requested he attend the next one. *The Beer and Whiskey League,* page 22.

p. 16 "Mr. Von der Ahe was proprietor of a pleasure resort . . ." *America's National Game* by A. G. Spalding, page 240.

p. 17 For a description of Von der Ahe's dress, demeanor, and visage, see *Baseball* by Robert Smith, pages 103–5.

p. 17 . . . he would personally parade the pile of coins and bills to a nearby bank. *Glory Fades Away* by Jerry Lansch, page 48.

p. 18 "Vy do they laugh at us?" *Baseball: An Informal History* by Douglas Wallop, page 67.

p. 18 ". . . pictures of the diamond's heroes in striking and catching attitudes." *St. Louis Critic,* April 11, 1885.

p. 18 He paid the fourteen players under contract a total of $32,000. *St. Louis Critic,* March 28, 1885.

For more on Von der Ahe, see also "Baseball's 'Boss President' Chris Von der Ahe and the Nineteenth Century St. Louis Browns" by Jim Rygenski, *Gateway Heritage,* Summer 1992, p. 42.

For a photo of Von der Ahe's saloon, see the *St. Louis Globe-Democrat,* August 3, 1958.

Chapter 3

p. 19 "First place is the only subject of conversation." *Commy,* page 80.

p. 19 "I have fought every point . . ." Ibid., page 316.

p. 19 ". . . as if hurled from a catapult." *The Sporting News,* May 24, 1886.

p. 19 "Von der Ahe's hoodlums." Ibid.

p. 20 "How'd do, Anse?" *Baseball* by Robert Smith, page 111.

p. 20 ". . . the disgusting mouthings of the clown Latham . . ." *Glory Fades Away,* page 79.

p. 20 ". . . will not be tolerated in Chicago."
Latham's bench jockeying was not only tolerated, but applauded by the St.

Louis press. That same day the reporter for the *St. Louis Post-Dispatch* wrote: "The only man on the Browns' side who failed to get a hit was Latham, but he more than made up for his weakness at the bat by his excellent coaching." *Glory Fades Away*, page 80.

p. 21 "The chalk lines . . ." *Judge Landis*, pages 74–75.

p. 22 "There was always good discipline . . ." *Commy*, pages 105–6.

p. 22 "He held himself responsible for the smallest detail . . ." Ibid., page 82.

p. 22 "He never went to sleep at night . . ." Ibid., page 103.

p. 23 "His marvelous memory . . ." Ibid., page 84.

p. 23 "A new opponent planted himself at the plate . . ." Ibid., pages 82–83.

p. 23 "Comiskey won pennants at St. Louis by his inventiveness . . ." *Touching Second* by John J. Evers and Hugh Fullerton, page 201.

p. 25 "[Dave Foutz is] tall, slim, good-natured . . ." *St. Louis Critic*, April 25, 1885.

p. 26 "I would not be on the level . . ." *Commy*, page 95.

Chapter 4

p. 29 "We will not even claim the forfeited game." *Glory Fades Away*, page 65.

p. 30 Spalding refused to ignore the forfeit. *The Beer and Whiskey League*, page 81.

p. 30 . . . cheating his players out of the $1,000 prize money. *Glory Fades Away*, page 66.

Chapter 5

p. 31 "He had heard their story that they were being abused . . ." *The National Game*, page 36.

p. 31 "an outrageous and unjustifiable claim on the freedom of players." Ibid., page 242.

p. 31 "There is a class of ball players . . ." *St. Louis Critic*, February 21, 1885.

p. 32 ". . . to get a good whack at a free lunch." *St. Louis Critic*, February 21, 1885.

p. 33 Reenactment of the siege of Vicksburg. *The Sporting News*, July 5, 1886.

p. 33 . . . disproving "the cranks harping that baseball is dying out." *The Sporting News*, July 12, 1886.

p. 33 For the fight between Sweeney and Dolan, see *The Sporting News*, May 10, 1886.

p. 34 Sweeney died of tuberculosis on April 4, 1902. *Glory Fades Away*, page 35.

p. 34 "On Monday, Henry V. Lucas, president of the St. Louis team . . ." *The Sporting News*, August 16, 1886.

p. 34 John T. Brush, an Indianapolis merchant. Brush would eventually own the New York Giants, managed by John McGraw.

p. 34 "Baseball was the rock on which Lucas's fortunes were wrecked." *St. Louis Post-Democrat*, November 16, 1910.

Chapter 6

p. 35 . . . the brainchild of Al Spink.

Within months of starting *The Sporting News,* Alfred saw he needed someone with business acumen to run the financial side of the paper, and he talked his brother Charles into coming onboard as business manager.

Recalled Al Spink, "The paper was having a hard row to hoe and made little headway until he took hold of its business management. From that day it prospered." From information provided by *The Sporting News.*

p. 39 "Bobby's got the heart disease bad." *Glory Fades Away* by Jerry Lansche, page 77.

p. 40 ". . . why it wasn't done I don't know." Ibid., page 82.

p. 41 "The White Stockings, with the exception of Cap Anson, seemed strangely undisturbed by their loss . . ." Ibid., page 84.

p. 41 Ned Williamson had pitched twice in relief during the regular season.

p. 41 "Admitting that base ball is a business conducted for pecuniary profit . . ." Ibid., page 87.

p. 41 ". . . on a warm, cloudy day before a grandstand full of men in high-crowned derbies . . ." *Baseball in the Afternoon* by Robert Smith, page 96.

p. 42 "Arlie was oddly silent . . ." Ibid., page 96.

p. 42 "He's got a flat bat." *Baseball* by Robert Smith, page 99.

p. 42 "Ten men . . ." Ibid.

p. 43 "Arlie did not miss this move." Ibid., page 100.

p. 43 "[Clarkson] took his stance again and, as he did . . ." *Baseball in the Afternoon,* pages 96–101.

p. 45 "We were beaten, and fairly beaten . . ." *A Ballplayer's Career* by Adrian Anson, 1900, page 137.

p. 45 ". . . he was the Boss Manager . . ." *Baseball,* page 103.

See also *The Baseball Story* by Fred Lieb.

Chapter 7

p. 46 "O, Jim O'Neill is a slugger bold . . ." *St. Louis Critic,* May 23, 1885.

p. 47 "I shall order my men on the field . . ." *St. Louis Globe-Democrat,* July 10, 1887.

p. 47 A close friend spoke on his behalf . . . Ibid., July 16, 1887.

p. 48 "The Browns stay awake all night gambling and fighting and . . ." *Glory Fades Away,* page 111.

p. 49 "Individually the team is playing strong ball . . ." Ibid., pages 109–10.

p. 49 "That was no game we played today . . ." Ibid., page 111.

p. 50 "Von der Ahe had built a row of apartment houses . . ." *Commy,* page 63.

p. 50 "Very few people know that the sale of Welch . . ." *The Beer and Whiskey League,* page 103.

p. 51 According to Jerry Lansche, who researched ambidextrous pitchers before the turn of the century, Tony Mullane also pitched lefty and righty in one game. But for the life of him, he cannot remember the name of the third pitcher to perform that feat in a nineteenth-century ball game. The player, he said, was not a standout like Chamberlain and Mullane.

Chapter 8

p. 51 "You can spend $50,000 on players . . ." *The Beer and Whiskey League,* page 113.

p. 54 "an affront to the community." Wallop, page 93.

p. 54 When Von der Ahe demanded $125,000, the deal fell through. *Where They Ain't* by Burt Solomon, page 128.

p. 55 On the train, the men revealed themselves as detectives hired by Nimick. *Baseball,* Smith, pages 106–7.

p. 55 "Von der Ahe was thrown into an Allegheny County jail . . ." Wallop, page 93.

p. 56 THE MAN WHO PUT ST. LOUIS ON THE MAP. *Judge Landis,* page 212.

Chapter 9

p. 57 Theodore P. Wagner's description of the first game of the new Browns. *St. Louis Post-Dispatch,* April 25, 1954

Though Wagner places the events during 1903, two of the players he mentions, Harry Niles and Jay "Nig" Clarke, didn't enter the league until 1906 and 1905.

p. 58 "I played six weeks in the summer of 1901 . . ." *The Glory of Their Times,* pages 39–40.

p. 59 Crawford jumped from Cincinnati in 1902 to Detroit in 1903; Lajoie from Philadelphia (N) to Philadelphia (A); Griffith from Cincinnati (N) to Chicago (A); Keeler from Brooklyn (N) in 1902 to New York (A) in 1903; Young from St. Louis (N) in 1900 to Boston in 1901; Chesbro from Pittsburgh (N) in 1902 to New York (A) in 1903; and Delahanty from Philadelphia (N) in 1901 to Washington (A) in 1902.

p. 60 "When I was with the Highlanders . . ." Ibid., pages 80–81.

p. 61 rookie third baseman John "Red" Corriden.

Corriden played four more years in the majors with Detroit and the Chicago White Sox, then became a coach with the Cubs (1932–40), the Dodgers (1941–46), and the Yankees 1947–48. In 1950 he was named the manager of the White Sox after Jack Onslow was fired.

p. 62 "I got the rap for the Lajoie affair . . ." *The Sporting News,* February 23, 1933.

p. 62 "I'll never forget my conference with Johnson . . ." Ibid.

p. 63 O'Connor sued the Browns for $5,000, the amount of the contract, and received judgment.

p. 63 "When I went to St. Louis . . ." *The Glory of Their Times,* pages 76–78.

p. 64 ". . . was at the University of Michigan as a teacher or a baseball coach . . ." *The American Diamond,* page 14.

p. 67 There was no fanfare and no official announcement . . . *American in Action* by Arthur Mann, page 66.

p. 67 "Let's get right, once and for all . . ." Ibid., pages 68–70.

p. 68 "Poor nothing . . ." Ibid., pages 71–72.

Chapter 10

p. 69 "I didn't wish to make it known at the time . . ." Mann.

p. 70 Rickey predicted that Huggins would copy his theories before he left St. Louis. Ibid., pages 75–76.

p. 70 "After a prolonged struggle . . ." Ibid., page 76.

p. 71 "Manager Branch Rickey's team is arousing the interest of the country . . ." *St. Louis Post-Dispatch,* June 9, 1914.

p. 71 "For who is going to trust you . . ." Mann, page 82.

p. 73 "Within a week after he came to the majors . . ." *The American Diamond,* page 16.

p. 73 "It all began back in the season of 1915 . . ." *Bill Stern's Favorite Baseball Stories,* pages 52–53.

p. 73 "He showed such promise of greatness as a hitter . . ." *The American Diamond,* page 16.

p. 75 "Roscoe Hillenkoelter brought Ball in . . ." Mann, page 84.

p. 75 "Many wanted the club . . ." Ibid., page 87.

p. 76 "Get it. I'll help you with the contract." Ibid., page 88.

p. 76 "He had made rough language a part of his gruff nature . . ." Ibid., pages 88–89.

p. 77 "I'll never work another day for you." Ibid, page 89.

p. 77 "I wish I had gone out of baseball at that moment." Ibid.

Chapter 11

p. 81 He had once been swindled out of $1 million by a corrupt broker. *Where They Ain't* by Burt Solomon, pages 192–93.

p. 81 McGraw and Robinson hated their year in St. Louis. Ibid., page 200.

p. 82 When he looked at the slips of paper, all had the same name on them: Branch Rickey. Lieb, page 60.

p. 83 "Unfortunately, the men who bought the shares knew . . ." Mann, page 92.

p. 83 Rickey would take the Knothole Gang concept with him to Brooklyn, where another generation of boys would become dedicated Dodger fans.

p. 84 What was the use of scouting under those circumstances? *The Sporting News,* January 24, 1935.

p. 85 "You do have a player I like." Mann.

p. 87 "I'll never forget those moments on the bench . . ." *The Gashouse Gang.*

p. 87 "They're yours for Hornsby . . ." Mann, page 102.

p. 87 "I said to myself that I could find other Hornsbys . . ." *The Gashouse Gang,* page 15.

p. 87 Mueller said he could run "like Ty Cobb . . ." Mann, page 105.

p. 87 "Blades's speed could be built on . . ." Ibid., pages 106–7.

p. 89 "I might want to see him in an automobile some day . . ." *The Fordham Flash.*

p. 90 Lambert thought the automobile business was "terrible." Bob Hood interview with Bill DeWitt, Sr., for his book *The Gashouse Gang,* published by William Morrow and Co., 1975. All interviews by Hood were conducted at this time.

p. 90 He sold the real estate to the Board of Education for $200,000. Today Beaumont High School stands on that spot.

p. 90 "Without [that money], we never could have made our early purchases . . ." Lieb, page 78.

p. 90 Blake Harper.

Later Harper would work for the Cards. He was their concessionaire, called "the Harry M. Stevens of the Mississippi." Lieb, page 83.

p. 91 "They got drunk together one night." Bill DeWitt, interviewed by Bob Hood.

p. 91 Charles "Chick" Hafey.

In 1923 Rickey brought the Cards to Bradenton, Florida. Rickey watched Hafey hit long drives during batting practice, and on the spot, against Hafey's protests, determined that he should become an outfielder.

BRANCH RICKEY: "We'll send you to Fort Smith, son. You'll strike out there, many times, and you'll be ashamed. But you have a God-given grace and quality in your swing that causes hitting power. You can run like a deer and throw as well as anyone in camp. A pitcher works once every four days. As an outfielder, you'll play every day and you'll play well, I'm sure." *American in Action*, page 121.

Hafey was the batting champion in the National League in 1931 in his last year with St. Louis. He hit .349. He was traded to Cincinnati, where he finished his career in 1937. Hafey was elected to the Hall of Fame in 1971.

p. 92 "I'm a married man with a family." *Times at Bat* by Arthur Daley, pages 72–73.

p. 93 "Hornsby was the greatest right-handed hitter that ever lived . . ." *The October Heroes*, page 90.

p. 93 "I'll never forget my first big league game. . . ." *The October Heroes*, pages 87–89.

p. 95 "What chance have we ever to win a pennant in St. Louis?" Lieb, page 96.

The Browns were helped that year by the suspension of Babe Ruth and Bob Meusel by Commissioner Landis for barnstorming after the 1921 World Series. Both were suspended the first part of the 1922 season and didn't return until May 30.

p. 95 The three-year overall profit was $374,000. *American in Action*, page 113.

Chapter 12

p. 96 "Rickey's players could not understand his ideas . . ." *The Gashouse Gang*, page 234.

p. 96 Hornsby lies about Rickey . . .

The Rajah was nothing if not consistent. When in 1953 Hornsby got into a similar public pissing match with Bill Veeck, Hornsby went to the papers and made up a nasty story about Veeck.

p. 97 "I have just read of Hornsby's statement . . ." Mann, pages 123–24.

p. 97 "Rogers Hornsby will not be sold or traded." Lieb, page 100.

p. 97 "That isn't right."

Hornsby lost the MVP by three votes. Each writer voted for the top ten selections, with ten points for first, nine for second, etc. When Sam Breadon poled the writers, he discovered that Jack Ryder of the *Cincinnati Enquirer* had left Hornsby off his ballot entirely. Ryder, who must have hated the Cards slugger, lamely explained: "Hornsby was valuable to himself, but not to the team. His .424 average had failed to lift the Cards above sixth place." Ted Williams, who had a bitter feud with several sportswriters in Boston, would lose an MVP title the same way in 1946.

p. 98 ". . . the only way I would be interested in becoming manager . . ."

Breadon was lucky because when Rickey was dropped as manager, he told the owner, "If I can't be manager of the club, I don't want to own any stock." Lieb, page 107.

Rickey later admitted he had acted hastily when he sold his stock.

p. 99 "He's got to go, Branch." Mann, page 143.

p. 100 "In 1926 we went to spring training . . ." Honig, pages 91–92.

p. 100 Rickey claimed Alexander at Hornsby's request.

In another version, Breadon says he claimed Alexander on waivers after he couldn't get a hold of either Rickey or Hornsby. Lieb, page 111.

It is more likely that Hornsby instigated the deal. Owners taking credit for important deals that turn out well has long been a baseball tradition. Walter O'Malley once boasted it was he who brought Jackie Robinson to the majors, breaking the color line, not Rickey.

p. 101 "Sometimes a fit would strike him while he was out on the mound . . ." "The Ups and Downs of Old Pete" by Jack Sher, *Sport,* April 1950, as reprinted in *The Baseball Chronicles,* edited by David Gallen, page 143.

p. 101 "Sometimes he'd have one of those spells . . ." *Two Spectacular Seasons* by Bill Mead.

p. 102 "Alex always thought he could pitch better with a hangover . . ." Gallen, page 143.

p. 102 "In June of 1926, Joe McCarthy, manager of the Chicago Cubs . . ." *My War with Baseball* by Rogers Hornsby, page 150.

p. 103 "I was a rookie on the Cardinals . . ." Honig.

p. 103 "I never saw a machine like him . . ." Hood, page 181.

p. 104 "[Alexander] liked to go out before a game . . ." Honig, pages 185–86.

p. 104 "I knew Alex liked his highballs . . ." *My War with Baseball,* pages 151–53.

p. 104 "He was the greatest man with the bat I ever faced . . ." *The Sporting News,* January 28, 1937.

p. 105 "You know, I sure like that young fellow . . ." *The Baseball Chronicles,* page 146.

p. 105 "I've heard a lot of ballplayers say he was a tough man to play for . . ." Honig, pages 90–91.

p. 105 "I ran into front-office bossing the second year I was manager . . ." *My War with Baseball,* pages 106–7.

p. 106 ". . . that certainly didn't help relations."

p. 106 "I came to the decision . . ." Lieb, page 127.

According to Frankie Frisch, "[Hornsby] suggested that Breadon make an utterly impossible disposition of all such contests." *The Fordham Flash,* page 70.

Translated, Hornsby told Breadon to shove his exhibition games up his ass.
p. 106 "We finished up in the East . . ." *The October Heroes,* pages 91–92.
p. 107 "We came to the Polo Grounds on September 24, needing just one more victory . . ." *My Greatest Day in Baseball* by John Carmichael, page 182.
p. 107 "Hornsby poured acid on us . . ." Ibid., pages 182-83.
p. 108 ". . . there was no score showing up for Cincinnati . . ." *The October Heroes,* pages 91–92.
Interview with Gene Karst.

Chapter 13
p. 108 "They've got a good ballclub . . ." Lieb, page 119.
Quotes from Les Bell come from *The October Heroes* by Donald Honig. Quotes from Grover Alexander and Aimee Alexander come from *The Baseball Chronicles,* edited by David Gallen, and from *My Greatest Day in Baseball* by John Carmichael. Quotes from Bob O'Farrell come from *The Glory of Their Times.* Quotes from Rogers Hornsby come from *My War with Baseball* by Hornsby.
p. 111 "If we don't do it today . . ." Lieb, page 123.
p. 114 "They said Alex was drunk . . ." Hood, page 181.
p. 117 "Gene, you can't possibly realize what this means to me . . ." Lieb, page 145.
Also see *The Sporting News* of January 28, 1937. John Carmichael interview with Alexander reprinted from the *Chicago Daily News.*

Chapter 14
p. 118 "If you two can work something out, I can handle him." Branch Rickey, page 147.
p. 119 "You can have him for Frisch and [pitcher Jimmy] Ring." Lieb, page 127.
p. 119 "Had I been in sole charge." Ibid.
p. 119 [The amount was reported to be $118,000.] Ibid., page 107.
p. 120 "Even though I had managed the Cardinals . . ." *My War with Baseball,* pages 157–58 and 45–46.
p. 121 "That winter the Cardinals up and traded . . ." *The Glory of Their Times,* pages 235–38.
p. 121 "Hornsby used to bet on the horses a lot . . ." *Even the Browns,* pages 57–58.

Chapter 15
p. 122 Frisch's record of 48 steals in a season for the Cardinals was far surpassed by Lou Brock and Vince Coleman, who each stole more than 100 bases in a season, but Frisch stole more bases than any other player during the years 1919 to 1960, before Maury Wills, Brock, Coleman, and Rickey Henderson changed the way speedsters stole bases. Frisch averaged 27 stolen bases a season. He was the fifth-best hitter during the 1920s, hitting at a .331 average from 1921 through 1930. And he rarely struck out—only 272 Ks in 9,112 at-bats!

p. 122 "cement head." *The Fordham Flash,* page 50.

p. 123 "I know what you can do . . ." *The Fordham Flash,* page 62.

p. 123 "Spring training with the Cardinals at Avon Park . . ." Ibid., page 61.

p. 123 "I knew after that year . . ." Lieb, page 131.

p. 125 "They were passing drinks to Alex so fast . . ." Lieb, page 132.

p. 125 "Tommy was a master . . ." *The Fordham Flash,* page 63.

p. 126 "He has brains and knows what it's all about." Lieb, page 133.

p. 127 "Billy Southworth had been one of the gang only two springs before . . ." *The Gashouse Gang* by Roy Stockton.

p. 128 On the gold band it said: ST. LOUIS CARDINALS, WORLD CHAMPIONS, 1926. *The Baseball Chronicles,* page 136.

Chapter 16

p. 129 As you can see, the issue of big market teams versus small market teams, the disparity which commentators say threatens the very sport itself today, has been with us for many, many years. Branch Rickey was smart enough to get around the rules that seemed to favor the big market teams in the 1920s. Today there seems to be no way a small market team can possibly compete with a team like the Yankees, the Dodgers, or the Braves.

p. 129 "From the start, the commissioner regarded [Rickey] as . . ." *Judge Landis and Twenty-Five Years of Baseball,* page 192.

p. 129 "chain gang." *Branch Rickey,* page 155.

p. 132 "That relieves God of a tremendous responsibility." *Branch Rickey,* pages 167–68.

Chapter 17

p. 134 "Dizzy went as far as the third grade in school . . ." Interview with Gene Karst.

p. 134 "Just get me to Houston . . ." *Branch Rickey,* page 161.

p. 135 "Don't you know who I am?" Ibid.

p. 135 "As long as we heard the clink of the coal . . ." Ibid., page 162.

p. 135 "That's be a pretty fur piece . . ." Ibid., page 163.

p. 135 "All I got was a lecture on sex . . ." Ibid.

p. 136 "I was in Florida with Rickey . . ." Interview with Gene Karst.

p. 136 "It's the first time a ballclub's ever lost 30 games in one day." Stockton, page 43.

p. 138 "I just can't help doin' favors for people . . ." Stockton, page 34.

Chapter 18

p. 139 "All right, Sammy. You get your wish . . ." Stockton.

p. 139 "Frisch was a high-ball hitter right-handed . . ." Interview with Bob Broeg.

p. 140 "You didn't smile . . ." *The Fordham Flash,* page 107.

p. 140 "Frisch was the best money player . . ." Hallahan, interviewed by Bob Hood.

p. 140 "Nobody was up there digging in against me . . ." Hood, page 168.

p. 141 "The tougher the going . . ." Ibid., page 173.

p. 141 "If I was a manager . . ." Hallahan, interviewed by Bob Hood.

p. 141 "Ray Blades and I and another player . . ." Ibid.

p. 142 "Meanwhile, I was still in considerable pain . . ." *The October Heroes,*
pages 187–89.

p. 143 "In the 1930 World Series . . ." Hallahan, interviewed by Bob Hood.

p. 143 "Oh, Connie Mack had sweet teams . . ." *Man in the Dugout,* pages
46–47.

p. 144 "There's no question in my mind . . ." *The Fordham Flash,* page 117.

p. 144 "I've seen a lot of great ballclubs . . ." Lieb, page 148.

p. 145 "I want to get into the game . . ." Ibid., page 150.

p. 145 "Pepper was a mess . . ." Interview with Bob Broeg.

p. 146 "We got hunk with the A's . . ." *Man in the Dugout,* pages 47–48.

p. 146 "I'm not a dignified man myself . . ." *My Greatest Day in Baseball,*
pages 142–46.

p. 148 ". . . my sombrero mightn't a fit me after all the luck I had." Ibid.,
pages 153–56.

p. 149 "The National League hadn't beaten the Americans . . ." Branch
Rickey, pages 169–70.

Chapter 19

p. 151 "On an Eastern trip . . ." *The Fordham Flash,* page 163.

p. 152 "I always ranked DeLancey . . ." Interview with Bob Broeg.

p. 152 "I had no power to enforce . . ." Interview with Gene Karst.

p. 155 "Gelbert would have been a Hall of Famer sure shot . . ." *The Fordham Flash,* page 113.

p. 155 "Will you deny this man the right to earn a living as a baseball
player?" *Branch Rickey,* page 176.

p. 155 ". . . they were murder." Tex Carleton, interviewed by Bob Hood.

p. 156 ". . . the air was blue . . ." *Who's Who in Professional Baseball,*
edited by Gene Karst, page 240.

p. 156 "You said a lot of things about me . . ." *Nice Guys Finish Last* by
Leo Durocher and Ed Linn, page 79.

p. 157 "Three days after a session with Mr. Rickey . . ." Ibid.

p. 158 "When he came to St. Louis . . ." *Bums* by Peter Golenbock, pages
37–38.

p. 159 "I was allergic to the sun . . ." Carleton, interviewed by Bob Hood.

p. 159 "He recommended three highballs before dinner . . ." Ibid.

p. 160 "You sat in the station . . ." Ibid.

p. 160 "After riding two buses and a streetcar . . ." Medwick, interviewed
by Bob Hood.

p. 161 "I could have come up my first year . . ." Ibid.

p. 163 "I can manage better than he can." *Branch Rickey,* page 180.

p. 163 "The baseball writers soured Gabby on the ballclub . . ." *The Fordham
Flash,* pages 145–146.

p. 165 "I'm through, Branch. I'm pushed." *Branch Rickey,* page 181.

p. 165 "I said, 'Mr. Breadon . . .' " *The Fordham Flash,* pages 166, 167.

Chapter 20
Interview with Gene Karst.

Chapter 21
p. 167 "cheap coolie labor" Dan Daniel in the *New York World-Telegram* of September 13, 1934.

p. 169 "Rickey and his business associate in St. Louis . . ." *The Fordham Flash,* pages 201–2.

p. 169 "Frankie was a New Yorker . . ." Tex Carleton, interviewed by Bob Hood for his book *The Gashouse Gang,* published by William Morrow and Co., 1975.

p. 169 "Carleton was offended by the behavior and big mouth of Dizzy Dean."
Carleton would demand and receive a trade at the end of the 1934 season to get away from Dean. He was sent to the Cubs.

p. 170 "I like Brooklyn . . ." *The Gashouse Gang* by Roy Stockton, pages 35–36.

p. 170 "We're gonna win between us 40 or 45 games . . ." Martin Haley, *St. Louis Globe-Democrat,* March 12, 1934.

p. 170 Sid Keener of the *St. Louis Star-Times* predicted that "Paul will be another Walter Johnson." March 17, 1934.

p. 170 "We used basically single signs . . ." *Baseball Is a Funny Game,* pages 80–81.

p. 171 ". . . they can go home." *St. Louis Post-Dispatch,* May 26, 1934.

p. 171 ". . . if you don't want to pitch, go home." *St. Louis Star-Times,* June 1, 1934.

p. 172 "Diz would just stand there nodding his head . . ." *Nice Guys Finish Last,* pages 85–86.

p. 172 "There were times when members of the Gashouse Gang . . ." *The Gashouse Gang* by Roy Stockton, pages 85–86.

p. 173 "There is reason to suspect . . ." *New York Post,* June 4, 1934.

p. 173 "The outcome seems to indicate . . ." *New York World-Telegram,* June 4, 1934.

p. 174 "Dizzy Gunga Din (If Mr. Kipling Doesn't Mind)" by Grantland Rice. *New York Sun,* July 20, 1934.

p. 175 "Florida," said Diz. *St. Louis Globe-Democrat,* August 14, 1934.

p. 176 "I'll leave it to you and the sports fans . . ." A letter published in the *St. Louis Post-Dispatch* on August 17, 1934.

p. 176 "Dizzy has been a source of worry . . ." *St. Louis Globe-Democrat,* August 18, 1934.

p. 177 "I'm not saying we are always right . . ." *St. Louis Star-Times,* August 20, 1934.

p. 177 "Hardly taking care of me an' Paul . . ." Ibid., August 22, 1934.

p. 178 "Writing about Dizzy Dean is what keeps the papers from going out of business." *Brooklyn Times-Union,* September 7, 1934.

p. 179 "The owners blame it on the town . . ." *New York Daily Mirror,* Sept. 18, 1934.

p. 179 "The day Paul pitched the no-hitter in Brooklyn . . ." Jim Mooney, interviewed by Bob Hood.

p. 180 "I sure was having a picnic with Frisch . . ." *The Gashouse Gang* by Roy Stockton, page 47.

p. 180 "Diz didn't pitch but one way . . ." Carleton, interviewed by Bob Hood.

p. 180 "Then we went out on the field . . ." Jim Mooney, interviewed by Bob Hood.

p. 181 "My curve was breaking good . . ." *St. Louis Post-Dispatch,* September 21, 1934.

Chapter 22

p. 182 "Tell that to Bill Terry." *New York Herald Tribune,* February 24, 1934.

p. 182 "We're going into the ninth inning, leading . . ." Jack Rothrock, interviewed by Bob Hood in 1974 for his book *The Gashouse Gang,* published by William Morrow and Co., 1975.

p. 182 " 'We're in the mon-ey . . .' " *St. Louis Post-Dispatch,* October 1, 1934.

p. 183 "Sit down . . ." Ibid., October 2, 1934.

p. 184 "Take the ballclub we had . . ." Jim Mooney, interviewed by Bob Hood.

Chapter 23

p. 188 "I don't want people to think I'm a big windbag . . ." *The Gashouse Gang* by Roy Stockton, page 26.

p. 189 "Frisch is sayin' that he don't know who's goin' to pitch that first game . . ." Ibid., page 55.

p. 189 "Hello, Mose . . ." Ibid., pages 64–65.

Said Leo Durocher, "The 'Mo' was just what you think it is, the casual anti-Semitism of the locker room. That was part of the era of the farmboy, too. What did it mean? Well, it meant what it meant . . . Outrageous, but never vicious." *Nice Guys Finish Last,* page 100.

p. 189 "He's guarding me." *The New York Times,* October 7, 1934.

p. 189 "It's my 'pennant trophy' . . ." *St. Louis Star-Times,* October 4, 1934.

p. 189 "Dizzy Dean talked Frisch into letting him go . . ." France Laux, interviewed by Bob Hood.

The quiet, low-key France Laux was "the Voice of the Cardinals and Browns" on KMOX for eighteen years between 1929 and 1946.

According to Leo Durocher, Dean had inserted himself into situations like that all season long without consulting Frisch. The first time he did it, Frisch asked Durocher, "Who sent him in?" Leo answered, "What difference does it make, Frank?" *Nice Guys Finish Last,* page 101.

It didn't, until Dean was beaned in Game 5 of the '34 Series.

p. 190 "The speeding ball . . . struck Dizzy Dean . . ." *New York Sun,* October 7, 1934.

p. 190 "Fortunately, Dizzy wasn't hurt badly . . ." *The Fordham Flash,* pages 173–74.

p. 190 "The Dean boys came through in storybook fashion . . ." Ibid., page 174.

p. 191 "We went back to Detroit to finish up." France Laux, interviewed by Bob Hood.

p. 192 "We had to come out through the Detroit dugout . . ." *Nice Guys Finish Last,* pages 104–5.

p. 192 "Don't think I don't still get a kick out of that last World Series game of mine." *The Fordham Flash,* page 175.

p. 192 " 'Frank,' Diz says, 'Do you think Hubbell is a better pitcher than me?" *The Fordham Flash,* page 108.

p. 193 "Eleven–nothing I got 'em . . ." *My Greatest Day in Baseball,* pages 7–8.

p. 193 "There was no mistaking Medwick's ideas . . ." New York *Daily News,* October 10, 1934.

p. 194 "It was really dangerous out there . . ." France Laux, interviewed by Bob Hood.

p. 194 "That goddamn Commissioner Landis . . ." Joe Medwick, interviewed by Bob Hood.

p. 194 "We're in the clubhouse, see, celebratin' . . ." *My Greatest Day in Baseball,* page 7.

p. 194 "I never knew a city to take a World Series defeat so bitterly . . ." *The Fordham Flash,* pages 176–77.

Chapter 24

p. 195 "The next afternoon we played before a large crowd . . ." *The Fordham Flash,* page 75.

p. 196 "You never knew what would happen . . ." Joe Medwick, interviewed by Bob Hood.

p. 196 "We're here to do it in aluminum . . ." *Nice Guys Finish Last,* page 92.

p. 196 "A Boy Scout meeting was in progress . . ." Ibid., page 92.

p. 197 "When I joined the team in '36 . . ." Interview with Don Gutteridge.

Chapter 25

p. 203 "Terry was absolutely great . . ." Interview with Don Gutteridge.

p. 204 "The first big blow . . ." *The Fordham Flash,* pages 207–8.

p. 205 By 1935 Dizzy Dean had become such a celebrity that his income outside baseball that year was $32,315. *The Gashouse Gang* by Roy Stockton, page 64.

p. 206 "I am lopsided on one shoulder from that wheel . . ." *The Gashouse Gang* by Roy Stockton, pages 66–67.

p. 207 "I was in a hell of a spot . . ." *My Greatest Day in Baseball,* pages 12–13.

p. 207 "I was at the game when Dizzy hurt his arm . . ." Interview with Don Gutteridge.

p. 208 "After the All-Star Game in '37 . . ." Jesse Haines, interviewed by Bob Hood.

p. 208 "It was my judgment that Dizzy ought to wait . . ." *The Fordham Flash,* pages 201 and 209.

p. 209 "I loved playing with Dizzy . . ." Interview with Don Gutteridge.

p. 209 "We don't want you players to feel we're letting you down . . ." *My Greatest Day in Baseball,* page 10.

p. 209 "Hell, I knew they couldn't win any ole pennant without Dizzy . . ." Ibid.

p. 210 "Leo and Frisch battled all the time . . ." Interview with Don Gutteridge.

p. 210 "I was traded because Frisch demanded that Rickey get rid of me . . ." *Nice Guys Finish Last,* page 114.

p. 210 "Frisch treated me very well . . ." Interview with Don Gutteridge.

p. 210 "During the latter part of the season, all of us were thinking . . ." Ibid.

Chapter 26

p. 212 "This was 1933 . . ." Interview with Don Gutteridge.

p. 213 "This was one of the best things . . ." *Branch Rickey,* pages 171–72.

p. 214 "We always had good ballclubs in St. Louis. . . ." *Baseball When the Grass Was Real.*

p. 214 "I'll tell you what the talk used . . ." Ibid., pages 105–6.

p. 215 "religious hypocrite . . ." *Judge Landis and Twenty-Five Years of Baseball,* page 292.

p. 215 "He always seemed to think that Rickey . . ." Ibid., page 232.

p. 215 "Was I being used as a stool pigeon . . ." *The Fordham Flash,* page 100.

p. 215 "Landis had Leslie O'Connor work on the Cedar Rapids case . . ." *Judge Landis.*

p. 216 ". . . if he knows the facts." Ibid., page 237.

p. 217 "The old guy has got a dictator complex . . ." Ibid., page 272.

p. 217 "They were not permitted to present their side of the case." *Branch Rickey* by Murray Polner, page 114.

To the day he died, Rickey swore there was nothing illegal about his arrangement with the Cedar Rapids club.

Though Rickey maintained his farm system even after Landis sanctioned him, the same was not true of the Detroit Tigers, who also were sanctioned by Landis. Tiger GM Jack Zeller, rather than fight Landis, sold all his farm teams. As a result, the Tigers were mediocre or worse for the next twenty years.

Chapter 27

p. 218 Slaughter's rabbit fever. *St. Louis Post-Dispatch,* September 8, 1949.

p. 224 "I was managing in the Southern League . . ." Bennie Borgmann, interviewed by Bob Hood.

Interviews with Enos Slaughter, Don Gutteridge, and Marty Marion.

Chapter 28

Interview with Max Lanier.

Chapter 29

p. 233 "Musial is the kindest, most modest famous person I have ever met."

Richard Petty, the winningest driver in NASCAR history, is the only other sports legend in Stan's class.

p. 237 "Moore called over to Mize, 'Hey, John . . .' " *Stan Musial* by Jerry Lansche, pages 26–27.

p. 237 "That kid is born to play baseball." Ibid., page 26.

p. 239 "I'm tearing it up, boy." Stan Musial, as told to Bob Broeg, page 55.

Interview with Stan Musial.

Chapter 30
Interviews with Marty Marion, Stan Musial, and Max Lanier.

Chapter 31
p. 247 Rickey's sales in the summer of 1940. *The Gashouse Gang* by Roy Stockton, page 172.
p. 247 "Breadon, a stickler for the rules . . ." Ibid., pages 231–32.
p. 248 "Sam, I will dig ditches . . ." *Branch Rickey* by Murray Polner, page 116.
Interviews with Max Lanier, Marty Marion, and Bob Broeg.

Chapter 32
p. 263 "The way you're playing, you ought to be sitting behind a post." *They Also Served,* page 153.
p. 264 "Ted Wilks's temperament . . ." *Baseball Is a Funny Game,* pages 90–91.
Interviews with Marty Marion, Stan Musial, Danny Litwhiler, and Max Lanier.

Chapter 33
p. 267 "So you want to quit?" *The Baltimore Orioles* by Fred Lieb, page 191.
p. 267 "Are you crazy, Sam?" Ibid.
p. 267 "I was a poor boy . . ." Ibid., pages 191–92.
p. 269 "One morning, when Ball happened to be in the neighborhood . . ." *Bill Stern's Favorite Baseball Stories,* pages 8–10.
p. 270 "Hornsby used to bet the horses a lot." *Even the Browns,* pages 87–88.
p. 273 The record of 12 RBIs in a game, set on September 16, 1924, by Jim Bottomley, was tied by the Cards' Mark Whiten on September 7, 1993. Whiten hit 4 home runs that day. Tony Lazzeri holds the American League record with 11.
p. 273 ". . . and one other." Mr. Giuliani could not remember the name of the fourth player.
Interview with Tony Giuliani.

Chapter 34
p. 274 Briggs hated Auker's underhanded delivery.
Auker was the only pitcher at the time in the major leagues to throw underhand. In the late 1940s, Russ Christopher of Cleveland threw underhand. In the 1950s, Ted Abernathy and Dick Hyde of the Washington Senators threw with an underhand motion, and in the 1970s, Kansas City's Dan Quisenberry and Pittsburgh's Kent Tekulve threw with that motion. The last submariner was Jeff Innis, who pitched with the Mets from 1987 through 1993.
p. 280 TWA arrangements. *St. Louis Post-Dispatch,* September 30, 1953.
p. 281 "It was kept very quiet . . ." *Even the Browns,* pages 33–34.
Interviews with Eldon Auker and Denny Galehouse.

Chapter 35
p. 283 "I felt then that I could take practically any ballclub . . ." *Man in the Dugout,* pages 265–66.

p. 289 Newsom rarely pitched on a pennant-winning ballclub. In 1940 Newsom won two games for the Detroit Tigers in the World Series, and in
the 1947 World Series he lost a game for the New York Yankees.
Interviews with Don Gutteridge and Ellis Clary.

Chapter 36
p. 300 "The Red Sox lost several key players . . ." Those players were Bobby
Doerr, Jim Tabor, Hal Wagner, and Cecil "Tex" Hughson.
p. 302 ". . . the last ball I ever hit in the major leagues." In 1945 Paul Waner
went up to bat once as a pinch hitter and walked.
p. 304 ". . . there are only six of us left . . ." Denny Galehouse died in 1998,
after my interview with Gutteridge and two weeks after my interview
with him.
Interviews with Ellis Clary, Don Gutteridge, and Denny Galehouse.

Chapter 37
p. 305 ". . . the third time the World Series was played in one ballpark." In
1921 and 1922 the New York Yankees and New York Giants played in
the Polo Grounds. The New York Americans moved into Yankee Stadium
the next season.
p. 305 "Now, you can come up." *Even the Browns,* page 183.
p. 307 ". . . Koufax and about four Yankees . . ." In Game 1 of the 1963
World Series, Sandy Koufax struck out 15 and three Yankee pitchers
(Ford, Williams, and Hamilton) struck out 10 to set a two-team record
of 25.
Interviews with Ellis Clary, Denny Galehouse, and Don Gutteridge.

Chapter 38
p. 309 "I was six or seven years old . . ." Pete Gray interviewed by Tony
Salin for his book *Baseball's Forgotten Heroes.*
p. 312 "When Three Rivers got in Organized Baseball . . ." Ibid.
Interviews with Don Gutteridge, Ellis Clary, and Denny Galehouse.

Chapter 39
p. 321 "We just have to limit ourselves to our incomes." "The Brothers
Who Boss the Browns" by Terry Dickson, *St. Louis Post-Dispatch,* June
15, 1950.
p. 324 ". . . had to play in that playoff . . ." On October 4, 1948, the Indians
defeated the Red Sox, 8-3. Player-manager Lou Boudreau hit two home
runs and two singles. Gene Beardon, who had been on the torpedoed
cruiser *Helena* and who had floated unconscious for twenty-one hours until
he was rescued, allowed five hits and got the win.
Interview with Eddie Pellagrini.

Chapter 40
p. 326 "Many critics were surprised . . ." *Veeck As in Wreck,* page 213.
p. 327 "All kids are tickled . . ." Ibid., page 12.

p. 327 "When I was with the Giants . . ." Unidentified newspaper of March 13, 1960.

p. 328 "I'm going to shoot you dead." *Veeck As in Wreck,* page 14.

p. 329 "You dead or alive, you're going in there." Ibid., page 16.

Interviews with Bill DeWitt, Jr., Bob Broeg, and Bill Miller.

See "The Sad Life of Baseball's Midget" by Jim Reisler in *The Perfect Game,* Mark Alvarez, ed., SABR Cleveland.

Chapter 41

Interviews with Ned Garver and Bill Miller.

Chapter 42

p. 340 "All players are alike to me . . ." *Veeck As in Wreck,* page 233.

Interviews with Marty Marion and Ned Garver.

Chapter 43

p. 345 "You can't do no winning in relief . . ." *Boston Daily Globe,* June 19, 1952.

p. 346 "ol' Sugar Cain." Distinguish Bob Cain, who pitched for the Chicago White Sox, Detroit Tigers, and St. Louis Browns from 1949 through 1953 from pitcher Merritt "Sugar" Cain, who pitched in the majors for the Philadelphia A's, St. Louis Browns, and Chicago Cubs from 1932 through 1938. The one referred to here is Bob.

Interviews with Marty Marion and Bob Broeg.

Chapter 44

Interview with David Lipman.

Chapter 45

p. 353 "I'll take him and pay him $200,000." *Veeck As in Wreck,* page 260.

p. 354 . . . the dimensions of the Coliseum seemed too crazy for baseball.

Bill Veeck was too much a baseball purist to play in the oddly shaped Los Angeles Coliseum and make a mockery of the game. Five years later, Walter O'Malley, the owner of the Brooklyn Dodgers, showed no such reluctance.

p. 354 "It's too close to the start of the season." Ibid., page 287.

p. 357 "I suggest you vote them in without any more delay." Ibid., pages 304–5.

Interviews with Bob Broeg, Marty Marion, Max Lanier, and Bill Miller.

Chapter 46

p. 368 "I was rooming with Max . . ." *Red,* page 48.

Interviews with Stan Musial, Danny Litwhiler, Max Lanier, and Marty Marion.

Chapter 47

p. 375 "Young man, that was awfully nice of you." *Holy Cow!,* page 81.

p. 375 "Well, consider this proof of that." Ibid., page 83.

p. 376 ". . . the first of two disastrous career calls . . ."

p. 377 Williams's second home run in the All-Star Game was against Truett "Rip" Sewell, who threw him his famous eephus, or bloop ball.

Interviews with Marty Marion, Bob Broeg, Danny Litwhiler, and Enos Slaughter.

Chapter 48

p. 384 "Some players on some teams . . ." *Red,* page 87.

p. 385 "I understand he was one of the few Cardinals . . ." *If I Had a Hammer,* page 104.

Interviews with Bob Broeg, Stan Musial, Marty Marion, and Danny Litwhiler.

Chapter 49

p. 390 Fred Saigh had the opportunity to buy Elston Howard from the Kansas City Monarchs, but passed. Recalled Bob Broeg, "Elston's house was a long, loud foul behind home plate, about three blocks away. That's where he lived with his mother, a dietician. They missed a hell of a player. It's hard to understand things as they were then."

Said Bing Devine, "The expectation that had been developed over a period of time was that this community wasn't ready for black players. It was that simple. It was kind of a Southern-place approach. Right or wrong, and obviously it was wrong, but that was the thought."

p. 393 . . . tryout with the Cardinals.

Gardella flied out in his only at-bat in 1950. He was sold to Houston in the Texas League. In 1951 he played with the Bushwicks in Brooklyn, and then quit the game.

p. 393 . . . more than $60,000, half of which went to his lawyer.

The Imperfect Diamond by Tony Lupien and Lee Lowenfish, page 167.

Interviews with Bob Broeg, Fred Saigh, Marty Marion, Stan Musial, and Max Lanier.

Chapter 50

p. 399 "Gussie Busch was my kind of guy . . ." *Holy Cow!,* page 135.

p. 399 "tyrannical, profane, prolific . . ." *Under the Influence,* page 123.

p. 400 When Anheuser-Busch tried to trademark the Budweiser name, it was challenged by a German brewery. In 1911, Adolphus Busch paid the brewery 82,000 kronen. He also paid the brewery in Budweiser. Under the agreement, Busch could sell Budweiser only in the United States. Even today, Budweiser cannot be sold in most of Europe. The Czechs have that exclusive right under the agreement of 1911.

p. 400 He had a debt of $300,000 . . .

Under the Influence, page 37.

p. 401 "Another bad trait in the American character . . ." The Charles Nagel papers, July 29, 1911, *Under the Influence,* pages 66–67.

p. 401 "Let every man do as he pleases." The Charles Nagel papers, February 18, 1911, *Under the Influence,* page 77.

p. 403 Al Capone bought his Miami home from Clarence Busch.

p. 403 "They were so bitter . . ." *Under the Influence,* page 132.

p. 403 "Beer, beer, we want beer . . ." *St. Louis Globe-Democrat,* date unknown.

p. 404 "We used to smell powder together . . ." *St. Louis Post-Dispatch,* July 10, 1979.

p. 405 . . . who had never been a baseball fan . . .

As Gussie Busch's ownership in the team developed, he would become a very big fan. He particularly loved Stan Musial and later Whitey Herzog. He liked to go out onto the field and work out with his players, who he would come to think of as family. When free agency and player agents became part of the equation, he felt very strongly that his "family" had turned on him.

p. 405 "There's a lot of standing around." *Under the Influence,* page 212.

p. 405 "This is one of the finest moves in the history of Anheuser-Busch." *Under the Influence,* page 213.

p. 405 "I'm ashamed to bring my friends out here." *St. Louis Globe-Democrat,* October 16–17, 1982.

p. 406 And it hasn't lost its crown yet.

In 1996 Anheuser-Busch sold the Cardinals to a group headed by Bill DeWitt, Jr., the son of the former owner of the St. Louis Browns and a partner of George Bush, Jr., in the oil and gas business. It will be interesting to see whether the sale of the team will hurt Anheuser-Busch's position in the industry.

Chapter 51

p. 407 The meeting between Busch and Stanky was witnessed by John Wilson, one of the Anheuser-Busch board members.

p. 407 Busch knew almost nothing about baseball at the time he began running the team. At a game early in his ownership, the Cards led after eight and a half. When the game ended, Busch asked why the Cards were not batting in the bottom of the ninth.

p. 407 "go out and find our own players." *St. Louis Globe-Democrat,* October 16–17, 1982.

p. 407 His full name was Thomas Edison Alston. He was born in 1926, the year Edison died.

p. 408 "I think we have a real player . . ." *Crossing the Line,* page 102.

p. 408 "Mr. Busch knew the Cardinals needed to have black players . . ." *Red,* page 78.

p. 409 "Being a Negro is an interesting life." *Crossing the Line,* page 114.

p. 414 "Stanky was fired in '55 . . ." Busch fired him as manager because the team lost two years in a row. Related Al Fleishman, "He told Eddie, 'I like you very much, and I'm very sorry to see you go.' Harry Walker was there two years. He hired them and fired them trying to get a winner."

Interviews with Bing Devine, Bob Broeg, and Brooks Lawrence.

Chapter 52

p. 417 "Al Fleishman had a hand in that." Related Al Fleishman, "When Mr. Busch learned that Frank Lane was going to trade Stan Musial, Busch said, 'We're not going to trade Stan Musial. That's all. Call him up and tell him.' Just as simple as that."

p. 418 . . . Lane upped and quit . . .
Another reason Lane quit was that he had asked for an extension on his
    contract, which had a year to run. Busch turned him down.
Interview with Bing Devine.

Chapter 53
Interview with Jim Brosnan.

Chapter 54
p. 434 "He said Gibby'd never make it . . ." *Oh Baby, I Love It!*, page 59.
p. 434 "Under Solly Hemus nothing worked out fine . . ." *The Way It Is,*
    pages 69–70.
p. 435 "Hemus must have been the only manager ever to have a problem
    handling Stan the Man . . ." *Stranger to the Game,* page 52.
p. 435 "Gibson, White, Crowe, and I . . ." *The Way It Is,* pages 70–71.
p. 436 Bill White has never forgiven the city of St. Petersburg for its racist past.
On August 7, 1992, it was announced that the San Francisco Giants were going
    to relocate to St. Pete and Tampa Bay. One month later, on September 7,
    baseball commissioner Fay Vincent resigned. Immediately White, the Na-
    tional League president, announced his opposition to the move to St. Pete.
    He said he was organizing an effort for the city of San Francisco to keep
    the Giants. On November 21, it was announced that the Giants had been
    sold to a group led by Peter Magowan and would remain in San Francisco.
    White had his revenge.
p. 437 "Everything in between [Omaha and St. Petersburg] was disgusting or
    degrading . . ." *From Ghetto to Glory,* page 42.
p. 437 "As I floated toward the baggage claim area . . ." *The Way It Is,*
    page 34.
p. 437 "I was at Ma Felder's because . . ." Ibid., page 35.
p. 437 "I was ready for High Point–Thomasville . . ." Ibid., page 37.
p. 438 "What had started as a chance to test my baseball ability . . ." Ibid.,
    pages 38–39.
p. 438 . . . seventeen businesses ended their discriminatory policies.
See . . . Baseball's Reluctant Challenge: Desegregating Spring Training Sites,
    1961–1964 by Jack Davis, Doctoral Candidate in History of American
    Civilization, Brandeis University, *Journal of Sports History,* Vol. 19, No.
    2, Summer 1992.
p. 439 "I think about this every minute of the day." UPI, March 18, 1961.
p. 439 "[White] had been raised in a basically white community . . ." *Stranger
    to the Game,* page 58.
p. 440 ". . . help [a St. Petersburg businessman] buy the two motels . . ."
According to David Halberstam, a wealthy friend of Gussie Busch bought the
    Skyway Motel, and the Cards leased it for six weeks and rented some
    rooms in the adjoining Outrigger Motel, so the entire team and families
    could stay together. *October 1964,* page 59.

p. 441 "Several of the white players . . ." Ibid., pages 58–59.

p. 442 "One night I decided to make a big impression on a girl . . ." *The Way It Is,* pages 76–77.

Interviews with Bing Devine, Stan Musial, Carl Warwick, Bill White, Al Fleishman, and Bill Davenport.

Chapter 55

p. 444 "It had often been written that Solly went too far toward being one of the boys." *Oh Baby, I Love It!,* pages 122–23.

p. 445 "The impact of a man like Musial . . ." *Oh Baby, I Love It!,* page 17.

p. 446 "Just outside the ballpark, in the players' parking lot . . ." *Holy Cow!,* pages 106–7.

p. 446 "You're the center fielder, Curt." *The Way It Is,* page 13.

p. 447 . . . Robert Cobb, the owner of the Brown Derby restaurant . . . *October 1964,* p. 30.

p. 448 "The best brain in baseball is sitting in Pittsburgh doing nothing . . ." *Branch Rickey* by Murray Polner, page 265.

Interviews with Bing Devine, Carl Warwick, and Nelson Briles.

Chapter 56

p. 456 "Presto. We were transformed." *Stranger to the Game,* page 85.

p. 456 "When they started to announce his name . . ." *From Ghetto to Glory,* page 97.

p. 457 "At the start of the season . . ." *Stranger to the Game,* pages 86–87.

p. 458 "When Keane was finished . . ." Ibid.

p. 459 "How about you becoming my general manager?" *Holy Cow!* pages 138–39.

p. 459 "Bing Devine is a great general manager, Gussie. Keep him." Polner, page 273.

p. 460 "I believe in you." Ibid.

p. 460 "I felt bad when Bing Devine left . . ." *From Ghetto to Glory,* page 93.

p. 460 "You're a number-one man . . ." *Holy Cow!* page 143.

p. 461 "If someone came to me and asked me to manage a team with some talent on it . . ." Ibid.

p. 462 "I have never known a loss that was harder . . ." *From Ghetto to Glory,* page 70.

Interviews with Carl Warwick, Bing Devine, and Bill White.

Chapter 57

p. 465 "What was poor Barney Schultz doing . . ." *Oh Baby, I Love It!,* pages 94–95.

p. 467 "The hitter was Bobby Richardson . . ." *From Ghetto to Glory,* pages 85–87.

p. 468 "It is probably the nicest thing that can be said . . ." *From Ghetto to Glory,* page 87.

p. 469 "I've made other plans . . ." *Holy Cow!,* pages 147–48.

Interviews with Carl Warwick and Bill White.

Chapter 58

p. 470 . . . he much preferred to coach than to manage.

The night after Johnny Keane's resignation, Red Schoendienst called Harry Caray to remind him to tell Gussie Busch that he had no ambitions to manage, that "he'd much rather spend the next twenty-five years as coach." Red didn't want to live under the axe-will-fall insecurity of managing. Coaching gave him the security he desired. But Caray avoided passing such messages to Busch whenever possible. Before hanging up, he told Red, "If you keep your nose clean with all the craziness that's going on here, you're going to wind up being manager of this club." Which is exactly what happened. *Holy Cow!,* page 149.

p. 471 "Stan's administrative gifts were not exactly apparent . . ." *The Way It Is,* page 66.

p. 473 "My father was eighty-six when he died . . ." *The New York Times,* December 11, 1965.

p. 476 "Branch Rickey was responsible for every St. Louis star . . ." *St. Louis Post-Dispatch,* December 10, 1965.

p. 476 "If he had been younger . . ." *St. Louis Post-Dispatch,* December 13, 1965.

Interview with Carl Warwick, Bill White, Nelson Briles, and Bob Broeg.

Chapter 59

p. 478 "Here I have complete charge . . ." Polner, page 278.

p. 479 "I went home after the 1966 season ended . . ."

For the full interview I had with Roger Maris in 1974, see *Dynasty,* pages 299–303.

p. 480 . . . he was a star who won wherever he played.

It seems a sin that Roger Maris is not in the Hall of Fame. The time is nigh to put him in there.

p. 482 "The speculation was if he didn't throw to the next hitter, maybe it wouldn't have been broken, only cracked." In 1937 Dizzy Dean was struck in the All-Star Game by a batted ball off the bat of Earl Averill. Because Dean came back too soon, he hurt his arm and was never the same pitcher. Forty years later when Clemente nailed Gibson, the big pitcher didn't make the mistake Dean made. When Gibson came back, he was better than ever, and the following year had one of the great seasons in baseball history.

p. 483 checked the scope of his hunting rifle.

Stranger to the Game, page 130.

p. 483 "Steve Carlton was always certain . . ." *The Way It Is,* page 95.

p. 485 "Cepeda had been traded to us . . ." Ibid., page 85.

p. 486 "The Cardinals of 1967 and 1968 . . ." Ibid., pages 86–90.

p. 486 . . . men were free of racist poison.

Curt Flood always felt great disappointment over the fact that the black-white harmony on the Cardinals never was written about in the newspapers. Said Flood, "If any hint of the team's interracial closeness was reported in the daily press, I never saw the clippings." Ibid., page 90.

Flood also was upset that the white reporters tended to spend most of their time with the white players. Said Flood, "Bob Burnes never interviewed me once during my twelve years with the team." Ibid., page 92.

Interview with Nelson Briles.

Chapter 60

p. 488 "I never saw a player have a season like that . . ." *Fenway*, page 313.

p. 490 "The St. Louis Cardinals are as bush as the beer company that owns them . . ." Ibid., page 315.

p. 492 "There was so little left of my fastball . . ." *Stranger to the Game*, page 148.

Interview with Nelson Briles.

Chapter 61

p. 494 "In the winter of 1967–68 . . ." *White Rat*, pages 80–81.

p. 495 "I don't give a fuck. I have a ball game to pitch." *Stranger to the Game*, page 199.

p. 495 "Get back there where you belong." *Oh Baby, I Love It!*, page 63.

p. 496 "During the game itself, he was at us constantly." *The Way It Is*, page 96.

p. 497 . . . second most behind Grover Cleveland Alexander's 16.

In 1910 Jack Coombs of the Philadelphia A's recorded 13 shutouts. Grover Cleveland Alexander (1915) and Christy Mathewson (1908) each had seasons in which they recorded 12 shutouts. Gibson was in rarefied company.

p. 498 "The 1.12 is the number that seems to have impressed a lot of people . . ." *Stranger to the Game*, page 196.

p. 500 The highlight of Game 5 of the 1968 World Series may well have been the soulful rendition of "The Star-Spangled Banner" by José Feliciano. Some fans loved it, others hated it. None would ever forget it.

p. 502 "It's nobody's fault." *Oh Baby, I Love It!*, page 59.

Interviews with Bill Devine and Nelson Briles. Tim McCarver interviewed by Bill Mead.

Chapter 62

p. 503 "It was curious to me and the other players . . ." *Stranger to the Game*, page 210.

p. 503 "The leading members of the Cardinals . . ." *The Way It Is*, pages 171–74, 180–82.

p. 505 "A few days later, the front office underlined . . ." *The Way It Is*, pages 171–75.

p. 506 "No offense is less forgivable than that . . ." Ibid., pages 85–86.

p. 506 "I knew in my bones . . ." Ibid., page 184.

p. 507 "To this day I'll always think that the trade contributed to the disintegration of the Cardinals . . ." *Oh Baby, I Love It!*, page 148.

p. 507 "I loved the Cardinals . . ." *Stranger to the Game*, page 217.

p. 508 "I am pleased God made my skin black . . ." *The Way It Is*, pages 197–98.

p. 508 "Nothing I said in interviews got through . . ." Ibid., page 198.

p. 508 "Flood suffered two losses . . ." *Oh Baby, I Love It!*, page 147.

Interviews with Nelson Briles and Marvin Miller.

Chapter 63

p. 512 "While Harry was still convalescing . . ." *Voices of the Game*, page 462.

p. 513 "I never raped anyone in my life." Ibid.

p. 513 "Broadcaster who antagonize wrong woman . . ." *The Way It Is*, page 94.

p. 514 "I love Harry Caray . . ." *This Time Let's Not Eat the Bones*, pages 181–82.

p. 520 "Let them strike." *Imperfect Diamond*, page 215.

p. 524 Bob Gibson struck out batter number 3,000 on July 17, 1974, the day Dizzy Dean died. I don't know what the cosmic connection is. I just thought the two events occurring on the same day seemed more than just a coincidence.

p. 526 Bob Gibson had counted on getting an Anheuser-Busch beer distributorship like Roger Maris had gotten. He was staking his business livelihood on it. Gibson and Gussie Busch had had a number of discussions about it. But after the strike of 1972, the subject was dropped for good.

Interviews with Rich Folkers and Bing Devine.

Chapter 64

p. 526 "Vern Rapp in St. Louis held some destructive ass-kickings . . ." *If at First*, page 128.

p. 527 "Don't worry about it. You're the man." Ibid., page 111.

p. 528 "I wondered where he'd been all my life." *White Rat*, page 116.

p. 528 "Beer was part of our food." Ibid., page 26.

p. 530 "I wanted him to do something about it." *St. Louis Globe-Democrat*, October 16–17, 1982.

p. 530 "Great." *White Rat*, page 120.

p. 530 "I've never seen such a bunch of misfits . . ." Ibid., pages 117–18.

p. 532 "All of a sudden I was a one-man band." Ibid., page 124.

p. 533 "Suppose that you are the new manager of an office . . ." *This Time Let's Not Eat the Bones*, pages 163–64.

p. 533 "By God, the Cardinals were ready . . ." *White Rat*, page 133.

p. 535 "So Tempy goes out and loafs . . ." Ibid., page 136.

p. 538 "I knew when we got him that he was good . . ." Ibid., page 138.

Interviews with Tommy Herr and Darrell Porter.

Chapter 65

p. 543 "No. Black and decker." *St. Louis Post-Dispatch*, October 21, 1982.

p. 546 pinch hitter extraordinaire.

Steve Braun finished his career with 113 pinch hits, seventh most in baseball history.

p. 549 "There were a lot of people around baseball . . ." *White Rat*, page 145.

Interviews with Darrell Porter and Tommy Herr.

Chapter 66

p. 554 "I'm not going to be general manager of the Cardinals . . ." *That's a Winner!* by Jack Buck, page 181.

p. 559 Whitey and Maxvill swung a deal to acquire Cesar Cedeno from Cincinnati. Jim Kaat, the Reds pitching coach, told Herzog that Cedeno and Reds manager Pete Rose weren't getting along. Herzog told Maxvill, and the Cards made the trade for him. Cedeno hit a home run the first time up as a Card and ignited the team. We hit .434 for the rest of the season.

Chapter 67

p. 567 "I was two-thirds of an inning from winning the ERA title . . ."
Magrane pitched 113⅓ innings. The American Association required a minimum of 114. Magrane was called up in September by the Cards, but he never pitched.
Interviews with Tommy Herr and Joe Magrane.

Chapter 68

Interview with Joe Magrane.

Chapter 69

p. 578 The new head, August Busch III, held no love for baseball.
It had been his wife with whom Harry Caray had had the affair.
p. 580 "There were ten players in the final year of their contracts . . ." *Red,* pages 188–89.
Interview with Joe Magrane.

Chapter 70

p. 582 Joe Torre was fired.
Walt Jocketty was so upset about having to fire Torre that after he went over to his manager's home to tell him the news, Torre ended up comforting Jocketty. According to Jack Buck, he gave Jocketty a bottle of wine when he left. *That's a Winner!* by Jack Buck, page 196. In 1998 Torre managed the New York Yankees to a world championship, winning 114 regular season games. He repeated in 1999.
p. 583 In July of 1997, Card GM made a trade . . . for . . . Mark McGwire.
At the time of the trade, McGwire had 363 home runs in 4,448 at-bats, a homer for every 12.5 at-bats. Only Babe Ruth, with one in every 11.76 at-bats, had ever been better.
p. 585 "Somewhere along the line up there in Alaska . . ." *St. Louis Post-Dispatch,* "Stadium Extra," September 8, 1998, page 17.
p. 587 "I did so much stupid stuff." *Sports Illustrated,* September 7, 1998, Vol. 89, No. 10, page 38.
p. 587 "I think there were too many things calling Mark's name . . ." Ibid.
p. 588 "I had to face the music . . ." Interviewed by Roy Firestone, "Up Close," ESPN, April 1, 1999.
Interviews with Bill DeWitt, Jr., and Sandy Alderson.

Chapter 71

p. 593 "Just when we needed it most . . ." *The New York Times,* "Sports Sunday," October 4, 1998.

p. 596 "If what McGwire accomplished had been about home run hitting . . ." *St. Louis Post-Dispatch,* "Salute to 62," September 11, 1998, page 4.

p. 598 "Dear Mark . . ." *Suburban Journal West County,* "A Tribute to Mark McGwire," messages from his fans, October 4, 1998.

p. 598 "Whichever way the season ends, so be it . . ." *The New York Times,* September 25, 1998.

p. 599 "I am a normal person who plays sports . . ." Ibid., September 26, 1998.

BIBLIOGRAPHY

Hank Aaron and Lonnie Wheeler, *If I Had a Hammer,* HarperCollins, New York, 1992.

Dick Allen and Tim Whitaker, *Crash: The Life and Times of Dick Allen,* Ticknor & Fields, New York, 1989.

Stephen Ambrose, *Undaunted Courage,* Simon & Schuster, New York, 1996.

Dave Anderson, *Pennant Races,* Doubleday, New York, 1994.

Will Anderson, *Beer, U.S.A.,* Morgan & Morgan, New York, 1986.

G. W. Axelson, *Commy,* Reilly and Lee Co., Chicago, 1919.

Stanley Baron, *Brewed in America: A History of Beer and Ale in the United States,* Little, Brown, Boston, 1962.

Bill Borst, *Baseball Through the Knothole,* Missouri Prank Press, 1980.

Jim Brosnan, *The Long Season,* Harper & Brothers, New York, 1960.

Jack Buck with Rob Rains and Bob Broeg, *That's a Winner!* Sagamore Publishing, Champaign, Ill., 1997.

Harry Caray with Bob Verdi, *Holy Cow!,* Berkley Books, New York, 1990.

John Carmichael, *My Greatest Day in Baseball,* Grosset & Dunlap, New York, 1963.

Charles Cleveland, *Baseball's Greatest Managers,* Thomas Y. Crowell Co., New York, 1950.

E. Merton Coulton, *The Confederate States of America 1861–1865,* LSU Press and The Littlefield Fund for Southern History of the University of Texas, Austin 1950.

Leo Durocher and Ed Linn, *Nice Guys Finish Last,* Simon & Schuster, New York, 1975.

Gerald Eskanazi, *The Lip: A Biography of Leo Durocher,* William Morrow & Co., New York, 1993.

Johnny Evers and Hugh Fullerton, *Touching Second,* Reilly and Britton, Chicago, 1910.

Ed Fitzgerald, *The National League,* Grosset & Dunlap, New York, 1959.

G. H. Fleming, *The Dizziest Season,* William Morrow & Co., New York, 1984.

Curt Flood with Richard Carter, *The Way It Is,* Trident Press, New York, 1971.

Frank Frisch, *The Fordham Flash,* Doubleday, New York, 1962.

David Gallen, ed., *The Baseball Chronicles,* Carroll & Graf, New York, 1991.

Joe Garagiola, *Baseball Is a Funny Game,* J. B. Lippincott Company, Philadelphia/New York, 1960.

Bob Gibson and Phil Pepe, *From Ghetto to Glory,* Prentice-Hall, Englewood Cliffs, N.J., 1968.

Bob Gibson with Lonnie Wheeler, *Stranger to the Game,* Penguin Books, New York, 1994.

Bill Gilbert, *They Also Served,* Crown, New York, 1992.

David Halberstam, *October 1964,* Villard Books, New York, 1994.

Keith Hernandez and Mike Bryan, *If at First,* McGraw-Hill Book Co., New York, 1986.

Peter Hernon and Terry Ganey, *Under the Influence: The Unauthorized Story of the Anheuser-Busch Dynasty,* Simon & Schuster, New York, 1991.

Whitey Herzog and Kevin Horrigan, *White Rat,* Harper & Row, New York, 1988.

Don Honig, *Baseball When the Grass Was Real,* Simon & Schuster, New York, 1975.

———, *The October Heroes,* Simon & Schuster, New York, 1979.

Bob Hood, *The Gashouse Gang,* William Morrow and Co., New York, 1975.

Rogers Hornsby, *My War with Baseball,* Coward-McCann, New York, 1962.

Bill James, *This Time Let's Not Eat the Bones,* Villard Books, New York, 1989.

MacKinlay Kantor, *Missouri Bittersweet,* Doubleday, New York, 1969.

Gene Karst, ed., *Who's Who in Professional Baseball,* Arlington House, New Rochelle, N.Y., 1973.

Jerry Lansch, *Glory Fades Away,* Taylor Publishing, Dallas, 1991.

———, *Stan the Man Musial,* Taylor Publishing, Dallas, 1994.

Frederick G. Lieb, *The Baltimore Orioles,* G. P. Putnam & Sons, New York, 1955.

———, *The St. Louis Cardinals,* G. P. Putnam & Sons, New York, 1945.

———, *The Story of the World Series,* G. P. Putnam & Sons, New York, 1949.

Lee Lowenfish, *The Imperfect Diamond,* Da Capo, New York, 1980.

Wes Lyle and John Hall, *Missouri: Faces and Places,* Regents Press of Kansas, Lawrence, Kan., 1977.

Arthur Mann, *Branch Rickey: American in Action,* Riverside Press, Cambridge, 1957.

Tim McCarver with Ray Robinson, *Oh Baby, I Love It!,* Dell, New York, 1987.

William B. Mead, *Even the Browns,* Contemporary Books, Chicago, 1978.

———, *Two Spectacular Seasons,* Macmillan, New York, 1990.

Marvin Miller, *A Whole Different Ball Game,* Birch Lane Press, New York, 1991.

Larry Moffi and Jonathan Kronstadt, *Crossing the Line,* University of Iowa Press, Iowa City, 1994.

John J. Monteleone, ed. *Branch Rickey's Little Blue Book,* Macmillan USA, New York, 1995.

Stan Musial as told to Bob Broeg, Doubleday, New York, 1964.

David Nemek, *The Beer and Whiskey League,* Lyons & Burford, New York, 1994.

Satchel Paige and David Lipman, *Maybe I'll Pitch Forever,* Doubleday, New York, 1962.

Murray Polner, *Branch Rickey,* Atheneum, New York, 1982.

Darrell Porter and William Deerfield, *Snap Me Perfect!,* Thomas Nelson, Nashville, 1984.

Branch Rickey and Robert Riger, *The American Diamond,* Simon & Schuster, New York, 1963.

Larry Ritter, *The Glory of Their Times,* Macmillan, New York, 1966.

Red Schoendienst with Rob Rains, *Red: A Baseball Life,* Sports Publishing, Champaign, Ill., 1998.

Curt Smith, *Voices of the Game,* Diamond Publishing, South Bend, Ind., 1987.

Robert Smith, *Baseball,* Simon & Schuster, New York, 1947.

————, *Baseball in the Afternoon,* Simon & Schuster, New York, 1993.

Burt Solomon, *Where They Ain't,* Free Press, New York, 1999.

A. G. Spalding, *America's National Game,* American Sports Publishing Co., New York, 1911.

J. G. Taylor Spink, *Judge Landis and Twenty-Five Years of Baseball,* Thomas Y. Crowell, New York, 1947.

Bill Stern, *Bill Stern's Favorite Baseball Stories,* Doubleday, New York, 1949.

J. Roy Stockton, *The Gashouse Gang and a Couple of Other Guys,* A. S. Barnes & Co., New York, 1945.

Frederick Turner, *When the Boys Came Back,* Henry Holt & Co., New York, 1996.

Bill Veeck with Ed Linn, *Veeck as in Wreck,* G. P. Putnam & Sons, New York City, 1962.

Douglas Wallop, *Baseball: An Informal History,* Norton, New York, 1969.

INDEX

Page numbers in italics refer to illustrations.